D1302290

PRINCESS OR PRISONER?

PRINCESS OR PRISONER?

Jewish Women in Jerusalem, 1840–1914

MARGALIT SHILO

Translated by David Louvish

Brandeis University Press

Waltham, Massachusetts

PUBLISHED BY UNIVERSITY PRESS OF NEW ENGLAND
HANOVER AND LONDON

Brandeis University Press

Published by University Press of New England,
One Court Street, Lebanon, NH 03766
www.upne.com
© 2005 by Brandeis University Press
Printed in the United States of America

5   4   3   2   1

Originally published in Hebrew as *Nesikhah o shevuyah: Hahavayah hanashit shel hayishuv hayashau biYerushalayim* by Hafia University and Zmora Bitan, 2003

This book was published by Brandeis University's Hadassah-Brandeis Institute, through the generous support of the Donna Sudarsky Memorial Fund and the Tauber Institute, and through the generous support of the Valya and Robert Shapiro Endowment.

Library of Congress Cataloging-in-Publication Data

Shilo, Margalit.
[Nesikhah o shevuyah? English]
Princess or prisoner? : Jewish women in Jerusalem, 1840–1914 / Margalit Shilo.—1st ed.
    p.   cm. — (Brandeis series on Jewish women) (The Tauber Institute for the Study of European Jewry Series)
Includes bibliographical references and index.
ISBN 1–58465–483–X (cloth : alk. paper) — ISBN 1–58465–484–8 (pbk. : alk. paper)
1. Jewish women — Jerusalem — History — 19th century. 2. Jewish women — Jerusalem — History — 20th century. 3. Jewish women — Jerusalem — Social conditions — 19th century. 4. Jewish women — Jerusalem — Education. I. Title: Princess or Prisoner? II. Title. III. Series.
HQ1728.5.S5413 2005
305.48'89240569442'09034 — dc22   2004027439

Shulamit Reinharz, General Editor
Joyce Antler, Associate Editor
Sylvia Barack Fishman, Associate Editor

The Brandeis Series on Jewish Women is an innovative book series created by the Hadassah-Brandeis Institute. BSJW publishes a wide range of books by and about Jewish women in diverse contexts and time periods, of interest to scholars, and for the educated public. The series fills a major gap in Jewish learning by focusing on the lives of Jewish women and Jewish gender studies.

Marjorie Agosín, *Uncertain Travelers: Conversations with Jewish Women Immigrants to America*, 1999

Rahel R. Wasserfall, editor, *Women and Water: Menstruation in Jewish Life and Law*, 1999

Susan Starr Sered, *What Makes Women Sick? Militarism, Maternity, and Modesty in Israeli Society*, 2000

Pamela S. Nadell and Jonathan D. Sarna, editors, *Women and American Judaism: Historical Perspectives*, 2001

Ludmila Shtern, *Leaving Leningrad: The True Adventures of a Soviet Émigré*, 2001

Jael Silliman, *Jewish Portraits, Indian Frames: Women's Narratives from a Diaspora of Hope*, 2001

Judith R. Baskin, *Midrashic Women: Formations of the Feminine in Rabbinic Literature*, 2002

ChaeRan Y. Freeze, *Jewish Marriage and Divorce in Imperial Russia*, 2002

Mark A. Raider and Miriam B. Raider-Roth, editors, *The Plough Woman: Records of the Pioneer Women of Palestine*, 2002

Farideh Goldin, *Wedding Song: Memoirs of an Iranian Jewish Woman*, 2003

Elizabeth Wyner Mark, editor, *The Covenant of Circumcision: New Perspectives on an Ancient Jewish Rite*, 2003

Rochelle L. Millen, *Women, Birth, and Death in Jewish Law and Practice*, 2003

Kalpana Misra and Melanie S. Rich, editors, *Jewish Feminism in Israel: Some Contemporary Perspectives*, 2003

Marcia Falk, translator, *The Song of Songs: Love Lyrics from the Bible*, 2004

Sylvia Barack Fishman, *Double or Nothing? Jewish Families and Mixed Marriage*, 2004

Avraham Grossman, *Pious and Rebellious: Jewish Women in Medieval Europe*, 2004

Iris Parush, *Reading Jewish Women: Marginality and Modernization in Nineteenth-Century Eastern European Jewish Society*, 2004

Shulamit Reinharz and Mark A. Raider, editors, *American Jewish Women and the Zionist Enterprise*, 2004

Tamar Ross, *Expanding the Palace of Torah: Orthodoxy and Feminism*, 2004

Margalit Shilo, *Princess or Prisoner? Jewish Women in Jerusalem, 1840–1914*, 2005

George L. Mosse, 1993
Confronting the Nation: Jewish and Western Nationalism

Daniel Carpi, 1994
Between Mussolini and Hitler: The Jews and the Italian Authorities in France and Tunisia

Walter Laqueur and Richard Breitman, 1994
Breaking the Silence: The German Who Exposed the Final Solution

Ismar Schorsch, 1994
From Text to Context: The Turn to History in Modern Judaism

Jacob Katz, 1995
With My Own Eyes: The Autobiography of an Historian

Gideon Shimoni, 1995
The Zionist Ideology

Moshe Prywes and Haim Chertok, 1996
Prisoner of Hope

János Nyiri, 1997
Battlefields and Playgrounds

Alan Mintz, editor, 1997
The Boom in Contemporary Israeli Fiction

Samuel Bak, paintings
Lawrence L. Langer, essay and commentary, 1997
Landscapes of Jewish Experience

Jeffrey Shandler and Beth S. Wenger, editors, 1997
Encounters with the "Holy Land": Place, Past and Future in American Jewish Culture

Simon Rawidowicz, 1998
State of Israel, Diaspora, and Jewish Continuity: Essays on the "Ever-Dying People"

Jacob Katz, 1998
A House Divided: Orthodoxy and Schism in Nineteenth-Century Central European Jewry

Elisheva Carlebach, John M. Efron, and David N. Myers, editors, 1998
Jewish History and Jewish Memory: Essays in Honor of Yosef Hayim Yerushalmi

Shmuel Almog, Jehuda Reinharz, and Anita Shapira, editors, 1998
Zionism and Religion

Ben Halpern and Jehuda Reinharz, 2000
Zionism and the Creation of a New Society

Walter Laqueur, 2001
Generation Exodus: The Fate of Young Jewish Refugees from Nazi Germany

Yigal Schwartz, 2001
Aharon Appelfeld: From Individual Lament to Tribal Eternity

Renée Poznanski, 2001
Jews in France during World War II

Jehuda Reinharz, 2001
Chaim Weizmann: The Making of a Zionist Leader

Jehuda Reinharz, 2001
Chaim Weizmann: The Making of a Statesman

ChaeRan Y. Freeze, 2002
Jewish Marriage and Divorce in Imperial Russia

Mark A. Raider and Miriam B. Raider-Roth, editors, 2002
The Plough Woman: Records of the Pioneer Women of Palestine

Ezra Mendelsohn, 2002
Painting a People: Maurycy Gottlieb and Jewish Art

Alan Mintz, editor, 2002
Reading Hebrew Literature: Critical Discussions of Six Modern Texts

Haim Be'er, 2002
The Pure Element of Time

Yehudit Hendel, 2002
Small Change: A Collection of Stories

In cherished memory of my parents
Professor Aron and Eva Bondi
Lovers of the Land of Israel

Contents

Acknowledgments

The female experience of the "Old Yishuv" in Jerusalem has been a most profound one for me. My first research, more than two decades ago, on the women's farm at Kinneret, led me slowly but surely to the central theme of my work: the history of women in the Jewish community of the Land of Israel toward the end of the Ottoman period. The study of the history of women and gender has provided me not only with a stimulating intellectual challenge but also with a means of forging contact with a great number of scholars, mainly women, who are investing all their efforts in this new field of research.

For lack of space, I cannot possibly list here all those persons who have listened to me and given me the benefit of their knowledge and their comments, critical or otherwise, helping me in a variety of ways to complete this project. Much of what they have told me is featured in the following pages. Much help has been forthcoming from people who have personal, family links with the Old Yishuv. Special mention must be made of Dov Genechovsky, economist and writer, who possesses a comprehensive and profound knowledge of the history of Jerusalem and kindly permitted me to use documents from his personal archives. I am particularly indebted to Professor Billie Melman, a foremost authority in women's history and gender, who read the manuscript and encouraged and assisted me in many ways.

Several funds provided the necessary financial aid: the Bar-Ilan University Research Fund; the Dr. Irving and Cherna Moskowitz Chair in Land of Israel Studies, Bar-Ilan University; and above all the Ingeborg Rennert Center for Jerusalem Studies and its chairman, Professor Joshua Schwartz, without whose help the study would never have been published. I owe particular thanks to several diligent and enthusiastic research assistants, in particular Tamar Schein, who were all extremely helpful in the collection of material. I am also indebted to David Sperber, who brought my attention to the painting reproduced on the cover of this book, and to Professor Jacob Wahrman, who graciously gave me permission to reproduce the original lithograph that was made over a hundred and fifty years ago. Haifa University awarded the original Hebrew version of this book—which it also published—the Ya'acov Bahat Prize for Outstanding Academic Books.

The present English translation is slightly shorter than the Hebrew original, where the footnotes are more detailed. Several institutions helped to finance the translation: the Koschitzky Family Fund; the Martin (Szuz) Department of Land of Israel Studies; the Rivlin Institute for the History of Eretz-Israel and Its Settlement; The Fanya Gottesfeld Heller Center for the Study of Women in Judaism; all at the Faculty of Jewish Studies, Bar-Ilan University; and the Lucius N. Littauer Foundation, New York. Support for the English edition was also provided by the Hadassah-Brandeis Institute and the Tauber Institute for the Study of European Jewry at Brandeis University. Thanks go to the translator, David Louvish, for his painstaking work.

My family all had a significant part in my work on this book. Special thanks are due to my husband, Shmuel Shilo, whose help was of immeasurable value, and to my youngest son, Yehiel, who read the manuscript, offered useful comments, and was always ready to help when my computer refused to submit to my blandishments. They all have my heartfelt love and gratitude.

Introduction

The Jerusalem Woman as Typifying the "Jewess of Erez Israel"

There is a folk legend about a remarkable woman of Jerusalem, who observed the commandments "like a man," recited prayers three times a day at the Western Wall, and kissed its stones. She was once hit by a stone thrown at her by a young Arab. Raising her eyes in supplication to heaven, she begged God to redeem the Holy Land from its shameful condition. In answer to her prayer, a mysterious man appeared to her in a cave just outside the city and told her when the Messiah would come. This intriguing female figure possesses cross-gender characteristics: while observing the commandments like a man, she embraces the stones of the Western Wall and weeps for the misery of the land, like a woman. Upon returning home the woman wanted to relate her experience to the local rabbi — representing the male establishment: "And lo, a hand emerged from heaven and struck her on the mouth, and the woman's soul left her body in a state of purity and sanctity."[1] The information she had received was for her ears alone, and her attempt to pass it on to a person of lesser spiritual stature sealed her fate.

Embodied in this folktale is an ancient popular belief in women's capacity to achieve supreme sanctity by dint of both personal excellence and devotion to the holy places.[2] Perhaps it attests to awareness among Jerusalem's Jews of the presence in their midst of a unique female figure, virtually personifying the sanctity of the Holy Land and of the community.[3]

The figure of the "Jerusalem woman" was discussed from a different viewpoint in Eleazar Ben-Yehudah's newspaper *Ha'or* in 1895. Hemdah Ben-Yehudah, his wife, drew a colorful portrait of a typical Jewish woman of Jerusalem:[4] a woman of the Ashkenazi community, living in the Old City, one of the thousands of women who immigrated to the Holy Land in the second half of the nineteenth century. Her external appearance was expressive of her inner nature: self-denying to the point of suppressing her own person; so modest that she seemed to despise the shape of her body; obedient, submissive to her husband, with her home the sum total of her life and her principal mode of worship. Ben-Yehudah writes in a rather critical tone, noting that her "Jerusalem woman" was bent on worshiping the Creator by external, material means. Unlike men, who could approach God through study or communal prayer, a woman's means of worship involved shaving her head (a stringent interpretation of the Halakhic injunction that married women have their hair covered in public); she wore special clothes, which were similar to shrouds; she began preparing for the Sabbath on Wednesday, and sometimes welcomed the Sabbath hours before sundown on Friday. Women were seen not only as representative of the physical world but as preoccupied with it.

As against the ascetic Ashkenazi woman, Ben-Yehudah drew a picture of the Sephardic woman as more enamored of life, an uneducated female figure obsessed with cleanliness. Implicit in her writing is disapproval of the Ashkenazi woman's quest for spiritual elevation:

[The Sephardic woman] is not overly modest; she is pious but not crazy; as far removed from education as east is from west; but nevertheless her movements are handsome . . . She is both handsome and beautiful . . . Her eyes are big, shining, brilliant and good-natured; she walks upright, with head thrown back, with roving eyes, attired in scarves and crescents and anklets, somewhat reminiscent of Isaiah's daughters of Zion [Isa. 3:18].

Ben-Yehudah rejected the figure of the woman determined to achieve sanctity through self-denial. She much preferred women whose appearance and personality embodied joy of life; this, she insisted, was "the real Erez Israel woman."

These three female figures represent different ways in which women dealt with the Jerusalem aura of sanctity: crossing the limits of gender; suppressing the physical aspect; or welcoming the physical world and rejoicing in life as it was. These descriptions attest to the multifaceted figure of the Jerusalem woman, also hinting at the ambivalent attitude of Jewish culture to women. They portray the Jerusalem woman as a faithful reflection of the highly variegated Jewish community — a portrayal to be gradually revealed in the coming chapters.

A good deal of scholarly work has been done in recent years, from a multidisciplinary standpoint, on Jewish cultural attitudes to woman, who, according to Orthodox Jewish tradition, was created by God "according to His will." My object in this volume is to uncover the diverse layers and characteristics of attitudes to Jewish women as represented in Jerusalem in the late years of the Ottoman Empire. Family life and education, religion and culture, are the major factors that shape the identity of both individual and society.[5] Jerusalem, the Holy City, the object of an entire nation's hopes and desires for spiritual experience, provided fertile ground for the creation of a unique society: synagogues and study houses shaped it as dedicated to sanctity and the study of sacred texts, while gender relations gave it pronounced features of austerity and asceticism. Both aspects left their indelible imprint on the individuals of whom it was made up and on their mutual relationships.

The members of the so-called Old Yishuv who lived in Jerusalem were shaped by a metamorphosis that generally began with their immigration to Erez Israel. On the one hand, their immigration was the first stage of a journey to spiritual perfection; on the other, it introduced them to a rocky path of harsh living conditions at the edge of the Ottoman Empire. It is my intention, through women's experience in Jerusalem, to reveal the hidden face of that unique society, most of which was made up of relative newcomers.

Immigration and Its Motives in the Nineteenth Century

The years from 1840 to 1914 were a time of relative prosperity and calm in Erez Israel.[6] After the brief reign of the Egyptian ruler Muhammad Ali (1832–1840), who had initiated the modernization and westernization of the Holy Land, Jerusalem enjoyed a period of energetic growth lasting until the outbreak of World War I,[7] which dealt the Jewish community of Erez Israel — the Yishuv — a mortal blow and was a veritable watershed in its history.[8] One of the major signs and outcomes of those "good" years was an increase in tourism, pilgrimage, and immigration.

The Holy Land was a preferred destination for tourists and pilgrims in the nineteenth century.[9] The political changes in the Ottoman Empire in general, and in Erez Israel in particular, combined with technological changes that facilitated both land and sea travel, brought about an impressive growth in the number of visitors to the Holy Land. More than twenty thousand tourists and pilgrims came annually to Jerusalem,[10] whose population on the eve of World War I was some seventy thousand souls. The feeling of security along both sea and land routes was an important catalyst in the development of tourism. In contrast to previous periods, a journey to the Holy Land was no longer considered a hazardous undertaking.[11]

While pilgrimage has been described as a circular trip,[12] returning to the point of departure, immigration to Erez Israel was a linear, one-directional undertaking. Despite the obvious difference between the two phenomena, they have much in common: both pilgrimage and immigration to Erez Israel before the Zionist era were spiritually motivated, based on what anthropologists call "spiritual magnetism."[13] Both pilgrims and immigrants were driven by a profound attraction to a holy place, a place characterized by "sacred geography"; they willingly endured dangers and affliction as an integral part of a process whereby they hoped to come nearer to God.

The pilgrims came both as individuals — Jewish pilgrims on their own — and in large groups, mainly from the Ottoman Empire.[14] However, in contrast to Christian pilgrims from Europe and the United States, whose object was to tour the country, see its biblical landscape, and partake of its sanctity,[15] most of the Jews who came in the nineteenth century came to stay.[16] Rabbi

Joseph Mansfeld, who immigrated from Kalisch in 1835, wrote to a relative: "You ask if I intend to return to my former homeland. This question amazes me very much. Do you think I set out on my long journey without troubles and wars . . . and how would it occur to me to exchange the holy ground on which I live today with the ground of the foreign country where I lived before?"[17]

Jewish tradition fanned the fires of the ancient prayers for the restoration of the Jews to Erez Israel. The primary homeland of any Jew living in the Diaspora was not his or her physical country, but the spiritual homeland — Zion. Jewish immigration was driven first and foremost by the desire to be in the Holy Land, to fulfill the commandment of settling there, to achieve spiritual and religious perfection and help to bring Redemption nearer.[18] Rabbi Eleazar Bergman, head of the first family to come from Germany to settle, wrote, in a letter requesting financial help to prepare for his immigration:

How great and special is the commandment to move from abroad to the Holy Land . . . And for that reason this commandment was indeed fulfilled, in the name of all Israel, in all periods of time, by individuals as well as families, whether out of danger or not.[19]

The mystical belief that the eschatological resurrection of the dead would take place in the Holy Land, and that the bodies of the deceased would have to be transported there through underground tunnels before being resurrected, was another motive for elderly immigrants, who came to the country mainly to die there and be buried in its soil.[20] Immigrants came from eastern and central Europe, from all parts of the Ottoman Empire, and from North Africa.[21] Among them were, on the one hand, distinguished scholars and wealthy individuals, and, on the other, simple men and women.[22]

Immigration to Erez Israel, unlike the major wave of Jewish emigration to the West in the nineteenth century, was driven primarily by religious and ideological motives, though there were also groups of Jews from Eastern countries who came to escape persecution.[23] A new motive was added to these traditional ones in the nineteenth century. Some eastern European Jews decided to flee from the *Haskalah* — the movement of secular Enlightenment in European Jewry, which they perceived as a threat to the traditional way of life — by immigrating to the Holy Land and creating there a Utopian society that would preserve what they believed to be true Judaism.[24] Besides those who came to the country for religious reasons, members of the lower classes also came in large numbers, hoping to benefit from the abundant charitable funds sent to Zion from all parts of the world.[25] These representatives of the lower rungs on the social ladder were not welcomed by other immigrants, who aimed to create a social elite in their new country.[26]

There were also various personal reasons for immigration, such as the hope to find a partner in marriage, fulfillment of a vow made on the occasion of some sickness or tragedy,[27] or the desire to escape troubled conditions in the home or the environment.[28] Such circumstances had provided the impetus for immigration for centuries, and the improved conditions of transport and enhanced security in the nineteenth century made it possible.

Unlike most emigrant societies, which are generally made up of a majority of unmarried men,[29] a typical feature of Jewish immigration toward the end of the nineteenth century and at the turn of the twentieth century, both to the West and to Erez Israel, was immigration of whole families.[30] However, in the wave of emigration to the United States, for example, it was the men who went there first alone, in order to earn enough money to bring over their families; in such cases, immigration involved separation from one's family, sometimes for several years.[31] In contrast, men who came to Erez Israel generally came with their families. Another special feature of Jewish immigration was the relatively high average age of the immigrants. Moreover, there were also a good number of women who came alone, mostly widows — a unique aspect of immigration to the Holy Land. According to Montefiore's censuses, the number of adult Jewish women was considerably larger than that of adult men.[32] Thus immigration to Erez Israel had a definite gender aspect.

The Old Yishuv: The Holy Community

The designation "Old Yishuv" for the Jewish communities in the four holy cities of Jerusalem, Hebron, Tiberias, and Safed is highly misleading. The Old Yishuv, which experienced accelerated growth from the 1840s up until the outbreak of World War I, was composed mainly of relative newcomers to the country. Immigration was indeed the formative experience of the Jewish community.[33] In the nineteenth century, Jerusalem was the major demographic center of the Jews of the Holy Land. The growth of the Jerusalem community also had a significant effect on the communal makeup of that community. At the beginning of the nineteenth century the small Jewish community had consisted almost entirely of the old Sephardic families,[34] but by the end of that century the Ashkenazim were the dominant group. Up to the 1880s most of the Ashkenazi community were Hasidim, but from that time on the *mitnagdim* (the opponents of the Hasidic movement) or, as they were called in Jerusalem, the *Perushim*, gained the upper hand.[35]

By the last years of the Ottoman period, Jerusalem was the largest city in Erez Israel. In 1840 its population had numbered only about 13,000, of whom 5,500 were Jews.[36] By 1914 the population had reached 70,000, more than half of whom — 47,000 — were Jews.[37] Demographic growth was not the only factor that made its mark in Jerusalem. As a city hallowed by the three monotheistic faiths, Jerusalem was a destination for religious emissaries and political representatives from many other countries. Jerusalem under Muhammad Ali, the Egyptian ruler who extended his rule over Palestine and Syria from 1832 to 1840, was more open to foreigners and foreign influence, and this openness, which was further reinforced by legal reforms (known as the Tanzimat),[38] promoted the development of the city as a lively religious and political center. In the second half of the nineteenth century, the Old City walls no longer constituted an obstacle, and construction began to take place outside the walls on a massive scale. On the eve of World War I, there were more people living outside the Old City than inside it. The many new buildings springing up in the New City presented architectural features drawn from a profusion of cultures — western and eastern Europe, Ethiopia, and of course Mediterranean, creating a fascinating and unique cultural mosaic.

The Jewish community — the largest religious community in the city — was divided into various congregations and *kolelim* (groups of people originating in the same European country or district, organized in order to distribute the funds collected in their countries of origin) and constituted a highly diverse society. Immigrants arrived from a great number of Diaspora countries: those of eastern and western Europe, the United States (*"Di goldene medine"*), the Ottoman Empire, North Africa, and even far-off Persia (Iran) and Buchara.[39] The foreign consuls who created a presence in Jerusalem beginning in the mid–nineteenth century provided welcome support for the Ashkenazi community, most of whose members retained their foreign citizenship,[40] while most of the Sephardim, as Ottoman citizens, were recognized as a *millet* (religious community).[41] Each community observed its own customs and looked up to its own rabbis, though only the rabbi of the Ottoman Sephardic community, the *hakham bashi* or *rishon leziyon*, was recognized by the authorities.

The Jews did not sever their ties with their countries of origin. Neither did all the Jews in Erez Israel speak the same language: the Ashkenazim, who had come from eastern Europe, adhered to Yiddish, while the Sephardim spoke Ladino or Arabic, depending on their origins. The cosmopolitan city of Jerusalem was a suitable arena for preservation of one's original practices. As expressed by Avraham Moshe Lifshitz, a teacher and scholar who came to the Holy City from Galicia just before World War I: "The communities of the Old Yishuv are like a great museum of living types from all corners of the Diaspora."[42] Reliance on foreign powers and on contributions sent from the Diaspora reinforced the immigrants' identification and contacts with the countries they had left. The immigrants, speaking different tongues, dressing differently, and affecting different customs, seemed to have little in common; on the face of it, the Jewish community of Jerusalem in the twilight of the Ottoman period was a mosaic of smaller communities, by no means a melting pot.[43] Nevertheless, there was a profound awareness of a special character,[44] which the Jews of Jerusalem tried to express through special ordinances.

One aspect of the special character was economic, namely, the almost exclusive reliance of the Jewish community on the *halukah*—the monetary contributions sent by Jews from all over the world to be distributed among their brethren in the Holy Land. The Old Yishuv, which subsisted on charity, considered itself an elite society with a special mission, a community that was holy by virtue of where and how it lived. "Acceptance of *halukah* funds was not seen as shameful in the Old Yishuv; they were theirs by right, not as charity—this psychology was a basic characteristic of the Old Yishuv."[45]

The various communities formulated various agreements as to the distribution of the funds that came in from all parts of the Jewish world. The distribution was not egalitarian, but preserved both the different ethnic identities and the ideologies of the immigrant groups. The Ashkenazim recognized the right of all their community members to receive *halukah* monies, since in their view any Jew living in the Holy Land was a representative of the entire nation, who had decided to devote his or her life to serving God. The Sephardim, however, distinguished between scholars and other members of the community, ruling that only people who had dedicated their lives to Torah study, or the destitute, were entitled to financial support. Women did not receive the added benefits due to scholars; they received *halukah* money in keeping with their family status and their husband's standing.[46]

The 1880s witnessed an increase in the flow of immigrants to Erez Israel, which now included, besides Jews who had set their sights on Jerusalem and the other holy cities, groups and individuals known as Hovevei Zion (Lovers of Zion)—the earliest advocates of the idea of returning the Jews to the Land of Israel. This new category of immigrants aimed to establish agricultural settlements and sustain themselves by the sweat of their brows. It was they, known collectively as the "New Yishuv," who coined the designation "Old Yishuv" for their predecessors, whom they considered as antagonists.[47] In their view, the "old-timers" were worthless idlers, bent on nothing but worship. The newcomers did not head primarily for Jerusalem and the other holy cities, but saw agricultural settlement as the supreme ideal of Jewish presence in Erez Israel. Few of them, therefore, settled among the people of the Old Yishuv in Jerusalem. The most prominent of them were educators and physicians, who added a new element to the diverse human mosaic of the city and tried to spread their views among the Jews of Jerusalem. Some of them, taking up as it were an intermediate position, were *maskilim* (proponents of the

Haskalah movement) but nevertheless observant Jews who recognized the importance of secular studies and Western culture in general.

Living conditions in Ottoman Palestine were particularly difficult. The *halukah* funds were insufficient for the many needs, and there was widespread poverty in Jerusalem. In addition, sanitary conditions were poor and medical institutions backward.[48] A shocking example of the methods of medical treatment common in the Holy City was reported in the Jerusalem newspaper *Hazevi* in 1900. A young pregnant woman died of smallpox, "but the fetus was still [alive] inside her. According to the custom here, it was necessary to kill the fetus. So the old women took a broom and struck the dead woman's belly many times, until they felt that the unborn baby was also dead."[49] It appears from the report that the woman had not died in a hospital and that the authorities took no interest, since the body was in the hands of "old women," associated with the *hevrah kadisha* (burial society); beating the woman's body with a broom was apparently the traditional, accepted practice. That the incident was reported together with an appeal to Jewish doctors to come to the rescue attests to some awareness of the need to modernize medical practices in the Holy City. Only on the eve of World War I did the situation improve,[50] expressing itself among other things in the natural demographic growth of the Jewish community in Jerusalem.

To go back to the Old Yishuv: As already indicated, the main instruments at the Jews' disposal in order to achieve religious and spiritual merit in the ancestral homeland were Torah study and communal prayer, as indeed recognized by Jews in all parts of the world. Reliance on the *halukah* was seen as a necessity in the existing circumstances, an economic mainstay that allowed male society to devote itself entirely to study. In a sense, the Old Yishuv maintained a paradoxical existence. On the one hand, it considered itself an intellectual elite, representative as it were of the Jewish nation, studying Torah and "guarding the walls of Jerusalem." On the other, it was a society in constant need, dependent on financial contributions from all corners of the Jewish world. Lofty spiritual aspirations, combined with constant reliance on charitable funds, created extreme intrasocietal tensions. Moshe Smilanski, a prominent author and publicist of the New Yishuv, writes of the disappointment this society caused its supporters: "Why does Erez Israel not supply the Diaspora with excellent rabbis? . . . We had hoped that Erez Israel would surely become a spiritual center for us!"[51] And he goes on, in despair: "It is not the curse of God that rests upon us . . . but the curse of the support . . . and wherever there is support, there is no natural life, and wherever there is no natural life, there is nothing." Menahem Friedman, who has made an extensive study of contemporary ultra-Orthodox society, refers to the same dilemma: "Was the very attempt to establish an entire society as a society withdrawing from the secular world, its economic sustenance completely dependent on another society, not an inner contradiction, which paradoxically created a preoccupation with physical needs and an increase in inner tension . . . ?"[52]

Aims of This Study and Methodological Questions

My voyage to the world of women in Jerusalem's Old Yishuv was essentially a voyage into the unknown. Chava Weissler, who has been studying the religiosity of Ashkenazi woman in Europe for more than a decade, confesses that, consciously or otherwise, she tried to glorify female religiosity and uncover its inherent cultural wealth.[53] Consciously, at least, I had no such goal. As a historian of modern Jewish settlement in Erez Israel, I saw my task to unveil a reality that has been almost completely ignored in historical research: women and gender in the Jewish community of Jerusalem in the nineteenth century. The Museum of the Old Yishuv Court in the Jewish Quarter of the Old City of Jerusalem offers rare museological evidence to the very presence of women in the Jerusalem Old Yishuv. However, even that evidence — a birthing mother's bed, handmade embroidery depicting the holy places, and photographs of women crowding together at the foot of the Western Wall or selling homemade baked products — is hardly indicative of the complex reality that I discovered in the course of my travels in those unknown parts.

Paraphrasing Billie Melman's assertion, "The colonial enterprise was regarded as *ipso facto* masculine,"[54] one might say that the life of the Old Yishuv in Erez Israel was considered wholly male. Jerusalem, like the Orient in general, has been pictured as a domain of masculinity. Life in the Holy Land was seen as a realization of imperatives directed exclusively at Jewish men: to study the Torah day and night, to engage in communal prayer at the holy places. This exclusion of women from the ultimate ideals of Judaism raises several questions. What was the nature of female existence in Jerusalem? Were women supposed to define male existence by their very absence? Perhaps one might say that the benediction pronounced daily by men, "Blessed be He . . . Who did not make me a woman," has always been a definition of Jewish masculinity, while the parallel benediction for woman, "Blessed be He . . . Who made me according to His will," implies that femininity is essentially defined as the lack of any intrinsic identity.[55]

The goal of this study is to reconstruct female existence in a male environment, as far as possible. Once women's lifestyles have been revealed, it transpires that women not only defined male society by their very essence but also shaped their own reality, thereby contributing to the shaping of society as a whole. While my attention will center on female society, I will not entirely ignore male society but will try to examine, in depth, the relationships be-

tween men and women and, even more, to determine the role of gender relations in the shaping of the Jewish community of Jerusalem.[56] Among the
subjects dealt with will be women's immigration experience and modes of expression of the female religious experience; the life cycle, including in particular marriage and the creation of the family unit, the female and universal
foundation experience; women's economic and philanthropic activity and
their incursions into public life; women's scholarship and the development of
modern education for girls in Erez Israel; social problems, some of which are
specific to women — widowhood, poverty, desertion (*aginut*), prostitution, religious conversion. I shall try to point out the social phenomena most common in the mid–nineteenth century and the changes that took place, mainly
toward the end of the period of this study.

My eagerness to research these subjects in all their ramifications came up,
at times, against a blank wall — the silence, or even absence, of documentation. Such areas as intimate relations between husband and wife, family violence, and birth of children outside the family framework are almost never
mentioned. The only possible conclusion is that the society under study re-
coiled from public discussion of sexuality and violence; the very silence of the
documents implies unwillingness to deal with such matters. Nevertheless,
those highly diverse topics that I have been able to study offer new points of
view and imply social insights that have as yet received no scholarly attention.
The experience of women immigrants throws new light on the religious experience of ordinary Jews, of "men who are like women."[57] My objective was
to draw a kaleidoscopic picture, enriched by authentic voices, that represents
the female reality of Jewish Jerusalem and through that medium illuminates
social reality as a whole. Given the unique features of the Jews living in the
Holy Land, it was my goal to study how their "holy life" shaped the lifestyles
of both women and men. The result has been a scholarly and literary representation of the lives of women in the Jewish community of Jerusalem.

The first task, the underpinning of the entire structure, was to assemble
documentation. It is a commonplace that women in traditional society are absent not only in research but also in documentation. Given my original assumption that their voice had been silenced for all time, the results of my
search were unexpectedly impressive.[58] Women's voices have been preserved
in a variety of documents: pamphlets written by three learned women in Yiddish; a fascinating travel journal translated from the Italian; travel literature
written by female tourists, Jewish and non-Jewish; memoirs;[59] stories based on
childhood memories; newspaper articles; letters to relatives and to philanthropists all over the world. This material, scattered in libraries and archives
both in Israel and in Europe, helped me listen to the female voice, to the beating of women's hearts and to the silences. The various documents revealed

the writers' innermost thoughts, sometimes showing how they accepted and internalized the male worldview. In keeping with feminist literary theory, I have examined women's writings with an attentive ear to the discourse of the double voice: the male voice that the writers had appropriated and the female voice that expressed their world, sometimes out of the very silence.[60] The many passages that I quote reveal the essence of that female voice, as interpreted by myself, a resident of Jerusalem at the turn of the twentieth century.

Putting together this collection of women's voices was indeed an adventure, but most women of the Old Yishuv in Jerusalem were illiterate, and I therefore searched for echoes of their voices in men's stories. Men also wrote diaries, memoirs, travel journals, stories, newspaper articles, letters to relatives and philanthropists, but the male voice is immeasurably more varied than the female one. Among the documents I used were also various regulations (*takanot*), books of Halakhic responsa, studies written by contemporaries, posters, poems, deeds, *ketubot* (marriage contracts), and even epitaphs on tombstones. The sources were written both by Jews resident in Jerusalem and by visitors — Jewish and non-Jewish tourists who documented women's lives in the Holy City.

The male voice documents women's lives and at the same time reflects male society's attitude to women. My intention was to glean from such sources both an idea of the reality and an indication of how women were seen by men. I have also tried to determine whether the reality implicit in female documentation differs from that reflected in male documentation, and to what extent the female world had internalized the male point of view. The more I continued to explore libraries and archives, the more I realized that the material is so abundant and varied that it is virtually impossible to reach each and every source. In some of the subjects treated, my discussion essentially paints a preliminary picture of the situation, which will surely have to be reexamined and refined by others.

Besides primary sources, I have of course drawn on scholarly publications concerning the ideological, demographical, organizational, legal, social, economic, and geographic aspects of the Old Yishuv in Jerusalem.[61] Various studies stress the highly variegated nature of that community, characterized as it was by considerable ethnic diversity. Immigration to Erez Israel involved cutting oneself off from one's home community, while at the same time transposing its way of life to the Holy City. I have tried to paint a precise picture of the two dominant communities in Jewish Jerusalem: Ashkenazim and Sephardim, on the one hand pointing out their common features, while on the other stressing their more distinctive qualities. In other words, my object has been to trace both the general outline and the distinguishing colors and nuances. I have not always succeeded in painting a sufficiently multicolored picture. The information was sometimes too fragmentary and inadequate to ensure statistical confirmation of some of my evaluations and conclusions.

The fields of research that I have engaged, some of which have been ignored in the historiography of the Old Yishuv, were new and fascinating for me: pilgrimage and tourism, folklore, anthropology, history of costume, study of family life, and so on. My desire to determine the extent to which various phenomena were unique to the Old Yishuv or common to traditional societies everywhere induced me to exercise particular caution. To enhance my understanding of the findings, I also used sources relating to the other holy cities—Hebron, Tiberias, and Safed—and read studies of different Jewish communities in the Ottoman Empire, as well as some studies focusing on earlier periods. Such comparisons, I trust, have helped me pinpoint the more characteristic aspects of the society I have been studying.

I have been much concerned with the methodological question of how to create the proper balance between the desire "to tell the story" and the need to place the findings in a proper theoretical framework. Peter Burke has written at length of the confrontation between narrative and theory in historiographical writing. In his view, one has to consider both sides of the equation: to immerse oneself in the flow of events, while at the same time examining them carefully and critically,[62] in other words, to "thicken the narrative" so as to encompass the theory as well. This approach is also advocated by Billie Melman, who holds that research will profit from a combination of such traditional and new attitudes.[63] Historical writing is not a mirror of reality, but an attempt to present and analyze that reality—in light of the voices and colors presented by the documentation, and the insights of an observant researcher.

Chapter 1

The Female Experience of Immigration

OUR QUEST FOR the nature of the female experience of immigration, as distinct from the male experience, was virtually exploration of an "unknown land." It was necessary to study the formation of the sacred experience in Erez Israel through channels that have generally been considered of secondary importance. An understanding of the unique experience of Jewish women immigrating to the Holy Land may help one to understand the very meaning of sanctity in Jewish society, through channels other than Torah study and communal prayer. Such "female" channels are not those of the social elite but the more popular ones. The female experience is not exclusively that of women; it is also largely the experience that shapes family life and makes an imprint on the education of the younger generation, the experience of men who lack intellectual ability, and in fact of the common person in general, of most people.[1] Examination of the female immigration experience is thus also an attempt to redefine Jewish religious experience as a whole.

Male Initiative: Immigration as Breakup or Unification of the Family

Immigration to Erez Israel toward the end of the Ottoman period ran counter to the central direction of Jewish migration, and was also exceptional from a family and human standpoint. Aviezer Ravitzky, discussing the ambivalent attitude to the Holy Land in Jewish sources, speaks of it as a land arousing both love and awe, even fear. Paradoxically, what was ostensibly the Jewish homeland instilled a sensation of exile in those whose immigration cut them off from their families.[2] When a woman immigrated to Erez Israel, she was essentially abandoning those under her care; the family home, which was also the central religious space of the Jewish woman, was replaced by the national home — the Holy Land.

The first price that immigrants, both men and woman, had to pay was separation from their childhood world, from parents, brothers, and extended family members in general. Though many of the immigrants brought their close families with them, the immigration experience was first and foremost one of separation; it was therefore difficult, even traumatic. As a rule, it was the man who initiated the bold step of immigration, notifying his family of the impending change as a fait accompli. This is aptly illustrated by the story of Judah Aaron Weiss:

One day, after a sermon about the Torah and Erez Israel, he [the father, Naftali Hertz] told my mother of the vow he had taken many years ago, to immigrate to Erez Israel . . . And after father had revealed his decision that I, too, should accompany him on his long journey, the words struck her like a heavy blow.[3]

The father, in a spiritual world of his own, had vowed to go to the Holy Land but had not shared his thoughts with his wife. She heard of his decision with no prior warning and, stunned as she might be, had no choice but to agree. Without suitable spiritual preparation, the enforced separation was immeasurably more difficult.

Rachel Yellin's grandmother had come to the Holy Land with her husband; when she first realized that she had been, as it were, exiled from her family in Lomza she asked herself: "What was she doing here, whom did she have here, having abandoned her family . . . and exiled herself to a wasteland . . . For what sin had she sentenced herself to exile?"[4] Such grieving voices are clearly heard in immigration stories describing how married women were separated from their parents[5] or parents from their children. Toive Pesil Feinstein, in her pamphlet *Sefer zikhron Eliyahu*, wrote of her pain at realizing she would never lead her children to the wedding canopy and, conversely, they would not accompany her bier when she passed away.[6] Parents' duties toward their children and children's obligations to their parents were brushed aside by immigration. Toive Pesil's entreaty not to be forgotten indicates the anguish of separation; as she wrote, "The pain of the spirit exceeds the pain of the body."[7]

An echo of the breach in one's family and soul caused by immigration may be discerned in the letters written by Syla Bergman, who came to the Holy Land in 1935 from Germany with her husband and children.[8] She describes the sorrow of parting at length: "I could shed many glassfuls of tears upon remembering our very difficult parting."[9] Her husband, Eliezer, had initiated the family's immigration, and Syla, like other wives, agreed. But even in Jerusalem — a city in which, as she wrote, it was "a great privilege" to live — she continued to refer to the town of her birth in Germany as "home."[10] The question of whether women agreed to immigrate out of obedience to their husbands or yearning for the Holy Land remains unanswered.

The wife's complete internalization of her husband's desire to immigrate is also obvious in the autobiography of a Jerusalem banker named Hayim Hamburger. His grandfather, he writes, was incensed by the reforms instituted in Pressburg in 1857 and, in a fit of rage, told his wife:

I have decided to travel to Erez Israel with our sons and daughters. Here a generation of ignorant people is growing up, throwing off the yoke of Judaism; while there in Erez Israel the air is holy and we shall rear a generation who know the Lord.[11]

The woman agreed to join her husband, and her answer, "Wherever you go, I will go" (Ruth 1:16), presents her as an embodiment of Ruth, great-grandmother of King David. The way the decision to immigrate was reached is a reflection of gender relations in the family: the husband makes all decisions, but the wife's needs are not even mentioned, let alone taken into consideration.

Rabbi Isaac Yeruham Diskin immigrated to Erez Israel in 1908 to head the orphanage that his father had founded in Jerusalem. His wife, Yente, accompanied him, as we are told: "She willingly abandoned her children, grandchildren, family and all her possessions and agreed to immigrate to the Holy Land, so that here, too, she would be able to help and support her learned husband in discharging his task."[12] This writer, too, agreed that the wife, by coming with her husband to the Holy Land, was abandoning her own world in the Diaspora for that of her husband in his chosen home.

However, following in the husband's footsteps was not the only model of women's immigration. Special circumstances brought some women, sometimes specifically in order to preserve the family unit, to come on their own initiative, or to agree wholeheartedly. "Sarah Beyla Hirshensohn harbored the unvoiced hope that, thanks to the merit of the Holy Land, she would be blessed with children."[13] However, the Hirshensohns' immigration was postponed for fear of the dangers of travel. "Days and years passed, and the children born to them in that time did not live long; they attributed this to the sin of delaying their journey."[14] Their children's death tipped the scales, and they set out for Erez Israel. The journey lasted a whole year (they reached Safed in 1847). Thus, the sanctity of the Land was seen not only as a vehicle of spiritual perfection but also as a means to guarantee the birth of children and build one's family.

This belief in the magical power of Erez Israel was not confined to Jews alone. The Spaffords, a Christian family whose children had died in a marine disaster off the shores of the United States, came to the Holy Land in 1881 in the hope that "perhaps the sojourn to Jerusalem and the Holy Land would help [them find solace]."[15] Paradoxically, living in Jerusalem, a city in which, in the nineteenth century, natural growth showed a negative balance, where child mortality was rife, was considered a means toward achieving life. Earthly Jerusalem presented a challenge to heavenly Jerusalem.

Life in Zion was fraught with danger. New immigrants were warned by Rabbi Moshe Nehemiah Kahanov, a Jerusalem rabbi with a secular education, in a propaganda tract he wrote in 1867 about settling in Erez Israel. The potential immigrant, he wrote, should weigh matters carefully before setting out, lest he or she later regret the decision.[16] Sometimes, indeed, the journey did not yield the expected results. Reitze, wife of Rabbi Zelig of Slonim, came to the Holy Land with her husband in 1867. In a pamphlet titled *Sefer mishpahat yuhasin*, she wrote that, before immigrating, she had given birth to four sons and three daughters, all of whom had died. This personal tragedy moved her to immigrate to Erez Israel: "I thought that perhaps I would have children there and that the Lord would have mercy upon me, but that was not to be."[17]

Immigration to Erez Israel, life there, and prayer in the holy places were thought to guarantee not only childbirth but also secure lives in the Diaspora. Rivkah Lipa Anikster, the first woman in Jerusalem to author a printed work, wrote that after her seven small children had died in Lithuania, she was concerned for the health of the survivors and hoped that if she immigrated together with her husband their lives would be spared, "and because of those troubles we were privileged to come here."[18] Her surviving children, though still minors, stayed behind in the Diaspora, and she wrote with profound sorrow of being separated from them (see also below).

Marion Kaplan has analyzed Jewish women's feelings about leaving Nazi Germany in the 1930s, emphasizing that, in the circumstances that had evolved there, women were quicker to opt for emigration than men. Her analysis seems to imply that women identified primarily with their families, whose security they placed above any other consideration.[19] Female immigrants' identification with their families was generally more important to them than their religious identity. However, when convinced that continued existence of the core family depended on immigration, they would leave their extended families.

Anthropologists Victor and Edith Turner have defined pilgrimage as a reaction to secularization.[20] This particular motivation for immigration to Erez Israel first came to the fore in the nineteenth century, when some traditional Jews, concerned by the increasing secularization of European Jewish society, saw immigration as the only way to ensure their spiritual well-being. Education in the Holy Land, they believed, would keep children safe in the bosom of their families and tradition and protect them from the *Haskalah* [Enlightenment] movement or secularization. Khina, mother of Avraham Moshe Luncz — one of the first Jews who made a scientific study of Jerusalem — vowed upon his birth to bring him to Erez Israel when he reached the age of thirteen, so as to ensure his health and keep him away from the *Haskalah*. His father, apprehensive of the dangers of travel, objected. Khina would not give up, and she set out without her husband, but the hardships along the way forced her to return home. After further entreaties, her husband relented, and the whole family left again for the Holy Land, this time reaching their destination.[21] Concern for her sons' education was also the main motive behind the immigration to Erez Israel of Shayna Rivkah Shaikowitz, a well-educated widow with some knowledge of Hebrew, who reached Palestine in 1857, believing that to be the best step for her small children.[22] The same was true of Freha Abukasir of Morocco, who came to the Holy Land in 1872 with her husband and two children.[23] Concern for spiritual welfare was no less important than concern for continued physical well-being.

These were the motives that promoted a thin trickle of immigration. For most Jews, life in the Diaspora was a permanent state of affairs; only a small minority saw in immigration to the Holy Land a way to preserve the family. Rabbi Yaakov Berlin, father of Rabbi Naftali Zvi Berlin (known as the "Neziv of Volozhin"), compared immigration to Erez Israel with a return to the "real" mother's bosom; as he wrote: "The Holy Land . . . shall be called 'mother.'"[24] In this way Rabbi Yaakov somewhat mitigated the pain of separation.

A woman's refusal to immigrate together with her husband raised weighty Halakhic questions, which throw light on the attitude of the rabbinical establishment toward women, on the one hand, and immigration, on the other. Halakhic tradition considers the love of Erez Israel to take precedence over love for one's wife. Accordingly, a man is entitled to divorce his wife without paying her *ketubah* (payment due a woman from her husband's estate upon being divorced or widowed), or to marry a second wife, if she refuses to immigrate to the Holy Land with him.[25]

Sometimes a woman's parents could not bear the anguish of parting and tried to prevent her immigration, even at the cost of divorce. While some women would nevertheless decide to accompany their husbands,[26] others preferred their parents and were indeed divorced as a result.[27] Judging from rabbinical responsa written in the nineteenth century, rabbis differed as to whether a husband could compel his wife to accompany him to Erez Israel. Rabbi Shlomo Kluger, one of the most prominent Halakhic authorities of the time, ruled that "if a person married a woman, it is his duty to live with her wherever she lives," implying that, since it was not accepted practice for men to immigrate, it was not justified to force a woman to do so.[28] Through the generations rabbis wavered between religious commitment to immigration, on the one hand, and pragmatic considerations such as contemporary conditions and the psychological effect of immigration on the family, on the other.[29] It would appear that, since most of the rabbis to whom such questions were addressed did not come to the Holy Land, they did not consider immigration as an immediate religious imperative. Their refusal to make divorce mandatory in such cases may attest more to an ambiguous attitude to immigration than to consideration of the needs of women who refused to immigrate.

Despite the increasing number of immigrants to Erez Israel in the nineteenth century, immigration was nevertheless far from common. Immigration of several families was a reasonable solution to the problem of separation, but only a few such large groups set out to become part of the Old Yishuv in the Land.[30] Large groups of students of the Vilna Gaon[31] and of Hasidim came to the country at the beginning of the nineteenth century in organized convoys,[32] perhaps inspiring Eliezer Bergman to try to organize a convoy of his own (though he failed).[33] In 1844, a caravan of some seventy people left the Moroccan city of Meknes for the Holy Land.[34] Jews from Georgia and Buchara also organized groups of immigrants to Jerusalem, in the second half of the nineteenth century,[35] as did a group of rabbis from Salonika.[36] The basic unit most common in immigration was the primary family cell: husband, wife, and small children, paying their own way.[37] On rare occasions, elderly parents joined their married children, or, alternatively, married sons or daughters came to the Holy Land to assist their parents.

The immigrant to the Holy Land, the spiritual home of the Jewish people, was essentially cut off from his or her physical home. The person not infrequently affected was the housewife, concerned as she was with the material aspect of family life. Given the demanding, harsh conditions of everyday life in Erez Israel, women at times became victims on the altar of their husband's spiritual life or on the altar of their children's future life.

Female Initiative: Immigration as a Quasi-monastic Experience

Tehilla, the heroine of a famous story by Nobel prizewinner S. Y. Agnon, is probably the most famous widow to immigrate alone to the Holy City: "[S]he is a saint, a saint plain and simple . . . [S]he was very rich indeed and conducted big affairs, but finally her sons died and her husband died and she went and abandoned all her affairs and came up to Jerusalem."[38] Tehilla, an archetype for women living alone in Jerusalem, a widow whose children had died in her lifetime, longing for a life of spirituality and good deeds, hoped to achieve her goal by living in Jerusalem, near the holy places. This widow, and others, were perhaps eager to forget their personal tragedies by exchanging their broken individual homes for the national home in Erez Israel.

It was a time-honored custom for elderly men and women to come to the Holy Land to be buried there; this was perceived as one way of achieving religious perfection.[39] Glückel of Hamelin (1635–1724), a Jewish widow of Germany who wrote a celebrated book of memoirs, aptly expressed the female desire to immigrate to Erez Israel: "I should have forsaken the vanity of this world and with the little left, gone to the Holy Land and lived there, a true daughter of Israel."[40] Glückel was here expressing the idea that a good, genuine life could be lived only in the Land of Israel. Anthropologist Susan Sered has confirmed the intensification in old age of the female desire for religious expression.[41]

Documentation from the sixteenth century onward indicates that there were more elderly women than men in the Holy Land.[42] The immigration of Jewish women to Erez Israel, which was a common phenomenon from that time on, is apparently unique in the history of emigration. Demographer and statistician Uziel Schmelz has summarized the information gleaned from various nineteenth-century censuses: "49 percent of all Jewish [adult[43]] women [in Jerusalem] in 1839 and 36 percent in 1866 were widows . . . There was a considerable excess of women over men in the adult population [of Jerusalem]."[44] According to Schmelz's calculations, based on a 1905 estimate, the number of Jewish women aged sixty and above was twice that of Jewish men in the parallel age group.[45] Schmelz attributes this to two factors: (i) widows immigrating to Jerusalem for religious reasons; (ii) male mortality (owing to the higher age of husbands compared with that of their wives, and women's longer life expectation). Toward the end of the nineteenth century there was a decline in the number of widows.[46] Besides these estimates, tombstones in the Mount of Olives cemetery provide ample evidence of single women, generally widows, who came to the country to spend the last years of their lives.[47] From the available evidence it is difficult to infer the proportion of widows who had been widowed prior to their immigration, but it was probably more than 7 percent of the total.[48] The large number of elderly women who immigrated to Erez Israel provides incontrovertible evidence, not only of the profound spiritual link they felt with the Land, but also of a uniquely female mode of participation in religious life.[49]

Only when a woman was widowed did she achieve freedom to fulfill any spiritual ambitions that she might have. In traditional Jewish society, widows were in a sense better off than daughters or wives, whose lives were entirely controlled by men — whether fathers or husbands.[50] A woman's primary commitment in traditional society was to her parents, her husband, and her children. Only when she had grown old, her parents and husband had died, and her children had grown to adulthood was she allowed to live out the rest of her life as she herself wished. Widowhood had a direct effect on women's status and sometimes even on their living conditions. It not infrequently implied the widows' moving from their own homes to those of their married sons or daughters, hence the need to change their living quarters. Could this possibly have been a catalyst for the decision to immigrate?[51] Since Jewish women were excluded from communal religious life, from communal prayer and Torah study, a Jewish widow, in her now empty home — the major site of religious observance within the family — was more or less faced with a religious-spiritual vacuum,[52] at the very stage of her life when the desire for religious fulfillment became stronger. Immigration to the Holy Land could fill the gap. Wealthy women who wanted to come to Erez Israel could do so independently, while poorer women could rely on organized support by the Jews of the Holy Land. Living in the Holy Land was an exhilarating religious experience, as Reitze of Slonim wrote in her pamphlet: "For when I traveled away from this Holy City . . . , I saw that one could neither flee nor hide from the Lord, whose glory fills the whole earth."[53]

Jewish old women were not the only ones who came alone to the Holy Land. Thousands of elderly Russian Christian women traveled to the country in the second half of the nineteenth century. Pilgrimage to the Holy Land provided these women, who were mostly abysmally poor and ignorant,[54] with the most important religious experience of their lives. In addition, many Christian women came to the Near East in general, and to Erez Israel in particular, in the nineteenth century. They saw a visit to the Holy Land, where Jesus had been born, as a kind of rereading of the Bible and an uplifting spiritual experience.[55] Similarly, pilgrimages by Catholic men and women from Austria have been explained as following in Jesus' footsteps and as achieving a spiritual experience of atonement; this experience would accompany the pilgrims in their minds as long as they were alive.[56] However, as against Christian women, who came as tourists for a limited time, the Jewish widows (who came alone, as individuals) settled in the country, intending to be buried there when their time came. For them, immigration was a journey that would end in the World to Come.

There is much evidence that widows' immigration was particularly common among women from the Balkans.[57] The spiritual conception of Erez Israel as a place where one could withdraw from the vanities of the physical world, where national redemption was bound up with personal salvation, may be found in the writings of Rabbi Eliezer Pappo, who lived in Bosnia in the nineteenth century.[58] Was he expressing moods that came to realization in the immigration of widows? We find numerous indications of special appreciation for women's attraction to the Holy Land, which exceed that of men. For example, we know of a group of women who had immigrated from Izmir together with their husbands but subsequently returned to their previous homes; however, once the husbands had died and been buried in the Diaspora, their widows immigrated again to Erez Israel, by themselves, to be buried there.[59] From an account of Izmir in the 1880s we learn that there was not one courtyard in that city from which some widow had not come to the Holy Land.[60] Another example of the particular desire of women to immigrate is that of the mother of the author of the responsa known as *Muzal me'esh*, who set out for the Land in her old age, apparently at the age of 110. An educated woman, who wanted to be sure to hear communal prayer in a quorum (*minyan*) even on the way to the Holy Land, she actually brought ten learned men and a Torah scroll with her on the journey.[61] Even at that advanced age, she was intent not only on coming to the realm of holiness but also on doing so in a state of sanctity. Jewish women who came alone from the Balkans were known in Ladino as *madrinas*, a word meaning particularly benevolent and caring women.[62]

European Jewish women were also among the lone immigrants, though in smaller numbers than their Sephardic sisters from the Ottoman Empire. They too, like Agnon's Tehilla, wanted to pray at the holy places and find their final rest in the hallowed ground of Erez Israel. Frume, wife of Rabbi Samuel of Kelm, who refused to immigrate together with her husband when at the prime of life, explained this as due to her refusal to live on charity; in her old age, however, she did immigrate, in fact against her doctors' advice.[63] Another remarkable story was told by the founder and first mayor of Ramat-Gan, Avraham Krinitzi, who came to Israel in 1905, about his grandmother Hadassah. After coming to the Holy Land on her own in the 1880s, she lived in Jerusalem, visited the holy places, and awaited her death. However, the separation from her family troubled her and, impatient at the long wait for death, she returned to her family. About thirteen years later, she suddenly felt that her end was near. Despite her children's entreaties, she again left her home, came back to Jerusalem — and died less than one month later.[64]

Widows who decided to immigrate were not always encouraged. Members of their communities in Europe were alarmed by such a bold enterprise. "The oppressed woman Sheyna Davis, widow of Rabbi Simhah b. David of London," in a letter she wrote requesting aid, related that when she had announced her intention to "approach the sanctuary," her disapproving relatives in London had tried to stop her, "but I, who have no children, decided to spend the rest of my days in the Holy [Land]."[65] One common reason for hesitating about setting out for Erez Israel was that it was impossible to estimate what capital would be necessary to maintain a widow until her death. Women thus set out on their own, responsible to no one but themselves and enjoying no support from their family members; in addition to profound religious sentiments, they were thus demonstrating spiritual power and independence.

Wealthier widows received a regular allowance from their families abroad and lived in well-appointed rooms, some even adopting "sons" from the Sephardic community who would care for their needs and mitigate their solitude; however, most of the *madrinas* were not rich, and they created a unique female (unisexual) community. They received some support from the Sephardic community. In 1875 the community established a hostel for such widows, known as Gevul Almanah (The Widows' Homestead). It comprised seventeen rooms, each room sometimes housing as many as seven women.[66] Poor Ashkenazic widows were housed in the basements of the Hurvah Synagogue, while richer ones found living quarters in the Batei Mahaseh Quarter;[67] women of the North African community, who were known for their poverty, lived in the *hekdesh* (endowed property) of the community or in a rented room.[68] The latter, like their Sephardic sisters, supported one another.[69] Sephardic folklore describes the relations among the widows as a form of kinship, almost a commune.[70] The *madrinas* and their associates also behaved charitably toward neighbors belonging to their community, helping them in the home with their families. North African Jewish families would generally "adopt" widows to mitigate their solitude, and encouraged them to work in numerous charitable institutions.[71]

The lifestyle of these women in the Holy Land largely embodied their religious ideals. Not content merely to live in the Land, they spent their time visiting the holy places at set times — a kind of immigration within immigration, or pilgrimage within pilgrimage (see below). On every *rosh hodesh* (the first day of the month in the Jewish calendar) they would gather by the Western Wall to hear the *moda'ah*.[72] The *moda'ah* (literally, announcement), written in Ladino, contained Maimonides' "Thirteen Principles of the Faith" and a description of the Day of Judgment. For these women, most of whom were illiterate, listening to the *moda'ah* being read out loud was a central religious experience: "They sat silently, their arms folded over their breasts, listening in awe and trepidation to the descriptions of the Day of Judgment and its gradual, inexorable approach."[73] These widows felt that such women's gatherings raised them to a higher spiritual plane, as if preparing them for the World to Come.

As Natalie Davis has written, examination of the characteristics of any religious culture gains breadth when compared with those of other religions.[74] The immigration of single Jewish women presents several highly significant characteristics: intensive preparation for the next world; abstention from family life and living instead in a kind of female community; devotion of one's life to a religious goal. Is the lifestyle of these women comparable to that of Christian nuns? Monastic life of women is indeed characterized by celibacy and devotion to divine service through prayer and charitable deeds,[75] qualities that, as we have pointed out, were also typical of the single female immigrants. One might perhaps view the harsh living conditions of the widows in Erez Israel as a parallel to the self-abnegation of nuns, who aim through such means to atone for their own ills and those of society at large. However, there is a major difference: the Jewish widows were all advanced in age, and it was only the last years of their lives that they wanted to devote to God.

The little evidence that exists of Jewish women who came to Erez Israel alone in their youthful years only bears out the unique quality of the widows. One of the more exceptional immigrants was the famed female *zaddik*, the "Maid of Ludmir," Hannah Rachel, who came to Erez Israel in the second half of the nineteenth century.[76] As far as we know, she had elected from her youth to live a celibate life and devote herself to the love of God. Married once and almost immediately divorced, she was a controversial figure: "Her love for the Holy Land exceeded all bounds."[77] Her immigration was, on the one hand, convenient for her community, which took exception to her behavior; on the other, it enabled her to express her religious experience as she wished, since "there in the Holy Land she would be able to worship God in her own way."[78]

Another young woman who came to Erez Israel, Flora Randegger, was also moved by religious feelings. As she traveled on her own from Trieste in 1856, her fellow passengers on board thought her a nun; and indeed she wrote in her diary, "I have withdrawn from the vanities of the world."[79]

Additional light on the phenomenon of what we have called quasi-monastic immigration comes from the case of a young woman who came to Jerusalem in the first half of the nineteenth century. This remarkable evidence of immigration as an act of withdrawal from the physical world in a quest for the spiritual comes from the recently discovered inscription on the tombstone of Malkah, daughter of Yizhak Babad of Brody. This woman, member of a distinguished family, was well known for her charitable acts. Although quite well off, she rejected her easy life in the Diaspora. "In her youth she spurned the joys of the world" and decided to immigrate to Erez Israel, to the "place of God's house" in Jerusalem. She arrived at some time in the first half of the nineteenth century, when travel was still extremely dangerous. Unlike the widows, who immigrated only after they had realized their femininity, young Malkah was apparently married only after she had returned from her pilgrimage.[80] Why did she return to her home town of Brody? The inscription on her stone alludes to the solution of the puzzle. Malkah had accomplished her goal — communion with God — but God had commanded her in a vision to return home. While she had immigrated on her own initiative, she returned under duress.[81]

Both acts, immigration and departure, figure in the inscription as praiseworthy expressions of obedience to God. Did the society in which Malkah was living disapprove of her immigration, though the latter was presented in a positive light? Perhaps the writers of the inscription believed that the proper place for a righteous young woman was the home; only "at the end of days would she face her destiny." Immigration to the Holy Land, as an act of withdrawal, was fit only for widows, nearing the end of their lives. Thus, Malkah

Babad's immigration and return to Brody were exceptional. The depiction of a ship, carved on the tombstone, is also extremely unusual in stones of Jewish women.

A similar quest for religious satisfaction, even at the cost of leaving one's family behind, is exemplified by the young Catholic women who left their homes in nineteenth-century Ireland to go to the United States. While it is true that emigration to America offered considerable economic advantages, the primary motive underlying these young women's emigration was religious. The girls, who had taken monastic vows, felt that God had called on them to spread His word, and that they would be able to live more satisfying lives in a new country than they could in Ireland.[82]

In sum, emigration in fulfillment of spiritual and religious aims was not unique to Jewish women in the nineteenth century. Nevertheless, immigration as a widow in old age was probably the sole opportunity available to a Jewish woman to dedicate the rest of her life to the fulfillment of her religious desires.

The Experience of Self-Sacrifice: Sanctification of Suffering

Syla Bergman, whose possessions were lost in a storm off the coast of Jaffa, described her situation as follows: "I have now lost everything that I possessed. I console myself . . . with the thought that I am in Jerusalem. For that is a great privilege . . . Nevertheless, I would not advise anyone not strong enough to attempt this: one must suffer a great deal."[83] This, in a nutshell, conveys the feminine experience in Jerusalem: a sensation of unavoidable suffering, to be endured as a sacrifice to God. Indeed, the word "sacrifice," which recurs again and again in women's immigration narratives, is cited in anthropological studies as one characteristic of pilgrimage.[84]

Flora Randegger, the young Italian-speaking Jewess mentioned previously, used the expression to describe her remarkable immigration: "God will remember our sacrifice, the willingness I have already shown twice to do something useful for our poor brethren in the Holy Land."[85] Sara Beyla Hirschensohn, according to her granddaughter's memoirs, had always dreamed secretly of going to the Holy Land, but her husband, who finally came in 1847, had been "reluctant to demand such a sacrifice from his wife."[86] Ita Yellin, daughter of Rabbi Yehiel Michel Pines and wife of the celebrated educator David Yellin, in her memoirs, described the difficulties experienced by her family when they immigrated to Erez Israel: they had been unable to take a Jewish maid with them to help them, for "no one could be found willing to make such a sacrifice and to travel."[87] Sheyna Davis of London, already mentioned above, described herself as a woman "who had offered up her old soul as a burnt-offering to the Lord, to approach the sanctuary."[88] The feeling that immigration to the Holy Land was in the nature of a sacrifice was common to women who immigrated unwillingly and to those who came of their own free will.

Men and women alike endured much affliction in the Land of Israel. Dr. Neumann, a Jewish physician active in Jerusalem in the second half of the nineteenth century, wrote: "No one who observes the life of the Jews of Jerusalem without prejudice . . . can deny that the motives that brought them there and their willingness to live lives of self-sacrifice are admirable."[89] Life in the Holy Land involved continual suffering; the attitude that it had to be endured as a real sacrifice or offering and thus contained a significant element of sanctity somehow made it easier to endure. Reitze, already mentioned previously, thanked God for her ability to bear her burden in silence: "It is enough for me that the good Lord endowed me with good sense so that I might quietly endure the hardships that have befallen me."[90]

A sensation of sacrifice also pervades Rivkah Lipa Anikster's pamphlet *Zekher Olam* (For Eternal Memory). This woman, who immigrated with her husband in 1862, indeed compared her immigration to Erez Israel to a sacrifice — no ordinary sacrifice, but comparable with Abraham's offering of Isaac on the altar: "You should know, my beloved children, that our journey to the Holy City of Jerusalem was very difficult, it was a test like the binding of the patriarch Isaac."[91] Rivkah Lipa was addressing her children, whom she had left behind in the conviction that her immigration to the Holy Land would grant them long life; she tried to explain to them how she had suffered since abandoning them. The story of the sacrifice of Isaac was thus being viewed in a feminized version, though it is not clear whether the "sacrifice" bound on the altar here was herself, distraught over leaving her children, or the abandoned children.

The perception of life in the Holy City as a sacrifice was more than a mere metaphor. Life in Jerusalem, with all its hardships (see below), not infrequently demanded the supreme price — life itself. Chronicles of Jewish life in Jerusalem refer to a good many cases of women murdered by Arab bandits. Syla Bergman, the immigrant who continued to refer to her hometown in Germany as "home," was murdered by Arabs in a dark lane, only a few years after coming to the country, and after some of her children had died of various diseases.[92] Pinehas Zvi Grayevsky, who lived in Jerusalem and studied its history, wrote an account of "our [six] sisters, sacred sacrifices, who were slaughtered, murdered, and killed on the altar of 'settlement in sanctity.'"[93] Hemdah Ben-Yehuda, Ben-Yehuda's second wife and sister of his first, also used the term "sacrifice" in reference to her sister's death, calling her "the wife of his youth, offered up as a sacrifice for him and for his idea."[94] The

women of the Old Yishuv were described as sacrifices to God, but Devorah
Ben-Yehuda was here called a sacrifice to her husband, or to the homeland.
The idea that both men and women in the Holy Land were sacrifices was
common to Old and New Yishuv alike.[95]

The idea of a woman's life as a means toward achievement of societal goals
is an integral part of society's perception of women and of women's self-
perception. While man is seen as fulfilling the basic purpose of creation, it is
woman who enables him to do so. However, immigration to Erez Israel
brought women to a higher spiritual level through suffering, which was interpreted as sacrifice and sometimes actually made the woman a sacrifice. In this
role, the woman was no longer a mere tool but was "promoted," as it were, to
the rank of a goal herself.

Identification with Jewish Historical Experience

When Sir Moses Montefiore made his sixth visit to Palestine, in 1866, he met
a young widow aged about twenty, with three infant children. Montefiore was
asked by well-wishers to help her and provide her with money to leave the
country, so that she could live close to her family in Germany. The widow,
however, whose name is not known, refused to accept his help and leave,
explaining her position as follows:

God has granted me the high privilege to breathe the hallowed atmosphere of the
land of our forefathers, Abraham, Isaac and Jacob. He has caused His grace and mercy
to descend upon me by bringing me, when an infant, unto this sacred spot . . . He has
permitted me to tread on that hallowed ground on which our prophets and our teachers lived . . . Am I now to leave it, and take my children away from Zion? . . . No; I
would rather starve together with my children, whilst kissing the dust in the Holy City
Jerusalem, than live in plenty elsewhere.[96]

The young widow's statement expresses profound identification with the historical past of the Jewish people, which was so palpably present everywhere
in Erez Israel. Unlike the expected figure of an ideal mother, who would
place her children's welfare above every other consideration, this Jerusalem
woman preferred to fulfill her spiritual ideal of life in the Holy Land.

British women writing in the nineteenth century show a similar tendency,
to identify with biblical figures. This has been attributed to feelings of inferiority on the part of women, who therefore seek their mirror images elsewhere.
Lacking familiarity with theological literature, women delved into the holy
scriptures to seek meaning in life.[97] Jewish women were also nourished first
and foremost by stories from the Bible. Books of penitential prayers (*tehinot*)
written for Jewish women reveal their deep spiritual ties with the Patriarchs

Jewish women at the Wailing Wall. Orna and Micha Bar-Am, eds. *Le-zayyer ba-or: Ha-hebbet ha-zillumi biyzirat E. M. Lilien* (Tel-Aviv, 1990), p. 130.

and Matriarchs of the nation.[98] Unlike men, whose spiritual world was deeply rooted in Halakhah, women built their world out of the scriptures and Aggadah, the glory of the historical past and hopes for the future.

Analyzing the migratory experience of Jewish women from shtetl to city in the nineteenth century, Charlotte Haver has pointed out the dual reality of both women and men in Jewish society: the reality of shtetl life as against the dream "reality" of visionary Jerusalem.[99] This profound internalization of the Erez Israel experience was intensified by the actual encounter with the Holy Land, and with it the encounter with the Jewish historical past. It was a triple encounter: the visionary Land confronted the desolate Land as it was in the nineteenth century, creating the link with the biblical Land. The experience found expression in the diaries of two exceptional educated Jewesses from western Europe: Judith Montefiore (wife of Sir Moses), who visited the country several times during the nineteenth century;[100] and the aforementioned Flora Randegger of Trieste, who immigrated on her own.[101] Both wrote their diaries in their mother tongues: Judith Montefiore in English, Flora Randegger in Italian. Both were influenced by reports written previously by Christian tourists, who frequently referred to the excitement of coming face to face with the land of the Bible.[102]

These women wrote not only for their own satisfaction but out of a sense of mission on behalf of the entire Jewish people. Judith Montefiore's diary was published while she was still alive, while Flora Randegger, who planned to disseminate her vision by establishing a girls' school in Jerusalem, wrote in her diary: "Perhaps these lines will convey to you at least some of the national enthusiasm that has almost consumed my soul, at least to the degree that you will wholeheartedly aspire to the resurrection of Israel."[103] Judith Montefiore was influenced by the degree to which pilgrimage had become fashionable in British high society[104] and was also motivated by her religious feelings for the Holy Land. Flora Randegger, however, decided to travel to Palestine in fulfillment of a vow she had made to her father, inspired in addition by an intense sensation of mission: "I am a tool in the hand of Providence . . . to restore the glory of Israel and its Torah."[105] Both women's ambitions were nourished by their love of the historical past, which aroused their hopes for a no less glorious future in the redeemed Land. Flora Randegger in fact believed that her efforts would actually help to bring on the redemption.

Judith Montefiore, writing of her first trip to Palestine in 1827, described the history of Jerusalem at length, dwelling on the different historical periods — from David and Solomon to the Ottoman Empire. The visit, she writes, was inspiring: "We are standing in the place where great events took place . . . and we feel a profound sense of worship." Upon visiting the Temple Mount, she wrote of her feeling "as if the building was still before us."[106] Such veneration of the past was infused with hopes for its restoration, and she ended her diary with one of Isaiah's prophecies of consolation (Isa. 35:10). During her second visit, in 1839, her visit to the Western Wall of the Temple Mount aroused in her intense yearning for redemption, signifying, she believed, that all hope was not lost. The day would surely come, she wrote in her diary, that all the nations would come to worship the God of Israel.[107] The solid stones of the Western Wall were thus both a token and a testimony to the fulfillment of Jewish hopes.

In contrast to the rather sedate style of Judith Montefiore's writing, Flora Randegger's diary is replete with revealing admissions of her innermost emotions. Traveling from Jaffa to Jerusalem, prayer book in hand, her heart full to overflowing, she spoke with no one, but "rejoiced to set foot on the holy soil of our ancestral land, full of yearning for those desirable regions."[108] The encounter with Jerusalem aroused in her thoughts of the origins of the Jewish bond with the Land of Israel. She imagined the Patriarchs, conquering the Land by peaceful means — concluding pacts, digging wells, and purchasing land — and the bands of warriors who had spilled their blood for the Land: "The miraculous victories of the chosen people pass before us, as they conquer the Land with the aid of the God of Hosts."[109] Stressing the right of the Jewish people to their Land as the basis for faith in the future redemption, she writes, "Who shall stand in our way if we wish to take it back?"[110] Drawing on this identification with the heroes and heroines of the nation, such as Sarah and Rachel, she issues an appeal not to await miracles but to initiate action that will bring on the redemption.[111] Obviously influenced by the Italian movement of national awakening, Flora clearly demonstrates the relationship between identification with the Jewish past and the desire for the restoration of Jewish independence in their own land.

Rivkah Lipa Anikster, the mother who compared her experience to Abraham's sacrifice of Isaac, seems to have felt differently. Her identification with the wretched present reality of the Holy Land brought about a sensation that redemption, if anything, was farther away. In her pamphlet she cites a parable of the relationship between the nation and its God: "To what may we now liken Erez Israel in its ruins and those of its sons who live in it? To a king whose sons have rebelled against him . . ."[112] The Jews had returned to Erez Israel in the nineteenth century, she believed, without permission from the King — God. The many departures from the country and the dependence of the remaining inhabitants on the *halukah* were decreed by God. Explaining the situation in this way, Rivkah Lipa was able to attribute her difficult economic situation to divine decree and thus to mitigate the shame of her impoverished condition. Thus, while Judith Montefiore and Flora Randegger drew from the past hopes for imminent redemption, Rivkah Lipa interpreted life in the present in the Holy Land as a sign that redemption was actually receding in time.

Another remarkable instance of identification both with the past and with the first steps toward the rebuilding of the national homeland is provided by the story of Esther Hadad of the island of Jerba, Tunisia, as told by her husband, Moshe David, who wrote a book in her memory.[113] The book — a rare testimony — describes the pilgrimage of the couple in 1911, four years after their marriage and eight months after the birth of their second son. Esther decided to join her husband on a visit to the Holy Land, "because of her overwhelming desire to visit the Land." The couple toured the country extensively, including the four "Holy Cities" and "the Jewish city of Tel-Aviv." They also visited tombs of many "holy men" and took part in the *hilula* (celebration) of Rabbi Simeon bar Yohai at Meron.[114]

Moshe David Hadad describes his wife's experiences, writing that she was "happy and infinitely satisfied and completely fascinated at the vision of the past and the present that she saw." The admiring husband writes how she took interest in everything she saw and demanded "to hear from me with intense desire of the thousand-year charter [of our people] in our ancient Land."[115] Acquaintance with the past intensified Esther's sense of national identification, and the light shining from her radiant face attested to her profound love of her people and her Land. The experience of her visit was so strong that she begged to stay in Erez Israel and not to return to Tunisia, suggesting that her husband return home alone and bring the family back. Moshe Hadad, however, refused, and the couple returned to Tunisia — there is no indication in his book of her disappointment.

While these female testimonies are exceptional, they nevertheless attest to the broader picture. The writings of these women give us a glimpse of the experience of the female immigrant, one characteristic of which was identification with the historical past of the Holy Land. Although most women did not express their feelings in writing (or, if they did, their writings have been lost), we can gauge their mood by studying their way of life. The immigrant experience, whether male or female, was not exhausted by the mere fact of arrival. It continued as the immigrants went on pilgrimages within the country, touring the holy places. Visits to the holy places became a central experience of the female immigrant, giving concrete expression to her unique identification with the major figures of Jewish history.

Pilgrimage to the Holy Places: Immigration within Immigration

For female immigrants, pilgrimage to the holy places (a sort of immigration within immigration[116]) was the ultimate realization of their longings for a life of sanctity. Edwin Ardener has pointed out that women's religious beliefs are expressed most characteristically through ritual and artistic action.[117] One learns from female immigrants' letters — particularly those of widows, no longer preoccupied with the needs of their families — that visiting holy places was a permanent feature of their lives. Thus, Rivkah Schwartz, widow of Rabbi

Judith Montefiore. Pinehas Grayevsky, *Benot Zion viYerushalayim* (Reprinted: Jerusalem, 2000), p. 113.

Yehosef Schwartz, writer, geographer, and one of the first immigrants from Germany, wrote her relatives as follows: "Today I was at the Western Wall, and next week, on the eve of *rosh hodesh* [the first day of the Jewish month], we will also be, God willing, at the tomb of the matriarch Rachel."[118] Toive Pesil Feinstein, in her pamphlet *Sefer zikhron Eliyahu* (see above), considered praying at the holy places to be the very center of her life.[119] Her contemporary Rivkah Lipa Anikster described her fears that her poor state of health would thwart her plans, but had nevertheless hoped, as she wrote, "that at any rate I shall reach Jerusalem while still living, be there two days, and be merited to visit the holy places." When she and her husband arrived, "we immediately went to the Western Wall and on the next day to the Mount of Olives and then we rode to Hebron and were able to visit the Cave of Machpelah three times. I also visited all the tombs of the *tanna'im* and *amora'im* [the sages of the Mishnaic and Talmudic period]."[120]

Pilgrimage, immigration, and the cult of holy places are "different manifestations of the same religious phenomenon — the practical religious relationship with Erez Israel."[121] Pilgrimage to the holy places was at the same time a repetition of the immigration experience and fulfillment of the desire for greater sanctity.[122] The holy place is, at it were, a person's cosmic space, and the mere fact of being there exposes one to the transcendental dimension.[123] The experience of visiting the holy places was largely a reconstruction and reinforcement of the immigration experience itself; sometimes, if a person was unexpectedly forced to leave the Holy Land, it guaranteed that he or she would ultimately return to Zion.[124]

Anthropologists have defined pilgrimage in such terms as "populist," "anarchic" and "anti-establishment."[125] In contrast to immigration, which is by its very nature an act culminating in a situation that lasts for the immigrant's entire lifetime, pilgrimage to a holy place involves an action that occupies a fixed time span, at most a few days. It is precisely because of the random nature and ceremonial freedom associated with visits to holy places that they provide fertile ground for the emergence of alternative modes of religious expression. The holy places in Erez Israel furnished opportunities for the expression of personal emotions and the development of individual ceremonies, distinct from the standard synagogue ceremonies practiced by the establishment, which were rooted in Halakhah. Unlike the synagogues, which were generally organized on a community basis, people gathering at holy places hailed from a variety of communities; the holy sites were therefore scenes of ethnic unity and shared ceremonies. In addition, they were open to members of both sexes, men and women alike, though they particularly attracted women.[126] Partha Chatterjee has written of women's experience of pilgrimage in India, pointing out not only the religious ecstasy but also the self-liberation achieved by female pilgrims who perceive themselves as closer to God.[127] Available sources on Jewish pilgrimage in Erez Israel in the nineteenth century do not conclusively imply that the number of women pilgrims to holy places exceeded that of men,[128] but they certainly indicate the importance of the phenomenon for women, their extensive participation in pilgrimage, and the formation of a unique female experience.

Over the centuries, hundreds of sites considered to possess special sanctity have been marked out on the map of the Holy Land.[129] Those in Jerusalem and Hebron relate particularly to Bible times, while the holy places in Tiberias and Safed are associated with the times of the Mishnah and the Talmud. Among these sites are many women's tombs.[130] The authenticity of the association of a particular site with a specific name and historical tradition cannot generally be proved.[131] Most of the holy places are tombs or sites thought to be the burial places of important personalities. An exception is the Western Wall, no doubt the most important Jewish holy site in Erez Israel. Although the creation of holy places is an ongoing process, pilgrims believe wholeheartedly in the authenticity of the places they visit.

Improved security conditions in Erez Israel in the second half of the nineteenth century, the slow improvement in road conditions, and the large numbers of visitors to the country, both immigrants and tourists, brought about a corresponding increase in the numbers of men and women who visited the holy places. As Syla Bergman wrote in a letter to her parents, "Now, in gen-

eral, all summer long, Jews continually go to all the tombs of our ancestors —
to Hebron, to Rachel our Mother, to the prophet Samuel . . ."[132] Such visits
were sometimes called *"mitzvah* trips."[133] Every holy place had its unique
flavor, deriving from the specific person whose name it perpetuated and from
its geographical location. Some places were associated with specific times,
and there were sometimes organized pilgrimages to the various tombs, both
from the Holy Land and from other countries.[134] Common to all the holy
places was that they were open to all and moreover that visiting them did not
involve any special ritual.[135]

The mere visit to a holy place, which sometimes required traveling along
bad or dangerous roads, was essentially an avowal of faith in the saints and
their tombs. Holy places were thought to have magical influence on those
visiting them,[136] and this was true particularly in regard to tombs; for example,
a visit to the tomb of a holy person within the country was thought to be a
remedy for barrenness, just like immigration from abroad to the Holy Land.
Childless men and women would frequent such tombs and pray for offspring.
Thus, Rabbi Vidal and his wife, a childless couple who immigrated from
Salonika in 1858, "went on a *ziyara* [organized pilgrimage] to Kefar Ramah to
the tomb of the prophet Samuel . . . and they of course prayed there that God
would grant them male sons, and his wife made a vow that, should God grant
them a son, they would call him Samuel; and that indeed happened."[137] The
woman's vow attested to her belief that she would please the prophet if the son
were named for him. Whereas in the synagogue women were distanced from
the focus of the prayer service, in a holy place they could achieve, as it were,
direct contact with the person buried there, who would help to fulfill their requests. Some tombs were supposed to have special properties. It was believed,
for example, that a visit to Elijah's Cave, at the foot of Mount Carmel, could
heal mental disorders, and sick persons, particularly women, were brought
there to be cured.[138]

The main activity during a visit to a holy place was prayer, but by no means
the routine, regular mode of prayer. Both men and women wrote of the
unique quality of prayer at a holy place, of the spiritual elation and exultation
that worshipers experienced there. Rabbi Menahem Mendel of Kaminetz, for
example, came to Erez Israel by way of Haifa in the 1830s, and immediately
set out for the nearby Elijah's Cave. Of his feelings there he wrote: "Our eyes
shed tears, for never before had I prayer thus, and it was then that I understood
that this is holy ground."[139] Rabbi Yosef Mansfeld, who came to the country
in the same decade and worshiped at holy tombs in and around Safed, wrote
his relatives in Kalisch: "I am sure that the prayer was accepted, because the
holy place inspires and one prays from the depth of one's heart."[140] Golda, his
wife, aptly expressed her appreciation of the efficacy of prayer at holy sites,

and in particular their economic significance: "The tombs of righteous men here are of great value; I hope in particular that through our prayers we will help more than having money at home."[141] Prayer at a holy place was imbued with a sensation of physical proximity to the divine emissary buried there, of confidence that one's prayers would be answered and miracles would take place.

Even where there was no obligatory ceremonial or ritual behavior, special prayers were sometimes devised. Prayers were composed for the most popular sites and later published in booklets. Many such booklets were printed beginning in the 1870s, some also with Yiddish and Ladino texts, indicating that they were used in particular by women.[142] However, the text itself never refers to a specific female experience; women's prayers were personal and private, never uttered in public or published.

Poor women would beg money from wealthy individuals, undertaking to offer up special prayers for them in holy places. Rivkah Lipa Anikster promised her relatives to pray for them at the Western Wall daily,[143] while her daughter Rachel wrote the officials in Amsterdam who were responsible for sending funds to the Holy Land: "I, your servant, will also mention your names constantly at the holy places—the Western Wall, the Tomb of our Mother Rachel, may her merit protect us."[144] A needy pilgrim would repay benefactors in the Diaspora by frequenting a holy place, praying there and mentioning their names.

Women visiting holy places also hoped that their prayers would have a magical effect on their lives. Toive Pesil Feinstein describes how she begged God in her prayers that her children would not stray from the right path like "lost sheep," and also prayed for national redemption.[145] Toive Pesil and her friends admitted freely that they were trying to stem the tide of Jewish secularization through their prayers. Women who had tended their children when young now, having grown old, expanded their conception of motherhood. Instead of physical welfare, they were now concerned for their children's spiritual well-being.[146] Prayer and the attendant manual gestures were seen as an act of worship, a way of influencing the world. On one special occasion—Queen Victoria's jubilee in the year 1887—women organized a special "women's service" at the Western Wall to express their appreciation of the British monarch.[147] The identification of Jewish women in Jerusalem with Queen Victoria's reign, and the expression it received at the Western Wall, indicate not only the powers that women believed were inherent in their prayers but also their freedom of action at the Wall.

Yehudah Yizhak Yehezkel writes of his grandmother's custom to go every Friday afternoon to the Western Wall, where she recited Psalms and the Song of Songs till candle-lighting time. "Sometimes only women were present there;

no person bothered or insulted the women that thronged that holy place."[148] The Western Wall, which was not used in the nineteenth century as just another synagogue, was not only considered the holiest site in Jerusalem but also the most accessible to Jewish residents of the Old City of Jerusalem; women were therefore among the most frequent visitors there.[149] Sephardic women, who were illiterate and therefore could not pray,[150] found alternative ways to worship God at the Western Wall. While prayer was the primary medium of communication between the upper and lower worlds, it was not the only one. Women frequenting the holy places devised their own means of communication, through which they expressed their special relationships with these places.

Women were concerned to maintain the proper atmosphere of the site and to care for its physical aspect. Accordingly, they kept the place clean and tended to visitors' needs. Women of the Sephardic and oriental communities would cast lots among themselves to determine who would have the honor of sweeping the floor of the Western Wall court.[151] A woman named Malkah de Parnas was known at one time as guardian of furniture and other equipment needed at the Wall, keeping chairs and benches in the courtyard of her home; she would also bring candles and water to those in need.[152]

We hear of women's capacity to arouse excitement among the worshipers at the Wall in Avraham Luncz's description of prayers at the Western Wall on the eve of the fast of the Ninth of Av: "These delicate creatures, upon whom nature has bestowed the power of weeping and mourning far more than upon men, summon up all their strength, each woman arousing her sister to mourn in loud, bitter shrieking."[153] Any prayer service at times of particular emotion, whether of sorrow or of joy, included ululations emitted by Sephardic women. Although the strictly Orthodox frown on listening to a woman's voices, these mourning women's voice were prominently heard, contributing to the general emotion.

As already mentioned, women also cared for the needs of the worshipers at the Western Wall. Some would stand at the entrance to the Wall area with a fragrant citron fruit or spices, offering them to passersby to enable them to recite the proper blessing (thereby completing their daily quota of one hundred blessings), to which they themselves would answer "Amen." Other women sat along the path leading to the Wall in the hot summer months, with cool water to refresh the visitors.[154] Another physical expression of love for the Western Wall was to kiss its stones: "On Friday after midday a Sephardic woman would push her way through the worshipers to the Wall, for she took care to kiss each and every stone separately."[155] The kiss created contact between the visitor and the site: she expressed her love for it, while at the same time some of its sanctity, as it were, adhered to her. Women's routine domestic role assumed, as it were, a ritualized form.[156] At the Western Wall, women were granted a degree of autonomy: it was they who determined the times of assembly, the style of prayer, and the care for the site.

The Western Wall and other holy places provided the opportunity for the development of female companionship. Visits to holy places, in particular to cemeteries, were not infrequently organized in groups. In addition to the above-mentioned sense of companionship, traveling in groups was conducive to a greater feeling of security. In addition, going out to the cemetery, which was outside the city limits, was in the nature of a refreshing walk,[157] while also assuming special significance in widows' lives.

Anthropologists have been hard put to distinguish between pilgrimage and tourism. The two phenomena are intertwined; pilgrimage involves an element of tourism, and it is not always possible to set the sacred apart from the secular. Nevertheless, one difference is clear: unlike tourism, the object of pilgrimage is the visit itself, whereas recreation is merely a by-product.[158]

The tragic tale of the widow of Rabbi Meir Auerbach, Hindel of Kalisch,[159] throws light on a custom of Jewish women (in fact, not only in the Holy Land) to visit graves and measure them. Measuring graves was seen as a way to arouse the dead to render assistance to the living.[160] In Jerusalem it was the custom for groups of women to visit graves of saintly people on the Mount of Olives.[161] Hindel of Kalisch, despite her advanced age and poor eyesight, joined such a group, but apparently lost contact with the other women, and searches sent out for her were fruitless. The story of her disappearance spread rapidly, and a rumor that she had been seen in one of the city's many convents aroused concern in the Jewish community of Jerusalem.[162] This was not the only disaster associated with visits to graves and cemeteries. Jerusalem newspapers reported other cases of women who had been bold enough to go up to the Mount of Olives.[163] The less institutionalized the site, the more involved women became, so that the desolate cemeteries attracted many women.

Among other things, women would pay their respects to the dead by whitewashing the tombstones. We find an illustration of this practice, albeit not in Jerusalem, in Safed: "In the holy city of Safed it is the custom that women go occasionally, particularly on the eve of the New Moon, to whitewash the tombs of the righteous men of God, and this custom is common among the Sephardim in the other holy cities as well."[164] Whitewashing tombstones may also be seen as an extension of women's role in caring for their relatives or the elderly members of the community.[165] Visits to cemeteries were particularly appropriate for elderly widows who considered their immigration as a preparation for the Next World and thus had, as it were, a direct relationship with the dead and with death. They saw death as a desirable goal, so that visiting graves was both a realization of their goals and a spiritual experience.

Hilulot: *Festivities at Saints' Gravesides*

A visit to a holy place was an individual event, in which each detail depended on the visitor him- or herself. A *hilula* (plural *hilulot*), however — special festivities held at the graveside of a saint or other righteous person on the anniversary of his or her death — was a group experience, generally involving a procession to the grave. The *hilula*, which began as a spontaneous ceremony, became a ritual, observed in accordance with fixed traditions. It was an opportunity to express spiritual affinity for the saint associated with the scene of the event, and to gather in large crowds — men, women, and children — to celebrate, eat, dance, and in general make merry. Anthropologists have pondered the question of the degree to which pilgrimage is a personal or collective experience: do the many pilgrims who come together form a *communitas?*[166] An examination of the characteristics of *hilulot* shows that the *communitas* formed at a *hilula* may be divided into two groups, men and women, and the *hilula* experience similarly occurs in two variations, the male and the female. Women may be present during a *hilula* as observers only; at other times, they may create a female event in parallel, but secondary, to the male one. We have here yet another aspect, on the one hand, of the exclusion of women from the center of activity but, on the other, of the alternatives that female society created for itself. Women's very exclusion from the central scene of action in fact enhanced their spiritual link with the sacred dimension.

The main *hilulot*, involving the largest number of participants, all took place on the minor festival of Lag ba-Omer, at four sites in different parts of the country. The custom of holding *hilulot* at tombs of holy men on this particular date probably dates from the sixteenth or seventeenth century, and it has taken various forms over the centuries.[167] Since the second half of the nineteenth century, *hilulot* have been held regularly at the tombs of Rabbi Simeon bar Yohai at Meron (near Safed), of Rabbi Simeon the Just in Jerusalem, of Rabbi Meir Ba'al haNess at Tiberias, and at Elijah's Cave near Haifa.[168] Since the best-known (and most heavily attended) *hilula* is that of Rabbi Simeon bar Yohai at Meron, it will be discussed in what follows. The celebrants — whose numbers, toward the end of the twentieth century, have reached thousands — hail from all communities: Sephardim, North Africans, Ashkenazim (both Hasidim and *Perushim*).[169]

The *hilula* began with a procession of men, women, and children to the holy site, carrying their food with them and playing musical instruments. Some came from great distances, traveling for several weeks in a kind of spontaneous family "happening," in which women took part as well as men.[170] However, upon arrival in Safed, when the ceremonies began, women were excluded from the central arena. The march from Safed to Meron was an exclusively male affair: the men carried Torah scrolls in their arms, while "the women watched from the windows, throwing candies and sprinkling those marching in the procession with perfumed water."[171] Similarly, when the procession reached the site, the men worshiped at the tomb itself, whereas women were allowed to pray only at a less important site — the niche marking the grave of Rabbi Simeon's son Rabbi Eliezer.[172]

The center of interest at the *hilula* was the kindling ceremony (the *hadlakah*). The first light was set to the bonfire by a man (who purchased the privilege for a price),[173] but women were probably among those who, as was the custom, threw clothes and valuables into the fire. Rabbi Yosef Mansfeld describes the excitement of the event in considerable detail:

To crowd close to the fire and throw into it a dress or a kerchief is considered as a meritorious deed; the kindling is particularly valued by the women, each of whom sees it as her duty to throw a dress, a kerchief or an apron into the fire. My wife, too, was so overjoyed that she took off her beautiful apron and threw it into the fire.[174]

The burning of clothing and the enthusiastic willingness of both men and women to donate valuable possessions for the holy occasion was likened to a "burnt-offering."[175] A midrash relating to the incident of the Golden Calf in the desert relates that women declined to contribute their jewelry to make the calf, because of their natural aversion to sin;[176] at Meron, however, women willingly took part in the holy ritual, throwing their clothing into the bonfire. The ecstasy was shared by all those present. While some rabbis protested that the burning of clothes was a transgression against the prohibition of purposeless waste, Rabbi Shmuel Heller of Safed argued that the ability to achieve real joy was conditional upon divesting oneself of corporeality, and one way to do this was to burn one's clothing, as a symbol of the physical body.[177] However, the spiritual jubilation at the *hilula* involved merrymaking, which was surely exclusively corporeal. Might one say that women's participation in throwing away their best clothing was a kind of protest?

While not excluded from the kindling, women were certainly excluded from the dances, which were reserved for men alone: "A chain of men would stand in a circle together . . . Two of them would fight a mock battle with drawn swords, one against the other."[178] Avraham Luncz of Jerusalem reports that women watched the events at Meron, or sat together while "the oldest of them told them of the actions and adventures of the tanna Rabbi Simeon ben Yohai."[179] According to this tradition, women were forbidden to dance and rejoice,[180] but achieved physical closeness to the saint by "throwing kisses" at the tomb and reciting a special formula. At Meron, women were segregated behind an isolating curtain; in the modest ceremony at Elijah's Cave, however, Sephardic women danced among themselves,[181] while the "Polish

women" danced "according to the Polish rite." To the degree that the ceremony became less spontaneous and became institutionalized, women's participation became more limited.

Another indubitably male ceremony associated with the *hilula* was the *halakeh*, in which three-year-old boys were given their first haircut. Their hair
was shorn, leaving only sidelocks, in accordance with the commandment
"You shall not round off the side-growth on your head" (Lev. 19:27).[182] This
hair-cutting ceremony is not an original Jewish rite but an element of pilgrimage ceremonials in general.[183] The *halakeh*, celebrated in an exclusively
male environment, has been defined as a male rite of passage, signifying the
child's removal from the exclusive charge of his mother.[184] Yosef Mansfeld, in
his 1836 letter to his relatives in Kalisch, notes: "This commandment is considered as important among the Sephardim as that of [circumcision]."[185] The
hilula at Meron, generally pictured as a merry family celebration, cultivated
and stressed masculinity to the extent that women were excluded from the
ceremony.

In other words, in contrast to individual or family visits to holy sites, the
hilula deliberately limited female participation. While women were physically present at the site, they were generally left in their own arena. Nevertheless, criticism of the atmosphere during the festivities indicates that women's
presence did leave its imprint on the *hilula*. We hear echoes of such criticism
in letters written in the sixteenth and seventeenth centuries,[186] and the complaints became louder in the nineteenth century: "One of the great lumi-
naries of this generation wanted to cancel, or may even have canceled, the
Lag ba-Omer festivities and the gathering of men and women, which he believed to be merely debauchery, heaven forfend."[187] Similar criticism was
aimed at the *hilula* at the tomb of Simeon the Just in Jerusalem, as we read
in a Jerusalem newspaper: "How many transgressions are committed by a Jew
who goes to 'Shim'on hazadik' on that day!"[188] Since women were considered
the root of immorality, they had to be removed.

In 1911 a ban was imposed on female participation in the *hilula* of Rabbi
Simeon ben Yohai, after a roof had collapsed on dozens of people at the site
of the Meron tomb, killing nine of them. In the wake of the tragedy, "everyone here unanimously decided to try and abolish the custom of lighting the
bonfire at Meron, or at least to forbid women to visit the place."[189] The text of
the ban excluding women from the festivities was based on the conception of
women as the root of all evil; the men, it was claimed, would be exonerated
only if women were removed from the scene.[190] However, the ban was not observed for very long. Ada Maimon, a young feminist but traditional-minded
pioneer, wrote in her memoirs of having gone with two friends to the *hilula*
in 1914 in defiance of the ban, and the ban was indeed soon lifted.[191]

However, the fact that women had no part in the central ceremonies of the *hilula* did not detract from their emotional affinity with the saint buried at Meron; on the contrary, they tended to feel even closer to him. The central protagonist in a pilgrimage or *hilula* is "the single believer, who faces the saint in the fullness of his [or her] individuality."[192] A book titled *Hilula de-Rabbi Shim'on bar Yohai* (the *Hilula* of Rabbi Simeon ben Yohai) presents a legendary tale that aptly pictures women's close relationship with the saint. In 1923, during the *hilula* at Rabbi Simeon's tomb, a young child, brought there for the *halakeh*, died. His mourning mother carried the body to the lower chamber of the tomb, lay him at its foot, and directly addressed "Rabbi Shim'on," reminding him that she had vowed to bring her son to Meron and had indeed kept her vow. She now entreated the saint to revive her son, both to prevent her being publicly shamed and, even more, to enhance his (Rabbi Simeon's) own reputation and sanctify God's name. Having completed her prayer, she left the chamber, closed the door, and left her dead son there on the floor — a miracle occurred, and the child came to life.[193]

The story, which is of course reminiscent of the biblical story of the prophet Elisha and the wealthy woman of Shunem (2 Kgs. 4:8–37), is told in several variations.[194] It typifies the profound attitude of women to saints' tombs:[195] their strong sensation of the presence of the deceased saint at the site; spiritual affinity with the saint; the importance of physical contact with the tomb;[196] implicit faith that a woman's tears, prayers, and actions have the power to influence the deceased saint; and faith in the saint's ability to influence events in the real world.[197] The atmosphere at the *hilula*, which permitted "egalitarian, direct, irrational, existential and spontaneous social relationships,"[198] also created a unique relationship between women and holy figures of the past.

Rachel's Tomb as the Culmination of Women's Immigration

Nowhere did the female desire for identification with the deceased saint and his or her spiritual message find more profound expression than at the tomb of the matriarch Rachel. Rachel's Tomb in Bethlehem, on the road to Hebron, some two hours' walk from the Old City, attracted frequent visitors,[199] particularly on the first day of every Hebrew month, in the month of Elul, during the Ten Days of Penitence, and on the eleventh of Heshvan, the supposed day of Rachel's death.[200] Visitors would pray for themselves and their benefactors, whose donations provided them with sustenance. Earth from the tomb was sent abroad regularly, and in times of drought people would pray there for rain.[201] The Jerusalem community had long been paying a tax to assure free access to the site.[202] In the nineteenth century, Jews purchased a plot

Rachel's Tomb. Ely Schiller, ed., *Jerusalem in Old Engravings* (Jerusalem, 1977), p. 82.

of land near the site.[203] Rachel's Tomb was one of the most frequented tombs in the Land of Israel, and in the nineteenth century it became a favorite pilgrimage site for women, both Jewish and non-Jewish.[204]

The story of Rachel — the beautiful favorite wife, afflicted with barrenness, her rivalry with her sister Leah, her early death on the road to Ephrath — provided plenty of opportunity for empathy and identification on the part of individual women. But that was not all. Rachel was not just one of the four Matriarchs: Jeremiah's famous words of consolation (Jer. 31:15–17), which credited her tears and prayer with supernatural powers to bring on the redemption of the nation, lifted her out of her historical context and placed her above and beyond time. She became the eternal mother of the nation, whose special merit was instrumental in bringing her children back to their homeland.[205]

Susan Sered has published several anthropological studies of the reestablishment of Rachel's Tomb as the site of a women's cult in the twentieth century.[206] There is no hard evidence as to the point in time when this cult first took shape. It was presumably not a sudden development but a slow, gradual process, which reached fruition as the number of immigrants and pilgrims increased and security and road conditions improved. Judith Montefiore first visited the site in 1827 without her husband, in the company of a group of women.[207] The few reports from the late nineteenth century indicate that women preferred to visit the site alone. Shim'on Berman, a traveler who visited the place in 1870, wrote, "Many people come to pray at the tomb, most of them women."[208] Mordecai Ben Hillel, an early Zionist, businessman, and intellectual who visited Erez Israel in 1889, describes the site as frequented by women.[209] Yizhak Ben-Zvi, the labor leader and historian who later became Israel's second president, gives a similar report.[210] The practice of visiting the tomb on the first day of the Hebrew month, when women traditionally refrained from labor, made the place particularly attractive for them.[211] One piece of evidence, though difficult to substantiate, concerning the development of the female cult at the site may be found in the memoirs of Ephraim Taubenhaus:

> Every New Moon the Maid of Ludmir would lead her admirers to Rachel's Tomb and hold a solemn prayer service, with impressive ceremony. At the Tomb of the matriarch Rachel the Maid would offer all the prayers and supplications that had accumulated over the past four weeks, in response to all those who had come to her for help.[212]

While men still came to visit Rachel's Tomb, there is no doubt that women were particularly attracted to the site. As we have pointed out, it became the focus of a unique ritual, comprising recitations, gestures, and symbolic acts[213] that were intended to express special affection for "the mother of the nation."

Accounts of pilgrimage to Rachel's Tomb speak of women's intimate relationship with the figure of Rachel, of their feeling that the venerated Matriarch would help all those who appealed to her. Rachel was perceived as the ultimate mother figure. Syla Bergman, who sorely missed her mother, referred to Rachel as "the beloved mother."[214] Judith Montefiore, who was childless, had special regard for Rachel as having been barren for many years, and called her "mother in Israel." With her husband's agreement, she gave instructions to enlarge the tomb structure and repair it.[215] In addition, the Montefiores built a mausoleum modeled on Rachel's Tomb in their home at Ramsgate in England. The students of the Evelina de Rothschild girls' school in Jerusalem donated a special curtain to the tomb to commemorate one of their number who had died.[216] A sharp-eyed visitor would have perceived that the women who frequented the place were largely "unfortunate and embittered women."[217] Rachel's Tomb was seen as a kind of substitute mother, lavishing love on all comers.

Besides being a mother figure, Rachel also personified the Diaspora. This was inspired by Jeremiah's description of Rachel weeping for her children's exile. The identification of femininity with exile is a well-known gender metaphor. Women, excluded from the centers of power,[218] are naturally in "exile." The identification of Rachel with Jewish history is echoed in Judith Montefiore's journal; in her view, Rachel's Tomb represented the march of

Jewish history with its centuries of suffering. She wrote of her excitement and gratitude to God at visiting the site, aware that she was one of six European women to have toured the Holy Land in a hundred years.[219]

The identification of Rachel with the Diaspora assumed special significance in the 1870s and 1880s, with the increased number of Jews settling in the Holy City and the first stages in the development of the New City of Jerusalem and of the rebuilding of the Land of Israel. In these decades, when the first neighborhoods to be built outside the Old City walls had taken root and Jews had become a majority in Jerusalem, voices were heard in the Old Yishuv as well, to the effect that these achievements were preliminaries to Redemption.[220] Both Old and New Yishuv were pervaded with the sensation that the exiles were beginning to return to their ancient homeland, as it were attesting to the success of Rachel's efforts on behalf of her people. Rachel thus became a symbol of the reawakening nation.

Eliezer Ben-Yehuda wrote of Rachel in *Havazelet*, the organ of the Old Yishuv, as a national symbol: "Of all the Matriarchs, Rachel was the one who came to signify the entire nation."[221] In contrast to the figure pictured by Jeremiah, of a woman trying to influence God through her weeping, Ben-Yehuda portrayed a forceful woman, urging God not to delay the redemption any further. Rachel Yanna'it Ben-Zvi, later prominent in the Zionist labor movement, who visited Bethlehem in 1908, wrote of her grandmother's faith in the matriarch Rachel's power to open the gates of the Land of Israel and admit the Jews who wanted to come — a popular belief that figured in numerous stories and folksongs.[222] The Matriarch was thus an object of both individual and national identification, signifying both the sorrows of the Diaspora and the joys of redemption.

There were many physical manifestations of this profound, complex attitude to Rachel. Syla Bergman described how she walked around the tomb, deeply affected by her very ability to touch it.[223] Some women used to embrace the tombstone: "Women would press up against the stone, sobbing and weeping."[224] It was also the custom to touch the tombstone not directly but with a symbolic object — a piece of string. Women would walk around the stone holding string of different colors (red, white, yellow, or green), which was then wound seven times around it. Such pieces of string were then considered to possess magical powers as remedies for barrenness and various diseases.[225] Hadassah, Avraham Krinitzi's grandmother (see above), brought her family such charms, which she had personally measured out at Rachel's tomb, and gave them to the children, saying, "Is there any better remedy in the whole world than these ribbons, which have touched the beloved ground of our mother Rachel?"[226] The belief in such pieces of string, which possessed the magical powers of the saint buried in the tomb, was not unique to Rachel's Tomb. The Jews of Afghanistan used to wind string around the tombs of holy men.[227]

Another way to connect with the tomb was to inscribe one's name on special plaques at the site. Judith Montefiore, for example, inscribed her name and that of her husband (who had not accompanied her to the tomb) on stone plaques at the site.[228] Another custom was to collect pebbles from the vicinity of the tomb, as these were supposed to have the capacity to alleviate birth pains.[229] The key to the tomb was also thought to have healing properties, especially for birthing mothers. Lighting the wicks in a lamp hanging at the site was also considered equivalent to touching the tombstone, assuring that one's wishes would be fulfilled.[230]

These customs attest to a deep spiritual need for physical contact with the site. This was achieved by bringing gifts to the tomb, helping to keep the surrounding area clean, and offering drinking water to the pilgrims.[231] Young Sephardic women used to bring various gifts: embroidered towels and curtains, mantles for the Torah scrolls. Such gifts, the fruit of considerable labor, deepened and reinforced the donors' relationship with the place.[232] Miriam Burla relates how she and her sister-in-law worked hard to scrub and clean the tomb area, and describes the feeling of spiritual elation their efforts gave them: "For many days I had a strange, pleasant sensation, as if I had been purified, as if something of the sanctity of the place had adhered to me, having been our mother Rachel's handmaiden for several hours."[233] In yet another expression of the affinity felt for the Matriarch, women used to gather together near the tomb structure and tell stories about her.[234] Summarizing the foregoing evidence of activities around Rachel's tomb, one can say that it was here that women's immigration experience reached its culmination: the experience of self-sacrifice and suffering (spiritual identification with Rachel's barrenness and personal tragedy); identification with Jewish historical experience and the perception of women as capable of hastening the redemption; and symbolic acts expressing physical affinity with the Matriarch and belief in her magical powers.

While the physical-ritual dimension was not unique to women, it was they who particularly nurtured it. The dichotomy between men and women is not as rigid in the area of popular ritual as it is in the synagogue or in the world of Halakha in general.[235] Physical contact with the tomb gave women a feeling of being close to supernal forces, of an encounter between personal and divine;[236] the identification with Rachel gave rise to identification with national destiny. The customs practiced at Rachel's Tomb point not only to the emergence of a new women's cult but also to a certain convergence of views between the Old Yishuv and the New, in relation to historical identification and the belief, common to both societies toward the end of the nineteenth century, that Redemption was imminent.[237]

A New Reality

The complex Jewish reality in Erez Israel also had certain feminine characteristics: a feeling of exile under the thumb of a foreign power, and insecurity because of the dangerous road conditions. The feminine images of the Holy Land, as "home" and "maternal bosom," express the many-sided reality of the country and the complex perception of femininity. This analysis of women's experience throws new light on Jewish fears of the Holy Land, which finds little expression either in the sources or in modern scholarship.[238] The immigration experience had an overwhelming influence — psychologically, among other things — on the immigrant's world. The phenomenon, which has received attention in anthropological studies,[239] is discernible in various testimonies of the metamorphosis experienced by the immigrants upon arrival in their new country. Jacob Goldman, a journalist of the Old Yishuv, described his mother-in-law's arrival in the Holy Land as follows:

When she came with her husband from Hungary, she arrived at the gates of Jerusalem dressed in her European clothes. She stood there and rent her garments as required [on beholding the ruins of Jerusalem]. Said she: I shall not enter the Holy City in these worldly clothes; rather, bring me a white sheet in which to wrap my whole body. For this was then the customary attire of Jewish women in Jerusalem.[240]

Men and women of European appearance totally altered their image.[241] The rending of one's garments — a familiar practice of visitors to the Holy Land, in mourning for the destruction — is described here as a woman's act, symbolizing the breaking of ties with the Diaspora and the start of a new era in the immigrant's life.[242] The European image was discarded immediately, as if to stress the immigrant's ardent desire for total identification with the values of his or her new home.

Immigration involved not only changing one's appearance but also acquiring a new reference group. The immigrants and the Jerusalem Jews who welcomed them felt like brothers and sisters. Veterans and newcomers alike sought to put down roots in the Holy City, creating as it were an extended family. This somewhat compensated the immigrants for being virtually cut off from their families in the Diaspora; it also helped them to acclimatize themselves to their new lifestyle. Seniora Gentil, who came from Greece in the late 1880s, described the reception accorded the immigrants in the following terms:

Women and men came out to welcome us. They stood around us and began to in-
quire of father where we had come from. Upon hearing that we were from Yanina,
people from families who had come from diverse Greek cities clung to us and began
to dance around us *as if we were relatives and family members.*[243]

This treatment of the immigrants as family, though not always realized,
signified the creation of a unique, intimate, all-embracing lifestyle that affected all areas of the immigrants' being.

Immigration to Erez Israel was the most important rite of passage in an immigrant's life, giving women among the newcomers an opportunity to shape
new lives for themselves. For some women, immigration was a traumatic experience, involving coercion and self-sacrifice; others saw it as offering new
prospects and challenges. In contrast to the canonical nature of masculine Judaism, shaped by the intellectual world of Halakhah, women's spiritual world
was shaped by a variety of practical aspects.[244] Excluded from the centers of
power and ritual of the religious establishment, women were inspired to find
alternative channels of activity: immigration on their own, development of
their own rituals at holy places, and even formation of a specifically female
holy place — Rachel's Tomb. Thus, immigration to the Holy Land, combining spiritual elation and sanctification, on the one hand, and suffering and
distress, on the other, was a corridor leading to earthly Jerusalem, which aspired to imitate heavenly Jerusalem. Analysis of the Jerusalem experience will
enable us to examine the contacts between the perception of sexuality and social gendering, on the one hand, and the formation of a holy community, on
the other.

Chapter 2

Princess or Prisoner?

Marriage as a Female Experience

"WHAT DID I know of love or marriage?" — so said Julia Chelouche's grandmother of her engagement and marriage at the age of eleven.[1] The wealth of available documentation enables us to draw a most detailed picture of the formation of new family units in Jerusalem, through all its stages. An account of the steps leading up to and including marriage will throw light on the woman's complex place in the family, pointing to the processes of change taking place in the Jewish community of the Holy City. Central to this account is the young girl's world and society's attitude to her.

The study of home and family, not as an appendix to history but as a fundamental institution, seminal for society as a whole, occupies an important position in contemporary historical theory. There is a growing demand to study the family not only from the male but also from the female viewpoint.[2] Studying the family also includes studying societal mentality in general. "By mentality we mean a worldview, not entirely explicit, shared by a large number of people in a given culture."[3] This particular worldview must be understood if one wishes to understand the variety of approaches to social institutions and processes. The myth of the strength of the traditional Jewish family, and the realization of its central place in Jewish life,[4] will be examined here on the basis of the unique situation in Jerusalem: growth of a family that was supposed to embody the desire for religious life and experience. Just as in the life of the individual a distinction has to be made between that individual's public personality and his or her private/family personality, the study of a society must differentiate between its public and its inner/familial face. Behavior within the family is a reflection, albeit sometimes very faint, of society's overt conventions. The family — society's most elementary institution — is as it were a laboratory in which society's innermost attitudes and desires are watered down and fused; but at the same time it is a paramount agent of change. The mentality and inner personality of a society, as manifested in family ceremonies, are not always explicitly expressed, and the societal "symbol language" requires interpretation.

Jacob Katz pointed out the contrast between the coercive power of what he called the natural institution of the family, on the one hand, and that of the family created by marital relationships, on the other.[5] The very fact of the contrast raises questions as to the nature of marriage: Is it a "natural" institution or a "volitional" one? Is the bride under the marriage canopy a princess or a captive? In a traditional society such as the Jewish community of Jerusalem, matches were made and marriages arranged by the parents, generally without any involvement of the couple themselves.

It is a commonplace in Judaism that the day of a woman's marriage, unlike her birth, is one of the peaks of her life, a day of unmitigated rapture. Does the bride indeed feel this? Traditional Jewish society's attitude to women is peculiarly paradoxical: Women in themselves are considered to be inferior creatures, ancillary to men; but their alleged negative influence is supposed to exceed men's powers.[6] A woman's marriage guarantees neutralization of that negative influence, on the one hand, but helps her to achieve completeness by union with a man, on the other. Male society's condescending attitude to women may be discerned in a system of mechanisms that, in the past, assured that she would ultimately be married.

Marriage as a Necessity: The Power of the Community

The Jerusalem community's involvement in the life of the individual was total. This unique character of the community was achieved by means of special regulations (*takanot*) enacted in the Holy City, known as the "Jerusalem Regulations." These regulations developed over several centuries; they were first published in print in Jerusalem in 1842. While intended for members of all the communities living in Jerusalem, they were never enforced in a uniform manner, and one discerns changes in their application, depending on prevailing conditions and, moreover, on the ethnic origin of the individuals in question. The regulations enjoyed Halakhic authority and reemphasized the status of Jerusalem as the Holy City.[7]

An instructive example is the so-called Bachelors Regulation, which dealt with family life in the community. A very old regulation, unique to Jerusalem, it was reconfirmed in the eighteenth century. It decreed that the right of any Jewish male aged from twenty to sixty to live in the Holy City was conditional on his family status:

As to the matter of bachelors aged twenty years and more, they shall not be allowed to live in the Holy City of Jerusalem, may it be rebuilt and reconstructed, without a wife . . . And if he is unable to do so, for he has found no time to wed a wife, he must depart forthwith from this Holy City and seek his life abroad. The community . . . is entitled, in regard to whomsoever should transgress these instructions of ours, to banish him from the land.[8]

The object of the regulation was to safeguard the moral fiber of the community, as it stated explicitly: "We have a tradition that there is no guardian against unchastity [Bab. Talmud, Chulin 11b]." That is to say, men are susceptible to seduction — specifically by women. The authors of the regulation did not mention the well-known Halakhic principle that the male is subject to the commandment of procreation; possibly, they refrained from doing so, on the assumption that the obligation was explicit and well known to all. At any rate, the regulation was aimed at bachelors coming to live in Jerusalem and attributing their unmarried state to lack of means. The regulation allowed them four (or six) months to find a spouse; otherwise, they had to leave the city, and in case of need the community leaders were entitled "to pursue them mercilessly."[9]

In Jerusalem, marriage was not only a personal religious obligation but also a public duty.[10] Married life was recognized as the best way to preserve society's purity. The lack of any reference to women in the regulation speaks for itself; it essentially expresses the view that women are no more than instruments, expected to come and get married at any time and under any conditions. There was no similar regulation concerning women — that would have been considered superfluous or impractical. Nonetheless, Flora, the teacher from Trieste described in chapter 1, wrote in her diary that from the day she arrived in Jerusalem she was pressured to marry, because "sin couches at the door of the unmarried state."[11] We have already noted that, because of the large number of adult women living alone in Jerusalem, the Jewish population of the Holy City suffered from a marked demographic imbalance. The proportion of married individuals among the Jewish men of Jerusalem was more than 90 percent.[12]

Was this regulation ever enforced in the case of a bachelor who refused to marry? A complaint issued in 1875 by Rabbi Akiva Yosef Schlesinger explicitly bewails the fact that it was not applied in his own lifetime: "In the early generations no one was allowed by any means to settle in the Land of Israel without a wife, be he even very old, so as to protect him from sin . . . But now no one demands or asks, every man who wishes to do so comes without a wife and lives alone . . ."[13] Schlesinger was giving voice to his fear that men's sinful thoughts would delay the redemption. However, the high proportion of married men in the Holy City indicates that, even if the community did not impose sanctions, men's marriage was an obligatory norm in Jerusalem.[14] Even second or third marriages, as in eastern Europe and elsewhere, were common.[15]

As Katz has shown, the system of hierarchic family relationships in Jewish society had remained constant for generations.[16] Given the attitude to women in Jerusalem society, which derived from the traditions of both eastern European and Ottoman Jewry, women were on the one hand subjugated, but on the other they shaped a unique experience in their homes.

Members of all communities in Jerusalem, as elsewhere in the Jewish and non-Jewish worlds, saw in marriage an almost magical guarantee for the maintenance of community life.[17] When death and disease ravaged the community, one way to prevail was to celebrate a wedding in the cemetery, of all places, symbolizing the victory of fertility and life over death. In 1866, for example, in response to a severe cholera epidemic that had broken out in Jerusalem, Rabbi Yosef Lutziner and his bride were married in the cemetery on the Mount of Olives, in a ceremony held "with a large crowd and great rejoicing."[18] In Safed it was the custom to marry orphans in the cemetery, since arranging marriages for orphans was thought to be a highly meritorious deed, which might avert the danger of famine.[19] In this case the victory over death was twofold, as it ensured the continuity of both the parents and, in the future, the orphans. The custom was taken up by the Yemenite Jews living in Jerusalem: following a spate of infant deaths in their community toward the end of the nineteenth century, they consulted with the rabbis of the Ashkenazic community, who suggested that they hold an orphans' wedding in the cemetery in the presence of a large crowd.[20] In sum, marriage was not only a means toward guaranteeing the moral and demographic well-being of both individual and society; it was also a magical act, ensuring the continued health and strength of society: "Whosoever establishes a household in Israel — it is as if he had rebuilt one of the ruins of Jerusalem" (Bab. Talmud, Berakhot 6b).

Marriageable Age

According to Jewish law, the minimal age for marriage is thirteen years for a boy and twelve for a girl (*Shulchan aruch, Hil. Piryah urviyah* 1:3). Marriage at a young age was the norm in most traditional societies[21] — it was one way in which society ensured that the young of the community would be dependent on their elders. This was standard in eastern European Jewry, and indeed became the hallmark of learned Jews — the so-called *sheyne yidn.*[22] In Yemen, where Jews were severely persecuted, and in the Mediterranean countries, it was customary to marry at an even younger age than decreed by Halakhah.[23] This usage was justified by a variety of excuses: the hardships of life in exile, the desire to guarantee sexual purity, economic pressures, and the shortage of suitable spouses. A Jerusalem regulation referring to the age at which the community's children should marry stated: "One should take care to marry one's children close to puberty, as is done by the people of the

Holy City . . . and whosoever does so even earlier is worthy of praise."[24] It may be presumed that the local practice of child marriage in the Land of Israel was also influenced by the usage of the local Muslim population, as well as that of the Jews of the Ottoman Empire.[25] The few immigrants reaching the country from western Europe noted that marriageable age in the Holy Land was less than had been customary in their countries of origin.[26]

As in the "Bachelors Regulation," marrying off one's children at an early age was also intended as a measure against succumbing to sexual desire before it could arise. Charles Netter, who visited Jerusalem in 1866 as representative of the Alliance Israélite Universelle, suggested that the practice resulted from parents' interest in enlarging the support received from *halukah* funds.[27] Moreover, the economic dependence that was the rule among the Jews of Jerusalem was not considered an impediment to establishing a new family. Marrying at the age of twelve and thirteen, children became part of the adult community, as it were omitting childhood and adolescence.[28] Such marriages were forced on the boy and girl; in the case of girls, the bride also became subordinate to a new master—her husband instead of her father.[29] Child marriages were an indication of the parents' wish to impose their will on their offspring. Fadwa Toukan, born around the beginning of the twentieth century in a distinguished Arab family in Nablus, writes in her autobiography of the oppressive education she received in childhood, practically destroying her ability to love, her self-awareness, and her femininity.[30] Lawrence Stone has pointed out how oppression of children may produce an emotionally crippled family. Child marriages were one way of ensuring the continued rule of society over the new generation, as well as an expression of society's attitude to that generation.[31]

The bride's youth guaranteed that she would be completely under the sway of her parents and husband, in a state of utter submission and resignation. Ya'akov Yehoshua, who belonged to the Sephardic community, quotes his mother's story of her first meeting with her future husband and in-laws when the marriage was being arranged: "I was sitting in the courtyard playing with my friends . . . My mother approached and invited me to come home. As I was still a child, with a pale face, my mother reached out with both hands and pinched my cheeks to redden them, so that my future father [*sic*] would like me."[32] Rachel Yellin-Danin-Sochowolsky, in her memoirs, clearly expresses the helplessness of a girl who, too young to understand the situation, could not respond: "Do I know?—I answered, embarrassed, my father's and brother's question. If you think this is a suitable match, so be it!"[33] Thus, in the mid–nineteenth century, marriage at a young age was the rule in Jerusalem, and when the Jerusalem educator and scholar Yeshayahu Press's mother came to the country in 1860, aged seventeen, she was considered an "old maid," to be married off as quickly as possible.[34] Boys were also married off, to ensure that they would "behave themselves." Avraham Moshe Luncz's mother, afraid that he might wish to travel to Europe to acquire an education, quickly found a wife for him.[35]

Jewish law, strictly speaking, frowns on marriage of minors aged less than twelve. However, the Jerusalem community found a way to evade the prohibition. The city elders enacted a regulation "that no girl aged less than twelve years should be married; and if a person should marry his daughter before she reaches the age of twelve, the wedding shall be celebrated outside the city, generally in the plot of land adjacent to the Tomb of Simeon the Just."[36] This regulation, which was actually observed in practice,[37] provided an avenue for those wishing to marry off their children at an early age. The desire to preserve morality in the community thus produced a rule contrary to Halakha.[38]

While the bride's young age was a major factor in ensuring her obedience, her ignorance was no less important.[39] Women, once grown to adulthood, would treat their own young daughters just as they themselves had been treated; it is, after all, well known that adults feel the need to reconstruct behavioral patterns that they have experienced in childhood, even when those patterns are negative. In nineteenth-century Jerusalem, matchmakers and parents alike were favorably disposed toward child marriage; this was common to rich and poor, Ashkenazim and Sephardim, Yemenites and North Africans.[40] A Swiss doctor named Titus Tobler tried to explain child marriages in Jerusalem against the background of the geographical and ecological circumstances of the Orient, which, he claimed, accelerate the maturing process in girls;[41] but his attempt is not convincing. After all, the practice had been common in seventeenth- and eighteenth-century eastern Europe as well. Sha'ul Stampfer noted that the Ashkenazic community of Jerusalem was the only eastern European community in which child marriage was still customary, an indication of the community's economic condition and its view of itself as a "holy community."[42]

An expression of the negative aspect of child marriage may be found in a collection of customs common in the Land of Israel: "In the year [5]490 [1729/30] an agreement was concluded by Rabbi Shlomo Abdullah and his [rabbinical] court that no woman should be married less than twelve years old, because the practice has caused considerable misfortune."[43] Nevertheless, the community's fear of the possible outcome if the marriageable age were postponed overcame the fear of "considerable misfortune."[44] Eliezer Ben Yehuda, a severe critic of the Old Yishuv society, considered marriage at a young age, particularly of children, an impediment to a healthy married life. Referring to an affair that had resulted from a child marriage in Jerusalem, he wrote that conjugal relations between a mentally immature boy and girl might turn the latter into a "wild animal."[45] As he wrote, society's eager-ness to preserve its own purity, even at the cost of child marriages, was having the very opposite effect.

Only around the turn of the century, when marriageable age was raised in eastern Europe and various educational institutions for girls were established in Jerusalem, was the age of marriage in the Holy City raised.[46] Avraham El-maliah, a member of the Jerusalem Sephardic community, writing in 1911, took note of the change: "Not long ago the Sephardim were accustomed to marry off their daughters aged thirteen and even twelve or eleven years, and the Moroccans — at age seven or eight. But from now on girls will be married at the age of seventeen and eighteen, and the boys will marry at the age of eighteen or twenty years."[47] In 1902, the Yemenite community, influenced by the customs of Jewish society in Jerusalem, enacted a regulation that girls should not be married before reaching the age of twelve, and "neither shall young girls be sold to old men."[48] The management of the Evelina de Roth-schild School — the first girls' school in Jerusalem, which was attended by girls of both Ashkenazic and Sephardic communities — was proud of having been instrumental in getting the marriageable age postponed.[49] However, the post-ponement caused anxiety among parents, fearful that their daughters would remain unmarried — a common phenomenon among Sephardic girls.[50] The changes that took place in Jerusalem toward the end of the nineteenth cen-tury were expressive of the inroads that the new outlook had made.

Matchmaking: A Deal, a Quick Look, and Agreement

In a marriage of minors, it was self-evident that the match would be initiated not by the couple themselves but by adult society. In Jerusalem, as every-where else where couples were married at a tender age, it was the parents' task to find partners for their children.[51] Prospective spouses were generally found through some intermediary, sometimes the rabbi or his wife but mostly a *shadchan* — a professional matchmaker.[52] The use of such matchmakers, male or even female, was common among Jews everywhere.[53] Sometimes the parents themselves would initiate the match, and a *shadchan* would mediate between them; sometimes parents would come to an agreement without out-side intervention.[54] Unusual marriages, such as intercommunal matches, were generally engineered by the parents. Orphans, of whom there were a great many in Jerusalem, were married by charitable associations established for that purpose. One of these, for example, was the Benot Zion association, headed by Sultana Navon, whose members "engaged mainly in marrying male and female orphans and helping them to establish respectable Jewish families."[55] Marriage was a project for which the entire community was responsible; it was to be left neither to the families of prospective brides and grooms nor to chance. "Independent" contacts between men and women became common only at the end of the period, when the marriageable age increased and the winds of modernity began to blow, bringing with them the idea of romantic love .

The nature of the first meeting of a prospective bride and groom was also indicative of the Jerusalem community's desire for the status of a "holy society." The couple had no prior contact—that was the rule. The first meeting of the two, before their engagement was announced, was known in Yiddish as *einkuken*, that is, "looking." The necessity of such a "first glimpse" was dictated by talmudic law: "A man may not betroth a woman before he sees her" (Kiddushin 41a). It ensured that the groom would see the bride before the engagement was concluded. The text of the Talmud implies that the "first look" was incumbent on the man, for the duty of marriage was imposed on him and not on the woman.[56] Rabbi Ben Zion Yadler, a popular Jerusalem preacher, wrote in his memoirs of the shyness and silence of a couple meeting thus for the first time.[57] When the meeting took place in the bride's parents' home, generally without the couple saying a word, the women would sit near the bride, while the men would stand around the groom: "If the boy and girl were rather bold, they would cast a few glances at one another, from a distance; thus ended the couple's first step toward cementing a bond for the rest of their life."[58] Crowded living conditions, shyness, and the ascetic quest for moral purity created yet another practice: the couple might exchange glances from a distance while taking an afternoon stroll on the Sabbath or the first day of the Hebrew month, in a narrow street, or in the plaza between the Armenian Monastery and the Zion Gate.[59] Even if a young man were quick to agree to a match without seeing his future bride, he would be directed to look at her first.[60]

There are various indications that the nature of this encounter changed toward the end of the nineteenth century, and that the children were occasionally brought together for a talk, and sometimes even asked for their agreement to the match.[61] Some exceptional families, such as the Pines family, would even allow girls to express their opinions about the choice of a husband.[62] In Europe, youngsters in non-Jewish high society had already, by the late seventeenth century, been given the right to veto a proposed match.[63] However, even when young people were allowed an opinion in regard to a suitable candidate, the largely economic negotiations between the parents were carried out without their participation, and only upon their successful conclusion were the couple informed of their engagement. Fifteen-year-old Ita Yellin wrote in her memoirs how, though knowing of the negotiations to betroth her to David Yellin, she was surprised to be told about her engagement, and remarked: "Both she [her mother] and myself were surprised at first to hear the news."[64] Economic affairs were placed squarely in male hands.

The considerations governing the choice of a spouse in the Jerusalem community were no different from those normal in the Jewish world in general and indeed in the non-Jewish world. Marriage was a business transaction, a socialization procedure, not a choice guided by love.[65] The desirable qualities were scholarly excellence in the groom,[66] diligence and a good nature in the bride,[67] and lineage and a suitable dowry in both families.[68] Unlike Diaspora communities, which were based on commercial relations and whose members often sought to expand business connections by marrying into families from other places, members of the Jerusalem community unequivocally preferred their children to marry other Jerusalemites; in general, it was considered preferable that the young couple should continue to live in the Holy Land. The father of the Hamburger family, who immigrated to the Land of Israel in 1857, considered himself particularly lucky: "Not one of his sons and daughters, daughters-in-law and sons-in-law, or even grandsons and granddaughters, went abroad throughout his lifetime; they all lived here and earned their livelihoods honestly."[69] Other reports refer to young girls immigrating in order to marry grooms resident in Jerusalem.[70] Hanna Leah, granddaughter of Rabbi Shmuel of Kelm, came to Jerusalem from Kovno with her mother, to marry a young man chosen for her by her grandfather. "Hannah Leah, educated and a high-school graduate, who played the piano and wore Paris fashions, with white gloves and a parasol," belonged to a family of scholars and seems to have lovingly accepted the imposed match.[71] Agreeing to one's parents' proposal was an act of obedience and respect for them; their word was not to be questioned.[72] Evidence from the period indicates that most girls indeed bowed to their parents' will; perhaps, given their education and the prevailing atmosphere of their environment, it was not in their nature to protest.

Cases of girls who refused matches were rare, and one's impression from the few documented cases is that their struggles were doomed from the start.[73] An 1891 issue of the newspaper *Ha'or* published the story of parents who had agreed on a match before their children were born, undertaking to marry the children when they reached maturity. The agreement was concluded on a night when the mothers, who had been childless till then, immersed themselves in the *mikveh* (ritual bath) as a quasi-magical measure to ensure that they would be granted children. Their wish was granted, but when the time came the girl refused to marry the prospective groom. The unhappy father would have liked to comply, but the leaders of the community could not countenance "such a sin" and threatened him that violation of the agreement was tantamount to bloodshed. The father "had mercy" on his daughter, who was brought forcibly to the wedding canopy.[74] The fact that the story was re-ported in the press indicates the rarity of such situations. The story was pub-lished not only as a report but also as a criticism of the patriarchal nature of Jerusalem society.

Personal choice of a marriage partner was not a significant element of the matching process among Jews, whether from western or eastern Europe, until the twentieth century, though a gradual shift in the attitude to romantic bonds was discernible in western Europe as early as the eighteenth century, and in eastern Europe in the nineteenth century.[75] As Jacob Katz put it, "there was no ideology whatever of marriage as a means toward personal hap-piness."[76] As already stated, beginning at the turn of the century, the mini-mum age for marriage gradually increased, and at the same time a new con-sideration gained weight in regard to choosing a spouse: the prospective couple's attitude toward one another. Ephraim Cohen-Reiss, who had been born in the Old Yishuv and spent several years studying in western Europe, reported that the then chief rabbi of Jerusalem, Rabbi Shmuel Salant, was aware of the new ideas. Before Cohen-Reiss's engagement, the rabbi congrat-ulated his future wife, wishing her "may you be favored to marry the partner you wish!"[77]

Young people of Jerusalem who had never left the city first heard of the concept of marriage for love through meetings with educated members of the New Yishuv and through romantic stories published in the local press or in specially printed booklets. David Yellin, an educated resident of Jerusalem who was also familiar with the European capitals, wrote love letters to Ita Pines, his fiancée. Some of these letters, which indicate the degree to which the new Western ideas had penetrated Jerusalem society, were published by Ita Yellin in her autobiography. Here is an example: "As a lovely seedling, a beautiful branch, do I find thy love; it is a delight to my soul . . . How plea-surable is thy nearness, friend of my soul . . . I see thee — and thou surpassest them all."[78] (The original letter was written in elegant, biblical Hebrew, which traditional interpreters of the Bible had appropriated from the sexual realm to express the love between God and Israel; the ancient words return here to their primary meanings.) In Jerusalem of the time, the young Yellin's sentiments were quite bold.

Hannah, Avraham Luncz's daughter, described the longing for love be-tween a man and a woman in a story published in 1911 about a young Yemenite girl: "I shall not marry until I reach the age of twelve, and then only to a man who finds favor in my eyes."[79] The new, modern ideas were slowly percolating into Jerusalem, till then closed and barred to outside influence, and the first to be affected were the residents who possessed a secular educa-tion, the *maskilim*.

Intercommunal Marriages as a Two-Way Street

Jerusalem was the scene of a unique encounter between people hailing from different Diaspora communities. Most studies of intercommunal relations in Jerusalem have dwelt on the question of institutional contacts between Sephardim and Ashkenazim,[80] but many aspects of the problem have hitherto received no attention; in particular, gender has rarely been utilized as a tool of research. "The relationship between the Sephardim and the Ashkenazim is very bad. They are marked by simmering hatred, ever since the Ashkenazim established a sizable permanent presence in the Land of Israel" — so wrote Avraham Shmuel Hirschberg, a critic who, treating the Eastern communities with condescension, traveled all over the country.[81] The tension between the communities was clearly expressed on the institutional level; on the personal level, however, hostility was sometimes offset by positive contacts between individuals, including intercommunal marriages.

By "intercommunal marriages" I mean, first and foremost, marriages between Sephardim and Ashkenazim, though there were also marriages between members of the different Eastern communities, such as Yemenites and Sephardim. Lacking statistics in this context, one can nevertheless surmise that such marriages became more common toward the end of the nineteenth century; the change affected all the communities, including Hasidim and *mitnagdim* among the Ashkenazim, and soon began to leave its mark on society as whole.[82]

The attitude to intercommunal marriages was complex and paradoxical, as if expressive of rejection and appreciation at the same time. In some cases such marriages were perceived as a magical remedy for some social misfortune. Once, when marrying orphans in the cemetery failed to have the desired results, the elders of the Yemenite community sought a solution by mystical means; on the basis of a dream, they decided that an "intermarriage" between Yemenites and Sephardim would remedy the situation,[83] and indeed it did. This evidence, dated to the late nineteenth century, indicates how rare marriages between these two communities were, so much so that they were considered to have special spiritual and supernatural qualities. Statistical data from a later period imply that the proportion of intermarriages among the Yemenites was higher in Jerusalem than elsewhere; the reason may lie in the practice outlined above.[84]

Intercommunal marriages provide a most intriguing angle for viewing Jerusalem society. On the one hand, members of every community that came to the Holy City did so out of a desire to conserve their own heritage; on the other, neighborly relations, and even more so intercommunal marriages, did much to reshape communal customs. Intermarriages were very rare in the middle of the nineteenth century. Elizabeh Finn, wife of then British consul James Finn, believed that Ashkenazim and Sephardim never intermarried.[85] However, Ludwig August Frankl, the secretary of the Jewish community in Vienna, who came to Jerusalem in 1856 and founded the Laemel school, wrote that "only the poor among them may marry one another."[86] Moses Montefiore founded the Mishkenot Sha'ananim neighborhood in 1860 for both Ashkenazim and Sephardim; it has been surmised that he intended to en-courage intercommunal marriages by offering a money prize, but there were no takers.[87] Montefiore's intentions do not seem to have had much appeal for many Jerusalem parents.[88] Nevertheless, in an entry in his diary in 1866 he noted that, happily, marriages between Ashkenazim and Sephardim were no longer so rare in the Holy Land.[89] The first to cross the intercommunity boundaries were apparently not the poor, as Frankl had suggested, but the rich, who sought spouses in conformity with their wealth and social standing. However, while there is ample documentation about the rich and distin-guished members of society, our information concerning the poor is rather sparse. The newspaper *Hazevi* reported in 1885 that intercommunal mar-riages of poor couples were a new and welcome phenomenon.[90]

Members of the Hod (Holland-Deutschland) *kolel*, who were among the more wealthy Ashkenazim, were apparently the first to forge ties of mar-riage with members of the Sephardic community.[91] Eliezer Bergman married his son Binyamin, whom he had brought with him as a boy in the 1830s, to Miriam Kulis, daughter of the saintly Rabbi Abdullah of Baghdad.[92] Eliezer boasted, in a letter to his relatives in Germany (1847), of the distinguished marriage his son had made: "The daughter of a well-born and distinguished family . . . The bride's mother, most blessed of women in tents, is a righteous and learned woman, and her daughter too, about 15 years old, is chaste and modest and most worthy."[93] Of course, the model of womanhood portrayed in this letter is in keeping with the values of western European Jewry. Another rare description of such a bride is that of Delicia, daughter of Rabbi David ben Shim'on, head of the Mughrabi *kolel*, who married Joseph Kraus, secre-tary of the Hungarian *kolel*:

She inherited from her father all his sterling virtues and good qualities, and while still young studied Torah and wisdom, being proficient in the Talmud and Halakhic liter-ature; she would always debate with her father's visitors on Talmudic texts and com-mentaries on the weekly portion of the Torah.[94]

Delicia was thus the daughter of a scholar who was herself a scholar. Rabbi Yizhak Oplatka, eager to join the Sephardic community, married a wellborn young Sephardic woman.[95] But marriages with Sephardic women were not confined to Jews influenced by western European culture. A member of the eastern European Porush family married the daughter of a rich man of Calcutta, who was just twelve years old at the time.[96] In sum, lineage and wealth were instrumental in bridging intercommunal differences.

Communication or, more precisely, the lack of a common language, was the first and most serious problem of intercommunal relations. Ashkenazic society spoke Yiddish; the Sephardim, Ladino; and the North African and Yemenite communities, different Arabic dialects. There is varied evidence from the mid–nineteenth century that everyday contacts among members of different communities were conducted in Hebrew; this was the lingua franca, the tongue that linked the Jewish residents of the city[97] (a fact that is known to have contributed to the revival of Hebrew as a modern language). Most Jewish women, however, had not studied any Hebrew. It is surely no accident that the earliest intercommunal marriages were of educated women who knew Hebrew. When an Ashkenazic man married a Sephardic woman of more common origins, they had no common language.

The normal situation — marriages of young children, complete strangers who had at most stolen a glance at each other — was thus further aggravated by an inability to communicate. This norm is evidence of the dominant perception in society that marriage in itself provided the means for living together. According to the traditional perception, people were not free to manage their own lives, but everything was dictated "from above," whether this meant God or His recognized partners — the parents. Intercommunal marriage provided an example of the total subordination of marrying couples to the authority of adult society.

Avraham Shmuel Hirschberg, examining the issue of intercommunal marriage in the context of gender, stated that the most successful matches were those in which an Ashkenazic man married a Sephardic woman. This, he argued, was because of the different communities' attitudes to women: "[A Sephardic woman,] accustomed from her parents' home to consider a woman as a maidservant enslaved to her husband, will be happy with her Ashkenazic husband, who will respect and love her with the respect and love that a husband owes his wife." Hirschberg, an educated but prejudiced European, aware of the importance of respect and love for the marital bond, believed that these features would determine the success of a marriage. As a Sephardic woman was inferior in status to her Ashkenazic sister, marriage to an Ashkenazic man would benefit her. On the other hand, "when an Ashkenazic woman marries a Sephardi, such a match will never succeed; for the Sephardi . . . cannot give his wife the respect that she deserves."[98] He inferred, from a conversation with a learned Sephardic man married to an Ashkenazic woman, that the lifestyle of Ashkenazic society was at variance with Sephardic practice. Sephardic mentality in the area of gender relations was quite different from that of the Ashkenazim. Nevertheless, despite such mental and cultural differences, intermarriage between different communities became a fact of life.

Such marriages provided a channel through which mutual influence could flow. Various customs trickled through from community to community, shattering established conventions and habits. Consideration of the two most famous intercommunal matches in Jerusalem confirms this statement. In both cases, the husbands were Yellins: Yehoshua Yellin married Serah, daughter of Shlomo Yehezkel Yehudah, scion of an Iraqi Jewish family; and his son, David Yellin, married Ita, daughter of Yehiel Michel Pines, who came from Ruzhany, Belorussia. Both marriages were arranged by the heads of the respective families, without the aid of *shadchanim*. Yehoshua's father-in-law stipulated two special conditions: his daughter would not shave her head, as the Ashkenazic brides used to do; and the young couple would live in his house so that the groom could learn his wife's family customs and language. From the second condition we learn that when the young Yehoshua married his wife, they had literally no common language. Shlomo Yehezkel, the rich, distinguished father of the bride, showed a profound understanding of the difficulties involved in adopting a new community. By insisting that his daughter would not shave her head or move out of her home, but continue to live for the first phase of her marriage with her biological family, he was essentially proposing that his young Ashkenazic son-in-law should adopt Sephardic customs.

The wedding, which took place in 1856, was apparently one of the first mixed ones in the Holy City in the nineteenth century. As the groom wrote in his memoirs: "The wedding was celebrated with pomp and circumstance, the like of which had never been seen by the people of Jerusalem at that time."[99] The magnificent wedding was tantamount to a declaration that intercommunal marriage was a respectable practice. The fact that the conditions affected not only economic matters but also religious custom (not shaving the head) and social practices (the couple's first home and spoken language) was proof that social change was possible. The nuptial ceremony was performed in a unique style, both Ashkenazic and Sephardic, indicating the formation of a new local custom, the core culture of Jerusalem.[100]

David Yellin, son of Yehoshua and Serah, was thus of "mixed," half-Sephardic, origins. His love letters to Ita Pines, his bride — daughter of Yehiel and Zipporah Pines and thus an Ashkenazi — reveal the difficulty experienced by the young couple in overcoming their respective communities' attitudes to gender relations. The fact that the educated David Yellin advocated new, European values merely complicated the already serious difficulties facing the "mixed" couple. For example, David was deeply hurt by his bride's refusal to sit beside him after their engagement. Here, too, the bride's father showed more understanding of the mental discrepancy between the two young people, and urged his daughter to adopt her groom's customs. The key to the success of an intercommunal marriage was the readiness of one party to the marriage to adopt at least some new practices.[101]

Naturally, most of our information on this issue concerns intercommunal matches that succeeded. There are a few reports of families that refused to permit such marriages,[102] such as that of a young Yemenite man who wanted to marry a young Sephardic woman and was refused on such grounds: "The parents denied his appeal, arguing that communities in Jerusalem were not accustomed to marrying one another, particularly since Hayim and his community had just arrived from distant climes [literally, from beyond the Dark Mountains] and no one was acquainted with their customs and nature."[103] In this case the would-be groom did not give in, and the girl agreed to marry him.

Immigration to the Land of Israel, one aim of which was to preserve one's heritage, was thus a cause of renewal as well. Although members of different communities generally lived in separate courtyards, the geographical proximity and, no less, the shared experience, combined with religious ideology, created fertile ground for the emergence of a society that, while institutionally fragmented, was held together by a multitude of connecting threads. Gender research has revealed the undoubted interest of Sephardic women in marrying Ashkenazic men. Intercommunal contacts not only created various unifying influences among the Jews of the Holy City but also promoted processes of change. In a society that firmly believed in the need for the preservation of traditional Judaism, intercommunal marriages proved how difficult it was to adhere to rigorous norms. Despite the many differences between Ashkenazic and Sephardic usages, family ties between the communities made it imperative to find some common ground. Examining the private and familial aspect of societal relations, one finds evidence of sometimes revolutionary change rumbling beneath the surface. The monolithic character of Jerusalem's Jewish community was slowly being replaced by a kind of cultural pluralism.

The Dowry

While finding a match is everywhere as difficult as the parting of the Red Sea, here in the Holy City it is even more difficult, for as your excellencies are aware, there is no commerce and trade here, this being a place exclusively devoted to study and prayer.[104]

So wrote David, son of Menachem Hakohen, son-in-law of the celebrated Rabbi Israel of Shklov, in a letter to the officials in Amsterdam responsible for distributing the *halukah* monies from western Europe, referring to the financial problems facing parents in Jerusalem who wished to find matches for their children. The all-important *nedunyah*, that is, dowry,[105] was entirely dependent on the parents; the young couple had no say in the matter. The importance of the economic arrangements prior to a wedding cannot be exaggerated, in view of both the poverty rampant in the Holy City and the fact that the couple were so young that they could not yet make their own way. The economic aspect of marriage, which was common to members of all religions,[106] generally guaranteed that bride and groom came from the same economic class. In Jerusalem, as in other Jewish communities, the dowry was contributed by both families. There were differences between Ashkenazim and Sephardim in this area too. The father of an Ashkenazic bride generally "bought" the marriage, that is, he paid the groom and undertook to provide for the couple during the first few years of marriage.[107] The custom of paying the groom (or his family) for his agreement to marry one's daughter and take her under his wing emphasizes the bride's inferior social status. In the Sephardic community, the groom's parents contributed a large sum to the parents of the bride, as compensation for the expenses incurred in rearing their daughter to marriageable age, and in order to guarantee payment of her *ketubah* should she be divorced. Both Sephardim and Ashkenazim considered the bride as an "object," to be passed from hand to hand and paid for — whether payment was given to her former "owner" or her new one. If the parents could not honor their commitments, for whatever reason, the engagement would be canceled.[108]

The dowry, whether in Jerusalem or elsewhere, could be divided into three components:

1. Sustenance paid to the couple in the first stage of their marriage (by the parents of either groom or bride, sometimes by both families). The duration of this stage varied from one to four years, sometimes even more.[109]
2. Money or jewelry given the bride by her father and/or her groom. In wealthy families the sums involved could be quite high.[110]
3. Household effects, including clothing and bedding for the bride — it was this component that was, strictly speaking, known in Hebrew as the *nedunyah*.[111]

As to the economic aspect of marriage agreements between poor parents, who could not support their children, the available documentation provides no information. However, the many existing letters begging for help to arrange matches, as we shall see below, are proof enough of the basic need for some contribution, minor though it might have been.[112]

Before the wedding, a bride would be occupied in various ways relating to the third part of the dowry (the *nedunyah*), which might be considered as a kind of "cushion," helping to ease the bride's departure from her maternal home. Rivkah Alper has described Rachel Yellin-Danin's feelings before her wedding: "I felt like a guest in my own parents' home, taking leave of my youth and embarking on a new life, which was as yet hidden and mysterious for me."[113] Preparations for the wedding were entrusted mainly to the women of the family, who took the opportunity to lavish love and attention on the bride before she left for her new life. The same was true of the *nedunyah* itself.

Among the Sephardim, preparation of the *nedunyah* was the main occupation of a young girl until her marriage: "Ask a Sephardic girl what she does all day . . . to prepare everything necessary for the *nedunyah*. While still young, she was already thinking night and day of the *nedunyah*."[114] These sentences, published in the newspaper *Hashkafah* in 1907, betray more than an element of criticism; the reporter, who signed himself "A young Sephardi," condemned the girls of his community for their lack of interest in anything except marriage, while Ashkenazic girls, whom he described as well educated, took an interest in national affairs as well.

Unlike other phases of the wedding preparations, for which the father alone was responsible, the bride herself was involved in preparing her household effects, thus gradually accustoming herself to the idea of departure from the parental home. Detailed accounts of the atmosphere in the large community of Salonika indicate that these preparations were a profound social experience for both the bride and her friends, who labored together with her, singing and chattering.[115]

It was customary among all Jerusalem communities to prepare detailed lists of the bride's accoutrements. The various objects were displayed in a kind of exhibition a few days before the wedding, and an assessor would estimate their value.[116] This exhibition was known as *ašogár*. Both men and women came to see it, and a professional scribe would meticulously record everything. The many such lists preserved in the depths of the Jerusalem archives furnish clear proof that this practice was not confined to Sephardim. Besides detailed lists in the typical "Rashi" script of the Sephardic scribes, one finds no less detailed lists in Yiddish, which, among other things, give us an idea of typical Jerusalem dress at the time.[117] Textiles and clothing were generally prepared by women, but the estimates of their value were always done by men — yet another example of women's labor being dominated by men.[118] The *ašogár* gave the bride's family an opportunity to flaunt their wealth and enhance their prestige.[119] However, this ostentation was sometimes suppressed, as in the case of the Bukharan community at the beginning of the twentieth century, whose rabbis, showing understanding for the feelings of poor brides whose parents were unable to procure them such finery, forbade any public demonstration of the bridal effects, urging that they be assessed in private "in accordance with the custom of Jerusalem."[120]

The bride would receive women's jewelry — constituting both wealth and artistic value — from her groom, as a sign of his admiration for her, as well as evidence of his economic standing. The descriptions of jewelry in the lists stand out in particular against the background of wretched poverty typical of the Holy City, whose Jews lived modest lives, and the Jerusalem regulation prohibiting the wearing of jewelry.[121] The Ashkenazic Ita Yellin, in her auto-biography, provides a lengthy description of jewelry she received from her half-Sephardic husband-to-be, whose family was known for its wealth and distinction:

> The gifts I received from the day of the *kinyan* till the wedding were: During the *kinyan*, ear-rings, a gold medallion on a chain, and a gold pin set with rubies. On the day of the *tena'im* I received a pin with precious stones; on Purim, strings of pearls and gold bracelets; for the festival of Shavu'ot, a gold ring set with pearls, a very valuable, artistically made gold chain, and a gold watch.[122]

This list incidentally indicates the stages involved in realization of the marriage contract: the *kinyan* (literally "acquisition," namely, the formal decision to marry the couple), the *tena'im* (stipulation of the terms of the match), and various festivals. The jewels were bestowed on the bride at set times, as decided by both sides, as befitted a business agreement.[123] The jewels were intended not merely to enhance the bride's appearance but also as a kind of deposit, stored away for use in time of need. The woman could use her valuables as security if necessary and thereby earn profit for the entire family.

In contrast to the bride's jewelry, which was displayed for all to see, the gifts given the groom were not shown. Paradoxically, it was the property of the woman, supposedly a symbol of domesticity and privacy, that was exhibited in public, while the man's possessions were considered his private property, not visible to the critical eyes of society. Society was thus spinning its manipulative web: Was this public exposure supposed to strengthen the woman's ties to her private property, or was the opposite true? The bride's effects, representing her private world, were shown for all to see before her marriage, ostensibly, in order to guarantee her economic security; in actual fact, perhaps it was just another manifestation of society's close supervision of women. A woman's privacy was violated in any case immediately after her marriage, when proof of her virginity was presented for all to see.[124] Male society sought to take charge of a woman's most intimate affairs: her virginity, her clothing, including her underclothing. In stark contrast to the conventional principal that a woman should remain at home, this exhibition of her personal belongings constituted an undoubted invasion of her privacy.

The feeling in the Jerusalem community at large, that the Jewish people throughout the Diaspora were duty bound to send it aid, found particular expression in the many requests for aid to prospective brides, a charity known in Hebrew as *hakhnasat kallah.* Underlying such requests was the idea that it was a religious duty, incumbent on the whole community, and not only on parents, to ensure that their children would be able to marry. This explains the large proportion of "begging letters" that specifically mentioned *hakhnasat kallah.*[125] Some parents would actually undertake to give a *nedunyah* beyond their means and later dispatch frantic letters to obtain help in meeting their obligations. These letters, which were very common,[126] attest to the desperate financial straits of the residents of Jerusalem, as well as to their conviction that this seemingly private area — their children's marriage — was the responsibility of the Jewish community worldwide. However, the practice was not confined to the poor but could be found even among the more distinguished Jews of Jerusalem. For example, such personalities as the scholar Avraham Moshe Luncz and Dr. Eleazar Gruenhut, director of the German Jewish orphanage in Jerusalem, penned letters asking for help to marry off their children.[127] Even those of the city's Jewish residents who possessed a secular education believed in the particular merit of helping Jews in the Holy Land, in particular young brides.[128]

The winds of progress also affected dowry practices. An echo of new ideas may be discerned, for example, in the words of an elderly woman, quoted referring to the mid–nineteenth century: "More than thirty years ago, before the Me'ah She'arim neighborhood was founded [in 1874], when we women were not as important as we are today, every young girl was obliged to bring a large *nedunyah* to her groom."[129] Paradoxically, the speaker was implying that the high dowry payments were an indication of women's inferiority. Toward the end of the century, when secular education began to make inroads and there was a greater appreciation for women, the sums of money involved were reduced. This may also be inferred from a letter written in 1903 by the above-mentioned Eleazar Gruenhut to Moses Gaster, *hakham* of the Sephardic community in London, who corresponded widely with many members of the community in the Land of Israel. Gruenhut appealed for help in defraying expenses incurred in celebrating his daughter's wedding and purchasing household effects promised to his son-in-law, noting that the sums involved were relatively modest: "This lad is well educated and devout, he finds favor in my eyes and my daughter has found favor in his, so he agreed to marry her without a dowry, on condition that I give him what he needs to spend on household effects."[130]

Despite the father's concern, he was finally able to meet his commitment, as we learn from a newspaper report in a 1904 issue of *Hashkafah,* according to which the wedding indeed took place: "Wedding of the fine young woman, Rivkah Regina, daughter of Dr. Gruenhut . . . A large crowd of distinguished members of the Jewish congregation, as well as Muslim and Christian notables, his excellency the Consul of Germany and his excellency the Consul of Austria, and physicians, colleagues of the groom, were present at the wedding ceremony."[131]

In sum, while the poverty common in Jerusalem presented young women's parents with a serious economic challenge, the feeling among Jerusalemites that Jews all over the world should support them through the channels of the *halukah* was effective.

The Engagement Ceremony

The engagement ceremony, generally held at the bride's home, was on the one hand a celebration of the new bond to be established but also, on the other, an act symbolizing the conclusion of a business deal.[132] As was customary in Jerusalem, men and women sat in different rooms. The meaningful part of the affair was conducted by the men: it was they who formulated the *tena'im*, as the terms of the agreement were called in Hebrew, and broke a dish to commemorate the destruction of the Temple; if the elders of the community were present, they would confirm the agreement.[133] The young couple did not always participate.[134] Hayim Hamburger, later a Jerusalem banker, told the story of a unique initiative on his own part: "While my 'last *tena'im*'[135] were being written, I went up to my grandfather's home, knocked on the door and entered uninvited. They were very happy to see me; the writing was already over, and they were busy eating bagels and drinking tea, and my future father-in-law said to his sons-in-law: 'The groom isn't lazy at all!'"[136]

The higher the economic standing of the couple, the more extravagant was the engagement party. When Ya'akov Valero, scion of a famous banking family, was engaged to be married in 1906, the proceedings were honored not only by the spiritual leaders of the Sephardic community but also by the pasha Rashid Bey, the municipal engineer Kaminian Effendi, and other Ottoman notables.[137] From the late nineteenth century on, Jerusalem newspapers carried numerous engagement announcements and congratulations.[138] This was a new custom, adopted by the more wealthy members of the community, as well as those known as its *maskilim*, that is, those having a secular education (though still remaining observant).

An old Jerusalem regulation decreed that the fiancé and fiancée should not meet before the wedding; among the Eastern communities, it was the custom that after the engagement a man should not visit his fiancée's home.[139] The accepted Ashkenazic custom, which in time assumed the force of a binding regulation, was that the couple did not meet at all. Flora Randegger, the young woman from Trieste who lived for a while in Jerusalem, wrote in her diary: "After the *tena'im* have been written, the couple remain far apart, like strangers."[140] The Jerusalem-born scholar Yeshayahu Press, in his memoirs, described his elder sister's confusion upon meeting her fiancé by chance in the street: "She was astonished and, calling out, 'There he goes!' quickly retraced her steps and ran home."[141] Her failure even to mention his name and her terror at seeing him attest to the alienation that she felt, perhaps hinting at the difficulties that might arise after the wedding, when, totally unprepared, they would begin to live together as a married couple. We may assume the confusion felt by the fiancée was matched by her husband-to-be. Thus, Ya'akov Orenstein discontinued his studies with Rabbi Shmuel Salant after becoming engaged to the latter's stepdaughter, in order to avoid seeing her upon coming to his teacher's home.[142]

This strict separation of the sexes was one of those stringent practices for which Jerusalem was famous. Underlying it was the fear of premarital relations between the future bride and groom. This fear was of course quite unmerited in the case of very young couples, who were not sexually mature. Another possible motive for the regulation was to prevent not only intimacy but any kind of acquaintance, even the most superficial, between the couple before their marriage, lest one or both of them decide to oppose the relationship that had been forced on them. Complete lack of information about one another would prevent any such eventuality. Only around the turn of the century, when the stringency of Ashkenazic engagement customs became somewhat weaker, was this demand for complete separation also relaxed, and couples began to meet while engaged.

In addition, around the same time, when the age of marriage rose, some couples refused to submit to social convention and blazed new paths. Thus, Yehuda Aaron Weiss, a printer later active in public affairs, having no relatives in the country, considered his future father-in-law's home as his own and ignored the local custom.[143] Ita Pines reported that her half-Sephardic fiancé, David Yellin, disobeyed the dictates of the Ashkenazi fanatics of Jerusalem and frequently visited her at her home. As she wrote, it was considered "very sinful" for the young couple to hold a conversation, but her parents and her future in-laws thought otherwise.[144]

Among the Sephardim, however, the atmosphere was more relaxed. On the contrary, it was the custom for a Sephardic groom to visit his fiancée on festival days and bring her gifts; he could thus have the pleasure of seeing her dress up in his gifts as an indication of the couple's new status.[145] These customs made the engagement period a time of psychological and material preparation for the marriage. However, as brides were often very young, such meetings did not always have the desired effect.[146] David Yellin's candid letters to his fiancée, Ita Pines, reveal something of the bewildered state of the young girl, unaccustomed to have any contact with boys or men and not properly capable of expressing her feelings. In these letters, David Yellin confessed his love for Ita, complaining of her shyness, which impeded his efforts to forge a relationship with her. Addressing her as "Meine liebe und leben"[147] (my love and life — Yiddish was the language in which they could converse), he admitted his confusion at her shyness: "At first I was pleased by your embarrassment, for I saw it as a sign of the purity of your soul and the depth of your chastity . . . But I would like the shyness to come to an end . . . If you knew, my soul's beloved, how my heart aches when I greet you and you do not answer; or when you rise from your seat to sit far away from me."[148] The extreme modesty created by the typical Ashkenazic education in Jerusalem was clearly evident in Ita Pines's manners and bashfulness, to the extent that she would refuse to sit beside her fiancé. David Yellin, accustomed to the greater freedom given to betrothed couples among Sephardim, was hurt. Ita, for her part, promised to try to overcome her shyness; her response reflects the degree to which Ashkenazic society was gradually becoming accustomed to new values and modes of behavior.

Another attestation of the new manners percolating into Jerusalem society is the New Year's card that Chayim Winograd sent his fiancée, Batsheva Koenig, with a personal printed message in flowery, poetic language: "Please accept my greetings . . . My soul is bound to your pure soul for all eternity."[149]

The Wedding Celebrations

The wedding, with its wealth of events and ceremonies, celebrated the beginning of a new life for bride and groom. Wedding celebrations differed in nature, depending on the country of origin of the couple being wed, though the basic components were of course the same.[150] Although the Jerusalem community as a whole was made up of many smaller communities, weddings in Jerusalem followed a common pattern, as was also evident in the design of the *ketubah*, the marriage contract.[151] Any culture considers the celebration of a wedding as a sacred rite, in fact the most important rite of passage in one's life.[152] The message conveyed by the ceremony was complex: Members of the two sexes that had been carefully kept apart, from childhood to maturity, came together in a covenant that would unite them from that time on. The ceremony performed under the wedding canopy, the *chupah*, permitted what was absolutely forbidden otherwise — commingling of the sexes. The goal of the union — to ensure the birth of a new generation — was not a private one but the concern of the whole community. The marriage covenant was a high point in the lives not only of the bride and groom but also of their parents and of the community. In contrast to contemporary society, in which both men and women freely choose their partners and make their own decisions with regard to the details of the ceremony, young couples in those times were guided at every step of the way by their families and by the community.

While the rapid growth of the community brought about added involvement of the community in private life, it also allowed the individual more independence.[153] However, the increase in individual freedom enhanced the community's coercive power. The wedding ceremony, which in the mid–nineteenth century had still been a small one, celebrated within the family, emerged from the four walls of the family home and took on a public aspect. The change is clearly illustrated by the way invitations to the wedding were issued.

In mid-nineteenth-century Jerusalem, a wedding would be announced publicly, the announcer inviting the entire community to attend.[154] In Safed, however, it was customary to draw up a list of guests and give it to the beadle of the *kolel*, who would invite the guests to the different parts of the ceremony.[155] Toward the end of the nineteenth century, the informal mode of invitation was supplanted by new customs. The rapid demographic growth of the community, the development of the local printing industry and of the local press — all these contributed to the emergence of printed invitation cards and newspaper announcements,[156] with or without ornamentation; this applied both to longtime residents and to newcomers.[157] As it happened, the members of the wealthy Bukharan community were among the first to try to keep out unwanted guests, and in 1904 they enacted a regulation stating, "No man may come to another's home for some celebration unless invited in writing."[158] Besides written invitations, there were also public announcements congratulating the bride and groom.[159] The use of the printing press and the newspaper attests to the change in the nature of the ceremony itself: it was no longer a small, modest affair, confined to the immediate family, but a public event, a joyful occasion in which large numbers of people were expected to participate. Private affairs had become the concern of the community, and the formal invitation became an integral part of the ceremony.[160]

The wealth of ceremonies associated with the wedding expressed, not only the desire for entertainment in a city that generally lacked such occasions,[161] but also emotional statements aimed at the bride and groom. The wedding ceremony was a kind of show, a rite of passage symbolizing the beginning of a new life. Because of the puritanical nature of society and the fact that the bride and groom were almost completely unprepared for married life, the various stages of the ceremony employed a special language of symbols. The various symbols, which could also be found in the different parts of the Diaspora, related above all to matters of sex and fertility.[162]

On the Sabbath before the wedding, an Ashkenazic groom in Jerusalem — as indeed anywhere else in the Ashkenazic Jewish world — was called up to read the Torah in the synagogue, while the bride's friends would visit her at her home.[163] This applied to Sephardic brides as well. The Ladino word *vizhita* (visit) was also adopted by Ashkenazic women, pointing up the fact that this feature was common to both communities.[164] These visits, which expressed women's eagerness to lavish attention on the bride, were quite modest in Jerusalem. In Salonika, however, the bride's female relatives and friends would throw a party on that Saturday evening, at which ancient love songs were sung to her.[165] In Hasidic communities in nineteenth-century Galicia, young women would gather at the bride's home on the wedding day and dance with her to raise her spirits.[166] All these occasions gave young women an opportunity to express their emotions and innermost feelings.

Once a couple had received their friends' approval, each of them separately would visit the rabbis of their community and request their blessing. Ita Yellin wrote: "Two days before my wedding day, my mother took me to Rabbi Shmuel Salant, of blessed memory, so that he would bless me on the occasion of my marriage."[167] Less distinguished brides would come to the rabbi's wife for a blessing.[168] After receiving the rabbinical blessings the bride and groom — still separate — would often visit the Wailing Wall: "According to Jerusalem custom, . . . a groom and bride on their wedding day . . . would come to the Wailing Wall and offer there a prayer of thanks and ask for mercy concerning the future."[169]

An occasion of great excitement for the bride was the visit to the *mikveh*, the ritual bath, on the night before the wedding. While a married woman's immersion in the *mikveh* is generally an entirely private act, performed far from the public eye, in Jerusalem, the same act of the bride before her wedding was carried out with much ado, in both Ashkenazic and Sephardic communities.[170] Again quoting Ita Yellin: "Women from both sides, that of the groom and that of the bride, came to accompany me to the bathhouse, . . . singing and playing, with drums and dancing . . . There were also condiments, coffee and delicacies."[171] The festive atmosphere was further increased by taking a roundabout route to the *mikveh* and carrying torches. The bride and her companions were greeted on the way to and from the *mikveh*, and showered with candies by the local women standing at their doors.[172] Some features of these proceedings would be duplicated at the wedding itself: the young woman, being led toward an unknown future, was supported by other women, headed by her mother and her friends; the ceremony was full of joy, accompanied by music, dancing, candles, and a large crowd.

Luncz describes similar proceedings for the benefit of the groom: On the eve of the wedding, his relatives and friends would gather at his home to cut his hair, again with musical accompaniment.[173] Cutting the hair, incidentally, is a well-known component of rites of passage that signify separation or farewell.[174] In some places the groom was also expected to bathe in a *mikveh* or in the sea.[175] At any rate, the groom's haircut and the bride's immersion in the *mikveh* were physical preparations for the great day; both were likened to "a newborn baby whose sins have been forgiven."[176] These preparations were gender-linked events, reemphasizing the separation of the bride and groom.

Jerusalem weddings were usually held on Friday afternoons, so that the wedding feast could be combined with the Sabbath meal.[177] "A ruling has been issued in the Holy Land that it is customary to marry young men and women on the eve of the Holy Sabbath, as has been permitted by the greatest Halakhic authorities, and so it should indeed be ruled."[178] The proximity of the wedding to the Sabbath also minimized the time "wasted" by Torah scholars away from their studies; but it also invested the proceedings with the special sanctity of the Sabbath.

As already noted, Bukharan Jews in Jerusalem at the turn of the century were particularly concerned to avoid needless ostentation, and this tendency was meticulously observed with respect to wedding celebrations. Thus, they ruled that some of the feasts that customarily preceded the actual wedding ceremony in Bukhara should be abolished: the community elders sought "to abolish bad customs that have been followed until today . . . and only the closest relatives should be invited."[179] Residence in the Holy City thus encouraged the maintenance of a modest, unostentatious lifestyle.

Wedding ceremonies in the mid–nineteenth century were held at the home of the parents of the bride or the groom; sometimes, if neither possessed a home with a sufficiently large room, the wedding canopy was set up in the synagogue courtyard by the cistern, as a symbol of good luck.[180] One compendium of "Land of Israel customs" reads as follows: "It is the custom to betroth the woman in the groom's home, but in the Land of Israel and elsewhere one betroths her when she is still in her parental home, on the eve of the wedding day, and at night she is led to the groom's home."[181] Performance of the wedding ceremony at the bride's parental home stressed the importance of the bride's father: he had arranged the match, it was in his house that she married her future husband, and from there she would leave for her new home. Some used to accompany the groom and his party in a procession from the synagogue to the bride's home.[182] Beginning in the 1880s, when new buildings were springing up in and around Jerusalem, weddings were held in halls; thus, the wedding of Albert and Henriette Antebi took place in the new Alliance Israélite School.[183] The private ceremony had taken on public features.

The differences between different ethnic groups were clearly expressed in bridal costume. Ashkenazic brides wore the large white *dektukh* (sheet), a

typical item of Ashkenazic women's clothing (in fact, this was also the costume of German Jewish brides in the fifteenth century).[184] White, the color
of the shrouds in which the dead were wrapped for burial, symbolized the serious nature of the occasion and was conducive to a more subdued atmosphere. Jewish brides in the Caucasus also wore mourning clothes, as if to express their sorrow at leaving their parents' homes.[185] Ashkenazic brides in
Jerusalem were forbidden to adorn themselves in any way, even to wear floral
wreaths, owing to the perpetual mourning for the destruction of the Temple.
This may be inferred from the account rendered by Ludwig August Frankl:
"There was no floral wreath on her uncovered hair, for since the destruction
of the Holy City the brides of Jerusalem do not wear such things."[186] All these
strictures were further examples of the Jerusalem proclivity, already noted
many times in these pages, for asceticism.[187]

Sephardic customs, however, were different. Sephardic brides dressed up
and wore elaborate finery, stressing their sexuality. "Diligent women decorate
the bride, painting her hands, hair and even feet with *hini*; her eyelids, eye-
brows, face and lips are painted with eye shadow, kohl, vermilion and nut-
shells."[188] Bridal costume expressed the different communities' attitudes to
life, marriage, and even to magic and sorcery. A knot in a woman's hair — hair
being an important component of her sexuality — was thought to possess magical powers; for that reason, a bride's hair was unbraided, so that "there should
be no knot, lest witches be able to bind the couple and prevent them coming
together."[189]

Improvements in economic conditions and in living conditions outside
the Old City walls also brought about changes in bridal costume. Ita Pines,
whose family customs, though Ashkenazic, were not those generally accepted
in Jerusalem, wore "a dress of light pink taffeta, made in keeping with the lat-
est fashion," but she concealed it under a white silk top.[190] Her sister-in-law
Rachel, daughter of a Sephardic mother and an Ashkenazic father, wore jewelry and wore a magnificent silk dress that her mother had brought from
India.[191]

Before the religious ceremony (the *kidushin*) the bride and groom were en-
wrapped together in a new *tallit* (prayer shawl), and in honor of the occasion
the groom recited the blessing over a new garment (*shehechiyanu*). Sometimes
the *tallit* was raised and spread like a canopy over the couple's heads,[192] symbolizing their coming together as one body and their sanctification through
the *tallit*. This ceremony, lasting some five minutes,[193] was also supposed to
have a spiritual effect on the couple. In one report, for example, we are told
of a young bride who stood beneath the canopy, "her eyes closed and her
hands tightly clenched."[194] On another occasion, Ludwig Frankl, a deeply
perceptive person, described the bride as having "the look of a marionette."[195]

The bride's stance surely attested to her feelings: the closed eyes and clenched fists were signs of helplessness and submission. Another element of the ceremony, her walking around the groom seven times, symbolized "her duty to take daily care of the head of the household."[196] Few young women showed any sign of rebellion: "In some circles the groom used to tread on the bride's foot to demonstrate his domination of her. But if the bride was smart she would act first, treading on his foot to show him that she would rule him."[197]

Judging from accounts by tourists, such as William Francis Lynch and Shim'on Berman, Jewish brides were better off than Muslim brides in the Holy Land. Lynch provides the following description of a Muslim bride walking beside her groom and his friends: "On each side was a man with a drawn sword in his hand, suggesting to the mind thoughts about a lamb led to the sacrifice."[198] Berman describes a Muslim bride exchanging a few remarks with her groom, but he beat her with his stick to demonstrate his power over her.[199] The fate of Christian brides was, it seems, not much better: "She must look heartbroken, as if reluctant to be married."[200] All these descriptions leave one with the impression of a young woman being delivered into the hands of a new master, a stranger, with a heavy heart.

The custom of breaking a glass under the wedding canopy, which is common to many communities, was given a magical significance. Since the glass shards were supposed to have a weakening influence on the groom's sexual prowess, the glass would be wrapped in a kerchief so that it would be possible to remove every fragment without leaving a trace.[201] After the *ketubah* had been read, it was customary to place before the couple a silver platter with gold-plated fish, symbolizing fertility, and the guests would congratulate them. The use of fish or seeds of grain was also common to many communities;[202] it took the place of an open injunction, which was apparently never actually enunciated, in regard to the meaning of the wedding and its spiritual and physical significance.[203] After the ceremony beneath the wedding canopy, the bride and groom would embrace their relatives; the groom's relatives would give the bride gold coins and her relatives would do the same to the groom. The Sephardim observed this practice on the day before the wedding ceremony: the bride-to-be sat in her home, in the middle of a room, wrapped in a veil, "and her parents and all her relatives would pass before her and throw her silver and gold coins."[204] In Salonika, the groom would give the bride rice, candies, and coins.[205] Such exchanges of gifts and money were a kind of temptation, or a compensation for the couple's agreement to walk an unknown path and unquestionably to obey various demands without having an inkling of their purpose.

During the nuptial banquet, care was taken to keep women and men strictly apart; in fact, the women were concerned to prevent the men even seeing them.[206] To entertain the bride and groom, verses were recited and sung, and *badchanim* (professional jesters) and dancers performed. The entertainers might be volunteer groups or even local rabbis, since entertainment of the bride and groom is considered a worthy occupation in Jewish tradition.[207] Among Ashkenazim, particular kabbalistic significance was attached to the *kosher tants*,[208] a dance in which men would take turns dancing with the bride, not touching her, of course, but holding one end of a kerchief whose other end was in her hand. According to one account, the bride's face was heavily veiled during the dance;[209] some authorities, however, forbade the *kosher tants* altogether, permitting women to dance only among themselves.[210] To introduce a more sedate atmosphere, the dance was preceded by the reading of a famous passage from the *Ethics of the Fathers* (3:1)[211] concerning the lowly origins and ultimate mortality of humanity, which is a regular part of the Jewish burial service. The basic idea was that the bride and groom had now completed one chapter of their lives and were setting out on a new one. The effort made by the men to engage the bride in the dance was intended to make her aware of her new situation and to ensure her active participation in the celebrations. At the same time, the fear of actual contact (or even a glance) between the two sexes was still present, and so the aforementioned kerchief, and perhaps also the veil over the bride's face, were an integral component of the dance. Similar practices have been observed among Christian brides in the East, who do not exchange one word or glance with their grooms during the ceremony. The rather gloomy atmosphere of such wedding ceremonies was indicative of the feelings of the bride and the other participants, all well aware of the gravity of the occasion.[212]

The desire to amuse the couple and entertain them was expressed in yet another custom. Bride and groom would sit in the middle of the room, each holding a burning torch; when one of the torches went out, the other would light it. Luncz, describing this custom, provides a psychological explanation: "The married couple are generally young boys and girls, who have never met before, and are too overcome by shyness even to look at one another. This custom was therefore devised, to draw them gradually closer to one another."[213]

In the second half of the nineteenth century, it was forbidden to play music at weddings; only drumming and singing in the women's section were permitted,[214] as if to emphasize the especially ascetic nature of Jerusalem, continually mourning the destruction of the Temple; it may also have been feared that music might arouse the guests' baser instincts. This new prohibition of the Ashkenazic community was enacted in the 1870s, the official reason being that it was unseemly to play music in the devastated Holy Land.[215] According to Luncz, however, the real reason was the fear that the musicians might steal a glance at the women, and in addition the desire to stress the simplicity and poverty of the Jerusalem community.[216] Thus, only drumming could be heard at an Ashkenazic wedding. Sephardic weddings, however, were accompanied by instrumental music and dancing.[217] Ultimately, the prohibition of instrumental music was enforced only within the Old City walls but not in the new neighborhoods outside the walls. Thus, an 1897 issue of *Hazevi* reports that Rabbi Shmuel Salant attended an Ashkenazic wedding in the New City, at which music was played.[218]

After the banquet, the couple's relatives, particularly the bride's mother, would accompany them to their room. When the bride entered her husband's home, her mother-in-law would distribute candies and cut a small *challa* loaf or cake over her head, as a symbol of fertility.[219] This symbolic act was common in various localities, in different variations. In Turkey, a marzipan cake was broken over the bride's head; the Jewish community of Baghdad cut a loaf of bread over the groom's head.[220] This symbolic language was designed to hint to the bride — who presumably knew nothing of the secrets of reproduction — that something was about to be torn, and that it was her duty to suffer willingly. The person conveying the hint was a stranger — her mother-in-law. Yehoshua Yellin relates that when he came to his room with his bride, a sheep was slaughtered on the doorstep "for atonement" and the meat given to the poor;[221] a similar practice was known in Baghdad.[222] The underlying idea was that the groom was as it were offering a sacrifice, since his wedding day was, for him, equivalent to the Day of Atonement.

The couple's first entrance to their shared quarters was an act of great significance for their relationship. Sephardic custom dictated that the bride should immediately sit on the groom's clothes, to confirm her dominant role.[223] This and other such symbolic acts — such as the bride treading on the groom's foot under the wedding canopy — were expressive of the considerable tension under which the young girl, apprehensive of her husband's "ownership" of her person, was laboring.[224]

On the morning after the wedding, the bride's and groom's mothers, as well as other relatives, would come early to the door of the nuptial chamber to express their feelings for the bride. They might also bring gifts, known as *shivchaya*, and help her to get dressed, for "dressing the bride on this day was considered to be a very meritorious deed."[225] Silently, just by means of bodily contact, the bride's relatives would try to inform her that her body had not been desecrated; rather, she had been raised to a new level, and the shower of gifts and personal help was intended to express feelings of intimacy and support.[226]

Another event was unique to Ashkenazic brides: a special celebration held when she had her hair shorn on the day after the wedding and wore the head scarf for the first time. The Sephardim, however, forbade the practice.[227]

Shaving and covering the head was an unequivocal declaration, aimed both at the bride and at her environment, that the young woman had undergone an essential change. Just as a three-year-old boy assumed his "Jewish shape" when his hair was cut for the first time, a young girl would be given her "Jewish shape" by having her head shorn, signifying a radical transformation of her personal status. This transformation of a woman's outer appearance further illuminates society's perception of masculinity and femininity: the male receives his proper "shape" as a Jew in childhood, but the female does so only upon marriage to a male.

While a married woman is required by Orthodox Halakhah to cover her head, shaving the hair is an additional, stringent measure, designed to prevent the exposure of the slightest wisp of hair.[228] The practice spread throughout eastern Europe in the eighteenth and early nineteenth centuries, somewhat declining in the second half of the nineteenth century.[229] In Jerusalem, however, it continued to be strictly observed, in keeping with the overall tendency to stress the austere atmosphere of the city. A special feast, known as *shlayer vorimes* (veiling lunch) or *shlayer vecheres* (veiling supper)[230] was held to mark the shaving of a new bride's head. The veiling feast was intended to cheer up the young woman and comfort her upon the loss of her hair.

Evidence as to the feelings of young brides upon having their heads shaved is rare. Hannah Trager, daughter of Zerach Barnett, one of the founders of the city of Petach Tikvah, who spent her childhood in Jerusalem, describes, on the one hand, the weeping bride, mourning for her beautiful hair, and, on the other, her joy over her head scarf.[231] Another report is cited in the memoirs of Ze'ev Leibowitz, of the New Yishuv. He describes a despairing young woman of Jerusalem who threatened to convert to Christianity to avoid having her head shorn:

They are about to lead me to the slaughter, shaving the locks of hair on my head, and I shall be delivered into the command of my mother-in-law . . . Come what may, I shall take this shameful, despicable step, as other women have done, abandoning their nation and their religion.[232]

For this young woman of Jerusalem, and perhaps also for others, shaving off the hair of her head was the last straw, which prompted her to rebel against being forced to marry a man she did not know.

Among the Sephardic communities it was the custom for the bride and groom to stay in their home for the entire week after the wedding, and this became a general practice in Jerusalem. Till the end of the "Seven Days of Feasting," the young couple would sit beneath the wedding canopy, which was made of curtains taken down from the Holy Ark in the synagogue. Here is Luncz's description: "This canopy is not taken down until after the Seven

Days of the Wedding Feast are over, and all those days the groom and bride sit beneath it. A similar canopy is made in the bride's home as well and a burning candle placed beneath it . . . No man will dare to sit there, it being considered a holy place."[233] Ya'akov Gellis calls this canopy a *sukkah*, thus likening it to the ritual structure, symbolic of the home, erected on the festival of Sukkot.[234] Ostensibly, the bride and groom remained home in order to be protected from the forces of evil that might try to harm them during the first week of their marriage. Another possible explanation of the custom might be to prevent "improper" reactions on the couple's part, following the dramatic events in their lives, for which they were inadequately prepared. The couple were thus placed at the center of attention, both to raise their spirits and to protect them as they embarked on their new life's journey together.

The celebrations continued for seven days, the guests partaking every day in two banquets.[235] Only on the Sabbath did the groom leave the house, to attend services at the synagogue, accompanied by his friends, like a king who goes nowhere alone.[236] At the synagogue, he was called up to the Torah reading, in the course of which chapter 24 in Genesis, which tells the story of the quest of Abraham's servant to find a wife for Isaac, would be read.[237] The point of reading this chapter was to convey the societal importance of family life. The congregants would sprinkle rosewater on the guests. Nevertheless, there was a constant fear that the merrymaking might get out of hand, and various precautions were therefore taken.[238] The main banquet took place on Saturday evening, after the end of the Sabbath; it was known as *nochada* (from the Ladino word for night).[239] Jesters would entertain the guests; in some communities it was customary to display the wedding gifts. During the entire seven-day celebration the couple's family and friends remained with them constantly, giving them continuous support (just as family keeps a mourner company during the seven days of mourning after the funeral, the *shiv'ah*).

In sum, the wedding ceremony was essentially an encounter of several opposing tendencies: separation of the sexes as against their union; rejoicing as against the couple's embarrassment and sometimes sadness; wearing finery as against austerity and remembrance of national destruction. One can hardly avoid the conclusion that the rejoicing and celebrations were in some ways a way of sweetening the pill: conjugal relations between a previously unacquainted man and woman, who had not been prepared; the beginning of an unfamiliar mode of life; the traumatic shaving of the bride's pride and joy — her hair. The new ideas that appeared at the turn of the century accentuated these apparent contradictions, bringing out the communal nature of what should have been a private ceremony. From a small ceremony, held within the family, the wedding developed into an impressive social affair. Printed invitations and large wedding halls signified the intrusion of the public domain into private life and, even more, the westernization of Jewish society in the Holy City.[240]

We have a detailed account from a Bukharan Jew named Sha'ul Me'ir Moshayoff of his wedding in 1908, in which the signs of processes of modernization penetrating Jerusalem society are clearly evident.[241] Moshayoff refused to obey the dictates of custom and marry at a young age, insisting on waiting until he had achieved economic independence to take a wife. As a twenty-two-year old bachelor, he fell in love with a young Ashkenazic woman. Having ascertained that she would agree to marry him, he appointed a friend as *shadchan* and enacted what appeared to be a "normal" matchmaking transaction. The wedding and all its appurtenances were in modern, Western style: printed invitations, orchestral music, and guests attired in Western-style clothes. After the wedding, the couple went off on a honeymoon in the Jericho district, not remaining in their family circles to celebrate the Seven Days of Feasting. Nevertheless, notwithstanding the modern ceremony, it was the groom who took the initiative and made all the arrangements, his bride adhering to the pattern of the passive woman: though relatively modern, the marriage still bore the patriarchal, masculine stamp, the main change being the shift of initiative from the parents to the younger generation.

Despite being an expression of conflicting tendencies, the wedding was sometimes also a unifying event. The 150 guests at the lavish wedding of David and Ita Yellin, for example, were representatives of all communities, as might be expected at a wedding where the groom was of mixed Ashkenazic-Sephardic parentage. Ephraim Cohen-Reiss, who married a daughter of the owner of the well-known Kaminetz Hotel, noted in his memoirs that members of all the communities had been invited to the wedding, which was "a kind of symbol of the Sephardim and Ashkenazim being drawn closer together."[242] A reporter for the Yiddish newspaper *Beis Ya'akov* used similar terms to describe the guests at the wedding of Rosa, daughter of Yosef Navon, as "desirous of furthering real unity between Sephardim and Ashkenazim."[243] The guests at weddings held by distinguished members of society generally included Muslim representatives of the authorities, as well as Christian consular staff.[244] At times, the poor were invited as an act of charity, to enhance the celebrations.[245] Hayim Hamburger, a banker, described his own wedding as a mass celebration, with the participation of thousands of guests of all religions.[246] These examples serve to underline our thesis that marriage was no longer a family or even community affair, with most attention being devoted to the young couple; it was now an opulent demonstration on the part of the hosts, a public affair that united religious and ethnic communities.[247]

Captive under the Wedding Canopy

It has long been the custom at Jewish weddings to break a glass under the wedding canopy in memory of the destruction of the Temple. The Ashkenazic community of Jerusalem added further customs for the same purpose: they forbade the bride to wear jewelry and prohibited the playing of instrumental music at the ceremony. This insistence on an ascetic lifestyle had a gender-based significance: it derived from the desire to preserve men's purity and resulted in various additional strictures on women. As if in contrast to their life-giving capacity, women were forced to practice abstinence and self-denial. Perhaps the increase in this trend, just when Jerusalem in general was experiencing heightened prosperity and building, was meant to convey the message that redemption could not be brought nearer and that false hopes should not be raised.

Marriage customs throw much light on the considerable difference in gender perception between the two main communities, Ashkenazim and Sephardim. Sephardic society was more open and life-loving than Ashkenazic society. It permitted affianced couples to meet, albeit under supervision, and also allowed brides to adorn themselves in jewelry at the wedding. After the wedding, Sephardic custom required the woman only to cover her hair as a sign of her new status, opposing the idea of shaving the head. The Ashkenazic community, by contrast, imposed various restrictions on newly married women, apprehensive of their effect on male society. Excess rejoicing and attention to femininity were thought to contradict the austere character of the Jerusalem society that they sought to preserve.

With all this in mind, it is even more striking that, throughout the complex elements and moves that made up the wedding ceremony—some of which were meant for the bride alone, such as Shabbat *kallah*, immersion in the *mikveh*, the reception on the morning after the wedding, and the "veiling feast"—nowhere could the bride's voice be heard. The circumstances surrounding the wedding ceremony, in all its phases, only reemphasized the bride's female passivity. While of course present at the ceremony, she had no active part in any phase. The young girl whose parents led her to the wedding canopy had no say in the matter but was essentially treated as a mere object. Owing to her tender age and lack of education, she generally remained under society's sway. Paradoxically, the wedding ceremony, symbolizing the girl's coming to maturity, worked to weaken rather than strengthen that process. One might say that the bride, by marrying, lost her own autonomous personality and became an instrument in the hands of her spouse.

Ludwig August Frankl, witnessing a Jerusalem wedding in 1856, remarked perceptively: "The impression created by the entire ceremony was painful.

The bridal pair looked like two puppets, with whom the adults were playing at weddings."[248] Frankl clearly observed the situation during the wedding, but he could not have known the next phase: While the groom was shown the way to a new chapter in his life, one of maturity and independence, his bride, having been released from her father's ownership, came under that of her husband. Princess or prisoner? To my mind, given the foregoing account of the wedding, in all its phases and ceremonies, there is only one possible answer to that question.

Chapter 3

Women at Home

"ALL GLORIOUS IS the princess within" (Ps. 45:14)—Jewish tradition, focusing on the word "within," interprets this biblical verse as proclaiming the Jewish woman's home to be her kingdom. By studying women in their homes and families, we may gain new insights into the conventional distinction between public and private domains. Separation of home life and public life, it turns out, is artificial, insofar as domestic affairs are a reflection, albeit at times in reverse, of social messages. The two realms cannot be considered in complete isolation, since each intrudes on the other. Everyday lifestyles in the home provide a new look at the internalized female world, at worldviews and values deeply embedded in the soul.[1]

The family unit prepares the individual for his or her life in society. While each family has its own special features, families do influence one another: the process of socialization, as acquired in the family unit, is what shapes the face of society.[2] But there is also a reverse process: society affects the family unit. Thus, the winds of change blowing in Jerusalem at the turn of the nineteenth and twentieth centuries were not stopped at the threshold of the home; the resulting changes in domestic life reveal that new, Western ideas were penetrating the very fortress of traditional Jerusalem society.

In the survey of domestic life offered below, we shall touch on a broad spectrum of topics: women's clothing, the interior and furnishing of the home, women's relationships with their husbands, the birth of children and women's attitudes to them, female friendship, and the dismantling of the family. Our discussion of what took place after the family had fallen apart, that is, the fate of widows and abandoned wives, will be deferred to the last chapter of this book, which will be devoted entirely to social adversity in the Holy City.

Women's Clothing: Private and Public Aspects

Bugajili, meaning "the day of the bundle," was the name given to one of the seven days of festivities following a wedding in the Sephardic community. The bride's mother would pack up all her daughter's clothes and have them removed to her new husband's home,[3] and the mother-in-law would keep a watchful eye that nothing was missing from her new daughter-in-law's possessions. At first sight this would seem to be nothing but a prosaic, personal, act; in fact, however, the clothes in the bundle were not just the wearer's personal expression but a social code, in Jerusalem as anywhere else.[4] While the usual definition of clothing is "anything that clothes the body, adorns it, or protects it from the environment,"[5] clothing is also a nonverbal language, a sensual code, an expression through which one presents oneself to the world and influences society's perception of oneself.[6] It is an expression of religion, ethnic identity, citizenship, status, gender, and personality.[7] In some cultures, clothes are a magical means to protect the wearer from evil influences.[8] Halakhic authorities[9] ruled that women exposing their bodies and/or hair ran a dual risk: they would give birth to unworthy children, and they would become poor. Clothing, like any other cultural expression, characterizes a certain group of people and shapes their group identity. A society, by obliging its members to dress similarly, is amplifying its power, enhancing its collective authority.[10] Standardization of clothing reflects the individual's obedience and the coercive capacity of the community.

Complex, equivocal attitudes to women's clothing are aptly expressed in the public notices posted on Jerusalem walls calling for modesty in women's dress, beginning in the late nineteenth century (and continuing today). Women's clothing, ostensibly their private affair, came to be considered as "the symbol of the chastity of our holy nation,"[11] that is, a social symbol. Thus, a poster published by the Hungarian *kolel* in 1908 attests to the social changes embodied in clothing habits, warning the public of the impending dangers:

Every one of the worshipers in our study house must conduct himself, and instruct his household, men and women alike, to conduct themselves . . . as our ancestors were accustomed for generations, with no innovation whatever . . . In particular, none of them, young or old, should wear immodest clothing.[12]

A woman wearing "immodest" clothing was committing not only a personal offense but a public one.[13] A private individual's transgression of chastity implied a public offense, and the punishment would accordingly be collective — extension of the Exile. Since the clothing of a Jewish woman in the Holy City was a national affair rather than a private one, she was expected to observe the rules of modesty in her dress for the entire nation's sake. Moreover, immodest clothing would arouse derision on the part of the non-Jewish residents of Jerusalem,[14] leading to defamation of national honor and hence, necessarily, to "desecration of the Holy Name."

Women in Jerusalem wore a characteristic costume, as described by many visitors to the city.[15] Ita Yellin, who immigrated to the Holy Land with her parents in the 1880s, wrote at length of her impressions while still abroad, as a child, of the costume of an emissary from Jerusalem, Hannah Novardikern, also describing the women's preparations of new clothing for their arrival in the Land of Israel. The family were aware of the need to change their daughters' style of clothing with their change of abode.[16]

The piece of clothing of most significance, both halakhically and socially, was the head covering. A Jewish woman's head covering was (and in certain circles still is) an indication of her marital status.[17] Custom dictated how women members of different communities should cover their heads: "The [Sephardic] bride never cuts her hair, but they take care that not a single strand of hair should show outside [the head covering], for their scarves cover the hair well. But Ashkenazic women always shave their heads."[18] Although the Halakhic basis for shaving off the hair is dubious at best,[19] advocates of this extreme measure considered its abandonment an act of rebellion and raised vociferous protests.[20] Women who refrained from shaving their heads had a metaphysical effect on the world, actually "preventing rain from falling."[21] On one occasion, the leaders of the Hungarian *kolel*, who administered the distribution of *halukah* funds from their headquarters in the Diaspora, threatened the husband of a woman who refused to comply with the custom that he would be "persecuted with all manner of persecution, both in respect of money and in respect of religion."[22] The most common — and convincing — threat in this connection was to withhold *halukah* payments from the families of recalcitrant women.

Even women raised their voices against others who were thought to violate these social constraints. Zipporah Pines, who refused to part with her wig, was called an "apostate" by her (female) neighbors, and on one occasion, when she visited the synagogue, "one woman fell upon her, spat in her face and screamed out loud that her dress and her wig were holding up the advent of the Messiah and defiling the Holy Land."[23] Women no less than men believed that changing one's clothing habits was simply "defilement" and could metaphysically affect the fate of the entire nation; hence it was their prerogative to insult the "sinners" and wage uncompromising war against those "the defilers of the land."

The desire to force women to shave off their hair was the cause of many "stumbling blocks and disputes between men and their wives . . . likely to lead, heaven forfend, to divorce."[24] The issue was repeatedly discussed in the local press. In one such discussion, *Hazevi* explained that the proponents of shaving the head were particularly incensed at the "luxury" and self-beautifying of women, which went against the grain in the Holy City. The more apprehensive the rabbis became of the new ideas, the more fanatical they were, and shaving the head became a central issue for the self-styled "guardians of the walls."[25] Rabbi Yosef Hayim Sonnenfeld, one of the most prominent hard-liners, forbade a father to lead his adopted daughter to the wedding ceremony because she refused to shave off her hair, arguing that "this might lead to lenience in the matter of shaving the hair in the family."[26]

This whole subject is characteristic of the most important elements in the attitude of male society to women's appearance: It was male society that established the Halakhic and social norms, regardless of women's own desires and feelings. The husband was seen as being responsible for his wife's appearance, and it was he, therefore, who was punished should she stray from the "correct" code. The supreme value was maintenance of the traditional face of Jerusalem society, even at the cost of domestic peace and tranquillity. A writer in the Jerusalem newspaper *Hazevi* surely spoke for many silenced women when he wrote, "Would that I had died an infant, rather than seeing how my head is now like a potsherd," or "How many hot tears have fallen from how many beautiful eyes this week because of those beautiful pigtails and braids?"[27]

The various headdresses were identifying marks of different groups: Young Ashkenazic girls, "on the morrow of their weddings, covered their heads with two kerchiefs. One was made of simple white cloth, and over this they wore a second kerchief made of wool or silk in different colors."[28] The "trademark" of the elderly Ashkenazic women who came to the Holy Land to end their days there was the so-called *knop*, literally, knot.[29] This, too, consisted of two kerchiefs — two, in order to guarantee that the cover would remain secure on the wearer's head. The fanatics of Jerusalem would not even countenance the idea of a woman covering her head with a wig; that was dismissed entirely and deplored as deceptive.[30] The Sephardic women, by contrast, were more colorful and vital in appearance. Syla Bergman refers to their appearance when describing her arrival in Jerusalem in the 1830s: "[On their heads they wore] a red cap with large blue fringes, as well as pretty scarves with many ducats [coins] worn around the forehead."[31] There was more variety in the Sephardic women's appearance. Young women wore a turban; older women wore a small black cap, known as a *toka*, and rabbis' wives were draped in a long, black, silk veil, adorned with flowers.[32] At the turn of the century, the veil covering the hair became thinner, and young women wore a *yazma* — a veil with fringes, on which flowers were drawn.[33] There were strict instructions as to the color and thickness of these various headdresses: women were constantly under the community's supervision.

Drawings and photographs, as well as memoirs and diaries, have immortalized the image of the Jewish woman of Jerusalem. "In Jerusalem, women go about in white sheets, wrapped in them from head to foot."[34] The women of Jerusalem, both Ashkenazic and Sephardic, probably wore this costume both in accordance with the ascetic ideals of the community, which always aimed to prevent any danger of temptation, and under the influence of Muslim women's clothing.[35] The sheet enveloped and concealed a woman's body and even face, as in the case of Muslim women, whose bodies and faces were concealed by their garb.[36] Most Jewish women did not hide their faces: "They do not wear a veil over their faces when walking out in the city."[37] Nevertheless, one report from the beginning of the nineteenth century notes that "all the women [including Jewish women] are veiled."[38] Yaakov Yehoshua relates that in his youth, at the beginning of the twentieth century, his mother would cover her face with a veil before going out to the Old City.[39]

Wearing the sheet, no less than covering the head, was obligatory. Jerusalem regulations decreed: "We have agreed with all force, by an overwhelming majority, and in fact unanimously, that no daughter of Israel, even elderly women, may walk in the market without a covering over the clothing (called *lizar*)."[40] The regulation sets out the prohibition in detail and warns that a woman should not even go from one courtyard to the next without a *lizar*, nor may she look out of the window of her home to talk to her neighbor unless both are covered. In addition, the regulation applied to any woman going out into the public domain, and any woman violating it would "become a proverb and a byword" (i.e., would earn public scorn and derision). With the coming of the twentieth century, women cast off the sheet, then the kerchief, even shortening the hems of their clothing until it became completely different.

Beneath the sheet women could wear whatever their personal preference, means, and ethnic origins dictated, depending of course on the season of the year.[41] Sephardic women — and, at the turn of the century, Bukharans in particular — were known for their colorful costumes, while the Ashkenazic women preferred the utmost simplicity, except for some embroidered pattern.[42] The latter were also careful to cover the legs in trousers and stockings, to ensure the maximum modesty.[43] Such clothing completely obscured the female figure. It was the outcome of a special regulation enacted by the rabbis of the Ashkenazic community in 1842: "Every God-fearing person should consider it his duty to obey this regulation meticulously, and his reward will be doubled and redoubled by He who awards, may His name be exalted."[44] European tourists considered these women a kind of vestige of the previous century.[45]

The American explorer William Lynch wrote in his travel journal: "To make up for [married women concealing their hair], the heads of the latter were profusely ornamented with coins and gems and any quantity of another's hair."[46] A woman's jewelry, worn for display, was the antithesis of the general tendency to camouflage her as far as possible behind veils and extra layers. Jewels were an avowal of wealth and status for the wearer; a bejeweled woman was a kind of walking savings plan.[47] The ornaments were displayed in prominent places, such as on the forehead or suspended from the ears. It was common to fashion a necklace out of valuable coins, "many ducats worn around the forehead."[48] Sephardic families took especial care to beautify their daughters from childhood with jewelry. Earlobes were pierced at an early age for earrings, and when infant girls grew older, "their arms were adorned with bracelets of colorful Hebron glass, thanks to which our sisters rustled as they went by—this was to attract our attention to them."[49] (Might one compare such "rustling" ornaments to the bells hung around sheep's necks in the flock?—for both were intended to attract attention and make it easier for the "shepherd" to protect them!)

Women wearing jewelry aroused complaints. In the eighteenth century, the rabbis of the Sephardic community decreed that women should refrain from arousing too much attention with their jewels: "In the year [1749] . . . the city rabbis agreed and laid down strict regulations in the matter of clothing . . . As to jewels, women should not go out in public with them."[50] These regulations, which were also accepted as binding by the Ashkenazim in the nineteenth century, imposed a sweeping injunction that forbade women to wear any jewelry whatever, even a bride on her wedding day. The previously mentioned 1842 regulation concerning modest clothing also forbade the wearing of jewelry: "Any manner of jewelry made of precious stones, in any way whatever, shall not be used for adornment at all, in any women from our community, even an unmarried woman . . . whether in their homes and their courtyards, on any festive occasion, nor on festivals when attending the synagogue."[51] Among the reasons given for this regulation was the desire to honor the intentions of Jews abroad who were supporting the Jews of the Holy Land.

This language of clothing was refined not only by male society but also by women themselves.[52] Rochke Lipales, daughter of Rivkah Lipa Anikster, never wore fashionable shoes but only wooden clogs, which were "a custom of the most venerable, specific to the residents of Jerusalem."[53] The clogs were essentially a medium through which Rochke Lipales and others like her were proclaiming their objections to the going fashions and identifying instead with the past. Sephardic women would make up their eyes as a sign to their husbands of their desire for sexual relations: "In the days of their purity they make up their eyes and paint their nails in red."[54] A sign of unwillingness in that respect, as it were signaling to her husband, was a white kerchief knotted around the forehead.[55] Zlata Alte Levi, of the Orenstein family, expressed her fervent messianic hopes by ironing her dress: she used to iron her dress regularly, once a week, in the hope that "perhaps the Messiah will come tomorrow . . . so I must have an ironed dress ready to receive him."[56] Thus, costume played a major communicative role: clogs symbolized asceticism and conservatism; facial makeup signaled readiness for conjugal relations; and an ironed dress meant that the wearer was ready at all times to greet the Messiah.

Beauty and physical culture aroused considerable interest among Sephardic women. Their colorful costume was exciting and arousing, wrote a certain reporter in *Haskafah*, but their face might be completely expressionless: "Her eyes arouse nothing, no sublime feeling." As to Ashkenazic women, on the other hand, "their participation in spiritual life is what makes their company so pleasant for the educated person."[57] Women's exposed faces were part of their appearance, part of their body language, which blended with the language of their clothing. The Ashkenazic observer did not always properly understand or appreciate the appearance of Sephardic women, but looked at them through his own personal lenses.

The social and spiritual changes that took place in the Jerusalem community toward the end of the nineteenth century had an effect, in particular, on women's headwear. Sometimes it was women themselves who initiated the change, sometimes men.[58] By the end of the nineteenth century, the women (albeit a small number) who did not conceal their hair clearly presented a challenge, which erected a social barrier between them and the rest of the community.[59] Fashionable clothes were thought to violate the codes of modesty: "The daughters of 'Montefiore' [the neighborhoods that had been built with the support of the Montefiore Fund] were considered more modern. They were so bold as to paint their faces . . . They went about in dresses with a *décolleté*."[60] Yaakov Yehoshua attributed these changes to not only religious but also social grounds: "They were afraid that their husbands might cast eyes on other women who exposed their hair."[61] The celebrated ultra-Orthodox preacher Ben Zion Yadler, however, highly disapproved of such practices as being shameless and provocative. To his mind, women who exposed their hair were thereby deriding the others, who adhered to tradition, and wished to influence the latter to abandon the old customs and adopt new ways.[62]

The more changes that occurred in female appearance, the more eager was society to impose stricter supervision on women. We have already seen that the Ashkenazic community was not averse to shaming "rebellious" girls,[63] in the hope that this could stem the rising tide. The rabbinical establishment declared that "according to the law of our sacred Torah, . . . the virtuous daughters of Israel shall ever conduct themselves as always, with not one change."[64] This principle became a sacred mission; the transformation taking place in the female image was seen as a violation of moral barriers and a challenge to Jerusalem society.

The Home: Physical Space and Its Influence on Women's Lives

"The Jerusalem Jews' frugality is amazing. In their modesty, they are content with one dark room, barely furnished . . . Because of the prevailing conditions, even the more wealthy immigrants are obliged to live simply and forgo the considerable pleasures and comfort to which they had been accustomed in their home countries."[65] This description by Bernhard Neumann, physician to the Jewish community of Jerusalem in the 1860s and 1870s, while setting out the functional role of the Jewish home in Jerusalem, namely, to serve as living quarters, also alludes obliquely to its symbolic role: to symbolize the nature of Jewish life in the Holy City. Most of the immigrants had not left behind lavish homes in their countries of origin, and their modest habits conformed to the austere nature of the city: "Ukrainian simplicity combined with Jerusalem modesty in complete harmony."[66] Difficult living conditions and lack of sanitation caused illnesses and fatalities that led to a negative demographic balance:[67] "Of all the congestion in human homes, ten measures of congestion and crowdedness came down to the Earth; nine of them were taken by the Jewish Quarter in Jerusalem, and the others—by all the ghettos in the world."[68] Wretched as the small, dark homes in the Jewish Quarter of the Old City were, the rent demanded by their Arab owners was not low, and it too contributed to the harsh conditions.[69] While the Hebrew term for "housewife," *akkeret habayit*, was traditionally thought to portray her as the major axis around which the home revolved, living conditions in the Holy City belied the idea: the miserable home made the mistress of the home miserable in her turn. Added to the poor living conditions were shortages of the most basic commodities, such as water. Contemporaries were well aware of their situation, noting that "life [was] a life of suffering."[70]

An apartment in the Old City generally consisted of a single room in which the whole family lived, with no privacy whatever.[71] In addition, newly married couples would often come to live with one or the other's parents (generally the groom's), as was customary in traditional societies.[72] Under such conditions, a bride coming to live with her husband could expect little privacy. Poverty and overcrowding sometimes inspired creative solutions, such as dividing a high-ceilinged room into two by building a low wooden ceiling, or hanging a curtain across the room to create a special corner for the newlyweds.[73] As to intimate relations between husband and wife — our documentation is entirely silent on that subject. Neither does the responsa literature pay any attention to the emotional aspect of conjugal relations.

In keeping with the home itself, the furniture was poor and meager.[74] Rabbi Moshe Blau, who was married in 1902, describes the furniture in his home as follows: "Planks supported on two iron bases — that was my bed, an old bed that I had inherited from my aunt . . . A bed for my wife, a table, a cupboard, two chairs."[75] In a Sephardic home there were usually no beds: "They lie down to sleep every night on mats spread on the floor, and by day they put the bedclothes away in closets in the wall."[76] Such "closets" were usually nothing more than niches in the wall. A Sephardic home, like a Muslim home, did not usually contain a dining table and chairs, except for a copper or bronze tray.[77] Given the constant shortages and lack of finished products, housewives had to exercise their ingenuity and work hard. Ita Yellin, who enjoyed above-average living conditions, both in her father's home and later in her own, described the complicated annual planning of a household in her time. The housewife had to take great care and exploit whatever was in season.[78] Only toward the end of the nineteenth century, with the arrival of more wealthy immigrants, was there an increase in the standard of living, and the gloomy "Jerusalem style" gradually began to change.[79]

The multifunctional courtyard housed, among other things, lavatories, kitchen, and laundry room-there was generally one common kitchen, with one stove per family.[80] On weekdays and, in particular, on festivals, "the courtyard became one big family. Women were busy day and night preparing food and the men, studying and eating."[81] The courtyard was also the scene of arguments and quarrels that broke out, often because of the poor hygienic conditions.[82] Not infrequently, those living in the same area were members of an extended family,[83] but sometimes they were members of different communities or even of different religious groups.[84] (In Jerusalem, as in other Mediterranean cities, people generally grouped together according to ethnic origin.) Relations with Arab neighbors are sparsely documented, generally in a negative connection.[85]

The neighborhood oven was in effect an extension of the home, use of which necessitated coordination among neighbors.[86] During the week housewives used it to bake the dough prepared in their kitchens, and on Fridays they placed the special Sabbath stew (*cholent* or *chamin*) there to cook slowly overnight.[87] I have found no references to any restrictions on the movements of men or women in the shared courtyard. Most probably, neighbors' sharp eyes were sufficient to warn against immodest behavior. However, the communal oven was considered to be a possible scene for forbidden encounters. In 1854, a special regulation was enacted, to the effect that "no woman aged less than fifty years shall go to the oven to bring bread or the like, neither shall she enter the oven door under any circumstances."[88] There were also restrictions on the selection of the baker's staff: "He shall not employ as a servant a young man, neither Jew nor non-Jew, but a married man or one with grown beard." Given the prohibition on women, married or otherwise, to enter the bakery, one may ask why the authors of these regulations were worried about unmarried laborers? Could they have feared the development of homosexual relations? In any case, the regulation concerning women obviously expressed the community's intent of limiting women's freedom of movement. It was children who benefited directly from these restrictions: "For we, the children, go to deposit [the stew] every Friday"; on the other hand, the women who prepared the food were at the bakers' mercy.[89] By the end of the nineteenth century, however, this regulation was apparently no longer observed, and in fact the trip to the oven become an exciting social event for women, and an opportunity for women of different communities, speaking different languages, to meet one another.[90]

Life in Jerusalem, the proximity of the holy places, and fervent longings for redemption inspired a sensation of extreme sanctity, particularly on Sabbaths and festivals. "It has become customary in the Land for women to recite the blessing over the *lulav* [i.e., the four species on the festival of Sukkot], and they should not be prevented."[91] This long-established Ashkenazic custom — Sephardic women did not normally observe this particular commandment — gained wide acceptance, providing an example of the desire to enhance one's religious faith. Such desires found expression, a fortiori, in religious practices that had long been considered a female prerogative, such as salting the meat (to render it ritually fit for consumption) and kindling the Sabbath lights. Some women experienced a feeling of spiritual uplift when performing these commandments and did not practice them merely by rote. Baruch Zevi Shur described how his grandmother Reitzl, after salting the meat, feeling responsible for the fitness of the meat, would utter a prayer, appealing in Yiddish to the four Matriarchs: "If I have not properly salted the meat, let Sarah, Rebecca, Rachel and Leah come and complete the work."[92] Everyday life was being lived not far from the very ground trodden by the Matriarchs or from their graves, creating a strong spiritual link with them, as if they were actual partners in the present. The concern for domestic needs, in particular the preparation of food, thus assumed a religious dimension. Sacred and profane came together to create a kind of female autonomy of sanctity.[93]

Passover, the festival of freedom, was of particular significance for women. While the preparation of the *mazzot* and the search for leaven are a male prerogative,[94] the cleaning and preparation of the home itself, to enable the family to celebrate the festival properly, are the women's responsibility. The women of Jerusalem were meticulous to an extraordinary degree. Sonya Diskin, a well-known rabbi's wife who was celebrated for her religious zeal, was famed far and wide for the little stockings she used to put on her cat's feet, lest it carry bread crumbs or the like from room to room.[95] Like other women, she believed that men could not be relied on in connection with the preparation of the home for Passover. Another of the many tales told about her is that when her husband, Rabbi Moshe Yehoshua Diskin, scolded her for her exaggeration, she replied: "If I rely on you and your *Shulchan Arukh*, we'll be eating *chametz* [leaven] on Passover!"[96] It was probably women's ignorance of Halakha that prompted their unbridled adoption of various and sundry stringent measures that they themselves had invented. Preparation of the home for Passover allowed them, at least temporarily, to take command of the whole home: The men became "superfluous throughout the house, their rule was suspended and their power weakened."[97] The home was essentially dominated by the women — mother, grandmother and sisters — while the younger sons were sent packing and barred from participation.[98]

It emerges from the many available accounts of Jerusalem homes that female society traced its own life cycle, separate from the male world. Men left home early in the morning for the synagogue and the study house, or for work, while the women were left with their lowly housework. Jewish women, like their Muslim counterparts, "maintained their own socioeconomic system . . . their interaction with the surrounding society did not pass through the male world, but through their own closed circles."[99]

Life in the closed realm of the home and the courtyard produced a kind of female companionship. This exclusively female world took shape either within the home and the family or among neighbors and friends. Opportunities for friendship arose both while housework was being done and on occasions when women had finished their routine chores.[100] Socializing could take place on Sunday evenings and on the first day of the Hebrew month. "Every Sunday, as the evening shadows fell, many residents of our city, and in particular women, take the air outside the city, along the road leading to Jaffa"[101] — this was largely because leftovers from the Sabbath meals were eaten on Sunday, since in those days food could not be preserved;[102] Christian neighbors also had some influence on the practice. As to the first day of the Hebrew month, *rosh hodesh*, it was (and still is) traditionally regarded as a minor festival for women,[103] allowing them a special day of rest and recreation: "Female neighbors and friends would meet, dine together and sing."[104] On rare occasions, ethnic barriers might fall, and women of neighboring Muslim households who knew some Ladino might participate. On these occasions, "every one of us would open up her heart." Besides intimate conversation, community singing was a major means of expressing specifically female feelings.

Another regular opportunity for female companionship and singing was the close of the Sabbath. At twilight, and even later, in the moonlight, women would sing sadly of their destiny: "A beautiful maid without luck — it were better for her if she had not been born."[105] Women would also unburden themselves in song during the exhausting hours of housework, for example, during the preparations for Passover. "The lives of our mothers and sisters were harsh . . . and they could cope with the labor only by singing constantly."[106] Mutual aid was the rule among women, in all areas of life:

giving advice about cooking or managing the household, caring for children, and even wet-nursing for a mother too exhausted to suckle her own child.[107]

Traditional Jewish society frowned on socializing per se. Jacob Katz explains that this disapproval stemmed from the suspicion that such activities "were considered religiously and ethically dangerous . . . There was even some ethical suspicion concerning social gatherings of members of the same sex. This was seen as temptation to engage in gossip, slander and quarreling."[108] Women's friendships sprang up naturally in the physical space of the home and the courtyard, with no male intervention. Writers tend to include in their memoirs descriptions of the pleasant aspects of their lives, suppressing quarrels and adversity.[109] The documentation at our disposal reveals extraordinarily little about women's feelings regarding their homes, families, friends, and environment, despite the importance in women's lives of female friendship — some consider it even more significant than family relationships.[110]

For a few people, the Jerusalem home, despite the poverty and wretched conditions, offered an opportunity for spiritual enrichment: "[Rivkah Anikster's daughter] Rochke savored the sanctity and mystery of the Hurvah [she lived in a basement of the famous Hurvah Synagogue]. She wished to extend this sanctity and be elevated with it."[111] But few individuals could see their poor living conditions as a way to achieve sanctity. Even wealthy women experienced hardship and grueling labor.[112] A reporter wrote in *Hazevi* of women's attitude to their housework: "The Ashkenazic woman does her work only for heaven's sake, as a sacred commandment," seeing in her efforts a kind of sacrifice to God; the Sephardic women, however, seemed to enjoy their labors immensely.[113]

If a person's home is his or her castle, in Jerusalem that castle could not adequately guarantee its residents' security or privacy. Nevertheless, a modicum of privacy was attempted. As was the rule in oriental cities, the windows of Jerusalem homes did not open onto the public thoroughfare, thus enhancing the residents' sensation of intimacy and security.[114] People necessarily reflect their environment, but one can only guess the psychological implications of living conditions in the Old City of Jerusalem for its Jewish residents. While clothing offered some sensation of physical privacy,[115] privacy in the sense of freedom from observation by others was apparently unattainable under such circumstances. The privacy of information conveyed by some of the documentary evidence surely does not reflect the everyday reality of the time. A change took place only when neighborhoods began to go up outside the walls of the Old City.[116] For the first time, crowded rooms and communal courtyards were replaced by homes permitting a lifestyle somewhat similar to that in the average European city.

Jewish Family in Mount Zion. Ely Schiller, ed., *Jerusalem in Old Engravings* (Jerusalem, 1977), p. 170.

Marital Relationships as a Mirror of Perception of Family

The medieval ban against bigamy, attributed to Rabbi Gershom "Me'or Hagolah," was never accepted as binding by the Sephardim and most of the oriental communities, including those in the Land of Israel.[117] Marriage with two wives, strictly forbidden in Ashkenazic Jewish society, had some currency in the Ottoman Empire in non-Jewish society[118] and also, though to a very small degree, among Sephardic Jews.[119] Yosef Mansfeld, who immigrated to the Holy Land in 1835 and recorded his impressions, reported that the Sephardim practiced bigamy and even levirate marriage.[120] However, Montefiore's 1855 census listed only three polygamous families in the Land of Israel.[121] Shim'on Berman, who toured the country in 1870 and heard of a Sephardic Jew who had three wives, speculated about the living conditions of women in a polygamous marriage: "One would like to know how three women married to the same man behave, and how a husband treats his three wives."[122] Hayim Sethon, the Sephardic rabbi of Safed, wrote in 1905: "[Rabbenu Gershom's] ban is not accepted in the Land of Israel."[123] Nevertheless, by the beginning of the twentieth century the practice of marrying a second wife had almost disappeared, except for a few cases in which the first wife was barren or had borne only daughters.[124]

A rare document dated to 1818, quoting Siniora Oro, wife of Meir Shlomo Farhi of Damascus, reveals the thoughts and feelings of a woman whose husband had taken a second wife: "I give him sufficient permission according to the law, of my own free will, for him to marry the wife that he has betrothed, and may he rejoice and live forever . . . Perhaps as a reward I shall have a son through her, with God's help, if she should bear male children." The religious court responded as follows: "We say that she has done her husband's will." [125] Siniora Oro, in her letter, stated that her husband had married a second wife because of his distress that she had borne him no male children. Expressing complete empathy, she declared that she bore him no grudge; on the contrary, she wished him well, hoping that his desire for a son would be fulfilled, in which case she would rejoice together with him. Did Siniora Oro's reaction reveal her internalization of the male point of view, or was it a mere legal convention? While justifying her husband's act, she could not tolerate her rival's everyday presence, and insisted that the second wife should not live in her home. Another document, from the archives of the Jaffa religious court, dated 1894, concerning marriage with a second wife, contains the husband's undertaking to allow his first wife to remain in her home "without the company of her rival." [126] Unlike Muslim women, who were accustomed to the idea of living in a harem and keeping company with other wives, these Jewish women refused to do so.

The wedding ceremony under the canopy, followed by entry into a family room, marked the first acquaintance of the young husband and his bride. As noted in a previous chapter, the strict separation of sexes from childhood had no little influence on the relationship between the newlyweds. [127] The relationship was also affected by the culture of separation between female and male society familiar from the local Muslim society in the Ottoman Empire. [128] Parents were charged with keeping the genders strictly apart from infancy: "Parents took great care that their [male] child should not play with little girls." [129] The effect on a young couple is graphically illustrated by the following description of the married life of a young Ashkenazic man and his Sephardic bride:

R. Mordechai . . . knew no Ladino, while his wife knew no Yiddish, but nevertheless the couple lived a quiet, calm life. At first they stammered and conversed like dumb people, with gestures and grimaces; but soon the husband learned a few words in Ladino and his wife a few words in Yiddish . . . They made do with conversation about necessary matters only. [130]

This account attests not only to the relationship between the husband and his wife but also to the perception of the writer, who considered such a life as "quiet" and "calm." The limitation of their conversation to the most necessary matters only confirms one's impression that the husband and wife were spiritually miles apart; they had no desire to engage in what we would consider today a meaningful relationship, but at most to cooperate in material, everyday affairs.[131] In *Sefer takhshitei nashim*, a Yiddish manual of ethical conduct, written in Jerusalem, we read the author's advice to his female readers to speak with their husbands as little as possible; this, he averred, would enhance their husbands' affection for them.[132]

One possible expression of the lack of any deep personal relationship between husband and wife was perhaps the latter's reluctance to refer to (or address) her husband by his given name, generally preferring the use of the third-person singular pronoun, "he/him." If a woman wished to report that she had told her husband something, she would say, "I told him"; "and she always had to address him in the third person, partly out of oriental-style respect and partly for fear of the evil eye"[133] (in which case this practice does not actually attest to the couple's relationship). Women's ignorance or lack of education also contributed to the gap between husband and wife. A rare admission on a father's part that his daughter's ignorance might impair her relationship with her new husband may be found in a letter from Yehiel Michel Pines to his future son-in-law, David Yellin, requesting the latter to be sure to improve his future wife's education.[134] Overcrowding was also an alienating factor. Haim Be'er, telling the story of his grandparents, notes the remoteness of their relationship, quoting his mother as saying, "That's how it is, when everybody — parents and grown children — sleeps in the same room."[135]

The bride, having left her parental home, came under the sway of her mother-in-law, who expected her to help in the housework and to have children. The groom, if a scholar, continued to frequent the study house, perhaps studying with his father-in-law or some other member of the family.[136] Moshe Blau describes a strict, harsh lifestyle, in which his wife had no part:

During the years of the *kest* I kept company with my grandfather . . . We ate together, went to services together, went to the *yeshiva* together, and went to sleep at one o'clock . . . My grandfather, who used to get up about two hours after midnight, would wake me up for the *vatikin* service [morning service at earliest possible hour].[137]

Husband and wife lived their lives on two parallel axes, which hardly ever met. Rising so early in the morning, absence from home till the late hours of the night or sometimes even for the whole night,[138] and dining separately on weekdays did not leave much room for the couple to meet and communicate. Reitze, daughter of Mordechai Chen, wrote in her pamphlet:

My husband, may his light shine, was never home, for by both day and night he was always in the study house, where he sat and studied. And when he came from the study house he would come after midnight, and [even] by night, if he went to study at some special night session, he would not come home all night.[139]

The subject also figures in the aforementioned ethical manual *Sefer takh-shitei nashim*. The author, with an eye to teaching young couples how to behave in married life, notes that young husbands refrained from coming home to sleep and preferred to spend the night in the study house.[140] This lifestyle was common among scholars in eastern Europe, as we read in the biography of Moshe Nehemiah Kahanov, who came to the Holy Land in the 1860s. Before immigrating, shortly after his marriage, Moshe Nehemiah left his hometown and his young wife for Vilna, where he spent his time studying Torah. He came home briefly for his son's circumcision but hurried back to Vilna. His biographer considered this praiseworthy behavior: "There [in Vilna] he resided for a few years, essentially a celibate, spending his time studying the Torah and worshiping God."[141]

Flora Randegger, the teacher from Trieste, described the marital relations of a Jerusalem couple with whom she was acquainted, the Constantinis: "A lofty, righteous couple," she wrote admiringly, "he lives for prayer and Torah study; and she is completely preoccupied with him — serving him, supplying all his needs as far as she can — that is her main goal in life."[142] In a will signed in Jerusalem in the 1880s, a husband thanks his wife for serving him "with all her might"[143] — clearly an expression of his profound appreciation of her efforts. The relationship was thus expressed primarily in the wife's providing her husband with all his physical needs, and in his acceptance of this service.

A Sephardic woman would "toil day and night to prepare her husband's favorite dishes," while the husband, whose task it was to distribute food at the table during Sabbath meals, would give his wife her favorite food.[144] While singing the biblical passage "A good wife who can find?" (Prov. 31:10–31) at the Friday night dinner table, in Jerusalem as anywhere else in the Jewish world, the husband might, with his eyes, take the opportunity to thank his wife for her devotion.[145]

If this distant relationship was the rule in a first marriage, it was surely most common in second or third marriages.[146] Such marriages, in which the couple were generally, of course, older and in most cases had known one another before the wedding,[147] were frequently purely functional in nature. Yosef Rivlin, describing his third marriage (his first two wives had died), wrote: "God gave me this wife . . . to enhance the honor of my home."[148] The prosaic, practical nature of the conjugal relationship is also brought out in a prenuptial agreement between the revered rabbi of Jerusalem, Rabbi Shmuel Salant, and his third wife. Salant made two conditions for his wife-to-be: first, he would allow her a fixed sum of money for household expenses, and she should make no further demands; second, she would be expected to cook for him every day.[149]

Conversely, we have no documentary evidence of a woman's expectations of her husband as to their relationship. It may be surmised that the remote nature of the relationship before marriage left its imprint on the relations that developed later.

The husband was considered not only his wife's guide and mentor; he was also held responsible for her behavior. As the medieval sage Maimonides ruled: "Whosoever does not supervise his wife and children and household, admonishing them and watching their conduct constantly, to ensure that they be free of any sin and transgression — that person is a sinner."[150] This ruling clearly emerges from the regulations enacted by the members of Kolel Ungarn (the Hungarian *kolel*), according to which, among other things, a man whose wife did not shave her head would not be allowed to rent a place in the study house.[151] A man who failed to impose his will on his family would be punished for their offenses.

Ashkenazic men's utter devotion to studying the Torah seems to have had the unquestioning backing of their wives. Grayevsky tells the story of Chayah Gitel Bassan, who was willing to endure hardship and live a life of poverty, on condition that her husband should study Torah all his life.[152] Chayah Gitel not only managed the household and raised her children; she was also the family's breadwinner and opened a grocery store for the purpose.[153] In another such story, Rabbi Zalman Grossman aspired to stay at the Hasidic "court" of Rabbi Israel of Stolin. His wife, "aware of his noble character" and of his desire for "a journey of spiritual elevation, to gain strength and scale the heights of Torah and Hasidim," persuaded him to go and devote his time to studying the Torah.[154] Her granddaughter, who told her story, described the wife's "satisfaction and enjoyment of the privilege granted her, to help her husband improve himself and fulfill his spiritual desires." Hayyim Hirschensohn, a scholar who spent his youth in Jerusalem, thanked his wife, Chavah, an educated woman, for enabling him to engage in his spiritual labors.[155] On the other hand, the husband's total immersion in his spiritual world, which was usually closed to his spouse, created yet another barrier between them. On the one hand, the wife supported her husband, but on the other, she was barred entry to his world. The two were separated by an almost unbridgeable abyss.

The Ashkenazic woman's responsibility for the family's daily bread was taken for granted by all concerned. Rabbi Yehoshua Yosef Lifschitz had no idea of the location of his wife's store; he was so engrossed in his studies that he paid no attention whatever to her worries. When she wanted to consult him about marrying off their daughters, she had to stay awake the whole night so as to "catch him."[156] An account of another family's life, published in the newspaper *Hazevi*, paints a picture of a scholar so cut off from his environment that he forgot that it was Friday, and that he was expected to bring his wife oil to light the Sabbath candles; she, for her part, paid no attention to him or to his thoughts.[157]

The lack of communication or cooperation between husband and wife was also taken for granted in relation to financial decisions. The husband was entitled to decide what to do with the dowry money that his wife brought with her, without her having any say in the matter. Shmuel Heller, the rabbi of Safed, married a second wife after his first wife had died in an earthquake, and she brought considerable wealth to the marriage. Rabbi Heller, who had lost his entire library in the quake, bought a new one with the dowry money; she knew nothing of the purchase until a convoy of camels reached Safed with the new books.[158] Ben Zion Yadler, the famed Jerusalem preacher, related that his mother had opened a store for her family's livelihood; heavy losses later forced her to sell it, but she told her husband nothing of this, so as not to trouble him. After he heard of her action, he secured a loan for her, and a religious court nullified the sale, which had been made on her initiative alone.[159] The economic relationship between husband and wife was often expressed in wills: some men appointed their wives as managers of their estate, and a few even left them all their property.[160]

Poverty and congestion helped to create a spartan family atmosphere, and there were few attempts to encourage any feeling of togetherness or mutual communication. We have a poignant description of the resulting alienation from the pen of Rachel Danin, David Yellin's sister, who married one Yehezkel Danin Socholowsky. She had barely known her husband before their marriage, and was from the start revolted by a relationship with a spouse with whom she had little in common:

Once, on Friday night, Yehezkel came late for Kiddush and I had to wait for him in vain; the table was set, the candles had already gone out, and the meal that I had cooked so lovingly was almost spoiled, and I was very upset. Finally, he arrived, with a visitor, with whom he was so deeply in conversation that he almost ignored my presence.[161]

Rachel clearly felt that they were like complete strangers, and later in fact ran away from home in a fruitless attempt to leave her husband. To the extent that any real personal relationship could develop, it was a long, slow process.

Hannah Trager, a Jerusalem-born woman who was educated in London, told a story of life in the Holy City, in which a young woman complains that her mother-in-law does not allow her to talk to her husband: "If she would only let me talk with my husband . . . When his mother is asleep, . . . he tells me stories from the Talmud and sometimes reads them to me aloud. I enjoy those hours immensely!"[162] The young woman's yearning to speak to her husband and be allowed into his spiritual world is indicative of the deficiency of marital relations in Jerusalem, expressed through the eyes of a person influenced by Western culture.

The utterly different spiritual worlds of husband and wife in Jerusalem sometimes brought about their separation even on Sabbaths and festivals. In his last will and testament, Rabbi Moshe Nehemiah Kahanov admonished his family to devote all their time, even on the Sabbath, to studying the Torah: "For we see that many people spend almost all the holy day in conversation and trivial matters . . . but he who plans his ways, and sees to it that his time is counted and his moments prepared, should be able to study on the holy Sabbath, night and day, some ten hours."[163] The father of the family was expected to spend his time studying even on the Sabbath, while his wife would read Psalms, *Zena ure'ena*, or *Ethics of the Fathers*;[164] some women spent the day teaching small children. Zemira Mani, the educated daughter of a well-known Hebron family, would gather children around her at home and teach them the Torah portion of the week and the *haftarah*.[165] During the festival of Hanukkah mothers and grandmothers would listen to the translation of a book named *Tokpo shel Yosef* (a romance written in the mid–nineteenth century by a kabbalist of the Land of Israel),[166] on Purim they would thrill to the story of Queen Esther,[167] and on Passover some recited the Song of Songs in Ladino.[168]

The sole occasion on which all family members would gather around the dinner table was apparently the Sabbath. Not only in Jerusalem did most families refrain from dining together on weekdays. Esther Hilwani-Steinhorn, in her book *Damascus, My City*, notes that "[Sabbath] is perhaps the only day when the family eat a meal together."[169] Gad Frumkin, scion of a well-to-do Hasidic family, relates in his memoirs that his father, constantly busy with his newspaper *Havazelet*, never dined with the rest of his family during the week, but only on the Sabbath did the whole family get together for meals.[170] Sometimes, on special occasions, families would enjoy an entertaining hour or two, generally around a festive table, accompanied by songs.[171] But relationships even within the family were organized in accordance with a clear-cut gender-based hierarchy. Even on the Sabbath, separation ruled for most hours of the day: at home, as in the synagogue, men gathered by themselves, while the women were restricted to their own area.[172] It was not customary for couples to take a walk together.[173] This gender-based division was strictly maintained, as we infer from the following account by Jerusalem-born Eliyahu Eliachar: "Studying together on the Sabbath was a joyful experience. All [male] members of the family took part, as well as rabbis who lived nearby . . . At the end, the women of the family would serve the participants sweetmeats and drinks."[174]

Marriage between members of different communities implied special problems for the couple: each had to learn a new language, a new mentality, and new modes of behavior. Yehoshua Yellin, describing his reception in his wife's parents' house, writes: "Upon coming into the home of my late father-in-law I saw before me a new world, the world of a new language, a world of clothing and food, customs and manners, which were foreign and new to me."[175] The Ashkenazic establishment, in keeping with the accepted Halakhic principle, ruled that it was incumbent on a woman to adopt her husband's customs, including whatever more lenient or stringent rules of conduct he followed, "for the woman is subject to her husband in her dwelling, it is she who must leave [her parental home] and live in his realm, and so she must follow his customs."[176] Despite the "housewife" designation *akkeret habayit*, already mentioned previously, the real center of the household was the man, and it was she who was obliged to move into his home and subordinate herself to his ways. Whether a bride adjusted to her husband's family easily or with difficulty was largely dependent on how the rest of the family treated her.[177]

The writer Avraham Shmuel Hirschberg, who made no secret of his harsh criticism of the Sephardic community, described how men of that community would gather not only in the study house but in cafés, where they also met young Arabs. Even if his account centers on a small group of people, it nevertheless points to the complexity of male society. The wives of those young men lived in their own isolated sphere: "The Sephardic woman, who for the most part never studied in her youth, . . . becomes lazy and indifferent after her marriage, spending her time seated on the floor with her legs folded beneath her, drinking coffee, smoking a *nargilah* and gossiping with her companions."[178] Hirschberg clearly believed, in keeping with Orientalist tradition, that the Sephardic family was less robust than the Ashkenazic, that the mutual commitment of Sephardic couples was weaker than that of Ashkenazim. Might one perhaps link this conclusion with his impression of the ignorance of Sephardic women? Did he believe that this ignorance increased the gap between them and their men?

Though Jewish Law enjoins men to treat their wives with love, respect and integrity,[179] reality was frequently otherwise: the man's absolute power sometimes tempted him to mistreat his wife.[180] Shim'on Berman, who made an attempt to found an agricultural colony in the Land of Israel ten years before Petah Tikvah, describes in his memoirs a Jew from Hebron who abused his young wife, justifying his behavior as consistent with the verse, "he shall rule over you" (Gen. 3:16).[181]

As elsewhere, Jerusalem was not unacquainted with cases of domestic violence. The editor of *Hazevi* wrote that domestic life in the Holy City was anything but holy, and admonished his readers: "Did you hear how last year a young scholar almost beat his wife to death . . . ? I know of many, many such cases, among both Ashkenazim and Sephardim."[182] In her memoirs, the celebrated nurse "Schwester Selma," who immigrated to the Holy Land during World War I, describes a violent practice that was common in the city: men returning from services on Friday night who were dissatisfied with their wives' Sabbath preparations would cut off their earlobes. Schwester Selma writes that she used to prepare a supply of bandages every Friday afternoon — her laconic account betrays no hint of surprise, let alone of protest.[183] Echoes of wife abuse may be heard in the responsa literature written in the country. Rabbi Rahamim Yosef Franco of Hebron refers disapprovingly in one responsum to a pregnant woman whose husband, attracted by another woman, beat her fiercely.[184] The editor of *Hazevi* published numerous stories of this kind in order to arouse public protest, in one case even reporting the murder of a Muslim woman motivated by "family honor."[185] While we may suppose that, given the overcrowded living conditions, such stories were well known, they were rarely mentioned in writing; this, too, may be yet another reflection of society's attitude to such cases.[186]

The honor of the family was the honor of the community, as is clearly demonstrated by the rare documentations of adultery. Yehoshua Yellin mentions a married woman who had an extramarital affair. When the affair became known to her neighbors, the man fled to Egypt, and the woman was summoned to the religious court. There she admitted her guilt and was condemned to be publicly disgraced in the synagogue. The congregation seems to have taken part eagerly and willingly in spitting in her face and putting her to shame: "Many of those gathered there threw rotten eggs, eggshells and rotten fruit, as well as dirty rags, at her, each trying to outdo the other."[187] After this public spectacle she was whipped and then released. In the perception of the Jerusalem community, forbidden relations detracted from the city's sanctity and honor; hence humiliating the woman was a fitting punishment, in effect "measure for measure."[188] The public disgrace had its effect, and the woman fled the city. The community had achieved its goal: punishment was meted out in full view, and the community was freed of the presence of the adulteress.

Conjugal relations or sexual desires were never discussed in public. Chava Weissler, in a study of women's penitential literature, points out the lack of any reference to female eroticism in the ethical literature of traditional Ashkenazic society in the nineteenth century, inferring that this literature was entirely informed by the male viewpoint, according to which women have no sexual urge.[189] This explanation was probably valid for the Jerusalem community as well. On the other hand, there are numerous references to the *mikveh* (ritual bath). Care for the *mikveh* was the responsibility of the community, and hygienic conditions there affected the users' health.[190] Women's visits to the *mikveh* took place, in accordance with tradition, in near-secrecy, in order to conceal them from the children and the prying eyes of the neighbors. "[The woman's] intimations were meant for her husband, and they alone were aware of their secret. It was a kind of heartfelt interchange, replete with modesty and lofty emotions, whose ultimate purpose was the sanctity of the family."[191]

Perhaps the only surviving evidence for the intimacy that might evolve between husband and wife, in a society where men and women inhabited parallel spheres that never intersected, lies in the facial expressions of couples in old, faded family photographs. Loving relationships were almost never mentioned; they were reserved for the innermost realms of the heart. A rare witness to a meaningful relationship between a man and woman joined in a prearranged marriage, as was the custom, is Hannah Luncz. She relates that her father, Avraham Moshe Luncz, who, while studying in a *yeshiva*, nevertheless acquired an extensive secular education, studied and read with his young wife, Devorah, to the extent that they became veritable soul mates. Her parents, writes Hannah Luncz, were thus able to create a shared spiritual world and become real partners in life.[192] Exceptional expressions of affection may be found in husbands' eulogies of their wives. The editor of *Havazelet*, Yisra'el Dov Frumkin, married Mindel, daughter of Yisra'el Bak, a pioneer of printing in Jerusalem, at the age of fourteen, only to lose her after a little more than ten years of marriage. He commemorated her in an emotional elegy titled *Evel yahid* (Private Mourning), in which he extolled their unique relationship: "Together with me, she endured and suffered life's labors, summoning up all her courage to help me, to calm my heart and spirit, with intelligence, with reverence for God, and with unusual and precious talents." Mindel was able to achieve a close rapport with her partner in all areas of life: "In her and in my darling children I have found consolation from all the many trials and tribulations that have come my way."[193]

The editor of *Havazelet* was not the only person to publish a eulogy of a beloved wife. The same newspaper published a heartfelt tribute by one B. D. Margaliyot, whose young wife had died: "The heavens over my head are darkened, and the stars' light has dimmed; there is no more joy in my wounded heart, for my virtuous wife has died, . . . plucked like a lily."[194] And Yaakov Asher Grayevsky wrote a moving dirge for his young wife, Nehamah: "What consolation [*nehamah*] can there be for Nehamah?" Grayevsky yearned for his deceased wife, mourning above all for the profound affinity he felt for her: "Our souls are linked forever."[195] The sincere words penned by such widowers, expressing deep sorrow for their loss, incidentally paint a portrait of the ideal Jerusalem woman: virtuous, loving, and God-fearing.

A unique story was told of Rabbi Yosef Hayyim Sonnenfeld, who refrained from idle conversation with his wife after their marriage, in keeping with the maxim from *Ethics of the Fathers*, "Talk not overmuch with women" (Avot 1:5):

Himmel-bett, the "Heavenly bed" on which Jewish women gave birth. Courtesy of "The Old Yishuv Court" Museum, the Jewish Quarter, the Old City, Jerusalem.

While studying he realized that his wife was pained by loneliness, which in turn pained him; but what could he do? speak trivial things with her?! He could not; but on the other hand he did not wish to leave her in her loneliness, and so he decided to give her a lesson in *Orah Hayyim* [the section of the *Shulhan Arukh* concerned with daily conduct] for half an hour each day.[196]

The story graphically illustrates the problematic nature of the relationship. On the one hand, there was a desire to maintain a loving relationship; on the other, men had been raised from infancy in the conviction that one should keep one's distance from women, who symbolized temptation, profane matter, and impurity. The desire for love was apparently a kind of Utopian idea, possibly achievable in the messianic era but not in real life. In everyday life, while husband and wife were confined to a small room (or two small rooms), they were actually living in two quite different spheres, which generally came together only in relation to a third entity: the younger generation.

Childbirth and the Newborn

Infant mortality was rife in nineteenth-century Jerusalem; every successful birth was therefore a major event. The tender age of the mothers,[197] the poor hygienic conditions, and the lack of modern physicians in the Holy City were contributory factors in the high rate of mortality among both mothers and babies.[198] Only toward the end of the century did Jerusalem's health services improve to some extent.[199] Treatment of birthing mothers included both medical treatment proper — as far as the available medical facilities would allow — and magical techniques to neutralize the forces of evil that were believed to threaten the lives of mothers and babies alike.[200] Such techniques were common throughout the Ottoman Empire. However, given the inadequate hygienic conditions, the religious tension pervading the Jewish community, and the variety of popular beliefs among the different communities, birth in Jerusalem had its own special features over and above its usual Middle Eastern characteristics.

Perhaps the only time in a Jerusalem woman's life when she was able to enjoy special attention and pampering was her pregnancy.[201] The consideration given to pregnant women was also a consequence of the fact that, since the child in her womb might well be a boy, she was potentially representing both genders for a while. The scene of the birth was the home. Present in the room besides the prospective mother herself were the midwife, as well as the birth stool — "a padded chair with two supports, one on either side, which the woman could clutch while giving birth."[202] A woman's joy after a successful birth knew no bounds. The elaborate canopied bed used by a woman recovering from the experience was known as the *himmel-bett*, that is, heavenly bed.[203] This bed was carried from house to house, as required. Memoirists frequently mentioned that Jewish birthing mothers were treated better than their Arab counterparts:

In Jewish families care was taken to pamper the mother and lay her in an iron bed rented for her for the seven days of birth. Arab women brought their babies into the world on a mattress spread on the floor, and Arab peasant women who chanced to be in the Jerusalem markets would give birth at the side of a narrow lane or under a gloomy arch, without midwife or iron bed.[204]

To make the birth easier, there were magic spells of many kinds, documented in numerous memoirs.[205] In the absence of preventive medicine, magical healing was the rule, in particular by means of charms and amulets; the basic motifs were common to Ashkenazim and Sephardim.[206] A pregnant woman would tie around her waist a length of red string that had previously been wound around a saint's tomb, as a "remedy" against miscarriage. When the woman was in labor, the string would be taken to the synagogue and its end wound around a Torah scroll, to ensure an easy birth.[207] During birth, the woman would be assisted by midwives, who were highly respected and in fact also tended non-Jewish women.[208]

"Happy is he whose children are males, and woe to him whose children are females" (Bab. Talmud, Kiddushin 82b) — in Jewish society as in other societies, the birthing mother's right to attention depended on the sex of her child. The woman herself was considered unclean after giving birth, her body a "source of filth," while the infant was seen as pure and sacred.[209] Birth of a son would enhance the mother's status, and she would enjoy special protection and treatment, designed above all to ensure her child's welfare. Not so if she gave birth to a daughter (though it should be emphasized from the start that the sex of the infant had no direct economic significance—the *halukah* paid the same allowance for a daughter as for a son).[210] Among the Sephardim, the very wording of the announcement of a daughter's birth was different: birth of a boy was greeted with *siman tov*, that is, a good sign; birth of a girl, with *mazal tov*, good fortune.[211] The birth of a daughter was a gloomy occasion: "How people's faces would fall and grimace upon hearing . . . *mazal tov!* Their hearts became cold and the joy was dimmed, the father's face darkened."[212] The mother's house became "a veritable house of mourning."[213] A popular saying among the Sephardim held that "Heaven and Earth also weep when a daughter is born."[214] Such expressions of sorrow, aimed at the mother who had just suffered the pangs of birth, graphically demonstrate both male and female perceptions of the time: a woman is an inferior creature, lacking self-respect.

The negative attitude was sometimes particularly cruel: when a daughter was born "there was no need for any means of protection and defense, since it was not feared that 'Habrosha' [the female demon Lilith] would come and take the daughter away."[215] However, Ita Yellin wrote in her memoirs that after she had given birth to a daughter, pages inscribed with prayers to protect the child and its mother were hung in her room.[216] There were two reasons that abduction of a daughter by the she-demon was not feared. First, many families were indifferent to loss of a daughter, and second, the demon herself, according to popular belief, was not interested in girls. Society thus projected its own negative attitude toward the female sex onto the demonic world. This negative attitude, as we have noted, was shared by men and women alike: "Each and every woman was eager to have male sons and noisily offered up prayers and visited saints' tombs, contributed to charity, sought magical remedies etc., just in order at least to have a male son."[217] Mothers had internalized the male desire for a son, and with it the perception of the female sex as the unwanted "other," the superfluous soul in whom no one, not even Lilith, was interested. Only the midwife who brought the little girl into the world would try to mitigate the general disappointment. Assuring everybody that the newborn baby girl was beautiful, she would add, "Wait and see what a handsome groom she will bring into your home!"[218] The only good thing about a daughter was that in the future she would bring another male into the home.

Evidence at my disposal indicates that the negative attitude to female babies was more pronounced in Sephardic society and less clearly expressed among the Ashkenazim.[219] Ita Yellin — an Ashkenazic woman married to a semi-Sephardic husband — briefly described her feelings after she had given birth to her firstborn, a daughter, in 1885, at the age of seventeen: "I felt particular joy at returning to life, the life of a helpmate and a mother in Israel and in the Land of Israel." At the peak of her personal joy, Ita was still acutely aware of her permanent place as ancillary to her male partner, an instrument of procreation. The baby was named in the presence of the family, and the refreshments served were more modest than in the case of a *brit milah* (circumcision ceremony).[220] It was only when a more educated religious element emerged in Jerusalem society, at the turn of the century, that the attitude to daughters gradually began to improve. Around that time, one finds newspapers publishing announcements by proud parents of the birth of a daughter, sometimes also giving the newborn a new, original name; there were also printed notices of congratulation to parents on the birth of a daughter.[221]

The birthing mother's home was thought to be haunted by sorcery: "'Habrosha' is the evil Lilith. She appears in the guise of an old woman . . . She takes the baby from its mother's breast, strangles it and returns it to the mother; but sometimes she slays the mother and eats the child."[222] The she-demon had a variety of guises, but she was originally simply the personification of woman as a symbol of the forces of evil. The birthing mother's room was closed off, and it was forbidden to remove anything from it, even only a flame.[223] The midwife would draw a black charcoal line on the walls, which evil spirits would supposedly be unable to cross.[224] It was also considered unlucky to praise the baby, for fear of the evil eye. Pieces of paper inscribed with charms and magic spells were hung in the room. In addition, a folded slip of paper with a suitable inscription might be placed on the mother's or the child's forehead.[225] Typical texts were "A charm and protection for burning and for the mother from any evil thing," "Protection for the child and its mother," or "Protection for the house and the mother."[226] Texts were also taken from the Bible, from the mystical Book of the *Zohar* and from popular spells against the evil eye. The texts were illustrated with a variety of drawings: the holy places, the *hamsa*, and so on. A lamp was kept burning by the mother's bed day and night, to banish the forces of evil.[227]

During the day the young mother's relatives would keep her company. The custom of visits by friends was particularly common among the Sephardim. In all respects, such visits were full-blown social affairs: the company smoked the *nargilah*, refreshments were served, stories and jokes were told, and the women sang and danced.[228] Practiced after the birth of a boy or a girl, this custom helped to encourage the mother after her birth experience and to lessen her fear of various harmful influences.

At night, when evil forces were thought to be more powerful, extra measures were taken to protect male children and mothers. The father would invite a *melammed* (elementary schoolteacher) with his pupils to gather around the mother's bed and recite the Shema and other verses aloud. With them were two adults, who studied Torah the whole night, "to guard against the coming of witches disguised as black cats to abduct the baby."[229] Only after circumcision was the child considered to be safe, and transferred from his mother's bed to the cradle. These intensive activities around the birthing mother's bed were representative of a highly gender-based perception. On the one hand, the male sector — little schoolboys and adult scholars — acted as a defensive wall; on the other, female figures engaged in sorcery threatened the lives of mother and child. The newborn baby was seen as a force of purity provoking the female forces of evil. The tension would peak on the night before the circumcision, at which time the protective measures were further intensified. This night, known as *Vakh nakht*, that is, Wakeful Night, was kept as a vigil in both Ashkenazic and Sephardic society.[230] Women would dance in the mother's room, men in the next room.[231] While these ceremonies were particularly popular among Jews of Mediterranean countries, in the Holy City they were also observed by members of the Ashkenazic community.

The *brit*, the circumcision ceremony, was a fairly modest affair in Jerusalem. An old regulation decreed that the number of participants should not exceed the requisite quorum (*minyan*) of ten men.[232] Women, wearing their best, prepared refreshments, brought the baby to the synagogue where the festive meal was to be held, and entertained the female guests.[233] Among the Yemenites, the women themselves did not bring the baby into the men's section, "for modesty's sake,"[234] but a man would bring him in for the ceremony. The mother herself, not to speak of the other women, was barred from the central arena of the ceremony, and could only watch from a distance.

More than any other event, the birth of a child is indicative of society's treatment of the woman in an instrumental rather than an independent role. The very attention that she enjoyed as a birthing mother expressed disparagement of her as a person. The preference for male children was deeply anchored in Jewish faith and culture. The very act of circumcision, making an imprint of Judaism on the male child's sexual organ, was in the nature of an unequivocal statement, reminding each of the sexes of its "proper" place in society.

Mothers and Children

Until the end of the nineteenth century, raising children in Jerusalem was an exhausting process, fraught with anxiety and uncertainty. Sickness and death were constant companions, palpable threats from infancy till youth. Besides the poor hygienic conditions and the lack of progressive medicine, many visitors named childhood marriages as a major reason for miscarriages and infant mortality.[235] In the late 1860s, Dr. Benjamin London, director of the Rothschild Hospital, published an item in the newspaper *Hamaggid* stating that most miscarriages were caused by the mothers' young age.[236] The same explanation had been given for infant mortality by an Alsatian physician who settled in Poland in the eighteenth century, who claimed that childhood marriage was having a deleterious effect on the health of Polish Jews.[237] Infant mortality was common in all sectors of Jerusalem's population, both Jewish and non-Jewish. During the first half of the nineteenth century, an average family in Jerusalem included four souls, but by the beginning of the twentieth century the figure had increased to seven.[238] Uziel Schmelz showed in a series of detailed studies that among children born in the mid–nineteenth century, the great majority died at a tender age; in 1866, about 22 percent of Ashkenazic and North African families in Jerusalem had no children.[239] Luncz wrote in 1901 that natural reproduction among Jews in the Land of Israel was less than that in most European Jewish communities.[240] Even in nineteenth-century Istanbul the Jews' demographic situation was far better than in Jerusalem; an average family there included three children.[241]

Given these conditions, parents' primary concern was naturally to ensure their children's physical well-being. The epitaph on the gravestone of Rachel, wife of Rabbi Yaakov Leib Levi, who lost two of her children in a single week, reads: "Here lies the righteous woman, one of the precious daughters of Zion, who had to endure bodily affliction and great, great sorrow in the raising of children."[242] Yizhak Shiryon, born in Jerusalem, in his memoirs describes his wife, three of whose children had died, as "suffused with sorrow for the first children who had died."[243] The death of several children in a single family was not uncommon,[244] and when plague hit the city there was unbearable tension; processions of parents and other family members could be seen accompanying their children on their last journey.[245] At such times the impression was that "there was not a home that the grave digger had not visited, a small plank in his hands, on which he laid the body of the child to carry him off alone for burial."[246] The frequency of infant deaths was also sometimes evident in the manner of burial. Justice Zevi Berenson, born in Safed in the first decade of the twentieth century, gave a detailed account of the death and burial of a younger sister: "A man . . . took her for burial without any ceremony or prayer, accompanied by no one."[247] Rami Yizre'el, in a study of gravestones on the Mount of Olives, notes that most children were not commemorated by gravestones; some of the stones that do exist state nothing more than "a child."[248] It was not, I believe, a matter of callousness, but the simple fact that the community was too familiar with death.

Rabbi Moshe Nehemiah Kahanov, in his book *Sha'alu shelom Yerusha-*

layim — written as a guide to life in the Holy Land — confessed that "it [was] difficult to raise them [children] in the Holy Land . . . and it is not within the power of a woman alone to endure and suffer everything."[249] Everyday management of the household, compounded by the need to care for sick children, was an unbearable burden. While people were deeply concerned for the living, they were reconciled to the miseries of reality. Reitze, daughter of Mordechai Chen, who lost her children before coming to the Land of Israel, bewailed her bitter fate in her book *Sefer mishpahat yuhasin:* "My children, O my children, how can you . . . look upon my great sorrow; woe is me, a bereaved and lonely woman, O my children, my children."[250] Paradoxically, the bereaved mother was here calling on her dead children to observe her sorrow. She found some consolation for her grief by founding Hakhnasat Orhim Society, namely a women's group that extended that hospitality to the needy, thus leaving a small mark on the city.

Since physicians and healers were of little avail, Jerusalemites adopted various tricks to frustrate the designs of the forces of evil. Parents would relinquish possession of a newborn baby, "selling" him or her to another family whose children had survived; or they might make a vow that till the age of seven the child would wear only clothes received as charity.[251] Underlying this practice was the belief that some factor associated with the parents might cause the child to die.[252] Fear of death was so strong that parents were willing to separate from their children, if only such a measure might guarantee that the children would remain alive. Rivkah Lipa Anikster as it were sacrificed her children by immigrating to the Holy Land and leaving them in the Diaspora, hoping that her sacrifice would ensure them continued life.[253]

On the other side of the coin, plagues and high mortality rates left large numbers of orphans, and voluntary, though informal, adoption of children was not uncommon in Jerusalem. Only in the 1880s and later, after the first orphanage had been established, did community institutions begin to care for homeless children. Jerusalem-born Eliyahu Eliachar relates that "many families used to adopt an orphan boy or girl, or abandoned children . . . who were considered as children in every respect: food, bed, clothing, education and even marriage."[254]

Studies of the history of the family have attempted to understand mothers' relationships with their children. One researcher has used the term "traditional indifference" for the attitude of the average European mother in the eighteenth century to her children.[255] In a patriarchal society, parent-child links were based more on the demand for obedience than on supportive love.[256] Does society's focus on the sex of the child and its chances of survival provide a key to understanding why parents so rarely expressed their feelings for their offspring? Can one interpret various gestures as revealing feelings?

The myth of the warmth of family life in Jewish society[257] also assumed such warm relations between parents and their children. A monk named Stanislaw Staszic penned an illuminating impression of Jewish society in eighteenth-century Poland: "One finds [among the Jews] loyalty between husband and wife and very strong love of children for their parents and parents for their children."[258] Are loyalty and devotion synonymous with love? Contrary to the conventional wisdom, according to which the child's place in traditional societies is marginal,[259] the Jewish community in the Holy City, with its high infant mortality rate, was highly attentive to children's needs, as far as education and child development were concerned.[260]

Once the child had grown and been weaned,[261] it was the mother's task to instill him or her with a proper sense of religious piety. The father's allotted task was to promote the child's intellectual abilities — in the case of a son, and in exceptional cases of a daughter as well; the mother's responsibility was the child's soul.[262] Ben Zion Yadler explained that when women were charged with kindling the Sabbath lights, the commandment had an inner meaning too: it was their mission to kindle the human soul, which was likened to a candle.[263] The mother cultivated the child's spiritual and emotional makeup, told it stories appropriate for its age, and made sure that no unclean language emerged from its lips. Telling stories, considered a woman's occupation, was recognized as an important means of education.[264] The mother was also responsible for inculcating good manners and proper relations within the family.[265] Cultivating the child's moral and emotional character also included preparing him or her for independent life. The mother was assisted in these tasks by the grandmother, who in fact sometimes assumed responsibility for raising the children — particularly when the mother was occupied in earning a livelihood.[266] When the child began to walk, the mother or grandmother would walk ahead with a glass of water and a knife. As the child drew near she would spill out the water and make motions with the knife as if cutting the water; this was supposed to symbolize severance of the bonds that had previously limited the child's movements: "Now they could walk by themselves."[267] It was after all the mother or grandmother who was constantly with the child from birth; hence it was her task to let the child know that, having grown up, he or she could go on with life independently.

The attitude to children was shaped not only by concern for their physical survival but also by regard for the spiritual character of Jewish society. As we have repeatedly pointed out, the Jerusalem community was dedicated to the creation of a uniquely sacred entity, a kind of model to be emulated by all of Jewry. Part and parcel of this perception was a far-reaching approach to education, which considered study of the Torah as the supreme goal.[268] Men and women who had immigrated to the Holy Land saw themselves as the emissaries of the whole Jewish world, responsible for its survival. Rare pamphlets published by educated women in Jerusalem give us a glimpse of the moral and educational message that they wished to impart to their descendants.[269]

Toive Pesil Feinstein came to the Holy Land on her own; her children had grown up and emigrated to the United States, and she was acutely anxious for their welfare, besides deeply regretting the separation from her family and apprehensive that, in those far-off parts, they might abandon religious observance. As far as the physical distance was concerned, one discerns in her words a tone of acquiescence; but she cannot accept the idea that they might distance themselves from traditional Judaism. She seems to be struggling with her words and thoughts to kindle the spark of Judaism in their hearts. Above all, she urges them to heed their spiritual rather than material welfare, pointing out that life is limited, and so it is every person's duty to take full advantage of his or her brief hours on this earth.[270]

The desire to guarantee one's children's survival and proper religious behavior did not necessarily entail an intimate relationship; it did, however, demand absolute devotion, sometimes accompanied by coercive pressure. Unlike modern society, which considers motherhood as an enriching emotional experience, Jerusalem society in the nineteenth century viewed the mother's raising of her children as a supreme religious mission.

Divorce: Dissolution of the Family Unit

"Have you seen the quarrels and disputes between man and wife, between parents and children, heard every day in the courtyard of the Hurvah and the *bet din* and everywhere? Have you seen the dozens and hundreds of divorces concluded every day?"[271]—so lamented "A Hebrew," writing in Eliezer Ben-Yehuda's newspaper *Hazevi*, presenting the Holy City as a city of strife and contention, not only in public but also in private life. Jerusalem newspapers indeed complained frequently of the ease with which divorces were granted.[272] Luncz, for example, noted on one occasion the high frequency of divorces and second matches in Jerusalem.[273] It appears that breaking up a marriage, no less than initiating a match, was considered to be a simple matter, requiring little if any investigation. A similar impression was recorded by many visitors to the city. Abraham Gruenbaum, an emissary of the German Jewish committee for the establishment of a hospital in Jerusalem, remarked during his 1885 visit that "there are numerous divorces here. Rabbi Salant alone deals with some forty [divorces] a year, and the total number exceeds one hundred."[274] A similar observation was made by Edwin Wallace, a non-Jewish tourist from the United States, toward the end of the nineteenth century: "Divorce among the Jews here is a very common occurrence and more easily obtained than in Oklahoma."[275] It is clear from such evidence[276] that the divorce procedure in itself did not carry any stigma. Moreover, I have found no hint of any difference between Ashkenazim and Sephardim in their attitude to divorce or, consequently, in the frequency of divorce in the two communities.[277] Lacking documentation from the Jerusalem rabbinical courts, we cannot of course attempt any statistical analysis of the extent of the phenomenon, and will have to content ourselves with rough estimates.

However, our evidence of family life in Jerusalem is not uniform. Alongside reports that paint a dark picture of frequent tension and altercations, which often ended in the breakup of a marriage,[278] we also possess evidence of contented, happy families. Yaakov Yehoshua, in his documentation of Sephardic society, described the disintegration of a Sephardic family as a rare event: "The concern to protect the family honor discouraged people from going to court . . . It was not easy to divorce one's spouse; divorce was considered as the end of the world, not as is the practice today."[279] According to Yehoshua, divorce was seen as a mark of disgrace for society, and religious court judges always tried to persuade the couple to reach a compromise. Even when domestic life was painful, women would gnash their teeth and pretend that nothing was wrong. They generally preferred to protect "the honor of the family and of our children."[280] The negative perception of divorce in the Ashkenazic community is clearly expressed in a hagiographic tract devoted to Rabbi Shmuel Salant, which paints an utterly different picture from that provided by the tourist Gruenbaum: the venerated rabbi — whose own first marriage ended in divorce — is portrayed as disapproving of divorces and trying to influence couples to settle their differences.[281] Clearly, one's image of Jerusalem depended on one's particular point of view.

Attitudes to divorce in Jewish communities in general were not uniform and indeed varied. When a German Jewish family heard that their daughter, then living in Jerusalem, was about to be divorced after ten years of a childless marriage — a halakhically binding motive for divorce — they tried to dissuade her: "It is not the practice in our place to divorce a woman for that reason."[282] In Baghdad, for example, divorces were quite rare,[283] but in the Holy City they were common in Muslim society too, in keeping with the treatment of the subject in Islam.[284] Dror Ze'evi's description of Muslim society in seventeenth-century Jerusalem also fits the situation in the nineteenth century: "One gets the impression that there was no dimension of obligatory sanctity in the institution of marriage; it was not a one-time, lifelong commitment. Such bonds were tied and untied with relative ease."[285] This atmosphere in Muslim society left its mark on Jewish society. Even in Jewish society in eighteenth- and nineteenth-century Istanbul, divorce, far from being seen in a negative light, was fairly common.[286]

Jerusalem society's attitude to married life was not consistent with the myth of the healthy Jewish family.[287] The tolerant attitude to divorce was also quite different from the standard approach of Jewish society in late medieval Europe, as outlined by Jacob Katz. Katz writes that the economic demands made on the divorcing husband, as well as the social and economic status of the divorced wife, were weighty obstacles to divorce.[288] In European Jewish society of the time, divorce was therefore quite rare. Another reason given for this situation was that family life is the only lifestyle recommended for adult Jews.[289] Such was also the accepted view among Jerusalem society, but the conclusion drawn there was different: instead of preventing divorces, it resulted in a high proportion of second and third marriages.[290]

Despite the view of divorce as a relatively routine matter, the religious courts made efforts to reestablish domestic harmony when the parties expressed their willingness to try. Three compromise agreements preserved in the archives attest to the court's efforts to settle differences peacefully. The first was concluded between an Ashkenazic couple, partners to a particularly stormy marriage; despite being parents of sons and daughters, their altercations sometimes involved physical assault. Yehudah, son of Rabbi Eliezer Bergman (already mentioned in these pages as the first immigrant to come from Germany with his family), and his wife Elka belonged to distinguished families and were quite well-to-do. In the agreement, concluded in 1851, both parties undertook to ensure that "from this day forward there shall be peace and calm between us, as is customary, without any quarrel or altercation, heaven forfend. And they shall not curse or insult one another in any way, heaven forfend, nor, a fortiori, raise a hand against one another."[291] If the document is an accurate representation of the facts, it would seem that the wife did not suffer passively but gave as good as she got. The agreement also included a financial arrangement in case the reconciliation should fail.

Another document records an agreement between two impoverished residents of the city, living at the very edge of society, who had quarreled over both financial matters and the husband's keeping bad company. The husband undertook to manage his financial affairs fairly, not to take up with "ruffians and scallywags," and not to suspect his wife. If he did not honor the agreement, he would have to divorce her.[292] The many conditions to which the husband agreed indicate that he was interested in maintaining the marriage and trying to better his ways. The third document mentioned also records a couple's agreement to make another effort to continue their married life.[293] Such compromise attempts, incidentally, also tell us something of the woman's silent voice: in all cases, she is eager to preserve the match and believes in the man's ability to change.

To what degree did the special conditions in Jerusalem affect the large number of divorces, and what conclusion may one draw as to the Jewish woman's position in Jerusalem? The sporadic reports in newspapers or in memoirs of families breaking up not infrequently indicate that the peculiar circumstances of married life in the Holy City were indeed among the factors that contributed to divorce. For example, the very young age of marriage is recognized as such a factor. The same Abraham Gruenbaum who took note of the high frequency of divorces explicitly blamed the phenomenon on the tender age at which couples were married: "I found that boys are already married at the age of 13, sometimes even earlier . . . This is the reason for the divorces."[294] A related factor was the ease with which matches were made in Jerusalem, no effort being made to get the bride and groom acquainted before the wedding. Thus, a young woman who was married and divorced shortly thereafter writes in a letter that she was married to a husband she barely knew: "I was married to a man whom I did not know and whom I had seen only twice before the wedding."[295]

Eliezer Ben-Yehuda laid the blame in general on the inferior status of women: "We still see the poor, humble woman here among us, deeply humiliated, likened to dust under the feet of her cruel, ignorant husband."[296] This status was associated, in turn, with women's general lack of education. Until the beginning of the twentieth century, only a minority of Jerusalem girls attended any sort of school, and many were completely uneducated. Young women's ignorance was often a source of alienation between husband and wife, and a fertile ground for tension: "Because of the difference and distance in advice and opinions between man and his wife, . . . and if girls do not come at least slightly to resemble the boys in their education, domestic life among us will suffer."[297] Women's inferior education enabled society to impose its will on them and exploit their weakness; in some cases, however, it aroused rebellious feelings.[298]

Paradoxically, the common tendency in Jerusalem to impose exaggeratedly stringent religious practices on women sometimes led to divorce when women refused to comply; conversely, some women adopted such practices themselves and made life impossible for their spouses.[299] This was one aspect of the indifference to a couple's spiritual and emotional life as a major motive for dissolution of the domestic unit. Emotional needs could be suppressed or disregarded, but they could not be simply erased. In sum, the desire to enhance the sanctity of life in Jerusalem, as expressed in the child marriages, the prevention of contact between members of opposite sexes, the humiliation of women, and their lack of education, contributed to the devastation of family life and the destruction of the family, the very warp and woof of society. The quest for sanctity essentially had the opposite effect.

Which of these various factors was uppermost in causing the dissolution of the domestic unit? We have already cited Eliezer Ben-Yehuda's belief that it was the social and cultural mismatch between the partners in the marriage, while Yaakov Yehoshua pointed to the economic factor as the prime culprit. Yaakov Goldberg, in a study of married life among Polish Jewry in the second half of the eighteenth century, noted the relation between economic instability and unhappy marriages. In his view, marriages of children aged less than fourteen were almost sure to fall apart, as the low age precluded the couple establishing a firm economic basis.[300] These explanations are all valid for the situation in Jerusalem. In many cases the couple had no assets — which in turn made divorce itself somewhat easier. In the surrounding Arab society, as well, the inferior socioeconomic status of young couples contributed to the ease with which the ties of marriage could be loosened.[301]

There were, of course, many other, more direct causes for divorce, as in any society anywhere: financial disputes,[302] bad health,[303] adultery,[304] male violence,[305] and barrenness. The functional attitude of society to marriage may be seen, not only in relation to the initial forging of marital bonds, but also in regard to the dissolution of those bonds. According to Jewish Law, a couple unable to bring a child into the world for ten years is obliged to separate.[306] A touching letter from one Hayim ben Elimelech describes his agony at being commanded by the *bet din* to divorce his wife of ten years: "Now I sit alone, without a wife, in poverty and destitution, and my life is bad and bitter in every way."[307] The fact that, according to some interpretations (not universally accepted), Halakhah requires a childless couple to dissolve their marriage, even if they wish to continue to live together, highlights the traditional Jewish definition of the primary goal of marriage: to produce children. In fact, not only the wife's barrenness was a valid reason for divorce, but even giving birth to girls only.[308] An article in the newspaper *Hashkafah* urges mothers of daughters only to consult with Professor Schenk in Vienna, who has found a way "to affect the fetus in the mother's womb so that it should be a male." The writer expresses his hope that the birth of a son would avert divorce.[309] Unlike the case of barrenness, enforced divorce of a woman for having only daughters was contrary to Halakhah; the very practice throws further light on women's inferior standing in Jerusalem society.

Luncz wrote at length on the ease with which religious courts[310] awarded divorces. The fee for arranging a divorce, he writes, was quite low, and the rabbi, who received no remuneration for his efforts, was generally content not to interrogate the husband too thoroughly as to his motives and reasons.[311] Matchmakers were also satisfied, since divorces dropped new customers into their laps as a matter of course. Given the alacrity with which the beadle of the *bet din* would draw up a writ of divorce, it seems clear that the spiritual and emotional aspect of dissolving the family unit was not taken into consideration at all.[312]

The act of divorce illuminates women's position vis-à-vis Halakhah from yet another angle. The right to initiate a divorce is generally reserved for the male partner alone;[313] in Islam, however, women are also empowered to initiate divorces, and as a result Jewish women occasionally appealed to the Muslim *shari'a* courts to release them from their marriages.[314] Men and women who wished to end their marriage could do one of several things: they could appeal to the *bet din* of the *Perushim*, the Hasidim, or the Sephardim; but as noted, they occasionally went to the non-Jewish courts.[315] Women who felt abused would leave their homes and might even present their own case to the court. A woman leaving her house generally had nowhere to go but back to her parents' home.[316] Divorce cases documented in the responsa literature clearly express the judges' cold indifference to a woman's plight. One responsum, written by Rabbi Rahamim Franco of Hebron, tells the tragic story of a young woman of Hebron who had been married to a young epileptic, after being assured that he had been cured. It turned out that she had been deceived, and after three years of suffering she sued for a divorce. The rabbis ruled, however, that since she had been able to endure her distress for three years, she should go on living with her invalid husband for another year or two, in the hope that he might recover; only then would they consider whether a compulsory divorce could be arranged.[317] It may be presumed that, had the situation been reversed, the judges would not have hesitated to grant a divorce. The ruling in Hebron was wholly in accord with attitudes in Jerusalem.

Women who were unable to extricate themselves from unhappy marriages felt trapped and were sometimes led to take desperate measures. We know of at least four cases, from Jerusalem, Safed, and Hebron, of women who committed suicide to escape their predicament. Two young women from Jerusalem and Safed who were refused a divorce poisoned themselves;[318] a young woman who could not stand her husband drowned herself in a Jerusalem cistern; and a North African woman from Hebron, at odds with her mother-in-law, also took her own life.[319] In Jerusalem, as anywhere else in the traditional Jewish world, dissolution of the family unit was conditional upon the husband's consent, so that the wife was practically a captive. The idea that marriages in Jerusalem were easily broken up is of course concordant with the male point of view. Edwin Wallace's observation, "Israel has always been noted for the purity of its home life . . . In the home, the wife is the equal of her husband,"[320] does not fit the picture of the Jewish family in Jerusalem that emerges from the above documentation.

The above account of the dissolution of family life clearly indicates that the means devised by society to enhance its purity took on, quite paradoxically, a destructive aspect. Indifference to women's needs was a natural consequence of society's refusal to consider the needs of the individual. Examination of the various tales of divorce, whether in the responsa literature or in other sources, not infrequently reveals the truth about matters sometimes defined as "social misfits": disappearance, abandoned wives, and the like. These will be considered in chapter 6, which is devoted in general to the margins of society. The well-known maxim that anyone establishing a Jewish family is considered as if rebuilding the ruins of Jerusalem had little effect on society's attitude to divorce. Even the fact that women constituted the demographic majority in Jerusalem could not improve their status or create better marriages; men were always in command.

The Gender-Shaping Aspect of Jerusalem Regulations[321]

Each of the diverse sources cited above in essence tells its own story; the mosaic we have tried to create is an artificial construct, a collage, aiming to reflect the spirit of the period as it emerges both from the documentary material and from the eyes of the observer. Did family life in Jerusalem possess any unique features, or was it just a variation on the theme of family life in an oriental traditional society? The visual images created by Jerusalemites, such as the illustrations of *ketubot* (marriage contracts), do point to a certain characteristic local style, confirming the presence of a special Jerusalem flavor.[322]

Members of the community themselves openly declared their interest in building a unique lifestyle. Over the centuries, local regulations were designed to enhance the community's sanctity, to preserve its special spiritual nature, to ensure its economic stability, and to influence the conduct of newcomers; the goal was to create uniformity rather than an "eclectic congregation."[323] Viewed individually, many of these regulations were similar to those enacted in the other three "Holy Cities," and in some cases even in Diaspora communities,[324] though some were indeed specific to the Holy City par excellence, Jerusalem. However, taken as a whole, the totality was unique to Jerusalem. It included several directives that directly affected women's life, home, and family. The primary responsibility of a Jew or Jewess living in Jerusalem was to conserve the city's peculiar character. The community saw itself as guardian of its members' conduct and activities, at home and in public. This was true not only in regard to various guidelines in areas not directly delineated in Halakhah; in some cases, the community saw fit to dictate behavior actually contrary to Jewish Law, in order to guarantee what the city rabbis considered to be the community's vital needs.[325] The good of the community outweighed the dictates of Halakhah.

Jerusalem's regulations were aimed first and foremost at ensuring men's moral conduct, guarding them against any possible temptation, in keeping with the idea that life in Jerusalem imposed special standards of sanctity on its residents. The easiest way to do this was of course by restricting women's behavior. The regulation regarding clothing made sure not only that a woman's body would be covered — practically disguised — but also that she would stand out from a distance in her white garb. The so-called *lizar* (white sheet) itself, however, was not sufficient to achieve complete separation, so additional rules were required. Women were forbidden to enter the synagogue at certain times and also to bring food for baking to the "oven." Even this was not enough. Ashkenazic women had to shave their heads and were not allowed to wear jewelry. A woman's gloomy external appearance was supposed to nullify any chance that men's desires might be aroused, and in addition to heighten the somber atmosphere of a city still in mourning for the destroyed Temple.

Another expression of the desire to avoid any kind of opulence or enjoyment were regulations that prohibited large-scale celebrations, whether for a wedding or the birth of a son; brides were supposed to wear relatively plain costumes, and music was forbidden at weddings. These regulations aimed at maintaining a modest, practically spartan, way of life.

The regulation requiring every man to marry, and that urging parents to marry off their children as soon as they reached puberty, ostensibly safeguarded the institution of the family. Almost all adult males in the Holy City, as a result, were married. On the other hand, women were perceived as an instrument of the male world, with no recognition of their own needs. Women's behavior was in fact also influenced by their own self-perception as "others," as excluded from the life of the "first" society and inextricably included in the "second" society. Family life in the Holy City was the embodiment of the perception of sanctity, providing a firm background against which the life of the next generation was shaped.

Toward the end of the nineteenth century, certain changes took place in home and family life in Jerusalem, under the influence of the new ideas filtering in from the outside world. Chinks began to form in the impassable barriers that the community had erected between men and women. A poster published in 1894 demonstrates the power of these innovations: "Young men and women go out dancing, Jews and gentiles, dancing and carousing together! Insolent and bold, in the public eye, quite openly . . . Who knows what will happen in the future because of this evil practice."[326] Mixed dancing, brought by immigrants from western Europe, symbolized the first cracks in the wall separating man and wife, the first infiltration of love and affection as a supreme value in relations between the sexes, or between parents and children.

An echo of the new relationships between the sexes may also be discerned in the book that David Spitzer wrote in 1913 as a guide to marriage for young Jerusalem girls. The author, insisting at the outset that a woman should think of her husband as her monarch, was well aware of the new moods filtering in from the Western capitals. In Paris, London, Berlin, Vienna, and America, he writes, the "new" men respected their wives, held their hands, addressed them as "Dear Madam" (*genedige froy*), and obeyed them. These, however, were foreign ways, suitable for gentiles or apostate Jews, and he roundly condemned them. In Spitzer's view, such "love" would ultimately lead to hate. Loving and equal relations between husband and wife were simply a threat to the stability and health of the family unit.[327]

Chapter 4

Women in the Public Sphere

Religious, Economic, and Philanthropic Involvement

The "Women's Section" as Symbol of Their Activity in the Public Sphere

THE LOCATION AND size of "women's sections" in Jerusalem synagogues "told the whole story."[1] Small, dark cubbyholes or attics, hidden from the male eye by iron grills,[2] defined women's space in the Jewish prayer house.[3] Women were thus placed outside the arena of religious activity, able only to watch the proceedings in the synagogue without the men even sensing their presence. In the larger and more magnificent synagogues in the Old City, the Churvah (also known as Bet Ya'akov) and Tif'eret Yisra'el, the women's sections were at a considerable distance from the male worshipers; and the situation was similar in synagogues outside the walls.[4] In addition, not all synagogues had any kind of women's section.[5] Women preferred to frequent holy places, such as the Western Wall, Rachel's Tomb, and tombs of saintly people, rather than attend the synagogue,[6] where they were clearly outside the pale.

The Jerusalem Regulations dictated women's behavior in the synagogue as well: "No woman should wait to hear the last Kaddish"[7] — for the obvious reason that women should make their exit before the men, lest they mingle with them. In 1854 the regulations were made even harsher: "No woman aged less than forty should attend the synagogue for the afternoon and evening services . . . whether on a weekday or on the Sabbath, with the exception of the New Year and the Day of Atonement."[8] The fear of any contact between the sexes was so great that women at their most fertile time of life — aged up to forty, when they are supposed to be sexually most active — were forbidden to hear the last Kaddish of the service on the Sabbath. They were allowed to stay in the synagogue only during the High Holy Days, "on which days they would wait in their section to permit the men to leave before them and prevent them meeting."[9] The elders of the Jerusalem community were afraid that men's desire might be aroused by the mere presence of women during prayers; the Gaon of Vilna, for his part, was anxious lest the women talk during the service, particularly as their conversations might contain gossip and slander, or discussions of fashions.[10]

Jewish Law exempts women from the obligation of public prayer, and indeed most women refrained from attending services, being too busy with their household work and, in addition, not always knowing enough (if any) Hebrew to follow the service and the reading of the Torah. The fragmentary evidence indicates that only a few old ladies attended synagogue. There is a detailed account of female involvement in synagogue affairs in Moshe Reicher's *Sha'arei Yerushalayim*, published in the second half of the nineteenth century: "[The women] stand outside and look in through the synagogue windows and the door, pointing their hands at the Torah scroll and then kissing their hands."[11] This picture of the women — and similar ones can be seen even today — reveals their profound craving to touch the holy. Old women were eager "to catch a few *Kedushot* and Amens,"[12] while others, living near the synagogue, followed the services from their apartments. Nevertheless, at certain times women would join the congregation: in the Hebrew month of Elul, before the New Year, when the *Selichot* (penitential hymns) are recited before dawn;[13] during the High Holy Days, when some kind of temporary women's section would be annexed to the synagogue; on Purim, for the reading of the Scroll of Esther;[14] and on a few other occasions. Pregnant women would come to synagogue "to hear holy things that might have an effect on the fetus,"[15] and learned women, sometimes moved to tears, would follow the translation while the Torah was being read.[16] On Saturday afternoon, when there were no services, women might gather in the synagogue to hear the *Ethics of the Fathers* or listen to an edifying sermon.[17]

Since women were excluded from participation in ceremonies in the male arena, they evolved their own activities, ranging from keeping the synagogue clean to preparing various ceremonial objects, such as embroidering a mantle for the Torah scroll or a Torah Ark curtain.[18] It was common among both Sephardic and Ashkenazic women to twist wicks for the synagogue lamps. Preparing the wicks was sometimes a job for the whole family: a specific lamp in the synagogue might be assigned to one or several families, whose women would twist the wick around a thin piece of straw. Eliahu Eliachar noted that "the wick was twisted and prepared with a sensation of being engaged in a sacred task . . . Preparation of the wicks was seen as a *mitzvah*."[19] Old women considered the task a vocation, and those dealing with it were nicknamed *korkhit* — from a Hebrew verb meaning "to wind, twist." The *korkhit* would recite psalms while working, thus combining two sacred occupations.[20] She knew precisely for which synagogue the wicks were being prepared, and would not think of trespassing on another woman's province. The beadle of the synagogue, upon reception of the wicks, would express his hope that the *korkhit* would someday be privileged to prepare wicks for the Temple. The wicks were prepared with precision and devotion, evidence of the women's desire to have their part in synagogue activities.[21]

The exclusion of women from the synagogue essentially symbolized their position in the Jewish public sphere in general. While women were not allowed to participate in the prayer service, some of them found their way into the synagogue notwithstanding: the poorer ones cared for the synagogue's physical needs, such as preparing the wicks; wealthier ones made donations and sometimes even financed the construction of synagogues. In 1913 there were six synagogues in Jerusalem that had been founded with the help of Jerusalem women's contributions and were in fact named for them.[22] Women's intrusion into the public sphere began as an extension of the domestic sphere and made a considerable contribution to the shaping of a unique feminine identity. Economic and philanthropic activities provided an opportunity for women to empower themselves while still under male domination.

Economic Life in Jerusalem

The reliance of Jerusalem's Jewish population on the *halukah* was responsible for its reputation as a city of idlers and good-for-nothings, male and female alike. "The Jews are not engaged in commerce, whether wholesale or retail. There are only a few artisans . . . Apart from the poverty, physical weakness and incapacity for work are rife."[23] Such were the impressions of the great Jewish historian Zvi Graetz, who paid a brief visit to Jerusalem in 1872. A different report is heard from Avraham Gruenbaum, a Jewish tourist who visited the country in 1885 and noted the large number of Jews working for a living. Gruenbaum had his explanation for the misleading image: "One should not forget that while even in our part of the world it is difficult for an artisan to provide for himself and his family, over there [in Jerusalem] it is almost impossible, for poverty is rife, . . . , there is little demand for goods."[24] In other words, the poverty of Jerusalem's residents was not an indication of laziness.

Historical research has shown that economic conditions in Jerusalem were very complex and variegated.[25] According to Alexander Schölch, there was no economic activity in Jerusalem in the years from 1856 to 1882, whether in production or in business.[26] However, the picture changed at the turn of the nineteenth to the twentieth century. A programmatic article by Avraham Moshe Luncz, published in 1899, provides varied and interesting documentation. Luncz writes of having taken great trouble to assemble information that would refute the negative image of Jerusalem's residents as "lazy and good-for-nothing." He draws up a detailed table, presenting the great diversity of professions and occupations in which the city's Jews made their livings. As he writes, "Almost nine-tenths of its residents are engaged in all manner of crafts and occupations, and only the minority, most of whom are old and infirm . . . , have no profession."[27] According to his calculations, around 80 percent of the Jewish population of Jerusalem were working for a living toward the end of the nineteenth century; a further 5 percent were living on their own capital, brought from abroad (like others, Luncz says nothing about women working). Luncz's observations are confirmed by Yehoshua Barzilai, an early Zionist of the First Aliya, later employed in the Anglo-Palestine Bank. Based on an estimate made at the beginning of the twentieth century, Barzilai concluded that almost half the Jewish population of Jerusalem worked for its living, while only one-tenth were dependent entirely on outside support.[28] Clearly, the variety of occupations and professions was not sufficient to supply the Jews' needs, so that the *halukah* was still necessary.

Around the turn of the nineteenth to the twentieth century, as the New City of Jerusalem began to grow and more capital came into the country, changes took place in the city's economy. Production, based till then on primitive domestic industry—which provided most of the city's needs—began to show signs of a transition to preindustrial conditions,[29] as well as the development of wholesale and retail business. European companies and firms established various new institutions and factories. However, since the increased economic activity did not have adequate financial backing, considerable turmoil was involved. From the beginning of the twentieth century to the outbreak of World War I (and even more so during the war) many residents left the city.[30] The unstable economic conditions were a major factor in this "negative emigration."

Halukah was intended to enable the men of Jerusalem to devote all their time to study and prayer. They were expected to frequent the study house every day, including Sabbaths and festivals. Woman are referred to in the *halukah* regulations in the following terms: "Whoever leaves the Holy Land for foreign parts, out of necessity, as long as he resides abroad he is not entitled to *halukah*, but his wife and children shall receive their part."[31] The sum of money assigned to daughters or women was equal to that for sons. Married women received *halukah* portions depending on their husband's position,[32] and when the husband went abroad his family would receive only its own portion, without the husband's allowance.[33] The actual allowance for wives of artisans or of "ordinary people" was decided by the directors of all the *kolelim* consulting together. These women, as well as divorced women and widows, were entitled only to half of the normal *halukah* allowance. The balance had to be made up by various nursing jobs, tending for the aged and the sick.

To what degree women were involved in economic life is not entirely clear. Housework was not valued as an economic resource, and statistical data relating to various occupations do not generally specify the subjects' sexes.[34] Western tourists generally report that women were excluded from any economic activity,[35] but recent research into the activities of Jewish women in the Middle East has revealed that they were engaged in business, handicrafts, services, and midwifery.[36] Montefiore's 1839 census lists some 57 percent of all widows in Jerusalem as self-supporting.[37] They were engaged, according to the census, in a great number of professions: seamstresses, laundrywomen, grinding grain and sifting flour, services, weavers, musicians, shopkeepers, bleaching, magical charms. While there are estimates of women's labor in eastern Europe — which show that, at the end of the nineteenth century, 28 percent of Jewish women were working for a living[38] — there are few similar data for the women of Jerusalem, and, as noted, it is difficult to evaluate the proportion of women active in the different economic sectors.

The *halukah* ideology provided the theoretical basis for the disposition allowing Torah scholars to be supported by their wives, contrary to the explicit Halakhic obligation of men to support their wives. The conception of women as breadwinners was mentioned in the context of ideas suggested for "productivization" of the city by introducing agriculture and industrialization. The proposal was raised in a letter from Mordechai Zoref to Montefiore in 1945, requesting the latter's aid to establish an agricultural village in which men would work one month a year, while "women of Jerusalem, widows, and orphans would be instructed in agricultural work"; women and orphans would "tend the sheep and milk the goats."[39] In another letter to Montefiore in 1849 from a few Jerusalem notables, the writers proposed that Montefiore establish in the Holy City an "*industriya*" in which the poor and the women would work, while the scholars would devote themselves entirely to Torah study. A similar proposal came sixty years later from a society of young Jerusalemites, called Kehilat Ya'akov, who wished to found an agricultural neighborhood in the outskirts of the city: "Our wives and daughters will occupy themselves in cultivating the garden and rearing the animals and fowl, which will provide one-half of our livelihoods, while we shall be free to labor in the Torah and supervise the education of our children in the manner of our ancestors."[40]

In the late years of the nineteenth century, Western ideas were making themselves felt in Jerusalem, and the idea of promoting the working woman met with two opposing ideological goals: on the one hand, the conception of women's work permitting the men to devote themselves to Torah study; on the other, the Western-philanthropic concept of educating young girls to recognize the value of working for one's living, in the hope that the idea would ultimately be internalized by boys as well when the girls grew up and had their own families.[41] These ideas soon bore fruit: the women of Jerusalem became involved in the city's economy.

Women in Business

"Here, too, it is not customary for women to sit in the shops."[42] Women's avoidance of commercial affairs was considered by some to be typical of the perfect, holy life lived in the Land of Israel. However, Ashkenazic women who came to Jerusalem, beginning in the mid–nineteenth century, rejected this perception and willingly bore the burden of supporting their families, out of the conviction that it was a woman's vocation to enable her husband to spend all his time studying the Torah. This was certainly a common situation in nineteenth-century Lithuania.[43] The wife of Elijah the Gaon of Vilna, who had supported her celebrated and revered husband, was a typical role model. "When I was a shopkeeper in Krakanawi [a small village in Lithuania], my dealings ran to the thousands, when I bought goods on credit in the city of Kaidan," as Rivka Anikster wrote in her booklet, *Kunteres zekher olam*, describing her life as a seasoned businesswoman before she immigrated to the Holy Land.[44] Immanuel Etkes has made the rather surprising point that no one in Lithuania ever questioned the consistency of women serving as breadwinners with the husband's duty to support his wife. He suggests that men's obligations toward their wives were superseded by society's excessive regard for Torah scholarship.[45] The generally offered excuse is that since one can legitimately renounce one's monetary rights, women were willing to give up what was theirs by right. If that was the case in Lithuania, how much more so in Jerusalem: in the Holy City, women's commitment to the support of scholars was no less than realization of the very goal of their immigration to the Land of Israel. In many cases, Ashkenazic women who had been active in commercial life in their countries of origin did so in Jerusalem as well, as a natural continuation of their previous lives.[46] Shops were opened by women exclusively as the result of Ashkenazic women's initiatives.[47] As in eastern Europe, business and trade constituted the most prestigious sector of the economy.

Unlike Ashkenazic women, who were accustomed to go out into the public domain, Sephardic women were excluded not only from selling activities but also from buying. In Jerusalem, as in the Islamic world in general, Muslim women did not normally leave their homes; only in the nineteenth century did Arab peasant women make their first appearance in the market to sell their produce.[48] In keeping with these oriental practices, Jewish women also refrained from going to the market, which was a male sphere: "When a woman comes to buy by herself, she is slighted by the Arab vendors, who do

not withhold insult and spittle from her."[49] Sephardic society sought to protect women from any contact with non-Jews and to keep them at home. In
Izmir, for example, women were not allowed to sit alone in a shop.[50] Only
around the end of the nineteenth century did Jewish women of the Eastern
communities in Jerusalem enter the business world.[51] Sephardic women
were not infrequently envious of their Ashkenazic sisters, whom they thought
were more diligent and hence well off. Supporting their families, as Jewish
Ashkenazic women from eastern Europe were used to doing in their home
countries (and later in the United States as well), must have enhanced their
image as being of a strong and independent nature,[52] unlike Ottoman
women, who were hedged in by a multitude of restrictions.[53]

The Jerusalem Regulations also dealt with women's place in business: "No
woman, whether widow or wife, shall sell wine and spirits to any man."[54] This
1854 regulation was worded in negative terms, but unlike the other regulations, it did not intend to restrict women's freedom but rather to extend it and
permit women to do business, with the sole exception of intoxicating beverages. Based on a similar ordinance in Lithuania,[55] this prohibition aimed at
limiting female activity in what was considered to be a dangerous area (although Muslims were ostensibly forbidden to drink wine). Avraham Freimann pointed out an early-eighteenth-century regulation that consisted of
just four Hebrew words: "No woman shall deal." He explained that, in the
eighteenth century, women were expected to remain entirely aloof from economic life. This prohibition is consistent with the fact that all Ashkenazic Jews
were expelled from Jerusalem in 1721. Once the Ashkenazic community began
to revive in the first half of the nineteenth century, this interdict could not be
upheld, and women were permitted to engage in business, with the sole exception of the sale of intoxicating beverages.[56] This is also confirmed by our information about Fruma, Rabbi Samuel of Kelm's wife, who had supported her
family in Lithuania and refused to immigrate to the country with her husband
in 1858,[57] fearful that she might have to appeal for charity in the Holy Land.
Thanks to the new, more permissive regulations, several women began to take
part in the city's meager economic life. Though the number of such women
was at first small, their numbers increased apace with the passing years.

Many Jerusalem families made their own wine, and it was only natural that
any surplus should be put on the market.[58] This was a decisive turning point,
and the regulation forbidding sale of wine by women was never imple-
mented. The pride of wine commerce in Jerusalem was the production of
sacramental (Kiddush) wine, which was then Jerusalem's main industry and
was primarily in female hands.[59]

As far as trading with non-Jews was concerned, however, the regulations forbidding women to do so remained in force. "An ordinary woman who has not

reached sixty years of age is not permitted under any conceivable circumstances to enter a non-Jew's home to trade in any commodity or perform any service."[60] In fact, Jewish women of Turkey and eastern Europe were not allowed any contact with the male non-Jewish population. This was no trifling matter: the few manufactured products that could be purchased in Jerusalem shops were generally made by Arabs, and if women were prevented from any dealings with non-Jews, they were thereby excluded from any kind of commercial activity. There is ample evidence, however, that this regulation was also effectively ignored. Jewish women worked behind the counter in their shops and sometimes engaged in vigorous negotiations with Arabs, whether producers or purchasers. Some of them even learned to speak Arabic,[61] and some would actually peddle their wares in the streets, selling them to passersby.[62]

Business openings in Jerusalem in the mid–nineteenth century were sparse indeed. Luncz gave a very clear account of the situation: "Trade and every profession were in a very poor state, because almost all residents of the city, except for the few Europeans, were living according to the custom of Eastern countries, their needs and demands being few and meager, and they made most of their household necessities by themselves."[63] There was an intimate relationship between production for the individual household and retail trade.[64] Women brought surpluses of domestic production to be sold to the public, such as baked goods, dairy products, and the like; without home industry, the shelves in most retail stores would have remained empty. Clothing, too, was manufactured domestically at all stages, from the actual spinning of the thread to the weaving and sewing of fabrics.[65] On rare occasions, women might establish a business partnership.[66] Generally, however, they worked independently, maintaining their own contacts with the various professionals — many of them Arabs — from whom they bought raw materials wholesale. Only toward the end of the century was machinery of various kinds, such as sewing machines, first seen in the Holy Land — a veritable technological breakthrough.[67]

Those women who did go in for business worked in a variety of areas: grinding and sale of flour;[68] production and sale of wine;[69] purchase of cotton wool to be spun, woven into thread, and sold;[70] manufacture of yeast;[71] sale of milk,[72] cakes, charcoal,[73] cloth,[74] coffee,[75] clothing, souvenirs from the Holy Land;[76] and more. The most common commercial areas in which women were active were precisely those typical of the Ashkenazic community toward the end of the nineteenth century.[77] It may be assumed that women's business activities did not take up all their time; only a few of them did such work as a full-time occupation.[78]

We find a typical description of a female shopkeeper in the preacher Rabbi Ben Zion Yadler's account of his parents' arrival in the Land of Israel in 1867 and their trials and tribulations. His mother, Malka, decided to open a shop, as she had done in the "old country."[79] The Yadlers' story includes several significant motifs: The father, Rabbi Yizhak Ze'ev, came to his wife's help when she had difficulty communicating with the local Arabs, acting as her interpreter in her first steps as a shopkeeper. Once she had established herself, he had no further involvement: "[My father] had nothing to do with her dealings." While not normally setting foot in her shop, he continued to help his wife to keep the accounts, working at home by night. Malka ran a food store, and one reason for her success was her ability to churn butter. As we have pointed out, there were no finished products in the 1870s, and shopkeepers were also manufacturers. As described by her son, Malka Yadler's establishment was not devoid of a miraculous dimension: the butter she made never ran out, as long as there were prospective customers: "The blessing was actually visible, like Elisha's jug of oil."[80] However, her impressive commercial success lasted only until she had made up the capital that the family had brought with them from abroad — as if that signified a final severing of ties with the "unclean" funds from the Diaspora; from now on, the family would have to be content with what the Holy Land could provide. A few years later, when the business failed, Malka decided to sell it, without informing her husband — communication between them was limited to what they considered the most crucial matters.[81] When Malka died, the epitaph that was engraved on her tombstone read: "She supported her husband and her household for thirty years."[82]

Malka Yadler's story illustrates an important aspect of the husband's attitude to his wife: God had entrusted the men with a mission — to fulfill their vocation in the Land of Israel[83] — and the women had indeed internalized these male values. As described by Grayevsky: "The relationship between her and her husband was like that between Zebulun and Issachar. She loved our sacred possessions [the Torah] with all her heart and soul."[84] This female attitude is also illustrated by the case of Miriam Yocheved Shifra, wife of Rabbi Naftali Zvi Porush-Glickman, who objected to his decision to leave the Torah world and support his family. She entreated him to leave the task of caring for the family's needs to her alone, while he continued with his studies at the Etz Hayim *yeshiva*.[85] The perception was that a woman, by supporting her scholarly husband, was in essence playing her own part in divine worship.

Gitel Dinovitz, who came to Jerusalem from Odessa with her husband in 1906, was probably the most successful and shrewd of these female businesswomen. Unlike the women whose sole object was to enable their men to study Torah, Gitel managed a wholesale grocery business close by the Churvah Synagogue, together with her husband. Pinehas Grayevsky, who eulogized her upon her death in 1939, noted that "for her, trade was not merely one more way of making a living, but a profession to which she was devoted."[86] Calling her a "man," he noted her piety, so intense that she recited the morning service every day before going to work and spent the Sabbath in prayer and study. After her husband's death, Gitel herself managed the business. After her death all the mourners stressed her "manly" qualities, nevertheless calling her "the mother of the Old City of Jerusalem."

Our information about the place of Ashkenazic women in the commercial world of Jerusalem is not adequate for a precise quantitative evaluation, but it nevertheless implies considerable female involvement in the public realm. Our puzzlement at the very ability of the Ashkenazic community in Jerusalem to subsist is somewhat mitigated by our knowledge of this additional economic resource.

Paradoxically, it was when women, who were supposedly "all glorious . . . *within*," left home, enabling their spouses to devote their lives exclusively to the Torah, that they gained the increased appreciation of society. In contrast to the domesticity that was the ideal of the western European woman in the nineteenth century,[87] the Ashkenazic woman of Jerusalem, of eastern European origin, earned admiration above all when she left her own private sphere for the world of commerce. One might think that this situation, with women engaged in business and men in Torah study, represents a case of gender reversal. That is not the case: the burden of supporting the Jews of the Holy City was borne primarily not by males but by those they considered in the category of the "other" and the "weak"—the Jews of the Diaspora, the source of *halukah* funds; but these are also the characteristics of femininity.

Women in Menial Occupations

The most common—and lowly—occupation of women in the Holy City was domestic service in others' homes.[88] This occupation was common in the nineteenth century both in the Ottoman Empire and in Europe. At that time, there was a considerable increase in the number of Jewish girls who were hired out as servants in both Jewish and non-Jewish homes in the Mediterranean countries.[89] In Eastern Europe as well, around the turn of the 20th century, Jewish girls entered service of this kind.[90] In contrast to shopkeeping and trade, which were held in some respect, menial work earned a paltry salary and was considered as rather humiliating. In Jerusalem, Ashkenazic women worked in business, but domestic servants were generally Sephardic women (and women of other oriental communities).

The aversion of Ashkenazic women in Jerusalem to menial work was deep rooted, to the extent that the leaders of the *kolelim* considered their refusal a most dangerous offense: "This is a matter of life and death. For there were some tender and weak women, as well as invalids, who needed some service, but they did not wish to help them or to work for them."[91] In order to induce Ashkenazic women as well to perform menial tasks, the officials responsible for distributing *halukah* funds to wives of artisans, and to divorced women and widows, decided to cut their allowances by half, thus obliging them to earn their own livelihoods.[92]

Owing to the wrenching poverty in mid-nineteenth-century Jerusalem, it was rare to find servants in private homes,[93] but with passing time, as more well-to-do immigrants came to the city, women found more employment of this kind, especially as extra help for pregnant mothers about to give birth.[94] Despite the general contempt for menial tasks, this was the most convenient opportunity for uneducated and needy women to make a living. In the difficult living conditions of Jerusalem, a servant was most welcome.[95] We do not have reliable information as to the numbers of women filling domestic positions in Jewish homes in Jerusalem. Some indication of the difficulty involved in locating such servants may be derived from a newspaper advertisement published at the beginning of the twentieth century and offering work to a female servant.[96] While domestic service in general was not confined to women,[97] at least one field was exclusively a woman's province — laundering. Washerwomen, who usually came from the very poorest classes,[98] were mostly from the Sephardic community,[99] with a few Ashkenazic exceptions — widows or divorcées.[100] Other professions in demand were wet-nursing,[101] as well as cooking, sifting flour, kneading dough, and baking,[102] whether in the worker's own kitchen or in the employer's home.[103] One prominent example is Krisha Berman, who came to the country in 1874 and soon began to bake rolls and sell them to Christian pilgrims. Her initiative was the first step in the establishment of the Berman bakery — the first bakery in Me'ah She'arim.[104]

In rare cases, when a useful service was backed up by capital, it might give rise to a profitable enterprise. This was the case with the hotel industry in the Holy City. As tourism increased, enterprising Jews established restaurants,[105] inns, and hotels, and women were active in this area. Tzipa, wife of Menachem Mendel Kaminitz, managed her husband's inn;[106] Sarah-Dinah, wife of their son Eliezer Kaminitz, the owner of the celebrated Kaminitz Hotel, managed the hotel kitchen and was its chief cook.[107] Esther Mendelevich of Hebron established an inn there and was known for her good cooking.[108] However, these were exceptions. Most of the women engaged in domestic work were poor, and even adoption of a regular profession did not extricate them from their poverty.

Women were able to go out and work in other homes only under strict male supervision. For example, responding to a request from the Yemenite community, the committee of the Sephardic community issued an appeal to Ashkenazic and Sephardic householders not to employ Yemenite women in their homes without their husbands' knowledge: "For such work may lead to misfortune, if they rebel against their husbands and find fault with their men and violate the commandment of procreation."[109] Yemenite women's employment as domestic servants was seen as having a negative effect on their devotion to their own families. Clearly, being exposed in Jerusalem to gender relations quite different from those customary in their country of origin, these women were inspired to make various demands of their husbands. The regulation forbidding Yemenite women to take domestic employment without their husbands' consent, together with the previously mentioned regulation forbidding women to deal in intoxicating beverages, clearly testify to the male sector's feeling of ownership vis-à-vis the female. However, neither regulation was ever enforced. The fact that their initiators lacked coercive force clearly testifies to women's economic power and the importance of their work for society.

Women in Health Services

Care for the sick, a traditional area of female concern, was also common in Jerusalem. There were midwives,[110] nurses, and even—by the twentieth century—a small number of women physicians. Until close to the end of the nineteenth century, nursing was not recognized as an independent profession,[111] and untrained women engaged in a variety of health-related occupations: healing with charms and amulets;[112] treatment of eyes;[113] pharmacists;[114] and home care for invalids.[115] In the second half of the nineteenth century, the number of Jewish hospitals in Jerusalem grew, and they began to acquire more modern medical equipment. The shortage of nurses did not affect the meager salaries paid to female nurses, which were about half those of male nurses.[116] At this time, the Ottoman imperial authorities still refused to permit women to work as physicians; the formality, however, did not prevent women from rendering professional help when needed and making their living in that field. On the eve of World War I there were a few women in Jerusalem who had completed their studies in European schools and were active in a variety of medical fields.[117]

Midwifery was exclusively a women's profession.[118] Jerusalem boasted a not inconsiderable number of Jewish midwives, who worked in both Jewish and Muslim homes,[119] though they lacked any modern professional training; some neglected to take the necessary hygienic precautions. Yaakov Yehoshua described them quite clearly: "The midwives were our neighbors, kindhearted old women who had attended women in childbirth many times and acquired considerable experience."[120] Ita Yellin wrote in similar terms of the first midwife who had helped her: "An old woman, wise, nimble and clean, with much experience in births."[121] Some of the midwives were also professional healers and used charms to ward off the evil eye.[122] Others came to the prospective mother's home a few days before the birth to help with easy domestic chores; some of these refused to take payment from poor women, considering their activities a religious duty. Medicine was a bridge between the various ethnic groups in Jerusalem, and the midwives' efforts were seen as a unique contribution to the improvement of intercommunal and interfaith relations.[123]

As health services in Jerusalem began to modernize, it became more common for midwives to undergo some sort of training. Before long, many Jewish women in Jerusalem — until World War I, women invariably gave birth in their homes[124] — began to prefer midwives with European diplomas. The first midwives who felt the need to update their professional knowledge did so with the assistance of Jerusalem doctors in the various new hospitals.[125] Toward the end of the nineteenth century, a few European-trained midwives arrived. Some of them were young women originally from Jerusalem, such as Rivkah de Freidis, daughter of a Jerusalem rabbi and kabbalist, who had traveled to Paris to study her profession,[126] and Frume Kestelman, a native of Safed, who had studied in Vienna.[127] Some midwives advertised their personal histories and professional education in the Jerusalem press;[128] also found in the newspapers are occasional notices of thanks from people who had used the midwives' services.[129] In 1898 the Jerusalem women's society Ezrat Nashim (see below) designated a fixed salary for a midwife with modern education, hoping thereby to enable people, especially the poor, to avail themselves of modern medical services.[130]

Women were welcomed in the field of nursing, and particularly as midwives; indeed, women's assistance at birth, the most exclusively female act of all, had always been common all over the world.[131] Female involvement in the medical field was appreciated, more than in any other economic area, by the non-Jewish population as well. The fact that, toward the end of the nineteenth century, at least two women of the Old Yishuv traveled to Europe to study midwifery in medical schools bears witness to the degree to which new Western ideas had penetrated Jewish society in the Holy Land. However, the most significant changes to take place in the Jerusalem community with regard to employment affected another area — that of domestic handiwork, embroidery and sewing.

From Domestic Handiwork to Home Industry

Women had traditionally done embroidering and sewing, not only in Europe but also in the Ottoman Empire.[132] However, poverty was so widespread in the 1840s that no one could afford to buy the products of their labors. A

Parisian philanthropist named Joseph Blumenthal gave some poor seamstresses cloth to sew clothes, paid them for their work, and distributed the products to those too poor to buy them; and Montefiore acted similarly.[133] In Jerusalem, arts and crafts were hardly profitable, and were not considered very highly.[134] As Yaakov Yehoshua wrote, "Our parents did not consider crafts a respectable profession."[135] Elizabeth Finn, wife of British consul James Finn, reported that when she came to Jerusalem in 1846 she found few Jewish seamstresses.[136] Nevertheless, Montefiore's 1839 census had reported a seamstress and a spinstress.[137] Dr. Neumann, a physician who spent some years in Jerusalem (1847–1862), refers to Jewish women who earned their living by sewing, embroidering, and knitting.[138] In the 1880s some mechanization arrived — until then the work had all been done manually.[139] The numbers of women employed in these professions cannot be estimated, since existing statistics make no distinction between men and women.

Both Ashkenazic and Sephardic women did needlework;[140] they could not always afford sewing machines. In 1900, Rivkah, daughter of the talmudic scholar Rabbi Nachman Nathan Coronel, one of the founders of Hod *kolel*,[141] appealed to the officials in Amsterdam in charge of distributing *halukah* funds, requesting aid to purchase a new sewing machine in place of the old one, which had been damaged, so that she could continue to earn her living.[142] A family named Mandelbaum, who immigrated to the Land of Israel in the 1890s, brought a sewing machine with them; in the realization that "the chaste daughters of Jerusalem will not go to other people's homes to work," they lent the machine to young women to work at their homes.[143] A few women "encroached" on male professions: Devorah Luncz helped her blind husband, Avraham Moshe Luncz, at his printing press; and Feige Weiss, daughter of a Jerusalem printer, was the first female typesetter in the Holy City.[144]

Worldwide changes in the textile industry not only brought women into the factory[145] but also increased awareness of the need to promote folk arts and crafts with national elements.[146] In the wake of the modernization and industrialization that were sweeping Europe, handiwork emerged from the domestic sphere into the public eye. The Arts and Crafts movement of the years 1850 to 1920, which was particularly popular in England,[147] developed as a reaction to the featureless, mass-produced objects of the industrial revolution and the suppression of individual expression on the part of the worker virtually chained to his or her machine. The movement promoted home crafts and, among other things, resulted in the introduction of sewing and embroidery as a recognized part of women's education. These ideas first reached the Holy Land at the turn of the nineteenth to the twentieth century, brought by various Jewish philanthropic organizations. Various and sundry reformers, eager to transform the economic basis of Jewish Jerusalem, targeted women first and foremost. The Rothschilds and the Montefiores were the first to work for women's vocational education as a major tool for the remaking of society. The schools they founded included sewing as an integral part of the curriculum.

The first attempt to establish home industry among Jerusalem women was apparently made in 1898 by the Jewish Colonization Association (JCA), founded by Baron Maurice de Hirsch, best known for its attempts to settle Jews on the land in various parts of the world; in the Land of Israel it also gave assistance to urban settlement.[148] In 1898 the directors of the association in Paris decided to purchase looms and knitting machines for the Jewish women of Jerusalem. The looms were set up in a large workshop, while ten knitting machines were given to women for home use in exchange for a monthly payment.[149] One year later a lace workshop was added, and two young Jerusalem women were sent to Belgium to learn the craft and impart it to others upon their return to the city. Home production began in 1901, and the products were marketed in the Holy Land and abroad.[150] One year later similar projects were launched in Safed and Jaffa, and later also in Gaza.[151]

Zionist organizations were also active in furthering home industries. Boris Schatz, who arrived in Palestine in 1906 and founded the Bezalel School of Art in Jerusalem, applied these ideas and advocated the modernization of Jewish art.[152] The Bezalel School was supported by the first representation of the Zionist Organization in the country, the Erez Israel Office, founded in 1908. Schatz's goal was to cultivate urban home industry as a means of reinforcing Jewish urban settlement, particularly in Jerusalem.[153] The drive to encourage Jewish "productivization" in Jerusalem was combined with the desire to cultivate Jewish arts and crafts. The female sector, in particular girls and young women as a cheap labor force, was seen as a suitable target for such efforts.

In the early twentieth century, the Bezalel School of Art, with its workshops, was the largest employer in Jerusalem. The workshops produced Jewish folk art. Its arts and crafts were fueled by Zionist fervor; for Schatz, Bezalel was no less important than the Western Wall in Jerusalem, "the property of the nation and symbol of its hope."[154] The invention of Hebrew art was a part of the new process of "inventing" a new national tradition. Schatz hoped that his Hebrew art would further the creation of the new "Hebrew man and woman," both as creators of a new aesthetics and as productive persons and lovers of labor.

In 1906, when Bezalel opened workshops for weaving and dyeing carpets, some four hundred women applied, but only forty-five were accepted.[155] Most of the workers at Bezalel were girls aged twelve, graduates of the Evelina de Rothschild School, who had received some basic training in their school years. Schatz described them, in a pamphlet he published in 1910, as follows:

> The women working in the carpet workshop . . . are not of the same age: they vary from jolly, carefree twelve-year-olds to elderly widows and deserted wives who have seen considerable suffering. The first thing that amazes you is the multitude of Jewish types: from "yellow," that is, Ashkenazic girls, to swarthy, curly-haired Yemenite women. This workshop is a miniature ingathering of exiles of the women of Israel.[156]

However, in contrast to Schatz's obvious enthusiasm, in Jerusalem as elsewhere, the weavers received only meager payment (as did nurses), totaling at most half the average salary of a male worker.[157]

Statistical data for the number of Bezalel employees in 1911 indicate that most of the workers in the workshops were women: in 1911 the total number of workers was 265, of whom 149 were young girls, employed mainly in weaving carpets and making lace.[158] The many surviving photographs show dour, unsmiling young women and girls demonstrating the fruit of their labors.[159]

Beginning in 1908, the Association of Zionist Women for Cultural Work in Palestine, affiliated with the Zionist movement, established lace workshops in various cities in the country.[160] The declared goal was to assure young women of a livelihood, but the association also aimed to make women's labor a way of life and not a mere means of sustenance.[161] The workshops, which produced lace, fabrics, and other textile products, provided employment for hundreds of girls and women in Jerusalem, Tiberias, Safed, Ekron, and Jaffa, particularly for women of the Eastern communities.[162] After working for eight hours, the girls were also offered an hour of Hebrew studies per day. Another developing industry in Jerusalem produced souvenirs, such as dried flowers, ritual articles, and the like; here, too, women were among those employed.[163]

Although the women employed in all these enterprises received very low pay, almost no profits were made, owing to marketing problems. Nevertheless, taken together, these diversified activities were proof positive that new modes of employment could be established using the most limited means. During World War I, a Committee for Women's Employment in Jerusalem was formed.[164]

The women employed in the Bezalel workshops exemplify the transformation that had taken place in female society in Jerusalem: hundreds of women, mainly from the Eastern communities, had entered the labor market. The fact that most of the workers were members of the Sephardic community indicates not only that community's inferior economic condition but also the changes that it had undergone, perhaps owing to the educational work of the Evelina de Rothschild School. Sarah Chinsky, in a recent article, complains of the absence of women from the scope of historical representation, referring to the Bezalel workers as "objects producing objects."[165] Schatz, she argues, described the girls in the same terms as he described their products: according to size, color, and price. The fact is that women's silent participation in the highly significant changes then taking place in the Old Yishuv was not confined to the economic realm. Their part in various other aspects of those changes is no less silent, and this applies in particular to the field of education. The historians are not alone in their silence on these points; they are merely reflecting the silence of their subjects, the people of the Old and New Yishuv alike, in Jerusalem.

Women in Education as a Channel of Modernization

The economy of Jerusalem in the nineteenth century was remote from the achievements of modernization elsewhere in the world, and women began only very slowly and gradually to enter the ranks of the labor force.[166] The field of education[167] is a good example of the slow rate of progress in Jerusalem society. European education was at this time in the throes of a femininization process,[168] but in Jerusalem women had only just begun to work as teachers. *Maestras*, as some of the early Sephardic elementary schoolteachers were known, and rabbis' wives helping their husbands did not really teach but were little more than babysitters. The number of Jewish schoolmistresses in the Holy City was small, in keeping with the small number of girls' schools. We have very little information about the number of teachers born and educated in Jerusalem. Fortuna Behar, a native of Jerusalem and principal of the Evelina de Rothschild School in the 1880s, was exceptional for her education and talents; nevertheless, the quality of the school during her term of office was low, because of the lack of suitable teaching forces in the city. Young women were not considered highly in Jerusalem. Two girls' schools founded around the beginning of the twentieth century by ultra-Orthodox circles (one for girls in general and one catering specifically to orphans) employed male teachers, only handwork classes being taken exclusively by women. The first Jewish kindergarten in Jerusalem, which operated under the aegis of the Evelina de Rothschild School, was run by a Christian teacher, educated in Germany, who essentially trained the first Jewish kindergarten teachers in the Land of Israel. Annie Landau, sent from London to Jerusalem in 1899 to head the school and improve its level of education, encouraged young single women to come from Europe and work as teachers. Only in the first decade of the twentieth century did the school begin to train its own graduates as teachers. However, those teachers trained in Jerusalem ultimately earned much less than those boasting a European education.

Educational institutions for girls not only provided a new profession for women wishing to earn a livelihood but also — and most importantly — accelerated the penetration of new ideas and Western culture in Jerusalem. The schools taught their graduates to work for a living and eschew the support of the *halukah*. The message issuing from the Evelina de Rothschild School at the turn of the century was the importance of educating girls to go out to work, as a step in reeducating society as a whole, men and women.

Wealthy Women

Women's wills[169] and various other legal documents, as well as endowment plaques, provide us with a glimpse of the amount of capital owned by Jewish women in the Holy Land. While most of Jerusalem's Jews were very poor, there were nevertheless some fairly wealthy women living in the city. They had generally acquired their wealth as an inheritance, from father or husband, and were entitled to do as they pleased with it.[170] In Jewish law, all of a woman's income, whether from property or from her own labor, is owned by her husband, but wealthy women usually took care of their own funds.[171] Islamic Law also allows women to own property and bequeath it to others.[172] The available evidence reveals a variety of assets owned by women: fluid capital — money, jewelry, and even a Torah scroll[173] — and real estate — a courtyard, an apartment, a shop.[174] While possession of property did not alter society's gender-based attitudes, it provided the owner with power and influence.

The last will and testament of a woman named Perel of Safed, widow of one Beinish of Satanov, who died in 1892, reflects the personality and property of a rich woman in the latter part of the nineteenth century.[175] In accordance with custom, the widow Perel appointed three executors to process her will and portion out her money and property when her time came. The testator left sums of money to be given to all those who, after her death, would prepare her body for burial (all the various functionaries were listed in detail). Further funds were left to pay the *minyan* (prayer quorum) who would hold prayer services for her during the thirty days after her passing and later on her *Yahrzeit* (anniversary of her death), and also to contribute to the poor, to Torah scholars, and to a few synagogues. Perel also requested that, throughout the first year after her death, Torah scholars hold a prayer service at her grave on the eve of every new moon. The executors she appointed sent telegrams to her five sons — who were living abroad — so that they could recite the Kaddish for their mother (other women, incidentally, expressed similar concerns).[176] The second part of the will was devoted to the distribution of her property. In Safed, as in late-nineteenth-century Jerusalem, every household item had its value.[177] She owned two pillows, a pillowcase, and various articles of clothing — these were left to the poor. The rest of the household goods were to be sold and the proceeds sent to her sons, who would divide them equally among themselves. As to the shop, house, and courtyard in her possession, these were to be either rented out or sold by her sons, and the proceeds disposed of in accordance with instructions specified in the will — some to the poor, some to finance the study of Mishnah at her father's grave on the anniversary of his death.

This detailed will clearly indicates an experienced businesswoman, carefully portioning out her assets, in full awareness of the value of her money and possessions. Also evident in her will is her commitment to the poor of Safed and to various communal institutions; her sons take second place in that regard. Perel was in complete command of everything she had, and clearly went about her business in a fully independent manner.[178]

Another interesting woman emerges from the letters of Chayah Rivka, widow of the geographer Yehosef Schwartz, which show her to have been well versed in financial matters, including varying rates of exchange between different countries. Thus, she carefully tells her relatives in Germany how to deal with her money.[179] On the other hand, the story of a woman from Safed who was attacked by Arabs after the earthquake[180] presents a woman who carefully concealed her riches and was able to save the group of people who escaped with her. These varied pieces of evidence yield portraits of women who contributed to the economy and public institutions of the four holy cities.

Exceptional for her wealth and generosity was Sarah Davis, who immigrated from the United States toward the end of the nineteenth century.[181] Her generosity to her fellow Jews in Jerusalem was unique; she seems to have been responsible for extensive contributions. Her obituary, published in *Hazevi* in 1893, describes her wealth and her generosity:

She decorated the Bet Ya'akov Synagogue in the Churvah of R. Yehudah the Pious, the expenses for which reached 35 Napoleons; she built a magnificent study house in Me'ah She'arim, which was dedicated on Friday the 11th of Elul (5)650 [1890]. She left twelve apartments in Me'ah She'arim to be distributed by lot to the poor of Jerusalem,[182] and similarly in the neighborhood of Nachalat Shiv'ah as well as the neighborhood of Sha'arei Moshe [also known as Batei Wittenberg]. Moreover, she frequently lent money and household utensils to anyone who requested them.[183]

Sarah Davis's house in Me'ah She'arim bears a plaque in her honor to this day, inscribed "*Ohel Sarah.*"[184] In her will she requested that her heirs not try to collect outstanding debts and even restore any items held as security to their rightful owners. She appointed three distinguished executors — Rabbi David Zalman Beharan, Rabbi Hayyim Sonnenfeld, and Rabbi Ya'akov Blumenthal — for her estate. Despite these activities, little is known about her, and she is not mentioned in any of the numerous books of memoirs written about the city's history.

While Sarah Davis's wealth and generosity were unique, the institutions that benefited from her donations were favored by other women as well. Hinda, daughter of Rabbi Moshe Kaplan, endowed the land in her possession for the benefit of the poor of the Vilna *kolel*.[185] Various women made contributions to synagogues and study houses, their wealth enabling them to encroach on the male sphere from which they had been excluded.[186] Sarah Beila Hirschensohn built a study house for the *Perushim* in Safed;[187] Esther Chavah Rimon paid the expenses of a synagogue for the Polish Hasidim;[188] Zelda Steinberg financed an elementary school (Talmud Torah) in the Yemin Moshe neighborhood of Jerusalem; we hear similar reports of Dinah, daughter of Rabbi Meir Libersman, and of other women.[189] Some women earmarked their contributions specifically for typical feminine institutions, such as ritual baths, orphanages,[190] or institutions giving aid to the sick. The first contribution to the first hospital in Safed was made in 1870 by a woman — Chanah, daughter of Rabbi Baruch of Mezhibozh. She not only gave of her own money but worked to persuade other women to follow suit.[191] This leads us to our next section: the funds that paved the way for women to engage in public activities led to another form of energetic activity, in the philanthropic sphere.

Philanthropy as Women's Path to the Public Sphere

In Jerusalem, receiving charity was a way of life;[192] those who provided it, on the other hand, saw it as a kind of sacrifice, establishing a bond of lovingkindness between them and God.[193] Helping the poor was an uplifting experience for donors, male and female alike. In contrast to these Jerusalem perceptions, Jewish philanthropists in Europe, while being committed to giving aid to the Jerusalem community, preferred instead to try to educate the needy, so that they would be able to help themselves and no longer depend on charity. Charles Netter, one of the founders and first leaders of Alliance Israélite Universelle, which was intensively engaged in such activities, accused the advocates of *halukah* of perpetuating poverty among the Jews of Eretz Israel. "Palestine," he wrote, "has been corrupted by charity."[194] The social ideas that wetsern European Jewish society had absorbed rejected poverty as a religious value and denounced it as a social evil to be eradicated,[195] whereas Jerusalem society considered poverty as part of the affliction by which the Land of Israel would be earned, to be borne with love.

In the nineteenth century a considerable number of charitable organizations were established in Europe and the United States, some by women, who were now "intruding" in areas previously considered exclusively male. With the rise of the middle classes and the appearance of the "lady of leisure" stereotype, many wealthy women turned to philanthropic activity. In fact, philanthropy came to be seen in the nineteenth century as a natural outlet for "ladies of leisure" to express themselves.[196] The usual explanation for women's attraction to charitable activities is that charity belongs to the essence of "female nature." In non-Jewish Western culture this phenomenon was supposed to derive from the supposedly "typical" female characteristics of empathy, generosity, and love, and from women's identification with Jesus.[197] Perhaps, in addition, the housewife's escape from the private sphere to philanthropic activity was something of a challenge to conventional ideas of the Victorian woman. Paula Hyman, who has studied the Jewish woman in the throes of modernization, believes that philanthropic organizations redefined what should be considered as "proper" activity for women.[198] In Jewish society, philanthropic activity was a modern means to intensify Jewish identity, which was closely associated with charitable acts.[199] However, despite women's considerable involvement in the various charitable organizations, modern research has clearly shown that women occupied a secondary place in the hierarchy of such organizations. Here again, as in the home, men were the directors, while women were left to do the hard work.[200] Hence one can hardly regard such activities as a challenge to the traditional gender-linked division of labor.[201]

We thus have a contrast between, on the one hand, the theory of women's increased adoption of philanthropic work in Europe and America in the second half of the nineteenth century and, on the other, the charitable activity of the women of the Old Yishuv in Jerusalem. To my mind, these two different mind-sets should be seen in the context of the two entirely different processes taking place in the West, on the one hand, and the East, on the other. The women of Jerusalem were not "women of leisure," and of course they had no intention of identifying with Jesus or, for that matter, emphasizing their Jewish identity. They were simply eager to find an outlet for their religious and social feelings. The concept of the Jewish woman as intent on contributing to others, to the family and to society,[202] was reinforced in the nineteenth century as a consequence of the proliferation of women's charitable organizations, Jewish and non-Jewish, all over the world. Jerusalem was a suitable arena for women's charitable activities, given its exceptional concentration of charitable institutions.[203]

Charitable Institutions: Women in Voluntary Social Work

Many Jerusalem women sought—and found—personal modes of activity, constituting as it were "one-woman" charitable institutions. We have a variety of evidence of charitable activity on the part of women of all circles—

A women's society for the aid of mothers of newly born children. Pinehas Grayevsky, *Benot Zion viYerushalayim* (Reprinted: Jerusalem, 2000), p. 71.

Ashkenazic, Sephardic, rabbis' wives,[204] and "ordinary" women. They found various channels for social action: cooking or in general providing food for the poor or for homeless immigrants;[205] collecting money for poor brides' weddings ("*hakhnasat kalah*");[206] visiting the sick and preparing medications;[207] helping in orphanages;[208] and even sewing *zizit* (the fringes attached to the four corners of special four-cornered garments worn by men in fulfillment of the biblical commandment in Num. 15:37–41).[209] Some women dedicated their efforts to helping the poorest of the poor — the little Yemenite Jewish community.[210] Others cared for the *madrinas* — elderly Sephardic women who came to the Holy Land on their own; in return, the *madrinas* would perform various tasks in the homes of their benefactors, such as caring for children, preparing food, and needlework.[211]

Women engaged in a great variety of unique activities. Malkah the washerwoman and Miriam Mizrahi washed clothes in particular for orphans, the old, and the solitary. Miriam Mizrahi took this upon herself from her very arrival in the Holy City. "She threw off her ornaments and jewelry and exchanged them for washing utensils . . . being one of those 'kindly washerwomen.'"[212] Just as some women found their own modes of worship in the synagogue, such as cleaning or preparing wicks for the lamps, others devised a kind of unique ritual of charity. One woman, known as Rivkah "who clothes the poor," would buy clothes in the market and distribute them to the needy;[213] while Tzipa "the shoemaker" supplied the barefooted poor, children in the Talmud Torah, and orphan brides with footwear.[214] These women's willingness to care for the poor and needy, sometimes investing considerable physical effort, shows a broad understanding of the concept of charity.

Besides these "one-woman" charities, which usually left women in their domestic surroundings, others burst out into the open, as it were, and joined existing charitable organizations. It was indeed customary in Jerusalem, as in Jewish communities the world over, for women to join the male-run charitable organizations and form a women's chapter.[215] They generally worked in areas that were out of bounds for men: purifying deceased women before burial (in burial societies), visiting sick women, and so on.[216] Women also established their own frameworks, sometimes aimed at other women alone but sometimes offering aid to men as well.[217] Most such activities were performed by Ashkenazic women;[218] only toward the end of the nineteenth century did Sephardic woman add their efforts.[219]

The oldest women's organization in Jerusalem was probably Hevrat Bikur Holim Vehakhnasat Kalah (Society for Visiting the Sick and Wedding [Poor] Brides). In Judith Montefiore's second visit to the Holy Land, in 1839, she was appointed an honorary official of the organization.[220] Jerusalem women's correspondence with Judith Montefiore, over many years,[221] reveals another important feature of female activity, namely, its reliance on women's financing.[222] Particularly worthy of attention is the philanthropic activity of the two well-known Jewish families, the Rothschilds and the Montefiores. In 1854, Albert Cohen, the Rothschilds' representative from Paris, established a fund in Jerusalem for the support of poor birthing mothers, on behalf of Betty Rothschild.[223] This fund was similar to the Paris fund, which had also been founded by the Rothschilds.[224] The support provided consisted of payment for two midwives and clothing for the mothers and their babies.[225] This charitable fund, known in Ladino as *pasidora* and accessible to women of all communities, is evidence of the prevalence of poverty in Jerusalem.[226] A similar institution, which financed babies' clothing and the mothers' meals, was founded by the Montefiores.[227]

The need for women to devote themselves to women's needs is clearly seen in an account we have of the establishment of a home for the aged in Jerusalem, called Bet Zekenim u-Zekenot — literally, house for old men and women (the official English name of the institution was Aged Needy Home).[228] In the 1880s a men's organization established a first shelter for elderly people. Despite the great number of solitary women in the city, a shelter was built for them only some ten years later, and the wing reserved for women contained many fewer places.

Only at the start of the twentieth century was the situation remedied. Just before that time, the Rothschild fund for the support of mothers after childbirth had been reorganized. In 1890 a local women's committee was set up in Jerusalem to administer the fund and determine its priorities. The sum of money offered as aid was cut in half but distributed to twice the number of women; support was provided to mothers in accordance with their economic standing; a special department for women giving birth was planned in the Rothschild Hospital in Jerusalem. These changes, however, were still inadequate to answer the many needs of women in Jerusalem. In 1908 a group of Ashkenazic women founded another organization, called Ezer Yoledot (Aid to Mothers). The preamble of the organization's regulations declared its intention to rely exclusively on donations from Jerusalem residents.[229]

The changes instituted over the years in the area of support for mothers after childbirth are evidence of pragmatism, of women's profound acquaintance with the prospective recipients of their aid, and of their desire to rely only on local donations. These initiatives of Jerusalem women had a significant local precedent in an enterprise known as Reitze's Hakhnasat Orhim.

Hospitality as Creation of Life

"I am the treasurer, here in the Holy City of Jerusalem, may it be speedily rebuilt and reestablished, in the Hakhnasat Orhim society."[230] This was how Reitze, daughter of Rabbi Mordechai Chen and wife of Rabbi Zelig of Slonim, described herself in her pamphlet *Sefer mishpahat yuhasin*, which provides a comprehensive description of her initiative. The Hebrew phrase *hakhnasat orhim* means "hospitality," in this context, in particular, hospitality extended as a charitable act to the poor and the underprivileged. In 1868, sometime after her arrival in Jerusalem, Reitze joined the Hakhnasat Orhim society,[231] which ran a soup kitchen for the needy. This was not the first institution of its kind in the Holy City: a few years before, the Bet Tavshil (Soup Kitchen) had been established by the Ashkenazic (male) establishment, with some help from Jerusalem women.[232] It would seem that Reitze took over this older establishment, which soon became the center of her life.

The soup kitchen extended its aid not only to hungry men but also to needy women. The treasurers of the society (all women) described their work as follows: "Whosoever enters hungry will depart satisfied. This is a matter of life and death for hundreds who depend on this — poor, elderly, scholars, widows, orphans, and proselytes."[233] The women prepared food for everyone. Wellborn poor people, reluctant to accept charity in public, would receive their meals in the privacy of their homes, thus preserving their honor.[234] The understanding that any hungry person deserves help was also expressed in the continuity of the work. Rabbi Nehemiah Kahanov wrote that the society's kitchens distributed two meals a day at no charge, on both weekdays and Sabbaths and festivals; more than fifty people required its services.[235] There was seemingly nothing more "natural" for women to do, being occupied seven days a week with managing their own households.

The house run by the Hakhnasat Orhim society differed from the men's Bet Tavshil, not only in its prospective clients and the frequency of the meals, but also in a highly significant administrative feature, indicative of its unique nature: all income to the Hakhnasat Orhim House was reserved for the poor alone. In light of this philanthropic concept, the women devoted themselves entirely to their charitable work. Reitze worked hard, appealing every week to donors in Jerusalem and abroad.[236] She took part in preparing food, distributing it to the poor, and providing the needy with beds and bedclothes.[237] In the Bet Tavshil, however, men did the administrative work, while the routine work was done by women hired for the job. Reitze and her colleagues considered any kind of labor — collection of funds, taking loans, feeding the hungry — as a holy undertaking. This was a new, different conception of giving: the initiators of the aid project personally helped the needy.[238]

Nevertheless, these women's innovative perception of the meaning of charity had no effect on their traditional understanding of their role as women. Like women's organizations throughout the Western world, the Hakhnasat Orhim society relied on male assistance; in this case the help came from Rabbi Shmuel Salant, the revered rabbi of the Ashkenazic community, who was the official recipient of contributions from abroad.[239] The founders of the society felt the need for male authority, as embodied in a well-known public figure, especially in the financial area.

Reitze, the life and soul of the enterprise, was known as "holder of the keys from paradise."[240] She had the help of five other *gaba'iyot* (collectors),[241] who were tirelessly devoted to the society. They repeatedly declared that "we women are doing this for the sake of heaven, not in the hope of any reward."[242] One of Reitze's neighbors took care of her household, so that she could devote all her time to her philanthropic work; this unique partnership, which Reitze used to refer to as the collaboration between "Issachar and Zebulun," was maintained for some fourteen years.[243] She considered her neighbor a full partner in her acts of charity and worthy of the same reward; the partnership, she believed, was like that between the Jews of the Diaspora and those of the Holy Land, or between women and their scholarly husbands.

In her pamphlet, Reitze writes at length of the special merit of the commandment of hospitality, which is associated in particular with the patriarch Abraham. Developing her own style of sermonizing, she pointed out how important it was to observe this commandment in the Holy Land in particular, "because people completing a journey are very tired . . . and if he has no place to come for the first time and dine for the first few days, he will feel very bad."[244] Reitze's society provided not only an inn or way station but also a kind of "absorption center" for new immigrants in search of somewhere to rest their weary bodies. This was how Rabbi Kahanov described the society: "It is impossible to commit the suffering of those solitary souls to writing . . . And for that reason the aforementioned esteemed women got together and rented a house, and they labor with all their strength."[245] The women's work was appreciated in the male sector; for example, it won praise from a writer in *Havazelet:* "Great is the worth of this charitable house and it takes precedence over all the charitable houses in our city."[246] The society's work was also recognized by Sir Moses Montefiore, who, in his last visit to the country (1875), met the women who were in charge and sang their praises as distinguished women, to be reckoned among the most valued and important people of Jerusalem.[247]

Reitze's children had all died while she was still living in the Diaspora, and her hope of having more children in the Holy Land was never fulfilled. For her, therefore, care for immigrants was not only a religious duty, a matter of life and death, but also a means to conserve her own mental health: "Know, that whosoever gives a person life by giving him something to eat, it is just as if he or she had created that person."[248] A lonely soul herself, she reaped much joy from her charitable work, and also considered it of metaphysical significance. She and her friends hoped to influence Divine Providence by virtue of their labors, cementing a kind of partnership with the men in their study of Torah. Like a wife plying her trade to enable her husband to study without concern, Reitze felt that her activities were enabling poor scholars "to sit and learn the holy Torah . . . so that they would not thereby reach a situation in which, because of having nothing to eat, they might have to interrupt their studies — an act which deserves severe punishment."[249] In other words, the fruit of female activity was the prime male activity: Torah study.

The women of the Hakhnasat Orhim society saw themselves as addressing the needs not only of the individual but of the nation as a whole. Reitze, convinced of the metaphysical value of their work, expected their efforts to hasten the advent of redemption and the resurrection of the dead. Again and again in her pamphlet she refers to the talmudic saying that "the first redemption will come about through righteous women, and so too shall be the redemption that will come about, God willing, speedily in our time."[250]

The story of the Hakhnasat Orhim society is a unique female statement, attesting to women's perception of themselves in Jerusalem. A "subversive" reading of the story reveals women challenging their social and religious inferiority. By including women among the recipients of charity, they were in a way putting women on an equal footing with men, albeit with both on a low level. On the other hand, the recognition of women's power to influence

God, to prevent any loss of Torah study, and above all to hasten the redemption, places them on a higher level than that of the male sector. This paradoxical position is well rooted in Judaism: just as the observance of a hitherto
neglected commandment enhances its importance in comparison with that
of a commonly observed commandment, it was this "inferior" female form of
activity, concerned as it was with physical needs, that could have the most
sublime spiritual results. The religious duty of hospitality, wrote Reitze, had
been neglected, and so, in keeping with tradition, whoever "redeemed" that
duty would be richly rewarded. In support of this view, she cited a midrash according to which a person extending hospitality would receive a greater reward than someone welcoming the Divine Presence itself.[251] Reitze believed
that God Himself had entrusted her with the duty of providing hospitality.

However, the supreme value that Reitze attributed to her role, as well as
economic problems and perhaps also the establishment of rival societies for
women, seem to have aroused jealousy and disapproval. She felt herself to be
"small" and "weak" in the confrontation with Jerusalem society. Throughout
her pamphlet she refers to the people of the Old Yishuv in the most negative
terms: "vengeful and malicious," "every one of them jealous of his brother,
hating one another greatly for no reason."[252] Charitable activity was not always enough to suppress intrigue. The Jerusalem newspaper *Havazelet* reported that the institution was experiencing financial difficulties.[253] Reitze appealed to her colleagues, begging them to disregard her detractors' unkind
words: "For our many sins, there is now much dispute among those of our
generation . . . I perceive the great hatred that is between us."[254] Considering
herself responsible only to God for her actions, she felt confident in her efforts to influence the Upper Worlds.

Reitze's gender conception is worthy of note. She proposed a channel of
female activity designed to influence the male sector, thus creating, she believed, a highly effective channel of female influence in supernatural affairs.
Earthly Jerusalem, she realized, was treating her with rejection, jealousy, and
hatred; but her religious efforts were aimed at heavenly Jerusalem. She was
convinced that her actions would make a significant contribution to national
redemption. The variety of her activities attests to a perception of female action, in all its diverse forms, as a means both to help society and to achieve
nearness to God.

Ezrat Nashim in Jaffa: The Beginnings of Women's Self-Organization

A women's society known as Ezrat Nashim (literally, Women's Aid), founded
in Jaffa in 1891, opened a branch in Jerusalem early in 1895. At first, it was
largely similar to the Hakhnasat Orhim society, aiming to help the lower

classes of society, men and women alike. Like philanthropic women's organizations in the West in general, Ezrat Nashim was established by women of the higher social echelons — wives of the city's leaders, eager to extend the scope of their domestic activity to the public sphere.

In the early 1890s, changes were taking place in Jaffa, then home to a small Jewish center with both traditional and new elements.[255] While the Jews of the coastal city did not receive *halukah* funds to the same extent as their brethren in the four "holy cities," their rabbi was nevertheless supported by the so-called Kolel of all the Kolelim.[256] The key figure in the organization of Jaffa's Jewish women was a former resident of Jerusalem, Chaya Tzipora (Tzipa) Pines, who had moved to Jaffa for a few years in the late 1880s and later returned to Jerusalem.[257] Her husband, Yechiel Michal Pines, thinker, writer, and one of the leaders of Hovevei Zion in Jaffa,[258] was considered an innovator by people of the Old Yishuv, but a conservative by the standards of the New Yishuv. The first initiative for the establishment of Ezrat Nashim probably came from Pines's friend Yizhak Eizik Ben Tovim, another leader of Hovevei Zion in Jaffa. As reported by Ben Tovim's son, it was he who encouraged Tzipora Pines and her friends to establish a women's organization, while she had been pessimistic about the project: "I am surprised at you, Rabbi Ben Tovim, for occupying yourself with illusions and hallucinations! Shall we get water out of this dry rock in Jaffa?!"[259] However, the memory of this male initiative was expunged from the records of the organization as recounted by Ita Yellin, Tzipora Pines's daughter: "Together, [the women of Jaffa] established the first society of women in the Land of Israel."[260]

To begin with, the new society set itself several traditional goals: aid to poor women giving birth, to widows, and to abandoned orphans.[261] In the wake of a serious epidemic in Jaffa, the women took under their wing all solitary persons in that city who had fallen ill. The society's strongest point was the absolute devotion of its members. Like the *gaba'iyot* of the Hakhnasat Orchim society, the women of Ezrat Nashim undertook all aspects of care for the sick: "But the good done by [the society's] money was outdone by its deeds, for the daughters of the society performed most worthily in going to visit the pitiful invalids in person, to bring them assistance with their own hands; before being called, they responded . . . and appeared like an unexpected saving angel."[262]

People in Jaffa were particularly impressed by the predominant part played by women in the society's activities: "[They] personally perform truly charitable acts with the poor; through their devotion, their warmth and their good taste they help the sick."[263] Or, as reported in another newspaper article: "They do this gently and pleasantly, as only a woman can do."[264] The most "natural" womanly occupation, namely, caring for their family's physical well-being, was thus transposed to the public sphere. The people of Jaffa sensed the women's profound commitment to their objective and their sincere desire to render assistance.[265] The psychological help given by these women was also deeply appreciated.[266] The rabbi of Jaffa, Naftali Hertz Halevi, was well aware of the unique value of the society's work; writing to the members, he repeated a well-known rabbinic saying: "Through the merit of righteous woman [the people of Israel] were redeemed in the past, and may we be so merited in our time too."[267] He also wrote letters of recommendation to prospective donors in the Diaspora, requesting their support for the society.[268]

Ezrat Nashim also stressed its exclusively female membership in its appeals for assistance. In the summer of 1893, when the society redoubled its activities in the wake of a serious epidemic in Jaffa, while its resources had dwindled, it issued an appeal to women in general, requesting donations.[269] In addition, the society provided a social outlet for many women. In the second half of the 1890s, a Hanukkah party was held, with musical accompaniment.[270]

Women's activities of this kind had a paradoxical aspect. On the one hand, they brought women into a hitherto exclusively male sphere of public work; on the other hand, they clearly demonstrated the unique nature of female activity, enhanced solidarity among women, and reinforced their self-awareness as female members of society. As women made an ever-increasing impact on charitable public action, they themselves were increasingly empowered by their own efforts. But Jaffa was a mere training ground for Tzipa Pines, who returned to Jerusalem in the middle of the 1890s and founded the Jerusalem version of Ezrat Nashim.[271] Unlike Reitze of Hakhnasat Orhim, Tzipa Pines and her colleagues were not concerned with the metaphysical significance of their work.

Ezrat Nashim in Jerusalem: Women for Women

Ezrat Nashim in Jerusalem presents a different pattern of organization: it was a women's organization that aimed to cure the ills of society in general, but devoted particular attention to helping women, in keeping with the literal meaning of the phrase *ezrat nashim*. Like the countless women's clubs that sprang up at the turn of the century in the United States,[272] this women's society in the Holy City concentrated its efforts on helping needy women, and in so doing redefined the public sphere. The concept of women rendering assistance to women, not only in the intimate realm, but in the entire variety of their needs — while being of course closely acquainted with those needs — gave birth to a new upsurge of activity. It seems clear from the contemporary press that the Jaffa Ezrat Nashim had made a great impression, and two societies laying claim to that title were founded in Jerusalem in 1895. The first, headed by Tzipa Pines, was founded on January 24, 1895; the other was founded a short while later by a woman named Esther Rachel Niminsky,[273] perhaps jealous of Tzipa's achievements.

Tzipa Pines's society in Jerusalem was originally formed to deal with the traditional tasks of women's charitable organizations: providing aid to birthing mothers and invalids.[274] Almost unintentionally, however, it branched out into an entirely new field, namely, care for the mentally ill. Tzipa Pines and her colleagues heard a report of three mentally impaired women and two elderly men in a public shelter in the Old City, who were in a desperate situation.[275] The "Kolel of all Kolelim" had rented a place for them to stay, with a guard; however, "since there was no woman's eye to keep the place clean and the like, these four or five wretched individuals were living in filth, in conditions that made their lives even more difficult."[276] The women of Ezrat Nashim came to the rescue and extended their protection over the five. They bathed them, rented premises for them, equipped them with basic furnishings, and hired a doctor to tend them.[277] The case clearly demonstrated the need for a suitable institution.

Ezrat Nashim soon established a shelter for the mentally ill—the first of its kind in the Land of Israel.[278] Modern treatment of mental disease in Europe dates from the first half of the nineteenth century, when it was realized that a distinction had to be made between patients in need of economic aid and those needing psychological help.[279] Prior to the end of the nineteenth century, mentally ill persons in the Land of Israel received no medical treatment; in that part of the world it was believed that such individuals had simply been possessed by devils.[280] The Ezrat Nashim society, however, treated mental sickness as a wholly medical problem, considering this part of its activity in the context of its concern with health in general—an area that was receiving much attention from women throughout the Western world.[281] The society's interest in the mentally sick was perhaps due to the fact that women accounted for a relatively large proportion of such patients. However, since there was no similar institution for men, Ezrat Nashim unhesitatingly put itself at the service of all comers, women and men.

A rare letter describing the situation in the institution in 1900 indicates that, indeed, the first inmates were exclusively women: "Raving women . . . , some of them screaming, some weeping, others emitting deafening peals of laughter . . . , [some] as if sunk in thought, as if completely unaware of their surroundings."[282] The patients' grave mental condition was doubly obvious against the background of the favorable conditions. Rabbi Yizhak Nissenbaum, who visited the place in the summer of 1905, approvingly noted "the exemplary tidiness and cleanliness."[283] The society's first building, designed for women, was built in 1902; only six years later, in 1908, another building was added for men.[284] The number of women in the institution exceeded the number of men.[285] Patients were referred to the hospital from the whole country;[286] as the institution grew in size, an increasing number of patients requested admittance.

The number of women active in Ezrat Nashim rapidly reached several dozen.[287] Luncz's Land of Israel almanac for 1896 published an appeal (in Yiddish) to women to support the society's efforts by donations or to join and become active in its ranks.[288] The women who devoted their time, effort, and often funds to Ezrat Nashim were generally the wives of distinguished personages: Matil, wife of Rabbi Chaim Berlin; Reizale Feinstein, whose husband, David Feinstein, was the secretary of the American Consulate; and Rasha Salant, wife of the chief Ashkenasic rabbi of Jerusalem.[289] The society was essentially part of the Ashkenazic elite, and few Sephardic women were members. The founders considered their society a suitable avenue for female achievement.[290]

"This institution is the only one in Jerusalem where all those in the management work for purely altruistic reasons, without expecting any payment or even thanks."[291] So wrote Zvi Yosef Carlebach, a German Jewish teacher who spent some years in Jerusalem, in a letter to his family in Germany. Carlebach commented on the industry, devotion, and love with which the women treated their patients. The women of Ezrat Nashim, like those of Hakhnasat Orhim, besides managing the institution, were deeply involved in all aspects of its operation. A reporter for the newspaper *Hazevi*, describing the society's activities, also highlighted the uniquely female nature of the patients' treatment: "as much as a woman's heart is capable of."[292]

Ezrat Nashim's members were also made aware of their unique contribution as women by male appreciation of their work: "Praise for the behavior of this house is on everyone's lips . . . and we have found that what we have heard is no exaggeration."[293] The local governor, Sa'adat Pasha, visited the place and expressed his admiration.[294] The committee of the "Kolel of all Kolelim" offered its full support and allotted a plot of land for a building to house the male and female patients.[295] The aid and contributions that this entailed made it possible to transfer the shelter outside the Old City walls, greatly improving the inmates' quality of life. The novelty of the shelter, "the like of which is unknown in all the Land of Israel, even among Christians and Muslims,"[296] was recognized by all. This recognition also found expression in the establishment of a similar philanthropic organization for men, aptly named Ezrat Ahim (literally, Aid to Brothers).[297]

Ezrat Nashim was a focus of many women's activities. Tzipa Pines, exploiting her contacts with members of the New Yishuv, appealed to the women of the *moshavot* (the new agricultural settlements) for financial aid.[298]

The feeling of female solidarity had its effect. Many of the younger women of Jerusalem took their cue from the women of the Old Yishuv and those of the *moshavot*. Fortuna Behar, principal of the Evelina de Rothschild School, held up the members of Ezrat Nashim as a role model for her students, encouraging them to help the institution in various ways.[299] Women in the Holy Land and elsewhere would contribute to Ezrat Nashim to celebrate various family occasions;[300] among the most famous such donors were Baroness Clara Hirsch and Baroness Adelaide (wife of Edmond) de Rothschild.[301] Women's committees collecting funds for the institution were established in various European cities.[302] Ezrat Nashim thus became an international organization. However, it was the people of Jerusalem who, despite their poverty, made the most extensive contributions to Ezrat Nashim around the turn of the nineteenth to the twentieth century.[303]

Ezrat Nashim as a Modernizing Force in Jerusalem

The Ezrat Nashim society, seeing its primary task as improving women's life in the Holy City, soon extended the scope of its activities to such areas as vocational training for girls.[304] Vocational training, for both boys and girls, was a common item on the agenda of philanthropic societies in Europe, Jewish and non-Jewish.[305] An upright citizen, it was believed, was one who earned his or her own living, and so training young people for a gainful profession was considered a most important goal. This was also the understanding of Ezrat Nashim. In October 1912 the society established a vocational school for Jewish girls in which the students studied domestic subjects such as sewing, dressmaking, and embroidery.[306] The school's declared goal was to provide needy young women with a profession, to enable them to support themselves rather than be forced to appeal to Christian missionaries.[307] The new school also aimed to provide a proper framework for fifteen-year-old girls who had not previously attended any educational institution. It was successful from the start, beginning with about seventy students.[308]

The Ezrat Nashim society declared that the vocational school for girls would operate according to the most stringent religious requirements,[309] its goal being to help to revolutionize economic conditions in the Holy City. While vocational training per se was not entirely new in Jerusalem,[310] Ezrat Nashim set itself a double goal: On the one hand, the women considered themselves an integral part of the Old Yishuv and remained strictly observant; on the other, they wanted to transform the economic basis of the Old Yishuv, to encourage people to support themselves rather than rely on *halukah* funds. Ezrat Nashim, not content merely to render aid to needy members of society, strove to reform that society and place it on a firm economic basis.[311]

There was yet another aspect to the Ezrat Nashim vocational school: it aimed not only to prepare the girls themselves for a useful life but, through them, to influence family life in Jerusalem. The school's regulations required students' parents to sign a commitment that they would not take them out of the school before two years had passed; otherwise, they would pay a fine. Among other things, the school was designed to discourage child marriages. Here, too, Ezrat Nashim was not the pioneer; the Evelina de Rothschild School, founded a few decades before, had set itself a similar goal. In addition, girls were required to deposit one-quarter of their salaries in a school savings fund until they completed their course of studies. This was yet another measure to discourage them from leaving school, while at the same time teaching them the value of saving. These initiatives of the Ezrat Nashim society were clear signs of the modernizing influences originating in the Western world.

Alongside the school, the society established a home for young girls, providing an alternative for parents who might otherwise abandon their children to the Christian mission.[312] This project was based on a precedent due to another women's society in Jerusalem — Bet Ya'akov. Bet Ya'akov, founded in 1897, was apparently the first Jewish society to establish a home for orphan girls in Jerusalem, it too was a refuge for girls who were in danger of falling into missionary hands. This was also the declared aim of an organization named Benei Yisra'el, founded by men around the same time.[313] While this early female initiative did not last long, it seems to have provided the impetus for the establishment of several orphanages for girls in Jerusalem.[314]

The scope of Ezrat Nashim's activities, including the creation of an international network of contributors,[315] clearly attests to the founders' talent and reputation. However, these female activists still felt the need for some kind of male patronage, and therefore appointed a supervisory committee consisting of men. At the same time, the society's leaders insisted on maintaining their own independent goals and modes of operation; the male patronage did not affect that independence.

In contrast to the founders of Hakhnasat Orhim, who believed that their society could influence both the real world and the supernal realm, the women of Ezrat Nashim invested all their efforts in reforming "earthly Jerusalem." Nevertheless, both organizations proved that independent female action outside the domestic sphere could win the appreciation of the male sector. The traditional understanding of the verse "All glorious is the princess within" (Ps. 45:14), implying that women should confine their activities to the home, was no longer appropriate: women who worked for a living now had men's admiration — on one occasion expressed in the epithet "Cossack."[316] On the one hand, women were now earning respect specifically by virtue of leaving their homes; on the other, to the extent that women's activities out-side their homes were more characteristically "female," marked by especial devotion, delicacy, and diligence, male appreciation for their efforts was en-hanced.

Economics and Philanthropy Pave the Way for Women in the Public Sphere

The formation of Ezrat Nashim societies in Jaffa and Jerusalem inspired sim-ilar organizations in other cities.[317] We have some interesting information about a society calling itself Ezrat Benot ha-Galil (literally, Aid to the Daugh-ters of Galilee), formed as a female branch of the men's organization Maskil el Dal, a charitable society established in Safed in 1897.[318] The male parent organization was a multicommunity society, whose purpose was to help needy invalids by supplying them with medication and nursing help; it also founded a shelter for the elderly and contended with the mission.[319] The women's or-ganization, constituted one year later, confined its activities mainly to assist-ing women; in name and mode of operation it resembled the Jerusalem Ezrat Nashim. Another women's organization formed under male supervision was Neshot ha-Galil (Women of Galilee);[320] its letters were accompanied by an appeal from Raphael Zilberman, the rabbi of Safed. The women of Safed nevertheless solicited contributions primarily from women, appealing to fe-male residents of Rosh Pinah and Yesud ha-Ma'alah.[321] The first of these or-ganizations tried to impress prospective contributors by using what it consid-ered modern elements: printed stationery, personal stamps for the society's officials, and a regular account register.[322] Its proudest achievement was a home for aged women, "for those elderly women who cannot take care of themselves,"[323] housing a few hundred patients. Thus, Ezrat Nashim pro-vided a model for intensive activity on the part of women who undertook var-ious tasks in the female sphere and created new areas of activity.

Both in the Land of Israel and elsewhere, work and philanthropy paved women's paths to new areas of employment, while their participation in in-dependent organizations prepared them for political action.[324] "Charitable work outside the home had another aspect: it gave women a way to escape from the limitations of domestic life, as well as a chance to create ties of fe-male solidarity, which later formed the basis for the feminist movements."[325] Philanthropy was the primary basis for exclusive women's organizations. Emergence from the domestic to the public sphere was fueled by a profound economic need, and it was bound up with a paradoxical sense of simultane-ous elation and inferiority: Women were working in order to enable men to study, as well as to fill other urgent social needs. The unique "female touch" in the field of mutual aid was in a sense an outcome of their inferior status, of the concept of women as destined to deal with material matters. Their aid to the needy was extended not in a condescending spirit but out of a feeling of equality. The idea that women had the advantage over men in such areas was accepted by their male counterparts, both in the world at large[326] and in the Jerusalem establishment.

The perception of the women's organizations that their efforts should be directed toward women heightened awareness of women's inferior status and of the need for improvement. Moreover, philanthropic action provided an additional channel for female comradeship.[327] When these organizations appealed to women to take part in educational initiatives or in antimissionary activities — such as establishing orphanages or vocational schools for girls — they were in effect creating new instruments of change. Educational projects in Jerusalem were influenced, directly and otherwise, by innovative educational ideas brought to the Holy City by Western Jewish philanthropic institutions,[328] some of which had been established by Jewish women in the Diaspora. Such women's organizations reinforced female self-awareness and created nuclei of female leadership.[329] This slow process, the transition from the status of an object to unique philanthropic activity, to independent action, took place in Jerusalem as well and influenced the character both of the Ashkenazic woman and of Jerusalem society.

Nevertheless, were we to ask whether public work brought about a revolution in the traditional image of the woman, the answer would have to be negative. Careful examination reveals that the basic Jewish perception of women as inferior remained unchanged. Whether one takes the context of the talmudic saying, "As the reward for the righteous women who lived in that generation were the Israelites delivered from Egypt" (Bab. Talmud, Sotah 11b), or the self-perception of Reitze of Jerusalem, it transpires that women had still not shed their "material" essence: the fact that women had raised themselves up through physical action aroused admiration mainly because of their low point of departure. The Talmud relates that the women in Egypt were called "righteous" because they encouraged their men to sleep with them so that they could become pregnant and have children; the women of Jerusalem, however, could attribute their achievement to the physical care they extended to the needy. Even this emergence into the sphere of public activity did not affect the traditional conception of the inherently inferior status of women.

Chapter 5

Scholarship, Illiteracy, and Educational Revolution

Learned Women in Jerusalem

"IN THIS WHOLE great community [Jerusalem] there is not one single good school for girls, and all the daughters of Zion grow up without any education, without good training, without knowledge of the language of their nation and its history, be it only the smallest part, and therefore their spirits are not raised and they remain in their lowly state."[1] This criticism, published in the newspaper *Hazevi* in the late 1880s, disregarded educational institutions already operating in Jerusalem and complained of the lack of a comprehensive educational network for women, and of the inferior spiritual level of the female sector. In contrast to this critique, the system of male education in the Holy City has received copious praise from historian Yosef Salmon: "It is doubtful whether there was any Jewish society in the world which placed such emphasis on the education of its [male] children as Ashkenazic society in the Land of Israel at this time."[2] The Jerusalem community, which had invested heavily in the education of its sons, showed little interest in educating its daughters.

Despite the definitive evaluation of Jerusalem women as illiterate, an in-depth study of contemporary sources reveals an impressive number of exceptional learned women in the Holy City community. The existence of "learned women" or "wise women" is a known phenomenon in the course of Jewish history in general and in the nineteenth century in particular, though we have no precise information as to how common it was. Within the Jewish community in Jerusalem, which numbered more than twenty thousand at the end of the century, we can enumerate more than thirty women, most of them Ashkenazic, who were knowledgeable in Hebrew and scriptures. Among them were three writers of pamphlets, which constitutes a unique Jerusalem phenomenon[3] — Jewish women with Jewish education who published their writings. In the nineteenth century we have no knowledge of works published by traditionally learned women[4] other than the three above-mentioned pamphlets. These three writers and the other Jerusalem learned women were not born in the Land of Israel; most of them acquired their Jewish education in the countries of their birth[5] — not in educational institutions but informally, at home, as a means of satisfying their deep desire to study.

The fact that there were Hebrew-speaking Jewish women in Jerusalem did not go unnoticed by visitors and has attracted scholarly attention. Our first report of Hebrew-speaking Jewish women is found in the writings of the apostate missionary Joseph Wolff in 1821.[6] There is a description in Moses Montefiore's diary of his meeting with a Hebrew-speaking Jerusalem woman in 1866,[7] and the visionary tourist Shim'on Berman, who had a dream of Jewish settlement in the Land of Israel, described a meeting with a Hebrew-speaking Jewish woman in Haifa in his travel journal of 1870.[8] Along with these reports we may also mention Sheine Rivka Sheikovitz, who spoke Hebrew on the Sabbath,[9] and Fruma Reizel Karlin, born in the Holy City, a fifth-generation descendant of Rabbi Zalman Zoref, who "religiously spoke Hebrew from childhood. In [5]659 [1898/9] she gave birth to a daughter and decided to speak to her only in Hebrew."[10] Devora Luncz too, the wife of the blind Jerusalem scholar Avraham Moshe Luncz, who served as his eyes, was famed for her knowledge of Hebrew, and her daughter recounted: "Among those zealous for the language she always spoke Hebrew."[11] Among Sephardic women, Rima Reina, wife of Rabbi Shlomo Yehezkel Yehudah, who came to the Holy Land in 1854 and spoke Hebrew while still in her paternal home, was outstanding for her erudition.[12] She was completely immersed in Torah literature.[13] It was she who prepared the Bar Mitzvah sermon of her grandson, David Yellin, and she spent most of her free time in Jewish religious studies. Yehudah Yitzhak Yehezkel dubbed his wife Baida, born in 1879, "the first mother among the oriental communities (Sephardim) who spoke Hebrew and raised her children in the language of her people."[14]

When the Safah Berurah society was founded in 1889, with the goal of spreading Hebrew as a spoken language, the founders declared: "The society will hire Hebrew-speaking women (there are a few in Jerusalem capable of doing this job)."[15] In 1893 Ben-Yehuda exulted that his vision of Hebrew-speaking women was being realized, and that even among the women of the Old Yishuv there were Hebrew speakers, "just where it would be least expected, women and girls not from the world of the *maskilim*."[16] Indirect evidence of women's knowledge of Hebrew is supplied by a news item from 1898 about the B'nai B'rith Library: Women knowledgeable in Hebrew were evicted from a lecture held at the library on the grounds that their presence was an infringement of modesty.[17] Indeed, most Jerusalem girls had no formal education, but there was a group of women in the city who provided conclusive proof of Jewish women's capacity to study and get an education.[18]

From the material at hand it transpires that the learned women studied on their own initiative;[19] some were daughters of rabbis and were taught by their fathers, others by their mothers. Learned women, Ashkenazic as well as Sephardic, who were fluent in Hebrew studied the Bible, and some also became proficient in the Oral Law.[20] Some women were accustomed to preach within the family circle, and some taught outside as well.[21] There were women who organized children's groups in their homes to teach the weekly Torah portion, and others would read prayers for themselves or for their friends from the prayer book.[22] Etka, daughter of Rabbi Shalom of Boysk, wife of Rabbi Benjamin Rivlin, "had already been educated in her father's home and continued to study in her husband's home . . . She also taught religious subjects in public. Her miserable room was a meeting place for women seeking religious inspiration on the Sabbath."[23]

A few women also dared to make Halakhic decisions: Rosha, the third wife of Rabbi Shmuel Salant, was described as being highly knowledgeable in Jewish Law . . . She used to make her own decisions on matters of kashrut, but nonetheless was careful to send questioners to her husband for a final ruling.[24] Indeed, Halakhic authority was always squarely in Rabbi Salant's hands, and his wife ruled under his aegis, but according to the teller of the tale, it is obvious that the rabbi esteemed his wife's erudition. The *rebbetzin* Sarah Sonia Diskin, wife of Rabbi Yehoshua Yehuda Leib Diskin and known for her considerable influence over him, was acknowledged in the Jerusalem community for her religious zeal and tendency toward the most stringent interpretation of the Law.[25] From the wealth of information available about her it is difficult to ascertain whether her authority stemmed from her erudition, her aggressive personality, or her husband's prestige. Whatever the case, Sonia Diskin, like Rosha, Rabbi Salant's wife, derived her power from that of her husband. Among the Sephardim, too, there was a woman who was capable of issuing Halakhic rulings: "Grandma Rivkula," whose memory is preserved in the stories of the community. Having come to the Land of Israel from Salonika in her youth, she refused to leave the country with her husband, preferring to have a divorce. Grandma Rivkula assisted her father in his Halakhic rulings and was renowned in her community.[26] These women, and others of their ilk, were highly esteemed in the male sector, belying the view that women's study of the Torah should be considered an offense.

Few women were proficient in Torah literature in Hebrew, but many were familiar with religious literature written in Yiddish, such as *Ts'ena ur'ena*, *Menorat hama'or*, and *Kav hayashar*, which were collections of midrashim and legends;[27] Sephardic women could read similar works written in Ladino, such as *Me'am lo'ez*.[28] The women of the Hirschensohn family were famous for their wide knowledge. Sarah Beyla, who came to the Land of Israel with her husband in the middle of the nineteenth century, was knowledgeable both in Yiddish women's literature and in Torah literature, including books on Jewish philosophy, liturgical poetry, and the Talmud.[29] She also succeeded in learning Arabic. Even Rabbi Shmuel Salant recognized her stature. Her daughter-in-law, Chava Sarah Hirschensohn, Rabbi Hayyim's wife, was born in Jerusalem and emigrated to the United States with her husband at the beginning of the twentieth century. She was extremely knowledgeable in Bible, Talmud, and Midrash. She was well known as the distributor of *Beis Ya'akov*, the first Yiddish newspaper for women published in the Land of Israel.[30] According to her husband, she was the first Jerusalem-born woman in the Land of Israel to speak Hebrew in her home.[31] She was an exceptional personality among the women of the Old Yishuv, and her home was frequented both by members of the Old Yishuv and by the new settlers.[32]

Women's newspapers in Yiddish began to appear in the second half of the nineteenth century, and they brought about a revolution in the reading habits of Jewish women in eastern Europe.[33] Previously accustomed to having others read for them, women could now read for themselves. The Yiddish newspaper *Kol Mevasser*, which appeared in Odessa in the 1860s, became a popular journal and expanded women's education. Jerusalem's first newspaper for women, *Beis Ya'akov*, already mentioned above, appeared as a biweekly for a year and a half, from 1892 to 1893. It was apparently intended mainly for readers abroad, but it also reflected the level of reading and interest of Ashkenazic women in the Holy Land.[34] An advertisement published in *Ha'or* states: "The object of the paper is to awaken positive interest among women; this object is certainly good and desirable, and we therefore wish this new newspaper long life and a female readership of uncountable numbers."[35] Nonetheless, the material published in the paper (about half of the issues have been preserved) included very little information about or for women. It is likely that the paper, which was published by Ben-Yehuda's *Hazevi* Press, "masqueraded" as a women's paper in order to justify its being in Yiddish and to circulate news of the Land of Israel among the Yiddish-speaking population abroad, both men and women.

A fascinating aspect of the cultural life of learned women in Jerusalem is evident in the three pamphlets published by women in the Holy City:[36] *Kunteres zekher olam* by Rivkah Lipa Anikster;[37] *Sefer mishpahat yuhasin* by Reitze, daughter of Mordechai Chen Tov and wife of Zelig of Slonim;[38] and *Sefer zikhron Eliyahu* by Toive Pesil Feinstein.[39] All three women dedicated their writings to their families. The pamphlets essentially form an independent literary genre, with three central characteristics: autobiographical fragments; ethical comments (a kind of spiritual legacy); and parables, legends, and quotes from a selection of religious literature. The women, who had no knowledge of classical literature, wrote in a personal-biographical rather than a literary-artistic style, committing their ideas to writing without any editing or styling.[40] It is evident that at least two of the writers knew each other,[41] worked together in various charitable enterprises, and learned from each other's writing.[42] *Sefer zikhron Eliyahu* is not only the longest of these but also the richest in terms of parables and legends, as well as in the use of a great variety of sources. The fact that printing presses in Jerusalem agreed to print pamphlets written by women indicates the esteem in which these writers were held.

The three women write of their great esteem for men's Torah scholarship and their deep admiration for innovative Torah commentary appearing in print. Their introductions breathe an air of self-effacement, as if to secure entry into the male domain and the public sphere.[43] The ability to write gave the women a feeling of belonging to the general public, to the community.[44] Rivkah Lipa Anikster declared that the primary aim of her pamphlet was to stimulate others to publish the writings of her father and brothers. Her book was written as a means to promote their books. She nevertheless admitted: "You know of and remember my habit of writing and publishing."[45] Alongside these pragmatic considerations, the three women perceived their writings as a kind of spiritual legacy of learned women who feared for the spiritual future of their families and their people. All three show considerable erudition in the world of Jewish thought and deal with issues of the utmost consequence, such as the partnership of body and soul, the merit of humility, hospitality as a religious duty, knowledge of God, the value of charity, and the relationship of Jews in the Holy Land to their brethren in the Diaspora. Their writings reveal proficiency in Bible, Midrash, and ethical literature. Toive Pesil also quoted extensively from such classical sources as Rabbi Bahya ibn Paquda's *Duties of the Heart* and *Sefer Hasidim* (philosophical and ethical works from the Middle Ages), as well as from Bible commentaries.[46] Despite the fact the all three wrote their pamphlets in Yiddish, it is quite evident that they knew Hebrew well.

There is an extraordinary description in the Zohar of women studying Torah in paradise. Similar descriptions (with variations) appear in homiletical and penitential literature written in Yiddish. Chava Weissler, who has written extensively on this subject,[47] notes that toward the end of the nineteenth century the motifs of women studying in paradise and possessing mystical powers became less prominent. She suggests that this decline of women's power and influence may be associated with the ascendancy of the middle classes at that time and the renewed emphasis on women's domestic role. In Jerusalem, however, this explanation for the fall in the number of learned women may well apply in reverse. The learned Ashkenazic women who came to the Holy City in the second half of the nineteenth century wanted to escape the ideas of the *Haskalah* then spreading throughout Europe. Possibly, just as they stubbornly continued the custom of shaving their heads, they also adhered to the picture of women studying the Torah in paradise and therefore strove to do so in Jerusalem, the place on earth closest to the Next World. The fact that Rivkah Lipa Anikster's book went through (at least) three editions and four printings, and that in its wake her two friends' pamphlets were written and published, attests to the unusual spiritual climate prevailing in the Holy City. Jerusalem, a magnet for Jewish women immigrants who sought to express their religious feelings, also encouraged them to express their scholarship. The publication of the pamphlets, perhaps incidentally and after the fact, represents an admission that rabbinic society did not object to women studying the Torah. Was this also a rejection of the celebrated view of Rabbi Eliezer in the Talmud, that women should not study the Torah (Bab. Talmud Sotah 21b; see below)?

Apart from these women, who were held in high esteem in both male and female sectors,[48] most of the female population in the city was poorly educated or uneducated, owing to the lack of an educational system. Might there have been two contradictory approaches to the education of Jewish women, one applying to the silent majority, who received no education, and another pertaining to the exceptions, who proved that some women were perfectly capable of learning?[49] It may be assumed that Jerusalem society did not consider women's learning as a norm, suitable for the female population in general. The well-known story of Beruriah, wife of Rabbi Meir, who excelled in Torah learning but failed in fidelity, is perhaps the key to understanding the approach of traditional Judaism to this phenomenon. The rabbinical establishment did not view the figure of the learned woman as an example to be followed, believing that there is an immanent contradiction between femininity and Torah study. Rayna Batyah, first wife of Rabbi Naftali Zevi Berlin, the Netziv of Volozhin, who lived far from Jerusalem, was known for her remarkable scholarship: "She could by no means reconcile herself to the aspersions cast against women and the disrespect in which they were held, inherent in the prohibition of Torah learning for them."[50] Despite her scholarship, Rayna Batyah identified with illiterate women.

The Education of Jewish Girls: Tradition and Revolution

The attitude of Halakhah to Torah study for women is debated in the Mishnah, in Tractate Sotah (3:4):

Professional letter writer with women. Ely Schiller, ed., *Jerusalem in Old Engravings* (Jerusalem, 1977), p. 186.

Ben Azzai [declared]: A man is under the obligation to teach his daughter Torah . . . R. Eliezer says: Whoever teaches his daughter Torah, it is as though he teaches her obscenity.

The Halakha as practiced over the centuries was based on Rabbi Eliezer's approach. Even authorities who permitted women's study limited it to matters within the scope of her activities, or to self-study.[51]

Rabbi Eliezer's opinion found its practical expression in the almost universal lack of regular educational institutions for Jewish girls throughout the generations, in all parts of the Diaspora. It was largely responsible for the stigma of ignorance usually attached to women. The explanations given for withholding education from women were varied: the study of Torah had a bad influence on a girl's character; alternatively, teaching girls had a bad influence on the character of the Torah: "Most women are not predisposed to study, but rather they apply the words of the Torah to profane matters" (Maimonides, *Hilkhot Talmud Torah* 1:13). Male society appropriated learning exclusively to itself, excluding women from places of study and depriving them of access to education. The perception of the intellectual inferiority of women was, as it were, a self-fulfilling prophecy, because of the circumstances it created. Nonetheless, a negative attitude to education and the lack of educational institutions do not necessarily bring about ignorance and illiteracy.[52]

In Islamic countries, most women were excluded from formal studies, although some highly intelligent Muslim girls were in the habit of learning the Koran by heart and were known as expounders of learning.[53] Jewish society in those countries adopted those conventions, and the level of education of Sephardic and Oriental Jewish women in the nineteenth century was lower, in general, than that of Ashkenazic women; most were in fact illiterate. While some educated women were able to read and write, they were the exception that proves the rule. Fierce opposition to women's education was clearly expressed by the eleventh-century scholar of Kairouan (Tunisia), Rabbi Nissim b. Ya'akov: "Therefore the Sages, of blessed memory, were opposed to fathers teaching their daughters Torah . . . , since according to Talmudic opinion this will cause them to fall into corruption, deception and cunning."[54] This explicit statement, and similar ones made throughout the centuries, are indicative of the attitude of Sephardic and oriental Jewish society toward women's education.[55]

The application of Rabbi Eliezer's opinion in Diaspora communities was not universal but was rather influenced by the environment. During the Middle Ages, Jewish women living in Christian countries were permitted to learn to read and write, since that was not defined as "Torah," and literate Jewish women were a very widespread phenomenon.[56] From the sixteenth century on, Yiddish literature for women became popular, a fact that testifies to the existence of a female readership.[57] Recent research on the level of knowledge of Jewish women in eastern Europe at the end of the nineteenth century indicates that, while few Jewish girls received a formal education, about 50 percent could read and write.[58] Since there were only a few *heders* (elementary schools) for girls or coeducational *heders* for boys and girls in eastern Europe, many were educated at home by their mothers or by private tutors.[59] However, at the approach of the twentieth century, the following statement could be found in the Halakhic work *Arukh hashulhan*: "We never taught them from a book, nor did we hear of this custom. Rather, every woman teaches her daughter and daughter-in-law the appropriate laws [i.e., laws pertaining specifically to women]" (*Arukh hashulhan, Yoreh de'ah*, 246, sec. 19).

A real change in all matters connected with women's education took place in western Europe in the eighteenth century. Schools for girls were slowly but surely established and became very popular. Proponents of women's education did not necessarily advocate identical education for men and women, but did want to assure basic education for girls. The educational establishments sought to model the "ideal woman" in the image of the perfect housewife.[60] Jewish girls, too, attended these schools, marking a highly significant turning point in Jewish society.

Up until the eighteenth century, the education of Jewish women was not inferior to that of their non-Jewish sisters, whether in the West or in the East; at times it was even superior. However, the advent of schools for non-Jewish girls placed Jewish girls in an inferior position. The Jewish *Haskalah* movement, which arose in the wake of the European Enlightenment, adopted the latter's positive attitude to basic formal education for girls and encouraged girls to close the gap between themselves and their non-Jewish neighbors. Toward the end of the eighteenth and beginning of the nineteenth century, the first Jewish schools for girls were established in Germany, France, and England.[61] By the end of the nineteenth century, innovative educational institutions for girls also appeared in eastern Europe.[62] The curricula and textbooks were substantially different from those in boys' schools, and the material taught was scant and superficial,[63] but nevertheless it was a genuine revolution: Jewish girls were now receiving a basic formal education.

Far-reaching innovations with regard to the education of girls occurred in the Mediterranean basin as well. The Alliance Israélite Universelle organization was the leader in the field; it established the first schools for girls in the Ottoman Empire in the 1870s,[64] thus initiating a breakthrough in the education of Jewish girls. The revolution also reached the Holy City, where it had a unique facet. Nonetheless, up to the first decade of the twentieth century, only a minority of girls had the opportunity to enjoy these innovations.[65] The educational revolution penetrated the Holy City only gradually.

Rothschild and Montefiore: First Experiments in Education

As early as the 1840s, leaders of the Jerusalem community were already expressing their staunch opposition to the establishment of new educational institutions for boys in Jerusalem: "They unequivocally and conclusively ruled that neither the hospital nor the school should come to be [in Jerusalem]."[66] These blunt words were uttered in reaction to an innovative plan to found a hospital and school in the plague-ridden city. The city elders expressed their overriding opposition to any change that smacked of *Haskalah* influence, including even plans to improve sanitation in the city. For immigrants from eastern Europe who had personally experienced the inroads of the *Haskalah* in their countries of origin, the Holy City was a refuge from the ravages of secularization.[67] The opposition to health institutions finally broke down, and Jewish hospitals were established. Opposition to modern schools, however, only intensified. The new educational institutions in Germany and Russia were a warning sign: "Because we have seen with our own eyes how secular studies in Germany and Russia became stumbling blocks . . . to the young sons of Israel, most of whom threw off the yoke of Torah and the commandments, . . . and they turned the hearts of the Jews to true heresy and apostasy."[68] The deep apprehension regarding schools was due not only to the curriculum but also to the possible influence of secularization.

Given the fierce opposition to the establishment of new educational institutions for boys, the very agreement to establish schools for girls was remarkable. The absence of any educational framework for girls provided fertile ground for innovations. The first initiatives for the establishment of schools for Jewish girls in the Holy City came from western Europe, which was a testing ground for educational innovations in society in general as well as among Jews.[69] The Rothschilds of France and the Montefiores of England saw women's education in the Land of Israel as one of their primary goals. As a matter of fact, the activities of Christian missionaries in Jerusalem, who pioneered the establishment of schools for Jewish girls in Jerusalem, provided the momentum for their activity in this field. We have two indications to that effect: the fact that Christian and Jewish efforts in that area were contemporaneous, and the frank admission of Jewish pioneers in the field that their support for Jewish schools for girls was indeed intended to stem the flow of Jewish girls to mission institutions.[70]

The philanthropist Albert Cohen, who represented the Rothschilds of Paris, founded the first girls' school in Jerusalem in the summer of 1854;[71] Sir Moses Montefiore established a similar institution a year later.[72] In his report on his activities in Jerusalem, Albert Cohen described the girls' school as follows: "A girls' school, where all girls of the Jewish community will be taught women's handicrafts, as well as religious and basic general subjects, has been established under the auspices of Baroness Nathaniel Rothschild."[73] Could it be that the mention of "women's handicrafts" as the first purpose of the school was intentional, in order to deflect attention from the theoretical studies at the institution or to minimize their importance? Perhaps, by presenting the situation in this light, the writer hoped to minimize male interest in the school and thus prevent it from becoming a focus of public dispute in the Holy City (as would happen two years later, when the Laemel school was founded).

Several issues, some procedural and some substantial, stand out in this concise report. Unlike the origins of traditional institutions founded by parents or teachers, the initiative for the establishment of both new schools came from outside the community. Moreover, unlike the then common community-oriented educational institutions for boys, the Rothschild School was open to girls of all Jerusalem ethnic communities. Underlying these differences were innovative educational concepts. Vocational training toward the womanly ideal of the housewife was presented as the school's primary goal, and so the most important subject was handicrafts — "sewing and spinning."[74] On the other hand, in the male sector, vocational education was traditionally intended only for poorer students. Traditional education for boys was directed exclusively toward religious education, whereas modern education directed the pupil to prepare him- or herself for life, to fulfill a role in society.[75] This innovation was applied in the girls' school. As a consequence of these educational approaches, basic studies for girls, that is, reading and writing skills, were presented as the last educational goal.

The desire to promote girls' religious piety by training them to read the prayers was also an innovation.[76] Unlike traditional practice, which discouraged women from attending synagogue services and prepared them only minimally for participation in prayer, the founders of the schools for girls recognized the need to teach them Jewish studies. Women in non-Jewish society in nineteenth-century western Europe were perceived as being religiously more observant than men,[77] whereas the standard-bearers of the Torah in Jewish society were men. Emphasis on girls' religiosity was an innovation, apparently due to the influence of European trends.

Despite all these innovative elements, Luncz wrote that the girls' school in its early days was more like a *heder* than a school.[78] And indeed, the first course of study was minimalistic. Nevertheless, the mere perception that formal education for girls was of importance, and the first practical steps based on that perception, planted the seeds for change.

In its early days the school's population comprised a few dozen girls, both Ashkenazic and Sephardic.[79] Ludwig August Frankl, who came to Jerusalem in the spring of 1856 in order to establish the Laemel School for boys, noted that the girls' school seemed desolate: "The school benches were so covered with dust that no pupil could have taken her place there for a long time, and the writing slates lay half-broken on the floor."[80] Frankl pointed out that the girls' parents had agreed to send them to the new school only because of the payment they received from the administration. The fathers, he wrote, did not recognize the importance of the school, considering it as something of a game. This negative approach was apparently responsible for the apathy that characterized the place.

The school founded by Montefiore in 1855 was very much like the Rothschild School.[81] Here, too, emphasis was laid on women's handiwork: sewing, embroidery, and household chores, along with instruction in reading and prayer. This school was also intended for both Ashkenazic and Sephardic girls, but there were separate classes according to ethnic origin.[82] The title page of the school register bore the mission statement of the school: "A school to teach the daughters of our brethren of Israel, living in the Holy Land, how to pray from the book and to know our ancestral God with heart and soul."[83] This seems to indicate adherence to the European outlook, which recognized the importance of religious observance among women.

Mary Eliza Rogers, an English tourist, visited the Holy Land in the 1850s, and her book about daily life in the Holy Land has become a classic. She describes the atmosphere in the school at great length. There were about fifty girls, aged seven through fifteen, some of whom were already engaged to be married. The (female) teachers were enthusiastic: "[O]ur guide exhibited to us, with evident pride and pleasure, a considerable stock of wearing apparel, the result of one week's work in that room."[84] The girls, too, "looked busy and bright," and some of them were proficient in reading Hebrew. [85] Competition between the two new schools was probably detrimental to both, but the opposition of the Ashkenazic establishment had more serious consequences.

In the 1850s, Ludwig August Frankl and the German Jewish newspaper *Allgemeine Zeitung des Judentums* reported that the Ashkenazic establishment in Jerusalem objected to the school: "Many people of the Ashkenazic community saw this school, too, as an affliction, for they said it would give an opening for the establishment of schools in which students would be taught not only our Holy Torah but also secular subjects."[86] The objections, it would appear, were not to education of girls per se, but rather to the precedent it might provide for the approval of secular studies for boys. The prohibitions placed on the female sector were thus shaped exclusively by the needs of the male realm. The school lasted for only a very short time, but the headmistress, Rachel Roshe, opened a private *heder* for girls and continued to teach.[87] By contrast, the school founded by the Rothschilds did not close down, its continued existence being incontrovertible proof of the real need for formal education of girls.

This desire to educate the daughters of Jerusalem also occupied Flora Randegger, a young woman who immigrated from Trieste to Jerusalem for that very purpose (see above, chapter 1). Flora, who had taught for several years in a girls' school founded by her father in Trieste, immigrated twice, in 1856 and in 1864/65. Flora openly expressed her hope to "spread the holy light of knowledge among our oppressed brethren there . . . moderate and positive knowledge, without exaggeration or deviations."[88] As opposed to the men working in girls' education, who stressed their desire to create faithful Jewesses and good housewives, Flora regarded the spread of education as a holy mission that would influence not only women but society as a whole.

Flora failed to achieve her goal on her first visit to the country, and confined her activities to free private lessons that she gave to several female pupils.[89] Her second visit was no more successful. She collected a few pupils and taught a little in the Rothschild School, but financial difficulties forced her to abandon her efforts.[90] The Ashkenazi establishment issued a writ of excommunication (*herem*) on the school, referring to "the woman who has come here to the Holy City to teach the young daughters of Israel crafts and writing and language." They called the school "a malignant leprosy that will flourish in the City of our Lord."[91] The Ashkenazic community, already burnt by the fire of the *Haskalah* movement in Europe, unequivocally opposed any institution that was called a "school."[92] The excommunication kept Ashkenazic girls away from the school, its income declined, and Flora was obliged to leave.[93]

The Rothschild School continued to function but apparently did not leave a lasting imprint on education in Jerusalem. From Flora's diary it transpires that the school was intermittently opened and closed, and it had few students, most of whom were Sephardic. The fact that the school was attached to the Rothschild Hospital ensured the interest of the directors of the medical institution. In 1868, fourteen years after its establishment, the school received a grant and support from the English branch of the Rothschild family, and from that time was known as the Evelina de Rothschild School.[94]

The vehement criticism of the school obscures its considerable importance and pioneering achievements. For the first time, Jewish girls in Jerusalem had become the target of conscientious and systematic educational efforts. The school was the first channel for the transmission of European educational and cultural conceptions and viewpoints, such as the need for formal education for women, for systematic training for domestic tasks, and for a basic religious education. Intended for all Jerusalem girls, it was particularly successful among Sephardic girls, who, up to this time, had been systematically excluded from any education whatsoever.[95] Subsequent developments support the evaluation that women's enterprise and action regarding this school had a decisive influence. Despite its meager achievements, the school blazed a new trail, although its importance was not recognized by all its contemporaries.

Educational Initiatives in Jerusalem

Akiva Yosef Schlesinger, a very pious Jew who had immigrated to Jerusalem from Hungary, proposed a program for reforming the educational system. In 1873 Schlesinger published his Utopian vision in a booklet titled *Hevrat ma-*

hazirei atarah leyoshnah (Association for Restoration of Former Glory). He wrote: "We must establish schools for Jewish girls where they will learn prayers and reading . . . as well as . . . domestic tasks . . . and speaking and writing in the holy tongue [Hebrew]."[96] Schlesinger proposed to make a girl's marriage conditional upon her possession of a certificate attesting to her knowledge of Hebrew reading, writing, and speech; prayer and its interpretation; and handicrafts. But this vision remained hidden in Schlesinger's pamphlet.

Sephardic women *maestras* (elementary schoolteachers) opened infant nurseries in their homes for children (mainly girls) of preschool age whose mothers had difficulty minding them.[97] The *maestra* had no educational program: the children sat in her home doing nothing, and she ruled them with an iron hand. "We sat quietly in our places so as not to disturb her in her many and various activities," as Jerusalem-born Ya'akov Yehoshua describes his experiences. He writes at length of the punishments meted out to the toddlers and of the low level of hygiene in these homes.[98] Hasya Feinsod-Sukenik, one of the first kindergarten teachers in the Land of Israel, describes little children with eye diseases, crowded together on mats in enforced idleness. When she asked the *maestra*, "What do they do all day?" the reply was: "Do these little children have to do anything?"[99] Nevertheless, there were also exceptional *maestras* who taught small girls to read and write in Ladino. The daughters of wealthy families studied with a religious teacher (*hakham*) who came to their homes, and in the newer neighborhoods some coeducational *heders* were opened, giving infant boys and girls an opportunity to obtain a basic education.[100] Sephardic girls were generally not admitted to the boys' *heders*; most of them, like their mothers, were illiterate. Hemdah Ben-Yehuda, drawing a picture of Sephardic young women in Jerusalem in 1896, described their ignorance: "They do not know how to read or write, and for the most part, not even how to pray . . . as remote from education as East is from West."[101] But Rachel Eliachar, daughter of a distinguished family, writes in her diary that her mother had attended a *heder* for Sephardic girls.[102]

An article published in *Havazelet* in 1875 expresses admiration for the educational achievements of Ashkenazic girls: "All Ashkenazic women know how to read the holy tongue, and a great many of them also know how to write Hebrew."[103] Even if this report is somewhat exaggerated, it may be assumed that the more literate Ashkenazic mothers created a spiritual atmosphere conducive to study. The biography of Rachel Yellin-Danin (David Yellin's sister), born in 1872 in Jerusalem, contains a description of an Ashkenazic *heder* for girls, run in the Old City by Rachel Roshe, whom we have already mentioned. Four- to eight-year-old girls were taught the alphabet there.[104] The teacher tried to provide them with the elements of reading, so that they would be able to read the prayer book, albeit without understanding the meaning of the words: "We learned reading, without any explanation, just so as to be able to pray; I understood not one word of Hebrew."[105] The students of the Ashkenazic girls' *heder* were taught not to understand but to believe.

Moses Montefiore continued to support girls' education in the Holy City, sending a modest sum of two pounds sterling for any teacher who taught girls the elements of reading in her own home.[106] In his last visit to Palestine, in 1875, he met Rachel Roshe and sixty of her students. The distinguished visitor and his party examined the girls' achievements; he took note of their neat appearance and their knowledge of Hebrew. Rachel Roshe showed him her *heder* with the four teachers who were helping her, and told him that she taught her pupils the meaning of the prayer texts. The translator of Montefiore's diaries summed up the visit as follows: "The test lasted several hours and [the girls] were found to excel in everything, in the best possible way."[107]

Rachel Roshe's primary goal was to teach her wards to read. This sharp distinction between the teaching of reading and of writing was common in *heders* both in the Holy Land and in eastern Europe, and in fact also in educational systems in other cultures.[108] Rachel Yellin's father hired a special tutor to teach his daughter to write Yiddish. The rarity of writing skills among Jerusalem women may be deduced from the fact that Rachel, while still a child, wrote letters for women who were unable to write their own letters to their husbands.[109] Rachel Yellin's educated grandmother, Rima Rayna, rounded out her granddaughter's education by reading her Torah stories from *Z'enah ur'enah* on Sabbaths. Despite this, Rachel was considered ignorant in her family.

A similar account may be found in the memoirs of Ita Pines-Yellin, Rachel Yellin's sister-in-law, who came to Jerusalem in 1882. In Russia, the Pines girls had received an elementary education in a non-Jewish school, studying religious subjects with a tutor in their home.[110] Their father, Yehiel Michel Pines, tried to continue their education privately in Jerusalem, but religious fanatics frustrated his intentions: they forbade his daughters to study with an educated single man, threatening to excommunicate the teacher's family and the Pines's. The private sphere was thus the focus of public surveillance.

A census taken in Jerusalem in 1876 counted some 120 girls in such private *heders*, similar to the number of students in the Evelina de Rothschild School that year. Ten years later Avraham Moshe Luncz listed about twenty girls' *heders* in addition to the classes in the Evelina de Rothschild School.[111] However, though the number of students had increased, there were many girls who received no education. Unfortunately, we have no statistical data as to the number of literate Ashkenazic girls in Jerusalem; it may be assumed that the proportion was similar to that in eastern Europe at the time.[112]

Eliezer Ben-Yehuda disapproved of the rudimentary level of the education offered to girls in Jerusalem. Writing in his newspaper *Hazevi*, his wife Hemdah described Ashkenazic young women in the city as follows: "They do not speak Hebrew, do not read, have no idea of what is going on in the world at large, . . . and many of them have not developed at all."[113]

Evelina de Rothschild School, 1868–1894: "Bits of Education" or a "Real School"?

The Evelina de Rothschild School was a major point of interest, a veritable "tourist site," for Jewish visitors concerned with change in the Jerusalem community. Evaluations of the institution varied from one extreme to the other, depending on the visitors' expectations. Thus, the closing words of a report published in *Halevanon* in 1869 were: "These institutions will deserve the name of 'school' only if the teachers will be learned women."[114] Alfred Goldsmid, a prominent member of the London Jewish community who visited Jerusalem in the 1880s, noted: "The want of a good Jewish girls' School is much felt in Jerusalem . . . the state of education amongst Jewesses is deplorable."[115] Alfred Cohn, representative of the Anglo-Jewish Association — a philanthropic organization founded by British Jews — examined the students in 1893 and concluded that the school's level was inferior to that of the mission school run by the Soeurs de Sion convent in Jerusalem.[116] And Olga d'Avigdor, a representative sent from England to assess the school in 1900, wrote, "We appear at present to have no school, only bits of one."[117]

In contrast to these critical comments, the school received a more favorable evaluation from the *hakham bashi* (the Sephardic chief rabbi of Jerusalem), who at one time publicly examined the girls. He openly declared his positive attitude to the school and to girls' education in general: "I am happy to say that I derived great pleasure from seeing the young girls successfully displaying their achievements, both in the study of our holy tongue and in their knowledge of its sacred commandments."[118] On another occasion, he admitted, "The Jews of Jerusalem have never had such a school for girls in Jerusalem."[119] He also expressed his admiration of the progress shown by the students in their studies of French and handicrafts, ending with the words, "One's heart is full of joy, pleasure and happiness." The Sephardic chief rabbi of the city was essentially expressing his own community's positive attitude to the school.

For the first thirty-four years of its existence, the school operated as a kind of branch of the Rothschild Hospital, being managed by the wives of the hospital doctors.[120] For reasons of modesty and tradition, most of the teaching staff were women. The number of students increased apace; about fifty in 1868, by 1872 the number of students, aged from four to sixteen, had exceeded two hundred, and it continued to grow.[121]

Girls playground, Evelina De Rothschild School, Jerusalem. The Anglo Jewish Association
Annual.

In 1888 the link with the Rothschild Hospital was severed, and the school
continued to operate under the firm hand of the new principal, Fortuna
Behar, sister of Nissim Behar, the principal of the Alliance Israélite Universelle boys' school.[122] Her appointment signaled a dramatic change in the
institution,[123] arousing considerable hopes both for an improvement in the
general level of studies and for the intensification of Hebrew studies.[124] Luncz
wrote that Fortuna Behar was making strenuous efforts to endow the institution with "the character of a school."[125] At the same time, the celebrated educator David Yellin believed that her strict discipline was harmful to the girls,
both mentally and physically.[126]

The school, originally in the Old City, moved to the New City immediately
after separating from the hospital, probably in 1884.[127] But the new location
soon proved too small to accommodate would-be students, and hundreds were
turned away. According to the newspaper *Havazelet,* as many as four hundred
applications were refused.[128] Most of the girls came from the Sephardic
community of Jerusalem, only a few being of Ashkenazic stock.[129] The school
was probably the only opportunity for Sephardic girls to get an education,
while Ashkenazic girls could at least learn the basic literacy skills from their
mothers or grandmothers at home. Moreover, as already mentioned, the writ
of excommunication issued by the Ashkenazic establishment deterred many
Ashkenazic parents from sending their daughters to the school.

Millinery sale room, Evelina De Rothschild School, Jerusalem. The Anglo Jewish Association Annual.

Over the years, the basic curriculum proposed when the school had been founded was expanded. When Albert Cohen, the founder, visited Jerusalem in 1870, he gave instructions that a European language and some science should be taught.[130] In 1876 the curriculum included, besides reading, writing, and sewing, also arithmetic, history, geography, and natural science. There was also a proposal to study "the local language [Arabic] and a European language [French]."[131] There was some criticism of Fortuna Behar for giving priority to French over Hebrew culture,[132] and Eliezer Ben-Yehuda expressed his surprise in his newspaper: "Is this tongue [French] really necessary for a girl born in Jerusalem, where she will be living all her life?"[133]

With the appointment of Devorah, Ben-Yehuda's first wife, as Hebrew teacher instead of a Sephardic *hakham*, the use of Hebrew as a spoken language in the school was guaranteed.[134] Devorah knew how to attract the girls to Hebrew speech, as her proud husband reported in 1889: "All their speech was in Hebrew . . . and there is no doubt that next year all these girls will speak Hebrew well, as one of the living languages of this country."[135] A few years later Hebrew had become the language in which religious subjects were taught, as well as the spoken language, "for the students were instructed to speak Hebrew among themselves."[136] Ben-Yehuda was overjoyed: "This house will produce Hebrew-speaking girls, conversant with our history and lovers of our nation, educated girls, Hebrew through and through."[137]

Another manifestation of modernity in the Evelina de Rothschild School was the staging of classical plays or biblical events.[138] Toward the end of the

Specimens of lace manufactured at the Evelina De Rothschild School, Jerusalem.
The Anglo Jewish Association Annual.

nineteenth century, theater was seen as an educational tool of the first stamp: "A play is the most wonderful instrument to implant the spirit of our nation's history in the heart . . . It is the one thing most necessary to breathe life into our nation and the most holy thing to implant the sensation of Judaism deep in people's hearts."[139]

Alongside theoretical subjects, progress was also achieved in practical studies. Instruction in sewing and embroidery was improved; a sewing machine was made available to the girls, and they also learned to make lace.[140] These handicrafts were associated specifically with women,[141] and proficiency in them was thought to be an important means toward enhancing the economic condition of society. More than a decade before the establishment of the Bezalel School of Arts and Crafts, the Evelina School promoted Jewish art. "We saw there embroidered items that are indeed most artistic, almost a real picture. In particular, the portrayal of the sacrifice of Isaac is most excellent. The girls who excel in their work receive payment from the school for their work."[142]

The school encouraged its students to take up teaching as a profession. Upon completing their studies, the best students became auxiliaries and teachers in the school.[143] In 1870 it was proposed that the most talented girls would be sent to Paris for advanced studies, after which they would become teachers in Jerusalem.[144] The first girl to do so went to France in 1876 to study French,[145] and upon her return she joined the school's teaching staff.

The girls' ethical principles, no less than their physical needs, were seen as the school's responsibility. Fortuna Behar accustomed her students to acts of charity; in the 1890s they used to sew clothing for needy women in the Ezrat Nashim hospital.[146] The school also granted extensive aid to its poorer students, exempting the poorest from tuition fees. The girls received textbooks, sewing materials, and food.[147] Jerusalem rabbis would distribute dresses and other clothing, as well as books, to girls who excelled at their studies, in an impressive ceremony.[148] Awarding of prizes was also a kind of appreciation on the part of the male establishment for the girls' intellectual abilities. Girls who had studied at least five years in the school received a grant of two hundred francs when they married.[149]

Fortuna Behar strictly supervised the girls' neatness and cleanliness: "They are all clean, their hair combed (without ornament), they sit in good order, polite, modest, their faces alive and intelligent."[150] Cleanliness and order were considered to be formative elements in feminine character and of paramount importance. Fortuna Behar was an avid believer in the adage "Cleanliness is . . . next to godliness."[151] Toward the end of the nineteenth century, cleanliness and hygiene were seen as the most indispensable realization of progressive values. The girls' school was also an important channel for the inculcation of European ideas about "the cult of true womanhood,"[152] that is, piety, devotion, compassion, and cleanliness.

From 1878 on, the girls of the Evelina de Rothschild School were examined in public twice a year in the presence of the chief rabbi, foreign consuls, the pasha, Jewish public figures, and "the fathers of the girls who receive instruction in this house like all lovers of their nation and lovers of good, straightforward education."[153] The public examination was an incentive for both teachers and students. However, rather than serving the inner needs of education, it constituted a display of learning. As David Yellin put it: "Studies are not held for the sake of studying, but in order to excel before visitors."[154] As already noted, the event was extensively covered by the local press — *Havazelet* — and the school thus became a focus of public attention in Jerusalem. The ceremony revealed not only the girls' progress but also the overall appreciation of the school itself and the new female image that it was shaping.

Whether consciously or unconsciously, the Evelina de Rothschild School for Girls instilled a sense of self-awareness. This was clearly expressed in a speech by one of the students, Bolisa Angel, at a school celebration in 1878. Beginning with an account of the story of Creation, she stressed how woman had been made from a man's rib. She was describing the conventional gender images — the man leaving his home to support his family was "clothed in

Kindergarten: building with wooden cubes, the Evelina De Rothschild School, Jerusalem.
The Anglo Jewish Association Annual.

magnificent garments," while the woman, staying at home to tend his needs, "is subservient." She clearly expressed jealousy of men, pointing to the shortage of girls' schools as an impediment to women bettering their social position.[155] Paradoxically, it was the acquisition of knowledge that opened her eyes and made her recognize her lowly position. As long as she had been denied any education, she did not realize her weakness. Were these thoughts of Bolisa Angel hers alone, or did they occur to her companions as well?

At a similar ceremony in 1890, one of the girls told the story of Beruriah, Rabbi Meir's scholarly wife, who lost her two children on the Sabbath but did not inform her husband until the Sabbath was over.[156] The reference to Beruriah attests to a deliberate effort on the part of the teachers to present the girls with a model of a learned woman.

The importance of girls' education for social progress as a whole was pointed out in an article in *Havazelet* in 1886: "We have a hard-and-fast rule that you cannot be sure of an idea's realization unless it is taken up by women, for it is they who educate their children and also manage their husbands."[157] The Evelina de Rothschild School was a trailblazer in women's education in the East. For all its pioneering role, it seems to have sent out a double message: a conservative outlook, on the one hand, but, on the other, faith in women's intellectual talents and their importance in the education and support of their families. Owing to the relatively small number of graduates and the management's desire to insist that "Evelina" was a conservative institution, its public image was that of a small, rather unimportant, school. However, its slow educational efforts in the course of forty years prepared the ground for a real educational revolution.

The Anglo-Jewish Association: Girls' Education as a Path to Western-Style Progress

Philanthropic involvement in girls' education received new impetus in 1894, when the Anglo-Jewish Association (AJA, known in Hebrew as Agudat Ahim, literally, Association of Brethren) took the Evelina de Rothschild School under its wing. The AJA. was founded in 1871 by British Jews who wished to emulate the French Alliance Israélite Universelle and to cooperate with it.[158] Conscious of their improved political position, the Jews of Great Britain were anxious to help Jews of other countries, and particularly those of the Ottoman Empire. The AJA set itself both political and educational goals.[159] Its declared objectives being "to aid in promoting the social, moral, and intellectual progress of the Jews," it was particularly concerned with the education of Jewish boys and girls in Eastern countries.[160] This profound interest in education was shared by all sectors of the Jewish community: Zionists and anti-Zionists, nationalists and assimilationists. The special relationship of the AJA with the Evelina de Rothschild School was established with the full knowledge and assent of the Rothschilds, who continued to provide financial support.[161]

In the nineteenth century, the idea that girls' education was a highly significant tool for social change fueled the activities of many philanthropic organizations, some motivated by colonialist and/or missionary ideals. "If we get the girls, we get the race"[162] was the motto of missionaries working intensively among young girls. Or, on the other hand, as expressed by AJA officials: "Give me the daughters, and the grandsons will look after themselves."[163] In fact, they considered educating girls to be more important than educating boys, particularly in Eastern countries, given the inferior status of women there.[164] It was generally accepted that "it is the mother who usually makes two-thirds of the man."[165] Women's public activities and girls' education were intimately connected, as witness the establishment of girls' schools all over the world.[166] As put by Billie Melman, "In the colonial nation-state, motherhood was perceived not merely as an expression of femininity, but as women's national social service to the empire."[167] Such perceptions were nourished by a variety of social movements that flourished in the nineteenth century and promoted women's education, women's training as teachers, the founding of kindergartens, and the ideal of domesticity. All these motives found their echo in Jewish girls' schools in England as well, and in the extensive development of a network, founded at the time by Jewish philanthropic organizations, of girls' education throughout the Ottoman Empire.

In contrast to the positive image of the Jewish woman in western Europe, the Jewish woman in the East was viewed in an unfavorable light even in comparison with her non-Jewish counterpart in that part of the world. An AJA visitor to the Ottoman Empire observed that in cities such as Damascus, and perhaps also other Muslim cities, Jewish women seemed to be inferior to both their Muslim and Christian counterparts.[168] The members of the AJA concurred with this evaluation, declaring that "the terrible influence of Islam upon the status and position of women must be checked and counteracted."[169] The official organ of the AJA openly spoke of the need to emancipate Jewish women in the East.[170]

The AJA directors were convinced that "the question of education, especially of Jewish girls in the East, is one of such paramount importance to the future of our race, that no efforts . . . should be spared to promote the sacred cause."[171] Their task, they believed, was to cleanse the corrupted Judaism of the Jews in Islamic countries and, above all, to cleanse the women, whom they believed to be a stain on Jewish society.[172] By purging this social blot — women — of its impurities, they would accomplish the regeneration of society as a whole (even these proponents of Western liberalism were not completely free of prejudice as to the "demonic" nature of women).[173] Their ideal of Jewish womanhood was the British Jewess, who possessed such admirable characteristics as obedience, love, loyalty, and cleanliness. The perception of the inferiority of women in the East prompted the conclusion that their social position had to be improved.

The declarations of the AJA representatives attest to a dual goal: "to give our Jewish boys and girls the virtues of the West without robbing them of the virtues of the East."[174] Oriental culture attracted and repelled them at one and the same time. On the one hand, they admired the religious piety of the Eastern Jews, but at the same time considered "Eastern" religion to be primitive, while seeing their own "Western" religiosity as of sterling value.[175] In contemporary England, such contradictory ideas were in tune with the prevailing colonialist thought. In keeping with the innovative ideas characteristic of nineteenth-century philanthropists, the AJA sought to arouse the Eastern Jews to help themselves and thereby to advance their own culture.[176]

In its early days, the Anglo-Jewish Association participated in the financing of educational institutions established by the Alliance Israélite Universelle; only in the late 1880s were teachers with modern training first sent to various communities in order to organize educational institutions there or to establish schools of their own.[177] The Jews of Jerusalem were a focus of worldwide attention, and the British Jews took a particular interest in them. Britain was the leading country in Europe in regard to involvement in the Holy Land,[178] and British Jews' concern with affairs in the country was in effect a continuation of the extensive interest taken by British Christians in the East as a whole. The AJA saw its work as a national mission,[179] directed at Jewish society in Jerusalem, most of which subsisted in abject poverty.[180] (The headmistress of the Evelina School referred to her students as "Oriental.")[181] Another reason for the AJA's special interest in Jerusalem was the activity in the Holy City of various missionary organizations.

Evelina de Rothschild School, 1894–1914: Flagship of the AJA

The women's committee of the Anglo-Jewish Association, formed in 1893, was guided by the motto "There is room for women from the West to help their sisters in the East."[182] It was involved in all the routine operations of the Evelina de Rothschild School and had a formative influence on it.[183] In this respect, the AJA was by no means exceptional: within the Ottoman Empire, wealthy Turkish women helped girls' schools and contributed to educational improvements.[184] While the management of the AJA was entirely in male hands, the Evelina de Rothschild School was remarkable from its very establishment for the intense involvement of women. It had been founded by women of the Rothschild family, was directed in its early stages by wives of physicians in the Rothschild Hospital and others, and in later years was a popular focus of pilgrimage for young women teachers from Europe, in particular from Germany. Girls' education provided an impetus for intensive female activity. The AJA directors did everything possible to guarantee that the school would provide a high level of education.[185] It indeed became the flagship of the association, accounting by the turn of the century for more than one-half of the association's budget.

The overt motive of this devotion to the Jerusalem school was the desire to remove a seemingly indelible blot on Jerusalem society—Jewish girls being educated in mission schools.[186] In the United States, too, in the nineteenth century, similar reasons led to increased support for Jewish educational institutions.[187] The annual meeting of the AJA in 1894 declared that the association was determined actively to oppose missionary activity in the Holy City.[188] About fifty of the school's students received direct economic aid—food and clothing—similar to that provided by mission schools; only a few were required to contribute to the minimal tuition fees.[189] However, even these incentives did not suffice, and the AJA was unable to prevent a steady flow of Jewish girls to Christian schools. Only in 1911, responding to an appeal from an antimissionary committee constituted by the teachers' associations, did the school take in a hundred new students.[190] Opposition to the mission was thus a primary incentive for the school's development.

A first manifestation of the AJA's generous supervision was the move to a spacious new building, which made it possible to admit many more students. In 1895 the association bought a magnificent house, known as Bet Mahana-yim (previously the home of a banker named Frutiger), comprising more than forty rooms.[191] The building earned considerable praise; for example, *Hazevi* wrote: "This building is one of the most beautiful in our city, and it has a large garden, beautiful, spacious and with sufficient space for a large school."[192] The girls used to call it "the Queen of Sheba's palace."[193] It was the first step in the AJA's intensive efforts to develop the school.

The number of girls studying in the school rapidly increased. However, even after the student population had doubled, mothers still came to the school's doors begging for their daughters to be admitted and given a chance to study. Adela Goodrich-Freer, an English tourist, described the hubbub at the school gates on the day of registration. The neighborhood was full of people, and fathers eager to have their daughters admitted literally threw them into the school courtyard over the fence.[194] The *Hashkafah* reporter was amazed at Jerusalem parents' determination to secure an education for their daughters: "Whoever has not seen the sight on the day of registration for the school cannot suppose or imagine how vigorous and strong that desire is among the Jews of our city, to give the girls a better education."[195]

The school was thus a roaring success. Despite efforts on the part of the management, the Ashkenazic establishment did not cancel the writ of ex-communication pronounced on the school: the city's rabbis, headed by Rabbi Salant, refused to change their position.[196] Nevertheless, the boycott weak-ened, and there was a significant increase in the number of Ashkenazic girls attending the school.[197] By the beginning of the twentieth century there were about 200 girls in the kindergarten (which was part of the school), and more than 300 in the school proper. The number peaked in the summer of 1913: 676 girls in the kindergarten and the school.[198] The school management lim-ited the students' age to fifteen at most, and the increase in school population leveled off, for lack of space.[199] Conditions in the Frutiger mansion were un-bearably crowded, and the AJA was concerned both to refurbish the existing building and to plan more construction work.[200] Despite the growth of the in-stitution, AJA officials were well aware that the profound problem of girls' ed-ucation in Jerusalem had not been solved, and that only some 15 percent of Jewish girls in Jerusalem received formal education.[201] Further philanthropic organizations went into action, beginning in 1905, and established new girls' schools in Jerusalem; but many girls had still not found their place in a suit-able educational framework.

Not only were the school's physical accommodations changed; the man-agement was also replaced. In 1900 the veteran headmistress Fortuna Behar was dismissed, and was soon replaced by Miss Annie Landau, brought espe-

cially from London.[202] The replacement entailed numerous other administrative changes designed to streamline the running of the school, and a variety of educational measures that sought to change the atmosphere.[203] Miss
Landau, as her pupils addressed her, made a decisive imprint on the school
and was instrumental in making it an innovative, influential institution.
Yehudit Harari, a teacher from Rehovot who joined the staff, described her
warmly as an "educated English Jewess, with her energy and good taste; . . .
bright, beautiful, gray eyes, childlike laughter and domineering voice."[204]
The new headmistress, who was to rule the school for forty-five years with an
iron hand, till her death in 1945,[205] was absolutely convinced that she was discharging a mission and moreover that she would be able to influence the
character of the Holy City.

The directors of the AJA were guided in all their educational projects by
three principles: combination of sacred and secular studies; priority for girls'
education over boys'; and cultivation of good citizenship, implying economic
independence.[206] These principles challenged traditional educational ideas
in Jerusalem, which had always shunned secular studies, given absolute preference to boys over girls, and relied on *halukah* funds. The AJA, and Annie
Landau in particular, had internalized the Western conception of religious
principles as associated particularly with women: obedience, love, loyalty,
and cleanliness.[207] For Annie Landau, these qualities were pillars of human
society and religion, as she herself wrote: "'Moral' lessons as such are not
given, but in any and every lesson and in every conceivable manner have the
fundamental principles of our Faith — obedience, love, honesty, cleanliness —
been brought home."[208] The AJA directors, in their paternalistic way, believed
in the superiority of Western religious conceptions; religion, they believed,
was based on intelligence and understanding, whereas "Oriental" religion
was based on prejudice and emotion and was therefore to be rejected. Ignorance keeps people away from religion, whereas education brings them closer
and deepens their religious consciousness.[209]

These conceptions were the basic elements underlying the varied curriculum. The school offered the study of English on the same level as a
British primary school,[210] and in addition lessons in Hebrew and Judaism. Its
objectives were largely achieved. Boyd Carpenter, an inspector working for
the AJA, examined the girls in 1904; he praised their English speech and their
accomplishments in mathematics, music, and physical training.[211] In 1902,
after three years of educational work in Jerusalem, Miss Landau proudly declared: "The School is entirely English now . . . The children have learnt to
express themselves in English, and they are also English in manner, which is
more appropriate to the Oriental temperament than French."[212]

The cultivation of typically English cultural concepts was combined with manifestations of English patriotism.[213] Nevertheless, it is evident from the curriculum that, despite the institution's professed equal treatment of Hebrew and English, the number of hours devoted to Hebrew actually exceeded the number of English hours, and the AJA admitted that Hebrew was indeed valued more highly by the Jews of Jerusalem.[214] Speaking Hebrew was considered a most important means of enhancing the unity of Jews of Jerusalem, who spoke a multitude of different tongues. Sacred subjects were certainly studied in Hebrew only. The girls readily expressed themselves in that language, which was the everyday language for many of them.[215] The study of Hebrew was valued and encouraged not for nationalistic motives but as a pragmatic measure: Hebrew was the only language common to the Jews of Jerusalem.[216]

The repeated declarations that the Evelina de Rothschild School brought its girls up to be "capable good Jewish women, worthy daughters, sisters, and mothers in Israel"[217] attests to the school's adherence to tradition in the perception of women as housewives, subservient to the needs of the family. The curriculum included not only sewing and embroidery but also cooking, domestic science, ironing, and laundering—all subjects developed in England in the second half of the nineteenth century.[218] Toward the end of the nineteenth century, Jewish educational institutions in Europe were offering courses in domestic science, which was recognized, among other things, as a means of cultivating family life.[219] While the level of academic studies was quite high, the school gave priority to practical subjects, and domestic science was recognized as being of greater importance than, say, geography.[220] The school had workshops for needlework and lace, and school management even took part in marketing the girls' products, both in the country and, for the main part, abroad.[221] Frequent exhibitions held in different parts of Europe were an efficient way of displaying the girls' accomplishments.[222] Annie Landau not infrequently expressed appreciation for her pupils' determination, intelligence, and perseverance.[223]

The first kindergarten in Jerusalem operated in a wing of the school.[224] A movement for the establishment of nursery schools, emerging in Germany in the mid–nineteenth century, advocated systematic education adapted to the needs and abilities of infants.[225] In contrast to the system of the *maestras*, which did not recognize the development potential of infants and preferred to suppress it, and to the traditional *heder*, which treated the child as a "little adult," the new movement placed the child at the center of attention, seeking to develop and cultivate him or her both physically and mentally.[226] Friedrich Froebel, originator of the movement, who revolutionized education, brought about a change in the perception of women as well: motherhood became a science.[227]

Teaching in the kindergarten was entrusted to Emma Jungnickel, who had studied under Froebel's followers in Germany and came to Palestine from Russia as a Christian pilgrim in 1890. Her visit, originally supposed to last only two weeks, was extended without limit after she had been offered regular employment at the "Evelina" kindergarten. However, the kindergarten, intended for four-year-olds, began to operate regularly only from 1896, when Emma Jungnickel was joined by a Jerusalem woman, a Miss Siton, as auxiliary teacher.[228] Some two hundred children attended the kindergarten, and it was immediately successful. In a letter to Rabbi Moses Gaster in London, with whom she was acquainted, Jungnickel wrote, "I have given my heart, soul and love to the little children of your people," noting that "the kindergarten system has developed and spread from our institution to the whole of Palestine."[229] When the kindergarten first began to function, its main language was English, but it was replaced by Hebrew at the turn of the century.[230] Perhaps the paucity of reference to this important institution in official histories of the Yishuv may be ascribed to the fact that during its early stages it operated in English rather than Hebrew, and moreover the founding teacher was not Jewish.[231]

An Integrative Educational Institution

The Evelina de Rothschild School sought to reshape Jewish society in the Holy City. The first successfully achieved objective was communal integration. The school provided for girls of all Jewish communities. Together with girls from Yemen, Morocco, Persia, and Georgia, there were Ashkenazic girls of eastern European families and "real" Sephardic girls from the Balkans.[232] Around the beginning of the twentieth century, about one-half of the students were Ashkenazic, the other half Sephardic and Eastern.[233] In the school's early years, girls of different ethnic groups were taught in separate classrooms, but by the end of the nineteenth century the classes were mixed. This constituted a challenge to the traditional separation of communities in Jerusalem, as well as a victory over the Ashkenazic ultra-Orthodox community's ban on the school. Unlike the Alliance Israélite Universelle girls' school in Galata, Istanbul, in which the curricula offered to rich and poor girls were different, the Evelina de Rothschild School aimed at complete integration.[234] The school regulations, like those of Alliance institutions, declared that it was open to non-Jews as well.[235] In fact, some Turkish officials sent their daughters to study at the school, a fact that testified to its high educational level and its ability to compete with Christian schools.

Another goal of the school was to raise the average marriage age of girls in Jerusalem. To achieve a good education, a girl had to spend more years in school. In a newspaper interview, Annie Landau told how her attention had been drawn to an earring worn by a Yemenite girl. Inquiries revealed that the girl was engaged to be married. The young bride's mother was astounded at the headmistress's intervention, but Miss Landau saw in postponing the girl's marriage a definite educational goal, which moreover also had a medical aspect.[236] Postponement of marriage would also make it possible to enhance the girl's intellectual and physical maturity.

The school also devoted itself to ramified activities in the field of preventive medicine, thus making an important contribution to the health of Jerusalem's inhabitants. The early contacts with the Rothschild Hospital provided a preliminary basis for these activities.[237] As already mentioned, the school saw cleanliness as a supreme value, to an extent that sometimes annoyed parents.[238] A nurse supervised the girls' health,[239] and a local dentist was responsible for dental hygiene. Methods of preventive medicine, which were widely applied after the First World War by representatives of Hadassah, were realized in a limited but nevertheless intensive manner by the AJA directors in the school.[240] The school established close connections with various institutions that were working to improve public health in Jerusalem: A German anti-malaria mission examined the girls; the school supplied quinine when necessary, and actively cooperated in the struggle to eradicate the various epidemics that periodically affected the city, such as scarlet fever, smallpox and cholera.[241] The eye disease trachoma was intensively treated, in collaboration with the Jewish American philanthropist Nathan Straus, the Lema'an Zion eye clinic, and the Daughters of Zion (which later became the Hadassah organization) from the United States.[242] The school administration was responsible for every aspect of the students' lives. This was also clearly manifest in the curriculum: health and hygiene were major objects of physical training lessons, and there are impressive photographs of modern gymnastic equipment installed in the school yard.

Another expression of the desire to influence Jewish life in Jerusalem was the public celebrations held in honor of the festivals of Hanukkah and Purim.[243] These celebrations were occasions for theater performances directed by the teachers and moreover provided an opportunity to display the girls' achievements in English and Hebrew before residents and visitors to Jerusalem.[244] The educational value of these performances was a matter of public debate. A reporter in *Hashkafah* wrote that they were a unique opportunity for the girls "to stand erect and let their voices ring out in song and speech . . . before an audience."[245] This was, however, contrary to the Halakhic prohibition on hearing a woman's voice in song (Bab. Talmud, *Berakhot* 24a) and on standing erect (ibid., 43b). The school also organized field trips in different parts of the country to acquaint the students with the country as well as to strengthen them physically and cultivate a spirit of adventure.[246]

As part of its efforts to impart lofty spiritual and social values, the school also aimed to shape its students' character and ethical qualities. Annie Landau believed in encouraging voluntary activities;[247] the girls established a group they called Benot Zion, (Daughters of Zion), whose members undertook to speak only Hebrew.[248] They also established a society for the prevention of cruelty to animals.[249] The desire to influence the girls' way of life in the future as well was the motive for establishing a graduates' association, whose members were encouraged to revisit the school and hold weekly meetings, at which they would discuss Hebrew and English literature, also talking about their lives after leaving school.[250]

The social agents of these innovative ideas were the school's teachers, who had been educated in the pedagogical traditions of western Europe. Annie Landau was the harbinger of several young Jewish women who came, mainly from Germany, to teach in the Holy City. They regarded their stay in the country as something of an adventure and a cultural mission at the same time, what one might term today "national service."[251] They lived in a teachers' hostel near the school, in a virtually closed social circle.[252] The teaching staff also included men and women long resident in Jerusalem, such as Yosef Meyuhas, an educated member of the Jerusalem Sephardic community, son-in-law of Yehiel Michel Pines and brother-in-law of David Yellin, who wrote the first textbook in the country designed specifically for girls, titled *Bat Hayil* (see below).[253]

The school management tried to cope with the shortage of appropriate teachers in the country by training some of its graduates as teachers.[254] This also provided a temporary solution for some of the graduates, who wanted to continue their studies or work for a living, whether in the kindergarten or in the school proper.[255] Thus, in 1911/12 the school introduced a special class for continued studies, essentially a kind of embryonic teachers' college.[256] The school took pride in its being the first institution in the Land of Israel to train teachers for kindergartens and schools in the *moshavot*.[257]

Evelina de Rothschild School: Society and Gender

The declared goal of the directors of the AJA was to leave a permanent imprint on Jewish society in Jerusalem.[258] Less than a decade after her arrival, Annie Landau could tell the *Jewish Chronicle* in an interview that the school had brought about a revolution in the girls' values: "I have been accused of making our girls unfit for their surroundings. I admit the impeachment. I was sent to Jerusalem to do that and I hope I may succeed."[259] The girls of "Evelina" underwent a veritable "spiritual metamorphosis," she said on another occasion.[260] "The Evelina School is even more than a school . . . It is something also of a home."[261] As early as 1911 Miss Landau was able to assert, "By educating the girls of Jerusalem, . . . , we are slowly but surely improving conditions in the Holy Land."[262] "Evelina de Rothschild" had become a tool of major significance for the reshaping of Jerusalem society, which was then in the throes of accelerated social transformation.

If one follows the curriculum and the headmistress's declarations, as quoted not infrequently in the Jewish press, one gets the impression that the Evelina de Rothschild School was conveying a rather complex, even paradoxical, message, in terms of both national-religious and gender concepts. Was the management aware that its declared educational ideals were fraught with inner contradictions? It may be assumed that the school's supervisors, imbued with a sense of superiority and patronage, were convinced that they knew best what was good for the Jerusalem community, and that they were ultimately leading the Jews of the Holy Land along the right path for them. However, one discerns a disparity between the new educational messages and the society they were supposed to serve.[263]

The headmistress, who was strictly observant, wrote explicitly of her conviction that "the education of the Jewish girls of Jerusalem must be animated by a deep and ardent religious spirit in order to produce strong Jewish personalities."[264] Her school, she declared, was ultra-Orthodox, and it was her intention to respect Eastern culture, not to denigrate it, for "East and West have still something to learn from and to give to each other."[265] However, her actions did not always fit her declarations. Miss Landau tried to introduce eastern European ultra-Orthodox society and Sephardic-Eastern society to Rabbi Samson Raphael Hirsch's ideas of *"Torah im derekh eretz"* — Torah study with secular culture.[266] The growing number of applicants for admittance to the school, she claimed, attested to parents' confidence in her methods.[267] Despite her religious principles, Miss Landau was in full agreement with Western Jews' criticism of the *halukah* and the ideology that it represented. The directors of the AJA called the *halukah* a "cancer eating away the vitals of Jerusalem."[268] The school aimed to help solve the problem by educating the girls to work for a living — not only as a response to a basic economic need, but as an educational value. The girls were taught to love labor and to value economic independence.[269] In this sense, "Evelina" set itself goals not dissimilar to those of the Christian mission. Can one define the Evelina de Rothschild School as a feminist institution, educating women to fend for themselves? The term "feminism" is ambiguous and anachronistic, and the answer to this question is complex. The hope that the girls would have families was combined with the hope that they would be responsible for their families' livelihoods. Annie Landau believed that educating the girls to seek economic independence would assure both their personal future and the future of the city. She envisaged a future marked by coexistence of industry and the Yeshivot.[270] The school was proud of its graduates, who earned their living, and the annual reports of the AJA meticulously listed their professions and places of work.[271] Every profession was seen as worthy of respect.

In one of her *Jewish Chronicle* interviews, Miss Landau stressed her belief that "it is every human creature's right to strive to reach the highest rung in the ladder of life."[272] This simple observation, offered with the utmost caution, ultimately produced the insight that every woman had the right to study, not only in order to achieve her goal as a mother, but also by the mere token of being human. Girls' education, originally intended to contribute to the improvement of society by preparing women to educate their sons properly, became an end in itself. It is worth devoting some attention to the way the consequences of an innovative educational enterprise sometimes cause the innovators themselves to revise their concepts.

The teaching of Hebrew, as a language that could facilitate communication and unity among the different communities of the Holy City, redirected the Anglo-Jewish Association toward an area that it had not aimed for at all: the development of the new "Hebrew" nationalism. While "Evelina" became known throughout the Jewish community as a bastion of the English language, the paradoxical fact is that it became a valuable source of efforts to promote the study of Hebrew as a spoken language. Around the turn of the century, Hebrew became the spoken language of the Jews in the Land of Israel; it in fact became the major factor in the gradual shaping of the new Hebrew society.[273] In the first two kindergarten classes, opened at that time, only Hebrew was used, but in the school proper English was a central element in the curriculum. In 1901 Annie Landau claimed that knowledge of Hebrew among the infant girls registered for the kindergarten was inferior to that of Jewish girls in England.[274] Even if this was an exaggeration, we may conclude that the infants did not know Hebrew in advance, but took their first steps in the language in the one institution that considered itself the flagship of English language and culture!

In view of the political dimension of Hebrew speech in pre–World War I days, the school management distanced itself somewhat from Hebrew and declared its view that English was more important, whether for the promotion of general culture or as a key for economic success in the future.[275] Some years after her arrival in the country, Annie Landau explained her complex attitude to the revival of the Hebrew language. Denying any connection with the Zionist movement, she identified with the ultra-Orthodox establishment, declaring: "I am only a Zionist in that I give my life's strength to my work in Zion."[276] The school directors were highly critical of those working for the revival of Hebrew, who saw in Hebrew the essence of their new identity; the latter were branded as "determined foes to Judaism"; they were "'National-ists,' . . . who call for a Hebrew nation without the Jewish religion."[277] She ve-hemently objected to any attempt to call "Evelina" a Hebrew school, arguing that the language was not sufficiently developed and its exclusive use would have a deleterious effect on the girls' spiritual development.[278] Ronald Storrs, the first governor of Jerusalem after the British occupation, wrote in his mem-oirs that Annie Landau was "more British than the English."[279] In perspective, one might suggest that she lacked faith: she did not believe that Jerusalem could become the Jews' main home, and feared that, sooner or later, the Jews would have to leave, whereupon they would need a foreign language in order to make their way in the world.[280]

Yehudit Harari, who taught at the school, writes in her memoirs of her amazement at the school's official attitude: "How can one be religious, love the land dearly, and yet oppose Jewish nationalism? [Miss Landau] prays every day for the rebuilding of Jerusalem and the return to Zion, and yet she op-poses those returning to Zion!"[281] Many students at the school, rejecting this complex message, identified with the national longing for the revival of He-brew and saw Hebrew as their mother tongue. Other graduates, however, left the country to work as nursemaids and nurses; the pride expressed by the school in their success in western Europe and the United States is indicative of its attitude to Jewish settlement in the Holy Land.[282]

The Evelina de Rothschild School prepared its graduates to participate in the Zionist enterprise not only by teaching them Hebrew but also by shaping the image of a new, rural woman. In 1900, the first Hebrew reader aimed specifically at girls was published: *Bat Hayil* (the Hebrew phrase, by analogy with the biblical phrase *eshet hayil*, generally translated as "woman of valor" or "capable wife" [Prov. 31:10], means "capable daughter"), subtitled *Torat Em* (A Mother's Lore), by one of the schoolteachers, Yosef Meyuhas. It throws some light on the other female model that the school was trying to foster. The figure of the young woman most prominent in the various readings that make up the book is one living in the country or a town girl who spends vacations in the country; she is diligent, cheerful, always ready to help in domestic chores. Girls are described milking cows, making cheese, preparing jam from fruit, and so on. At sight, *Bat Hayil* seems to be a conservative figure: "a gra-cious crown to her husband and a good mother to her children."[283] Closer at-tention, however, makes it obvious that she was modeled on an ideal portrait of young women in the newly founded *moshavot*; this is also evident from the names of the protagonists, such as Naamah or Abigail the Jezreelite. The por-trait of a young woman as drawn by Meyuhas is nothing like the girls of Jeru-salem: she is a proud Hebrew woman in the renascent Land of Israel.

Various committees constituted by the AJA to examine the educational work done at the Evelina de Rothschild School speculated as to the school's influence on the Jewish population of Jerusalem.[284] The question was indeed frequently asked. As Annie Landau herself said, "I have been asked about the girls' future when they leave the school."[285] She was a domineering, charismatic personality, and well aware of it.[286] Graduates of the school remembered her in later years as being "a revered figure." "That wonderful woman had a kind of magical power, so much so that her very appearance put the fear of God into us."[287] On the tenth anniversary of her assumption of the office of principal, the "Iron Lady" of Evelina de Rothschild School summed up the achievements of the school's graduates in the previous three years: About one-half were working in workshops run by "Bezalel," the Jerusalem School of Arts and Crafts, or by the school itself. One-quarter had married and were now housewives. About 10 percent had left the country, some with their parents, others on their own, seeking a living; a similar number were working in Hebrew kindergartens in various parts of the country; and still others were continuing their studies in new Hebrew schools.[288] Economic independence, home industry, domestic life, Hebrew education, emigration, further study — this picture reflects the influence of the school's complex educational message.

The reform of the East as envisaged by the Evelina de Rothschild School was riddled with contradictions. The new woman shaped within its walls was at one and the same time an observant Jewess, a "real" European woman, and a new Hebrew woman. Her declared mission was to care for her family and work for the good of society and the nation, while at the same time being an independent human being, entitled to self-realization. The ideal girl was perceived first and foremost to be performing her tasks in the family and in the community, and education was considered a primary tool in guaranteeing her success as a wife and a mother.[289] The decision to give priority to the education of girls was a revolutionary element of Jewish educational thought in general, and in particular in Jerusalem.

Ultra-Orthodox Education for Girls before Beis Ya'akov

A new society, educated and preaching moderation in religious matters, sympathetic toward the new schools being established in Jerusalem, was emerging alongside the old, conservative society, which jealously adhered to its institutions and its customs. The growing number of boys and girls attending the new educational institutions, founded by the Rothschild and Laemel families, as well as associations such as Hilfsverein der deutschen Juden (Relief Organization of German Jews, Esra in Hebrew), AJA, and Alliance Israélite Universelle, were indisputable evidence of that new society. The ban pronounced in 1903[290] on the new Hebrew kindergarten did not deter mothers:

"A month has passed, the bans have been forgotten, and the kindergarten is thriving," wrote the noted educator David Yellin, one of the kindergarten's founders.[291] In light of the increasing demand for girls' education, the European associations active in the city established two new schools. The German-Jewish philanthropic association Esra founded a girls' school in 1905,[292] as did the French Alliance in 1906.[293] For Annie Landau, headmistress of "Evelina," this was just further proof that her efforts had not been in vain.[294]

Shortly before the establishment of the new girls' schools, the very circles that had previously declared war on modern education began to realize the importance of girls' education. The same establishment that had opposed the girls' schools now espoused some of its opponents' ideas and methods. Jerusalem, already unique for its many learned women, became the pioneer of formal education for girls in the ultra-Orthodox community. Almost fifty years elapsed from the establishment of the first girls' school in the Holy City until the idea of such a school was accepted by circles that had previously deplored it as a dangerous threat. Their acceptance was so complete that in time the identity of the original spiritual mentors of the idea was forgotten.

In 1902, two new institutions for the education of girls were founded: a Talmud Torah (elementary school) for girls called Bet Hinukh Yeladim, directed by Nahum Arieh Zelniker;[295] and an orphanage for girls, Bet Mahaseh Hinukh Yetomot, run by David Weingarten.[296] The founders did not use the Hebrew term *bet sefer* for school, since such institutions had, after all, been banned; they circumvented the ban by the semantic device of calling their schools *"bet hinukh"* (literally, house of education). Bet Hinukh Yeladim was simply a girls' class added to a boys' Talmud Torah; it had the approval of the ultra-Orthodox religious court, and was located just opposite the eastern gate of the Me'ah She'arim neighborhood. The orphanage was nearby. These schools were not a worldwide educational network, as "Beis Ya'akov" [literally, House of Jacob] was to become later;[297] nevertheless, they preceded it by nearly two decades — it was the first step toward institutionalized education of girls in the ultra-Orthodox community.

The rabbinical approval for the girls' school clearly attests to the radical change that had occurred in Jerusalem. Rabbi Shmuel Salant admitted that "I, too, [feel] that we are still suffering in the Holy City from the lack of [such] a worthy and necessary enterprise."[298] The directors of the girls school, writing two decades after its establishment, declared that the girls' could not be left "to grow up wild like animals" and that "the enterprise [was] worthy and necessary."[299] As to the boys' school, however, nothing had changed, and the ban remained in force.

The curriculum drawn up for girls' education included only the most basic subjects. In Bet Hinukh Yeladim it comprised "praying and reciting blessings grammatically, cutting and sewing all sorts of clothes, artificial flower arrangement, writing letters, and arithmetic."[300] In the girls' orphanage the curriculum was "learning to write, grammar, a special workshop for sewing and embroidery."[301] This elementary curriculum was strikingly similar to that introduced in the Evelina de Rothschild School in its early years. In the orphanage's visitors' book, its educational ideal was presented as follows: "Girls with good manners and behavior, girls that will come to know and value their nation and their Torah, and their good customs; and when they grow up and become mothers of children, they will endeavor to impart to their sons and daughters all the most admirable virtues."[302] Education was thus recognized as an important means toward shaping the traditional figure of a woman: a loyal daughter of her people, a mother devoted to her children.

Documentation of both these schools is extremely sparse. Nevertheless, comparing them with the Evelina de Rothschild School, one clearly gets the impression that the founders derived their ideas directly from the latter. Both schools were established, the founders claimed, not so much because of the need for education per se, but primarily because of the threat of the mission schools.[303] The latter also offered Jewish girls, in addition to financial help, education and professional training; the competition more or less defined the educational goals of the Jewish schools. The *bet hinukh*, while aiming to prepare the girls for their traditional role, also taught them new skills that would help them to support their families: "The girls educated in this school will become Hebrew mothers, faithful to their religion and nation, and will be able to make their livings in this enterprise."[304]

Since these new girls' schools were also insufficient to meet the demand for educational institutions, in October 1912 the members of the Ezrat Nashim society (see above, chapter 4) established the House of Study of Handiwork for the Daughters of Israel, designed first and foremost to combat poverty and the threat of the mission by teaching girls to sew and knit. Here, too, the "offensive" term *bet sefer* was avoided, calling the institution a *bet limud* — literally, house of study. The "house of study" offered the girls the basic skills of reading and writing in Hebrew, a little arithmetic, and vocational training. Its goal was to encourage "work that will earn one a respectable livelihood . . . and perhaps also a real revolution in the economic condition of the Holy City."[305] The founder, Ita Yellin, in an interview given to the *Jewish Chronicle* in 1913, pointed out that "the old 'orthodox' prejudice against girls' schools is gradually dying down in Jerusalem."[306] The school did not intend to compete with existing institutions; its level of study was low, as was the degree of professional sophistication, and its products were meant mainly for the Jerusalem market.[307] It was apparently intended for girls who had not yet gone to any school or acquired even the most basic skills. The institution's name, as well as the fact that most of the students were Ashkenazic,[308] would seem to imply that they came from circles that had hitherto refused to send their daughters to the existing schools but were nevertheless desperate for some sort of education, vocational training, and economic independence.

After the British occupation in 1917, when crippling poverty drove a few hundred Jewish girls in Jerusalem to prostitution,[309] Amitah Pinchover, the director of a Hebrew school for girls, pointed out that the best preventive in that respect was a woman's ability to earn her living. Clearly, the connection between education and the economic and spiritual state of society had been fully understood.

All the educational institutions for girls also accepted the idea that the place of learning was an intercommunal institution; they freely admitted both Sephardic and Ashkenazic girls. This was not, however, because integration was considered to be an educational goal; rather, it was a necessity. Paradoxically, the harbingers of progress — education and integration — were perceived by the conservative society of Jerusalem as measures more appropriate for its inferior, marginal elements, not fit for the social elite — the Torah-learning community.[310]

A letter about Bet Hinukh Yeladim, written almost two decades after its foundation, presented it as "an ancient institution, many years old."[311] This description seems to imply that the city's rabbis preferred to prevent any impression that the school was an innovation.[312] However, Eliezer Ben-Yehuda's newspaper, *Hashkafah*, left no room for doubt:

First of all, . . . this is a breach in the fence, and any breach in the fence of time-honored customs is a step on the road to progress. Second, . . . the directors of the school for girls surely decided not to violate the Sages' words, saying that anyone who teaches his daughter Torah, it is as though he teaches her obscenity. But the natural force of the matter will do the job . . . and gradually the restrictions will be lifted and our daughters will learn."[313]

Thus, formal education for girls had been adopted by all sectors of the Jerusalem community.

Did this mean that the responsibility for educating children had shifted from father to mother?[314] Talmudic law excludes Jewish mothers from the obligation of teaching their children Torah; Jewish tradition assigned them the responsibility for their children's moral character but not for their intellectual education.[315] However, changing attitudes to women's learning at the turn of the twentieth century also burdened them with new responsibility, namely, for their sons' intellectual and not only moral character.[316] We have evidence of this transformation in various letters written by members of the Old Yishuv in the very first years of the century. Thus, a letter about the orphanage published in *Havazelet* in 1904 states quite openly: "In many kinds of charity women are superior to men . . . For she is the housewife and all Jewish children's education depends on her."[317] Or, in a letter to the Education Committee after World War I from the Supervisory Committee of the ultra-Orthodox Jewish Girls' School, the writers admit that "the woman is . . . always . . . the standard-bearer of religious education, who accustoms and educates her children in the observance of Torah and religion."[318] In other words, all the responsibility for children's Jewishness was placed on the mother.

The Western conception of the woman as responsible for the family's spiritual welfare was thus accepted and applied by the Old Yishuv as well. Nevertheless, their patriarchal perception of male superiority remained unchanged: the man was still the spiritual figure, while the woman was an inferior creature, "who by her nature is not given to profundity and is easily influenced."[319] Even the fact that women now had the opportunity of education had not altered the gender perceptions of Old Yishuv Jewish society. Just as shouldering the yoke of supporting the household had caused no change in the woman's status in the domestic realm, the new responsibility for educating her children had not modified her portrayal as an inferior being. These contradictions naturally raise such questions as, How could a person described as "easily influenced" exert crucial influence on the education of her children? And how could a person defined as being spiritually inferior be charged with shaping her children's spiritual character? These questions remain unanswered. Despite the acceptance of formal education for girls, the concept of male superiority remained intact. The basic gender perception of the superiority of male society was axiomatic.

Chapter 6

On the Margins of Society

Poverty, Widowhood, Husband Desertion, Prostitution, Missionary Efforts

A City of Poverty

CONCEALED BEHIND THE conventional picture of Jerusalem as a haven of mercy and compassion was a different reality, of poverty and want.[1] The growth of the city's population entailed a concomitant increase in the number of poor.[2] Despite the many improvements made in the city in the course of the nineteenth century and the beginning of the twentieth, the number of poor did not fall but rather rose, and poverty became the salient characteristic. What is generally considered marginal elements of society were at the center in Jerusalem. From the ledgers of the Sephardic community, "*Hamoreh lizdakah*," it transpires that the number of beggars in 1903 was double the figure for the previous decade.[3] Mrs. Georgiana Dawson Damer, a tourist who toured the city in the late 1830s, wrote: "Nothing can exceed the misery and desolation of the lower classes of Jews in the Holy City."[4] And James Finn, the well-known British consul, wrote that he had never seen such misery as that of the city's Jews: "[In] . . . 1854, . . . we became aware, as we had never before been aware, that there is among the Jews of Jerusalem an amount of misery and hopeless poverty, inconceivable to those who have not been eye-witnesses of the condition of this unfortunate people."[5] Along with the hardships of the Jews, the tourists who flooded the city did not ignore the similar condition of non-Jews.[6] But tourists were not alone in spreading the word of Jerusalem's poverty abroad, for its paupers too, who assiduously sent begging letters all over the world, "defame the city and present it as a city of paupers preying on the benefactors of the people."[7]

Scholarly studies of poverty worldwide associate poverty with a variety of factors: old age; hardship due to immigration, ethnocentrism, or racism; crime; dependence on charity, frugality, asceticism, sanctity, and religious observance.[8] The phenomenon of poverty has two poles: on the one hand plumbing the depths, and on the other hand disregard of the material in favor of the spiritual. An extreme expression of the positive evaluation of poverty is found in the talmudic maxim "the Holy One, blessed be He, went through all the good qualities in order to give [them] to Israel, and He found only poverty" (Bab. Talmud, Hagigah 9b). Jewish tradition considers charity as one way of achieving closeness to God: "Whosoever provides food and drink for the poor and the orphaned in his home, should he call upon the Lord, the Lord will answer him and take pleasure in him."[9]

As seen in previous chapters, the Jews of Jerusalem were perceived on the one hand as superior to all other Jews but on the other hand as beggars, for whose needs Jews the world over were obligated to provide, and who took the charity of their compatriots as their due. The monies of the *halukah*, which were considered as a special form of charity, were not allocated on an equal basis and were not even given to everyone.[10] Talmudic scholars who spent all their time in study received special support, and their families benefited from their prestige.[11] In most of the *kolelim*, however, it was impossible to subsist on *halukah*,[12] so that the city's Jews were forced to seek additional sources of income. An ideology that discouraged people from going to work, combined with the sparse opportunities for gainful employment in Ottoman Jerusalem, condemned the Jews to abject poverty.

Time and time again, various and sundry catastrophes undermined the already shaky economic infrastructure of the city and further aggravated the situation. Years of drought brought hardship, since the only drinking water in Jerusalem was rainwater collected in underground cisterns. A dry year immediately caused the price of water to rise, soon to be followed by a rise in food prices. A letter signed by Rabbi Shmuel Salant and sent by the Jerusalem General Committee (Va'ad Hakelali) clearly reveals the writers' distress, "being troubled by the oppressively high cost of all necessities of life, owing to the shortage of water and failure of field crops during the past year."[13] Famine resulted in plagues, which greatly exacerbated the situation of the Jerusalemites, whose despair is graphically expressed in many sources: "Our hearts are torn to shreds . . . There were never such difficult times as at the present time . . . , for the Angel of Death has broken into the city and terrible diseases are wreaking havoc."[14] As festivals approached, particularly on the Eve of Passover, when special commodities had to be acquired, the distress was strongly felt.[15] Human oppression further compounded natural disasters: the authorities insisted on prompt payment of taxes,[16] while the *halukah* funds often arrived late because of pogroms or wars.[17]

The condition of the Yemenites was the most difficult. The Yemenite community council in Silwan (Shiloah) village described the community's suffering in detail: "We are located in the midst of Arab wolves in fear and trembling, surrounded by predatory animals and armed robbers who hound us night and day." The remote village on the outskirts of the city was a notorious trouble spot. According to the writers, the Arabs would enter their homes during the night, breaking open their doors or coming via the roofs, robbing and beating them mercilessly. The source of their distress was not only from the persecution of the neighborhood Arabs but also a result of poverty and deprivation, and particularly the lack of cooking ovens. "Because we have no ovens we are obliged to send our wretched wives and children to scavenge in the streets and markets for straw and garbage with dung from oxen and donkeys, in shame and humiliation."[18] The most ignominious task — collecting garbage — was relegated to the women and children.

Of all those living in these wretched conditions, women were the most humiliated. As difficult as the situation was in the male sector, the situation of the female sector was far worse. Jerusalem was a poor city with an absolute majority of women; and most of the poor were women. The identification of poverty with femininity was so self-evident that an anonymous writer from Safed wrote of his city that it was "all women, weak hands of women, and whence shall our relief come?"[19]

Begging Letters

The abject poverty produced an interesting phenomenon: Jews of Jerusalem, of all sectors, sent letters to the four corners of the world appealing and begging for assistance. A survey of the letters reveals that most of the writers were women. Even without scientific, statistical analysis, it seems obvious that these letters were sent, for the most part, by lone women, mainly widows, sometimes orphans[20] or divorcées.[21] The *kolelim* and other organizations founded by Jerusalemites did not possess the funds to combat the all-pervasive poverty.[22] The existing institutions, many of which were founded by private individuals,[23] could not provide enough relief. Despite the image of the Holy City as a place of charitable and benevolent societies, of soup kitchens and refuges, they could not meet the insurmountable needs. Historian Yisra'el Bartal attributes this situation not only to the economic condition of the city but also to the prevailing elitist view of the lower classes as "a superfluous social element in Jerusalem."[24] The many begging letters attest not only to the difficult economic situation but also to the fact that appeals to benefactors outside the city were almost the only means left to the needy. Only a few hardy souls had the courage to travel abroad and seek support for themselves and their families.[25]

The number of letters from the Holy City in the archives of the administrators of the *halukah* in Amsterdam reaches the thousands, and there are a

not insignificant number in other collections.[26] Famous families and personalities such as Rothschild, Montefiore, Hirsch, and Gaster also received large
numbers of letters. Women not infrequently appealed particularly to famous
women such as Judith Montefiore, Baroness Clara de Hirsch,[27] Baroness
Betty de Rothschild,[28] and others. The plethora of letters attests to the positive
response of these benefactors and to the dispatch of many donations. Avraham Moshe Luncz once noted that Montefiore never refused an appeal from
a Jerusalem resident.[29]

Rabbis and community leaders also sent many letters seeking support for
their communities in general, acting as spokesmen for their congregants: "We
are approached by multitudes of destitute Sephardim, Yemenites, *Mugrabim*
[North African Jews], Persians, etc., etc., multitudes of widows beseeching help
and abandoned and oppressed orphans."[30] The fact that so many private individuals, men and women, felt the need to write such letters indicates a realization that they had to fend for themselves. The hundreds of letters are extremely
varied, some impressive, some scribbled offhandedly, some written on scraps
of paper whose pitiful appearance brought home the misery of their senders.[31]

The women of Jerusalem, many of whom were illiterate, sent many letters
written by men (who in fact often did not bother to use the feminine gender
in writing), and moreover the names indicate that most of the writers were
Ashkenazic. In view of the more abject economic situation of the Sephardic
community, this is rather striking. Was the illiteracy of Sephardic women the
explanation for the paucity of letters sent by them? Was there a charge for
writing and sending letters, which Sephardic women could not afford to pay?
Is it possible that Sephardic women, unlike their Ashkenazic sisters, were
more reconciled to their situation? A description of the state of Jewish widows
in Aden may provide a clue to the behavior of the Sephardic women in Jerusalem: "A woman whose husband has died puts the remainder of her life on
hold and as it were dies herself."[32] Did Sephardic widows consider their husbands' deaths as the beginning of their own demise, therefore giving up the
struggle to improve their own economic situation? A begging letter sent by
Persian Jews living in Jerusalem describes their poverty with emphasis on the
passivity and wretched condition of the widows of the community.[33]

Perhaps the letter-writing efforts of the Ashkenazic women may be compared with the initiative of other Ashkenazic women who participated in the
economic life of the city. It seems plausible that the more active measures
taken by Ashkenazic women were promoted by their function in supporting
the family, while the passivity of Sephardic women was in keeping with their
failure to enter the job market. Did any changes occur in the behavior of
Sephardic women as the times changed? An item in the *Hazevi* newspaper in
the summer of 1888 reports that Sephardic women were trying to fight their

situation through a new strategy, namely, organization. Some eighty widows and orphans approached Eliezer Ben-Yehuda with a request that he write about their hardships in his newspaper. According to them, the *kolel* coffers were empty, and they sought an alternate source of relief.[34]

The begging letters were similar in their makeup.[35] The opening phrases invariably heaped praises on the recipient; for example: "Men of kindness! Wise men of goodness . . . Being convinced of the loving-kindness so deeply rooted in your hearts. . . ."[36] Next the writers would undertake to pray for their benefactors at the Wailing Wall and at Rachel's Tomb in exchange for their assistance.[37] The writers would introduce themselves, their own lineage, and the lineages of their fathers and their husbands. The husband was generally extolled: "His counsel is the counsel of the Torah," whereas the writer described herself as being in a desperate situation: "A wretched woman, unhappy, storm-tossed; and I have not a thing, and I have no power except the words of my mouth"; or: "My house is empty of all belongings, and I have not so much as a thread or a sandal strap."[38] The writers would sign their letters with various titles descriptive of their situation: "Lying on my deathbed all day," "the bitter-souled woman," or the like.[39] In a letter written jointly by several widows, they presented themselves as "widows of Jerusalem . . . , fainting from hunger on its streets, awaiting death that does not come."[40] Some women wrote of their disabilities. Hinka, widow of Rabbi Shlomo Elba, wrote that she was blind; another called herself "the cripple of Tiktin" and complained that she was therefore unable to beg in the streets; while the widow of Rabbi Yitzhak Ratzferter spoke of having had an accident that left her penniless, owing to the cost of medical treatment, so much so that she was reliant on help from others.[41] The various women writers represented the most injured and pained members on the margins of society.

The descriptions of suffering were not always accurate. *Hazevi* published a warning about "a woman from the Holy City who signs her letters as the *rebbetzin* [rabbi's wife] and sends hundreds of letters with every postal dispatch from here to Germany. Would that we were able to determine the identity of this *rebbetzin*."[42] The writing of begging letters was apparently a very lucrative "profession," which also led to fraud. A woman named Hannah Aboliski published a letter in the *Hashkafah* newspaper denying that she had written to an American newspaper bemoaning her poverty and her children's distress. Hannah requested those who were sending donations to desist, insisting, "I am not poor, Thank God . . . and I do not, Heaven forfend, need charity."[43] Many begging letters were countersigned by distinguished representatives of the Yishuv, as a confirmation of their authenticity.[44]

Many Jerusalemites were embarrassed by the need to rely on the benevolence of others. Some expressed dismay regarding their condition and felt the need to apologize for seeking charity: "I never tried to ask anyone for anything, for when my husband was alive, I enjoyed great blessings and lacked for nothing."[45] Even within such a large community of charity seekers there were those who were deeply humiliated. Worthy of mention is an unusual letter of "a poor and wretched widow," as she called herself, who did not appeal for charity but rather for work as a servant. She sent her letter to philanthropists who were said to be planning to found a hospital in Jerusalem. The woman, who wanted to support herself by her own efforts rather than rely on charity, ended her letter with the words: "You will thereby achieve the true purpose of charity."[46]

While the women's requests were varied and sundry, worry about the material needs of their children came first and foremost. Widows left with many children stressed the recipients' obligation to help them to raise their children, describing their children as naked, starving, and in need of urgent help.[47] Requests for aid in marrying children off were very common, and even people who could by no means be considered poor were not ashamed to ask various philanthropists for assistance.[48] Widows also sought donations to help them pay rent or requested permission to live in endowed properties (hekdesh).[49] The loss of a husband or parents sometimes left women grief-stricken, and their relatives might try to assist them by writing letters for them.[50]

The donations were generally sent to the address of a distinguished person of authority, such as Rabbi Shmuel Salant, who was known for his righteousness and integrity,[51] or Dr. Yitzhak Schwartz, a doctor at the Rothschild Hospital.[52] The donors seem to have preferred to send contributions to the address of a known person, to ensure some sort of supervision. However, the donation did not always reach its destination with the requisite speed. For example, in 1889 Hazevi published the complaint of a widow who claimed that the rabbi of Brisk—or, more precisely, "the ga'on whose wife rules over him [!]"—had withheld money that had been meant for her and caused her great suffering.[53] The thousands of letters that have been preserved attest to the depth of poverty and destitution in Jerusalem, and the widows, who were surely the weakest of the women, account for the largest number.

Widows

The portrayal of Jerusalem as a widow derived its force not only from its state of physical destruction but also from the large number of widows in the city.[54] In 1839, widows comprised 22.8 percent of the Jewish community in Jerusalem;[55] of these, a considerable majority were accounted for by Sephardic as against Ashkenazic widows.[56]

The life stories of many of these widows have come down to us in the hundreds, if not thousands, of begging letters that have been preserved (see above). While most of the widows must remain nameless, some were distinguished and well-known widows of prominent leaders of the Old Yishuv, such as Yuta Beila, widow of the Rabbi Israel of Shklov, one of the first disciples of Rabbi Elijah of Vilna to immigrate to the Holy Land;[57] Elka, granddaughter of Rabbi Israel of Shklov and widow of Rabbi Nathan Neta Natkin;[58] and Leah, widow of Rabbi Yosef Rivlin, the pioneering builder of neighborhoods outside the Old City.[59] Rivka Lipa Anikster, author of the pamphlet *Kunteres zekher olam*, and her daughter Rachel, who was an *agunah* (see below), were also prolific writers of letters requesting charity.[60] In 1882, in the wake of anti-Jewish pogroms that had swept Russia in 1881, a group of eight widows and their children arrived in Jerusalem, claiming that in the years prior to their immigration they had given generous help to the poor.[61] The fact that widows of community leaders should have been reduced to living on charity is evidence both of the extent of poverty in Jerusalem as well as of the feeling that appealing for charity was a matter of routine, so much so that some supplicants published their requests in the press.[62]

Unlike needy widows who had no alternative but to rely on the goodness of philanthropists abroad, wealthy widows were considered by the community to be capable of bearing the economic burden. Moreover, their wealth was often considered a communal resource. Declaring themselves to have the status of relatives of a deceased person who died intestate, the leaders in Jerusalem enacted the so-called inheritance regulation, which transferred ownership of such property to the community.[63] According to the regulation, the property of a deceased person with no heirs resident in Jerusalem would be "inherited" by the community; members of his family residing abroad would be dispossessed, contrary to the Halakhic laws of inheritance. In other words, the needs of the community overruled the dictates of Halakhah. Similarly, the community appropriated the property of wealthy widows during their lifetimes. The "Jerusalem Regulations" established that if women immigrating to the Holy City had "an annual allowance . . . , the clerks will collect five per one hundred each year. And from two hundred and up they will collect at the rate of eight per hundred; but if less than one hundred, they will not take even a penny."[64] A similar sense of assumed ownership of a widow's property by the community is discernible in a regulation according to which "if a widow who has no heirs should move away from Jerusalem, she must continue to pay taxes for three years."[65] A widow who rebuilt her life and remarried was considered to have caused the community to lose income, and was therefore required to give compensation; she was required to pay the *kolel* one-fifth of the capital that she brought to her new husband.

Needy widows, however, were seen as an economic burden. Thus, for example, a letter from the Hebron community requesting help to establish a
local hospital gave a rather unexpected reason for the need: since the journey
from Hebron to Jerusalem took eight hours, the absence of a local hospital
was responsible for the high mortality of the population, and a heavy economic burden thus lay on the community's shoulders, "because we are obligated to support the deceased's widows and orphans."[66] Clearly, the community leaders were more concerned about the forthcoming economic burden
than about the loss of life itself. The disregard for the widow's emotional condition, the lack of empathy toward her, the exclusive focus on the economic
aspect of her life — all these typified the attitude of the establishment in the
four "holy cities" to widows. This is the evaluation not only of a modern
scholar studying the mentality of the period but also of the widows themselves; as one of them put it: "They [the community leaders] seek only their
own benefit, not that of the poor and of the widows."[67]

A long letter from Sima, widow of Zvi Hirsch Perlman, renders an account of the torment and suffering she went through in her dealings with
Warsaw Kolel after her husband died. As a result of his illness and the excessive costs of his medicine, Sima had signed promissory notes drawn on her
husband's *halukah* allocation. After his death, however, the *kolel* directors refused to give her and her children their allocation, because of her debt to the
kolel. Sima strongly protested, arguing that "it is as clear as daylight that charity intended for support of orphans cannot be mortgaged to a creditor . . . and
halukah money is never mortgaged to a creditor."[68] Her letter, written in Hebrew (probably by a scribe), supplies references to the relevant clauses of the
Shulchan Arukh, according to which a debt may not be collected from charitable funds. Sima was saddened not only by economic hardship but also by
the perceived injustices done her: "I have dipped my quill in my blood and
my heart bleeds whenever I speak of this great injustice." Her words give us a
glimpse of the world of a widow, left alone with no support, forced to appeal
in her distress to the principals of Warsaw Kolel abroad.

A similar story emerges from letters written by women whose husbands
were on their deathbeds, some of whom sent desperate letters to benefactors
abroad, whether to the administrators of the *halukah* in Amsterdam or to
members of their own families. Haya Rivka, widow of the scholar Yehosef
Schwartz, discussed her husband's illness at length and her own difficulties.
Schwartz died in a plague that broke out in 1865. At first his widow refused to
inform his family of the tragedy, but later, when she had to cope with her
daughter's illness and with further expenses, she sought help from the family
and informed them of her situation: "Now the burden is too much for me to
bear . . . and now that all the debts are a heavy weight around my neck, I have

decided to inform you."[69] Letters like these constitute a mirror that clearly reflects the weakness of single women facing the male establishment.

"A Widow's Cry" (*Za'akat almanah*) — this was the title given by the widow Sarah Sheindel Nechmad (Nahmat) of Tiberias to her letter to the editor of the *Havazelet* newspaper.[70] Sheindel's story, both in her own version and that of the heads of the Tiberias community in their reply to her, chronicles the lack of communication between the recently widowed woman and the local establishment. Her letter reveals the story of a woman from Jerusalem, orphaned in childhood, who was married for the first time at the age of twenty to a wealthy resident of Tiberias, who had divorced his previous wife because she had not borne him sons.[71] The wealthy Tiberian pampered his new wife with the best of everything — clothing, food, and jewelry — but he fell ill and died about two months after their marriage. The leaders of the Sephardic community lost no time and, already during the seven days of mourning (*shiv'ah*), "confiscated everything in the house, leaving practically nothing," even removing jewelry from around the widow's neck, claiming that her husband had left many debts and that the creditors' rights took precedence over those of the widow.[72] She, however, complained that the community representatives had not only robbed her but also beaten and injured her. In her misery, "for I have no one to lean on," the widow published her life story in the Jerusalem *Havazelet* newspaper. Her story did not go unnoticed. A letter dated 25 Tamuz 5640 [July 4, 1880][73] from the rabbis of Tiberias, backed by a letter from Rabbi Ya'akov Shaul Eliachar, the *hakham bashi* of Jerusalem, rejected the woman's claims. The woman had called the rabbis of Tiberias "vipers, deaf men, . . . murderers, . . . swindlers and hypocrites." The Tiberias rabbis, however, insisted that they had treated her leniently, and sent all the deceased man's promissory notes to Rabbi Eliachar to prove the truth of their claims. Since the deceased had many debts, they argued, the wife was entitled to receive only the monetary worth of her *ketubah* (the statutory sum provided for in the marriage contract). They admitted that immediately upon his death they had sent two emissaries to the house and instructed them to "close every open closet and lock every open box with a wax seal [i.e., essentially to take possession of the deceased's property and deny the widow access], but to permit the widow and the heiress to stay in the house and to provide sufficient grain, bread and food, beds and bedding, utensils and clothing, necessary for seven days." The emissaries had acted in the spirit of the regulation that required the widow to reveal all her assets to the *kolelot*, including the most insignificant.[74] The mourner was supplied with sufficient food for the week of mourning only. According to Jewish law, the creditors have priority over the widow, and if the husband's assets are mortgaged, she forfeits her *ketubah*, all or part; after the mourning period, the rabbinical court will compensate the creditors and award the widow one-third of her *ketubah* payment in exchange for her signed undertaking to relinquish the rest of her *ketubah* payment. In the case of the widow Nechmad, the rabbis accused the widow of maligning them and heaping ridicule on the rabbis of Tiberias: "All her words are lies and libel . . . while they treated her generously and justly." The Ashkenazic rabbis joined the widow's accusers, as did the publisher of *Havazelet*. The story of Sarah Sheindel Nechmad illustrates both society's attitude to widows and her helpless state and total dependence on the male establishment.[75] The only recourse left her was the right to cry out.

In view of this appalling episode, one may well ponder the contradiction between the treatment of widows and the verse "The Lord watches over the stranger; He gives courage to the orphan and widow" (Ps. 146:9). The city of Jerusalem is compared in the Bible to a widow — "She that was great among nations is become like a widow" (Lam. 1:1) — but widows who lived in Jerusalem were treated with anything but compassion.

Agunot *(Deserted Wives)*

"There was an ancient custom in Jerusalem. When the bride and groom stood under the bridal canopy, among other things, the groom would give his word to the rabbi who was conducting the ceremony that he would not leave the country without the permission and agreement of the woman who was about to become his wife."[76] The various measures in Jewish law that were designed to avert the eventuality of a wife being deserted, by prohibiting her husband from going abroad without his wife's agreement, were thus additionally reinforced in Jerusalem. Nevertheless, even this ancient custom was inadequate. In Jewish law, a married woman whose husband has deserted her, or whose whereabouts are unknown for any reason, is known as an *agunah* (pl. *agunot*), a Hebrew word meaning literally a chained woman; an *agunah* is still considered to be married and cannot remarry until she receives a writ of divorce (*get*) — which only her husband can give her — or until proof of her husband's death be presented. No such law applies to men. The disappearance of family members — husbands from wives, children from parents — was a common occurrence, especially toward the end of the nineteenth century and beginning of the twentieth, as a consequence of the mass emigration movement of which the Jewish people were a part. The high incidence of *agunot* became an oppressive problem in Jerusalem and in general throughout the Land of Israel.

Mark Baker, in a study of the voice of the *agunah* as expressed in the journal *Hamaggid*, has identified economic motives as the main reason that husbands left home.[77] Poverty, he wrote, was created by child marriages, for when the young husbands were unable to support their families, they simply abandoned their equally young wives. Reena Sigman Friedman, who has studied the problem of wife desertion in American Jewish society, has called it the "poor man's divorce."[78] While attributing desertion by husbands to a variety of causes — dislike of one's wife and infatuation with another woman; economic hardship; family quarrels; or the desire for adventure — she nevertheless claims that the bond between the couple is the most important factor in a family crisis. Whatever the case, whether the reason for desertion was economic or psychosocial, the *agunah* was invariably the victim, a passive participant in a phenomenon that shaped her life.

The voices of *agunot* were first heard in the first modern Hebrew newspaper, *Hamaggid*, which was published in Lyck, eastern Prussia. In 1867, on the initiative of the editor, Eliezer Lipmann Silbermann, the last page of the newspaper was devoted to the appeals of *agunot* to locate their husbands. The appeals provide a rare opportunity to learn about their world.[79] Mark Baker, who has studied the pleas printed on that page, has estimated that most of the women did not actively search for their husbands, concentrating instead on publishing their names and trying to locate them from their own place of residence. Wide circulation of the runaway husband's name might not only help to locate him but would also punish him by embarrassing him in public. This was in fact the only punitive measure available to *agunot*. Does the large number of letters imply that this measure had some practical value, and that it had the desired effect? Or is it simply evidence of the writers' sense of frustration and helplessness? According to Baker, only 1 percent of cases of *agunot* were publicized; most cases remained unknown. Judging from the information at my disposal, very few of the runaways were ever found and gave their wives the sought-after divorce.

The large number of *agunot* all over the Jewish world in the second half of the nineteenth century attests to a crisis in Jewish family life and also to a dearth of authoritative leadership. *Hamaggid*, in addition to serving as a channel for publication of appeals, also provided as it were a "Wailing Wall" for women whose cries had gone unheard. Silbermann not only gave them a page in his newspaper but also wrote articles about their problem. The private domain, the home, had thus become a distinctly public concern.

The phenomenon of *agunot* in Jerusalem is reflected in letters, responsa, and the pages of local newspapers.[80] The hundreds of classified advertisements published in these papers demonstrate the suffering of the *agunot* then living in the Holy Land, who, like their sisters in the Diaspora, lacked the tools to deal with the problem. A typical example, an appeal by an official of the hakhnasat orhim society to the editor of *Ha'or*, expresses the writer's helplessness and profound loneliness: "Therefore, my dear sir, . . . , I pour out my tears before your honor, beseeching you to sympathize with my distress and come to my assistance"[81] — as if the editor was a wizard, who might be able to locate her husband through his many contacts. In another case, the publisher of *Havazelet* appealed in his paper to the publisher of *Hamaggid* to publish in his newspaper the name of a man who had escaped to Galatz (Galati) in Rumania.[82] In addition to such appeals by the *agunot* themselves, parents requesting assistance for their deserted daughters also advertised in the newspapers.[83] The announcements were not all of one cloth: some were laconic, giving only basic information,[84] while others told their sad stories in detail.

Emigration and economic hardship also caused children to abandon their parents. Mothers and fathers placed advertisements in Jerusalem newspapers, begging their sons and daughters for help.[85]

Very few *agunot* actually searched for their husbands. One of those few, as we learn from a letter to Moses Gaster, was the wife of Rabbi Nathan Halevi of Safed: "She has already journeyed to certain places in search of him, but to her dismay she has found no information as to his whereabouts."[86] Albert Antebi, the Jerusalem representative of Alliance Israélite Universelle, helped to finance the journey of an *agunah* from Jerusalem to Marseille to look for her husband.[87] The lack of means, plus the need to provide for little children, and the absence of any information whatsoever as to the whereabouts of the husband, prevented most women from taking that step.

The story of the *agunah* Rachel, daughter of Meir and Rivkah Lipa Anikster, mentioned previously, proves that everyone, not only the poor and socially deprived, could be affected by this particular problem. In addition, it demonstrates that there was no single main cause for husbands deserting their wives, financial or emotional. Rachel Anikster was born into a privileged family: her father was a public figure, her mother a highly literate woman, writer of the pamphlet *Kunteres zekher olam*. Rachel, the youngest child, who was born in Jerusalem, was described by Jerusalem memoirist Hayim Hamburger as an unpleasant woman: "She was a great nuisance, an incessant talker, and confused those who were praying in the community house."[88] (Was he trying to hint at some mental problem?). Her marriage was not successful, and her husband, Rabbi Shabbetai Fein, abandoned her, leaving her with their two children.[89] Hamburger wrote in his memoirs that Fein had left her "because he couldn't stand her," but Rachel herself wrote that economic problems had prompted him to leave home: "When my husband experienced trouble and hardship in my home, he wandered to faraway lands and abandoned me as a living widow."[90] Desertion was often caused by a combination of personal difficulties and economic hardship. The deserted Rachel compared herself to the city of Jerusalem as portrayed by the prophet Jeremiah in the book of Lamentations: "I [Rachel] am considered a living widow just [as] Jerusalem was considered a widow with none to comfort her."[91]

Rachel's story is told in her letters and those of her mother, which were sent to the Amsterdam administrators of *halukah* funds requesting help. Finding it difficult to raise her children on her own, Rachel bewailed her troubles: "My young son . . . is diligently learning Torah but I have not the wherewithal to provide him with bread. And my daughter, a child orphaned of her father, needs doctors and medicine and my house is bare."[92] Her widowed mother took care of Rachel and her children, who lived with her in Jerusalem: "I get bickering and grief from my flesh and blood, my *agunah* daughter. My son-in-law Shabbetai saw the difficulty at home and feared that the orphans would be a weight around his neck."[93] Only after many years did Rachel secure a divorce from her husband, but this did not improve her economic situation.

Clearly, then, husband desertion was likely to occur in all strata of society, communities, and sectors. The higher the social status of the *agunah*, the greater and more profound was the fall.

Another instructive example is provided by an official (*gabbai'it*) of the Hakhnasat Orhim society in Jerusalem, which extended aid to many of Jerusalem's poor, whose husband deserted her. She expressed her fear that she would become "an object of scorn and ridicule among my enemies and detractors, who are seeking any opportunity to harm me and rejoice in my troubles."[94] The study house known as Bet Midrash ha'Agunah [literally, Study House of the Agunah"] in the Old City attests to the incidence of this plague even among the wealthy. The house was donated by a wealthy but childless *agunah* who had immigrated to Jerusalem with her husband, but he disappeared. The first floor of the house served as a haven for the poor, and the study house was on the top floor.[95]

As to the "deserting husband," here too there was no "typical" profile. Mark Baker has described the average eastern European "deserting husband," on the basis of the *Hamaggid* newspaper, as a young man between the ages of twenty and thirty-five, a craftsman, married for only a few years.[96] The average type that emerges from Jerusalem newspapers is of a man aged between twenty and forty, married for only a few years and unemployed, who had gone off to some unknown destination.[97] A good many of these deserting husbands were unscrupulous rogues. For example, a newspaper item of 1897 reports one Moshe b. Yosef Halevi who abandoned not only his first wife but also his second wife.[98] One document concerning an *agunah* who lived in Safed describes the husband in harsh language: "A man of wicked deeds, of whom it has been told that he fell into bad ways"[99] — this person sought refuge under the aegis of Christian missionaries. Another husband from Safed turned out to be a professional forger of documents;[100] yet another robbed his wife of her jewelry and disappeared.[101] On the other hand, perfectly respectable members of society could also abandon their wives on occasion. Among such offenders were an emissary (*shadar*) of the North African community, Yosef

Abuhav, who traveled to England and the United States;[102] an emissary (*shadar*) of the Hebron community, R. Zalman b. R. Menachem, who disappeared on the way to Constantinople;[103] and a Torah scribe who made leather boxes (*batim*) for phylacteries.[104] We also have reports of distinguished scholars, converts to Judaism, and a blind scholar from Hebron.[105]

One of the prime reasons for husbands' desertion was of course a souring of the relationship between husband and wife. Many of the stories are similar: a Sephardic couple who were known for their quarrels;[106] a shoemaker who became rich, took a fancy to another woman, stole his wife's belongings, and went off to Europe;[107] a man who, constantly bickering with his wife, was ordered by the Sephardic religious court to pay her upkeep, and soon ran off.[108] Sometimes other family members were responsible for conflicts between couples.[109] In some cases, the husband was mentally ill.[110]

Leaving home was not always understood as an escape or as an irreparable rift. At times the abandoned wife felt empathy for her husband, believing that he had left the country with the honest intention of finding a source of income for his family.[111] A woman named Toive Zissel declared that her husband had not left her willingly but because of a disaster: "Not in a rebellious or treacherous fashion does my unfortunate husband refrain from writing to me. Only his misfortune has brought about this situation and he is in a very terrible state." She related that he had traveled to his family in Dinaburg but lost his money on the way, and this "seriously affected his state of mind and impaired his sanity."[112] In a letter written in 1912 by Dr. Yitzhak Levy, director of the Anglo-Palestine Bank in Jerusalem, about soup kitchens in the city, he mentions that hundreds of men had left their families because of compulsory army service, and their families were practically starving.[113]

There were many destinations for runaway men: Cairo,[114] Marseille, Amsterdam, England, Rumania, North Africa, the American continent. The Land of Israel was also a destination for escape, for instance, for Reuben, a resident of Edirna, who threatened the religious court in Jerusalem that, should they refuse his demand to divorce his wife, who had remained in his home, he would abandon her without granting her a divorce.[115] The wife of Eliahu, a convert from the Caucasus, thought he was living in one of the settlements of the Upper Galilee, which later indeed became a haven for converts from that region.[116]

As far as we can tell from the various newspaper items and letters, the husband's absence varied in duration from one to several years.[117] In one case a disappearance lasting thirteen years was reported.[118] Even after more than ten years, women did not lose hope that their husbands would be found. As to the size of the families of *agunot*, the wording of the appeals for help does not help to determine even an average figure. One would expect that, the greater the suffering of the *agunah*, the greater would be her efforts to publicize her sorry fate. However, a woman with children would frequently have her hands full in merely coping with her difficult condition, so that she had little time to engage in "public relations" and quickly became accustomed to a life of dependence. The trauma of her companion's disappearance without a trace could embitter and disappoint the woman, and at times even impair her mental health.[119] *Agunot* generally returned to their parental homes, and even when they managed to earn a meager living on their own,[120] they were still living in straitened circumstances.

Most of the women did not seek their husband's return home but rather a divorce.[121] As the wife of Nathan Halevi of Safed told the local rabbis, she would forgo the alimony and obligations of her *ketubah* if he could not afford it, because her only desire was to be released from the bonds of her status as an *agunah*.[122] A wealthy *agunah*, a Sephardic woman of Jerusalem whose Ashkenazic husband had absconded, managed to buy her writ of divorce "by wasting large amounts of money and bribes."[123] Sometimes the man was found, divorce proceedings were initiated, but he again ran off and the search began anew.[124] Perhaps the few *agunot* who asked to have their husband return home did so only as a matter of course, but did not really expect that to happen in reality.[125]

Both in the Land of Israel and elsewhere, *agunot* found themselves in a desperate situation: deep poverty, which sometimes brought them to the brink of prostitution (in their case — adultery) and abandonment of their children, who were put into orphanages.[126] A Halakhic question sent from Tiberias tells the story of an *agunah* whose husband went to a foreign country, and rumor had it that she had become a prostitute.[127]

In 1905, a Committee for the Protection of Deserted Wives and Children was established in the United States. Its purpose was to locate men who had disappeared and if possible ensure their return home and effect a reconciliation; if this proved impossible, the committee would try to obtain a divorce for the wife and give her financial help. Jewish law considers the "release" of *agunot* a sacred obligation: "Whosoever releases an *agunah*, it is as though he has rebuilt one of the ruins of Jerusalem."[128] At times the religious court allied itself to the *agunah*'s plea, and at times it published an appeal of its own.[129] Newspapers frequently referred to *agunot* as "that miserable woman."[130] At the beginning of the twentieth century, as the authorities were able to exert greater control over sea travel, when suspicion arose that a husband might attempt to escape via Jaffa Port, the court would appeal to the Ottoman government and request that he be detained.[131] As a rule, however, the religious courts in Palestine, as in other places, were powerless.

The Halakhic status of the *agunah* is an example of a gender-related phenomenon par excellence: the man takes off, leaving the woman helpless at home. The reverse, where the woman abandons her husband without notice or without leaving an address, is extremely rare. A letter published in *Havazelet* under the headline "To Restore a Merciful Mother to Her Children" sought to locate a mother for the sake of her children in Kovno. Bluma, daughter of Rabbi Zevi, had left her husband and children and gone to her relatives to seek financial help, and they had since lost trace of her. Her family appealed to the readers of *Havazelet*, in the belief that Bluma had headed for the Land of Israel.[132] Another case is evident from an item published in 1895 in *Hazevi*. A woman of about seventy came to Palestine as a lone immigrant, introduced herself as a widow, and was married in Safed. However, the Hasidic rabbi of Vizhnitz made it known that her husband was alive, and that she had left home after quarreling with him.[133] These two pieces of information are the only evidence I have found of abandoned men, as against most copious evidence of *agunot*. To my mind, women's reluctance to leave their husbands cannot be attributed to fear of the dangers of travel; hundreds, if not thousands, of single women set out for the Holy Land in the nineteenth century, undeterred by the hazards. Rather, one might say that the phenomenon of the *agunah* is incontrovertible evidence of a woman's absolute commitment to her family. Thus, women's most admired and valued quality, their loyalty to their families, was also their greatest vulnerability.

Shlomo Naftali Hertz Jonas, Eliezer Ben-Yehuda's father-in-law, published a poem titled *"Hokhmat nashim"* (Wisdom of Women) in the journal *Ha'or*, in which he pointed out the status of women in the conjugal relationship: The decision as to whether a marriage should be continued or not is exclusively in the husband's hands. It is the man who gives his wife a divorce — or goes off and disappears in the far reaches of the universe. The poem likens women to servants, bending the knee before their husbands, who rule over them. Their only consolation is the thought that "perhaps some day they may become widows."[134] By implication, marital life is compared to chains on a woman's hands, and desertion by her husband is merely a padlock on those chains. A husband, having deserted his wife, can totally cut himself off from his family and friends, from his past, his country, and his profession. It is not unusual, even today, for a runaway husband to change his name and take on a new identity. On the one hand, desertion is an indication of weakness, of inability to grapple with reality; on the other, it is also a kind of show of strength, the beginning of a new life. His unfortunate wife, however, remains where she is, and her identity acquires an additional attribute: being an *agunah*. While her husband, as already mentioned, may not infrequently adopt a new identity, remarry, and establish a new family, his wife is barred from opening a new chapter in her life. For women, desertion by the husband was a one-way street.

One journalist portrayed Jerusalem as a city of mourning, not because of the destroyed Temple, but rather because of the ruined households within its confines. Among the tales of desertion and privation that he published were those of a young woman, with a babe in arms, whose husband abandoned her and went off to Africa; of elderly parents whose son left them to go to America; and of an *agunah* with five children whose husband set sail for Australia.[135]

In sum, the breakup of a family was also a sign of social disintegration. Desertion of one's family was also desertion of the Land of Israel, that is, emigration. The ancient Jerusalem custom mentioned at the beginning of this section, requiring the bridegroom to undertake under the bridal canopy never to leave the city without his bride's permission, proved to be a rather ineffective solution. One's impression from the available evidence is that the lack of any positive emotional bond between the couple was the basic reason for such breakdowns, but material hardship provided the fuel that lit the fire. The insight of the editor of *Hamaggid*, based on his survey of the contemporary Jewish press, regarding the nature of the crisis that seized Jewish society in eastern Europe in the nineteenth century was also valid for the Holy Land: "Corruption, poverty, and ignorance thus started in the home and were transmitted like a disease from parent to child."[136] These words have a special resonance in view of the declared aim of Jerusalem's leaders to create a unique, sacred society.

Prostitution

Prostitution is a complex human phenomenon, almost an embodiment of feminine passivity and weakness. Not always engaged in out of necessity, it is sometimes a result of choice.[137] The practice of prostitution provides, as it were, female confirmation of the traditional male perception of women as essentially materially oriented, hence also unequivocal support for the perception of women's sensual power. Prostitution is simply the transfer of those feminine-materialistic forces from the private to the public domain. The prevailing opinion is that prostitution is intimately connected with a crisis situation. Scholarly studies of the phenomenon do not always indicate a link with a specific communal or cultural background; there is generally, however, a background of poverty, immigration, family crisis, and a low level of intelligence.[138] At the same time, prostitution is not associated with a negative stigma all over the world. The perception that sex drive is an expression only of masculinity is consistent with the idea that, in some cases, prostitution is a feminine form of exerting power, of defiance, of building a new identity. Whatever the case may be, however, women turning to prostitution were ostracized by the community and relegated to the fringes of society.

Immigration, transition from one culture to another, and impoverished living strengthened the phenomenon of prostitution in Jewish society in eastern Europe and in the New World toward the end of the nineteenth century and beginning of the twentieth.[139] Scholars dealing with this phenomenon stress that, despite the moralistic image of Jewish society, prostitution existed and was even common among Jews in modern times. However, many Jewish communities have denied its existence.[140] Studies of the subject among Jews the world over reveal that the proportion of Jewish women working in this "profession" was high as compared with that of non-Jews, perhaps owing to the urban character of prostitution and of Jewish society. White slavery was highly developed in the Jewish world; it brought Jewish girls from eastern Europe to North and South America, to East Asia, and to the Mediterranean region. Awareness of the severity of the problem at the beginning of the twentieth century prompted the founding of specialized Jewish organizations in London and Germany that applied themselves to the issue.[141] Prostitution being of course a distinctively gender-related phenomenon, the treatment of the problem was initiated primarily by women, but they depended on male support.

Echoes of the worldwide scourge of Jewish prostitution were also heard in the Holy City, and the topic came up for discussion in the Jerusalem press.[142] The publishers of the information intended to warn the local community, "so that our brethren of Israel may know to watch out and be warned of this trap set to catch their daughters by evildoers who, to our great dismay, come from our own Jewish people."[143] However, this attempt to bring the problem of prostitution within Jerusalem society into the open was almost inevitably doomed to failure. The subject is absent from almost all memoirs written over the period in question, and was only very meagerly documented in the press. The story of prostitutes in the Holy City is the story of a cover-up, and I cannot possibly estimate the extent of the phenomenon. We may assume that it was wider than what might be thought from the few sources that have been preserved. The fall into prostitution was such a profound blot on the community that everyone refrained from mentioning it. Jerusalem society was concerned first and foremost with its public image.

An example of the way Jerusalem society handled illicit sexual behavior is revealed in the report of a rape incident in *Hashkafah*. In November 1903 the paper published a report of a Yeshivah student who raped a seven-year-old girl in Jerusalem. Contrary to what might have been expected, the child's mother, far from remaining silent, brought her complaint to the rabbis, obliging them to deal with it.[144] This action in itself attests to the mother's initiative and courage. The usual veil of silence was in this case replaced by condemnation. A week later, *Hashkafah* reported on reactions to the article. The publication of the rape indeed rocked the community — not because of the incident itself, but rather because of the publicity. According to the journalist, readers feared that "since all the Hebrew press copy its reports [of *Hashkafah*] . . . and it will be publicized throughout the world, and the name of the Holy City will be defamed [deprecated], it must be denied in this same *Hashkafah*, so that the whole world will know that it is untrue." The readers clearly thought that the true story should be denied, lest the good name of the Holy City be dese-crated, and in fact it was suggested that the editor of the journal be punished: "The wicked editor of the journal who has published this thing and brought insult to Jerusalem should be excommunicated . . . and outlawed." The jour-nalist condemned this demand to suppress the news, unpleasant as it was. The city's good name, he suggested, was not sullied by the sin of one individ-ual, but by any attempt to conceal the deed "in order to defend the honor of one person."[145]

The newspaper also pointed out that, in keeping with biblical law, not the daughter but rather her father would be indemnified. Everything about this event exemplifies the complete and utter disregard of the Jerusalem commu-nity for the female victim and the physical and emotional violence done to her, and society's instinctive tendency to mask its shady fringes and present it-self as a pure and holy community.[146]

The disregard of a woman's plight, the concentration of attention exclu-sively on male society, is characteristic of the ultra-religious community's at-titude toward a woman practicing prostitution. The prevailing opinion was that a woman who had strayed from the path should be severely punished and expelled from the city. Evidence of this approach is found in a letter sent in 1865 by the heads of Kolel Galicia to the Austrian consul, reporting the case of a woman with Austrian citizenship who was receiving strange men in her home. The *kolel* obtained travel money for her and requested the consul to help them ensure that she left the city. The *hakham bashi*, Rabbi Hayim David Hazan, attached his own request to the letter, reasoning that "in cases such as these . . . we are commanded to eradicate wickedness from our midst and banish her from the country."[147] The community had apparently been loath to punish the woman themselves, as she was an Austrian citizen; expul-sion, however, was an accepted procedure and was carried out in coordina-tion with the authorities.[148] As far as ensuring sexual morality was concerned, the Jewish community and the Ottoman authorities were in complete agree-ment — a rare situation in itself.

Such cooperation is also evident in a story about women who had opened a bar that functioned as a house of prostitution, thus violating the moral prin-ciples of the local society, both Jewish and Muslim. A rabbinical court was convened, and the women were summoned and ordered to close the establishment; their heads were shaved as a sign of disgrace.[149] Unlike the punishment meted out to an adulteress, the punishment was not carried out in public; only "a few men and women from the market gathered and stood" to watch old women shave the offending women's heads. The proceedings were supervised by police officers, to ensure that the crowd would not physically assault the humiliated women. The attitude of the community to women who violated the norm was thus reiterated: since they had injured the Holy City's good name, there could be only one verdict — they had to suffer injury. The Ottoman authorities cooperated with the Jewish community and helped them to send away these women.[150]

Nonetheless, punishment and banishment could not eradicate prostitution, and the press, which had taken upon itself the responsibility for reforming Jerusalem society, had no scruples about publishing further news items and thereby besmirching the name of the Holy City. In autumn 1906 it reported the existence of a Jewish house of prostitution: "Two prostitutes of our people have had a brothel on the Street of the Jews for several years."[151] The laconic item indicates merely that the two women had been in business for several years. No attention was given to the human aspect of the story but only to the successful cooperation between the head of the Lay Committee of the Sephardic community and the local police in order to banish these women from the city. The story ends with a kind of sigh of relief: "Shame and disgrace have been removed from the Jewish community in Jerusalem." The columnist identified with the typical Jerusalem attitude: wanting to rid the city of this scourge, paying no attention whatever to the problem of the women.

A similar tale is told in Sha'ul Angel-Malachi's anthology of folk stories. A young woman of Jerusalem opened a brothel on the Street of the Karaites in the Old City, and the community was abuzz. The young woman had connections with the authorities, and the Jewish community did not have the power to expel her. Only the intervention of a charismatic rabbi had an effect on the young woman and, following his request, she left the Old City. Angel-Malachi puts the following words in the rabbi's mouth: "My daughter, you are aware that Jerusalem is a holy city, and your establishment violates the sanctity of the place. I beg you to leave the city for the sake of the honor of the Torah."[152] This folk story indeed describes — for the first time — a personal appeal to a prostitute; nevertheless, the rabbi's concern is for the city, not for the young woman. Once again, the Holy City rejects those who dishonor its sanctity; possibly, the young woman's agreement to move indicates that she, too, accepts this approach.

Only at the beginning of the twentieth century did society begin to consider the plight of such women and consider ways of preventing prostitution. Public consciousness was presumably aroused due to the deterioration of the situation, as well as reports of similar activities overseas. The letterhead of the General Orphanage for Girls, founded in Jerusalem in 1902, lists among the institution's aims saving "Jewish orphan girls from starvation, from being sold into prostitution and disgrace, and from conversion."[153] The problem had become so serious as to warrant the formulation of new methods to deal with such girls. The foundation of the school was a preventive, since it cared for the girls' material needs, as well as providing them with a basic education. Research into the causes of prostitution in modern times has revealed that besides poverty and processes of emigration, an important factor in the development of prostitution has been a lack of education.[154] The founders of the first orphanage for girls in Jerusalem regarded education, be it only the most basic, as a primary weapon for the prevention of prostitution. However, even though the first signs of a shift in attitudes to prostitution were evident, there was no overall solution.

The Threat of the Mission

Poverty, widowhood, and wife desertion were a kind of slippery slope that often led to crime or conversion. On one occasion, for example, the religious court of the *hakham bashi* dealt with the case of "two poor women who were neighbors, both widows, the firstborn son of one of whom was wicked and evil and wavered from the straight path . . . and stole some things . . . and converted."[155] This unusual story points to the potential for moral deterioration inherent in poor and single-parent families. Poverty, widowhood, desertion, and prostitution provided fertile ground for extensive missionary activity in the Holy City, some aimed specifically at women.

Ludwig August Frankl, the secretary of the Vienna Jewish Community, who visited the Land of Israel in 1856, was horrified by the scene he witnessed: "So where else can you find a community of Jews anywhere in the world, even one of the largest, which could compete in this respect with the city of Jerusalem, so that one sees there one hundred and thirty-one apostate Jews assembled in one Christian school?"[156] The large number and prominence of converts in the Holy City, some of whom had come to the Land of Israel as workers and emissaries of the mission, incensed Frankl, but he was no less infuriated by the forgiving attitude of Jerusalem society toward them. He blamed the Jews of the city for not going all out against the phenomenon of apostasy and for the fact that their families did not cut off relations with them: the apostate would visit his or her family, eat with them, and they would refer to him or her respectfully with a Hebrew name, as if nothing had happened.[157]

Frankl was not alone in his impression.[158] An article in *Hazevi* also denounced this attitude: "Behold! Elsewhere, it is prohibited to have any contact whatsoever with apostate inciters, and even the lowest of the low would not associate with them; but here in our Holy Land, apostates and in-citers . . . visit our homes and the homes of our scholars, they are our physicians and our confidants, they are the consolers of our widows and those who protect and raise our orphans."[159] And indeed, the missionary Moses Friedlander remarked that his work was practically undisturbed by the Jewish community. Should this apparently forgiving attitude be understood in light of the rapid increase of conversion in eastern Europe in the nineteenth century, or only against the background of local difficulties?[160]

The religious tension experienced by immigrants to the Holy City, combined with their considerable emotional and economic distress, provided fertile ground for missionary influence. Such a high concentration of missionary institutions and of men of the cloth longing to spread the Christian message was unique to Jerusalem. Messianic sentiments, particularly in the evangelistic Christian sects, both in Europe and in the United States in the nineteenth century, had a tremendous impact on religious activity in the Holy Land. The establishment at that time of many consulates in Jerusalem also provided an incentive for the intensive Christian activity.[161]

The Ottoman regime prohibited conversion to Christianity of Muslim citizens, but not of foreign nationals or of its non-Muslim citizens.[162] The establishment of the London Society for Promoting Christianity amongst the Jews at the beginning of the nineteenth century intensified Christian activity among the Jews of the Land of Israel, which was common to all the Christian denominations.[163] The continual increase of the Jewish population in Jerusalem offered a golden opportunity for the many Christian institutions operating in the region.[164] Many mission workers came to Israel, among them a not insignificant number of Jewish converts. The newcomers did not come empty-handed, and the funds they brought with them to the Holy City made their mark. The journal *Tidings from Zion*, a missionary paper published in Jerusalem, unabashedly admitted that assistance was given in order to encourage the needy to convert to Christianity.[165] Nevertheless, as remarked by the Arab historian Tibawi: "the missionaries . . . did not seek, and apparently, did not gain immediate converts. They merely hoped that those who received material benefits might become 'more accessible to Christian missionary influence.'"[166] Both contemporary visitors to the country and later scholars, who have devoted little attention to the subject, agree that, despite the gargantuan efforts of the mission, the number of converts was relatively small, though one should not belittle its impact.[167] The mission was active in three areas: medicine, financial assistance, and education. Its most significant influence was on the neediest population: the poor, the sick, and the lonely. The wave of immigrants that came to the Holy Land at the beginning of the 1880s was a target for intense missionary activity that even produced an agricultural settlement at Artuf (Har Tuv)-which was abandoned after a short time.[168]

The mission's concentration on the weakest link in society — women — answered to the needs of the target as well as to those of the missionaries themselves, who sought to demonstrate their ability.[169] Missionary work among Jewish women was often the work of women, whether of female missionaries working on their own or of male missionaries' wives.[170] Several organizations targeting Jewish women in the East were founded by female missionaries in the nineteenth century. This activity stemmed from the prevailing notion that women are agents for change.[171] The conversion of women was considered to be particularly significant, as a preliminary to the eventual conversion of the entire Jewish people.

Jewish women's appeals to missionary institutions had contradictory aspects: On the one hand, they had no scruples about accepting favors from the mission, whether medical aid or education for their children in mission schools. On the other hand, they did not regard such actions as necessarily implying conversion. In all matters concerning conversion to Christianity, the general assumption, both of contemporaries and of later scholars, was that women in particular were less willing to take this extreme step than men. This dual attitude to missionary activity may also explain the complex attitude of male society in Jerusalem to the ramified Christian activity. The Jews of the Holy City, who were always dependent on outside help, did not consider accepting aid as a form of submission or obligatory dependence. Their motto was "Take whatever's given," and they felt no special obligation to the givers. Their belief in their unique merits reinforced their belief that they would not sink into the missionaries' clutches.

Help from the Mission: Medicine, Employment, Education

Medical institutions were the crowning achievement of the mission in the Land of Israel.[172] Inadequate sanitation, combined with epidemics and other illnesses, as well as a lack of doctors and medications, characterized the Jewish community right up to the end of the Ottoman period. It is true that beginning in the 1840s, in the wake of missionary activity, Jewish doctors financed by European philanthropists did come to the Holy City, but this was not sufficient.[173] Avraham Gruenbaum, as mentioned before, visited the Land of Israel in 1885 in order to found a Jewish hospital. At the time, there were already three functioning Jewish hospitals in the city. He deplored the large numbers of Jews who sought the services of the English Mission Hospital: "Unfortunately, our wretched brethren are still obliged to find refuge in the English Mission. I visited this institution and found almost all of the beds occupied. On days when outpatient clinics are open, it is almost impossible to pass on the street because of the crowds of people coming for treatment."[174] A year later, a reporter for *Hazevi* gave a similar description of the crowds lined up in front of the physician's room at the English Hospital.[175]

The preference for the medical institutions of the mission was due to quite prosaic reasons: medical treatment and medications were dispensed free of charge, and the staff's attitude was friendly and welcoming.[176] Christian nuns, too, were not averse to any kind of communal medical activity; they would go as far as Silwan (Shiloah) village to treat the Yemenites living there and to distribute medicines free of charge.[177] The mission workers were mindful of the specific religious requirements of Jews: there were *mezuzot* on the doors of the English Hospital, the food was kosher[178] and prepared by Jews, the staff included Jewish nurses; there was even a small synagogue on the premises. During the Sukkot festival a *sukkah* (booth) was built for the patients, and the four species (the plants needed for the festival ritual) were distributed to those interested.[179] Missionary activity was not always obvious, and only the presence of New Testaments hinted at the nature of the institution.[180] The goal of the mission — to attract Jews to its institutions — was accomplished in no small degree.[181] In Galilee, too, hospitals were established to attract Jews to Christian institutions.[182] Despite the sharp disapproval of the missionaries constantly expressed by Jewish leaders, the Christian hospitals fulfilled an important purpose for the Jewish community, men and women.[183] Since medical services were directed at men and women alike, it is difficult to ascertain to what extent there may have been a difference in men's and women's dependence on them. Unlike medical services, however, vocational training and educational institutions were organized on a gender basis, thus providing a more far-reaching view of women's dependence on the mission.

Both the missionaries and the British consul believed that the Jews of Jerusalem should be accustomed to work for their living.[184] Ellen Clare Miller, a British woman who toured the East in the second half of the nineteenth century, expressed this policy unequivocally: "There is perhaps hardly any agency, after the school, which might do so much for the elevation of the country as mothers' meetings and sewing schools for the women."[185] And indeed, a not insignificant number of Jewish women participated and worked daily over a period of many years in Miss Caroline Cooper's workshop, which was innovative in many ways. In her memoirs, Elizabeth Finn, the energetic wife of the British consul, documented her first meeting with Miss Cooper — a convert to Christianity — who put the following question to her: What could she do in the Holy City? Caroline Cooper answered her own question, undertaking to open a sewing and embroidery workshop for Jewish women.

Cooper opened a workshop, where Jewish women with no previous knowledge of sewing could acquire a new profession.[186] The idea of encouraging women to leave their homes for a public workshop, located in a special building, in order to earn money from their craft, was quite revolutionary.[187] Their handiwork was sold in a special store, the profits being used to cover the costs of production. In her memoirs, Elizabeth Finn emphasizes the women's high work ethic: they reported for work at sunrise and worked diligently until midday.[188] Miss Cooper was not content merely to work with these women, and she opened a school on the premises for their daughters in the afternoon hours, teaching them general studies and sewing.[189] There was a dormitory adjacent to the school where students received kosher food and clothing. However, productivity, financial assistance, and education were not Miss Cooper's only goals. While the Jewish women were busy working, her assistants would read them chapters from the New Testament in Hebrew, Ladino, and Arabic.[190] Within a short time there were thirty women in the workshop. Its success raised the ire of the rabbis, and they issued a *herem* (writ of excommunication) against the institution.[191]

Elizabeth Finn, who described the events, noted that such actions followed a regular pattern: initiative and innovation on the part of Christians was inevitably followed by an attack by the rabbinic establishment. In the first stage the attackers held sway, but the women recovered rapidly and frequently won out in the end. Finn quotes the working women's reaction in her memoirs: "We cannot let our children starve if there is work to be done."[192] While the basic object of the workshop was to bring about a revolution in women's lives, enabling them to leave home, work for their living, and engage in religious studies,[193] there was an added dimension, namely, a revolt against the male-rabbinic establishment.

Surprisingly, we find no mention at all of Miss Cooper's workshop in memoirs written by contemporary Jews. If the institution was indeed a harbinger of revolution for Jerusalem women, why is there no trace of its influence? And if its influence was minimal, how can that be explained? And what can we learn from the relatively silent opposition of the rabbinic establishment?[194] The answer probably lies in the relatively small scope of the project, and even more so in the nature of the population of women who frequented the place. Judging from the evidence in Consul Finn's memoirs, it appears that the salary of a young woman who worked there was barely sufficient to buy food, certainly not to buy herself new clothes.[195] The workshop, which was self-sufficient in its first years and did not depend on support from the mission,[196] provided work for women but did not effect the hoped-for change in their social condition.

Up until the 1880s, the languages spoken at Miss Cooper's workshop were Ladino and Arabic, indicating that the workers were illiterate Sephardic women and women of the Eastern communities.[197] In Billie Melman's view, the evangelists believed that the Sephardic Jews were the true descendants of the Jews of biblical times. We may assume that the New Testament readings had only a minimal influence on their religious beliefs. As to Miss Cooper and the London Society, which took over the institution after her death, they clearly believed that women's education was a primary means toward social progress in general. However, their efforts did not bring about a revolution in Jerusalem society, nor, indeed, were they an effective agent for innovation. While Miss Cooper's workshop impressed occasional visitors from England,[198] the Jews dismissed it as a project for the socially inferior.

Cooper's workshop was the most prominent Christian enterprise targeting the women of the Old Yishuv, but not the only one. Various other missionary initiatives sought to provide gainful employment for Jewish women in Jerusalem.[199] The missionaries' wives also looked for other avenues to attract Jewish women in the Holy City. They toured the remotest and poorest neighborhoods, befriended Jewish women in order to attract their children to Christian schools,[200] and gave money to men and women in difficulty, widows, and the poor.

The journal *Hazevi* gives us an idea of the feelings of Jewish women employed by the mission and of their families. A reporter describing a visit to the home of a poor family who worked for the mission indicates that the family was indeed somewhat ashamed, but less so than families of young women employed as servants in Jewish households. According to women who worked making lace, their chances of making a "good match" were better than those of girls who worked as housemaids: "We will do work . . . of any sort, but we will not be servants."[201]

In 1913 the *Jewish Chronicle* published a description of a procession of Jewish girls wearing crosses on their chests, accompanied by their teacher, a nun, at one of the mission schools in Jerusalem. The description focuses attention on what had become a routine phenomenon: hundreds of Jewish girls were attending Christian schools in the Holy City.[202] In the 1880s, British consul Noel Temple Moore reported that there were more educational institutions, of every type, in Jerusalem than in any other city of similar size in the entire Ottoman Empire.[203] Girls' education was indeed one of the guiding principles of missionary policy worldwide.[204] The London Society's school was so eager to acquire Jewish pupils that it provided kosher meals, Jewish prayer, and Hebrew lessons.[205] Teachers at the Soeurs de Sion Catholic School, however, were more explicit in their efforts to teach the basics of Christianity.[206] In addition, they also offered courses in general studies, in English and French, as well as handicrafts and domestic science. Tuition, food, and clothing were free of charge, and further financial assistance was also sometimes forthcoming. Alfred Cohen, representative of the Anglo-Jewish Association, who visited Jerusalem in 1894, also surveyed the mission schools. He had the impression that the Protestant schools of the London Society were making no direct efforts to convert the girls against their parents' wishes. Nevertheless, he pointed out the profound moral degeneration of young girls whose education was guided by neither Jewish nor Christian principles but by "constant hypocrisy."[207]

The various Christian schools in Jerusalem toward the end of the nineteenth and beginning of the twentieth centuries were attended by about two hundred Jewish girls each year.[208] From a survey of the abundant information published in the Hebrew press just before the First World War, it is clear that the number of Jewish girls attending mission schools was somewhat higher than the number of boys.[209] It would seem that since the obligation to study Torah did not apply to girls, their parents had no scruples about sending them to Christian schools. While at that time several Jewish schools for girls were already active, all the Jewish communities were nevertheless represented at the mission schools: Sephardic, Ashkenazic, and Eastern communities.[210]

Undoubtedly, the most common motivation for sending girls to the mission schools was financial, and indeed, most of the students came from poor families, Sephardic and Eastern: "It is well known that the girls . . . are all from the most poverty-stricken, degraded families, daughters of the rabble."[211] David Weingarten, director of the Jerusalem Orphan Home for Girls, was familiar with the situation: "For the net of the Mission is abundantly spread throughout the Holy Land, and there are abandoned Jewish orphan girls with no-one to support them. Hence they were easily caught in the net of those accursed evil-doers."[212] We may assume that the male and female converts among those who studied in mission educational institutions were mainly homeless and had been entrusted to the nuns at an early age.

Single women, especially divorcées or *agunot* (and at times also single men), found that sending their daughters (or sons) to the mission could solve their financial difficulties with regard to the education of their children.[213] There were also cases of orphans or abandoned girls who reached the gates of the mission on their own initiative.[214] Parents' willingness to send their daughters to mission schools was also fueled by the lack of space in Jewish schools, as well as high esteem for the quality of Christian education.[215] In her memoirs, Julia Chelouche, who attended Christian schools in Jaffa, describes a well-endowed institution, which gave its students private lessons if necessary, as well as enrichment studies in musical instruments and singing.[216] Some parents even *preferred* to send their daughters to Christian schools, rather than expose them to the *Haskalah* (Jewish Enlightenment) in a Jewish school that had been banned.[217] In fact, disapproving accounts of the mission in the

Jerusalem press seemed to consider sending girls to such schools as less critical than sending boys.[218] Presumably, underlying the permissive attitude to
the education of Jewish girls in mission institutions was the traditional Jewish
disregard for girls' education.

Were parents indeed not afraid that their daughters' attendance at Christian
schools might lead to their conversion? The principal of the London Society
school admitted that about 10 percent of the girls attending the school converted to Christianity, and that in the Catholic school the conversion rate was
higher.[219] Nevertheless, the missionary Moses Friedlander told the story of an
immigrant couple who sent their children to a mission school because the
mother was not apprehensive of Christian influence and felt that her children
would remain Jews.[220] In contrast, *Havazelet* published reports of parents who
regretted having taken that step, once they realized that the missionaries had
alienated their children from themselves and their fellow Jews.[221]

Parents began to have reservations about educating their children in mission schools only after realizing that what they had thought to be an innocent
step was but the beginning of a path of no return, namely, conversion to
Christianity. By the time they had reached this bitter conclusion, they were
powerless. Economic hardship, which was common to all members of the
Jewish community in Jerusalem, seems to have blinded both communal leaders and parents.

Conversion

According to various estimates, the number of Jews who converted in Jerusalem during these years can be counted in the hundreds.[222] Conversion to
Christianity in Jerusalem was interpreted by the Christians as proof positive
of the justice of their path, by the Jews as a shameful religious failure. Ludwig
August Frankl pointed to the payment offered by Jerusalem missionaries to
potential converts, adding that these payments were higher in the Holy City
than anywhere else in the world.[223] The common metaphor for missionary
activity was "golden nets," which were spread out to "catch rotten fish."[224]
This metaphor reflects the modus operandi of the missionaries and the general opinion of the personality of the converts. Most Jews who converted were
described in accounts written by Jews as marginal men and women, who saw
in Christianity or (very few) in Islam[225] a means of improving their material
lot in this world: only very few were thought to be seeking to save their souls
in the World to Come.[226] A comparison of the motivation for conversion of
Jews in the Holy Land with the motivation for conversion in czarist Russia
during the same period indicates that in Russia, too, most of the converts

came from the margins of society, desperate people who sought relief for their distress in the Christian society that accepted them.[227] The question as to whether women were "easier prey" than men for missionaries in Jerusalem is clearly answered by Mordechai Eliav, in his study of the lives of several famous Jerusalem converts. He points out that, in many cases, the wife was not prepared to follow her husband and was more devoted than he to Judaism.[228] This positive evaluation of the piety of Jerusalem Jewesses recalls similar evaluations of the deep loyalty of women to Judaism during the years of the Inquisition in Spain and even after the Expulsion.[229]

The conversion of Jewish women in Jerusalem to Christianity reflects not only on their religious piety but also on family life — their relationships with their husbands, their children, and their parents. Many were the channels that led Jewish women to Christianity. A few arrived on their own initiative, others chose the step out of desperation, and still others simply trailed along after members of their families. Willing female converts determined not only their own fate but also that of their families. The available documentation on Jewish women who converted to Christianity is not from primary sources but from contemporary chronicles, such as consular correspondence or newspaper reports. The female voice in the story of conversion, which is by nature personal and confidential, is hidden and practically unheard.

An interesting case, uncovered a few decades ago by Mordechai Eliav, is that of the mother of a girl named Sarah Steinberg. Sarah's parents immigrated to the Land of Israel in the middle of the nineteenth century, suffered considerable privation, and decided to convert to Christianity. After a short while they returned to Judaism, but later sent Sarah's elder sister to a mission school and converted again to Christianity. These contradictory decisions bespeak a family struggling with internal conflicts regarding their religious beliefs. It was in point of fact the mother who wanted to return to Christianity before her death, while the father died a Jew.[230] The sources do not make it clear whether Sarah's mother experienced a religious revelation on her deathbed, or whether she simply believed that the mission might provide more reliable economic support for her family after her death. (The fate of Sarah herself will be discussed below, in the next section.)

Were differences between husband and wife over conversion more acute when the motivation for conversion was religious or ideological rather than economic? In families where the husband initiated conversion for purely religious reasons, the wife usually held back, not participating in the religious experience. In several known cases, wives refused to join their husbands in the act of conversion. Emilia, wife of Shimon Rosenthal, the first Jew known to have converted in Jerusalem in the nineteenth century, refused for years to leave her home town in Wallachia, until she finally gave in and agreed to come to the Land of Israel with him and convert with him.[231] Emilia Rosenthal was sincere both in her Jewishness, which she was loath to relinquish, and in her new Christian faith. She became a devout Christian, to the extent of trying to influence other Jewish women to emulate her example. Her husband, however, who was apparently rather unstable, returned to Judaism after twenty years as a Christian — but then changed his mind and returned to Christianity after only ten days. The newspaper *Hamaggid*, reporting the affair, noted that Rosenthal's return to Judaism had amazed not only his environment but also his wife, who had fainted upon hearing of his action.[232] The story of the Rosenthal couple clearly indicates a lack of communication between husband and wife regarding their religious experience.

Similar differences between husband and wife emerge from the separate stories of three rabbis, Eliezer Lurie, Binyamin Goldberg, and Avraham Nissan Wolpin, who in 1840, acutely disappointed and disconsolate that the predictions of the Messiah's advent in that year had failed to materialize, decided to convert to Christianity.[233] These cases illustrate, not only the wives' influence on their husbands' indecision as to whether to undergo baptism, but also their mutual relations as a married couple. Eliezer Lurie, for example, was determined to convert to Christianity, but told the missionaries that he could not talk to his wife alone because they were living in his father-in-law's house. The women's refusal to convert may be attributed, on the one hand, to their devotion to the Jewish religion, their parental homes, and their community, and, on the other, to the lack of communication between them and their husbands. While the women did not really seem to trust their husbands, the latter were eager for their wives and children to join them in their new lives. The fact that the couples did not have a common spiritual world did not affect their mutual loyalty and attraction. The men, bent on conversion out of religious conviction, nevertheless suggested that their wives continue to lead a Jewish life. Their wives, however, rejected this proposal and begged them to return to their homes and resume their previous lives. Once it became clear to the men that conversion would lose them their families, they elected to return home, even at the cost of compromising their religious beliefs. But their return to their families did not mend the breach between them and their wives. Two of the vacillators, Binyamin Goldberg and Eliezer Luria, decided to leave home and divorce their wives. The overt religious differences between husband and wife sealed the fate of their relationship. In the case of Eliezer Luria, his wife's feelings for the husband of her youth had not abated; two and a half years after his conversion, she too was baptized and returned to him. We do not know whether her love for her husband exceeded her love of Judaism, or whether religious conviction played a part. In contrast, Avraham Nissan Wolpin changed his mind, decided not to convert, and sought a reconciliation with his wife; she, however, rejected his contrition and the breach between them failed to heal.

The descriptions of the males' paths to Christianity clearly implies that their wives had no part in that venture. The missionaries themselves attributed the women's attachment to Judaism to their poor education and immersion in superstition and ignorance.[234] Could this lack of education have indeed made the women incapable of entertaining an intellectual preference for Christianity? Could this be the root of their deeper emotional commitment to Judaism than to their husbands? The fact is that women's ties to Judaism did in general seem to be stronger than their ties to their husbands, as the following cases imply.

The stories of the wives of Yehudah Levy, Mendel Diness, and Daoud Rahman, who also converted to Christianity out of conviction, illustrate the dilemma due to absence of religious and ideological harmony between husband and wife. Levy's wife was first unwilling to leave her husband, who had converted. She tried to live with him as a Jewess, declaring that she was determined to adhere to her religion. However, the attempt to maintain conjugal relations between a Christian and a Jew did not succeed; the rabbis persuaded her to leave her husband, and Levy married a woman who had converted like himself.

Sheindel Raizel, wife of the convert Mendel Diness (famed as the first photographer of Jerusalem[235]), was also not a partner to his conversion. Sheindel Raizel was influenced by her father, a Chabad Hasid from Hebron, who demanded that she divorce her husband. Diness refused to divorce her in accordance with Jewish law, hoping that she would return to him; but she refused to convert, and after considerable difficulties finally obtained the desired divorce.

The marriage of Daoud Rahman and his wife, both of the Mughrabi (North African) community, also failed because of the husband's conversion. His wife demanded a divorce and refused to live with him.

In sum: When their spouses converted out of religious conviction, women generally showed greater attachment to Judaism than men. But when economic factors brought the family to the missionaries' doors, there seems to have been less reluctance to espouse Christianity.

Children of single-parent families were much more likely to be baptized than those who had the benefit of two parents. Single mothers handed their children over to the mission as an act of desperation, being incapable of supporting and caring for their offspring. *Hazevi* reported the story of a Sephardic widow who wanted to put her three-year-old only son into a mission school so that he would not be a burden on her, but she changed her mind.[236]

The dormitories of the mission in Jerusalem were a magnet not only for the local needy but also for Jews from Egypt.[237] While the placing of children in Christian boarding schools far from home was not an explicit act of conversion, it essentially meant acceptance of this eventuality in advance.[238] Were such children brought to the Holy City because of the large number of available mission institutions there, or because of the parents' wish to conceal their move from the community? Whatever the case may be, conditions in the Holy City were such that young Egyptian children were regularly admitted to mission schools. The practice was vigorously decried in the press, giving Egyptian Jews a bad name.[239]

Women's threats to appeal to the mission if their demands were not met were sometimes an effective way of getting what they could not get by other means. In 1913, for example, *Hashkafah* published the story of a few women who claimed that they had not received the *halukah* allocation to which they were entitled. They threatened those responsible: "If you do not give us . . . here is our decision: We will go to the mission, yes, to the mission!"[240] The writer of the article was oblivious to the women's obvious distress; he held their threats in contempt, as did the rabbis. A similar threat was made by a young woman who refused to marry her appointed groom: "Whatever happens, I will take the disgraceful and contemptible step, as others have done, saying farewell to their people and their religion."[241] For a young woman in Jerusalem with no profession and no income, there was no other alternative. As opposed to suicide, which was a point of no return, the approach to the mission afforded a new and perhaps easier way of life.

In some cases conversion was not only an opportunity for material aid but also an escape from domestic violence. An elderly woman from Tiberias who was regularly beaten by her adult children appealed to the Muslim ruler of the city for asylum in his home and religion. However, she refused to eat his nonkosher food. After the rabbis of the Jewish community promised her their assistance, she returned home.[242]

Love for a non-Jewish man was seldom a reason for converting, especially given the way marriages were arranged among the young people of Jerusalem. At the same time, Jewish Arabic-speaking girls of the Eastern communities might well form ties with local Arab men, in view of the common language and residence in close proximity. Ya'akov Yehoshua wrote in his memoirs: "Among the Muslims there were a few men of means who exploited the poverty of Jewish women and seduced them."[243]

In 1889, *Hazevi* reported two love affairs between mixed couples. The first occurred in Jerusalem. Three young girls of the Mughrabi community converted to Islam because of their desire "to marry their Arab lovers."[244] From this short item it transpires that rabbis, acting under the protection of the pasha (who was of course a Muslim), tried to persuade the girls to reconsider, but the three were not to be deterred and refused as one to obey the rabbis. The other affair occurred in Hebron: "A Jewish girl from Hebron was seduced by a young Arab and succumbed to his advances."[245] In this case, too, an attempt was made, under the auspices of the pasha, to persuade the girl to relent, but again to no avail. The involvement of the pasha in preventing the conversion to Islam of Jewish girls was perhaps based on Ottoman law, which prohibited the conversion of minors; alternatively, perhaps it reflected society's disapproval of such a display of independence by the young women, who wanted to marry by their own choice, contrary to accepted norms in their communities (and of course his intervention may have been based on both of these factors). Another case that received publicity, and even aroused diplomatic interest, was that of a woman named Flora Motro, who wanted to marry a young Muslim and convert to Islam.[246]

As against our previous instances of married women refusing to follow their husbands and convert to Christianity, the willingness of young girls to abandon everything they had for their Muslim lovers is astonishing. The documented cases of love affairs between Jewesses and non-Jews in Jerusalem are too few[247] to imply any hard-and-fast conclusions, but they do pinpoint the question: to whom were women primarily faithful — to their God or to their husband?

Further light on the question of conversion is shed by the extraordinary story of the wife of a Rabbi Meir Auerbach, who disappeared after a visit to the Mount of Olives; a suspicion arose that she had been kidnapped by nuns of the Soeurs de Sion Convent. This suspicion was surely stimulated, on the one hand, by people's conviction that missionaries would not recoil even from kidnapping a helpless, elderly woman, and on the other by the apprehension of Jerusalemites regarding willing conversions. The disappearance of the rabbi's wife remained unsolved, but the population's far-fetched imagination reflects the popular perception of the missionaries as vultures constantly on the lookout for prey and the fear that they might indeed succeed.[248]

Conversion presents a fascinating opportunity to examine the question of whether women were motivated primarily by domestic obligations or by ideological considerations. A survey of the not insignificant number of cases of Jewish women of Jerusalem who converted to Christianity lends credence to the estimation that female conversion was generally due, not to a profound religious experience, but rather to domestic desires and economic exigencies. Nevertheless, the cases of women who refused to embrace Christianity shed additional light on Jewish women's devotion to Judaism.

Combating the Mission: Society's Attitude to Its Periphery

The intensity of opposition to the mission varied in accordance with the different goals. Communal leaders in Jerusalem found themselves in an impasse: on the one hand, they were loath to publicize the fact that a good number of Jews in the Holy City were enjoying the support of the mission; on the other, they were unable to assist the many needy persons who sought their help. This impasse was largely responsible for the shaping of a policy that sent a double message, namely, relative disregard of the dangers of missionary efforts, coupled with covert but constant dependence of Jews from the margins of society on the benevolence of Christian emissaries.[249] This policy was effective whenever all that was concerned was the acceptance of material assistance, but was totally abandoned when it came to conversion of Jews. Conversion, considered a cardinal sin, provoked open, no-holds-barred war.

Since women followed their menfolk's lead and rarely took the initiative, the arduous struggles to prevent conversion, which often went as far as kidnapping, generally concerned women. Women were regarded as "children taken captive,"[250] whom it was imperative to save at any cost, and attempts to do so were not hampered by any ideological scruples. To save a person's soul, his or her body had to be saved. To prevent a woman from converting her sister, a husband his wife, or a father his children — in all these cases the rabbis considered any means legitimate. Ottoman law, which prohibited conversion against a person's will, worked in the rabbis' favor, though the European consuls generally cooperated with the missionary institutions. Several cases provoked international incidents and were extensively documented in consular reports and in the press.

Outside intervention was particularly intense in the cases of the three rabbis' wives whose husbands decided to convert in 1840.[251] The leaders of the Ashkenazic community of Jerusalem maintained contacts with the rabbis and their wives and closely followed the details of their arguments. A distinguished delegation of elders of the *Perushim* community in Jerusalem even went to the home of the missionary where the recalcitrant husbands were staying, in order to speak to them and dissuade them from taking the crucial step. An appeal was made to the various consuls to prevent the abduction of the three rabbis by the English Mission. Similar intervention occurred when Yehudah Levy's family refused to join him after his conversion. The members of his family were smuggled out of the country with the help of the rabbis in order to prevent their conversion.

We have already mentioned the story of thirteen-year-old Sarah Steinberg.[252] After the death of Sarah's parents and brother, her elder sister Devorah, who had converted and married a convert's son, demanded custody over her. Devorah probably meant to take advantage of her relationship with her sister to convert a "lost soul" to Christianity; the Jewish community were determined to prevent this. The rabbis abducted the girl and hid her from her sister. The Prussian consul suspected Rabbi Arieh Marcus, one of the directors of the *kolel* of "German and Dutch Jews" (Kolel Hod), and he was badly beaten and thrown into jail. The heads of the Yishuv appealed for help to the Jewish press worldwide, the administrators of the *halukah* in Amsterdam, the Rothschilds, and other philanthropists. These efforts were finally successful; Sarah was not handed over to her sister and was not converted.

Parents who had sent their children to the mission, but later regretted that decision when their children expressed an interest in conversion, also became engaged in antimission struggle. In several instances parents tried to take their children out of mission dormitories but were too late, and had to kidnap them in order to bring them home.[253] They were not always successful: sometimes the children refused to return with them.[254] As already intimated, bodily abduction of boys or girls whom the mission refused to return to their parents was considered legitimate.[255]

On one occasion, two women attempted to remove their daughters from the mission school but were refused by the nuns. The women decided to trick the nuns. They proposed that the nuns take their daughters to a photographer, to have their pictures taken before taking leave of them. Under cover of the crowd assembled near the photographer's studio, the mothers seized their daughters and managed to escape.[256] Once again, they were able to keep their daughters in their custody thanks to Ottoman law, which, as mentioned above, prohibited the conversion of minors.

Jewish parents did not always succeed, however, and at times the missionaries, supported by the European consuls, had the upper hand. Sometimes, young girls refused to return to their families, having become attached to the nuns and to Christianity.[257] Conversion was not only a religious transformation for such girls; it also caused a rift in the family, and preventive efforts were for the most part argued not on religious grounds but usually involved various and sundry deceptive actions or attempts by other members of the family to change the girls' minds by persuasion.

The determination, resolve, and actions employed to prevent conversion are striking, particularly in light of the generally tepid reaction of the rabbinic establishment to Jews' acceptance of various benefits offered by the mission. This almost apathetic attitude was deplored by the journal *Hazevi*.[258] Ada Fishman (later Maimon), a young female socialist who worked as a teacher in Safed on the eve of the First World War, wrote bitterly: "The mission has so thoroughly penetrated all ranks of the Jewish community in Safed that they consider it holy."[259] The Yishuv had probably internalized the double message broadcast by the rabbis: while people who received benefits from the mission were ostracized, such receipt of benefits was nevertheless not absolutely forbidden. The missionaries' strategy — to try to endear themselves to the Jewish community by various means — was relatively successful.

The increased involvement of the mission among the Jews of Jerusalem with the coming of a large wave of immigrants in 1882, the establishment of the *moshavah* Artuf (Hartuv), and the dedication of the new building of the English Mission Hospital[260] aroused sharp reactions on the part of Jerusalem's rabbis. The leaders of the community resorted to well-tried measures, namely, excommunication both of workers in the hospital and of those receiving treatment. The writ of excommunication, signed by the rabbis of both communities, (Ashkenzic and Sephardic), declared that whoever received aid from the mission or earn a living through it — even as payment for preparing kosher meals — would be considered beyond the pale: their children would not be circumcised, and when they died, the purification rites would be denied them and they would not be buried as Jews.[261] Similar rabbinical reaction was observed in New York at the beginning of the twentieth century, in the wake of widespread missionary activity among the Jewish immigrant community there.[262] The writ of excommunication was in fact upheld, and in several cases Jews who died did not receive proper burial. Even an appeal to the Austrian consul was of no avail.[263] Infuriated Jews, who needed the support of the mission and whose deceased family members had been rejected by the Jewish burial societies, resorted to violence; not finding Rabbi Shmuel Salant at home, they spent their rage on his wife, and the beadle of the Warsaw Kolel, who was in the courtyard, was hit by a stone and killed.[264] Clearly, the families demanding Jewish burial for their relatives were convinced that accepting aid from the mission did not entail a break with Judaism; they therefore considered the sanctions imposed by the rabbis as unjust in the extreme.

The struggle against the mission and those who benefited from its support was exacerbated toward the end of the nineteenth century, when a writ of excommunication was again pronounced on people appealing to the mission for medical assistance. A young Sephardic widow who had come to Jerusalem from Jaffa took sick and was hospitalized at the Misgav Ladakh Hospital. As her condition worsened, determined to fight for her life, she turned to the English Hospital, but died there. The young woman's family was explicitly warned not to allow her to appeal to the Mission Hospital, but she had refused to obey. Even though the deceased woman had not converted, the rabbis of the community ruled that she would not be given a Jewish burial. In the British Consulate's report of the case, mention was made of "the extremely hostile attitude of the Chief Rabbi, who is said to be instigated by several European Jews of Socialist tendencies."[265] Despite the intervention of the con-

sulate, the Religious Court stood fast, and the burial society refused to bury
the young woman. The event became an international diplomatic affair, and
even the pasha's intervention was of no avail.[266] Hundreds of Jews, men and
women, took the part of the rabbis and surrounded the hospital, preventing
the removal of the body from the premises. With no other alternative, the
woman was buried in the mission's plot on the Mount of Olives.[267] The rabbinical position was in his case backed by the community; it was to recur a
year later, when another woman died at the Mission Hospital.[268]

In his memoirs, David Yellin wondered what had moved the rabbis to take
such an unforgiving stand: Were they motivated by "feelings of revenge, or
hatred for the lonely soul?" He suggested that the rabbis wished to distance
the community from Christian institutions and to educate them not to lose
their dignity for the sake of material gain. However, the refusal to grant Jewish burial punished the family first and foremost.[269] We may assume that punishment of the family was part and parcel of the general policy of the Jerusalem rabbis to attend first to the city's image and only afterward to its residents.
No distinction was made among those sullying the community's good name,
be they prostitutes or patients of the Mission Hospital. The community of Jerusalem, regarding itself as sacred, felt an obligation only to people who
helped to maintain that sanctity. Others were rejected, with no consideration
whatsoever for their distress. This attitude also dictated the attitude of the rabbinic establishment toward the female sector.

An inevitable consequence of the rabbis' attitude to education for girls was
their attitude to girls' attendance at mission schools. From time to time, the
rabbis and community leaders would issue a public outcry against these
schools,[270] and posters forbidding Jews to attend appeared again and again.[271]
The influence of these objections, however, was meager, as confirmed by
many of the relevant reports in the Jerusalem press: "Little by little, the practice is becoming common; there are increasing numbers of [Jewish] girls in
these schools, and no man gives it thought."[272]

The Sephardic rabbis had a less rigid attitude to girls studying at mission
institutions, and did not always agree to cooperate with the Ashkenazim.[273] A
news item in *Haherut*, the organ of the Sephardic circles, reported that the
granddaughters of the *hakham bashi* (Sephardic chief rabbi), Ya'akov Eliachar, were sent to a Catholic school.[274] Similarly, a decree issued by the
Sephardic rabbis against the Christian women who were visiting Jewish
women in their homes was considered to be mere lip service, and the *Hazevi*
writer who reported this commented, "How terrible it is that even now they
have not issued a total prohibition against the hospitals and schools of the in-
citers."[275] Even the Hasidic (Ashkenazic) leaders were not always quick to
raise their voices against the attendance of Jewish girls in Christian schools.[276]

Some insight into the prevailing attitudes is provided by a press report, published in *Hashkafah*, of a rumor that Rabbi Salant had openly remarked that, since those attending the mission's schools were Sephardic girls, "What does this problem have to do with us—what do we have to do with *them*?!"[277] While the journalist added that Rabbi Salant denied having said such a thing, the story is most revealing in regard to the rather indifferent attitude of the rabbinic establishment in this connection. What Sephardic girls were doing was no threat to the honor of the Ashkenazi community; and in any case, what girls did was of little real importance.

Paradoxically, it was not religious fanatics who took up arms against the beneficiaries of mission institutions in Jerusalem, but rather the common people,[278] the intellectuals and secular leaders of the New Yishuv. In the autumn of 1883 a number of persons, headed by Eliezer Ben-Yehuda,[279] founded a benevolent society called Ezrat Nidahim (literally, Aid to the Abandoned).[280] As far as we know, the society extended help only to men and took no notice of women's difficulties. Nonetheless, it was the first time that a group of Jerusalemites sought not only to condemn the needy, who were liable to fall into missionary hands, but also to try to help them.

The Jerusalem newspapers also joined the campaign, exposing the multifaceted dangers of the mission.[281] The battle was led by the writers of *Hazevi* and *Hashkafah*, who gave prominence to reports on people approaching the mission for medical assistance. The prominence given to these reports was aimed both at condemning such actions and at stimulating the community leaders to help those in need, rather than leave them to the mercies of what they called the "inciters."[282] The feeling that the rabbinic establishment was not sufficiently committed to the struggle against the mission also aroused the youth to organize.[283] These variegated initiatives are evidence of the feeling that the struggle against the mission was not being handled properly and therefore not producing the desired results.

A first attempt to attend to the particular problems of the female sector who used the mission's services was made—by women—toward the end of the nineteenth century. A society named Bet Ya'akov, founded in 1897 by women of the Old Yishuv, decided to establish a Jewish orphan home for girls, which would offer a real solution to the situation of girls forced to stay in the mission boarding schools in the absence of any suitable Jewish institution.[284] Unlike the men, whose efforts entailed mainly threats and punishment, the women of Bet Ya'akov realized the urgent need for material help.[285] The blame lay, they argued, not on the girls who fell prey to the mission, but on the poverty that forced them to do so. Similar ideas had been expressed in the United States, at a Congress of Jewish Women in Chicago in 1893, where it was declared that persons experiencing hardships should not be condemned, but rather the society that did not extend help to the needy.[286] For the male sector, a person who had been reduced to poverty was a sinner who deserved punishment; the female sector, in contrast, aimed at dealing with the root causes of that poverty. This was the ideology underlying establishment of the first orphan home for girls in Jerusalem and the attached workshop, which provided work and basic education for young girls.

A similar approach, namely, to deal with the problem rather than seek to punish the unfortunate, also characterized the members of the Teachers' Association (as distinct from teachers in the ultra-Orthodox educational system) and the Committee for Defense against the Mission,[287] who saw themselves at the forefront of the campaign against Christian educational institutions. As they put it, "Jerusalem is overwhelmed by the most terrible and inconceivable disgrace,"[288] and new avenues had to be explored. In 1913 the association organized the departure of about two hundred Jewish girls and teachers from mission schools and arranged their admission to Jewish schools, mainly Evelina de Rothschild.[289] The struggle for the preservation of the good name of the Holy City was replaced by a constructive struggle for Jewish education for girls.

Women: The "Margins" of the "Margins"

Should one ask, Are gender differences obscured or otherwise in what is perceived as the margins of society? — the answer is unambiguous: on the contrary, the differences are heightened. A journey to that social realm, generally passed over in silence in historical research, reveals that women have a special place and special representation. In addition to "ordinary" poor women and poor widows, who exceeded widowers in number, there are two sectors of the social periphery that are invariably made up of women: prostitutes and deserted wives. The fact that the Jerusalem community, like all other Jewish communities, was hard put to deal with these phenomena speaks for itself. Women did not constitute the mainstream of a society that saw its sacred, all-embracing goal in studying the Torah in the Holy Land. It was women's task to enable men to fulfill their destiny, and when, for various reasons, they were incapable of discharging that duty and were forced to rely on help from society, they had to look for it elsewhere. The poor of the Holy City, and particularly the poor women, were obliged to appeal privately to donors the world over and beg for their help. The formal network of the *kolelim* itself relied on support received from Jews in the Diaspora, and was not capable of giving charity to poor men and women.

The Jerusalem community's self-perception as an elite community inevitably shaped its attitude to the destitute, and particularly to those seen as violating accepted norms. Women who were forced to take to the streets were banished from society and expelled from the city. Men and women who died in the Mission Hospital were denied a proper Jewish burial. Since the primary goal was to uphold Jerusalem's image as a Holy City, its people closed their eyes to the existence of such afflictions as prostitution and apostasy within its gates. "All who admired her despise her, for they have seen her disgraced" (Lam. 1:8). The fear of disgrace falling on the city was the determining factor.

Among the many biblical depictions of Jerusalem, we find personifications of the city as the most wretched of women: prostitute, widow, and abandoned. "Alas, she has become a harlot, the faithful city," mourned Isaiah (Isa. 1:21). "She that was great among nations is become like a widow," was Jeremiah's lament (Lam. 1:1), and he continued: "Jerusalem has greatly sinned, therefore she is become a mockery" (Lam. 1:8). Women, the ultimate "other," became the symbol of the destroyed city, destitute and humiliated. Such terms as widow, prostitute, and abandoned, with all their implications, symbolize in masculine parlance destruction, humiliation, punishment, and loneliness. "These symbols have the power to influence us and fashion our point of view."[290] The masculine language was a message that perpetuated the tragedy of these unfortunate women, obviating any possibility of effecting a change. The lot of *agunot* and prostitutes was deeply rooted in the biblical image of the Holy City.

The Female Experience in Jerusalem

Honing Historical-Cultural Insights

I S OUR OUTLINE of the world of women in Jerusalem toward the end of Ottoman period only a kind of "complementary history"? Alternatively, might it offer a new vantage point for our understanding of Jerusalem society and the processes that molded the Old Yishuv in the Holy City? Scholars concerned with the methodology of women's history in general focus on two aspects: (a) the presentation of the women's historical narrative, namely, "what they did, what they felt, what they created, how they reacted to their situation, and how they tried to come to grips with it"[1] ("herstory" as opposed to history); (b) the attempt to write new history through focusing on gender, in terms of the material and symbolic significance of masculinity and femininity, and telling the separate women's story. The concept of gender focuses our attention on areas that have hitherto been almost totally ignored in research, and it also constitutes an invaluable principle for analyzing processes, institutions, and central structures in society that have hitherto been considered entirely apart from the concepts of masculinity and femininity. These directions of research may present gender as another, new and different, explanation for certain phenomena that have been studied in the past.[2]

My object in the present book, an account of the female experience of the Jerusalem woman in the Old Yishuv, was to sketch the feminine historical narrative and determine if, and to what extent, it is reshaped by the gender approach. Looking back, I would like to point out especially two insights that run all through the book: the unique Jerusalem character, and another look at the perception of women in Judaism. I would also like to propose the use of gender as yet another explanation for the fall of the Old Yishuv and as a link between the Old and New Yishuv.

The Unique Jerusalem Character

New light is shed on the unique quality of life in Jerusalem both by our description of the religious experience beyond the walls of the study halls and by the attention devoted to the common people, the deprived sectors of society. In other words, our study of the feminine experience has helped us to redefine the unique character of Jerusalem.

Life in the Holy City presented the opportunity to participate in the experience of striving toward holiness and thereby accelerating the advent of the Redemption, even for those who were excluded from the elite, that is, the learning community. While Jerusalem did not become a world Torah center,[3] it was able to establish its sanctity in the private domain, in the family unit, in everyday life. Secular life in "earthly Jerusalem" became a means of achieving "heavenly Jerusalem." (Perhaps the rabbinical establishment's realization of its inability to attain the desired level of Torah scholarship prompted it to focus all its attention on the life of the individual and on relations between the sexes.) As a result of the patriarchal Jewish perception of women as "inevitably linked with nature and its uncontrollable cyclical forces,"[4] the sanctity of life in the Holy City was particularly emphasized with respect to women in their daily lives. Since women were associated in male perception with material matters, they were subordinated to male society, and their oppression was also justified by spiritual and metaphysical motives. A close examination of the ways in which the community safeguarded its sanctity helps us to understand the many inconsistencies in the Old Yishuv society. Our study of women's experience also broadens one's normal view of religious experience as a whole.[5]

While refining our understanding of the aura of sanctity of life in Jerusalem, we also form a new perception of the multiethnic character of society in the Holy City. It is a commonplace in the scholarly literature that the Jewish community in Jerusalem was the most varied in the Jewish world.[6] The conventional view that the city was the home of two communities, Ashkenazim and Sephardim, who differed from each other in every way — in ideology, organization, language, and neighborhood — is given a slight twist when one considers women. It turns out that the differences between the communities, which have been extensively dealt with in the literature,[7] were becoming blurred in certain areas, and the Jews in the city were beginning to evolve a unique "core culture" all their own. As opposed to the synagogues (where the distinctions were clearly delineated), in the area of folkways, always closely identified with women — tombs of holy men, nonestablishment places of worship — there were clear signs of intermingling, and consequently even of customs copied from one another.

The poverty of the city and its dependence on donations sent from all corners of the earth produced a modest "Jerusalem" lifestyle. This was true of all communities and was even legalized in the city's regulations (*takanot*). The demand for modest living was common to all, and although it was usually directed at the female sector, it was not always expressed in a unified way. The Ashkenazic bride was not allowed to wear jewelry; the number of participants at family events was restricted; and the wealthy Bukharan community ruled in the early twentieth century that its members should not celebrate weddings extravagantly but should limit the scope of the festivities, contrary to the custom in Bukhara. While the elders of the city strove to preserve Jewish tradition in all its details, they promulgated regulations that were designed to give the city a unique uniform character.[8]

"Mixed marriages" meant marriages between members of different communities. These began to occur in the Yishuv little by little with the arrival in Jerusalem of the first Ashkenazim of the Dutch-German *kolel* (Kolel Holland veDeutschland). The detailed description we have of the wedding of Yehoshua and Serah Yellin confirms that such marriages contributed not only to more cordial relations among the various communities but also to the creation of a new, multicultural, local pattern of behavior. The girls' attendance at the bride's home on the Sabbath before the wedding, known as the *"vizhita,"* was a Sephardic custom that became part of Ashkenazic practice — the word even entered the Yiddish language. Another Jerusalem custom that was adopted by all the communities was for the bride and groom to go (separately) to the Western Wall before the wedding. Marriage contracts (*ketubot*) designed in Jerusalem also stood out in their unique simplicity.[9]

Customs common to the different communities also evolved in connection with childbirth. Ashkenazic women called the birthing bed a *himmel-bett* (German and Yiddish for a four-poster bed), after its canopy. This bed would be passed from woman to woman, with no ethnic distinctions made; Ya'akov Yehoshua, who extensively documented life in the Sephardic community, described it in detail. The amulets and other magical means used to protect the birthing mother and child also had a distinct and uniform local character. Upon the birth of a child, the same amulets and magic spells were hung in the rooms of Ashkenazic and Sephardic mothers. The fear that a woman might die in childbirth, or that the infant might die, was so great that any preventive means were considered legitimate by women of all communities.

Intercommunal integration was an official objective of the new educational institutions established in the city, in girls' and later also in boys' schools. Sir Moses Montefiore also favored closer relations between the communities; in Mishkenot Sha'ananim, the first Jewish neighborhood outside the Old City walls (built in 1860), half of the first twenty homes were reserved for Ashkenazim and half for Sephardim. Communal integration was also a goal of the first *maskilim* (secular intellectuals) in the Holy City. The local Jerusalem ethos was created primarily by the intermingling and blending of various community traditions in daily life. In both public and domestic domains, a unique Jerusalem character began to take shape; it sought to promote excessive sanctity among people by educating them toward a modest, ethical lifestyle and by creating a quasi-collective experience, weaving the various community customs together in one multicolored cloth. Gender studies shed new light on these trends.

The Female Jerusalemite: Another Look at the Perception of Women in Judaism

The characteristic features of the Holy City, the meeting of "heavenly Jerusalem" and "earthly Jerusalem," the contrast between the heights of holiness and the earthly reality, poverty, and oppression — all these provide fertile ground for reflections on the perception of women in Judaism. The dichotomies of the Holy City exacerbate the inherent dichotomies involved in the perception of women in Judaism. The "Jerusalem Regulations," which imposed strictures on women's dress, their ability to frequent the public domain and make contact — or mainly refrain from contact — with the male sector, highlight the traditional Jewish conception of women perceived as a source of temptation and sin and, as such, a constant danger to elite (i.e., male) society.[10] Many laws and regulations established women as inherently impure, to be kept away from Jewish learning and prohibited from participation in religious activities — in the synagogue or in the study hall. Nonetheless, women in Jerusalem sometimes took extraordinary measures to ascend to spheres of holiness.

Paradoxically, it was the inferior status, the bottomless well in which women were embedded as a consequence of the way they were perceived by society and indeed by themselves,[11] that enabled them to reach unexpected heights. Against the very background of their identification with the purely material, their image as seductresses and temptresses, women's achievement of spiritual greatness is all the more impressive. Since the basic female experience is always "inferior," women's special, unique ability to rise above and overcome that experience attracts immediate attention.

Life in Jerusalem offered women not a few opportunities to excel. Their very act of immigrating to the Land of Israel, particularly when they did so alone, gave them a unique arena for a life of holiness, namely, the chance to visit holy sites and shape their own paths of religious observance. Women, identified as they were with the materialistic aspect of life, evolved rituals that for the most part were their very own. They achieved religious merit mainly through physical work, such as caring for the stones of the Western Wall and whitewashing tombstones, supporting husbands who devoted themselves to Torah learning, opening soup kitchens for new immigrants and the poor to enable them to devote their time and effort to Torah learning. This elation that women felt, by virtue of their ability to express themselves and connect with the Almighty, fortified their religious experience.

By leaving the privacy of their homes and entering the public domain, the Jewish women of Jerusalem empowered themselves, enhancing the regard in which they were held by the male sector, so much so that they were seen as factors in bringing about Redemption. Both men and women in Jerusalem were in the habit of quoting the talmudic saying: "As the reward for the righteous women who lived in that generation were the Israelites delivered from Egypt" (Bab. Talmud, Sotah 11b). While this well-known saying seems, on the face of it, to compliment women, a closer examination of its context shows that such is not the case. As a matter of fact, the talmudic text is praising the wives of the Israelites in Egypt for seducing their husbands, exhausted from hard labor, to have sexual relations with them, thereby ensuring the continuity of the people of Israel. Evidently, there had been little change in the traditional Jewish perception of the feminine essence from the time of the Talmud until the nineteenth century. Both in antiquity and in the Old Yishuv, the material essence of women was responsible for their unique piety.

Women's religious superiority was also expressed in their refusal to convert when their husbands did so, in their devotion to Judaism even when their faith might lose them their families. What was the source of this religious piety? Some have attributed it to their ignorance, but perhaps the analogy between the Holy City and the perception of femininity suggests a new insight. Just as the inherent holiness of Jerusalem persists, despite the desperate condition of its residents, the inherent materiality of women is not affected by their ability to achieve sanctity. It is woman's very ability to rise above her natural essence that reinforces the perception of women as essentially material. Her ability to achieve exceptional heights is doubly significant, given her inherent "naturalness" and so-called inferiority. Perhaps women's universal resignation to their fate may be attributed to their awareness of their incomparable ability to overcome.

Gender and the Fall of the Old Yishuv: The Link between the Old and New Yishuv

The study of the female sector and the use of gender methodology offer new explanations for major phenomena such as the exceptional demographic gap between men and women in Jerusalem, the economic life of the city, how

Western ways penetrated traditional society, and many other topics that have been discussed throughout this book. In addition, the isolationism and emphasis on strict Orthodoxy typical of the Old Yishuv toward the end of the nineteenth century[12] find their expression in the private sphere and in new perceptions of masculinity and femininity. I suggest that the decline of the Old Yishuv in Jerusalem during the last years of the Ottoman regime in the Land of Israel may also have been associated with the changes that occurred in the feminine sector.

In the decade prior to the First World War, Jerusalem experienced crises in several areas — economy, leadership, and organization. The prestigious Torat Hayim Yeshiva went bankrupt. The stone industry and other branches of construction were on the verge of disaster.[13] The *halukah* monies, never plentiful, were no longer sufficient for the growing population of the poor city, where employment opportunities were lacking. The two rabbinical leaders who for decades had authority over both communities (Rabbis Ya'akov–Eliachar and Shmuel Salant) passed away, and the communities were unable to elect a new leadership of stature.[14] The most prominent symptom of the crisis was massive emigration from the country.[15] As in the case of emigration to the West from eastern Europe, those who left were usually young men, bachelors or family men, who sought their fortunes all over the world: in the United States, Australia, and South Africa.[16] The local press contains repeated reports of the number of departures and arrivals at the port of Jaffa, sometimes short and to the point, sometimes accompanied by expressions of anguish, such as: "Such a situation has never occurred in Jerusalem, and there is no doubt that the Yishuv is now in a crisis situation."[17] There was a general feeling that the trend affected every single household. This was the case not only in Jerusalem but in the other "holy cities" as well.[18]

I would like to suggest that the new education of girls in Jerusalem could have been a factor in the crisis of emigration from the Land of Israel. At the Evelina de Rothschild School, girls learned to speak European languages and were educated to regard dependence on charity as shameful. One might perceive here a direct or indirect incentive to emigration, as if the window of opportunity for Western education encouraged rejection of the norms of the Jerusalem lifestyle and their exchange for the New World. In view of the dearth of detailed statistics of the emigration, such conjectures cannot be verified. Nevertheless, there is no doubt that the school served as a catalyst for the infiltration of innovative values and ideas into Jerusalem society.

Our unfolding of the feminine narrative indicates that, far from being of secondary importance, it is a central, hitherto ignored, component of the historiography and hence of our basic historical narrative. The experience of the immigration of the women of the Old Yishuv suggests a new insight into the

Zionist yearnings of the first waves of immigration to arrive in the Land of Israel at the close of the Ottoman period. The ethos of first pioneers (*haluzim*),
who for the most part were educated in traditional homes, was very similar to
the immigration experience of the women of the Old Yishuv. The values on
which those women of Jerusalem based their new lives — self-sacrifice, frugality to the point of asceticism, and a deep identification with the national
history — were also the guiding values of the new immigrants who established
the New Yishuv. The foregoing account of the immigration experience of the
women of the Old Yishuv *reveals* that this was also the cultural infrastructure
and ideology of the people of the first waves of immigration, and hence a
bridge between the Old Yishuv and the New Yishuv in its earlier stages, before the First World War. The subsequent social confrontation between these
two societies to a great extent blurred their cultural common ground.

The perception of life in the Holy Land as no less than an ongoing sacrifice
convinced the women of the Old Yishuv of the inevitability of their sacrifice
and gave them the strength to bear their trials and tribulations. The poetess
Rachel, who came to the Land of Israel in 1909, worked as a pioneer, and
identified herself with the matriarch Rachel ("for her blood flows in my veins,
her voice sings with me"[19]), spoke of the collective experience of willingness
to sacrifice: "We yearned for sacrifice, for suffering, for the chains of prohibition with which we will publicly sanctify the name of the homeland."[20] The
sacrificial motif is repeatedly presented as the price that life demands of
haluzim (pioneers) in the Land of Israel. Readiness for sacrifice is an overt act,
a means of realizing an idea and one of the qualities of the "sabra," the myth-
ical image of the new Jew shaped in the Land of Israel.[21]

As mentioned, among other things, abstemiousness was a major feature of
life in nineteenth-century Jerusalem. The abject poverty that was the rule
among both women and men was perceived as a means of sanctifying material things and achieving a high level of spirituality. The *haluzim*, too, regarded frugality and self-denial as essential attributes in the face of life in the
Land of Israel, as values to be cherished. The poet David Shim'oni clearly
pictured this idea in his idyll "Monument" (*Matzevah*), which deals with the
pioneers of the Second Aliyah: "What is self-denial? . . . and Catriel sang the
copious praises of that *mitzva* [religious duty] and the tremendous reward
that it earned."[22] Observance of these values was for the pioneers on a par with
the observance of *mitzvot*, religious commandments. Their perception of
their daily activities as an act of holiness was similar to the sensation of spiritual uplift felt by the women of Jerusalem in the face of their unbearably
difficult situation.

Identification with the Jewish historical experience was a central component of the modern national reawakening,[23] and a familiar popular phenom-

enon, common for many generations among all parts of the nation, and particularly among women. The profound empathy of the women of the Old
Yishuv with the holy sites, especially with the matriarch Rachel, who seeks
the redemption of her children, is an indication of their deep affinity with
Jewish history. A similar empathy was also at the core of the nationalist feelings of the first pioneers. Eliezer Ben-Yehuda considered the matriarch Rachel
as "symbol of the Mother of the whole nation."[24] Concentration on her memory, her suffering, and her national meaning as the quintessential mother also
nourished the conscious and subconscious trends that brought the pioneers
to the Land of Israel.

Our discovery of the world of women in Jerusalem hones our vision of the
complex experience of the Old Yishuv, men and women alike, and of the
unique Jerusalem experience. As Partha Chatterjee has argued, the female
experience is an experience not of the margins of society, but rather a definitive experience that influences society's definition of itself.[25]

Notes

Introduction (pp. xvii–xxviii)

1. Pinehas Grayevsky, *Benot Zion viYrushalayim*, vols. 1–9, 1929–1932, reprinted in a single volume (Jerusalem, 2000), p. 237.

2. Ibid., p. 241.

3. For an example from Hebron see *Hevron ir hakodesh: Leket misihot ume'igrot ha'admor mi-Lyubavitch* ([Israel], 1998), pp. 190, 231.

4. "Ezrat Nashim," by "Hidah," *Ha'or* 25 (1896).

5. Partha Chatterjee, "Their Own Words?" in Edward Said and Michael Sprinker (eds.), *A Critical Reader* (Oxford, 1992), pp. 194–220.

6. Mordecai Eliav, *Erez Yisra'el veyishuvah bame'ah ha19 1777–1917* (Jerusalem, 1978); Arnold Blumberg, *A View from Jerusalem: The Consular Diary of James and Elizabeth Ann Finn* (London and Toronto), 1980; Yehoshua Ben-Arieh, *Jerusalem in the 19th Century: The Old City* (Jerusalem and New York, 1984); idem, *Jerusalem in the 19th Century: Emergence of the New City* (Jerusalem and New York, 1986).

7. Shim'on Shamir, "*Matay hithilah ha'et hahadashah betoledot Erez Yisra'el?*" *Cathedra* 40 (1986), pp. 138–158; Hagai Erlich, *Mavo lahistoriyah shel hamizrah hatikhon ba'et hahadashah* (1987); Donna Robinson-Divine, *Ottoman Palestine: The Arabs' Struggle for Survival and Power* (London, 1994).

8. Natan Efrati, *Mimashber letikvah — Hayishuv hayehudi bemilhemet ha'olam harishonah* (Jerusalem, 1991).

9. For example, Yehoshua Ben-Arieh, *Erez Yisra'el bame'ah ha19: Giluyah mehadash* (Jerusalem, 1970); Billie Melman, *Women's Orients — English Women and the Middle East, 1718–1918: Sexuality, Religion and Work*, 2nd ed. (Ann Arbor, Mich., 1995).

10. Alexander Schoelch, *Palestine in Transformation, 1856–1882 — Studies in Social, Economic and Political Development* (Washington, D.C., 1986), pp. 119–120.

11. For the Halakhic implications of this perception see Eliezer Bashan, "*Al yahasam shel yehudei Maroko bame'ot ha18–19 lehovat ha'aliyah leErez Yisra'el,*" in H. Z. Hirschberg (ed.), *Vatikin — Mehkarim betoledot hayishuv lezikhro shel R. Yosef Rivlin* (Ramat-Gan, 1975), p. 37; idem, "*Hakesharim hamasortiyim beyn yehudei hamizrah layishuv hayehudi beErez Yisra'el,*" *Pe'amim* 6 (1979), pp. 15–22; Yosef Tobi, "*Shorshei yahasah shel yahadut hamizrah el hatenuah haziyonit,*" in Shmuel Almog et al. (eds.), *Temurot bahistoriyah hayehudit hahadashah — Kovez ma'amarim shay liShmuel Ettinger* (Jerusalem, 1988), p. 183.

12. Yoram Bilu, "*Rega dahus shel ahavah gavrit bil'adit,*" *Haaretz*, May 23, 1997, p. D1; idem, "*Pulhanei kedoshim va'aliyot limkomot kedoshim ketofa'ah universalit,*" in Rivkah Gonen (ed.), *El kivrei zadikim — Aliyot likvarim vehilulot beYisra'el* (Jerusalem, 1998), pp. 11–25.

13. James J. Preston, "Spiritual Magnetism: An Organizing Principle for the Study of Pilgrimage," in Alan Morinis (ed.), *Sacred Journeys: The Anthropology of Pilgrimage* (Westport, Conn., 1992), pp. 31–46, esp. p. 18.

14. For example Zvi Yosef Carlebach, *Mikhtavim miYrushalayim* (Jerusalem, 1996), p. 66.

15. Billie Melman, *"Hamasa la'orient bekhitvei nashim angliyot bame'ah ha-19,"* *Zemanim* 24 (1987), pp. 49–61; Johann Krammer, "Austrian Pilgrimage to the Holy Land," in Marian Wrba (ed.), *Austrian Presence in the Holy Land in the 19th and Early 20th Century* (Tel Aviv, 1996), pp. 66–80.

16. On Jewish pilgrims see Ya'akov Barnai, *Yehudei Erez Yisra'el bame'ah ha19 bahasut pekidei Kushta* (Jerusalem, 1982); Shalom Bar-Asher, "The Jews of North Africa and the Land of Israel in the Eighteenth and Nineenth Centuries: The Reversal in Attitude toward Aliyah," in Lawrence A. Hoffman (ed.), *The Land of Israel: Jewish Perspectives* (Notre Dame, Ind., 1986), pp. 297–315; Schoelch, *Palestine in Transformation*, p. 120.

17. Yisra'el David Bet Halevi, *Toledot yehudei Kalish* (Tel Aviv, 1961), p. 330.

18. Immanuel Etkes, *Lita biYrushalayim — Ha'ilit halamdanit beLita ukehilat haperushim biYrushalayim le'or igrot umikhtavim shel R. Shemuel miKelm* (Jerusalem, 1991), pp. 85–90; Eliezer Bashan, *"Zikatam shel yehudei haMagreb vehatikvah hameshihit bekhitvei nozerim beyn hame'ot ha17 veha20,"* *Bar Ilan Yearbook* 14–15 (1977), pp. 160–175; Aryeh Morgenstern, *Meshihiyut veyishuv Erez Yisra'el bamahazit harishonah shel hame'ah ha19* (Jerusalem, 1985); cf. also idem, *Ge'ulah bederekh hateva bekhitvei haGra vetalmidav* (Jerusalem, 1989).

19. Eliezer and Syla Bergman, *Se'u harim shalom — Mikhtevei masa va'aliyah 1834–1836* (Jerusalem, n.d.), p. 23.

20. Dov Hakohen, *"Ha'aliyah me'Izmir bame'ah ha19"* (seminar paper, Hebrew University of Jerusalem, 1991); Henry Toledano, *"Yoman masa shel Rabbi Yizhak Toledano leErez Yisra'el,"* *Mimizrah umima'arav* 3 (1981), pp. 141–157.

21. Eliav, *Erez Yisra'el veyishuvah*, pp. 75, 99.

22. Barnai, *Yehudei Erez Yisra'el bame'ah ha19*, p. 71.

23. Ya'akov Barnai, *"Ha'edah hama'aravit biYrushalayim bame'ah ha19,"* in Yehudah Ben Porat et al. (eds.), *Perakim betoledot hayishuv hayehudi biYrushalayim* (Jerusalem, 1973), pp. 129–140; Yisra'el Bartal, *Galut ba'arez — Yishuv Erez Yisra'el beterem Ziyonut* (essays and studies) (Jerusalem, 1995), pp. 49, 63; Y osef Tobi, *"Hareka hamedini, hakalkali vehahevrati la'aliyot miTeman bashanim [5]641–[5]678" Tema* 3 (1983), p. 69. But see also Sergio Della Pergola, "Aliya and Other Jewish Migrations: Toward an Integrated Perspective," *Scripta Hierosolymitana* 30 (1986), p. 199.

24. Bartal, *Galut ba'arez*, pp. 49, 63; Netanel Katzburg, *"Pulemus hahinukh bayishuv hayashan," Shanah beshanah* vol. 6 (1966), pp. 299–312.

25. Yisra'el Bartal, *"Al demutah harav-adatit shel hahevrah hayehudit biYrushalayim bame'ah ha19,"* *Pe'amim* 57 (1994), p. 116.

26. Bartal, *Galut ba'arez*, p. 56; Alter Druyanov and Shulamit Laskov (eds.), *Ketavim letoledot Hibbat Zion veyishuv Erez Yisra'el*, vol. 3 (Tel Aviv, 1984), pp. 117, 129.

27. For example Avraham Yaari, *Zikhronot Erez Yisra'el*, vol. 1 (Ramat-Gan, 1974), p. 150; Rivkah Alper, *Korot mishpahah ahat* (Tel Aviv, 1967), p. 13; for a theoretical discussion see S. Everett, "Theory of Migration," *Demography* 3/1 (1996), pp. 51–52.

28. Barnai, *Yehudei Erez Yisra'el bame'ah ha19*, p. 46.

29. Nahum Karlinsky, *"Hahevrah hahasidit shel Zefat bamahazit hasheniyah shel hame'ah ha19 kehevrat mehagerim — hebetim demografiyim vegibush hevrati,"* in *Jerusalem Studies in Jewish Thought* 15 (1999), Immanuel Etkes et al. (eds.), p. 171.

30. Aryeh Gartner, *"Hahagirah hahamonit shel yehudei Eiropah 1881–1914,"* in Avigdor Shin'an (ed.), *Hagirah vehityashevut beYisra'el uva'amim* (Jerusalem, 1982), p. 363.

31. Arodys Robels and Susan Watkins, "Immigration and Family Separation in the U.S. at the Turn of the Twentieth Century," *Journal of Family History* 18/3 (1993), pp. 191–211.

32. See below, chapter 1.

33. Immigration to Erez Israel is known in Hebrew as *aliyah*, which literally means "ascent"; on the other hand, leaving the country is known as *yeridah*, "descent" — it presents problems from the point of view of Halakha (Jewish Law) and is halakhically permitted only under certain circumstances. See *Talmudic Encyclopedia*, 2 (1956), 223–225 (in Hebrew).

34. In 1839 the Sephardim made up 85 pecent of the Jewish population, the Ashkenazim only 15 percent; see Aya Shoham, *"Almenot Yerushalayim al pi mifkad Montefiore 1839 — Nituah statisti"* (M.A. seminar paper, Bar-Ilan University, Ramat-Gan, 2000).

35. Karlinsky, *"Hahevrah hahasidit shel Zefat,"* pp. 155, 156.

36. Zvi Karagila, *Hayishuv hayehudi be'Erez Yisra'el bitkufat hakibush hamizri (1831–1840)* (Tel Aviv, 1990), pp. 17, 19.

37. In 1839, 47 percent of the Jews of Erez Israel lived in Jerusalem, and the growth rate of the Jewish community in the Holy City was higher than in any other Jewish community in the country, reaching an average of 7.7 percent per annum; see Shoham, *"Almenot Yerushalayim,"* p. 4.

38. David Kushnir, *"Hador ha'aharon leshilton ha'Uthmanim beErez Yisra'el, 1882–1914,"* in Moshe Lissak et al., *Toledot hayishuv hayehudi beErez Yisra'el me'az ha'aliyah harishonah* (Jerusalem, 1990), pp. 1–74.

39. Uziel Schmelz, *"Be'ayot musagiyot bamehkar al adot Yisra'el,"* *Pe'amim* 56 (1993), pp. 125–139.

40. Alex Carmel, *"Pe'ilut hama'azamot beErez Yisra'el, 1878–1914,"* in Lissak et al., *Toledot hayishuv hayehudi beErez Yisra'el,* pp. 143–213.

41. Most of the westerners had French citizenship; Natan Efrati, *Ha'edah haSefaradit biYrushalayim,* [5]600–5677 (1840–1917) (Jerusalem, 2000).

42. Avraham Moshe Lifshitz, *Ketavim,* vol. 3 (Jerusalem, 1957), p. 142.

43. Bartal, *"Al demutah harav-adatit,"* pp. 114, 124; Karlinsky, *"Hahevrah hahasidit shel Zefat."*

44. For another view see Bartal, *Galut ba'arez,* esp. pp. 11, 22.

45. Lifshitz, *Ketavim,* vol. 3, p. 143.

46. See below, chapter 4.

47. For the terms "Old Yishuv" and "New Yishuv" see Yisra'el Bartal, *"'Yishuv yashan' ve 'yishuv hadash' — hadimuy vehamezi'ut,"* *Cathedra* 2 (1977), pp. 3–19; Yehoshua Kaniel, *"Hamunahim 'yishuv yashan' ve 'yishuv hadash' b'eynei hador (1882–1914) uve'eynei hahistoriyografiyah,"* *Cathedra* 6 (1977), pp. 3–19; Ya'akov Katz, *"Od al hayishuv hayashan vehayishuv hehadash,"* *Cathedra* 12 (1979), pp. 31–33; Yisra'el Kolatt, *"Miyishuv edot vekolelim leyishuv le'umi,"* *Cathedra* 12 (1979), pp. 34–39; Hannah Herzog, *"Hamusagim 'yishuv yashan' ve 'yishuv hadash' behe'arah soziologit,"* *Cathedra* 32 (1984), pp. 99–108; Yosef Salmon, *"Hayishuv ha'Ashkenazi ha'ironi beErez Yisra'el, 1880–1903,"* in Lissak (ed.) *Toledot hayishuv hayehudi be 'Erez Yisra'el,* pp. 539–620; Jehuda Reinharz, "Old and New Yishuv: The Jewish Community in Palestine at the Turn of the Century," *Jewish Studies Quarterly* 1 (1993), pp. 154–171.

48. Nissim Levi, *Perakim betoledot harefu'ah beErez Yisra'el, 1799–1948* (Haifa, 1998).

49. *Hazevi* 62, 20 Elul [5]660 [14 September 1900].

50. Zvi Shiloni, *"Hadildul ba'ukhlusiya hayehudit biYrushalayim bitkufat mil-hemet ha'olam harishonah,"* in Yehoshua Ben-Arieh et al. (eds.), *Mehkarim bege'o-grafiyah historit-yishuvit shel Erez Yisra'el*, vol. 1 (Jerusalem, 1988), pp. 128–151.

51. Moshe Smilanski, *"Nig'ei hayishuv,"* *Ahiassaf, Me'asef sifruti* (1905), pp. 97–109.

52. Menahem Friedman, *"Yeshivot hayishuv hayashan beshilhei hatekufah ha-Uthmanit — mosadot o batei ulpena?"* in Immanuel Etkes and Yosef Salmon (eds.), *Perakim betoledot hahevrah hayehudit biymei habeynayim uva'et hahadashah* (Jeru-salem, 1980), p. 375; idem, *Hevrah bemashber legitimaziyah — Hayishuv hayashan ha-Ashkenazi 1900–1914* (Jerusalem, 2001).

53. Chava Weissler, *Voices of the Matriarchs* (Boston, 1998), p. 174.

54. Melman, *Women's Orients*, p. xxii.

55. Gili Zivan, *"'Barukh . . . she'asani ishah / yisre'elit' — al hazorekh hadahuf betikun haberakhah,"* in Naham Ilan (ed.), *Ayin tovah: Du siah upulemus betarbut Yisra'el: Sefer yovel . . . Tovah Ilan* ([Tel Aviv], 1999), pp. 278–301.

56. For a general discussion of the impact of gender studies on Judaic studies see Miriam Peskowitz, "Engendering Jewish Religious History," in Miriam Peskowitz and Laura Levitt (eds.), *Judaism since Gender* (New York and London, 1997), pp. 17–39.

57. Weissler, *Voices of the Matriarchs*, p. 38.

58. The documentation will be surveyed in detail in the course of the volume.

59. Rivka Alper's book, *Korot mishpahah ahat*, should also be classed as a mem-oir; on this issue see Rivkah Alper, *"Ekh nirkam hasefer,"* *Devar hapo'elet* 22/10 (1956), p. 275.

60. Elain Showalter, "Feminist Criticism in the Wilderness," in idem (ed.), *The New Feminist Criticism: Essays on Women, Literature and Theory* (New York, 1985), p. 263; Hannah Naveh, *"Leket, pe'ah veshikhhah: Hahayim mihuz lakanon,"* in Daf-nah Yizre'eli et al. (Eds.), *Min, migdar upolitikah* (Tel Aviv, 1999), pp. 49–106.

61. The scholars on whose works I have relied for the most part are (in alphabeti-cal order) Ya'akov Barnai, Yisra'el Bartal, Yehoshua Ben-Arieh, Mordecai Eliav, Ben-Zion Gat, Yehoshua Kaniel, Aryeh Morgenstern, Tudor Parfitt, Yosef Salmon, Uziel Schmelz, and Alexander Schölch. Studies of the history of the family in the Diaspora are also of great interest, i.e., ChaeRan Y. Freeze, *Jewish Marriage and Divorce in Im-perial Russia* (Hanover, N.H., 2002).

62. Peter Burke, "History of Events and the Revival of Narrative," in idem (ed.), *New Perspectives on Historical Writing* (University Park, Pa., 1991), pp. 232–248.

63. Melman, *Women's Orients*, p. 22.

Chapter 1. The Female Experience of Immigration (pp. 1–34)

1. Susan Starr Sered, *The Religious Lives of Elderly Jewish Women in Jerusalem* (New York, 1992), pp. 145–146, note 4.

2. Aviezer Ravitzky, *"Erez hemdah vaharadah: Hayahas hadu-erki leErez Yisra'el bimkorot Yisra'el,"* in idem (ed.), *Erez Yisra'el bahagut hayehudit ba'et hahadashah* (Jerusalem, 1988), pp. 1–41.

3. Yehudah Aaron Weiss, *Bish'arayikh Yerushalayim* (Jerusalem, 1949), pp. 8–9; N. Ben-Avraham, *Sipurim Yerushalmiyim* (Jerusalem, 1994), p. 282.

4. Alper, *Korot mishpahah ahat*, p. 17.

5. E.g., Yizhak Ya'akov Yellin, *Avoteinu — Pirkei historiyah vehavay, demuyot vesi-*

purim mehayei bonei hayishuv harishonim (Jerusalem, 1966), p. 73; Ita Yellin, *Leze'eza-'ay—Zikhronotay*, vol. 1 (Jerusalem, 1938), p. 27.

6. Toive Pesil [Feinstein], *Sefer zikhron Eliyahu* (Jerusalem, 1895), p. 32. [Margalit Shilo, *Hakol hanashi haYerushalmi: Kitvei lamdaniyot min hame'ah ha-19* (Jerusalem, 2004), p. 260.]

7. Feinstein, *Sefer zikhron Eliyahu*, p. 196. [Shilo, *Hakol hanashi*, p. 248.]

8. Avraham Bartura, *Belev kashuv—Toledot R. Eliezer Bergman ish Yerushalayim* (Jerusalem, 1983); Mordechai Eliav, *Ahavat Ziyon ve'anshei Hod—Yehudei Germaniyah veyishuv Erez Yisra'el bame'ah ha19* (Tel Aviv, 1971), pp. 232, 238.

9. Bergman, *Se'u harim shalom*, p. 32.

10. Ibid., p. 21.

11. Hayim Hamburger, *Sheloshah olamot*, vol. 1 (Jerusalem, 1939), p. 14.

12. Grayevsky, *Benot Zion viYrushalayim*, p. 13.

13. Nima Adlerblum, "Sarah Beyla Hirshensohn," in Eliyahu [Leo] Jung (ed.), *Noterei moreshet—Parashiyot hayim* (Jerusalem, 1968), p. 82; idem, *Memoirs of Childhood: An Approach to Jewish Philosophy*, ed. Els Bendheim (Northvale, N.J., and Jerusalem, 1999), pp. 5–12.

14. Grayevsky, *Benot Zion viYrushalayim*; cf. also Bashan, "*Zikatam shel yehudei haMagreb*," p. 172.

15. Bertha Spafford Vester, *Our Jerusalem* (Jerusalem, 1950), p. 59; Ruth Kark, *The American Colony* (Jerusalem, 1998).

16. Moshe Nehemiah Kahanov, *Sha'alu shelom Yerushalayim* (Odessa, 1867; repr. Jerusalem, 1969), pp. 124–125.

17. Reitze, daughter of Rabbi Mordechai Chen Tov, *Sefer mishpahat yuhasin* (Jerusalem, 1885), p. 6. [Shilo, *Hakol hanashi*, p. 131.]

18. Rivkah Lipa Anikster, *Kunteres zekher olam* (Jerusalem, 1891), p. 1. [Shilo, *Hakol hanashi*, p. 92.]

19. Marion A. Kaplan, "Jewish Women in Nazi Germany: Daily Struggles, 1933–1939," *Feminist Studies* 16 (1990), pp. 592–605.

20. Victor and Edith Turner, *Image and Pilgrimage in Christian Culture* (New York, 1978), p. 18.

21. Hannah Luncz[-Bolotin], *Me'ir netivot Yerushalayim—Hayyei Avraham Moshe Luncz* (Jerusalem, 1968), p. 11; Avraham Moshe Luncz and Gedaliah Kressel (eds.), *Netivot Zion viYrushalayim—Mivhar ma'amarei Avraham Moshe Luncz* (Jerusalem, 1961), p. 13; Hannah Luncz[-Bolotin], "*Hayyei avi*," *Yerushalayim* 13 (1919), pp. 330–331.

22. Grayevsky, *Benot Zion viYrushalayim*, p. 257; see also Yizhak Shiryon, *Zikhronot* (Jerusalem, 1943), p. 49.

23. Grayevsky, *Benot Zion viYrushalayim*, p. 172.

24. A. R. Malachi, *Perakim betoledot hayishuv hayashan* (Tel Aviv, 1971), p. 254.

25. Natan Efrati, *Mishpahat Elyashar betokhekhei Yerushalayim* (Jerusalem, 1975), pp. 88–89; Leah Bornstein-Makovetzky, "*Nisu'in vegerushin bahevrah hayehudit be'Istanbul bame'ot hashemoneh-esreh vehatesha-esreh*," *Michael* 14 (Tel Aviv, 1997), p. 148.

26. Yosef Yoel Rivlin, "*Mishpahat Rivlin beErez Yisra'el*," in H. Z. Hirschberg (ed.), *Yad Yosef Yizhak Rivlin—Sefer Zikaron* (Ramat-Gan, 1964), p. 51; Shmuel Even-Or-Orenstein, "*Hanashim bemishpahat Orenstein*," *Leveit Avotam* 3–4 (1990), p. 35; Ya'akov Gellis, *Midemuyot Yerushalayim* (Jerusalem, 1962), pp. 174–175.

27. Binyamin Rivlin, *Yizhak Zvi Rivlin* (Jerusalem 1961), p. 14.

28. Shlomo Kluger, *She'elot uteshuvot ha'elef lekha Shlomo*, pt. 3, *Even ha'ezer* (Bilgorai, 1904), nos. 106, 118, 119; Shalom Mordechai Shwadron, *She'elot uteshuvot Maharsham*, pt. 1 (New York, 1962), no. 116, p. 66b.

29. Menahem Mendel Rabin, *Masa leMeron* (Jerusalem, 1983 [1889]), p. 224; Shmuel Heller, *She'elot uteshuvot shem miShmuel* (Jerusalem, 1979), no. 19, p. 85.

30. Henry Toledano, "Yahadut Maroko veyishuv Erez Yisra'el . . . ," in M. Zohari and A. Tartakover (eds.), *Hagut Ivrit be'arzot ha'Islam* (Jerusalem, 1981), pp. 228–252.

31. Morgenstern, *Meshihiyut veyishuv Erez Yisra'el*, pp. 66, 93.

32. Yaari, *Zikhronot Erez Yisra'el*, vol. 1, pp. 146–148; Yosef Yoel Rivlin, "Mishpahat Rivlin beErez Yisra'el," p. 48.

33. Bartura, *Belev kashuv*, p. 63.

34. Michal Ben-Ya'akov, "Olot le'Erez Yisra'el — Defusei hagirah shel nashim mizefon Afrikah leErez Yisra'el bame'ah hatesha-esreh," in Margalit Shilo et al. (eds.), *Ha'ivriyot hahadashot — Nashim bayishuv uvaZiyonut bir'i hamigdar* (Jerusalem, 2002), pp. 76–77.

35. Victoria Vida Valero, *Zikhronot* (Tel Aviv, 1991), p. 13.

36. Sha'ul Angel-Malachi, *Beterem reshit — misipurei Yerushalayim, mehayyei hakehilah hasefaradit biYrushalayim beme'ah hashanim ha'aharonot* (Jerusalem, 1977), p. 17.

37. See, e.g., Yosef Yoel Rivlin, "Mishpahat Rivlin beErez Yisra'el," pp. 47, 77.

38. Shmuel Yosef Agnon, "Tehilla," trans. I. M. Lask, in *Hebrew Short Stories: An Anthology*, selected by S. Y. Penueli and A. Ukhmani, vol. 1 (Tel Aviv, 1965), pp. 24–52 (quote from pp. 37–38). For differing approaches to this story see Sarah Halperin, "Al haperushim hasotrim lasipur 'Tehilla' leSh. Y. Agnon," in Dov Rapel, *Mehkarim bamikra uvahinukh mugashim liProf. Moshe Arend* (Jerusalem, 1996), pp. 236–258; Dov Fishelov, "Tehila aduyah bezemah, amusah be'oz: Halakhah uma'aseh befarshanut hasifrut," *Alpayim* 11 (1995), pp. 129–148.

39. Meir Menahem Rothschild, "Hahalukah" kevituy leyahasah shel yahadut hagolah layishuv hayehudi beErez Yisra'el bashanim 1810–1860 (Jerusalem, 1986), p. 37; Zevi Zohar, "Benei palatin shel melekh: Ta'am hahayim hayehudiyim beErez Yisra'el . . . ," in Aviezer Ravitzky (ed.), *Erez Yisra'el bahagut hayehudit ba'et hahadashah* (Jerusalem, 1988), pp. 343–344.

40. *The Life of Glückel of Hamelin, 1646–1724, Written by Herself*, trans. and ed. Beth-Zion Abrahams (London, 1962), p. 149.

41. Sered, *Religious Lives*, p. 9.

42. Ruth Lamdan, *A Separate People: Jewish Women in Palestine, Syria and Egypt in the Sixteenth Century* (Leiden, 2000), p. 198; Yaron Ben Na'eh, "Siyu'ah shel kehilat Istanbul liyhudei Erez Yisra'el bame'ah hasheva-esreh ukshareha imam," *Cathedra* 92 (1999), pp. 88–89; S. D. Goitein, *A Mediterranean Society*, vol. 3: *The Family* (Berkeley, Calif., 1978), p. 337.

43. That is, from the minimum marriageable age (generally 12–14) and older.

44. Uziel Schmelz, "Kavim meyuhadim bademografiyah shel yehudei Yerushalayim bame'ah hatesha-esreh," in Menahem Friedman et al. (eds.), *Perakim betoledot hayishuv hayehudi biYrushalayim*, vol. 2 (Jerusalem, 1976), pp. 66–67; Samuel Montagu and A. Asher, Letter to the Committee of the Sir Moses Montefiore Testimonial Fund, 13 May 1875, reproduced in Ya'akov Kellner, *Lema'an Zion —*

Hahitarevut hakelal-yehudit bimzukat hayishuv [5]630–[5]642, 1869–1882 (Jerusalem, 1977), p. 188.

45. Uziel Schmelz, *Population of Jerusalem's Urban Neighborhoods According to the Ottoman Census of 1905* (Jerusalem: Institute of Contemporary Jewry, Hebrew University of Jerusalem, 1992).

46. Shoham, *"Almenot Yerushalayim,"* p. 2.

47. Rami Yizre'el, *"Beyt ha'almin hasefaradi hakadum behar hazeytim,"* *Ariel* 122–123 (1997), pp. 41–42; Dov Hakohen, *"Ha'aliyah me'Izmir bame'ah ha19,"* p. 13.

48. Shoham, *"Almenot Yerushalayim,"* p. 21.

49. It has been suggested that communal leaders in the Diaspora encouraged widows to immigrate in order to avoid having to support them; see Ben-Ya'akov, *"Olot le'Erez Yisra'el,"* p. 79.

50. Lamdan, *A Separate People*, pp. 146–201; Cheryl Tallan, "The Medieval Jewish Widow: Powerful, Productive and Passionate" (M.A. thesis, York University, Toronto, 1989).

51. Susan Starr Sered, "The Synagogue as a Sacred Space for the Elderly Oriental Women of Jerusalem," in Susan Grossman and Rivkah Haut (eds.), *Daughters of the King* (New York, 1992), pp. 206–211; David I. Kertzer and Nancy Karweit, "The Impact of Widowhood in Nineteenth-Century Italy," in David I. Kertzer and Peter Laslett (eds.), *Aging in the Past: Demography, Society and Old Age* (Berkeley, Calif., 1995), pp. 229–248.

52. Sered, *Religious Lives*, pp. 106–108. On women's silence in religious ritual in the Pale of Settlement see Natalie Rein, *Daughters of Rachel: Women in Israel* (Harmondsworth, Eng., 1980), pp. 19–20.

53. Reitze, *Sefer mishpahat yuhasin*, p. 35. [Shilo, *Hakol hanashi*, p. 160.]

54. Natan Shor, *Sefer ha'aliyah leregel leErez Yisra'el — Toledot ha'aliyah leregel leErez Yisra'el mehatekufah haBizantit ve'ad hame'ah hatesha-esreh* (Jerusalem, 1994), pp. 98–99.

55. Melman, *Women's Orients*, pp. 172, 183.

56. Krammer, "Austrian Pilgrimage to the Holy Land," pp. 66–80.

57. Luncz-Bolotin, *Me'ir netivot Yerushalayim*, p. 24; Avraham Elmaliah, *Harishonim leZion, toledoteyhem u-f'ulatam* (Jerusalem, 1970), p. 168; Shoham, *"Almenot Yerushalayim,"* pp. 4, 9–10.

58. Ravitzky, *"Erez hemdah vaharadah,"* pp. 35–37.

59. Dov Hakohen, *"Ha'aliyah me'Izmir bame'ah ha19,"* p. 14; see also Sha'ul Angel-Malachi, *Hayei Yerushalayim, misipurei ha'ir* (Jerusalem, 1987), p. 69.

60. Dov Hakohen, *Ha'aliyah me'Izmir bame'ah ha-19*, p. 21, note 66.

61. Ya'akov Segal, *Midemuyot Yerushalayim* (Jerusalem, 1962), p. 259.

62. Joseph Nehama, *Dictionnaire du Judéo-Espagnol* (Madrid, 1977), p. 335.

63. Etkes, *Lita biYrushalayim*, pp. 87–88; Etty Lubochinsky-Lavi, *Mishpahah Yisre'elit — Toledot Shoshanah Nehemiah Yisre'elit: Yerushalayim, London, Petah Tikvah 1858–1982* (Tel Aviv, 1995), p. 5.

64. Avraham Krinitzi, *Bekhoah hama'aseh* (Tel Aviv, 1950), p. 12.

65. Letter written by Sheyna Davis, 5 Elul [5]647 [August 25, 1887], Jerusalem, to *Va'ad hapekidim veha'amarkalim*, Amsterdam, Bibliotheca Rosenthalia, Pekidim and Amarakalim Archives, Amsterdam, 51.

66. *Havazelet*, no. 14, 24 Tevet [5]636 [January 21, 1876].

67. Avraham Bartura, *Yerushalayim be'eynei ro'eha — Toledot batei hamahaseh la'aniyim vehakhnasat orehim al Har Ziyon* (Jerusalem, 1970), p. 111.

68. Binyamin Kluger, *Yerushalayim shekhunot saviv lah* (Jerusalem, 1979), unpaginated.

69. Y. Ben-Haggai, "Aniyim vekabzanim biYrushalayim ha'atikah milifnei dor," *Yeda Am* 10 (1965), p. 108.

70. Angel-Malachi, *Beterem reshit*, p. 43.

71. Ya'akov Yehoshua, *Yaldut biYrushalayim hayeshanah — Pirkei havay miyamim avaru*, 5 vols. (Jerusalem, 1965–1978), vol. 2, p. 169; idem, *Yerushalayim temol shilshom — Pirkei havay* (Jerusalem, 1977–1983), vol. 3, pp. 25–31.

72. Yehoshua, *Yaldut biYrushalayim*, vol. 5, pp. 121–122.

73. Yehoshua, *Yerushalayim temol shilshom*, vol. 1, p. 116.

74. Natalie Davis, "From Popular Religion to Religious Culture," in Steven Ozment (ed.), *Reforming Europe: A Guide to Research* (St. Louis: Center for Reformation Research, 1982), pp. 321–341.

75. Shulamit Shahar, *Ha'ishah behevrat yemei habeynayim — hama'amad harevi'i* (Tel Aviv, 1990), pp. 28–57.

76. Ephraim Taubenhaus, *Bintiv hayahid — Hayei lohem veholem be'ir hamekubalim* (Haifa, 1959); Ada Rappaport-Albert, "On Women's Hassidim: S. A. Horodecky and the Maid of Ludmir Tradition," in Ada Rappaport-Albert and Steven J. Zipperstein (eds.), *Jewish History: Essays in Honour of Chimen Abramsky* (London, 1988), pp. 495–525; Mordechai Biber, "Ha'almah miLudmir," *Reshumot* 2 (1946), pp. 69–76; Yohanan Twersky, *Habetulah miLudmir* (Jerusalem, 1949); Shoshana Pantel Zolty, *"And All Your Children Shall Be Learned": Women and the Study of Torah in Jewish Law and History* (Northvale, N.J., and London, 1993), pp. 250–252.

77. Taubenhaus, *Bintiv hayahid*, p. 41.

78. Yosef Hagalali, "Ma'amadah shel ha'ishah batenu'ah hahasidit," in idem, *Hashomerim laboker* (Meron, 1992), p. 159.

79. Daniel Carpi and Moshe Rinot, "Yoman mas'oteha shel morah yehudiyah miTrieste liYrushalayim, [5]617–[5]625," in *Kevazim letoledot hahinukh hayehudi beYisra'el uvatefuzot* 1 (1982), pp. 133, 141.

80. Aryeh Morgenstern, "MiBrody leErez Yisra'el vahazarah," *Zion* 58/1 (1992–1993), pp. 107–113; quotes on p. 108.

81. Morgenstern (in a lecture) related Malkah's departure to the revolt of the fellahin in Galilee in 1834, in the course of which the Jewish women of Safed were raped.

82. Suellen Hoy, "The Journey Out: The Recruitment and Emigration of Irish Religious Women to the United States, 1812–1914," *Journal of Women's History* 6/4–7/1 (1995), pp. 64–98.

83. Bergman, *Se'u harim shalom*, pp. 78–79.

84. Colin Turnbull, "Postscript: Anthropology as Pilgrimage," in Alan Morinis (ed.), *Sacred Journeys: The Anthropology of Pilgrimage* (Westport, Conn., and London, 1992), pp. 252–274.

85. Carpi and Rinot, "Yoman mas'oteha shel morah yehudiyah," p. 153.

86. Adlerblum, "Sarah Beyla Hirshensohn," p. 82.

87. Ita Yellin, *Leze'eza'ay*, vol. 1, p. 27.

88. See above, note 65.

89. Bernhard Neumann, *Ir hakodesh veyoshevei bah*, trans. from German (*Die

heilige Stadt und deren Bewohner [Hamburg, 1877]) by Benzion Gat (Jerusalem, 1949), p. 74.

90. Reitze, *Sefer mishpahat yuhasin*, pp. 16–17. [Shilo, *Hakol hanashi*, p. 141–142.]

91. Anikster, *Kunteres zekher olam*, p. 4b. [Shilo, *Hakol hanashi*, p. 99.] Rivkah Anikster has received considerable scholarly attention; see Yosef Yoel Rivlin, "Zur mehzavto shel Yosef Luriya z"l," in D. Kimhi (ed.), *Nefesh leDr. Yosef Luriya z"l* (Jerusalem, 1938), pp. 55–56; Yizhak Ya'akov Yellin, *Avoteinu*, pp. 172–173; Dov Genechovsky, *Sipurim Yerushalmiyim* (Jerusalem, 1989), pp. 119–123; Yael Levin-Katz, "Nashim lamdaniyot biYrushalayim," *Mabua* 26 (1993), p. 106; Pinehas Grayevsky, *Zikhron lahovevim harishonim*, vols. 1–2 (repr. Jerusalem, 1992), pp. 54–55; idem, *Benot Zion viYrushalayim*, pp. 7, 9.

92. Bergman, *Se'u harim shalom*, p. 22.

93. Grayevsky, *Benot Zion viYrushalayim*, p. 123.

94. Hemdah Ben-Yehuda, *Ben Yehuda — Hayav umif'alo* (Jerusalem, 1940), p. 42.

95. Oz Almog, *Hazabar — dyokan* (Tel Aviv, 1997), pp. 48–49.

96. Louis Loewe (ed.), *Diaries of Sir Moses and Lady Montefiore*, vols. 1–2 (facsimile of the 1890 edition) (London, 1983), vol. 2, p. 179.

97. F. K. Prochaska, *Women and Philanthropy in Nineteenth-Century England* (Oxford, 1980), p. 14.

98. Weissler, *Voices of the Matriarchs*, pp. 140–141.

99. Charlotte Haver, "Vom Schtetl in die Stadt," *Zeitschrift für Geschichte und Kultur der Juden* 5 (1995), pp. 331–358.

100. Yizhak Trivaks and Eliezer Steinman, *Sefer me'ah shanah — Anshei mofet vahaluzim rishonim beErez Yisra'el bemeshekh me'ah shanah vama'lah* (Tel Aviv, 1938), pp. 53–96; Sonia L. Lipman, "Judith Montefiore: First Lady of Anglo-Jewry," *The Jewish Historical Society of England Transactions* 21 (1962–1967), pp. 287–303.

101. Carpi and Rinot, "Yoman mas'oteha shel morah yehudiyah."

102. Israel Bartal, introduction to photographic reproduction of Judith Montefiore, *Private Journal of a Visit to Egypt and Palestine*, originally published in London, 1836 (Jerusalem, 1975).

103. Carpi and Rinot, *Yoman mas'oteha shel morah yehudiyah*, p. 133; and see below, chapter 5.

104. Sha'ul Sapir, "Sheloshet mas'otav harishonim shel Moshe Montefiore leErez Yisra'el," in Yehoshua Ben-Arieh et al. (eds.), *Mehkarim bege'ografiyah historityishuvit shel Erez Yisra'el*, vol. 1 (Jerusalem, 1988), pp. 30–31.

105. Carpi and Rinot, *Yoman mas'oteha shel morah yehudiyah*, pp. 134–135.

106. Judith Montefiore, *Private Journal*, p. 195.

107. Trivaks and Steinman, *Sefer me'ah shanah*, p. 79 (Hebrew translation; this particular part of the Montefiore journals cannot be traced).

108. Carpi and Rinot, *Yoman mas'oteha shel morah yehudiyah*, p. 139.

109. Ibid., p. 140.

110. Ibid., p. 146.

111. Ibid., p. 150.

112. Anikster, *Kunteres zekher olam*, p. 3b. [Shilo, *Hakol hanashi*, p. 114.]

113. Moshe David Hadad, *Sefer ma'amar Ester* (Jerba, 1946).

114. Ibid., pp. 8a, 11b, 13b.

115. Ibid., p. 15a.

116. For the concept of immigration in this context see Sered, *Religious Lives*,

pp. 19–20. For the similar characteristics of immigration to the country and pilgrimage within the country itself see also Julie Rivlin, "'Leyl kedoshim' — Aliyah lekivrei zadikim ke'erua shel te'atron sevivati" (M.A. thesis, Hebrew University of Jerusalem, 1997).

117. Edwin Ardener, "Belief and the Problem of Women," in Shirley Ardener (ed.), Perceiving Women (New York, 1975), p. 3

118. Letter from Rivkah, widow of Yehosef Schwartz, to her brother-in-law [date illegible, probably in the 1850s], CAHJP 7227 (2–4).

119. [Feinstein], Sefer zikhron Eliyahu, p. 24. [Shilo, Hakol hanashi, p. 252.]

120. Anikster, Kunteres zekher olam, p. 5a. [Shilo, Hakol hanashi, p. 100.]

121. Elchanan Reiner, "Aliyah va-aliyah leregel leErez Yisra'el 1099–1517" (Ph.D. dissertation, Hebrew University of Jerusalem, 1988), p. 1.

122. Bilu, "Pulhanei kedoshim," p. 11.

123. Myrcia Eliade, The Myth of the Eternal Return (New York, 1954); Ravitzky, "Erez hemdah vaharadah," pp. 14–17 and notes ibid.

124. Mordechai Levanon, Toledot hayay, [5]648–[5]746 (Jerusalem, 1997), p. 11; Angel-Malachi, Beterem reshit.

125. Turner, Image and Pilgrimage, p. 32; Thomas A. Idinopulos, "Sacred Space and Profane Power: Victor Turner and the Perspective of Holy Land Pilgrimage," in Bryan F. LeBeau and Menachem Mor (eds.), Pilgrims and Travellers to the Holy Land (Omaha, Neb., 1996), pp. 9–20.

126. For a parallel phenomenon among Muslim women in the seventeenth century see Deror Ze'evi, "Hame'ah ha'Uthmanit — Sanjak Yerushalayim bame'ah ha-sheva-esreh" (Ph. D. dissertation, Tel Aviv University, 1991), p. 326.

127. Chatterjee, "Their Own Words?" p. 205.

128. Avraham Stahl, Minhag ha'aliyah leregel lekivrei kedoshim vehityahasut elav behadrakhat metayelim (Har Gilo, 1981); Avraham Moshe Luncz, "Ha'em vehabat," Luah Erez Yisra'el (Jerusalem, 1911), p. 130.

129. Ze'ev Vilnay, Mazevot kodesh beErez Yisra'el, 2 vols. (Jerusalem, 1985–1986); Shraga Weiss, Atarim kedoshim beErez Yisra'el (Jerusalem, 1986); Zvi Ilan, Kivrei zadikim beErez Yisra'el (Jerusalem, 1997).

130. Avraham Moshe Luncz, Yerushalayim, vol. 1 (Vienna and Jerusalem, 1882), pp. 80, 83, 84, 87, 94, 97, 117, 120; Toledano, "Yoman masa shel R. Yizhak Toledano," p. 154; Grayevsky, Zikhron lahovevim harishonim, vol. 1, p. 471.

131. Avi Sasson, "Masoret vege'ografiyah, megamot vetahalikhim behitkadeshut kevarim bemishor hof Yehudah," in Eyal Regev (ed.), Hidushim beheker mishor hahof . . . (Ramat-Gan, 1997), pp. 97–113.

132. Bergman, Se'u harim shalom, p. 101; Moshe Reicher, Sefer sha'arei Yerushalayim (Lemberg, 1870), Sha'ar 9, unpaginated.

133. Gad Frumkin, Derekh shofet biYrushalayim (Tel Aviv, 1955), p. 70.

134. Vilnay, Mazevot kodesh, 1, p. 40.

135. Alan Morinis, Sacred Journeys: The Anthropology of Pilgrimage (Westport, Conn., 1992), p. 8.

136. James J. Preston, "Spiritual Magnetism."

137. Grayevsky, Zikhron lahovevim harishonim, vol. 2, p. 75.

138. Shim'on Berman, Mas'ot Shim'on — Erez Yisra'el 1870, trans. from Yiddish by David Niv (Jerusalem, 1980), p. 99; Yehudah Aaron Weiss, Bish'arayikh Yerushalayim, p. 59; Grayevsky, Benot Zion viYrushalayim, p. 363.

139. Avraham Yaari, *Mas'ot Erez Yisra'el shel olim yehudim* (Tel Aviv, 1946), p. 357.

140. Bet Halevi, *Toledot yehudei Kalish*, p. 314; for a similar reaction see Moshe Altbauer, "Iggerot haRav Yehoshua Zelig Hakohen mishnat [5]613 al odot aliyato arzah," *Cathedra* 1 (1976), pp. 109–110.

141. Bet Halevi, *Toledot yehudei Kalish*, p. 317.

142. Shoshanah Halevi, *Sifrei Yerushalayim harishonim [5]601–[5]651* (Jerusalem, 1976), nos. 74, 202, 606.

143. Anikster, *Kunteres zekher olam* (1884 ed.), p. 4b. [Shilo, *Hakol hanashi*, p. 116.]

144. Letter from Rachel Anikster to *Va'ad hapekidim veha'amarkalim*, Bibliotheca Rosenthalia, Pekidim and Amarkalim Archives, Amsterdam, IV, 61 (41–239).

145. [Feinstein], *Sefer zikhron Eliyahu*, pp. 3a, 33a. [Shilo, *Hakol hanashi*, pp. 232, 260.]

146. Sered, *Religious Lives*, p. 18.

147. Grayevsky, *Benot Zion viYrushalayim*, p. 180.

148. Yehudah Yizhak Yehezkel, "Kotel ma'aravi," *Me'asef Zion* 3 (1929), p. 141.

149. S. C. Bartlett, *From Egypt to Palestine through Sinai: The Wilderness and the South Country* (New York, 1977 [1874]), p. 438.

150. Bet Halevi, *Toledot yehudei Kalish*, p. 314.

151. Mordechai Hakohen, *Hakotel hama'aravi* (Ramat-Gan, 1968), p. 91.

152. Grayevsky, *Benot Zion viYrushalayim*, p. 363; Ya'akov El'azar, *Diyur uklitah bayishuv hayashan, [5]602–[5]679* (Jerusalem, 1981), pp. 43–44.

153. Luncz, *Yerushalayim*, vol. 1, p. 56.

154. Mordechai Hakohen, *Hakotel hama'aravi*, p. 91.

155. Avraham Shmuel Hirschberg, *Be'erez hamizrah* (Vilna, 1910; repr. Jerusalem, 1977), p. 397.

156. Sered, *Religious Lives*, pp. 27, 32–33, 117.

157. Luncz, *Netivot Zion viYrushalayim*, p. 202.

158. Erik Cohen, "Pilgrimage and Tourism: Convergence and Divergence," in Morinis (ed.), *Sacred Journeys*, pp. 47–61.

159. Grayevsky, *Zikhron lehovevim rishonim*, vol. 2, p. 257; Hayim Michal Mikhlin, *Bir'i hadorot* (Tel Aviv, 1950), p. 39; Shoshanah Halevi, *Parashiyot betoledot hayishuv* (Jerusalem, 1989), pp. 178–182; *Havazelet*, no. 1, 12 Tishri [5]641 [September 17, 1880], p. 8; ibid., no. 2, 1 Marheshvan [October 6, 1880], p. 15; ibid., 24 Marheshvan [October 29, 1880], p. 36.

160. Weissler, *Voices of the Matriarchs*, pp. 133–139.

161. Meron Benvenisti, *Ir hamenuhot — Batei ha'almin shel Yerushalayim* (Jerusalem, 1990), pp. 57–85.

162. Dov Genechovsky, *Misipurei hahevrah hagevohah ve'od me'ah sipurim yerushalmiyim* (Jerusalem, 1993), pp. 202–204.

163. *Hazevi*, no. 35, 29 Elul [5]655 [September 18, 1895]; *Hashkafah*, 14 Heshvan [5]667 [November 2, 1906].

164. Luncz, *Yerushalayim*, vol. 1, p. 58; Mordechai Aaron Ginzburg, *Devir*, I (Warsaw, 1884), p. 61.

165. Sered, *Religious Lives*, p. 22.

166. Yoram Bilu, "The Inner Limits of Communitas: A Covert Dimension of Pilgrimage Experience," *Ethos* 16 (1988), pp. 302–325; see also Turner, *Image and Pilgrimage*, p. v.

167. Meir Benayahu, "Hanhagot mekubalei Zefat beMeron," *Sefunot* 6 (1962),

p. 11; idem, *"Ha'aliyah leMeron,"* in Eli Schiller (ed.), *Sefer Ze'ev Vilnay*, vol. 2 (Jerusalem, 1987), p. 330.

168. Avraham Yaari, *"Toledot hahilula beMeron,"* *Tarbiz* 31 (1962), pp. 73–101; Aharon Bir, *"Kever Shim'on hazadik biYrushalayim,"* *Mahanayim* 116 (1968), pp. 102–105; Shim'on Hayat, *"Te'udot hadashot al hayishuv hayehudi biYrushalayim batekufah haUthmanit,"* *Sinai* 83 (1978), pp. 177–180.

169. The description that follows aims to represent the main components of the ceremony and in particular to analyze the place that it assigned to women.

170. Luncz, *Yerushalayim*, vol. 1, p. 49.

171. Vilnay, *Mazevot kodesh*, vol. 2, p. 143.

172. Bet Halevi, *Toledot yehudei Kalish*, p. 324; Carlebach, *Mikhtavim miYrushalayim*, p. 64.

173. Avraham Menahem Mendel Mohr, *Mevaseret Zion* (Jerusalem, 1880), p. 17.

174. Bet Halevi, *Toledot yehudei Kalish*, p. 325.

175. Reicher, *Sefer sha'arei Yerushalayim*, Sha'ar 9, "Minhagei ha'arez," unpaginated.

176. *Midrash Tanhuma*, Ki tisa 19.

177. Zeyde Avraham Heller, *Harav hamanhig veharofé. Toledot hayav ufo'alo shel Rabbi Shmuel Heller . . .* ([n.p.], 1989), pp. 203–210; Shmuel Heller, *She'elot uteshuvot*, nos. 38–42.

178. Yaari, *"Toledot hahilula beMeron,"* pp. 99–101.

179. Luncz, *Yerushalayim*, vol. 1, p. 50.

180. Hannah Trager, *Pictures of Jewish Home-Life, Fifty Years Ago* (London, [n.d.]), p. 58.

181. Berman, *Mas'ot Shim'on*, p. 100.

182. Mohr, *Mevaseret Zion*, p. 18.

183. Morinis, *Sacred Journeys*, p. 14.

184. Yoram Bilu, *Ha-aretz*, May 23, 1997, p. D1.

185. Bet Halevi, *Toledot yehudei Kalish*, p. 325.

186. Lamdan, *A Separate People*, pp. 129–130.

187. Yaari, *"Toledot hahilula beMeron,"* p. 100.

188. *Hazevi*, no. 19, 23 Iyar [5]648 [May 4, 1888].

189. *Moriah*, supplement to no. 85, 21 Iyar [5]671 [May 19, 1911].

190. *Hazevi*, no. 19, 23 Iyar [5]648.

191. Ada Maimon, *Le'orekh haderekh* (Tel Aviv, 1972), pp. 13–17.

192. Bilu, *"Pulhanei kedoshim,"* p. 20.

193. *Sefer mesos kol ha'arez* (Jerusalem, 1967), pp. 22–25.

194. Vilnay, *Mazevot kodesh*, vol. 2, p. 138.

195. Weissler, *Voices of the Matriarchs*, p. 133.

196. Bilu, "The Inner Limits of Communitas," p. 312.

197. Vilnay, *Mazevot kodesh*, vol. 1, p. 42.

198. Reiner, "Aliyah va-aliyah leregel," p. 15.

199. Pinehas Zvi Grayevsky, *Ziyun lekever Rahel imenu — Miginzei Yerushalayim* (Jerusalem, 1932).

200. Carpi and Rinot, *"Yoman mas'oteha shel morah yehudiyah,"* p. 145.

201. Rahel Yanna'it Ben-Zvi, *Anu olim* (Jerusalem, 1969), p. 129; Luncz, *Netivot Zion viYrushalayim*, p. 224; Etkes, *Lita biYrushalayim*, p. 135; Yehoshua Barzilai, "Be-

sha'arei Yerushalayim," in Yafah Berlovitz (ed.), *E'ebrah-na ba'arez — Masa'ot beErez Yisra'el shel anshei ha'aliyah harishonah* (Tel Aviv, 1992), pp. 84–85.

202. James Finn, *Stirring Times, or Records from Jerusalem Consular Chronicles of 1853 to 1856* (London, 1878), pp. 118–119.

203. Ben-Arieh, *Jerusalem . . . the New City*, pp. 124, 436–437.

204. Angel-Malachi, *Beterem reshit*, p. 11; Shraga Weiss, *Atarim kedoshim*.

205. For the figure of Rachel in a special mother's prayer composed in the nineteenth century see Weissler, *Voices of the Matriarchs*, pp. 121–125; Jody Elizabeth Myers, "The Myth of Matriarchy in Recent Writings on Jewish Women's Spirituality," *Jewish Social Studies* 4/1 (1997), pp. 7–11.

206. Susan Starr Sered, "Rachel's Tomb: Societal Liminality and the Revitalization of a Shrine," *Religion* 19 (1989), pp. 27–40; idem, "Rachel, Mary and Fatima," *Cultural Anthropology* 6 (1991), pp. 131–146; idem, "The Synagogue as a Sacred Space"; idem, *Religious Lives*.

207. Sha'ul Sapir, "*Sheloshet mas'otav harishonim,*" p. 18.

208. Berman, *Mas'ot Shim'on*, p. 72.

209. Yaari, *Mas'ot Erez Yisra'el*, p. 691.

210. Yizhak Ben-Zvi, *Zikhronot ureshumot mehane'urim ad 1920* (Jerusalem, 1969), p. 129.

211. Shmuel Yosef Zevin, *Hamo'adim bahalakhah* (Tel Aviv, 1957), pp. 143–144.

212. Taubenhaus, *Bintiv hayahid*, p. 38.

213. Daniel Sperber, *Minhagei Yisra'el*, pt. 4 (Jerusalem, 1994), pp. 113–114.

214. Bergman, *Se'u harim shalom*, p. 105; see also Miriam Burla, "*Ha'ziyara' bekever Rahel imenu: Pirkei zikhronot,*" *Bama'arakhah* 175 (1975), pp. 14–15.

215. Montefiore, *Private Journal*, p. 206.

216. *Hazevi*, 11th year, no. 16, Iyar [5]655 (Spring 1895).

217. Yaari, *Mas'ot Erez Yisra'el*, p. 691.

218. Sered, *Religious Lives*, p. 36.

219. Montefiore, *Private Journal*, p. 206.

220. Druyanov and Laskov, *Ketavim letoledot Hibbat Zion*, pp. 117–131; Margalit Shilo, "*Hashekhunot hahadashot — hemshekh hayashan o reshit hehadash?*" in Michael Shashar (ed.), *Sefer Yeshurun* (Jerusalem, 1999), pp. 261–269.

221. *Havazelet*, 12 Heshvan [5]642 [November 4, 1881].

222. Rachel Yanna'it Ben-Zvi, *Anu olim*, pp. 30–32.

223. Bergman, *Se'u harim shalom*, p. 105.

224. Yehoshua, *Yaldut biYrushalayim*, vol. 3, p. 43.

225. Rachel Furst, "Red Strings: A Modern Case of Charms," in Micha D. Halpern and Chana Safrai (eds.), *Jewish Legal Writings by Women* (Jerusalem, 1998), pp. 259–277.

226. Krinitzi, *Bekhoah hama'aseh*, p. 12.

227. Sperber, *Minhagei Yisra'el*, pt. 4, p. 317.

228. Sha'ul Sapir, "*Gishatah ve'ofi terumatah shel hakehilah hayehudit biBritanyah lehitpatehut hayishuv hayehudi be'Erez Yisra'el bame'ah ha-19*" (Ph.D. dissertation, Hebrew University of Jerusalem, 1989), p. 262.

229. Shraga Weiss, *Atarim kedoshim*, p. 14.

230. Burla, "*Ha'ziyara' bekever Rahel imenu,*" p. 15; Weissler, *Voices of the Matriarchs*, pp. 133–138.

231. Grayevsky, *Benot Zion viYrushalayim*, p. 204.
232. Shraga Weiss, *Atarim kedoshim*, p. 10.
233. Burla, "*Ha'ziyara' bekever Rahel imenu*," p. 15.
234. Angel-Malachi, *Beterem reshit*, p. 11.
235. Weissler, *Voices of the Matriarchs*, p. 65.
236. Sered, *Religious Lives*, pp. 139–140.
237. This perception will be discussed in detail in the concluding chapter.
238. Ravitzky, "*Erez hemdah vaharadah*," p. 4.
239. James J. Preston, "Spiritual Magnetism," p. 43.
240. Grayevsky, *Zikhron lahovevim harishonim*, vol. 1, p. 45.
241. Yehudah Raab, *Hatelem harishon — Zikhronot 1862–1930* (Jerusalem, 1988), p. 46.
242. Barbara Schreier, "Becoming American: Jewish Women Immigrants, 1880–1920," *History Today* 44/3 (1994), p. 26, describes a similar reaction in emigrants reaching America.
243. David Siton, "*Sipurah shel shekhunah Yerushalmit*," *Shevet va'am* 6 (1971), p. 44 (my emphasis).
244. Sered, *Religious Lives*, p. 60.

Chapter 2. Princess or Prisoner? Marriage as a Female Experience (pp. 35–68)

1. Julia Chelouche, *Ha'ez vehashorashim* ([n.p.], 1982), p. 28.
2. Yisra'el Bartal and Yeshayahu Gafni (eds.), *Eros, Erusin ve'isurin — Miniyut umishpahah bahistoriyah* (Jerusalem, 1998), pp. 7–14; Chatterjee, "Their Own Words?" p. 208; Tamara K. Hareven, "The History of a Family as an Interdisciplinary Field," in Theodore Rabb and Robert Rothberg, *The Family in History: Interdisciplinary Essays* (New York, 1973), pp. 211–226; Shulamit Magnus, "'Out of the Ghetto': Integrating the Study of the Jewish Woman into the Study of 'The Jews,'" *Judaism* 39/1 (1990), p. 35.
3. Shulamit Shahar, "*Al toledot hamishpahah*," in Bartal and Gafni (eds.), *Eros, Erusin ve'isurin*, p. 23.
4. Paula E. Hyman, "Introduction: Perspectives on the Evolving Jewish Family," in Steven M. Cohen and Paula E. Hyman (eds.), *The Jewish Family: Myths and Reality* (New York, 1986), p. 7; idem, "The Modern Jewish Family: Image and Reality," in David Kraemer (ed.), *The Jewish Family: Metaphor and Memory* (Oxford, 1989), p. 180.
5. Jacob Katz, *Tradition and Crisis: Jewish Society at the End of the Middle Ages*, trans. Bernard Cooperman (New York, 1993), pp. 113ff.
6. Blu Greenberg, "Woman," in Arthur A. Cohen and Paul Mendes-Flohr (eds.), *Contemporary Religious Thought* (New York and London, 1987), pp. 1039–1053; David Kraemer (ed.), *The Jewish Family: Metaphor and Memory* (Oxford, 1989), p. 5; Nitza Abarbanell, *Havah veLilit* (Ramat-Gan, 1994); Avraham Grossman, *Hasidot umoredot: Nashim yehudiyot be'Eiropah biymei habeinayim* (Jerusalem, 2001), pp. 232.
7. Meir Benayahu, "*Sefer takanot leminhagim shel Yerushalayim*," *Kiryat Sefer* 22 (1945), pp. 262–265; Avraham Lavski, "*Takanot Yerushalayim lemin tehilat hame'ah ha16 ve'ad lemahazit hame'ah ha19*" (M.A. thesis, Bar-Ilan University, Ramat-Gan, 1974).

8. Moshe David Ga'on, *Yehudei hamizrah beErez Yisra'el* (Jerusalem, 1928), vol. 1, pp. 112–113; for a similar regulation see Ya'akov Goldberg, *"Nisu'ei hayehudim be-Polin hayeshanah beda'at hakahal shel tekufat hahaskalah,"* *Gal'ed* 4–5 (1978), p. 27.

9. Lavski, *"Takanot Yerushalayim,"* p. 67.

10. Akiva Yosef Schlesinger, *Hevra mahazirei atarah leyoshnah* (Jerusalem, 1870), p. 9b.

11. Carpi and Rinot, *"Yoman mas'oteha shel morah yehudiyah,"* p. 152.

12. Uziel Schmelz, *"Ha'ukhlusiya ba'azorei Yerushalayim veHevron bereshit hame'ah ha'esrim,"* *Cathedra* 36 (1985), p. 144.

13. Akiva Yosef Schlesinger, *Bet Yosef hehadash* (Jerusalem, 1875), p. 94.

14. For some exceptions see Eliav, *Ahavat Ziyon*, p. 215; Lavski, *"Takanot Yerushalayim,"* p. 67; Aryeh Leib Frumkin, *Toledot hakhmei Yerushalayim* (Jerusalem, 1969), vol. 4, p. 22; Goitein, *Mediterranean Society*, vol. 3, pp. 48–53.

15. Sha'ul Stampfer, "Remarriage among Jews and Christians in Nineteenth-Century Eastern Europe," *Jewish History* 3/2 (1988), pp. 85–114.

16. Jacob Katz, *Le'umiyut yehudit, Massot umehkarim* (Jerusalem, 1979), p. 159.

17. Y. Shmuel Glick, *Hazikah shebeyn nisu'in leminhagei avelut bemasoret Yisra'el* (Jerusalem: Schechter Institute, 1998).

18. Eliyahu Porush, *Zikhronot rishonim* (Jerusalem, 1963), p. 39.

19. Reicher, *Sefer sha'arei Yerushalayim*, *Sha'ar* 7, unpaginated.

20. Yehudah Razahbi, *"Parashat hitnahalut yehudei Teiman biYrushalayim,"* in *Yerushalayim: Riv'on leheker Yerushalayim vetoledoteha* vol. 1 (Jerusalem, 1948), p. 118.

21. *First Marriages: Patterns and Determinants* (New York: United Nations, 1988), p. 11.

22. Sha'ul Stampfer, *"Hamashma'ut hahevratit shel nisu'ei boser bemizrah Eiropah bame'ah ha-19,"* in Ezra Mendelson and Chone Schmeruk (eds.), *Studies on Polish Jewry: Paul Glikson Memorial Volume* (Jerusalem, 1987), pp. 65–77.

23. Nissim Binyamin Gamlieli, *"Hayei ha'ishah hayehudiyah beTeiman uma'amadah hahevrati,"* *Tema* 6 (1998), pp. 133, 140, 149.

24. Ya'akov Gellis, *Minhagei Erez Yisra'el, halakhot vahalikhot, dinim uminhagim shenahagu lefihem benei Erez Yisra'el bekhol hadorot vehazemanim umehem hanehugim ad hayom* (Jerusalem, 1968), p. 326.

25. Avraham Stahl, *Mishpahah vegidul yeladim beyahadut hamizrah* (Jerusalem, 1993), p. 64.

26. Bartura, *Belev kashuv*, p. 169.

27. Netter's report to the alliance directors, quoted in Kellner, *Lema'an Zion*, p. 179.

28. Ilanah Krausman-Ben Amos, *"Defusei hitbagrut be'Angliyah ba'et hahadashah hamukdemet: Hamikreh shel Edward Barlow,"* in Bartal and Gafni (eds.), *Eros, Erusin ve'isurin*, pp. 145, 149.

29. For a description of a Bar Mitzvah celebration followed on the same day by the boy's marriage see Trivaks and Steinman, *Sefer me'ah shanah*, p. 418.

30. Fadwa Toukan, *Derekh hararit*, trans. into Hebrew by Rachel Halvah ([n.p.], 1993), p. 103.

31. Lawrence Stone, *The Past and the Present Revisited* (London, 1987), pp. 311–326.

32. Yehoshua, *Yaldut biYrushalayim*, vol. 2, p. 59.

33. Alper, *Korot mishpahah ahat*, p. 98.

34. Yeshayahu Press, *Me'ah shanah biYrushalayim* (Jerusalem, 1964), p. 55.

35. Luncz[-Bolotin], "*Hayei Avi,*" p. 332.

36. Luncz, *Yerushalahim,* vol. 1 (1882), p. 57.

37. Porush, *Zikhronot rishonim,* p. 82.

38. The same is true of a regulation concerning decedents' estates; see Yehoshua Kaniel, "*Ma'avakim irguniyim vekalkaliyim beyn ha'edot biYrushalayim bame'ah ha19,*" in Menahem Friedman et al. (eds.), *Perakim betoledot hayishuv hayehudi biYrushalayim,* vol. 2 (Jerusalem, 1976), pp. 97–126.

39. Press, *Me'ah shanah biYrushalayim,* p. 55.

40. For example, Hamburger, *Sheloshah olamot,* vol. 1, p. 56; Moshe Blau, *Al homotayikh Yerushalayim* (Benei Berak, 1967), p. 20; Bartura, *Belev kashuv,* p. 198; William Francis Lynch, *Narrative of the United States Expedition to the River Jordan and the Dead Sea* (Philadelphia, 1849), p. 159; Montefiore, *Private Journal,* p. 203; David Siton, "*Sipurah shel shekhunah Yerushalmit,*" p. 45; Gamlieli, "*Hayei ha'ishah hayehudiyah.*"

41. Shim'on Stern, "*Te'ur harefu'ah biYrushalayim be'emza hame'ah ha19 al yedei Dr. Titus Tobler,*" in Ephraim Lev et al. (eds.), *Harefu'ah biYrushalayim ledoroteha* (Tel Aviv, 1999), p. 12.

42. Stampfer, "*Hamashma'ut hahevratit,*" p. 77.

43. Gellis, *Minhagei Erez Yisra'el,* p. 327.

44. For one attempt to abolish the practice see Yizhak Avishur, *Hahatunah hayehudit beBaghdad uvivnoteha* (Haifa, 1990), pp. 33–35.

45. *Hazevi* 12, no. 18, 9 Shevat [5]656 [January 24, 1896].

46. Stampfer, "*Hamashma'ut hahevratit,*" pp. 74–75.

47. Avraham Elmaliah, "*Mehayei haSephardim,*" *Hashiloah* 24 (Odessa, 1911), p. 266.

48. Yehudah Razahbi, *Bo'i Teiman — Mehkarim ute'udot betarbut yehudei Teiman* (Tel Aviv, 1967), p. 326.

49. Jerusalem mission schools made similar attempts; see Inger Marie Okkenhaug, "Civilization, Culture and Education: Anglican Mission, Women and Education in the Holy Land during the Nineteenth and Twentieth Centuries," in Anthony O'Mahoney (ed.), *The Christian Communities of Modern Jerusalem* (University of Wales Press, forthcoming).

50. Yehoshua, *Yaldut biYrushalayim,* vol. 3, p. 225.

51. David Spitzer, *Sefer takhshitei nashim* (Jerusalem, 1913), p. 16a; see also Freeze, *Jewish Marriage,* p. 13.

52. *Sefer Torat Rabenu Shmuel Salant,* ed. R. Nisan Aharon Tokachinsky (Jerusalem, 1998), vol. 2, p. 79.

53. Mendel Lewittes, *Jewish Marriage, Rabbinic Law, Legend and Custom* (Northvale, N.Y., 1994), p. 41.

54. Hamburger, *Sheloshah olamot,* vol. 1, pp. 15, 19.

55. El'azar, *Diyur uklitah bayishuv hayashan,* p. 48.

56. For a similar custom in Yemenite Muslim society see Gamlieli, "*Hayei ha'ishah hayehudiyah,*" pp. 135–137.

57. Ben Zion Yadler, *Betuv Yerushalayim* (Benei Berak, 1967), p. 53.

58. Press, *Me'ah shanah biYrushalayim,* p. 55.

59. Luncz, *Netivot Zion viYrushalayim,* p. 202.

60. Yehuda Aaron Weiss, *Bish'arayikh Yerushalayim,* p. 59.

61. Ben Zion Binyamin (ed.), *MeHodu liYrushalayim: Sipur shenei masa'ot meHodu leErez Yisra'el* (Jerusalem, 1993), p. 137.

62. Ita Yellin, *Leze'eza'ay*, vol. 1, pp. 59–61, 97–99.

63. Stone, *Past and Present Revisited*, p. 333.

64. Ita Yellin, *Leze'eza'ay*, vol. 1, p. 100.

65. *First Marriages*, p. 9.

66. Yehuda Aaron Weiss, *Bish'arayikh Yerushalayim*, p. 58.

67. Hamburger, *Sheloshah olamot*, vol. 3, p. 7.

68. Yehoshua, *Yaldut biYrushalayim*, vol. 3, p. 225.

69. Hamburger, *Sheloshah olamot*, vol. 1, p. 15.

70. Elmaliah, *Harishonim leZion*, p. 230.

71. Aryeh Leib Frumkin, *Masa Even Shmuel: Masa le'erez hakodesh bishnat 5631* (Petah Tikvah, 1979), pp. 52–53.

72. David Siton, "*Sipurah shel shekhunah Yerushalmit*," p. 45.

73. Berman, *Mas'ot Shim'on*, p. 80. For the futility of any attempt by a girl to refuse a suggested match see Puah Rakovsky, *My Life as a Radical Jewish Woman: Memoirs of a Zionist Feminist in Poland*, trans. Barbara Harshav, ed. Paula E. Hyman (Bloomington, Ind., 2002), pp. 33–37.

74. *Ha'or*, no. 16, 28 Shevat [5]651 [February 6, 1891].

75. Avraham Stahl, "*Ahavah kegorem bivhirat ben hazug bahistoriyah, basifrut uvafolklor*," *Mehkerei Hamerkaz leheker hafolklor* 4 (1974), pp. 125–136.

76. Jacob Katz, "*Nisu'im vehayei ishut bemoza'ei yemei habeynayim*," *Zion* 10 (1945), p. 42.

77. Ephraim Cohen-Reiss, *Mizikhronot ish Yerushalayim* (Jerusalem, 1967), p. 139.

78. Ita Yellin, *Leze'eza'ay*, vol. 2, p. 8.

79. Hannah Luncz[-Bolotin], "*Ha'em vehabat*," *Luah Erez Yisra'el* [5]671 [1910/1911], p. 138.

80. Yehoshua Kaniel, "*Hayahasim hahevratiyim beyn ha'Ashkenazim laSephardim bayishuv hayashan biYrushalayim bame'ah ha*19," in H. Z. Hirschberg (ed.), *Vatikin*, pp. 47–65.

81. Avraham Shmuel Hirschberg, *Be'erez hamizrah*, pp. 384–385.

82. For a marriage between Hasidim and *mitnagdim* see Yosef Rivlin, "*Minhagei Pesah biYrushalayim*," *Mahanayim* 44 (1960), p. 121; for marriage between Jews of the Old Yishuv and residents of the *moshavot*, Jaffa and Haifa, see *Hashkafah*, no. 1, 21 Tishri [5]658 [October 22, 1897]; ibid.., no. 4, 24 Heshvan [5]658 [November 19, 1897]; *Hazevi*, no. 34, 20 Sivan [5]658 [June 10, 1898].

83. Genechovsky, *Misipurei hahevrah hagevohah*, pp. 64–65.

84. Razahbi, "*Parashat hitnahalut yehudei Teiman biYrushalayim*," p. 117, note 11.

85. Elizabeth Ann Finn, *Reminiscences of Mrs. Finn* (London and Edinburgh, 1929), p. 55.

86. Ludwig August Frankl, *Nach Jerusalem! Palästina*, vol. 2 (Leipzig, 1858), p. 55.

87. Moshe David Ga'on, "*Moshe Montefiore veda'agato legoral benei adat hayehudim hama'aravim biYrushalayim*," *Minhah le'Avraham* (Jerusalem, 1959), p. 178.

88. Angel-Malachi, *Beterem reshit*, pp. 38–40.

89. Montefiore, *Private Journal*, p. 180.

90. *Hazevi*, No. 35, 20 Tamuz [5]645 [July 3, 1885].

91. Kaniel, *"Hayahasim hahevratiyim,"* esp. pp. 56–59.

92. Bartura, *Belev kashuv*, p. 142.

93. Ibid., p. 166.

94. Grayevsky, *Benot Zion viYrushalayim*, p. 38.

95. Grayevsky, *Zikhron lahovevim harishonim*, vol. 2, p. 392.

96. Porush, *Zikhronot rishonim*, p. 82.

97. Uzzi Ornan, "Hebrew in Palestine before and after 1882," *Journal of Semitic Studies* 29 (1984), pp. 225–253; Tudor Parfitt, "The Use of Hebrew in Palestine," *Journal of Semitic Studies* 17 (1972), pp. 237–252.

98. Avraham Shmuel Hirschberg, *Be'erez hamizrah*, pp. 397–398.

99. Yehoshua Yellin, *Zikhronot leven Yerushalayim* (Jerusalem, 1924), p. 25.

100. Peninah Talmon-Morag, *"Hishtalvutah shel edah vatikah behevrat mehagrim — Ha'edah haSefaradit beYisra'el"* (Ph.D. dissertation, Hebrew University of Jerusalem, 1980), p. 129.

101. Ita Yellin, *Leze'eza'ay*, vol. 2, p. 10.

102. Yehoshua, *Yaldut biYrushalayim*, vol. 3, p. 95.

103. El'azar, *Diyur uklitah bayishuv hayashan*, p. 67.

104. Letter written by David b. Menachem Hakohen, 8 Iyar [5]659 [April 18, 1899], Bibliotheca Rosenthalia, Pekidim and Amarkalim Archives, Amsterdam.

105. For the legal aspect of this concept see Ben Zion Sharshevsky, *Dinei mishpahah* (Jerusalem, 1993), p. 93.

106. Judith E. Tucker, "Marriage and Family in Nablus, 1720–1856: Toward a History of Arab Marriage," *Journal of Family History* 13/2 (1983), pp. 165–179.

107. Katz, *"Nisu'im vehayei ishut,"* pp. 25–26.

108. Yehoshua, *Yaldut biYrushalayim*, vol. 2, p. 63.

109. Ita Yellin, *Leze'eza'ay*, vol. 2, pp. 1–2.

110. Yehoshua Yellin, *Zikhronot leven Yerushalayim*, p. 25.

111. Mark Glazer, "The Dowry as Capital Accumulation among the Sephardic Jews of Istanbul, Turkey," *International Journal of Middle East Studies* 10 (1979), pp. 373–380.

112. See below, chapter 6.

113. Alper, *Korot mishpahah ahat*, p. 103.

114. *Hashkafah*, no. 91, 13 Elul [5]667 [August 23, 1907].

115. David Benvenisti, *Yehudei Saloniki badorot ha'aharonim: Halikhot hayim, masoret vehevrah* (Jerusalem, 1973), p. 52.

116. Elmaliah, *"Mehayei haSepharadim,"* p. 266.

117. Municipal Archives, Jerusalem, Old Yishuv, 280.

118. Archives of the Jerusalem *Va'ad adat hasefaradim*, Municipal Archives, Jerusalem, 1000a–b.

119. Glazer, "The Dowry as Capital Accumulation," p. 379; Esther Juhasz (ed.), *Yehudei Sefarad ba'imperiyah ha'Uthmanit* (Jerusalem, 1989), p. 200.

120. Regulations of the Bukharan community in Jerusalem, 1904, NHUL, L 820.

121. Barnai, *Yehudei Erez Yisra'el bame'ah ha19*, p. 205.

122. Ita Yellin, *Leze'eza'ay*, vol. 2, p. 3.

123. Yehudah Aaron Weiss, *Bish'arayikh Yerushalayim*, p. 59.

124. Ya'akov Yehoshua, *Yerushalayim hayeshanah ba'ayin uvalev* (Jerusalem, 1988), p. 207.

125. R. Shmuel Engel, *Responsa* (in Hebrew), vol. 3 (Yaroslav, 1926), no. 26 (p. 45).

126. See, e.g., letter written by Shalom Mizrahi Adani to Moses Gaster in 1904, Gaster Papers 178/77; further examples may be found in numerous archives.

127. A. M. Luncz to Moses Gaster, 14 Kislev [5]666 [December 12, 1905], Gaster Papers 200/42; for Gruenhut see below, note 130.

128. E.g., letter written in 1903 by Yehuda Shalem, Soranga Collection, CAHJP, 612.

129. Menachem Getz, *Kakh nifrezu hahomot, Kakh hem hayu* (Jerusalem, 1981), p. 159.

130. Letter written by Eleazar Halevi Gruenhut to *Hakham* Gaster in London, December 12, 1903, Gaster Papers 176/14; *Haskhafah*, 15 Kislev [5]664 [December 4, 1903].

131. *Hashkafah*, no. 25, 2 Nisan [5]664 [March 18, 1904].

132. Shiryon, *Zikhronot*, p. 132.

133. Oded Avisar (ed.), *Sefer Hevron* (Jerusalem, 1970), p. 373.

134. Stahl, *Mishpahah vegidul yeladim*, pp. 99–100.

135. Bezalel Landau, "*Miminhagei yahadut Ashkenaz (Perushim) beErez Yisra'el,*" in Asher Wasserteil (ed.), *Yalkut minhagim miminhagei shivtei Yisra'el* (Jerusalem, 1980), p. 83.

136. Hamburger, *Sheloshah olamot*, vol. 2, p. 74.

137. *Hashkafah*, no. 93, 24 Elul, [5]666 [September 14, 1906].

138. *Hashkafah*, no. 29, 3 Shevat [5]666 [January 29, 1906].

139. Avraham Hayim Freimann, "*Takanot Yerushalayim,*" in Izhak Baer et al. (eds.), *Sefer Dinaburg* (Jerusalem, 1949), p. 213; Nissim Binyamin Gamlieli, *Ahavat Teiman: Hashirah ha'amamit haTeimanit: Shirat hanashim* (Tel Aviv, 1979), p. 136.

140. Carpi and Rinot, "*Yoman mas'oteha shel morah yehudiyah,*" p. 148.

141. Press, *Me'ah shanah biYrushalayim*, p. 56.

142. Even-Or-Orenstein, "*Hanashim bemishpahat Orenstein,*" p. 41.

143. Yehudah Aaron Weiss, *Bish'arayikh Yerushalayim*, p. 59.

144. Ita Yellin, *Leze'eza'ay*, vol. 2, p. 2.

145. Yehoshua, *Yaldut biYrushalayim*, vol. 2, pp. 41, 60, 62.

146. Ibid., p. 60.

147. Ita Yellin, *Leze'eza'ay*, vol. 2, p. 7.

148. Ibid., p. 9.

149. Dov Genechovsky, Personal Archive.

150. Menachem Hakohen, *Sefer hayei adam: Kelulot* (Jerusalem, 1986).

151. Yonatan Benjamin, "*Kegan elohim poreah: Ketubot me'utarot meErez Yisra'el,*" *Rimonim* 4 (1994), pp. 44–49; Shalom Sabar, "*Livhinat hashoni bayahas shel haSefaradim vehaAshkenazim le'omanut hazutit beErez Yisra'el beshilhei hatekufah ha'Uthmanit,*" *Pe'amim* 56 (1993), pp. 92–93.

152. Arnold van Gennep, *The Rites of Passage* (London, 1977), p. 116.

153. For examples see Avraham Hayim Freimann, *Seder kidushin venisu'in* (Jerusalem, 1964), pp. 276–285; *Hazevi*, No. 4, 17 Heshvan [5]658 [November 12, 1897].

154. Angel-Malachi, *Beterem reshit*, p. 29.

155. Elimelech Weissblum, *Havay Zefat* (Tel Aviv, 1969), p. 73.

156. Gaster Papers, 14/120.

157. Chayim Hamburger (*Sheloshah olamot*, vol. 3, p. 75) relates that more than 4,000 (!) invitations were printed for his wedding.

158. Regulations of the Bukharan community in Jerusalem, 1904, NHUL, L 820.

159. *Hazevi*, no. 7, 1 Kislev [5]661 [November 23, 1900].

160. Tehiyah Sapir, "*Ma'arekhet simanim veheksheram hatarbuti bekartisei haz-manah lahatunah beErez Yisra'el mit'hilat hame'ah ve'ad yameinu*" (M.A. thesis, Hebrew University of Jerusalem), 1997.

161. Bergman, *Se'u harim shalom*, p. 58.

162. Katz, "*Nisu'im vehayei ishut*," p. 43; Lewittes, *Jewish Marriage*, p. 87.

163. Elmaliah, "*Mehayei haSepharadim*," p. 267; Bergman, *Se'u harim shalom*, p. 58; Yehudah Elzet, "*Inyenei tena'im vahatunah*," *Reshumot* 1 (1925), p. 356.

164. Kaniel, "*Hayahasim hahevratiyim*," p. 60.

165. David Benvenisti, *Yehudei Saloniki*, p. 53.

166. Philip and Hanna Goodman, *The Jewish Marriage Anthology* (Philadephia, 1965), p. 136.

167. Ita Yellin, *Leze'eza'ay*, vol. 2, p. 17.

168. Avraham Shmuel Hirschberg, *Be'erez hamizrah*, p. 378.

169. Mordechai Hakohen, *Hakotel hama'aravi*, p. 91.

170. Goodman, *Jewish Marriage Anthology*, p. 124; Yehoshua, *Yaldut biYrusha-layim*, vol. 2, p. 67.

171. Ita Yellin, *Leze'eza'ay*, vol. 2, p. 20.

172. Yehoshua Yellin, *Zikhronot leven Yerushalayim*, p. 25; Elmaliah, "*Mehayei haSepharadim*," p. 266.

173. Luncz, *Yerushalayim*, vol. 1, p. 6.

174. Van Gennep, *Rites of Passage*, p. 53.

175. Yehoshua, *Yaldut biYrushalayim*, vol. 2, p. 67; Goodman, *Jewish Marriage Anthology*, p. 123.

176. Letter from Yizhak Mattityahu to Nahum Etrog of Safed, 1897, CAHJP, Safed Collection, SA/IL ii/9/a (based on Jerusalem Talmud, Bikkurim 3:4 [65d]).

177. Porush, *Zikhronot rishonim*, p. 39.

178. Gellis, *Minhagei Erez Yisra'el*, p. 328.

179. Regulations of the Bukharan community in Jerusalem, 1904, NHUL, L 820; Municipal Archives, Jerusalem, 4902.

180. Porush, *Zikhronot rishonim*, p. 39.

181. Gellis, *Minhagei Erez Yisra'el*, p. 330.

182. Neumann, *Ir hakodesh veyoshevei bah*, p. 43.

183. *Hazevi*, no. 27, 7 Nisan [5]657 [April 9, 1897].

184. Bezalel Landau, "*Miminhagei yahadut Ashkenaz*," p. 84.

185. Philip and Hanna Goodman, *Jewish Marriage Anthology*, pp. 122, 129; Elzet, "*Inyenei tena'im vahatunah*," pp. 357–358.

186. Frankl, *Nach Jerusalem!* p. 128.

187. Sabar, "*Livhinat hashoni*," p. 93; Sperber, *Minhagei Yisra'el*, pt. 4, pp. 143–148.

188. Elmaliah, "*Mehayei haSepharadim*," p. 267; Shim'on Geridi, "*Hahalbashah ha'ivrit beTeiman*" (handwritten notebook, Jerusalem, 1937), NHUL, Kadesh Collection, V1253.

189. Hamburger, *Sheloshah olamot*, vol. 3, p. 7.

190. Ita Yellin, *Leze'eza'ay*, vol. 2, p. 21.

191. Alper, *Korot mishpahah ahat*, p. 104.

192. Luncz, *Yerushalayim*, vol. 1, p. 7; Sperber, *Minhagei Yisra'el*, pt. 2, p. 87.

193. Gellis, *Minhagei Erez Yisra'el*, p. 337.

194. Neumann, *Ir hakodesh veyoshevei bah*, p. 43.

195. Frankl, *Nach Jerusalem!* p. 129.

196. Carpi and Rinot, *"Yoman mas'oteha shel morah yehudiyah,"* p. 148.

197. Yehoshua, *Yaldut biYrushalayim,* vol. 2, p. 68.

198. Lynch, *Narrative of the United States Expedition,* p. 448.

199. Berman, *Mas'ot Shim'on,* p. 120.

200. Ellen Clare Miller, *Eastern Sketches: Notes of Scenery, Schools and Life in Syria and Palestine* (Edinburgh, 1871; repr. New York, 1977), p. 41.

201. Luncz, *Yerushalayim,* vol. 1, pp. 7–8.

202. Yadler, *Betuv Yerushalayim,* p. 29; Sperber, *Minhagei Yisra'el,* pt. 4, pp. 150–153; Philip and Hanna Goodman, *Jewish Marriage Anthology,* p. 133.

203. I owe my information about the lack of any sex education among the Ashkenazim in Jerusalem to conversations with a contemporary descendant of the "Old Yishuv."

204. Elmaliah, *"Mehayei haSephardim,"* p. 267.

205. Philip and Hanna Goodman, *Jewish Marriage Anthology,* pp. 124–125.

206. Rachel Ne'eman, *Yomanah shel ganenet vatikah* (Tel Aviv, 1960), p. 39.

207. Cohen-Reiss, *Mizikhronot ish Yerushalayim,* p. 38.

208. Ya'akov Mazor and Moshe Taube, "A Hassidic Dance: The Mitsve Tants in Jerusalemite Weddings," *Yuval: Masorot yehudiyot shebe'al peh* 10 (1994), p. 208.

209. Shiryon, *Zikhronot,* p. 104.

210. Spitzer, *Sefer takhshitei nashim,* p. 13.

211. Bezalel Landau, *"Miminhagei yahadut Ashkenaz,"* p. 86.

212. Miller, *Eastern Sketches,* p. 43.

213. Luncz, *Yerushalayim,* vol. 1, pp. 8–9, note 20.

214. Zevi Friedhaber, *"Hamahol bayishuv hayehudi biYrushalayim lifnei milhemet ha'olam harishonah,"* *Jerusalem Studies in Jewish Folklore* 11–12 (1989–1990), p. 145.

215. For a report of the previous situation (when music was permitted) see Minna Rosen, *Hakehilah hayehudit biYrushalayim bame'ah ha17* (Tel Aviv, 1984), p. 246. For the more recent prohibition see Gellis, *Minhagei Erez Yisra'el,* p. 337.

216. Luncz, *Yerushalayim,* vol. 1, pp. 9–10, note 21.

217. Ita Yellin, *Leze'eza'ay,* vol. 2, p. 22.

218. *Hazevi,* year 12, no. 6, 12 Heshvan [5]657 [October 21, 1896].

219. Elmaliah, *"Mehayei haSephardim,"* p. 267; Ann Bridgewood, "Dancing the Jar: Girl's Dress at Turkish Cypriot Weddings," in Joanne B. Eicher (ed.), *Dress and Ethnicity* (Oxford, 1995), p. 40.

220. Philip and Hanna Goodman, *Jewish Marriage Anthology,* p. 127.

221. Yehoshua Yellin, *Zikhronot leven Yerushalayim,* p. 25.

222. Avishur, *Hahatunah hayehudit,* vol. 2, p. 198; Clinton Bailey, "Bedouin Weddings in Sinai and the Negev," *Mehkerei hamerkaz leheker hafolklor* 4 (1974), pp. 126–127.

223. Elmaliah, *"Mehayei haSephardim,"* p. 268.

224. Philip and Hanna Goodman, *Jewish Marriage Anthology,* p. 136.

225. Elmaliah, *"Mehayei haSephardim,"* p. 268.

226. For a similar custom in Salonika see David Benvenisti, *Yehudei Saloniki,* p. 57.

227. Gellis, *Minhagei Erez Yisra'el,* p. 337.

228. Yadler, *Betuv Yerushalayim,* p. 56.

229. Louis M. Epstein, *Sex Laws and Customs in Judaism* (New York, 1967), pp. 50–55; Shalem Yahalom, *"Giluah harosh le'ishah nesu'ah"* (seminar paper, Hebrew University of Jerusalem, 1995); Pauline Wengeroff, *Rememberings: The World of*

a Russian-Jewish Woman in the Nineteenth Century, trans. Henny Wenkart, ed. with an afterword by Bernard D. Cooperman (Bethesda, Md., 2000), pp. 96–104; see also below, chapter 3.

230. Press, *Me'ah shanah biYrushalayim*, p. 21; Bezalel Landau, "*Miminhagei ya-hadut Ashkenaz*," p. 86.

231. Trager, *Pictures of Jewish Home-Life*, p. 107.

232. Ze'ev Leibowitz, *Ba'aliyah uvabeniyah: Zikhronot umasot* (Jerusalem, 1953), p. 68.

233. Luncz, *Yerushalayim*, vol. 1, p. 6.

234. Gellis, *Minhagei Erez Yisra'el*, p. 337.

235. Shiryon, *Zikhronot*, p. 105; Philip and Hanna Goodman, *Jewish Marriage An-thology*, pp. 124–125, 128; Avraham Hayim Elhanani, "*Hayei David Yellin*," *Shevet va'am* 7 (1973), pp. 215–233.

236. Gellis, *Minhagei Erez Yisra'el*, p. 339.

237. Neumann, *Ir hakodesh veyoshevei bah*, p. 44.

238. Ga'on, *Yehudei hamizrah*, vol. 1, p. 115.

239. Gad Frumkin, *Derekh shofet biYrushalayim*, p. 94.

240. On similar changes observed in Arab society see Robinson-Divine, *Ottoman Palestine*, p. 123.

241. Sha'ul Me'ir Moshayoff, *Betokhekhei Yerushalayim, [5]646–[5]734* (Jerusa-lem, 1978), p. 29.

242. Cohen-Reiss, *Mizikhronot ish Yerushalayim*, p. 139.

243. *Hazevi levet Ya'akov*, year 2, 14 Adar [5]653 [March 2, 1893].

244. *Hazevi*, no. 30, 19 Av [5]655 [August 9, 1895].

245. Ibid., year 12, no. 6, 14 Heshvan [5]657 [October 21, 1896].

246. Hamburger, *Sheloshah olamot*, vol. 3, p. 75.

247. Yizhak Alfasi, *Mimizrah shemesh: Toledoteihem shel hamishim mime'orei orot hamizrah* (Jerusalem, [1990]), pp. 234–235.

248. Frankl, *Nach Jerusalem!* p. 129.

Chapter 3. Women at Home (pp. 69–107)

1. Harvey E. Goldberg, "Family and Community in Sephardic North Africa: His-torical and Anthropological Perspectives," in David Kraemer (ed.), *The Jewish Family: Metaphor and Memory* (Oxford, 1989), p. 149.

2. Hareven, "The History of a Family," p. 214.

3. Yehoshua, *Yaldut biYrushalayim*, vol. 2, p. 66.

4. Elizabeth Wilson, *Adorned in Dreams: Fashion and Modernity* (London, 1985); Yedida K. Stillman and Nancy Micklewright, "Costume in the Middle East," *Middle East Studies Association Bulletin* 26/1 (1992), pp. 13–38.

5. Daniel Roche, *The Culture of Clothing* (Cambridge, 1994), p. 4.

6. Joanne B. Eicher (ed.), *Dress and Ethnicity: Change across Space and Time* (Oxford, 1995), p. 1.

7. Bet Halevi, *Toledot yehudei Kalish*, p. 319; Schreier, "Becoming American"; Michael Hakohen and Avraham Yaakov Brawer, *Zihronot av uvno* (Jerusalem, 1966), p. 448; John A. Hostetler, *Amish Society* (Baltimore, 1963), pp. 134–135; Roche, *Cul-ture of Clothing*, pp. 3–22.

8. Zipporah Sibahi-Greenfield, *"Bigdei kalah yehudiyah mikefar Muswar shebe-Teiman kimeshakef emunah"* (M.A. thesis, Hebrew University of Jerusalem, 1993), p. 108.

9. Dov Frimmer, *"Ilot gerushin ekev hitnahagut bilti musarit . . ."* (Ph.D. dissertation, Hebrew University of Jerusalem, 1980).

10. Roche, *Culture of Clothing*, pp. 228, 239.

11. Menahem Mendel Gerlitz (ed.), *Sefer mara de'ar'a Yisra'el: Masekhet hayav shel . . . Maran Yosef Hayim Sonnenfeld* (Jerusalem, 1980), p. 162; Julie M. Peteet, "Authenticity and Gender: The Presentation of Culture," in Judith E. Tucker (ed.), *Arab Women: Old Boundaries, New Frontiers* (Bloomington, Ind., 1993), p. 53.

12. Binyamin Kluger, *Min hamakor: Hayishuv hayashan al luah moda'ot*, vol. 2 (Jerusalem, 1980), p. 13.

13. Menachem Getz (ed.), *Lesha'ah uledorot: Osef keruzim umoda'ot*, vol. 2 (Jerusalem, 1971).

14. Undated poster, probably 1920s, NHUL, V1817.

15. Rosen, *Hakehilah hayehudit*, pp. 251–254; Alfred Rubens, *A History of Jewish Costume* (London, 1973), pp. 46–49.

16. Ita Yellin, *Leze'eza'ay*, vol. 1, p. 27.

17. Frimmer, *"Ilot gerushin,"* pp. 46, 139; Razahbi, *Parashat hitnahalut yehudei Teiman bi'Yrushalayim*, p. 125.

18. Reicher, *Sefer sha'arei Yerushalayim, Sha'ar* 9, unpaginated.

19. Avraham Naftali Zevi Roth, *"Al minhag giluah sa'arot ha'ishah beleyl nisu'eha,"* Yeda Am 16 (1972), pp. 14–21.

20. *Havazelet*, no. 29, year 8, 13 Sivan 5638 [June 14, 1878].

21. *Hazevi*, no. 10, 1 Shevat 5648 [January 14, 1888].

22. *Hazevi*, no. 12, 26 Kislev 5656 [December 13, 1895].

23. Ita Yellin, *Leze'eza'ay*, vol. 1, pp. 35, 52.

24. *Hazevi*, no. 12, 26 Kislev 5656 [December 13, 1895].

25. *Hazevi*, no. 15, 17 Tevet 5656 [January 3, 1896].

26. Gerlitz, *Sefer mara de'ar'a Yisra'el*, p. 85.

27. *Hazevi*, no. 38, 9 Tamuz 5653 [June 23, 1893].

28. Ital Yellin, *Leze'eza'ay*, vol. 1, p. 50.

29. Hamburger, *Sheloshah olamot*, vol. 1, p. 13.

30. Ben-Avraham, *Sipurim Yerushalmiyim*, p. 283.

31. Bergman, *Se'u harim shalom*, p. 57; Sibahi-Greenfield, *"Bigdei kalah,"* p. 52.

32. Montefiore, *Private Journal*, p. 203; Yehoshua, *Yerushalayim temol shilshom*, vol. 2, p. 140; Ya'akov El'azar, *Harova hayehudi biYrushalayim ha'atikah* (Jerusalem, 1975), p. 165.

33. Yehoshua, *Yaldut biYrushalayim*, vol. 2, pp. 34, 35, 41; idem, *Sipuro shel habayit haSefaradi barova hayehudi ba'ir ha'atikah shel Yerushalayim* (Jerusalem, 1976), pp. 114–115; Esther Yuhasz (ed.), *Yehudei Sefarad ba'imperiyah ha'Othmanit* (Jerusalem, 1989), p. 139.

34. Reicher, *Sefer sha'arei Yerushalayim, Sha'ar* 9, unpaginated; Avraham Grossman, *"Hazikah beyn halakhah vekhalkalah bema'amad ha'ishah hayehudiyah be'Ashkenaz hakedumah,"* in Menachem Ben-Sasson (ed.), *Dat vekhalkalah: Yahasei Gomelin* (Jerusalem, 1995), p. 152; Rosen, *Hakehilah hayehudit*, p. 252.

35. Montefiore, *Private Journal*, p. 211; Menashe Mani, *"Bahazar hayehudim be-Hevron,"* Shevet va'Am 5 (1960), p. 117; Yehoshua, *Yaldut biYrushalayim*, vol. 3, p. 225.

36. Reicher, *Sefer sha'arei Yerushalayim*, *Sha'ar* 9, unpaginated.

37. Ginzburg, *Devir*, vol. 1, p. 61.

38. Bergman, *Se'u harim shalom*, p. 58.

39. Yehoshua, *Yaldut biYrushalayim*, vol. 2, p. 34. On the veil and the protection it afforded in nineteenth-century Istanbul see Godfrey Goodwin, *The Private World of Ottoman Women* (London, 1997), p. 168.

40. Ya'akov Sha'ul Eliachar (ed.), *Sefer hatakanot vehaskamot minhagim hanohagim . . . Yerushalayim* (Jerusalem, 1883; repr. 1969), p. 45a–b; Ga'on, *Yehudei hamizrah*, vol. 1, p. 113.

41. Yehoshua, *Yaldut biYrushalayim*, vol. 1, pp. 106–108; Ephraim Davidson, "*Malbushei Shabbat uma'akhalei Shabbat,*" *Mahanayim* 85–86 (1964), pp. 158–165.

42. Lynch, *Narrative of the United States Expedition*, p. 159; Avraham Shmuel Hirschberg, *Be'erez hamizrah*, p. 342; Ita Yellin, *Leze'eza'ay*, vol. 1, p. 51.

43. Shmuel Avitzur, *Hayei yom yom be'Erez Yisra'el* (Tel Aviv, 1973), pp. 56–57.

44. Grayevsky, *Ziyun lekever Rahel imenu*, pp. 8–9.

45. Henry Baker Tristram, *The Land of Israel: A Journal of Travels in Palestine* (London, 1865), p. 568.

46. Lynch, *Narrative of the United States Expedition*, p. 159.

47. Luncz, *Netivot Zion viYrushalayim*, p. 218.

48. See above, note 38.

49. Yehoshua, *Yaldut biYrushalayim*, vol. 2, p. 41.

50. Barnai, *Yehudei Erez Yisrael bame'ah ha-19*, p. 205.

51. Grayevsky, *Ziyun lekever Rahel imenu*, pp. 8–9.

52. Rosen, *Hakehilah hayehudit*, p. 253.

53. Yizhak Yaakov Yellin, *Avoteinu*, p. 173; Porush, *Zikhronot rishonim*, p. 58; Tikvah Sarig, *Ima agadah* (Tel Aviv, 1980), p. 32.

54. Menachem Mendel of Kaminetz, *Korot ha'itim liYshurun be'Erez Yisra'el* (Jerusalem, 1839), p. 83.

55. Yehoshua, *Sipuro shel habayit haSefaradi*, pp. 31–32.

56. Even-Or-Orenstein, "*Hanashim bemishpahat Orenstein,*" p. 37.

57. *Hashkafah*, no. 81, 13 Elul 5667 [August 23, 1907].

58. Ita Yellin, *Leze'eza'ay*, vol. 2, p. 31; Hamburger, *Sheloshah olamot*, vol. 1, p. 57.

59. Ita Yellin, *Leze'eza'ay*, vol. 1, p. 52.

60. Yehoshua, *Yaldut biYrushalayim*, vol. 2, p. 35.

61. Ibid.

62. Yadler, *Betuv Yerushalayim*, p. 56.

63. Heller, *Harav hamanhig veharofé*, p. 257.

64. Gerlitz, *Sefer mara de'ar'a Yisra'el*, p. 28; Lola Landau, *Pesah Hevroni* (Jerusalem, 1972), p. 61.

65. Neumann, *Ir hakodesh veyoshevei bah*, p. 74; see also Ben Zion Gat, *Hayishuv hayehudi be'Erez Yisra'el, 1840–1881* (Jerusalem, 1923; photogr. repr. 1974), p. 127. While this account fits most Jews in the Holy City, there were also a few more sumptuous dwellings; see, e.g., Ruth Kark and Yosef Glass, *Yazamim Sefardim be'Erez Yisra'el: Mishpahat Amzaleg 1816–1918* (Jerusalem, 1993), pp. 65–67.

66. Ben-Avraham, *Sipurim Yerushalmiyim*, p. 281.

67. Schmelz, "*Kavim meyuhadim.*"

68. Avraham Shmuel Hirschberg, *Be'erez hamizrah*, p. 282.

69. Reicher, *Sefer sha'arei Yerushalayim*, *Sha'ar* 7, unpaginated.

70. Shiryon, *Zikhronot*, p. 101. For the domestic culture of the non-Jewish population around this time see Ron Fuchs, "*Habayit ha'aravi be'Erez Yisra'el: Iyun mehudash*," *Cathedra* 90 (1999), pp. 53–86, esp. p. 56.

71. For the lack of privacy in other nineteenth-century societies see Glenna Matthews, "*Just a Housewife*": *The Rise and Fall of Domesticity in America* (New York, 1987).

72. *First Marriages*, p. 10.

73. Yehoshua Ophir, *Hoter migeza* (Jerusalem, 1998), p. 28.

74. Wills are a sometimes useful source of information about the movables in typical homes; see, e.g., the last will and testament of Moshe Blau, son of Yaakov, 1850, CAHJP, J/10; will of Moshe Hillel, son of Yaakov, Jerusalem 1893, ibid., J/44; list of movable property of Baruch Odesser, ibid., J/46.

75. Blau, *Al homotayikh Yerushalayim*, p. 23; see also Porush, *Zikhronot rishonim*, pp. 34–36; Hamburger, *Sheloshah olamot*, vol. 3, pp. 11–15. The Old Yishuv Museum in Jerusalem's Old City has a permanent exhibition of typical furnishings of this period.

76. Avraham Shmuel Hirschberg, *Be'erez hamizrah*, p. 392.

77. David Yellin, *Ketavim*, vol. 2 (Jerusalem, 1973), p. 243.

78. Ita Yellin, *Leze'eza'ay*, vol. 1, esp. pp. 40–43; vol. 2, p. 47.

79. Dror Wahrmann, *Habukharim ushkhunatam biYrushalayim* (Jerusalem, 1992); Valero, *Zikhronot*, pp. 16–19.

80. Hamburger, *Sheloshah olamot*, vol. 2, p. 15.

81. Siton, "*Sipurah shel shekhunah Yerushalmit*," p. 46.

82. Simcha Mandelbaum, *Asarah dorot be'Erez Yisra'el: Matayim shanah, 1794–1994*, vol. 2 (Jerusalem, 1995), pp. 129–130.

83. Even-Or-Orenstein, "*Hanashim bemishpahat Orenstein*," p. 39.

84. Yehoshua, *Sipuro shel habayit haSefaradi*, pp. 21–22; Kaniel, "*Hayahasim hahevratiyim*," pp. 61–63.

85. Porush, *Zikhronot rishonim*, p. 58.

86. Trager, *Pictures of Jewish Home-Life*, pp. 43–44.

87. Shiryon, *Zikhronot*, p. 97.

88. Luncz, *Yerushalayim*, vol. 1, p. 67; Ga'on, *Yehudei hamizrah*, vol. 1, p. 114; Eliachar, *Sefer hatakanot*, p. 45b.

89. Y. Ben-Haggai, "*Purim ezel benei adot hamizrah biYrushalayim*," *Mahanayim* 77 (1963), p. 79.

90. El'azar, *Diyur uklitah bayishuv hayashan*, p. 39.

91. Ya'akov Sha'ul Eliachar, *Sefer hatakanot* (in the year 1908), no. 11, p. 143b.

92. Ben-Avraham, *Sipurim Yerushalmiyim*, p. 268.

93. Luncz, *Yerushalayim*, vol. 1, p. 33; Neumann, *Ir hakodesh veyoshevei bah*, p. 35; Avraham Hayim Freimann, "*Takanot Yerushalayim*," p. 214; Sered, *Religious Lives*, pp. 89, 102.

94. Gad Frumkin, *Derekh shofet biYrushalayim*, 83–85; Porush, *Zikhronot rishonim*, p. 43.

95. Nehama Ariel, "*Ishah behanhagat hayishuv hayashan bame'ah ha19: Harabanit Sonya Diskin, harabanit miBrisk*," *Talelei Orot* 2 (1990), p. 45. This story and the following one are probably apocryphal; similar tales have been told of many Jewish housewives.

96. Weissblum, *Havay Zefat*, p. 34.

97. Yehoshua, *Yaldut biYrushalayim*, vol. 1, p. 74.

98. Ibid., pp. 74–77.

99. Ze'evi, *"Hame'ah ha'Uthmanit,"* p. 339; and see in general Melman, *Women's Orients.*

100. Yehoshua, *Yaldut biYrushalayim*, vol. 2, p. 11.

101. Luncz, *Yerushalayim*, vol. 1, p. 36.

102. Yehoshua, *Sipuro shel habayit haSefaradi*, p. 52.

103. Yom Tov Levinsky, *Sefer hamo'adim*, vol. 5: *Yemei mo'ed vezikaron* (Tel Aviv, 1954), pp. 58–59; Avraham Arzi, *"Hag rosh hodesh,"* *Mahanayim* 90 (1964), pp. 12–15.

104. Yehoshua, *Yaldut biYrushalayim*, vol. 1, pp. 119–121.

105. Ibid., p. 125.

106. Ibid., p. 75.

107. Ibid., vol. 2, pp. 11–14.

108. Katz, *Tradition and Crisis*, p. 136.

109. Shiryon, *Zikhronot*, pp. 96–100; Yehoshua, *Yerushalayim hayeshanah ba'ayin uvalev*, pp. 197–198; Angel-Malachi, *Beterem reshit*, p. 79.

110. Carol Rosenberg, "The Female World of Love and Ritual: Relations between Women in Nineteenth-Century America," *Signs* 1/1 (1975), pp. 1–29.

111. Yizhak Yaakov Yellin, *Avoteinu*, p. 179.

112. Bergman, *Se'u harim shalom*, p. 58; Ita Yellin, *Leze'eza'ay*, vol. 2, pp. 82–83.

113. *Hazevi*, no. 18, 11 Nisan 5649 [April 12, 1889].

114. Shim'on Stern, *"Yerushalayim ke'ir mizrahit,"* *Ariel* 57–58 (1988), pp. 96–97.

115. Ze'evi, *"Hame'ah ha'Uthmanit,"* pp. 320–321.

116. Ben-Arieh, *Jerusalem . . . the New City*, passim.

117. Gellis, *Minhagei Erez Yisrael*, p. 333; Yehosef Schwartz, *Besha'arei Yerushalayim: Te'udot letoledot Yerushalayim vetoshaveha*, ed. Bezalel Landau (Jerusalem, 1969), pp. 19–34; D. Z. Neiman, *Haga'on sheniskah: R. Anshil Neiman ufrakim al aliyatam shel yehudei Hungariah le'Erez Yisra'el bereshit hithadeshut hayishuv* (Jerusalem, 1982), p. 280; Lamdan, *A Separate People*, pp. 139–156.

118. Alan Duben and Cem Behar, *Istanbul Households: Marriage, Family and Fertility, 1880–1910* (Cambridge, 1991), p. 148; Donald Quataert, "Ottoman Women, Households, and Textile Manufacturing, 1800–1914," in Nikki R. Keddie and Beth Baron (eds.), *Women in Middle Eastern History: Shifting Boundaries in Sex and Gender* (New Haven, Conn., 1992), p. 162.

119. Yehudah Razahbi, *"Rishonei olei Teiman ba'aliyat 5642,"* *Mahanayim* 77 (1963), p. 74; Leah Bornstein-Makovetzky, *"Hamishpahah hayehudit be'Istanbul bame'ot ha-18 veha-19 kiyhidah kalkalit,"* in Bartal and Gafni (eds.), *Eros, erusin ve'isurin*, pp. 316–317.

120. Bet Halevi, *Toledot yehudei Kalish*, pp. 319–329; see also Bartura, *Belev kashuv*, p. 132.

121. 1855 Census, Montefiore Archives, no. 592, pp. 2, 3, 7; Frankl, around the same time, counted six bigamous marriages among the Jews of Jerusalem: Frankl, *Nach Jerusalem!* p. 132–133.

122. Berman, *Mas'ot Shim'on*, p. 93.

123. Hayyim Sethon, *Sefer erez hayyim* (Jerusalem, 1982), p. 243.

124. Elmaliah, *"Mehayei haSepharadim,"* p. 266; see also Frankl, *Nach Jerusalem!* p. 132.

125. Eliav Shohetman, *"Mekorot hadashim lefarashat izvono shel ha'sar' Hayim Farhi,"* *Asufot* 11 (1998), pp. 285, 298, 300–301.

126. Avraham Hayyim (ed.), *Te'udot min ha'osef shel Eliyahu Eliachar* (Jerusalem, 1971), p. 80; Yehoshua, *Yaldut biYrushalayim*, vol. 3, p. 231.

127. Stone, *Past and Present Revisited*, p. 313.

128. Goitein, *Mediterranean Society*, vol. 3, p. 313; Duben and Behar, *Istanbul Households*, p. 223.

129. Yadler, *Betuv Yerushalayim*, p. 49.

130. David Siton, *"Sipurah shel shekhunah Yerushalmit,"* p. 50; Ophir, *Hoter migeza*, p. 28.

131. Stahl, *Mishpahah vegidul yeladim*, pp. 89–97; Duben and Behar, *Istanbul Households*, pp. 87–121.

132. Spitzer, *Sefer takhshitei nashim*, p. 19b, no. 7.

133. Elmaliah, *"Mehayei haSepharadim,"* p. 355; Duben and Behar, *Istanbul Households*, p. 225.

134. Shalom Kassan, *David Yellin, hamehanekh vehamanhig* (Tel Aviv, 1980), p. 38 (note).

135. Haim Be'er, *Havalim* (Tel Aviv, 1998), p. 59.

136. Among the Ashkenazim all men were expected to continue their studies, but Sephardic society made this demand only of scholars; see Eliav, *Erez Yisrael veyishuvah bame'ah ha-19*, p. 125.

137. Blau, *Al homotayikh Yerushalayim*, pp. 23–24.

138. Eliezer Yehezkel Grossman, *Kovez degel hazahav, "Der Goldener Fahn"* (n.p., n.d. [1991?]), p. 17.

139. Reitze, *Sefer mishpahat yuhasin*, p. 29. [Shilo, *Hakol hanashi*, p. 154.]

140. Spitzer, *Sefer takhshitei nashim*, p. 4b.

141. Bezalel Landau, *"Letoledot Rabbi Moshe Nehemiah . . . Kahanov,"* in R. Moshe Nehemiah Kahanov, *Siftei Yeshenim* (Jerusalem, 1968), p. 37.

142. Carpi and Rinot, *"Yoman mas'oteha shel morah yehudiyah,"* p. 141.

143. Last will and testament of Binyamin Rivlin, 1886/7, CAHJP, J111.

144. Yehoshua, *Yaldut biYrushalayim*, vol. 3, p. 94; Eliahu Eliachar, *Lihyot im yehudim* (Jerusalem, 1981), p. 78; Trager, *Pictures of Jewish Home-Life*, p. 108.

145. Y. Ben-Haggai, *"Shabbat ezel adot hamizrah biYrushalayim ha'atikah,"* *Mahanayim* 85–86 (1964), p. 187; Eliahu Eliachar, *Lihyot im yehudim*, p. 78.

146. Hamburger, *Sheloshah olamot*, vol. 1, p. 19.

147. El'azar, *Harova hayehudi*, p. 118; Gamlieli, *"Hayei ha'ishah hayehudiyah,"* p. 134.

148. Yosef Rivlin, letter written on 17 Elul 5632 [September 20, 1872], CAHJP, unnumbered.

149. Yizhak Yaakov Yellin, *Avoteinu*, pp. 75–76.

150. *Mishneh Torah*, Hilkhot Sotah, 4:19.

151. Binyamin Kluger, *Min hamakor*, p. 13.

152. Grayevsky, *Benot Zion viYrushalayim*, pp. 325–326.

153. See below, chapter 4.

154. Eliezer Yehezkel Grossman, *Kovez degel hazahav*, pp. 100–101.

155. Hayyim Hirschensohn, *Malki bakodesh*, vol. 1 (Saint Louis, 1919), p. 127; Alderblum, *Memoirs*, pp. 307–316.

156. Ben-Avraham, *Sipurim Yerushalmiyim*, p. 301.

157. *Hazevi*, no. 3, 29 Tevet 5655 [January 25, 1895].

158. Shmuel Heller, *She'elot uteshuvot*, pp. 131–132.

159. Yadler, *Betuv Yerushalayim*, p. 287.

160. Naftali Herz Huttner appointed his wife as executor, Sivan 5647 (spring 1887), CAHJP, J108; Aher b. Zevi Eisenstein, 11 Adar I 5643 [February 18, 1883], CAHJP, J35.

161. Alper, *Korot mishpahah ahat*, p. 115.

162. Trager, *Pictures of Jewish Home-Life*, p. 108.

163. Kahanov, *Sha'alu shelom Yerushalayim*, p. 9.

164. Yehoshua, *Yaldut biYrushalayim*, vol. 1, pp. 96–97, 132–133.

165. Avraham Hayyim Elhanani, *Ish vesiho* (Jerusalem, 1966), p. 73.

166. Yehoshua, *Yaldut biYrushalayim*, vol. 1, p. 47.

167. Ibid., p. 72.

168. Ibid., p. 98.

169. Esther Hilwani-Steinhorn, *Damesek iri* (Jerusalem, 1978), p. 24; but not so in Baghdad, cf. Avraham Ben Yaakov, *Minhagei yehudi Bavel hadorot ha'aharonim*, vol. 1 (Jerusalem, 1993), p. 274.

170. Gad Frumkin, *Derekh shofet biYrushalayim*, pp. 65–66.

171. Yehoshua, *Yaldut biYrushalayim*, vol. 1, pp. 47, 96–97.

172. Luncz, *Yerushalayim*, vol. 1, p. 36.

173. Alper, *Korot mishpahah ahat*, p. 66.

174. Eliahu Eliachar, *Lihyot im yehudim*, p. 79.

175. Yehoshua Yellin, *Zikhronot leven Yerushalayim*, p. 25.

176. Yehiel Michal Tokacinski, *Ir hakodesh vehamikdash*, vol. 3 (Jerusalem, 1969), p. 336.

177. On customs relating to mutual family visits see Ita Yellin, *Leze'eza'ay*, vol. 2, p. 26; David Siton, "*Sipurah shel shekhunah Yerushalmit*," p. 45.

178. Avraham Shmuel Hirschberg, *Be'erez hamizrah*, pp. 384–385, 392–393.

179. Maimonides, *Mishneh Torah*, Hil. Ishut 15:19.

180. Naomi Graetz, *Silence Is Deadly: Judaism Confronts Wife Beating* (Northvale, N.J., 1998).

181. Berman, *Mas'ot Shim'on*, p. 80.

182. *Hazevi*, no. 17, 5 Av 5655 [July 26, 1895].

183. Selma Mayer, *Hayay beSha'arei Zedek* (Jerusalem, n.d.), p. 13.

184. Rahamim Yosef Franco, *Responsa Sha'arei Yerushalayim* (Jerusalem, 1902), vol. 2, *Even ha'Ezer* 5, *Ishut*, no. 11.

185. *Hazevi*, no. 15, 4 Nisan 5648 [March 16, 1888]; ibid., no. 15, 5 Shevat 5657 [January 8, 1897]; ibid., no. 16, 12 Shevat 5657 [January 15, 1897]. According to Yaakov Yehoshua, wife abuse was particularly common in his own Sephardic community; Yehoshua, *Yerushalayim hayeshanah ba'ayin uvalev*, pp. 211–212.

186. Naomi Graetz, *Silence Is Deadly*, pp. 152–157.

187. Yehoshua Yellin, *Zikhronot leven Yerushalayim*, pp. 21–22.

188. Zeyde Avraham Heller, *Harav hamanhig veharofé*, p. 59.

189. Weissler, *Voices of the Matriarchs*, p. 46.

190. Letter in the name of the Ashkenazic religious court, 24 Tevet 5642 [January 15, 1882], CAHJP, J30; *Haskafah*, no. 43, 29 Tamuz 5663 [July 24, 1903]; Binyamin, *MeHodu liYrushalayim*, p. 85.

191. Yehoshua, *Yaldut biYrushalayim*, vol. 3, p. 19.

192. Luncz[-Bolotin], "*Hayyei avi*," p. 332.

193. *Havazelet*, nos. 18/19, 7 Adar 5636 [March 3, 1876].

194. *Havazelet*, no. 17, 12 Shevat 5637 [January 26, 1877].

195. Yaakov Asher Grayevsky, *Mazevet zikaron leNehama*, private archives of Halevi family.

196. Blau, *Al homotayikh Yerushalayim*, p. 13.

197. Stern, *"Te'ur harefu'ah biYrushalayim,"* p. 117.

198. Helena Kagan, *Reshit darki biYrushalayim* (Tel Aviv, 1982), p. 45.

199. On occasion husbands published messages of thanks to physicians who had tended their wives, e.g., *Ha'or*, no. 41, 24 Elul 5652 [September 16, 1892]; *Hazevi*, no. 7, 24 Heshvan 5652 [November 25, 1891].

200. Hamburger, *Sheloshah olamot*, vol. 3, pp. 7–11.

201. Yehoshua, *Yaldut biYrushalayim*, vol. 2, p. 79.

202. Yehoshua, *Yerushalayim temol shilshom*, vol. 1, p. 141.

203. One such bed is exhibited in the Old Yishuv Museum in the Old City of Jerusalem.

204. Yehoshua, *Yerushalayim temol shilshom*, vol. 1, p. 139.

205. Stahl, *Mishpahah vegidul yeladim*, pp. 30–33, esp. note 6; Yissachar Ben-Ami, *"Minhagei herayon veleidah bekerev haSefaradim ve'edot hamizrah,"* *Yeda Am* 26 (1995), pp. 37–49.

206. Hagit Matras, *"Ki mal'akhav yezaveh lakh lishmorkha bekhol derakhekha: Keme'ot layoledet velayeled biYrushalayim beyameinu,"* *Rimonim* 5 (1997), pp. 15–27.

207. Elmaliah, *"Mehayei haSepharadim,"* p. 264; Avisar, *Sefer Hevron*, pp. 370, 386.

208. On midwives see chapter 4.

209. Mark Zobrowski and Elizabeth Herzog, *Life Is with People* (New York, 1952), p. 133; Yadler, *Betuv Yerushalayim*, p. 50.

210. Salmon, *"Hayishuv ha'Ashkenazi,"* pp. 566–569, and see also references cited there.

211. Menashe Mani, *"Bahazar hayehudim beHevron,"* *Shevet va'Am* 2 (1958), p. 94.

212. Menashe Mani, *Hevron vegiboreha* (Tel Aviv, 1963), p. 83.

213. Elmaliah, *"Mehayei haSepharadim,"* p. 264.

214. Ibid.

215. Yehoshua, *Yaldut biYrushalayim*, vol. 2, p. 82; Luncz, *Yerushalayim*, vol. 1, p. 2.

216. Ita Yellin, *Leze'eza'ay*, vol. 2, p. 35.

217. Yehoshua, *Yaldut biYrushalayim*, vol. 2, p. 91; Gershon David Hundert, "Jewish Children and Childhood in Early Modern Central Europe," in David Kraemer (ed.), *The Jewish Family, Metaphor and Memory* (New York, 1989), p. 86.

218. Yehoshua, *Yerushalayim temol shilshom*, vol. 1, p. 48.

219. Bartura, *Belev kashuv*, p. 198.

220. Ita Yellin, *Leze'eza'ay*, vol. 2, pp. 35–37; Michele Klein, *A Time to Be Born: Customs and Folklore of Jewish Birth* (Philadelphia, 1998), pp. 188–192.

221. For example, *Hazevi*, no. 17, 19 Shevat 5658 [February 11, 1898], supplement; *Hashkafah*, no. 33, 29 Tevet 5665 [January 6, 1905].

222. Elmaliah, *"Mehayei haSepharadim,"* p. 265.

223. Reicher, *Sefer sha'arei Yerushalayim*, Sha'ar 9, unpaginated.

224. Luncz, *Yerushalayim*, vol. 1, p. 27.

225. Hamburger, *Sheloshah olamot*, vol. 3, p. 8; Elmaliah, *"Mehayei haSepharadim,"* p. 267.

226. NHUL, Kadesh Collection, V183/1002; rare book collection, National and Hebrew University Library; see also Hagit Matras, *"Segulot urefu'ot be'ivrit: Tekhanim*

umekorot" (Ph.D. dissertation, Hebrew University of Jerusalem, 1998); Eli Davis and David A. Frankel, *Hakame'a ha'ivri: Mikra'i, refu'i, kelali* (Jerusalem, 1995).

227. Hamburger, *Sheloshah olamot*, vol. 3, p. 7.

228. Mani, *Hevron vegiboreha*, p. 83.

229. Hamburger, *Sheloshah olamot*, vol. 3, p. 9; Yadler, *Betuv Yerushalayim*, p. 48; Joshua Trachtenberg, *Jewish Magic and Superstition* (New York, 1970), pp. 42, 169.

230. Cohen-Reiss, *Mizikhronot ish Yerushalayim*, pp. 42–43.

231. Zevi Friedhaber, *Hamahol be'Am Yisra'el* (Tel Aviv, 1984), p. 80; idem, *"Hamahol bayishuv hayehudi,"* pp. 150–151.

232. Aryeh Leib Frumkin, *Toledot hakhmei Yerushalayim*, vol. 3, p. 151; Bezalel Landau, *"Miminhagei yahadut Ashkenaz,"* pp. 86–87.

233. Reicher, *Sefer sha'arei Yerushalayim*, Sha'ar 9, unpaginated.

234. Razahby, *"Parashat hitnahalut yehudei Teiman bi'Yrushalayim,"* p. 125.

235. Zevi Graetz, *Darkhei hahistoriyah hayehudit* (Jerusalem, 1969), p. 279.

236. *Hamaggid*, 19 Heshvan 5629 [November 4, 1868]; see Levi, *Perakim betoledot harefu'ah*, pp. 58–59.

237. Ya'akov Goldberg, *"Nisu'ei hayehudim bePolin hayeshanah,"* pp. 32–33.

238. For the statistics for Safed see Karlinsky, *"Hahevrah hahasidit shel Zefat,"* pp. 164–165; Natan Shor, *Massa el he'avar, massa al he'avar* (Jerusalem, 1998), pp. 336–340.

239. Schmelz, *"Kavim meyuhadim,"* p. 66.

240. Luncz, *Yerushalayim*, vol. 5, p. 184, note 1.

241. Bornstein-Makovetzky, *"Hamishpahah hayehudit,"* p. 312.

242. Grayevsky, *Zikhron lahovevim harishonim*, vol. 2, p. 267.

243. Shiryon, *Zikhronot*, p. 45.

244. For example, Bartura, *Belev kashuv*, p. 134; Eliav, *Ahavat Ziyon*, p. 249; Gellis, *Midemuyot Yerushalayim*, p. 6.

245. *Havazelet*, no. 14, 29 Tevet 5639 [January 24, 1879]; ibid., no. 28/29, 14 Sivan 5639 [April 7, 1879].

246. Yehoshua, *Yaldut biYrushalayim*, vol. 2, p. 91.

247. Zevi Berenson, *"Pirkei hayyim vezikhronot,"* in Aharon Barak and Hayyim Berenson (eds.), *Sefer Berenson*, vol. 1 (Jerusalem, 1997), p. 42.

248. Yizre'el, *"Beyt ha'almin,"* pp. 39–40.

249. Kahanov, *Sha'alu shelom Yerushalayim*, p. 67.

250. Reitze, *Sefer mishpahat yuhasin*, p. 31. [Shilo, *Hakol hanashi*, p. 156.]

251. Avisar, *Sefer Hevron*, p. 385.

252. Ben-Ami, *"Minhagei herayon veleidah."*

253. Anikster, *Kunteres zekher olam*, p. 14. [Shilo, *Hakol hanashi*, p. 99.]

254. Eliahu Eliachar, *Lihyot im yehudim*, p. 82; Yehoshua Yellin, *Zikhronot leven Yerushalayim*, p. 8.

255. Edward Shorter, *The Making of the Modern Family* (New York, 1975), pp. 168–190.

256. Matthews, *"Just a Housewife,"* p. 4.

257. Hyman, "The Modern Jewish Family."

258. Ya'akov Goldberg, *"Nisu'ei hayehudim be'Polin hayeshanah,"* p. 29.

259. Stahl, *Mishpahah vegidul yeladim*, p. 37; Jack Goody, *The Oriental, the Ancient and the Primitive: Systems of Marriage and the Family in the Pre-industrial Societies of Eurasia* (Cambridge, 1990), pp. 424–425.

260. Yosef Salmon, "*Hahinukh ha'Ashkenazi be'Erez Yisra'el beyn 'yashan' le'hadash,*'" *Shalem* 6 (1992), pp. 281–301.

261. Levi, *Perakim betoledot harefu'ah*, p. 22.

262. Kassan, *David Yellin*, pp. 38 (note), 26ff.

263. Yadler, *Betuv Yerushalayim*, pp. 48–50; Hadad, *Sefer ma'amar Ester*, p. 5b.

264. Tamar Alexander[-Fraser], introduction in Angel-Malachi, *Hayei Yerushalayim*, p. 24.

265. Angel-Malachi, *Beterem reshit*, p. 25.

266. Yadler, *Betuv Yerushalayim*, p. 24.

267. Hamburger, *Sheloshah olamot*, vol. 3, p. 10.

268. Hundert, "Jewish Children and Childhood," p. 87.

269. Shilo, *Hakol hanashi*.

270. [Feinstein], *Sefer zikhron Eliyahu*, p. 4. [Shilo, *Hakol hanashi*, p. 248.]

271. *Hazevi*, no. 27, 27 Tamuz 5655 [July 19, 1895].

272. Ibid., 26 Kislev 5656 [December 13, 1895].

273. Luncz, *Netivot Zion viYrushalayim*, p. 21; Freeze, *Jewish Marriage*, pp. 131–132, 148.

274. Mordechai Eliav, "*Masa liYrushalayim bishnat 5645,*" *Sinai* 50 (1970), p. 157.

275. Edwin Sherman Wallace, *Jerusalem the Holy* (New York, 1977 [1898]), p. 304.

276. Avraham Shmuel Hirschberg, *Be'erez hamizrah*, p. 388; Raab, *Hatelem harishon*, pp. 50–52.

277. On divorce in Yemen see Gamlieli, "*Hayei ha'ishah hayehudiyah,*" p. 148.

278. On immigration to the Land of Israel as a cause for divorce see Franco, *Responsa Sha'arei Yerushalayim*, vol. 2, no. 32, pp. 114b–115a; Hayyim David Hazan, *Sefer nediv lev* (Jerusalem 1876), no. 21, pp. 47b, 48a.

279. Yehoshua, *Yaldut biYrushalayim*, vol. 3, pp. 54–55.

280. Alper, *Korot mishpahah ahat*, pp. 115–116.

281. Yaakov Gellis, *Shiv'im shanah biYrushalayim: Toledot hayyav shel . . . Rabbenu Shmuel Salant* (Jerusalem, 1960), p. 62; for Gruenbaum's account see above, n. 274.

282. Ben-Avraham, *Sipurim Yerushalmiyim*, p. 79.

283. Avishur, *Hahatunah hayehudit beBaghdad*, vol. 1, p. 151.

284. Amnon Cohen, *Yehudim be'veyt hamishpat hamuslemi: Hevrah, kalkalah ve'irgun kehilati biYrushalayim ha'Othmanit, Hame'ah hashemoneh esreh* (Jerusalem, 1996), pp. 461–470.

285. Ze'evi, "*Hame'ah ha'Uthmanit,*" p. 334.

286. Bornstein-Makovetzky, "*Nisu'in vegerushin,*" p. 149.

287. Menachem M. Brayer, *The Jewish Woman in Rabbinic Literature: A Psychological Perspective* (Hoboken, N.J., 1986), p. 54.

288. Katz, *Tradition and Crisis*, pp. 122–123.

289. Katz, "*Nisu'im vehayei ishut,*" p. 43.

290. For a case of a man remarrying his divorced wife see a document dated 14 Elul 5648 [August 21, 1888], CAHJP, (3) 2551.

291. Agreement between Yehudah b. Eliezer and Elka Bergman, 1 Kislev 5612 [November 25, 1851], Jerusalem, CAHJP, J52.

292. Compromise agreement, 2 Adar 5658 [February 24, 1898], NHUL, Eliachar Archive, 4* 1271 665.

293. Agreement between R. Nahum Etrog and his wife, 13 Sivan 5666 [June 6, 1906], Safed, CAHJP, Safed Collection, IL/Sa.

294. Eliav, "*Masa liYrushalayim,*" p. 157.

295. Hidah [Hemdah Ben-Yehuda], "*Mikhtavim miYrushalayim,*" in *Hazevi,* no. 28, 6 Kislev 5657 [November 11, 1896].

296. *Hazevi,* no. 22, 27 Tamuz 5655 [July 19, 1895].

297. Ibid., no. 7, 29 Tevet 5645 [January 16, 1885].

298. Ibid., no. 28, 5 Av 5655 [July 26, 1895].

299. Ibid., no. 17, 2 Shevat 5656 [January 17, 1896].

300. Ya'akov Goldberg, "*Nisu'ei hayehudim bePolin hayeshanah,*" p. 31.

301. Tucker, "Marriage and Family in Nablus," p. 178.

302. Spitzer, *Sefer takhshitei nashim,* p. 17b.

303. Ya'akov Sha'ul Eliachar, *Responsa Benei Binyamin vekerev ish,* vol. 1 (Jerusalem, 1876), no. 33, p. 55a; Franco, *Responsa Sha'arei Yerushalayim,* vol. 2, no. 27, p. 32b.

304. Avraham Shmuel Hirschberg, *Be'erez hamizrah,* p. 388; *Havazelet,* no. 15, 2 Shevat 5636 [January 28, 1876].

305. Yehoshua, *Yaldut biYrushalayim,* vol. 3, p. 55.

306. Bab. Talmud, Yevamot 64a; see Hamburger, *Sheloshah olamot,* vol. 2, p. 74.

307. Letter, Hayyim b. Elimelech in Jerusalem to the Amsterdam offices of the *halukah,* 4 Nisan 5659 [March 15, 1899], Bibliotheca Rosenthalia, Amsterdam, Pekidim and Amarkalim Archives 163.

308. Yehudit Toporowski, *Me'ah she'arim sheli: Korot mishpahat Shalom uMalkah Azulay bishkhunat Me'ah She'arim ke'aspaklariyah lehayei hayishuv hayashan beyn hashanim 1919–1924* (Jerusalem, 1994), p. 30.

309. *Hashkafah,* no. 12, 213 Tevet 5658 [January 6, 1898].

310. Yehoshua Kaniel, "*Batei hadin shel ha'edot biYrushalayim bme'ah ha19,*" in *Shanah beshanah* (Jerusalem, 1976), pp. 325–335.

311. Luncz, *Netivot Zion viYrushalayim,* p. 221.

312. Schmelz, "*Kavim meyuhadim,*" p. 64.

313. Sharshevsky, *Dinei mishpahah,* pp. 278–281.

314. Amnon Cohen, *Yehudim be'veyt hamishpat hamuslemi,* p. 461.

315. *Havazelet,* no. 29, 21 Iyar 5637 [May 4, 1877].

316. Beyla Kenig, letter to the offices of the *halukah* in Amsterdam, 14 Elul 5664 [August 25, 1904], Bibliotheca Rosenthalia, Amsterdam, Pekidim and Amarkatim Archives, 183.

317. Rahamim Yosef Franco, *Sefer Sha'arei Yerushalayim* (Jerusalem, 1881), pp. 48a–50a.

318. *Ha'or,* no. 31, Rosh hodesh Adar 5651 [May 8, 1891]; *Hashkafah,* no. 16, 2 Iyar 5662 [May 9, 1902].

319. *Hazevi,* no. 27, 27 Tamuz 5655 [July 19, 1895].

320. Wallace, *Jerusalem the Holy,* pp. 302–303.

321. Margalit Shilo, "*Takkanot Yerushalayim kime'azvot migdar,*" in Tovah Cohen and Yehoshua Schwartz (eds.), *Ishah biYrushalayim: Migdar, hevrah vadat* (Ramat-Gan, 2002), pp. 65–77.

322. Sabar, "*Livhinat hashoni,*" p. 102.

323. R. Yaakov Sha'ul Eliachar, approbation (*haskamah*) for the 1883 edition of *Sefer hatakanot,* before p. 1.

324. Lavsky, "*Takanot Yerushalayim,*" pp. 271–316.

325. Kaniel, "*Ma'avakim irguniyim.*"

326. Binyamin Kluger, *Min hamakor,* vol. 1, p. 91.

327. Spitzer, *Sefer takhshitei nashim,* p. 7a–b.

Chapter 4. Women in the Public Sphere: Religious, Economic,
and Philanthropic Involvement (pp. 108–142)

1. Ya'akov Pinkerfeld, *Batei haknesiyot beErez Yisra'el* (Jerusalem, 1946), p. 51; see also Tristram, *The Land of Israel*, pp. 503–504; Sara Mathilda Barclay, *Hadji in Syria, or Three Years in Jerusalem* (Philadelphia, 1858), p. 264.

2. Yehoshua, *Yaldut biYrushalayim*, vol. 1, p. 26.

3. For conditions in earlier periods see Shmuel Safrai, *"Ha'im haytah kayemet ezrat nashim bevet hakeneset batekufah ha'atikah,"* *Tarbiz* 32 (1963), pp. 329–338; Hanokh Ahiman, *"Ha'azarot bevet hakeneset,"* in Yeshayahu Ilan et al. (eds.), *Mikdash me'at: Kovez ma'amarim bish'elot izuv penim shel batei keneset* (Jerusalem, 1975), pp. 57–62.

4. Amiram Harlap, *Batei keneset beYisra'el miymei kedem ve'ad yamenu* (Tel Aviv, 1985), pp. 91–93; Aharon Bir, *"Mosedot torah utfilah beyn hahomot,"* in Mordechai Na'or (ed.), *Harova hayehudi ba'ir ha'atikah biYrushalayim* (Jerusalem, 1987), pp. 130, 143; Naomi Feuchtwanger, *Bet Ohel Moshe: Me'ah shanah lashekhunah ulvet hakeneset shelah* (Jerusalem, 1984), pp. 47–53.

5. *Havazelet*, no. 5, 8 Tevet [5]638 [December 14, 1877].

6. Sered, *Religious Lives*, p. 208.

7. Avraham Hayim Freimann, *"Takanot Yerushalayim,"* p. 210.

8. Ibid.; Luncz, *Yerushalayim*, vol. 1, p. 66.

9. Yehoshua, *Yaldut biYrushalayim*, vol. 1, p. 19.

10. Avraham Weiss, *Women at Prayer: A Halakhic Analysis of Women's Prayer Groups* (Hoboken, N.J., 1990), p. 44, note 5; Rabbi Elijah of Vilna, letter in Eliezer Steinman, *Sefer hama'alot: Parshiyot mehayei anshei shem beYisra'el: Megilot, te'udot vezava'ot* (Tel Aviv, 1956), p. 119.

11. Reicher, *Sefer sha'arei Yerushalayim*, Sha'ar 9, unpaginated.

12. Hamburger, *Sheloshah olamot*, vol. 3, p. 17.

13. Neumann, *Ir hakodesh veyoshevei bah*, p. 36.

14. Gad Frumkin, *Derekh shofet biYrushalayim*, pp. 73, 75; Yehoshua, *Yaldut biYrushalayim*, vol. 1, p. 17.

15. Yadler, *Betuv Yerushalayim*, p. 48.

16. Yehoshua, *Yaldut biYrushalayim*, vol. 1, p. 18.

17. Ibid., p. 187.

18. Susan Freiman, *"Nashim yehudiyot italkiyot keyozerot tashmishei kedushah,"* *Motar* 5 (1997), pp. 97–102.

19. Eliahu Eliachar, *Lihyot im yehudim*, p. 78; see also Chava Weissler, "The Religion of Traditional Ashkenazic Women: Some Methodological Issues," *AJS Review* 12 (1987), p. 80; idem, *Voices of the Matriarchs*, p. 136.

20. Hamburger, *Sheloshah olamot*, vol. 3, p. 17.

21. Bracha Yaniv, *"Seker batei hakeneset hasefaradiyim biYrushalayim,"* *Mehkerei Yerushalayim befolklor yehudi* 5–6 (1984), pp. 201–208.

22. Nahum Dov Freimann, *Sefer hazikaron haYerushalmi* (Jerusalem, 1913), pp. 79–87.

23. Zvi Graetz, *Darkhei hahistoriyah hayehudit*, pp. 278–279.

24. Eliav, *"Masa liYrushalayim,"* p. 151.

25. Gat, *Hayishuv hayehudi*, pp. 34–47; Shmuel Avitzur, *"Hamelakhah vehata'asiyah hayehudit biYrushalayim lifnei kom hamedinah mishilhei hatekufah ha'uthmanit ve'ad tom hamandat habriti,"* in Menachem Friedman et al. (eds.), *Perakim betoledot hayishuv hayehudi biYrushalayim*, vol. 2 (Jerusalem, 1976), pp. 266–272.

26. Schoelch, *Palestine in Transformation*, p. 124.

27. Luncz, *Luah Erez Yisrael*, vol. 4, pp. 163–164.

28. Yehoshua Barzilai, "*Mikhtavim me'Erez Yisra'el IV*," *HaShiloah* 24 (1911), pp. 273–275.

29. Shmuel Avitzur, *Haroshet hama'aseh: Kovez letoledot hata'asiyah ba'arez* (Tel Aviv, 1974).

30. Ben-Arieh, *Jerusalem . . . the New City*, pp. 413ff.; Yehoshua Kaniel, "*Memadei hayeridah min ha'arez bitkufat ha'aliyah harishonah vehasheniyah*," *Cathedra* 73 (1994), pp. 115–138.

31. Eliezer Rivlin, "*Takanot hahalukah shel 'Kolel haPerushim' be'Erez Yisra'el mishenat 5583*," *Me'asef Zion* 2 (1927), p. 159.

32. Luncz, *Yerushalayim*, vol. 9, p. 61.

33. Aryeh Leib Frumkin, "*Sipur hathalat yishuv ha'Ashkenazim hanikra'im Perushim*," *Me'asef Zion* 2 (1927), pp. 141–142.

34. Ben-Arieh, *Jerusalem . . . the New City*, pp. 393–395.

35. Ze'evi, "*Hame'ah ha'Uthmanit*," pp. 334–340.

36. Eliezer Bashan, *Sefer mimizrah shemesh ad mevo'o: Perakim betoledot yehudei hamizrah vehaMaghreb: Hevrah vekhalkalah* (Lod, 1996), pp. 147–167.

37. Shoham, "*Almenot Yerushalayim*," p. 22.

38. Susan A. Glenn, *Daughters of the Shtetl: Life and Labor in the Immigrant Generation* (Ithaca, N.Y., 1990), p. 15.

39. Eliezer Rivlin, "*Mikhtav me-R. Mordechai Zoref le-aviv R. A. Sh. Zalman, z"l, mi-shenat [5]605 [1845]*," *Me'asef Zion* (1926), p. 73.

40. *Kehilat Ya'akov* (Jerusalem, 1908), p. 6.

41. See below, chapter 5.

42. Rothschild, "*Hahalukah*," p. 39.

43. Glenn, *Daughters of the Shtetl*, p. 15.

44. Anikster, *Kunteres zekher olam*, II, p. 2. [Shilo, *Hakol hanasi*, p. 112.]

45. Etkes, *Lita biYrushalayim*, p. 83.

46. Ibid., pp. 74–80; Shlomo Ashkenazi, "*Ha'ishah hayehudiyah bameshek uvakalkalah*," *Mahanayim* 2 (1992), p. 180.

47. An undated request for charity, in the Montefiore Archives, no. 575, p. 53, also mentions that the writer, Sara, widow of R. Asher Zelig, had kept a shop.

48. Shmuel Avitzur, "*Hayei yom yom umelakhot masortiyot ba'ir ha'atikah*," *Ariel* 57/58(1988), p. 92.

49. Avraham Shmuel Hirschberg, *Be'erez hamizrah*, p. 340; Yehoshua, *Yaldut biYrushalayim*, vol. 3, p. 94.

50. Bashan, *Sefer mimizrah shemesh ad mevo'o*, p. 155; idem, "*Helkah shel ha'ishah hayehudiyah behayei hakalkalah shel yehudei zefon Afrikah*," *Mikedem umiyam* 1 (1981), pp. 67–84.

51. Luncz[-Bolotin], "*Ha'em vehabat*," p. 136.

52. Maxine Schwartz-Seller, "The Upbringing of the Twenty Thousand: Sex, Class and Ethnicity in the Shirtwaist Makers' Strike of 1909," in Dirk Hoerder (ed.), *"Struggle a Hard Battle": Essays on Working-Class Immigrants* (DeKalb, Ill., 1986), p. 267.

53. Ian C. Dengler, "The Turkish Woman in the Ottoman Empire: The Classical Age," in Lois Beck and Nikki Keddie (eds.), *Women in the Moslem World* (Cambridge, Mass., 1978), p. 230.

54. Luncz, *Yerushalayim*, vol. 1, p. 66; Ga'on, *Yehudei hamizrah*, vol. 1, p. 114.

55. Avraham Hayim Freimann, *"Takanot Yerushalayim,"* p. 212.

56. Ibid.; Lamdan, *A Separate People*, p. 125.

57. Etkes, *Lita biYrushalayim*, p. 86.

58. Luncz, *Netivot Zion viYrushalayim*, p. 216.

59. Alper, *Korot mishpahah ahat*, p. 43.

60. Luncz, *Netivot Zion viYrushalayim*, p. 67; see also ibid., p. 155.

61. Yehoshua, *Yaldut biYrushalayim*, vol. 3, p. 211.

62. Chaya Sara, daughter of Elchanan, letter (1839), Safed, Montefiore Archives, no. 575, p. 45.

63. Luncz, *Netivot Zion viYrushalayim*, p. 205.

64. Quataert, "Ottoman Women," p. 162.

65. Avitzur, *Haroshet hama'aseh*, p. 171.

66. Alper, *Korot mishpahah ahat*, p. 41.

67. Yehoshua Ben-Arieh, *"Hanof hayishuvi shel Erez Yisra'el erev hahityashvut hazionit,"* in M. Lisak et al. (eds.), *Toledot hayishuv hayehudi be'Erez Yisra'el* (Jerusalem, 1990), p. 128.

68. Yadler, *Betuv Yerushalayim*, p. 358.

69. Ophir, *Hoter migeza*, p. 51.

70. Naftali Porush-Glickman, *Sheloshah dorot biYrushalayim: Pirkei Zikhronot* (Jerusalem, 1978), p. 60; Philip and Avi Goodman, "R. Simchah Yaniver Diskin," *Ariel* 100–101 (1998), p. 35.

71. Alper, *Korot mishpahah ahat*, pp. 42–43.

72. Porush, *Zikhronot rishonim*, p. 44.

73. Yehoshua, *Yaldut biYrushalayim*, vol. 3, p. 211.

74. Gad Frumkin, *Derekh shofet biYrushalayim*, p. 46.

75. Hamburger, *Sheloshah olamot*, vol. 2, p. 37.

76. Luncz[-Bolotin], *Me'ir netivot Yerushalayim*, p. 86.

77. Ben-Arieh, *Jerusalem . . . the New City*, p. 395.

78. Nachum Rakover (ed.), *Shorashim va'anafim: Lidmutam shel Aba ve'Ima, R. Hayim veHanah Malkah (leveit Mandelbaum) Rakover* (Jerusalem, 1996), p. 20.

79. Ben Zion Yadler, *Sefer ben yekhabed av* (Jerusalem, 1948), p. 9.

80. Ibid.; Yadler, *Betuv Yerushalayim*, p. 283.

81. See also above, chapter 3, text at note 159. For a similar figure see Gellis, *Midemuyot Yerushalayim*, p. 149.

82. Yadler, *Betuv Yerushalayim*, p. 288.

83. Dov Nathan Bar-Yakar, *"A[doni] A[vi] uM[ori] R. Ya'akov be-R. Zevi Netz z"l,"* *Luah Yerushalayim*, 12th year, 1952, p. 294.

84. Grayevsky, *Benot Zion viYrushalayim*, p. 340. According to the Midrash, Zebulun the merchant provided for his brother Issachar, thus enabling him to study Torah; the relationship between Issachar and Zebulun thus became the prototype of the relationship between the Torah scholar and his benefactors.

85. Porush-Glickman, *Sheloshah dorot biYrushalayim*, p. 60.

86. Pinehas Grayevsky [Ben Ya'ir], *Eshet hayil hageveret Gitel Dinovitz* (Jerusalem, 1939), p. 6.

87. Matthews, *"Just a Housewife."*

88. Devorah Bernstein, *Ishah beErez Yisra'el: Hashe'ifah leshivyon bitkufat hayishuv* (Tel Aviv, 1987), pp. 52–53; Bat Sheva (Margalit) Stern, *"Tenu'at hapo'alot*

be'Erez Yisra'el: Mo'ezet hapo'a lot 1920–1939" (Ph.D. dissertation, Haifa University, 1997), p. 177.

89. Bashan, *Sefer mimizrah shemesh ad mevo'o*, pp. 166–167.

90. Glenn, *Daughters of the Shtetl*, p. 17.

91. Aryeh Leib Frumkin, "*Sipur hathalat yishuv ha'Ashkenazim*," p. 142.

92. Shoham, "*Almenot Yerushalayim*," p. 22. See also above, at note 33.

93. Bergman, *Se'u harim shalom*, pp. 46, 106; Gad Frumkin, *Derekh shofet biYrushalayim*, pp. 17–20.

94. Letter from Feyge "die Varterin," Amsterdam, Bibliotheca Rosenthalia, Pekidim and Amarkalim Archives 62.

95. Ita Yellin, *Leze'eza'ay*, vol. 2, p. 82.

96. *Hashkafah*, no. 53, 25 Nisan [5]666 [April 20, 1906], advertisement.

97. Ben-Arieh, *Jerusalem . . . the New City*, p. 394.

98. Shiryon, *Zikhronot*, pp. 97–98.

99. Grayevsky, *Benot Zion viYrushalayim*, p. 295.

100. Letter from Gitel Hirsch, 4 Tamuz [5]659 [June 12, 1899], Amsterdam, Bibliotheca Rosenthalia, Pekidim and Amarkalim Archives 171; Yehoshua, *Yaldut biYrushalayim*, vol. 3, p. 94.

101. Letter from Yisra'el Yehudah Ze'ev Saminet, 2 Av [5]644 [July 24, 1884], Amsterdam, Bibliotheca Rosenthalia, Pekidim and Amarkalim Archives 65.

102. Mandelbaum, *Asarah dorot*, vol. 2, p. 128.

103. Aryeh Morgenstern, *Ge'ulah bederekh hateva: Talmidei haGra beErez Yisra'el, 1800–1840, Mehkarim umkorot* (Jerusalem, 1997), p. 350; Genechovsky, *Misipurei hahevrah hagevohah*, p. 262.

104. Galyah Gavish, *Nizanei ta'asiyah biYrushalayim* (brochure, Old Yishuv Museum, Jerusalem, n.d.).

105. Yehoshua, *Yaldut biYrushalayim*, vol. 2, p. 161.

106. Trivaks and Steinman, *Sefer me'ah shanah*, p. 117.

107. Yosef Barkan, "*Letoledot melon Kaminitz biYrushalayim*," Ariel 119–120 (1997), pp. 65–72; Elizabeth Ann Finn, *Reminiscences of Mrs. Finn* (London and Edinburgh, 1929), p. 185.

108. Avisar, *Sefer Hevron*, pp. 210, 396.

109. Razahbi, *Bo'i Teiman*, p. 326.

110. Levi, *Perakim betoledot harefu'ah*, p. 93.

111. Robert Dingwell, Ann Rafferty, and Charles Webster, *An Introduction to the Social History of Nursing* (London, 1988), pp. 4–18, 145–172.

112. Yehoshua, *Yaldut biYrushalayim*, vol. 2, pp. 129–130.

113. Ibid., pp. 110–113; idem, *Yerushalayim hayeshanah ba'ayin uvalev*, pp. 179–188.

114. Mandelbaum, *Asarah dorot*, vol. 1, p. 21; Shiryon, *Zikhronot*, p. 157.

115. Ben-Haggai, "*Aniyim vekabzanim.*"

116. Menachem (Meni) Shor, "*Bet haholim Sha'arei Zedek biYrushalayim bishnotav harishonot*" (seminar paper, Bar-Ilan University, Ramat-Gan, 2000).

117. *Haskafah*, nos. 57–58, 10 Iyyar [5]667 [April 24, 1907]; Kagan, *Reshit darki.*

118. Ben-Arieh, *Jerusalem . . . the New City*, p. 394; Shim'on Stern, "*Te'ur harefu'ah biYrushalayim*," p. 126.

119. Mani, *Hevron vegiboreha*, p. 82; idem, "*Bahazar hayehudim beHevron*," p. 93.

120. Yehoshua, *Yaldut biYrushalayim*, vol. 2, p. 85.

121. Ita Yellin, *Leze'eza'ay*, vol. 2, p. 34.

122. Hamburger, *Sheloshah olamot*, vol. 3, p. 110.

123. Yehoshua, *Yerushalayim temol shilshom*, vol. 1, pp. 141–142.

124. Eliyahu Auerbach, *Me'erez ha'av le'erez avot: Harofé hayehudi harishon be-Heyfah* (Jerusalem, 1977), pp. 256–257.

125. Yehoshua, *Yaldut biYrushalayim*, vol. 2, p. 86.

126. Ibid., vol. 3, p. 71.

127. Shiryon, *Zikhronot*, p. 157.

128. *Ha'Or*, no. 4, 2 Kislev [5]651 [November 14, 1890]; ibid., no. 5, 12 Heshvan [5]653 [November 2, 1892].

129. *Hazevi*, no. 1, 5 Tishri [5]654 [September 15, 1893].

130. David Yellin, *Ketavim*, vol. 1, pp. 197–198; Jacquelyn Litt, "Mothering, Medicalization and Jewish Identity, 1928–1940," *Gender and Society* 10 (1996), pp. 185–198.

131. Ya'arah Bar On, "*Milhemet haminim bikehilah mikzo'it — meyalledot umeyalledim bePariz shel hame'ah hasheva esreh*," *Historiyah* 3 (1999), pp. 79–102.

132. Quataert, "Ottoman Women"; Dengler, "The Turkish Woman," pp. 230–231.

133. Grayevsky, *Zikhron lahovevim harishonim*, vol. 1, p. 454; Luncz, *Yerushalayim*, vol. 2, p. 117.

134. Schölch, *Palestine in Transformation*, p. 124; Yisra'el Hanani, "*Po'alim uva'alei melakhah biYrushalayim*," *Yerushalayim* 3 (1951), p. 164.

135. Yehoshua, *Yaldut biYrushalayim*, vol. 2, p. 192.

136. Elizabeth Ann Finn, *Reminiscences*, p. 55.

137. Shoham, "*Almenot Yerushalayim*," p. 22.

138. Neumann, *Ir hakodesh veyoshevei bah*, p. 32.

139. Ita Yellin, *Leze'eza'ay*, vol. 2, p. 12; Leibowitz, *Ba'aliyah uvabeniyah*, pp. 67–68.

140. Avitzur, *Haroshet hama'aseh*, p. 173; Even-Or-Orenstein, "*Hanashim bemishpahat Orenstein*," 3–4 (1990), pp. 39–40; Efrati, *Mishpahat Elyashar*, p. 53; Grayevsky, *Benot Zion viYrushalayim*, pp. 23–24.

141. Eliav, *Ahavat Ziyon*, pp. 249–250.

142. Letter from Rivka, daughter of R. Nachman Nathan Coronel, 16 Elul [5]660 [September 10, 1900], Amsterdam, Bibliotheca Rosenthalia, Pekidim and Amarkalim Archives 184.

143. Rakover, *Shorashim va'anafim*, p. 18.

144. Yosef Olitzky, *400 shanim le'umanut hadefus be'Erez Yisra'el* (Ramat-Gan, 1973), p. 260.

145. Quataert, "Ottoman Women"; Ingeborg Glambek, "One of the Age's Noblest Cultural Movements: On the Theoretical Basis for the Arts and Crafts Movement," *Scandinavian Journal of Design History* 1 (1991), pp. 47–76; Anthea Callen, *Angel in the Studio: Women in the Arts and Crafts Movement, 1870–1914* (Great Britain, 1979).

146. Dalit Thon, "*Batei sefer limlekhet teharim beErez Yisra'el bereshit hame'ah ha20*," in Nina Benzur (ed.), *Tahara* (Haifa [Museum for Music and Ethnology], 1994), pp. 18–21; Rafi Thon, *Hama'avak leshivyon zekhuyot ha'ishah: Sipur hayeha shel Sarah Thon* (Tel Aviv, 1996), pp. 51–71.

147. Steven Adams, *The Arts and Crafts Movement* (London, 1987); see also Callen, *Angel in the Studio*.

148. Yisra'el Kolatt, "*Yerushalayim be'einei nezig JCA — Albert Antebi*," in Yosef Katz (ed.), *Hahevrah lehityashvut yehudim (JCA), me'ah shenot pe'ilut, 1891–1991* (Jerusalem, 1995), pp. 35–44; Theodore Norman, *An Outstretched Arm: A History of the Jewish Colonization Association* (London, 1985), pp. 54–67.

149. *Jewish Chronicle*, June 6, 1900.

150. Sha'ul Sapir, *"Terumat hevrot hamisyon ha'anglikaniyot lehitpattehutah shel Yerushalayim beshilhei hashilton ha'Uthmani"* (M.A. thesis, Hebrew University of Jerusalem, 1979), p. 25; *Jewish Chronicle*, September 5, 1902, p. 35.

151. Ibid., August 14, 1903; September 29, 1904; July 14, 1905.

152. Sarah Chinsky, *"Rokemot hataharah miBezalel,"* *Teoriya uvikoret* 11 (1997), pp. 179–183.

153. Shilo, *Nisyonot behitashevut: Hamisrad ha'Erezyisre'eli 1904–1918* (Jerusalem, 1988), pp. 190–193.

154. Binyamin Tamuz et al. (eds.), *Sipurah shel omanut Yisra'el miymei Bezalel be1906 ve'ad yamenu* (Tel Aviv, 1991), p. 27.

155. *Jewish Chronicle*, June 6, 1907, pp. 18–19; Luncz, *Luah Erez Yisra'el*, vol. 12 ([5]667), p. 99.

156. Boris Schatz, *Bezalel, toledotav, mahuto ve'atido* (Jerusalem, 1910), pp. 9–10.

157. Ruth A. Frager, *Sweatshop Strife, Class Ethnicity and Gender* (Toronto, 1993), pp. 121–124.

158. Yosef Luria, "Bezalel," *Ha'olam*, 5th year, no. 1, 19 Tevet [5]671 [January 19, 1911].

159. Nurit Shilo-Cohen (ed.), *Bezalel shel Schatz, 1906–1929* (Jerusalem, 1983), pp. 156–163.

160. *Jewish Chronicle*, January 28, 1910, p. 8; Margalit Shilo, "The Women's Farm at Kinneret, 1911–1914: A Solution to the Problem of the Working Women in the Second Aliyah," in Deborah S. Bernstein (ed.), *Pioneers and Homemakers* (Albany, N.Y., 1992), pp. 119–143.

161. Letter from Sarah Thon to Education Committee, August 15, 1915, CZA S2/744.

162. Gideon Ofrat-Friedlander, *"Tekufat Bezalel,"* in Shilo-Cohen (ed.), *Bezalel shel Schatz*, p. 60; Rafi Thon, *Hama'avak leshivyon*, p. 62.

163. Luncz[-Bolotin], *Me'ir netivot Yerushalayim*, p. 87.

164. Protocol of the Committee for Women's Employment in Jerusalem, 24 Av [5]677 [August 12, 1917], CZA S2/427.

165. Chinsky, *"Rokemot hataharah miBezalel,"* pp. 190, 200–201.

166. Luncz, *Luah Erez Yisrael*, vol. 14 (1909), pp. 63–64.

167. For a detailed discussion, see chapter 5.

168. Jo Anne Preston, "Gender and the Formation of a Women's Profession: The Case of Public School Teaching," in Jerry A. Jacobs (ed.), *Gender Inequality at Work* (Thousand Oaks, Calif., 1995), pp. 379–407.

169. Grayevsky, *Benot Zion viYrushalayim*, pp. 276–277; Avraham Hayyim (ed.), *"Mekorot ute'udot letoledot ha'edah hasefaradit biYrushalayim ha'Uthmanit,"* *Shevet va'am* 7 (1973), p. 167; idem, *Te'udot . . . Eliachar*, nos. 96, 100.

170. Letter of Zevi Hirsch Grover of Kitov to Moses Montefiore, 1839, Montefiore Archives 575, p. 7.

171. Bashan, *Sefer mimizrah shemesh ad mevo'o*, p. 158.

172. Ze'evi, *"Hame'ah ha'Uthmanit,"* pp. 335–336; Amnon Cohen, *Yehudim be'veyt hamishpat hamuslemi*, p. 461.

173. Money: Engel, *Responsa*, vol. 5, no. 7 (p. 9); jewelry: *Ha'or*, no. 42, 1 Elul [5]652 [August 24, 1892]; Torah scroll: R. Yizhak Elchanan Spector, *Responsa Ein Yizhak* (New York, 1965), Orah Hayim, no. 9.

174. *Havazelet*, no. 4, 1 Tevet [5]638 [December 7, 1877].

175. Last Will and Testament of Perel of Safed, 2 Av [5]652 [July 26, 1892], NHUL, Kadesh Collection, 4* 1261/38.

176. Similar provisions were made by the widow of the philanthropist David Reiss: *Havazelet*, no. 11, 29 Kislev [5]637 [December 15, 1876].

177. Similarly, for example, in the will of Ita Hena Sachs, 3 Kislev [5]671 [December 4, 1910], courtesy of Dov Genechovsky, Personal Archive.

178. A business transaction between two women, Yocheved, wife of Yizhak Hayat of Kolel Habad, and Esther Sarah, wife of Binyamin Bernstein, is attested by a deed dated Nisan [5]662 [March–April 1902], in the NHUL, Kadesh Collection, V57.

179. Letter of Chayah Rivkah Schwartz, 3 Shevat [5]633 [January 31, 1873], collection of her letters in CAHJP.

180. Letter to Montefiore on his visit in 1839, Montefiore Archives, no. 574, p. 29.

181. Yehoshua Ben-Arieh, *Ir bir'i tekufah: Yerushalayim hahadashah bereshitah* (Jerusalem, 1979), pp. 220, note 70, p. 678 (index) [this reference does not appear in the slightly abridged English translation, *Emergence of the New City*]; Eleazar Hurwitz, *Mosad hayesod Yerushalayim* (Jerusalem, 1958), p. 263, note 12.

182. Luncz, *Luah Erez Yisrael*, vol. 8 (1903), p. 70.

183. *Hazevi*, no. 43, 8 Av [5]653 [July 21, 1893].

184. Shelomit Langbaum, "*Hitpatehut takanot Me'ah She'arim kimshakefot tahalikhei shinuy bashekhunah 1874–1995*" (seminar paper, Hebrew University of Jerusalem, 1995), pp. 2, 52.

185. Last Will and Testament of Hinda, daughter of R. Moshe Kaplan, 4 Shevat [5]664 [January 21, 1904], courtesty of Dov Genechovsky, Personal Archive.

186. Yosef Yoel Rivlin, *Me'ah She'arim* (Jerusalem, 1947), p. 82; idem, "*Mishpahat Rivlin be'Erez Yisrael*," pp. 63–64.

187. Grayevsky, *Benot Zion viYrushalayim*, pp. 271–272.

188. Ibid., p. 340.

189. Ibid., p. 121.

190. Document of the Supreme Religious Court of the Ashkenazim in Jerusalem, 10 Av [5]668 [August 7, 1908], NHUL, 4* 1203/75.

191. Grayevsky, *Benot Zion viYrushalayim*, p. 365.

192. Charles Netter, Report to Alliance Israélite Universelle, 1869, reproduced in Kellner, *Lema'an Zion*, p. 178.

193. Bronislaw Geremek, *Poverty: A History* (Oxford and Cambridge, Mass., 1994), p. 250.

194. Charles Netter, Report to Alliance Israélite Universelle, reproduced in Kellner, *Lema'an Zion*, p. 183; Faith Rogow, *Gone to Another Meeting: The National Council of Jewish Women, 1893–1993* (Tuscaloosa, Ala., 1993), p. 131.

195. Geremek, *Poverty*, p. 243.

196. Prochaska, *Women and Philanthropy*, p. 5; Selma Berrol, "Class or Ethnicity: The Americanized German Jewish Woman and the Middle-Class Sisters in 1895," *Jewish Social Studies* 47 (1985), pp. 21–32; Beth S. Wenger, "Jewish Women and Voluntarism: Beyond the Myth of Enablers," *American Jewish History* 79/1 (1989–1990), pp. 16–19.

197. Prochaska, *Women and Philanthropy*, p. 15.

198. Paula E. Hyman, "The Volunteer Organizations: Vanguard or Rear Guard?" *Lilith* 5 (1978), p. 16; idem, *Gender and Assimilation in Modern Jewish History: The Roles and Representation of Women* (Seattle, 1995).

199. Sabine Knappe, "The Role of Women's Associations in the Jewish Community: The Example of the Israelitisch-humanitarer Frauenverein in Hamburg at the Turn of the Century," in *Leo Baeck Institute Year-Book,* (London, 1994), pp. 153–178.

200. Prochaska, *Women and Philanthropy,* p. 17.

201. Rogow, *Gone to Another Meeting,* p. 157.

202. Naftali Toker, *"Eshet hayil vedarkhei kishurah leleilot Shabbat,"* *Mehkerei Hag* 3 (1992), pp. 44–63.

203. Barzilai, *"Mikhtavim,"* p. 276.

204. Yehoshua, *Yaldut biYrushalayim,* vol. 3, pp. 24–29.

205. Grayevsky, *Benot Zion viYrushalayim,* pp. 36–53, 41, 181, 278.

206. Ibid., p. 266; Mani, *"Bahazar hayehudim beHevron,"* 5 (1960), p. 118.

207. Grayevsky, *Benot Zion viYrushalayim,* pp. 177, 353.

208. Even-Or-Orenstein, *"Hanashim bemishpahat Orenstein,"* vol. 3–4, p. 39.

209. Yosef Yoel Rivlin, *"Zur mahzavto shel Yosef Luriya z"l,"* p. 60.

210. Grayevsky, *Benot Zion viYrushalayim,* p. 264; Ben-Avraham, *Sipurim Yerushalmiyim,* p. 78.

211. Yehoshua, *Yaldut biYrushalayim,* vol. 2, p. 133; idem, *Yerushalayim temol shilshom,* vol. 3, pp. 25–30.

212. Grayevsky, *Benot Zion viYrushalayim,* pp. 61, 185.

213. Ibid., p. 205.

214. Ibid., p. 279.

215. See, e.g., Brachah Rivlin (Erdos), *Arevim zeh lazeh bagetto ha'Italki, hevrot gema"h 1516–1789* (Jerusalem, 1991), pp. 22, 104–122.

216. Wenger, "Jewish Women and Voluntarism," p. 21.

217. Ledger (*pinkas*) of the Linat Zedek Association, Montefiore Archives 527; *Havazelet,* no. 20, 10 Adar I [5]654 [February 16, 1894]; Grayevsky, *Benot Zion viYrushalayim,* pp. 71–73.

218. Yehuda Aaron Weiss, *Bish'arayikh Yerushalayim,* p. 74; Trager, *Pictures of Jewish Home-Life,* p. 87.

219. *Ha'or,* no. 42, 1 Elul [5]652 [August 24, 1892].

220. Letter from Devorah Malkah, granddaughter of R. Yaakov Emden, and others, to Judith Montefiore, n.d., among letters dated to 1839, Montefiore Archive 574, p. 69.

221. Poem in honor of Judith Montefiore, Montefiore Archive 574, p. 59.

222. Franz-Michael Konrad, *Würzeln jüdischer Sozialarbeit in Palästina: Einflüsse der Sozialarbeit in Duetschland auf der Entstehung moderner Hilfesysteme in Palästina, 1890–1948* (Weinheim and München), 1993, pp. 113–127.

223. Mordechai Eliav, *Bahasut mamlekhet Austria 1849–1917* (Jerusalem, 1986), p. 80, note 1.

224. Shifrah Schwartz, *"Histadruyot nashim lema'an imahot beErez Yisra'el . . . ,"* *Bitahon Soziali* 51 (1998), pp. 57–81.

225. Luncz, *Netivot Zion viYrushalayim,* p. 305; Neumann, *Ir hakodesh veyoshevei bah,* p. 57; Luncz, *Luah Erez Yisrael,* vol. 11 (1906), pp. 190–191.

226. Grayevsky, *Benot Zion viYrushalayim,* p. 182.

227. Luncz, *Netivot Zion viYrushalayim,* p. 281.

228. Shiryon, *Zikhronot,* p. 154; Shmuel Hakohen Kook, *"Moshav zekenim uzkenot me'uhad biYrushalayim,"* *Luah Yerushalayim* 10 (1950), pp. 235–241; Yehoshua, *Yerushalayim temol shilshom,* vol. 3, pp. 122–123.

229. Grayevsky, *Benot Zion viYrushalayim,* p. 73.

230. Reitze, *Sefer mishpahat yuhasin*, p. 4. [Shilo, *Hakol Hanashi*, p. 129.]

231. Grayevsky, *Zikhron lahovevim harishonim*, vol. 2, p. 125.

232. See *Komitee für Volksküchen in Palästina* (Berlin, 1907), CAHJP.

233. Letter from Chayah Rachel of Kremenzug and Reisel of Slutsk, 8 Shevat [5]659 [January 19, 1899], Amsterdam, Bibliotheca Rosenthalia, Pekidim and Amarkalim Archives, X 160 (53–130).

234. Grayevsky, *Zikhron lahovevim harishonim*, vol. 2, p. 125.

235. Kahanov, *Sha'alu shelom Yerushalayim*, p. 66.

236. Among the organizers of foreign contributions were the Amsterdam *pekidim* and *amarkalim*, the Rothschilds, and the Salvendis. The contributions were made out in the name of Rabbi Shmuel Salant (see below).

237. *Havazelet* no. 29, 3 Sivan [5]642 [May 21, 1882].

238. Prochaska, *Women and Philanthropy*, p. 223.

239. Mandelbaum, *Asarah dorot*, vol. 2, p. 118.

240. *Havazelet* (see note 237 above).

241. Grayevsky, *Benot Zion viYrushalayim*, p. 7.

242. Letter from Chayah Rachel of Kremenzug and Reisel of Slutsk, 11 Sivan [5]659 [May 20, 1899], Amsterdam, Bibliotheca Rosenthalia, Pekidim and Amarkalim Archives, X 170 (53–231).

243. Reitze, *Sefer mishpahat yuhasin*, p. 37. [Shilo, *Hakol hanashi*, p. 162.] For "Issachar and Zebulun," see above, note 84.

244. Reitze, *Sefer mishpahat yuhasin*, pp. 13–14. [Shilo, *Hako hanashi*, pp. 138–139].

245. Kahanov, *Sha'alu shelom Yerushalayim*, p. 66.

246. *Havazelet*, year 12, no. 40, 10 Elul [5]642 [August 25, 1882].

247. [Moses Montefiore], *Sippur Mosheh viYrushalayim*, trans. A. Amshewitz (from the original diaries) (Warsaw, 1876), p. 45.

248. Reitze, *Sefer mishpahat yuhasin*, p. 36. [Shilo, *Hakol hanashi*, p. 161.]

249. Ibid., p. 8. [Shilo, *Hakol hanashi*, p. 133.]

250. Ibid., p. 11. [Shilo, *Hakol hanashi*, p. 136.]

251. Ibid., p. 15. [Shilo, *Hakol hanashi*, p. 140.]

252. Ibid.

253. *Havazelet*, no. 39, 26 Av [5]642 [August 11, 1882].

254. Reitze, *Sefer mishpahat yuhasin*, p. 25. [Shilo, *Hakol hanashi*, p. 150.]

255. Ruth Kark, *Yafo: Zemihatah shel ir, 1799–1917* (Jerusalem, 1985); Chanah Ram, *Hayishuv hayehudi beYafo ba'et hahadashah: Mikehilah Sefaradit lemerkaz Zioni* (Jerusalem, 1996).

256. Ruth Kark, *"Aliyatah shel Yafo kemerkaz hayishuv hehadash — Hebetim tarbutiyim vehevratiyim,"* in Mordechai Eliav (ed.), *Sefer ha'aliyah harishonah*, vol. 1 (Jerusalem, 1982), pp. 301–302.

257. *Hazevi*, no. 18, 23 Iyar [5]655 [May 17, 1895].

258. Yosef Salmon, *"Yehiel Mikhal Pines — Demuto hahistorit,"* in *Milet: Kovez mehkarim betoledot Yisra'el*, vol. 1 (Tel Aviv, 1983), pp. 261–272.

259. Grayevsky, *Benot Zion viYrushalayim*, p. 163.

260. Ita Yellin, *Leze'eza'ay*, vol. 2, p. 89.

261. *Ha'or*, no. 31, 28 Adar [5]651 [1891].

262. Ibid., no. 19, pp. 85–86, 12 Adar [5]652 [March 11, 1892].

263. Ibid., no. 19, 12 Adar [5]652 [March 11, 1892].

264. Ibid., no. 13, 4 Tevet [5]653 [December 23, 1892].

265. Ibid., no. 19, 12 Adar [5]652 [March 11, 1892].

266. Ibid., no. 6, 19 Heshvan [5]652 [November 20, 1891].

267. Ibid.

268. Undated letter signed by Rabbi Hertz Halevi, Gaster Papers, 86/14; *Ha'or*, no. 19, 12 Adar [5]652 [March 11, 1892].

269. *Havazelet*, year 23, 23 Tamuz [5]653 [July 7, 1893].

270. *Hazevi*, no. 10, 29 Kislev [5]658 [December 24, 1897].

271. According to the Jerusalem society's stationery in the 1920s (CZA, S 25/576), it was headed by Tzipa Pines and Rosa Feinstein.

272. William Toll, "A Quiet Revolution: Jewish Women's Clubs and the Widening Female Sphere, 1870–1920," *American Jewish Archives* 41 (1989), pp. 7–26.

273. *Havazelet* 25 (21), 5 Adar [5]655 [March 1, 1895]; see also David Yellin, *Ketavim*, vol. 1, pp. 429–430.

274. David Yellin, *Ketavim*, vol. 4, p. 65.

275. Ibid., vol. 1, pp. 105, 272.

276. *Hazevi*, no. 31, 26 Av [5]655 [August 16, 1895].

277. Ita Yellin, *Leze'eza'ay*, vol. 2, pp. 92–93.

278. The first recognized mental hospital was established in Spain in the fifteenth century: Franz G. Alexander and Sheldon T. Selesnick, *The History of Psychiatry: An Evolution of Psychiatric Thought and Practice from Prehistoric Times to the Present* (New York, 1966), p. 65.

279. Dingwell, Rafferty, and Webster, *Social History of Nursing*, pp. 123–144.

280. Norbert Schwake, *Die Entwicklung des Krankenhauswesens der Stadt Jerusalem vom Ende des 18. bis zum Beginn des 20. Jahrhunderts* (Herzogenrath, 1983), pp. 654–655; Miri Shefer, "*Rofe'im uvatei holim bahevrah ha'Uthmanit*," *Zemanim* 62 (1998), pp. 38–48.

281. Toll, "A Quiet Revolution," p. 19.

282. Letter from Lydia Einsler, February 3, 1900, CZA A109/126.

283. Yizhak Nissenbaum, *Alei heldi [5]629–[5]689* (Jerusalem, 1969), p. 239.

284. Letter from Ita Yellin to Colonel Kisch, 18 Adar [5]687, CZA S576/25); the information derives from the stationery.

285. Nahum Dov Freimann, *Sefer hazikaron haYerushalmi*, pp. 28.

286. *Moriah*, no. 342, 6 Tishri [5]674 [October 7, 1913].

287. Luncz, *Netivot Zion viYrushalayim*, pp. 366–367; [Yosef Yo'el Rivlin], *75 shanah le'Ezrat Nashim, 1895–1970* (Jerusalem, 1970), unpaginated.

288. Luncz, *Luah Erez Yisrael*, vol. 1, p. 25.

289. [Yosef Yo'el Rivlin], *75 shanah*, unpaginated.

290. *Hazevi*, no. 38, 22 Tamuz [5]656 [July 3, 1896].

291. Carlebach, *Mikhtavim miYrushalayim*, p. 24.

292. *Hazevi*, no. 31, 26 Av [5]655 [August 16, 1895].

293. [Yosef Yo'el Rivlin], *75 shanah*, unpaginated.

294. *Hashkafah*, no. 10, 14 Adar II [5]660 [March 15, 1900].

295. Yosef Yo'el Rivlin, "*Mishpahat Rivlin beErez Yisrael*," p. 27.

296. Unsigned manuscript, perhaps by Pines, undated, CZA A109/126.

297. Founded 1904; brochure of Ezrat Ahim society, Municipal archives, Jerusalem, Old Yishuv material, no. 151.

298. Appeal to the women of Rishon Lezion, *Hazevi*, no. 19, 1 Sivan [5]655 [May 24, 1895].

299. *Hazevi*, no. 36, 4 Tamuz [5]658 [June 24, 1898].

300. Supplement to *Hazevi*, no. 16, 5 Shevat [5]658 [January 28, 1898].

301. *Jewish Chronicle*, June 16, 1899.

302. Luncz, *Luah Erez Yisrael*, vol. 12 ([5]667 [1907]), p. 44.

303. David Yellin, *Ketavim*, vol. 1, p. 428.

304. See below, chapter 5.

305. Lee Shai Weissbach, "The Jewish Elite and the Children of the Poor: Jewish Apprenticeship Programs in Nineteenth-Century France," *AJS Review* 12/1 (1987), pp. 123–142.

306. Correspondence relating to the school, CZA A 243/153; Ita Yellin, *Leze'eza-'ay*, vol. 2, pp. 93–94.

307. On the Christian mission in Jerusalem see chapter 6.

308. Nahum Dov Freimann, *Sefer hazikaron haYerushalmi*, p. 28.

309. *Jewish Chronicle*, May 30, 1913; June 13, 1913.

310. Ibid., June 20, 1913, p. 16.

311. David Yellin, *Ketavim*, vol. 1, p. 198.

312. [Yosef Yo'el Rivlin], *75 shanah*, unpaginated.

313. Luncz, *Luah Erez Yisrael*, vol. 4 (1899), p. 17.

314. See below, chapter 5.

315. *Jewish Chronicle*, May 1, 1914, p. 35.

316. Mandelbaum, *Asarah dorot*, vol. 2, p. 129.

317. David Yellin, *Ketavim*, vol. 1, p. 171.

318. Grayevsky, *Benot Zion viYrushalayim*, pp. 179–180.

319. Luncz, *Luah Erez Yisrael*, vol. 3 (1898), pp. 14–15.

320. Taubenhaus, *Bintiv hayahid*, pp. 100–101.

321. *Hazevi*, no. 39, 9 Tamuz [5]657 [July 9, 1897].

322. Letter from Ezrat Benot ha-Galil, 26 Shevat [5]659 [February 6, 1899], Amsterdam, Bibliotheca Rosenthalia, Pekidim and Amarkalim Archives 165.

323. Letter from Rachel Zilberman and Chaya Moshayoff, Amsterdam, Bibliotheca Rosenthalia, Pekidim and Amarkalim Archives XII, 198 (57–60).

324. Prochaska, *Women and Philanthropy*, p. 227.

325. Shoshanah Siton, "*Beyn feminizm leZionut: ma'avak hagananot ha'ivriyot lehakarah mikzo'it*," *Zemanim* 61 (1997), p. 27.

326. Prochaska, *Women and Philanthropy*, p. 226.

327. Bet Ya'akov, printed page with a Purim song, Rare Book Collection, NHUL, L2093.

328. Luncz, *Luah Erez Yisrael*, vol. 4 (1899), p. 17.

329. Wenger, "Jewish Women and Voluntarism," pp. 16–19.

Chapter 5. Scholarship, Illiteracy, and Educational Revolution (pp. 143–180)

1. *Hazevi*, no. 7, 29 Tevet [5]648 [January 13, 1888].

2. Salmon, "*Hahinukh ha'Ashkenazi*," p. 287.

3. Levin-Katz, "*Nashim lamdaniyot*"; Shilo, "*Hakol hanashi*."

4. Irit Parush, *Nashim kor'ot: Yitronah shel shuliyut* (Tel Aviv, 2001).

5. See, e.g., CAHJP, Letters of Rivka Schwartz.

6. Parfitt, "Use of Hebrew," p. 243.

7. Loewe, *Diaries*, vol. 2, p. 180; Parfitt, "Use of Hebrew," p. 243; Ornan, "Hebrew in Palestine," p. 234.

8. Berman, *Mas'ot Shim'on*, p. 93.

9. Grayevsky, *Benot Zion viYrushalayim*, p. 257.

10. *Bamishor*, 30 Av [5]705 [August 9, 1945], year 6, nos. 263–264, p. 11.

11. Luncz[-Bolotin], *Me'ir netivot Yerushalayim*, p. 89.

12. Grayevsky, *Benot Zion viYrushalayim*, pp. 84–85.

13. Alper, *Korot mishpahah ahat*, p. 44.

14. *Me'assef Zion* 3 (1928/29), p. 95.

15. *Lashon ve'Ivrit* 3 (1990), pp. 28–29.

16. *Hazevi*, no. 40, 23 Tamuz [5]653 [July 7, 1893].

17. Avraham Shmuel Hirschberg, *Be'erez hamizrah*, pp. 323–327.

18. *Hashkafah*, year 3, no. 19, 23 Iyar [5]662 [May 30, 1902].

19. Biber, "*Ha'almah miLudmir*," pp. 70–71.

20. Grayevsky, *Benot Zion viYrushalayim*, pp. 14–15, 38–39, 242, 274–275; Yosef Mashash, *Otzar mikhtavim*, vol. 1 (Jerusalem, 1968), p. 14.

21. Gellis, *Midemuyot Yerushalayim*, p. 259; Elhanani, *Ish vesiho*, p. 73; Yehoshua, *Yaldut biYrushalayim*, vol. 1, pp. 98–99.

22. Yehoshua, *Yaldut biYrushalayim*, vol. 3, p. 82.

23. Binyamin Rivlin, *Zekher av* (Jerusalem, 1992), p. 46.

24. Even-Or-Orenstein, "*Hanashim bemishpahat Orenstein*," 5–6 (1990), pp. 2–23.

25. Levin-Katz, "*Nashim lamdaniyot*," pp. 104–105.

26. Angel-Malachi, *Beterem reshit*, p. 17; idem, *Hayei Yerushalayim*, pp. 24–25; Tamar Alexander[-Fraser], *Ma'aseh ahuv vahezi: Hasipur ha'ammami shel yehudei Sefarad* (Jerusalem, 2000), pp. 122–124.

27. Yisra'el Zinberg, *Toledot Sifrut Yisra'el*, vol. 4: *Sifrut Iddish mereshitah ve'ad tekufat hahaskalah* (Tel Aviv, 1958), pp. 67–76; *Menorat Hama'or*, ed. Yehuda Preis Horev and Moshe Katzenellenbogen (Jerusalem 1961), introduction, p. 8.

28. Yehoshua, *Yaldut biYrushalayim*, vol. 3, pp. 25, 187.

29. Adlerblum, "Sarah Beyla Hirshensohn."

30. The newspaper's name alternated between *Beis Ya'akov* and *Hazevi Beis Ya'akov*. The available information is insufficient to assess Chava Hirschensohn's part in the enterprise.

31. Hayyim Hirschensohn, *Sefer musegei shav veha'emet* (Jerusalem, 1932), end of book, unpaginated.

32. Levin-Katz, "*Nashim lamdaniyot*," p. 110.

33. Shmuel Verses, "*Kol ha'ishah bashevu'on beYiddish 'Kol Mevasser,'*" *Hulyot* 4 (1997), pp. 53–82.

34. Arieh L. Pilovsky, "*Itonut Yiddish beErez Yisra'el mitehilatah ve'ad hofa'at Neivelt (1934)*," *Cathedra* 10 (1979), pp. 79–81.

35. *Ha'Or*, no. 23, 16 Iyar [5]653 [May 2, 1893].

36. Halevi, *Sifrei Yerushalayim harishonim*, nos. 395, 450, 514; Shilo, *Hakol hanashi*.

37. Published in three editions: 1882, 1884, and 1891.

38. Published in 1885.

39. Published in 1895.

40. Alyse Fisher Roller, "In Their Own Words: The Literature of Ultra-Orthodox Jewish Women" (M.A. thesis, Hebrew University of Jerusalem, 1996), p. 22.

41. Ita Yellin, *Leze'eza'ay*, vol. 1, p. 50.

42. Yosef Yoel Rivlin, "*Zur mahzavto shel Yosef Luriya z"l*," p. 60.

43. Tamar Schechter, "*Dyoknah shel ishah maskilit beGalizia*" (M.A. thesis, Bar-Ilan University, Ramat-Gan, 1987), p. 23.

44. Fisher Roller, "In Their Own Words," p. 22.

45. Anikster, *Kunteres zekher olam* (1884), p. 1b. [Shilo, *Hakol hanashi*, p. 92.]

46. Weissler, *Voices of the Matriarchs*, p. 43.

47. Ibid., pp. 76–85.

48. Shlomo Ashkenazi, *Ha'ishah be'aspaklariyat hadorot* (Tel Aviv, 1943).

49. Deborah Weissman, "*Hinukh banot datiyot biYrushalayim bitkufat hashilton haBriti . . .*" (Ph.D. dissertation, The Hebrew University of Jerusalem, 1994), pp. 7–9.

50. Barukh Epstein, *Mekor Barukh* (Vilna, 1928), p. 977; Don Seeman and Rachel Kobrin, "Like One of the Whole Men: Learning Gender and Autobiography in R. Baruch Epstein's *Mekor Barukh*," *Nashim* 2 (1999), pp. 52–94; Brenda Bakon, "*Benot Zelofhad vesivlah shel Rayna Batyah*," in Margalit Shilo (ed.), *Lihyot ishah yehudiyah* (Jerusalem, 2001), pp. 287–293.

51. Eliakim Ellinson, *Ha'ishah vehamizvot: Yalkut hore'ot hakhamenu ufiskei halakhot* (Jerusalem, 1974), pp. 160–171; Weissman, "*Hinukh banot datiyot,*" p. 113; Parush, *Nashim kor'ot*, pp. 14–17.

52. Deborah Weissman, "Education of Jewish Women," *Encyclopedia Judaica Yearbook* (1986–1987), col. 29.

53. Hagai Erlich, *No'ar upolitikah baMizrah haTikhon: Dorot umashberei zehut* (Tel Aviv, 1998), p. 19; Dengler, "The Turkish Woman," p. 231.

54. Bashan, *Sefer mimizrah shemesh ad mevo'o*, pp. 149–150.

55. Rachel Simon, "Jewish Female Education in the Ottoman Empire" (unpublished, n.d.).

56. Judith R. Baskin, "Some Parallels in the Education of Medieval Jewish and Christian Women," *Jewish History* 5/1 (1991), pp. 41–51; idem, "*Hinukh nashim yehudiyot vehaskalatan biymei habeynayim be'arzot ha'Islam vehaNazrut,*" *Pe'amim* 82 (2000), pp. 31–49; Avraham Grossman, *Hasidot umoredot*, pp. 266–303.

57. Havah Turnianski, "*Iberzetzungen un be'arbetungen fun der 'Ze'enah ure'enah,*'" in Shmuel Verses (ed.), *Sefer Dov Sedan* (Jerusalem, 1977), pp. 165–190.

58. Shaul Stampfer, "*Yedi'at kero ukhtov ezel yehudei mizrah Eiropah batekufah hahadashah,*" in Shmuel Almog et al. (ed.), *Temurot bahistoriyah hayehudit hahadashah* (Jerusalem, 1985), pp. 459–483; idem, "Gender Differentiation and Education of the Jewish Woman in Nineteenth-Century Eastern Europe," *Polin* 7 (1992), pp. 63–87; Sabina Levin, "*Batei hasefer ha'elementariyim harishonim liyladim benei dat Moshe beVarshah bashanim 1818–1830,*" *Gal'ed* 1 (1979), p. 68.

59. Avraham Gruenbaum, "'*Heder habanot' uvanot beheder habanim beMizrah Eiropah,*" in Rivkah Feldhai and Immanuel Etkes (eds.), *Hinukh vehistoriyah* (Jerusalem, 1999), pp. 297–303; A. M. Lifshitz, "*Haheder, tekhunato ve-shitato,*" *Hatekufah* 7 (1923), pp. 340–352.

60. Shmuel Feiner, "*Ha'ishah hayehudiyah hamodernit: Mikreh mivhan beyahasei hahaskalah vehamodernah,*" *Zion* 58 (1993), pp. 453–499; Barbara Welter, "The Cult of True Womanhood, 1820–1860," *American Quarterly* 28 (1966), pp. 151–174; Matthews, "*Just a Housewife.*"

61. Mordechai Eliav, *Hahinukh hayehudi beGermaniyah biymei hahaskalah veha'emanzipaziyah* (Jerusalem, 1961), pp. 271–279; Thomas Woody, *A History of Women's Education in the U.S.*, vols. 1–2 (New York, 1966 [1929]); Zosa Szajkowski, *Jewish Education in France, 1789–1939*, Jewish Social Sciences Monograph Series 2 (New York, 1980), pp. 4–9; James C. Albisetti, "The Feminization of Teaching in the Nineteenth Century: A Comparative Perspective," *History of Education* 22/1–4 (1993), pp. 253–263.

62. Zolty, "*And All Your Children Shall Be Learned*," pp. 238–241.

63. Stampfer, "Gender Differentiation," pp. 71–72; Iris Parush, "The Politics of Literacy: Women and Foreign Languages in Jewish Society of 19th-Century Eastern Europe," *Modern Judaism* 15 (1995), pp. 183–206.

64. Aharon Rodrig, *Hinukh, hevrah vehistoriyah: "Kol Yisra'el Haverim" viyhudei agan hayam haTikhon 1860–1929* (Jerusalem, 1991), pp. 34–39; Simon, "Jewish Female Education"; Frances Malino, "The Women Teachers of the Alliance Israélite Universelle, 1872–1940," in Judith R. Baskin, *Jewish Women in Historical Perspective*, 2nd ed. (Detroit, 1998), pp. 248–269; idem, "Prophets in Their Own Land? Mothers and Daughters of the Alliance Israélite Universelle," *Nashim* 3 (2000), pp. 56–73.

65. Letter from Sarah Thon to Education Committee, August 15, 1915, CZA S2/744.

66. Letter from the *hakham bashi* [chief rabbi] to the Amsterdam officials, 1849, quoted by Ben Zion Dinaburg, "*Me'arkhiono shel hehakham-bashi R. Hayim Avraham Gagin*," *Me'assef Zion* 1 (1926), p. 111; see also Getzel Kressel, *Potehei hatikvah: MiYrushalayim lePetah Tikvah* (Jerusalem, 1976), pp. 88–90; Morgenstern, *Meshihiyut veyishuv Erez Yisra'el*.

67. See above, chapter 1.

68. Letter to Baron Rothschild and Samuel Montagu, unsigned, no date, CZA A153/137.

69. Josephine Kamm, *Hope Deferred: Girls' Education in English History* (London, 1965), pp. 152–165; Jane Martin, *Women and the Politics of Schooling in Victorian and Edwardian England* (London, 1998), pp. 75–84.

70. See below, chapter 6.

71. The school was sponsored by the French Rothschilds until 1868, when it came under the protection of the English branch of the family.

72. Luncz, *Yerushalayim*, vol. 2 (1887), pp. 121–122.

73. Eliav, *Bahasut mamlekhet Austria*, p. 98. The reference is to Charlotte, daughter of James (Jacob) Rothschild of Paris and wife of Nathaniel Rothschild of the London branch.

74. Letter from Albert Cohen to the Austrian emperor, July 28, 1854. In Eliav, *Bahasut mamlekhet Austria*, p. 298; Rachel Elboim-Dror, *Hahinukh ha'ivri be'Erez Yisra'el*, vol. 1 (Jerusalem, 1986), pp. 80–82, 86–89.

75. Erlich, *No'ar upolitikah*, p. 25.

76. Sha'ul Sapir, "*Gishatah ve'ofi terumatah*," p. 269, note 2.

77. Prochaska, *Women and Philanthropy*, p. 14.

78. Luncz, *Luah Erez Yisra'el*, vol. 11, pp. 194–199.

79. Carpi and Rinot, "*Yoman mas'oteha shel morah yehudiyah*," p. 126; Eliezer Mannenberg, "Modernization and Educational Change: A Case Study in the Transition of a Jewish Community Antedating the Israeli Society," *Jewish Social Studies* 40 (1978), pp. 293–302.

80. Frankl, *Nach Jerusalem!* p. 110.

81. Sonia and Vivian David Lipman, *The Century of Moses Montefiore* (Oxford, 1985), pp. 307–308.

82. Luncz, *Netivot Zion viYrushalayim*, p. 285.

83. Luncz, *Yerushalayim*, vol. 2, p. 122.

84. Mary Eliza Rogers, *Domestic Life in Palestine* (London, 1862), p. 336 (quoted in Loewe, *Diaries*, pp. 48–49).

85. Rogers, *Domestic Life.*

86. Luncz, *Yerushalayim,* vol. 2, p. 122.

87. Grayevsky, *Zikhron lahovevim harishonim,* vol. 2, p. 119.

88. Carpi and Rinot, *"Yoman mas'oteha shel morah yehudiyah,"* p. 153.

89. Ibid., p. 142.

90. Ibid., p. 153.

91. *Sefer ma'aseh avot: Kinus lazadikim . . .* (Jerusalem, 1901), pp. 73–74.

92. Katzburg, *"Pulemus hahinukh"*; Yehoshua Kaniel, *"Miba'ayot hahinukh biYrushalayim bame'ah hatesha'-esreh,"* in H. Z. Hirschberg (ed.), *Zekhor le'Avraham . . . lezekher Avraham Elmaliah* (Jerusalem, 1972), pp. 140–168.

93. Letter from the *pekidim* and *amarkalim* of Amsterdam, quoted in Yosef Yoel Rivlin, *"Mishpahat Rivlin beErez Yisra'el,"* pp. 67–68.

94. Sha'ul Sapir, *"Gishatah ve'ofi terumatah,"* pp. 169–172. Evelina was the youngest daughter of Lord Lionel Nathan Rothschild of London and the wife of Ferdinand Rothschild of Paris; she died in childbirth in 1866; *AJA 23rd Annual Report* (1893–1894), p. 32.

95. *Havazelet,* no. 39, 27 Tamuz [5]635 [July 30, 1875].

96. Schlesinger, *Hevrah mahazirei atarah leyoshnah,* p. 14.

97. Press, *Me'ah shanah biYrushalayim,* p. 53; Ben-Yehuda, *Ben Yehuda,* p. 49.

98. Yehoshua, *Yaldut biYrushalayim,* vol. 2, p. 93; David Yellin, *Ketavim,* vol. 1, p. 92.

99. Hasya Feinsod-Sukenik, *Pirkei gan: Zikhronot uma'as* (Tel Aviv, 1966), p. 32.

100. Alper, *Korot mishpahah ahat,* p. 46.

101. *Hazevi,* no. 25, 28 Adar [5]656 [March 13, 1896].

102. Rachel Eliachar, *Album mishpahti* (Jerusalem, 1990), pp. 1–3.

103. *Havazelet,* no. 39, 27 Tamuz [5]635 [July 30, 1875].

104. Eliezer Mannenberg, "The Evolution of Jewish Educational Practices in the Sançak (eyalet) of Jerusalem under Ottoman Rule" (Ph.D. dissertation, University of Connecticut, 1976), p. 100.

105. Alper, *Korot mishpahah ahat,* p. 48.

106. Luncz, *Yerushalayim,* vol. 2, p. 138.

107. [Montefiore], *Sippur Mosheh viYrushalayim,* pp. 47–48.

108. Stampfer, *"Yedi'at kero ukhtov,"* pp. 480–481.

109. Alper, *Korot mishpahah ahat,* p. 50.

110. Ita Yellin, *Leze'eza'ay,* vol. 1, pp. 44–45.

111. Joachimsen Report to the Board of Delegates of American Israelites, 1876, in Kellner, *Lema'an Zion,* p. 208.

112. See Stampfer, "Gender Differentiation."

113. *Hazevi,* no. 20, 23 Shevat [5]656 [February 7, 1896], p. 76.

114. *Halevanon,* no. 20, 14 Sivan [5]629 [May 23, 1869].

115. Captain Albert E. W. Goldsmid, "Report on Jewish Schools in Palestine," *AJA 12th Annual Report* (1882–1883), p. 48.

116. *AJA 23rd Annual Report* (1893–1894), p. 55.

117. Secret report by Olga d'Avigdor, February 1900, Southampton Archives, AJ95/ADD/3.

118. *Havazelet,* no. 42, 28 Elul [5]641 [September 22, 1881].

119. Supplement to *Hazevi,* no. 17, 1890; see also *AJA 13th Annual Report* (1883–1884), p. 28.

120. *AJA 14th Annual Report* (1884–1885), appendix e, p. 74.

121. Kellner, *Lema'an Zion*, pp. 179, 208; *Havazelet*, no. 27, 21 Iyar [5]641 [May 20, 1881].

122. David Tidhar, *Enziklopediyah lahaluzei hayishuv uvonav*, vol. 1 (Tel Aviv, 1947), pp. 75a–76, s.v. "Nissim Behar" (entirely ignoring Fortuna and her achievements!).

123. Supplement to *Hazevi*, no. 17, 26 Adar II [5]649 [March 29, 1889].

124. *Hazevi*, no. 29, 19 Av [5]648 [July 27, 1888].

125. Luncz, *Luah Erez Yisra'el*, vol. 11 (1906), p. 195.

126. David Yellin, *Ketavim*, vol. 4, p. 123.

127. Sapir, "*Gishatah ve'ofi terumatah*," p. 177. See also Ben-Arieh, *Jerusalem . . . the New City*, pp. 265–266.

128. *Havazelet* no. 27, 21 Iyar [5]641 [May 20, 1881]; see also *Hazevi*, no. 3, 7 Heshvan [5]649 [October 12, 1888].

129. Sapir, "*Gishatah ve'ofi terumatah*," pp. 172–175.

130. Luncz, *Luah Erez Yisra'el*, vol. 11 (1906), pp. 194–195; [Montefiore], *Sippur Mosheh viYrushalayim*, p. 48.

131. *Havazelet*, no. 2, 30 Tishrei [5]636 [October 29, 1875].

132. *Hazevi*, no. 38, 9 Tamuz [5]653 [June 23, 1893].

133. *Havazelet* no. 3, 4 Marheshvan [5]642 [October 27, 1881]; *Hazevi*, no. 18, 11 Nisan [5]649 [April 12, 1889].

134. *Hazevi*, no. 39, 16 Tamuz [5]653 [June 30, 1893].

135. Ibid., no. 1, 14 Tishrei [5]649 [September 19, 1888], pp. 5–6.

136. Ibid., no. 5, 10 Heshvan [5]654 [October 20, 1893].

137. Ibid., no. 1, 14 Tishrei [5]649 [September 19, 1888]. p. 6.

138. Ibid., pp. 5–6.

139. Ibid., no. 34, 17 Elul [5]655 [September 6, 1895].

140. *AJA 24th Annual Report* (1894–1895), p. 39.

141. Rozsika Parker, *The Subversive Stitch: Embroidery and the Making of the Feminine* (London, 1996).

142. *Hazevi*, no. 25, 22 Adar II [5]657 [March 26, 1897].

143. Grayevsky, *Benot Zion viYrushalayim*, p. 267.

144. Sapir, "*Gishatah ve'ofi terumatah*," p. 173.

145. *Havazelet*, no. 10, 21 Kislev [5]637 [December 7, 1876].

146. Ibid., 10 Heshvan [5]658 [November 5, 1897].

147. Ibid., no. 2, 30 Tishrei [5]636 [October 29, 1875].

148. Supplement to *Hazevi*, no. 17, 1890.

149. Sydney Montagu Samuel, *Jewish Life in the East* (London, 1881), pp. 144–145.

150. *Hazevi*, no. 10, 17 Tevet [5]649 [December 21, 1888].

151. *AJA 23rd Annual Report* (1893–1894), p. 54.

152. Welter, "Cult of True Womanhood."

153. *Havazelet*, no. 43, 23 Elul [5]639 [September 11, 1879].

154. David Yellin, *Ketavim*, vol. 4, p. 150.

155. *Havazelet*, no. 21, 2 Nisan [5]638 [April 5, 1878].

156. Supplement to *Hazevi*, no. 17, 1890.

157. *Havazelet*, no. 43, 26 Av [5]646 [August 27, 1886].

158. The school came under AJA management on July 1, 1894; see *AJA 24th Annual Report* (1894–1895), p. 24; see also Sapir, "*Gishatah ve'ofi terumatah*," pp. 182–186; *AJA 23rd Annual Report* (1893–1894), p. 32.

159. *AJA 35th Annual Report* (1905–1906), p. 50.

160. *AJA 1st Annual Report* (1871–1872), Appendix a, p. 21.

161. Southampton Archives, AJ95/ADD/2.

162. Carol Devens, "'If We Get the Girls, We Get the Race': Missionary Education of Native American Girls," *Journal of World History* 3/2 (1992), p. 219.

163. *AJA 43rd Annual Report* (1913–1914), p. 47.

164. *AJA 30th Annual Report* (1900–1901), p. 47.

165. *AJA 31st Annual Report* (1902–1903), p. 51.

166. M. A. Scherer, "A Cross-Cultural Conflict Reexamined: Annette Akroyd and Keshub Chunder Sen," *Journal of World History* 7/2 (1996), pp. 231–257.

167. Billie Melman, *"Re'alot shekufot: Kolonializm vegender — likrat diyun histori mehudash,"* *Zemanim* 62 (1998), p. 96; see also Nancy B. Sinkoff, "Educating for 'Proper' Jewish Womanhood: A Case Study in Domesticity and Vocational Training, 1897–1926," *American Jewish History* 77 (1987), pp. 572–599.

168. *AJA 23rd Annual Report* (1893–1894), pp. 49–51.

169. *AJA 30th Annual Report* (1900–1901), p. 47.

170. *AJA 25th Annual Report* (1895–1896), p. 34.

171. *AJA 24th Annual Report* (1894–1895), p. 38.

172. *AJA 23rd Annual Report* (1893–1894), p. 49.

173. Abarbanell, *Havah veLilit*, pp. 25–40.

174. *AJA 30th Annual Report* (1900–1901), p. 47.

175. *AJA 31st Annual Report* (1902–1902), p. 46.

176. *AJA 3rd Annual Report* (1873–1874), Education Scheme, pp. 56–58.

177. *AJA 9th Annual Report* (1879–1880), pp. 61–62; *AJA 11th Annual Report* (1880–1881), pp. 48–49.

178. Barbara Tuchman, *Bible and Sword: England and Palestine from the Bronze Age to Balfour* (New York, 1956).

179. *AJA 3rd Annual Report* (1873–1874), p. 21.

180. *Jewish Chronicle*, June 16, 1911.

181. Ibid., October 30, 1903.

182. *AJA 39th Annual Report* (1909–1910), p. 48; see also Southampton Archives, AJ95/ADD/2, circular dated December 3, 1893.

183. The committee was headed for many years by Rachel Adler, wife of the British chief rabbi: *Jewish Chronicle*, January 12, 1912. For the committee's ongoing influence on the school see, e.g., Southampton Archives, AJ/34/1/4; *AJA 40th Annual Report* (1910–1911), p. 25.

184. Dengler, "The Turkish Woman," p. 238.

185. *Hazevi*, no. 56, 1 Av [5]660 [July 27, 1900]; *AJA 41st Annual Report* (1911–1912), pp. 41, 29; *Jewish Chronicle*, January 12, 1912, p. 14.

186. Eliav, *Erez Yisra'el veyishuvah*, pp. 61–65; see also below, chapter 6.

187. Jonathan D. Sarna, "Christian Missions and American Jews," in Todd M. Endelman (ed.), *Jewish Apostasy in the Modern World* (New York, 1987), p. 241.

188. Southampton Archives, AJ95/ADD/2, circular dated February 4, 1894; *AJA 24th Annual Report* (1894–1895), p. 38.

189. For example, the *30th Annual Report* (1900–1901), p. 35, reports the distribution of 30,153 meals to two hundred needy girls, many of whom were daughters of "chained" wives (*agunot*). In winter the girls were given hot meals; in summer they received fruit. Clothing and shoes were also distributed. See *AJA 33rd Annual Report* (1903–1904), p. 31; *AJA 43rd Annual Report* (1913–1914), p. 28.

190. Yo'av Silbert, *"Megamot behitpat'hut histadrut hamorim, 1903–1913"* (Ph.D. dissertation, Tel Aviv University, 1991), pp. 181–184; *AJA 42nd Annual Report* (1912–1913), p. 26. See also chapter 6 below.

191. David Yellin, *Ketavim*, vol. 1, pp. 6–7; Alex Carmel, *"Letoledotav shel Johannes Frutiger, bankai biYrushalayim,"* *Cathedra* 48 (1988), pp. 49–72.

192. *Hazevi*, no. 35, 1 Tamuz [5]656 [June 12, 1896].

193. *Jewish Chronicle*, October 11, 1912, pp. 20–21.

194. Adela Goodrich-Freer, *Inner Jerusalem* (London, 1904), p. viii; Natan Shor, *Sefer hanose'im le'Erez Yisra'el bame'ah ha19* (Jerusalem, 1988), pp. 216–217.

195. *Hashkafah*, no. 16, 2 Iyar [5]662 [May 9, 1902].

196. Southampton Archives, AJ95/ADD/3, letters dated October 20, 1901; January 12, 1902; March 2, 1902; see also *Jewish Chronicle*, January 17, 1902, p. 11; February 14, 1902, p. 15.

197. *Jewish Chronicle*, July 24, 1903, p. 11.

198. Figures for the total number of students in the school, as supplied by the yearly *AJA Reports* for 1900–1914, are as follows:

1901: 292 in the school, 225 in the kindergarten; total 517
1902: total 606
1903: total 600
1905: total 620
1912: total 530
1913: 426 in the school, 250 in the kindergarten; total: 676 students.

199. Resolutions of AJA Committee, Southampton Archives, March 13, 1900, AJ95/ADD/3.

200. Mordechai Eliav, *Britain and the Holy Land, 1838–1914: Selected Documents from the British Consulate in Jerusalem* (Jerusalem, 1996), pp. 385–386; Southampton Archives, MS137 AJ 37/14.

201. *AJA 33rd Annual Report* (1903–1904), p. 59.

202. Resolution of the London Women's committee, December 3, 1899, Southampton Archives, AJ95/ADD/3 (decision to dismiss Behar). Annie Landau first came to Palestine in March 1898; see Albert M. Hyamson, *The British Consulate in Jerusalem in Relation to the Jews of Palestine, 1838–1914* (London, 1941), vol. 2, p. 548.

203. Southampton Archives, February 1900, AJ95/ADD/3; David Yellin, *Ketavim*, vol. 4, p. 150.

204. Yehudit Harari, *Beyn hakeramim* (Tel Aviv, 1947), vol. 1, pp. 83–84.

205. Yehudit Harari, *Ishah va'em beYisra'el mitekufat haTanakh ve'ad he'asor limdinat Yisra'el* (Tel Aviv, 1959), pp. 271–272; Tidhar, *Enziklopediyah*, vol. 1, pp. 802–803; *AJA 44th Annual Report* (1914–1915), p. 16.

206. *Jewish Chronicle*, December 15, 1911.

207. *AJA 31st Annual Report* (1901–1902), p. 28; see also *AJA 39th Annual Report* (1909–1910), p. 47; Welter, "Cult of True Womanhood."

208. *AJA 31st Annual Report* (1901–1902), p. 29.

209. *AJA 32nd Annual Report* (1902–1903), p. 50.

210. *AJA 33rd Annual Report* (1903–1904), p. 30; *AJA 39th Annual Report* (1909–1910), p. 28.

211. Southampton Archives, AJ95/ADD/3, report of H. G. Boyd Carpenter, p. 9, dated March 1904.

212. *Jewish Chronicle*, September 12, 1902, p. 9.

213. *Jewish Chronicle*, July 7, 1911.

214. *Jewish Chronicle*, February 9, 1900, p. 15; *AJA 39th Annual Report* (1908–1909), p. 28; *Jewish Chronicle*, June 16, 1911, p. 17.

215. *Jewish Chronicle*, May 16, 1913, p. 15; see also ibid., June 16, 1911, p. 17; October 11, 1912, pp. 20–21.

216. Secret report by Olga d'Avigdor, February 1900, Southampton Archives, AJ95/ADD/3.

217. *AJA 31st Annual Report* (1901–1902), p. 54.

218. *Women in Education: Transactions of the Educational Section of the International Congress of Women* (London, 1900), pp. 113–119; *Jewish Chronicle*, December 1, 1911, pp. 25–26.

219. Knappe, "Role of Women's Associations," pp. 168–169.

220. Annie Landau, letter to students' parents, 11 Heshvan [5]663 [November 11, 1902], CZA A153/114; *Jewish Chronicle*, June 7, 1907, p. 21.

221. The products were marketed in Jerusalem, Jaffa, and Beirut: *Jewish Chronicle*, November 8, 1907.

222. *Jewish Chronicle*, December 1, 1911, pp. 25–26; ibid., December 22, 1911, p. 9. For the probable influence of the Arts and Crafts movement in England on the development of these subjects see Gillian Nayor, *The Arts and Crafts Movement* (London, 1971).

223. *AJA 38th Annual Report* (1908–1909), p. 26.

224. The first plan for a kindergarten in Jerusalem was proposed by Elisa von Laemel in 1856; see Yeshayahu Press, *Eleh toledot bet hasefer leha'azil levet Laemel biYrushalayim* (Jerusalem, 1936), pp. 8–12.

225. See Donna M. Bryant and Richard M. Clifford, "150 Years of Kindergarten: How Far Have We Gone?" *Early Childhood Research Quarterly* 7/2 (1992), pp. 147–154; Roberta Wollons, "The Black Forest in a Bamboo Garden: Missionary Kindergartens in Japan, 1868–1912," *History of Education Quarterly* 33/1 (1993), pp. 1–35.

226. Caroline Witerer, "Avoiding a 'Hothouse System of Education': Nineteenth-Century Early Childhood Education from the Infant Schools to the Kindergartens," *History of Education Quarterly* 32/3 (1992), pp. 289–314.

227. Wollons, "Black Forest"; *Women in Education*, pp. 26–29.

228. Emma Jungnickel, letters to Rabbi Moses Gaster, Gaster Papers, 17/215, 13.

229. Emma Jungnickel to Gaster, May 23, 1903, Gaster Papers, 229/93 (translated from German); Jungnickel to Gaster, March 23, 1907, Gaster Papers, 17/215, 13.

230. Harari, *Beyn hakeramim*, vol. 1, pp. 77–84.

231. For example, it is not mentioned in Shoshanah Siton's comprehensive study, "*Beyn feminizm leZionut*."

232. *AJA 34th Annual Report* (1904–1905), p. 28.

233. *Jewish Chronicle*, June 28, 1901, p. 8.

234. Esther Benbassa, "Education for Jewish Girls in the East: A Portrait of the Galata School in Istanbul, 1879–1912," *Studies in Contemporary Jewry* 9 (1993), pp. 163–173.

235. School regulations, para. 5, Gaster Papers, 14/274.

236. *Jewish Chronicle*, April 21, 1911, p. 10.

237. *AJA 34th Annual Report* (1904–1905), p. 30; *Jewish Chronicle*, December 2, 1906, pp. 23–24.

238. *AJA 40th Annual Report* (1910–1911), p. 24; *AJA 41st Annual Report* (1911–1912), p. 29.

239. *AJA 42nd Annual Report* (1911–1912), pp. 27–28.

240. Henrietta Szold, the founder of Hadassah, was also involved in the project; see Southampton Archives, AJ37/1/4, MS 137, letter dated May 24, 1914.

241. *Jewish Chronicle*, February 10, 1905, pp. 12–13; ibid., January 24, 1908, p. 12.

242. *Jewish Chronicle*, May 29, 1914, p. 16; Orit Navot and Avraham Gross, "Hamil-hamah bagar'enet: Reshit beri'ut hazibur be'Erez Yisra'el," *Cathedra* 94 (2000), pp. 89–114.

243. *AJA 31st Annual Report* (1901–1902), p. 29; *Hazevi*, no. 10, 6 Tevet [5]661 [December 28, 1900]; *AJA 34th Annual Report* (1904–1905), p. 28.

244. *Hashkafah*, no. 55, 21 Adar II [5]665 [March 28, 1905]; ibid., no. 38, 5 Adar [5]666 [March 2, 1906].

245. Ibid., no. 39, 9 Adar [5]666 [March 6, 1906].

246. Ibid., no. 38, 11 Tamuz [5]664 [June 24, 1904]; *AJA 31st Annual Report* (1901–1902), p. 29.

247. *Havazelet*, 10 Heshvan [5]658 [November 5, 1897].

248. Hannah Yellin, letter to the Russian-Jewish children's weekly *Olam Katan* 2 (1902), p. 36; Harari, *Beyn hakeramim*, vol. 1, p. 107.

249. *AJA 41st Annual Report* (1911–1912), p. 29.

250. *Jewish Chronicle*, June 16, 1911, p. 17.

251. Ibid., November 11, 1910, pp. 1–2.

252. Ibid., December 11, 1908, pp. 16–17.

253. Yosef Meyuhas, *Bat Hayil, o torat em: Sefer mikra livnot Yisra'el*, pt. 1 (Jerusalem, 1900).

254. *AJA 30th Annual Report* (1900–1901), p. 34.

255. *Jewish Chronicle*, June 28, 1901, p. 8.

256. *AJA 42nd Annual Report* (1912–1913), p. 26.

257. *AJA 32nd Annual Report* (1902–1903), p. 36.

258. *Jewish Chronicle*, October 25, 1901, pp. 2–3.

259. Ibid., June 7, 1907, p. 21.

260. Ibid., March 30, 1903, p. 21. See also ibid., October 30, 1903.

261. *AJA 42nd Annual Report* (1912–1913), p. 41.

262. *Jewish Chronicle*, June 16, 1911, p. 18.

263. Secret report by Olga d'Avigdor, February 1900, Southampton Archives, AJ95/ADD/3.

264. *Jewish Chronicle*, June 16, 1911, p. 17.

265. *AJA 37th Annual Report* (1907–1908), p. 48; *Jewish Chronicle*, May 19, 1911, p. 20.

266. See, e.g., Eliezer Stern, *Ishim vekivunim: Perakim betoledot ha'ide'al hahinukhi shel "Torah im derekh erez"* (Ramat-Gan, 1987).

267. *AJA 33rd Annual Report* (1903–1904), p. 58.

268. Ibid.

269. Ibid., p. 54.

270. *Jewish Chronicle*, June 16, 1911, p. 17.

271. *AJA 35th Annual Report* (1905–1906), p. 31.

272. *Jewish Chronicle*, June 7, 1907, p. 21.

273. See, e.g., Zohar Shavit (ed.), *Beniyatah shel tarbut Ivrit be'Erez Yisra'el*, vol. 1 (vol. 3/1 in a series titled *Toledot hayishuv hayehudi be'Erez Yisra'el me'az ha'aliyah harishonah*) (Jerusalem, 1999).

274. *Jewish Chronicle*, October 25, 1903, p. 3.

275. Ibid., May 12, 1911, p. 18.

276. Ibid., June 7, 1907, p. 21.

277. Ibid., May 19, 1911, p. 20.

278. Ibid., July 7, 1911, p. 28.

279. Sir Ronald Storrs, *The Memoirs of Sir Ronald Storrs* (New York, 1937), p. 442.

280. *Jewish Chronicle*, June 7, 1907, p. 21; this attitude was criticized in *Hashkafah*, no. 36, 17 Shevat [5]667 [February 1, 1907].

281. Harari, *Beyn hakeramim*, vol. 1, p. 84.

282. *Jewish Chronicle*, November 8, 1907, p. 17.

283. Meyuhas, *Bat hayil*, p. 2.

284. *Jewish Chronicle*, December 7, 1906, p. 24.

285. Ibid., June 16, 1911, p. 18.

286. *AJA 33rd Annual Report* (1903–1904), p. 57; *Jewish Chronicle*, December 20, 1901, p. 19; *Hashkafah*, no. 1, 12 Adar II [5]662 [March 21, 1902].

287. *Renanim* 17 [journal of the Evelina de Rothschild State Religious School, issue published in spring 1964 in honor of the school's centenary], p. 22.

288. *Jewish Chronicle*, June 16, 1911, p. 18.

289. *AJA 33rd Annual Report* (1903–1904), p. 49.

290. NHUL, V2232. The ban was first issued in the spring of 1903.

291. David Yellin, *Ketavim*, vol. 1, p. 231.

292. Moshe Rinot, *Hevrat ha'ezrah liyhudei Germaniyah bayezirah uvama'avak* (Jerusalem, 1972), p. 90.

293. Rodrig, *Hinukh, hevrah vehistoriyah*, p. 36.

294. *Jewish Chronicle*, June 7, 1907, p. 21.

295. Getz, *Lesha'ah uledorot*, p. 22; Nahum Dov Freimann, *Sefer hazikaron ha-Yerushalmi*, p. 38.

296. Ya'akov Weingarten, *Ish hesed biYrushalayim: Masekhet hayav shel avi hayetomot Rabbi David Weingarten z"l* (Jerusalem, 1979), pp. 175–203.

297. Deborah Weissman, "Bais Ya'akov: A Historical Model for Jewish Feminists," in Elizabeth Koltun (ed.), *The Jewish Woman: New Perspectives* (New York, 1976), pp. 139–148.

298. Poster issued in the name of Rabbi Shmuel Salant, 1902, NHUL, Eliachar Collection, 4* 1271 532.

299. Letter from directors of Bet Hinukh Yeladim to members of the Education Committee, 3 Heshvan [5]679 [October 9, 1918], CZA S2/427.

300. Getz, *Lesha'ah uledorot*, p. 24; see also CZA A9/203.

301. Stationery of Bet Hayetomot Hakelali, CZA S2/427.

302. Weingarten, *Ish hesed biYrushalayim*, p. 179.

303. Stationery of Bet Hayetomot Hakelali; letter from David Weingarten to the directors of the Erez Israel Office, 28 Adar [5]678 [March 12, 1918], CZA S2/427.

304. Supplement to poster about children's education, NHUL, Eliachar Collection, 4* 271 532.

305. Report, *"Bet limud melakhot livnot Yisra'el biYrushalayim,"* 1912/13, p. 4.
306. *Jewish Chronicle*, May 23, 1913, p. 20.
307. Ibid., June 13, 1913, p. 15.
308. In 1913 the school had sixty-five students, of whom forty-nine were Ashkenazic, ten Sephardic, and the rest from Syria, Georgia, and Yemen: *"Bet limud melakhot livnot Yisra'el biYrushalayim,"* 1912/13, p. 4.
309. Margalit Shilo, "Women as Victims of War: The British Conquest (1917) and the Blight of Prostitution in the Holy City," Nashim 6, 2003, pp. 72–83.
310. See letter from the Jerusalem Home for the Blind, 25 Av [5]667 [August 5, 1907], Gaster Papers, 20/220.
311. Letter from Bet Hinukh Yeladim, 3 Heshvan [5]679 [October 9, 1918], CZA S2/427.
312. Raphael Schneller, *"Zemihato vehitpat'huto shel hinukh habanot ba'Edah haHaredit,"* in Mordechai Gilat et al. (eds.), *Mikhtam leDavid* [Memorial Volume for David Ochs] (Ramat-Gan, 1979), pp. 322–333.
313. *Hashkafah*, no. 5, 7 Adar II [5]662 [February 14, 1902].
314. Norma Baumel Joseph, "Jewish Education for Women: Rabbi Moshe Feinstein's Map of America," *American Jewish History* 83/2 (1995), pp. 205–222.
315. Yisra'el Zevi Gilat, *"Hayahasim shebeyn horim viyladim bamishpat ha'Ivri — zekhuyot vehovot"* (Ph.D. dissertation, Bar-Ilan University, Ramat-Gan, 1994), p. 233; Shmuel Glick, *Hahinukh bir'i hahok vehahalakhah* (Jerusalem, 1999), p. 91.
316. Gilat, *"Hayahasim shebeyn horim viyladim,"* p. 321; idem, *"Al ma'amad ha'em bezikah liyladeha — beyn dinei haTorah lamishpat hanoheg beYisra'el,"* in Aharon Barak and Menashe Shava (eds.), *Minhah leYizhak* (Jerusalem, 1999), pp. 167–188.
317. *Havazelet*, 2 Tevet [5]664 [December 21, 1903], quoted in Weingarten, *Ish hesed biYrushalayim*, p. 176.
318. Letter from the Supervisory Committee of the Haredi Talmud Torah for Jewish Girls to Dr. Luria, chairman of the Education Committee, 9 Adar [5]679 [1919], CZA S2/425.
319. Ibid.

Chapter 6. On the Margins of Society: Poverty, Widowhood, Husband Desertion, Prostitution, Missionary Efforts (pp. 181–220)

1. Malkah Cohen, *"Yerushalayim vekabzaneha,"* Yeda' Am 21 (1982), p. 121.
2. In the seventeenth century poor people from Amsterdam were encouraged to immigrate to the Land of Israel; see Yisra'el Bartal and Yosef Kaplan, *"Aliyat aniyim me'Amsterdam le'Erez Yisra'el bereshit hame'ah hasheva-esreh,"* Shalem 6 (1992), pp. 175–193; letter of R. Avraham Gaguin to Montefiore, 1 Elul 5605 [September 3, 1845], Montefiore Archives, no. 587, pp. 94, 257.
3. *Sefer shimru mishpat va'asu zedakah: Takanat ge'onei hazeman shel adat ha-Sefardim* (Jerusalem, 1903), p. 3.
4. Mrs. G. L. Dawson Damer, *Diary of a Tour in Greece, Turkey, Egypt and the Holy Land* (London, 1841), vol. 1, p. 310.
5. James Finn, *Stirring Times*, vol. 2, p. 62.
6. Ben-Haggai, *"Aniyim vekabzanim,"* p. 109.
7. *Hashkafah*, no. 13, 5 Shevat [5]660 [January 5, 1900].
8. David Kertzer, "Toward a Historical Demography of Aging," in David Kertzer

and Peter Laslett (eds.), *Aging in the Past: Demography, Society and Old Age* (Berkeley, Calif., 1995), pp. 363–383; Geremek, *Poverty.*

9. Maimonides, *Mishneh Torah, Hil. Matnot Aniyim* 10:16. For a discussion of the historical problematics of the Jewish attitude to charity see Elimelech Horowitz, *"'Veyihyu aniyim (hagunim) benei beitkha . . . ,"* in Menachem Ben-Sasson (ed.), *Dat vekhalkalah: Yahasei gomelin* (Jerusalem, 1995), pp. 209–232.

10. See above, preface.

11. Eliav, *Erez Yisra'el veyishuvah,* pp. 110–129.

12. Yehoshua Kaniel, *Hemshekh utmurah: Hayishuv hayashan vehayishuv hehadash bitkufat ha'aliyah harishonah vehasheniyah* (Jerusalem, 1982), pp. 62–64.

13. Letter from the Jerusalem General Committee to Hakham Moses Gaster, London, 15 Tevet [5]668 [December 20, 1907], Gaster Papers, 224/72.

14. Letter from R. Shmuel Salant and R. Shaul Eliachar to the officials in Amsterdam, 2 Kislev [5]661 [November 24, 1900], Bibliotheca Rosenthalia, Pekidim and Amarkalim Archives, 187.

15. Letter from Sephardic and Ashkenazic leaders to Hakham Gaster, 1 Shevat [5]667 [January 16, 1907], Gaster Papers, 214/86; letter (March 1914) from General Committee of the Sephardic community to London Board of Deputies, Greater London Record Office, ACC 3121/E3/67/1.

16. Letter from Rabbi Salant to Hakham Gaster, 15 Av [5]662 [August 18, 1902], Gaster Papers, 160/32.

17. Letter from Mughrabi (North African) community to Gaster, [5]659 [1898/9], informing him that riots in Morocco had resulted in cessation of flow of funds from there; Gaster Papers, 106/49.

18. Letter from the General Committee of the "Silwan" Yemenite community, Gaster Papers, undated material (both quotations).

19. Letter from Safed community to Montefiore, Heshvan (autumn) 1846, Montefiore Archives, no. 587, p. 302.

20. Letter from the orphan daughter of R. Avraham Baer Schnitzer, 22 Sivan [5]659 [May 31, 1899], Bibliotheca Rosenthalia, Pekidim and Amarkalim Archives, 171.

21. Letter from Reizel Reuvens, 26 Av [5]647 [August 16, 1887], Bibliotheca Rosenthalia, Pekidim and Amarkalim Archives, 50.

22. Brochures titled *Shemesh zedakah,* published by the General Committee (Knesset Israel) of the Ashkenazic community, beginning in 1846, give the details of the allocation of charitable funds; most support was given to men.

23. Gat, *Hayishuv hayehudi,* pp. 146–158; Eliav, *Erez Yisra'el veyishuvah,* pp. 238–239.

24. Bartal, *Galut ba'arez,* pp. 56–57.

25. Yosef Baumgarten, letter from Vienna to the administrators of the *halukah* in Amsterdam., 3 Elul [5]670 [September 7, 1910], CAHJP, IL/SA XI/1C.

26. It has been conjectured that even these letters comprise only a small part of the original archives, most of which were lost in the Second World War; see Yehudit Ilan-Underoizer, *"Helko shel Irgun haPk.v.Am. me'Amsterdam behahzakatan uvekiyuman shel kehilot Zefat uTeveryah bemahalakh hame'ah ha19 uvithilat hame'ah ha20"* (M.A. thesis, Tel Aviv University, 1993), pp. 65–81. Parts of the Archives of the pekidim ve'amarkalim, besides what remains in Amsterdam, are scattered in other collections: the Jewish National and Hebrew University Library, the Central Archives for the His-

tory of the Jewish People, and the Yad Ben-Zvi Archives, all in Jerusalem, as well as various private collections.

27. Letter of the widow Leah Hirschensohn to Gaster, Gaster Papers, undated material.

28. *Havazelet*, no. 13, 5 Adair I [5]638 [February 8, 1878].

29. Luncz, *Yerushalayim*, vol. 2, p. 138.

30. Undated letter from R. Ya'akov Shaul Eliachar and R. Ya'akov Meir, Gaster Papers, 148/61.

31. Ilan-Underoizer, *"Helko shel Irgun haPk.v.Am."*

32. Razahbi, *Bo'i Teiman*, p. 169.

33. Letter from Persian Jewish community in Jerusalem to Gaster, Gaster Papers, 218/100.

34. *Hazevi*, no. 27, 27 Tamuz [5]648 [July 6, 1888].

35. Aryeh Morgenstern, *"Tik hahakirah shel Sh.Z. Plonsky vehaPerushim be'Erez Yisra'el,"* *Zion* 61 (1996), p. 459.

36. Letter from Zviyah, daughter of Yehosef Schwartz and widow of R. Eliezer Ralbag, 11 Av [5]659 [July 18, 1899], Bibliotheca Rosenthalia, Pekidim and Amarkalim Archives, X 164 (53a–173).

37. For example, letter from Tzirel Estreicher in Yiddish, German, and English, undated, courtesy of Dov Genechovsky, Personal Archive.

38. Letter from Mayta Lidleverin, 1 Tamuz [5]647 [June 23, 1887], Bibliotheca Rosenthalia, Pekidim and Amarkalim Archives, IV, 66 (41–485).

39. "Death bed": letter from Lova Baumgarten, 1 Elul [5]659 [August 7, 1899]; "bitter-souled woman": letter dated 11 Elul [5]659 [August 17, 1899]; both letters in Bibliotheca Rosenthalia, Pekidim and Amarkalim Archives, 162.

40. Letter written in "Rashi script," signed by several dozen widows, received on 18 Adar [5]650 [March 10, 1890], courtesy of Dov Genechovsky, Personal Archive.

41. Hinka: letter dated Tishri [5]59 [September/October 1898], Bibliotheca Rosenthalia, Pekidim and Amarkalim Archives, 161; "Cripple of Tiktin": letter dated 27 Av [5]647 [August 18, 1887], ibid., IV, 52 (41–632); Widow Ratzferter: letter dated [5]665 [1904/1905], courtesy of Dov Genechovsky, Personal Archive.

42. *Hazevi*, no. 8, 11 Kislev [5]646 [November 20, 1885].

43. *Hashkafah*, no. 78, 20 Sivan [5]665 [June 23, 1905]; ibid., no. 79, 24 Sivan [5]665 [June 27, 1905].

44. For example, a letter from Sarah Rivkah, daughter of Avraham, dated 29 Kislev [5]641 [December 2, 1880], was also signed by Elkanah b. Moshe Sachs and Azriel Zelig Hausdorf, who were senior officers of Kolel Hod, NHUL, Kodesh Collection, 4* 1203.

45. Letter from the widow of "the *zaddik* [righteous man]" Yehoshua Bezalel, 13 Tamuz [5]642 [June 30, 1882], Bibliotheca Rosenthalia, Pekidim and Amarkalim Archives, 62.

46. Letter from Esther Burdaki, 18 Tevet [5]645 [January 5, 1885], courtesy of Dov Genechovsky, Personal Archive.

47. Letter from Sheindl Wertheimer, 11 Iyar [5]645 [April 26, 1885]; letter from widow of Raphael Lama Pizanti to Amsterdam officials, 1 Adar II [5]654 [March 9, 1894]; both courtesy of Dov Genechovsky, Personal Archive.

48. See chapter 2.

49. Sheine Esther, widow of R. Aharon Jaffe, letter dated 27 Iyar [5]659 [May 7,

1899], Bibliotheca Rosenthalia, Pekidim and Amarkalim Archives, 170; letter from Hannah, widow of Moshe Nehemiah Kahana, 25 Sivan [5]647 [June 17, 1887], ibid., IV, 66 (41–500).

50. Ben-Zion b. Avraham requesting help for his just widowed mother, 22 Adar [5]661 [March 13, 1901], Bibliotheca Rosenthalia, Pekidim and Amarkalim Archives, 195; a mother requesting help for her widowed son, Hayim Zalman Vershner, in a letter to the Amsterdam officials, 17 Elul [5]654 [September 18, 1894], unnumbered material, NHUL; letter from Beila Kenig, 15 Elul [5]660 [September 9, 1900], Bibliotheca Rosenthalia, Pekidim and Amarkalim Archives, 184.

51. *Havazelet*, no. 29, 21 Iyar [5]637 [May 4, 1877].

52. Supplement to *Hazevi*, no. 16, 12 Adar II [5]649 [March 15, 1889].

53. Letter from R. Shmuel Salant, dated 8 Kislev [5]661 [November 30, 1900], confirming receipt of funds for invalids and poor people, Bibliotheca Rosenthalia, Pekidim and Amarkalim Archives, 191.

54. On widowhood in general see Kertzer and Karweit, "Impact of Widowhood"; widows in Safed: Karlinsky, "*Hahevrah hahasidit shel Zefat*," p. 195.

55. Shoham, "*Almenot Yerushalayim*," p. 1.

56. Ibid., pp. 2–7, 13.

57. Letter from Yuta Beila to Montefiore, 18 Av [August 9] 1839, Montefiore Archive, 574, no. 87.

58. Letter from Elka, daughter of R. Yeshayah Bardaki and granddaughter of R. Israel of Shklov, 21 Iyar [5]660 [May 20, 1900], Bibliotheca Rosenthalia, Pekidim and Amarkalim Archives, 183.

59. Letter from Leah, widow of Yosef Rivlin, 12 Elul [5]661 [August 27, 1901], Bibliotheca Rosenthalia, Pekidim and Amarkalim Archives, 184.

60. Letters from Rivka Lipa Anikster, 28 Shevat [5]647 [February 22, 1887], Bibliotheca Rosenthalia, Pekidim and Amarkalim Archives, IV, 54 (41–865); 2 Sivan [5]647 [May 25, 1887], ibid., IV, 66 (41–521); letter from Rachel Anikster, 21 Tevet [5]659 [January 3, 1899].

61. Letter from the widows to the Amsterdam officials, 1 Iyar [5]642 [April 20, 1882], NHUL, unsigned.

62. For example, "*Za'akat ha-Almanot*" (The Widows' Cry), *Hazevi*, no. 8, 19 Kislev [5]649 [November 23, 1898].

63. Lavski, "*Takanot Yerushalayim*," p. 90; Kaniel, "*Ma'avakim irguniyim*."

64. Ga'on, *Yehudei hamizrah*, vol. 1, p. 115.

65. *Sefer takanot vehaskamot* (Tel Aviv, 1969; photogr. repr. of ed. Jerusalem, 1883), p. 34b.

66. Letter from the Sephardic *kolelot* in Hebron, undated, to Gaster, Gaster Papers, undated material.

67. Letter from Sheindl, widow of Avraham Nisan Weinstein, 15 Sivan [5]659 [May 24, 1899], Bibliotheca Rosenthalia, Pekidim and Amarkalim Archives 163.

68. Letter from Sima, widow of Zvi Hirsh Perlman, to principals of the Warsaw Kolel, dated 10 Adar II [5]643 [March 19, 1883], Municipal Archives, Jerusalem, Old Yishuv Collection, folio 201.

69. Letter of Rivka Schwartz, 24 Nisan [5]626 [April 9, 1866], CAHJP, Collection of letters of Schwartz's widow.

70. "*Za'akat almanah*," *Havazelet*, year 10, no. 33, 25 Sivan [5]640 [June 4, 1880], p. 250.

71. *"Lehazdik zaddik,"* *Havazelet* no. 36, 16 Tamuz [5]640 [June 25, 1880], pp. 271–274.

72. For the rule that payments to the community take precedence over a widow's compensation, see Aryeh Karlin, *Torat even ha'ezer* (Jerusalem, 1950), pp. 176–177 and references cited there.

73. Quotations below are from the two *Havazelet* items cited in notes 69 and 70 above.

74. Lavski, *"Takanot Yerushalayim,"* p. 91.

75. If a widow was unable to mange her own financial affairs — whether because of illiteracy or a lack of self-confidence — the rabbinical court would appoint a male guardian; see letter from the guardians of the estate of R. Yosef Rivlin, dated 3 Elul [5]660 [August 28, 1900], Bibliotheca Rosenthalia, Pekidim and Amarkalim Archives, 184.

76. Yehuda Aaron Weiss, *Bish'arayikh Yerushalayim,* p. 96.

77. Mark Baker, "The Voice of the Deserted Jewish Woman, 1867–1870," *Jewish Social Studies: History, Culture, Society,* new series 2/1 (1995), pp. 98–123.

78. Reena Sigman Friedman, "'Send Me My Husband Who Is in New York City': Husband Desertion in the American Immigrant Community, 1900–1926," *Jewish Social Studies* 44 (1982), p. 4.

79. Baker, "Voice of the Deserted Jewish Woman," p. 99.

80. Jerusalem periodicals also publicized the names of men who had fled from Europe to the Holy Land; see, e.g., *Havazelet,* no. 4, 12 Heshvan [5]642 [November 4, 1881]; ibid., no. 37, 12 Av [5]642 [July 28, 1882].

81. *Ha'or,* no. 12, 23 Kislev [5]653 [December 12, 1892].

82. *Havazelet,* no. 32, 4 Tamuz [5]639 [June 25, 1879].

83. *Hashkafah,* no. 14, 6 Kislev [5]666 [December 4, 1905]; letter from the parents-in-law of Hayim Fogel, 5 Elul [5]660 [August 30, 1900], Bibliotheca Rosenthalia, Pekidim and Amarkalim Archives, 185.

84. *Havazelet,* no. 21, 3 Sivan [5]643 [June 8, 1883].

85. A mother searching for her son, who had run off with a large sum of money to India, *Havazelet,* no. 4, 17 Heshvan [5]631 [November 11, 1870]; a father seeking his only son, ibid., no. 32, July 4, 1878].

86. Letter from Safed rabbis to Gaster, 27 Av [5]663 [August 20, 1903], Gaster Papers, 172/79.

87. *Hashkafah,* no. 49, 12 Elul [5]663 [September 4, 1903].

88. Hamburger, *Sheloshah olamot,* vol. 3, p. 101.

89. Letter from Rachel Anikster, Nisan [5]647 [spring 1887], Bibliotheca Rosenthalia, Pekidim and Amarkalim Archives, 58.

90. Letter from Rachel Anikster, Lag ba'Omer [5]644 [May 13, 1884], Bibliotheca Rosenthalia, Pekidim and Amarkalim Archives, IV, 61 (41–239).

91. Letter from Rachel Anikster, 2 Shevat [5]647 [January 27, 1887], Bibliotheca Rosenthalia, Pekidim and Amarkalim Archives, 54.

92. Ibid.

93. Letters from Rivka Lipa Anikster, 2 Sivan [5]647 [May 25, 1887], Bibliotheca Rosenthalia, Pekidim and Amarkalim Archives, IV, 66 (41–521); 7 Shevat [5]647 [February 1, 1887], ibid., IV, 54 (41–865).

94. *Ha'or,* no. 12, 23 Kislev [5]653 [December 23, 1892].

95. Gad Frumkin, *Derekh shofet biYrushalayim*, p. 34; Hamburger, *Sheloshah olamot*, vol. 2, p. 79.

96. Baker, "Voice of the Deserted Jewish Woman," p. 103; see also Sigman Friedman, "Send Me My Husband," p. 5.

97. *Hazevi*, no. 6, 29 Kislev [5]657 [December 4, 1896].

98. Ibid., no. 43, 8 Av [5]657 [August 6, 1897].

99. Handwritten notebook about a deserted wife, undated, Raphael Silbermann Archives, Safed, CAHJP, IL/SA ii/7/9-d; see also Ya'akov Sha'ul Eliachar, *Responsa*, no. 18, p. 35a.

100. *Hashkafah*, no. 79, 5 Av [5]666 [July 27, 1906].

101. *Havazelet*, no. 35, 22 Tamuz [5]636 [July 14, 1876].

102. Rabbi Nachman Batito of the North African Jewish community, letter to Moses Gaster, Gaster Papers, undated material.

103. *Sefer Torat Rabenu Shmuel Salant, Kunteres hatarat agunot*, no. 99, p. 293.

104. *Havazelet*, year 35, 9 Adar II [5]665 [February 14, 1905], p. 88.

105. *Havazelet*, 15 Kislev [5]631 [December 9, 1870], pp. 6, 24; letter from Nechama Danskik, 3 Adar [5]659 [February 13, 1899], Bibliotheca Rosenthalia, Pekidim and Amarkalim Archives, 165; Eliahu "the convert," *Hazevi*, no. 3, 9 Heshvan [5]657 [October 16, 1896].

106. *Hazevi*, no. 22, 6 Tamuz [5]648 [June 15, 1888], and subsequent issues (nos. 26, 27, 31).

107. *Havazelet*, no. 45, 6 Elul [5]635 [September 6, 1875].

108. Supplement to *Hazevi*, no. 27, 28 Iyar [5]658 [May 20, 1898].

109. Supplement to *Ha'or*, no. 29, 29 Sivan [5]652 [June 24, 1892].

110. Mordechai Ze'ev Ettinger, *Sefer ma'amar Mordechai (Responsa)* (Jerusalem, 1968; photogr. repr. of 1852 ed.), no. 27, p. 38a; *Sefer Torat Rabenu Shmuel Salant, Kunteres hatarat agunot*, no. 260.

111. Supplement to *Hazevi*, no. 16, 12 Adar II [5]649 [March 15, 1889].

112. *Havazelet*, no. 6, 23 Heshvan [5]637 [November 10, 1876].

113. *Jewish Chronicle*, August 23, 1912, p. 13.

114. *Hazevi*, no. 43, 8 Av [5]657 [August 6, 1897].

115. Ya'akov Sha'ul Eliachar, *Responsa*, vol. 1, no. 8, p. 13b.

116. *Hazevi*, no. 3, 9 Heshvan [5]657 [October 16, 1896]; Yuval Dror, "*Hagerim harusiyim baGalil bereshit hame'ah ha'esrim*," *Cathedra* 10 (1979), pp. 34–71.

117. Letter from the committee of the Sephardic community, 27 Av [5]663 [August 20, 1903], Gaster Papers; *Hashkafah*, no. 19, 18 Kislev [5]667 [December 5, 1906].

118. *Havazelet*, no. 5, 24 Heshvan [5]651 [November 7, 1890].

119. Yonatan Shunari, "*Atirot nedavah umattan lehassi kallah vehatan*," *Jerusalem Studies in Folklore* 4 (1974), p. 123.

120. *Havazelet*, no. 45, 6 Elul [5]635 [September 6, 1875].

121. Supplement to *Ha'or*, no. 29, 29 Sivan [5]652 [June 24, 1892].

122. Letter from Safed rabbis to Gaster, 27 Av [5]663 [August 20, 1903], Gaster Papers, 172/79.

123. Ya'akov Sha'ul Eliachar, *Responsa Benei Binyamin*, vol. 1, no. 18, p. 35a.

124. *Hazevi*, no. 9, 19 Kislev [5]646 [November 27, 1885].

125. Ibid., no. 27, 27 Nisan [5]656 [April 10, 1896]; ibid., no. 13, 10 Tevet [5]657 [December 15, 1896].

126. Sigman Friedman, "Send Me My Husband."

127. R. Shlomo Drimmer, *Responsa Beit Shlomo* (New York, 1962), no. 66, p. 84b (written in 1854).

128. Joel Sirkes, *She'elot utshuvot Bayit Hadash ha-Hadashot* (Koretz, 1785), no. 64 (quoted by numerous Halakhic authorities).

129. *Hazevi*, no. 36, 4 Tamuz [5]658 [June 24, 1898]; ibid., no. 43, 8 Av [5]657 [August 6, 1897]; *Hashkafah*, no. 79, 5 Av [5]666 [July 27, 1906].

130. *Hazevi*, no. 22, 6 Tamuz [5]648 [June 15, 1888].

131. Letter to R. Shmuel Salant from Rabbi Yosef Hayim Sonnenfeld, 25 Tamuz [5]661 [July 12, 1901], Eliachar Collection, NHUL, 4* 1271 665.

132. *Havazelet*, nos. 11/12, 27 Shevat [5]638 [January 31, 1878].

133. *Hazevi*, no. 10, 9 Adar [5]655 [March 5, 1895].

134. *Ha'or*, no. 24, 23 Iyar [5]652 [May 20, 1892].

135. *Hashkafah*, no. 25, 5 Av [5]662 [August 8, 1902].

136. Baker, "Voice of the Deserted Jewish Woman," p. 110.

137. Judith R. Walkowitz, *Prostitution and Victorian Society: Women, Class and the State* (Cambridge, 1980).

138. Avraham Stahl, "*Zenut bekerev yehudim ketofa'at levay lema'avar mitarbut letarbut*," *Megamot* 24 (1978–79), pp. 209, 222.

139. Edward J. Bristow, *Prostitution and Prejudice: The Jewish Fight against White Slavery, 1870–1939* (Oxford, 1982); Yehudah Rimerman, *Hazenut vehana'arah hasotah* (Tel Aviv, 1977), pp. 42–45.

140. Lara Marks, "Jewish Women and Jewish Prostitution in the East End of London," *Jewish Quarterly* 34/2 (1987), pp. 6–10.

141. Ibid., p. 10.

142. *Hashkafah*, no. 88, 29 Av [5]663 [August 22, 1903].

143. *Hazevi*, no. 2, 2 Heshvan [5]657 [October 9, 1896].

144. *Hashkafah*, no. 9, 5 Kislev [5]664 [November 24, 1903].

145. Ibid., no. 10, 15 Kislev [5]664 [December 4, 1903].

146. See Bertha Pappenheim, *Leben und Schriften* (Frankfurt a/M, 1963), p. 54.

147. Eliav, *Bahasut mamlekhet Austria*, pp. 134–135.

148. Supplement to *Hazevi*, no. 18, 16 Iyar [5]648 [April 27, 1888].

149. Yosef Rivlin, *Mivhar ma'amarim ureshimot* (Ramat-Gan, 1966), pp. 163–165.

150. Muslim society treated prostitutes as having abandoned Islam, and they were severely punished. See Dengler, "The Turkish Woman," p. 233; cf. also Eliahu Eliachar, *Lihyot im yehudim*, pp. 83–84.

151. *Hashkafah*, no. 6, 14 Heshvan [5]667 [October 2, 1906].

152. Angel-Malachi, *Beterem reshit*, pp. 59–62; quote on p. 62.

153. Letter from David Weingarten to the Erez Israel Office, dated 28 Adar [5]678 [March 12, 1918], CZA, S2/427.

154. Stahl, "*Zenut bekerev yehudim*," p. 219; Nanette J. Davis, "Feminism, Deviance and Social Change," in Edward Sagarin (ed.), *Deviance and Social Change* (London, 1977), pp. 247–276.

155. Ya'akov Sha'ul Eliachar, *Responsa*, no. 35, p. 81.

156. Frankl, *Nach Jerusalem!* p. 70; see also Brawer, *Zihronot av uvno*, p. 460.

157. Frankl, *Nach Jerusalem!* pp. 75–76.

158. See, e.g., Samuel, *Jewish Life in the East*, p. 134.

159. *Hazevi*, no. 2, 30 Tishri [5]646 [October 9, 1885]; see also *Havazelet*, no. 37,

13 Tamuz [5]635 [July 16, 1875]; Hyamson, *British Consulate*, vol. 1, p. 134; David Sarid, *"Mezukat hayishuv ufe'ilut hamisyon biTveryah bashanim, 1884–1914," Mituv Teveryah* 2 (1983), p. 29.

160. Steven J. Zipperstein, "Heresy, Apostasy and the Transformation of Joseph Rabbinovich," in Todd M. Endelman (ed.), *Jewish Apostasy in the Modern World* (New York, 1987), pp. 207–208.

161. Blumberg, *View from Jerusalem*; Eliav, *Britain and the Holy Land*, pp. 45–59.

162. Leah Bornstein-Makovetzky, *"Pe'ilut hamisyon ha'Amerika'i bekerev yehudei Istanbul, Izmir veSaloniki bame'ah hatesha-esreh,"* in Minna Rosen (ed.), *Yemei hasahar: Perakim betoledot hayehudim ba'Imperiyah ha'Othmanit* (Tel Aviv, 1996), pp. 280–281.

163. W. T. Gidney, *The History of the London Society for Promoting Christianity Amongst the Jews (1808–1908)* (London, 1908); Ben-Arieh, *Jerusalem . . . the Old City*, and idem, *Jerusalem . . . the New City*, index, s.v. "missionaries."

164. Mordechai Eliav, *"Mumar, ba'al teshuvah vehozer lesuro (parashat Shim'on Rosenthal),"* *Cathedra* 61 (1992), pp. 113–132; Sha'ul Sapir, *"Terumat hevrot hamisyon"*; Shalom Ginat, *"Pe'ilut hahevrah haLondonit lekidum hanazrut beyn hayehudim"* (M.A. thesis, Haifa University, 1986).

165. *Tidings from Zion*, July 17, 1882, p. 7.

166. Abdul Latif Tibawi, *British Interests in Palestine, 1800–1901: A Study of Religious and Educational Enterprise* (Oxford, 1961), pp. 206–207.

167. Michael Ish Shalom, *Mas'ei nozerim leErez Yisra'el: Reshumot ve'eduyot letoledot hayishuv hayehudi* (Jerusalem, 1965), pp. 166–167; idem, *"Al hayishuv hayehudi beHevron lefi mekorot nozriyim," Sefunot* 9 (1965), p. 351; Ginat, *"Pe'ilut hahevrah haLondonit,"* p. 121.

168. Yisra'el Klausner, *Behit'orer am: Ha'aliyah harishonah meRusiyah*, vol. 1 (Jerusalem, 1962), pp. 307–321; Yosi Ben Arzi, *"Har Tuv — moshavah niskahah beharei Yehudah," Ofakim bege'ografiyah* 3 (1977), pp. 123–140; idem, *"Haperek hanozri betoledot Har Tuv," Nofim* 9–10 (1978), pp. 14–144.

169. For missionary activity in Turkey see Bornstein-Makovetzky, *"Pe'ilut hamisyon,"* p. 276; for England see Missionary Committee, Report of the Executive Committee to the General Committee, 1912, Greater London Record Office, ACC 3121/E3/28.

170. Melman, *Women's Orients*, p. 178.

171. See Devens, "If We Get the Girls."

172. Eliav, *Britain and the Holy Land*, p. 52.

173. See Shifra Schwartz, *"Histadruyot nashim"*; Morgenstern, *Meshihiyut veyishuv Erez Yisra'el*; Yisra'el Freidin, *"Hevrot hesed bayishuv hayashan ha'Ashkenazi biYrushalayim bame'ah ha19"* (M.A. thesis, Hebrew University of Jerusalem, 1987); Ben-Arieh, *Jerusalem . . . the Old City*, pp. 336–339; idem, *Jerusalem . . . the New City*, pp. 247–254; Schwake, *Entwicklung des Krankenhauswesens*; Levi, *Perakim betoledot harefu'ah*; Amalie M. Kass, "Sir Moses Montefiore and Medical Philanthropy in the Holy Land," in Manfred Waserman and Samuel S. Kottek (eds.), *Health and Disease in the Holy Land* (Lewiston, N.Y., 1996), pp. 207–229.

174. Eliav, *"Masa liYrushalayim,"* p. 152.

175. *Hazevi*, no. 8, 12 Kislev [5]646 [November 20, 1885].

176. Moshe Rivlin to Montefiore, letter criticizing the first Jewish physician in Jerusalem, 5 Tevet 5606 [January 3, 1846], Montefiore Archive, 587, no. 33; see also *Moriah*, no. 313, 19 Adar II, [5]673 [March 28, 1913].

177. *Moriah*, no. 414, 11 Tevet [5]674 [January 9, 1914].

178. David Yellin, *Ketavim*, vol. 1, p. 172.

179. Samuel, *Jewish Life in the East*, p. 137.

180. Moshe Sofer-Federman, "*Milhamtenu bamisyon haProtestanti biYrushalayim*," *Yeda Am* 10 (1965), p. 95; William Ewing, *Our Jewish Missions*, vol. 1: *The Holy Land and Glasgow* (Edinburgh, 1913), p. 33; Eliav, *Bahasut mamlekhet Austria*, pp. 194–195.

181. *Hashkafah*, no. 28, 7 Iyar [5]664 [April 22, 1904].

182. Sarid, "*Mezukat hayishuv*"; Yaron Bar El and Nissim Levi, "*Reshitah shel harefu'ah hamodernit be'arei haGalil, 1860–1900*," *Cathedra* 54 (1989), pp. 96–106.

183. Ewing, *Our Jewish Missions*.

184. *Hashkafah*, no. 7, 10 Heshvan [5]663 [November 10, 1902]; Eliav, *Britain and the Holy Land*, p. 52; James Finn, *Stirring Times*, vol. 1, p. 120.

185. Miller, *Eastern Sketches*, p. 150.

186. James Finn, *Stirring Times*, vol. 2, p. 72.

187. Melman, *Women's Orients*, p. 184.

188. Elizabeth Finn, *Reminiscences*, p. 75.

189. Sha'ul Sapir, "*Terumat hevrot hamisyon*," pp. 28–29.

190. Ish Shalom, *Mas'ei nozerim*, p. 674.

191. James Finn, *Stirring Times*, vol. 2, p. 73.

192. Elizabeth Finn, *Reminiscences*, p. 75.

193. Ginat, "*Pe'ilut hahevrah haLondonit*," pp. 82–83; *Hazevi*, no. 23, 29 Sivan [5]655 [June 21, 1885].

194. Ginat, "*Pe'ilut hahevrah haLondonit*," p. 83.

195. James Finn, *Stirring Times*, vol. 2, p. 323.

196. Miller, *Eastern Sketches*, p. 127.

197. Sha'ul Sapir, "*Terumat hevrot hamisyon*," p. 71; Melman, *Women's Orients*, pp. 184–187.

198. Miller, *Eastern Sketches*, pp. 150–151.

199. *Tidings from Zion*, October 1883; see also Sha'ul Sapir, "*Terumat hevrot hamisyon*," p. 112.

200. *Hazevi*, no. 15, 28 Adar I [5]649 [March 1, 1889].

201. *Hazevi*, no. 1, 4 Tishri [5]657 [September 11, 1896].

202. *Jewish Chronicle*, July 25, 1913, p. 20.

203. Tibawi, *British Interests*, pp. 154–155. See also Ben-Arieh, *Jerusalem . . . the Old City*, pp. 233–234.

204. Devens, "If We Get the Girls."

205. Samuel, *Jewish Life in the East*, pp. 138–139; Chelouche, *Ha'ez vehashorashim*, p. 64; *Hazevi*, no. 5, 21 Heshvan [5]646 [October 30, 1885]; Ginat, "*Pe'ilut hahevrah haLondonit*," p. 79.

206. AJA *23rd Annual Report* (1893–1894), p. 54.

207. Ibid., p. 53.

208. Rachel Ariel, "*Hamilhamah bamisyon bir'i haherut 1913–1914*" (seminar paper, Bar-Ilan University, Ramat-Gan, 1994); Eran Otztar, "*Hamilhamah bamisyon bir'i Hamoriah*" (seminar paper, Bar-Ilan University, Ramat-Gan, 1993); *Jewish Chronicle*, July 25, 1913, p. 20.

209. Ariel, "*Hamilhamah bamisyon*."

210. *Moriah*, no. 474, 24 Adar [5]674 [March 22, 1914]; *Haherut*, no. 125, 7 Adar I

[5]673 [February 14, 1913]; ibid., no. 131, 14 Adar I [5]673, [February 21, 1913]; David Yellin, *Ketavim*, vol. 4, p. 123.

211. *Moriah*, no. 152, 18 Tevet [5]672 [January 8, 1912]; ibid., no. 318, 8 Nisan [5]673 [April 15, 1913].

212. Letter from David Weingarten to Moses Gaster, 3rd day of the Torah portion "Pinehas," [5]673 [July 1913], Gaster Papers.

213. *Moriah*, no. 152, 18 Tevet [5]672 [January 8, 1912], pp. 1–2; Moshayoff, *Betokhekhei Yerushalayim*, p. 30.

214. *Tidings from Zion*, May 1884.

215. *Havazelet*, no. 27, 21 Iyar [5]641 [May 20, 1881]; Avraham Ben Petahyah, "*Reshit hinukh haMizrahi be'Erez Yisra'el*," in Y. L. Hacohen Maimon (ed.), *Yovel haMizrahi* (Jerusalem, 1952), p. 190.

216. Chelouche, *Ha'ez vehashorashim*, pp. 60–65.

217. *Moriah*, no. 152, 18 Tevet [5]672 [January 8, 1912]; Brawer, *Zihronot av uvno*, p. 452,

218. *Haherut*, no. 179, 13 Nisan [5]673 [April 20, 1913].

219. *AJA 23rd Annual Report* (1893–1894), pp. 53–54; *Hazevi*, no. 3, 29 Tevet [5]655 [January 25, 1895]; Sha'ul Sapir, "*Terumat hevrot hamisyon*," p. 74.

220. *Tidings from Zion*, March 1884, p. 137.

221. *Havazelet*, no. 37, 13 Tamuz [5]635 [July 16, 1875]; ibid., no. 2, 1 Heshvan [5]636 [October 30, 1875].

222. See Ginat, "*Pe'ilut hahevrah haLondonit*," p. 121, who puts the number at some four hundred souls.

223. Frankl, *Nach Jerusalem!* p. 71.

224. Mordechai Eliav, "'*Bizkhut nashim'—mekomah shel ha'ishah bema'amazei hanizur shel hamisyon haBriti biYrushalayim*," *Cathedra* 76 (1995), p. 98, note 8.

225. Yosef Tobi, "*Hit'aslemut bekerev yehudei Teiman tahat hashilton haZayidi—emdot hahalakhah haZayidit, hashilton ha'Umayyi vehahevrah hamuslemit*," *Pe'amim* 42 (1990), pp. 105–126.

226. On similar motivation for conversion up to the seventeenth century in Germany see Binyamin Ze'ev Kedar, "*Hemshekhiyut vehidush bahamarah hayehudit beGermaniyah shel hame'ah hashemoneh-esreh*," in E. Etkes and Y. Salmon (eds.), *Perakim betoledot hahevrah hayehudit* (Jerusalem, 1980), pp. 154–170; Eliav, "*Mumar, ba'al teshuvah*."

227. Michael Stanislawski, "Jewish Apostasy in Russia: A Tentative Typology," in Todd M. Endelman (ed.), *Jewish Apostasy in the Modern World* (New York, 1987), pp. 189–205.

228. Eliav, "*Bizkhut nashim*," p. 100; Ginat, "*Pe'ilut hahevrah haLondonit*," p. 67.

229. Nadya Zeldes, "'*Kevorahat mipnei hanahash'—hitmodedut nashim yehudiyot beSiziliyah bedor hagerush im hamarat ba'aleihen*," *Pe'amim* 82 (2000), pp. 52–63.

230. Mordechai Eliav, "*Parashat Sarah Steinberg: Perek bema'avak hayishuv neged hamisyon*," *Sinai* 64 (1969), pp. 78–91; idem, *Hayishuv hayehudi be'Erez Yisra'el bir'i hamediniyut haGermanit* (Tel Aviv, 1973), pp. 14–21; *Tidings from Zion*, October 1883, pp. 162–163.

231. Eliav, "*Mumar, ba'al teshuvah*."

232. *Hamaggid*, 28 Tishri [5]622 [October 2, 1861], quoted by Eliav, "*Mumar, ba'al teshuvah*," pp. 123–125.

233. With the exception of text accompanying note 234, all the information in the following five paragraphs is taken from Eliav, *"Bizkhut nashim,"* passim.

234. Report of the London Society, 1891, quoted by Eliav, *"Bizkhut nashim,"* p. 101.

235. Dror Wahrman, *"Hazalam haYerushalmi hamikzo'i harishon?" Cathedra* 38 (1985), pp. 115–120; Nizah Braun-Rozovski and Karni A. S. Gavin, *"Hayav va'avodato shel Mendel John Diness: Zalam, misyoner, metif umesaper sipurim," Cathedra* 75 (1995), pp. 69–91.

236. *Hazevi,* no. 34, 21 Sivan [5]646 [June 24, 1886]; for a similar story see *Hashkafah,* no. 23, 21 Adar [5]663 [March 20, 1903].

237. *Hazevi,* no. 20, 14 Adar I [5]646 [February 19, 1886]; *Moriah,* no. 152, 18 Tevet [5]672 [January 8, 1912].

238. *Hazevi,* no. 6, 28 Heshvan [5]649 [November 2, 1888].

239. Hyamson, *British Consulate,* p. 65.

240. *Hashkafah,* no. 18, 16 Shevat [5]663 [February 25, 1903].

241. Leibowitz, *Ba'aliyah uvabeniyah,* p. 68; see also Freeze, *Jewish Marriage,* p. 17.

242. *Hashkafah,* no. 91, 18 Tamuz [5]665 [July 21, 1905].

243. Yehoshua, *Yerushalayim temol shilshom,* vol. 1, p. 138.

244. *Hazevi,* no. 20, 17 Iyar [5]649 [May 18, 1889].

245. Ibid., no. 19, 3 Iyar [5]649 [May 4, 1889].

246. Eliav, *Bahasut mamlekhet Austria,* pp. 368–369.

247. Frankl, *Nach Jerusalem!* p. 71.

248. See chapter 1; see also Avraham B. Rivlin, *Zeh karah be'Erez Yisra'el: Eru'im ufarashiyot* (Jerusalem, 1993), pp. 38–40.

249. Yosef Rivlin, *Mivhar ma'amarim ureshimot,* p. 66.

250. [A Halakhic category, signifying a person so innocent as not to be legally responsible for his or her actions. — Trans.]

251. See above, text at note 232. For the details here see again Eliav, *"Bizkhut nashim."*

252. See above, text at note 229, and Eliav, *"Parashat Sarah Steinberg."*

253. *Havazelet,* no. 37, 13 Tamuz [5]635 [July 16 1875]; ibid., no. 2, 1 Heshvan [5]636 [October 30, 1875]; David Yellin, *Ketavim,* vol. 1, p. 260.

254. Moshayoff, *Betokhekhei Yerushalayim,* p. 30.

255. Supplement to *Hazevi,* no. 28, 7 Iyar [5]658 [April 29, 1898].

256. *Hazevi,* no. 36, 21 Sivan [5]657 [June 21, 1897].

257. Hyamson, *British Consulate,* vol. 2, pp. 491–493.

258. Taubenhaus, *Bintiv hayahid,* pp. 96–97.

259. *Haherut,* no. 107, 12 Tamuz [5]674 [July 6, 1914].

260. Eliav, *Hayishuv hayehudi,* p. 133; document on p. 164.

261. Undated writ of excommunication, CAHJP, J41.

262. Jeffrey S. Gurock, "Influences on the Lower East Side, 1900–1910," in Todd M. Endelman (ed.), *Jewish Apostasy in the Modern World* (New York, 1987), p. 266.

263. Eliav, *Bahasut mamlekhet Austria,* pp. 201–202; Genechovsky, *Misipurei,* pp. 160–165.

264. Weingarten, *Ish hesed biYrushalayim,* pp. 204–205.

265. Hyamson, *British Consulate,* vol. 2, pp. 505–508.

266. *AJA 27th Annual Report* (1897–1898), pp. 16–17.

267. David Yellin, *Ketavim,* vol. 1, pp. 171–173; Sofer-Federman, *"Milhamtenu bamisyon,"* pp. 95–96; Shiryon, *Zikhronot,* p. 40; Eliav, *Hayishuv hayehudi,* pp. 133–134; Wallace, *Jerusalem the Holy,* p. 308.

268. David Yellin, *Ketavim*, vol. 1, pp. 269–271; *Hashkafah*, no. 2, 10 Heshvan [5]658 [November 5, 1897].

269. David Yellin, *Ketavim*, vol. 1, pp. 271, 307.

270. *Hashkafah*, no. 58, 2 Nisan [5]665 [April 7, 1905].

271. Ibid., no. 2, 10 Heshvan [5]658 [November 5, 1897].

272. *Ha'or*, no. 10, 15 Tevet [5]651 [December 26, 1890]; *Hazevi*, no. 12, 10 Tevet [5]646 [December 18, 1885].

273. *Hazevi*, no. 13, 26 Iyar [5]647 [May 20, 1887].

274. *Haherut*, no. 231, June 30, 1913.

275. *Hazevi*, no. 15, 28 Adar I [5]649 [March 1, 1889].

276. *Ha'or*, no. 20, 26 Adar I [5]651 [March 6, 1891].

277. *Hashkafah*, no. 41, 2 Adar II [5]665 [March 9, 1905].

278. *Tidings from Zion*, October 1882, p. 82.

279. Yosef Lang, "*Itonut Eliezer Ben Yehuda ve'emdoteha be'inyenei hayishuv hayehudi vehatenu'ah hale'umit [5]645–[5]675 1884–1914*" (Ph.D. dissertation, Bar-Ilan University, Ramat-Gan, 1993), pp. 337–341.

280. Freidin, "*Hevrot hesed*," pp. 53–57, esp. p. 56 n. 7; Eliav, *Ahavat Ziyon*, pp. 305–397; Getzel Kressel, *Mivhar kitvei Yisra'el Dov Frumkin* (Jerusalem, 1954), pp. 196–201.

281. Lang, "*Itonut Eliezer Ben Yehuda*," pp. 337–341.

282. *Hazevi*, no. 20, 14 Adar I [5]646 [February 19, 1886]; ibid., no. 43, 18 Elul [5]645 [August 29, 1885].

283. Taubenhaus, *Bintiv hayahid*, pp. 99–101.

284. On the women of Bet Ya'akov, see chapter 4. This preceded the girls' orphanage mentioned in chapter 5 by some five years. For earlier efforts by Jewish women in Beirut see *Hazevi*, no. 19, 7 Adar I [5]646 [February 12, 1846].

285. *Hashkafah*, no. 5, 8 Kislev [5]658 [December 3, 1897].

286. Sarna, "Christian Missions and American Jews," pp. 240–241.

287. Circular letter from the committee, NHUL, Kadesh Collection, V1568; Silbert, "*Megamot*," pp. 181–184.

288. *Moriah*, no. 319, 14 Nisan [5]673 [April 21, 1913]; Letter from committee of the Jerusalem Branch of the Association of Hebrew Teachers in the Land of Israel, dated 8 Nisan [5]673 [April 15, 1913], CZA, A9/202.

289. Z. Buchman, "*Hamilhamah bamisyon*," *Pirkei Hapo'el Haza'ir* 12 (1938), pp. 61–63. A similar antimission campaign was organized in England; see Archives, Mission Committee Report, in the files of the Board of Deputies, Greater London Record Office.

290. Tamar Ross, "*Ha'od mesugalot anu lehitpalel le'avinu shebashamayim?*" in Naham Ilan (ed.), *Ayin tovah: Du siah upulemus betarbut Yisra'el: Sefer yovel . . . Tovah Ilan* ([Tel Aviv], 1999), p. 264; Rachel Elior, "*Almah yafah she'ein lah eynayim?*" in David Yoel Ariel et al., *Barukh she'asani ishah?* (Tel Aviv, 1999), pp. 37–56.

Epilogue. The Female Experience in Jerusalem: Honing Historical-Cultural Insights (pp. 221–228)

1. Devorah Bernstein, "*Heker nashim bahistoriographiyah haYisre'elit: Nekudot moza, kivunim hadashim vetovanot shebaderekh*," in Margalit Shilo et al. (eds.), *Ha'ivriyot hahadashot—Nashim bayishuv uvaZiyonut bir'i hamigdar* (Jerusalem, 2002), pp. 12–14.

2. Yosi Ben Arzi, *"Ha'im shinu heker nashim umigdar et yahasenu lahavanat hahistoriyah shel ha'aliyah vehahityashevut?"* in Margalit Shilo et al. (eds.), *H'ivriyot hahadashot—Nashim bayishnv uvaZiyonut bir'i hamigdar* (Jerusalem, 2002), pp. 26–44; Lawrence Stone, "The Revival of Narrative: Reflections on a New Old History," *Past and Present* 85 (1979), pp. 3–24 (reprinted in idem, *Past and the Present Revisited*, pp. 74–96).

3. Friedman, *"Yeshivot hayishuv hayashan"*; idem, *Hevrah bemashber legitimaziyah.*

4. Elior, *"Almah yafah,"* p. 46.

5. Sered, *Religious Lives*, p. 141.

6. Jeff Halper, *Between Redemption and Revival: The Jewish Yishuv of Jerusalem in the Nineteenth Century* (Boulder, Colo., 1991).

7. Yehoshua Kaniel, *"Hayahasim beyn haSepharadim veha'Ashkenazim bayishuv hayashan biYrushalayim (mehityashevut talmidei haGra ad shenot ha-80 shel hame'ah ha19)"* (M.A. thesis, Bar-Ilan University, Ramat-Gan, 1970); Salmon, *"Hayishuv ha'Ashkenazi"*; Margalit Shilo, *"Nidbakh hadash bikhtivat toledot hayishuv,"* *Cathedra* 58 (1990), pp. 60–69.

8. Shilo, *"Takkanot Yerushalayim."*

9. Sabar, *"Livhinat hashoni,"* p. 93.

10. Sherry B. Ortner, "Is Female to Male as Nature Is to Culture?" in M. Z. Rosaldo and L. Lamphere (eds.), *Woman, Culture and Society* (Stanford, Calif., 1974), pp. 67–87.

11. Vimala Jayanti, "Women in Mea Shearim: A Different Reality" (M.A. thesis, Hebrew University of Jerusalem, 1982).

12. Yisra'el Bartal, *"Hayezi'ah min hahomot—hitpashetut hayashan o reshit hehadash?"* in: Hagit Lavski (ed.), *Yerushalayim batoda'ah uva'asiyah hazionit* (Jerusalem, 1989), pp. 17–34.

13. Ben-Arieh, *Jerusalem . . . the New City*, pp. 413ff.; Friedman, *Hevrah bemashber legitimaziyah.*

14. Rachel Shar'abi, *Hayishuv haSepharadi biYrushalayim beshilhei hatekufah ha'Uthmanit, 1893–1914* (Tel Aviv, 1989).

15. Ben-Arieh, *Jerusalem . . . the New City*, pp. 413ff.; Kaniel, *"Memadei hayeridah."*

16. Letter from America, *Moriah*, no. 84, May 16, 1911; for emigration to South Africa see *Haherut*, August 19, 1913; Australia: *Moriah*, no. 115, September 1, 1911.

17. *Moriah*, May 5, 1911, pp. 2–3.

18. *Moriah*, October 16, 1911, p. 2; emigration from Safed: ibid., May 2, 1911; from Hebron: ibid., May 16, 1911.

19. Rachel [Bluwstein], *Shirei Rachel* (Tel Aviv, 1970), p. 59.

20. Ibid., p. 209.

21. Almog, *Hazabar*, pp. 49–50.

22. David Shim'oni, *Sefer ha'idilyot* (Tel Aviv, 1964), p. 256. The poem is dated 1926–1935.

23. Shlomo Avineri, *Hara'yon hazioni legvanau* (Tel Aviv, 1980), pp. 13–24.

24. *Havazelet*, 12 Heshvan [5]642 [November 4, 1881].

25. Chatterjee, "Their Own Words?" p. 205.

Bibliography

Archives

Beit HaMe'iri Archive, Safed
Bibliotheca Rosenthalia, University of Amsterdam, Amsterdam
Central Archive for the History of the Jewish People, Jerusalem (CAHJP)
Central Zionist Archives, Jerusalem (CZA)
Dov Genechovsky, Personal Archive, Jerusalem
Gaster Papers, Mocatta Library, University of London, London (Gaster Papers)
Greater London Record Office, London
Hartley Library, Southampton University, Highfield, Southampton, England (South-
    ampton Archives)
Haus-Hof und Staatsarchiv, Vienna, Austria
Jews' College Library, Montefiore's Papers, London (Montefiore Archives)
Municipal Archives, Jerusalem
National and Hebrew University Library Archives (NHUL), Jerusalem

Books and Papers

Abarbanell, Nitza. *Havah velilit.* Ramat-Gan, 1994.
Adams, Steven. *The Arts and Crafts Movement.* London, 1987.
Adlerblum, Nima. *Memoirs of Childhood: An Approach to Jewish Philosophy*, ed. Els
    Bendheim. Northvale, N.J., and Jerusalem, 1999.
——. "Sarah Beyla Hirshensohn," in Eliyahu Jung, ed., *Noterei moreshet —
    Parashiyot hayim*, pp. 81–111. Jerusalem, 1968.
Agnon, Shmuel Yosef. "Tehilla," trans. I. M. Lask, in *Hebrew Short Stories: An An-
    thology*, selected by S. Y. Penueli and A. Ukhmani, vol. 1, pp. 24–52. Tel Aviv, 1965.
Ahiman, Hanokh. "*Ha'azarot bevet hakeneset*," in Yeshayahu Ilan, Avraham Stahl,
    and Zvi Shteiner, eds., *Mikdash me'at: Kovez ma'amarim bish'elot izuv penim shel
    batei keneset*, pp. 57–62. Jerusalem, 1975.
Albisetti, James C. "The Feminization of Teaching in the Nineteenth Century: A
    Comparative perspective." *History of Education* 22/1–4 (1993), pp. 253–263.
Alexander, Franz G., and Sheldon T. Selesnick. *The History of Psychiatry: An Evolu-
    tion of Psychiatric Thought and Practice from Prehistoric Times to the Present.* New
    York, 1966.
Alexander[-Fraser], Tamar. Introduction in Sha'ul Angel-Malachi, *Hayei Yerusha-
    layim, misipurei ha'ir*, pp. 17–44. Jerusalem, 1987.
——. *Ma'aseh ahuv vahezi: Hasipur ha'ammami shel yehudei Sefarad.* Jerusalem,
    2000.
Alfasi, Yizhak. *Mimizrah shemesh: Toledoteihem shel hamishim mime'orei orot
    hamizrah.* Jerusalem, [1990].
Almog, Oz. *Hazabar — dyokan.* Tel Aviv, 1997.
Alper, Rivkah. "*Ekh nirkam hasefer.*" *Devar hapo'elet* 22/10 (1956), p. 275.
——. *Korot mishpahah ahat.* Tel Aviv, 1967.
Altbauer, Moshe. "*Iggerot haRav Yehoshua Zelig Hakohen mishnat [5]613 al odot aliy-
    ato arzah.*" *Cathedra* 1 (1976), pp. 109–110.

Angel-Malachi, Sha'ul. *Beterem reshit — misipurei Yerushalayim, mehayyei hakehilah hasefaradit biYrushalayim beme'ah hashanim ha'aharonot.* Jerusalem, 1977.

———. *Hayei Yerushalayim, misipurei ha'ir.* Jerusalem, 1987.

Anikster, Rivkah Lipa. *Kunteres zekher olam.* Jerusalem, 1891. [Shilo-Hakol Hanashi, pp. 91–125.]

Ardener, Edwin. "Belief and the Problem of Women," in Shirley Ardener, ed., *Perceiving Women,* pp. 1–17. New York, 1975.

Ariel, Nehama. "Ishah behanhagat hayishuv hayashan bame'ah ha19: Harabanit Sonya Diskin, harabanit miBrisk." *Talelei Orot* 2 (1990), pp. 41–64.

Ariel, Rachel. "Hamilhamah bamisyon bir'i Haherut 1913–1914." Seminar paper, Bar-Ilan University, Ramat-Gan, 1994.

Arzi, Avraham. "Hag rosh hodesh." *Mahanayim* 90 (1964), pp. 12–15.

Ashkenazi, Shlomo. *Ha'ishah be'aspaklariyat hadorot.* Tel Aviv, 1943.

———. "Ha'ishah hayehudiyah bameshek uvakalkalah." *Mahanayim* 2 (1992), pp. 172–183.

Auerbach, Eliyahu. *Me'erez ha'av le'erez avot: Harofe hayehudi harishon beHeyfah.* Jerusalem, 1977.

Avineri, Shlomo. *Hara'yon hazioni legvanau.* Tel Aviv, 1980.

Avisar, Oded, ed. *Sefer Hevron.* Jerusalem, 1970.

Avishur, Yizhak. *Hahatunah hayehudit beBaghdad uvivnoteha.* Haifa, 1990.

Avitzur, Shmuel. "Hamelakhah vehata'asiyah hayehudit biYrushalayim lifnei kom hamedinah mishilhei hatekufah ha'uthmanit ve'ad tom hamandat habriti," in Friedman et al., eds., *Perakim betoledot hayishuv hayehudi biYrushalayim,* vol. 2, pp. 266–285.

———. *Haroshet hama'aseh: Kovez letoledot hata'asiyah ba'arez.* Tel Aviv, 1974.

———. *Hayei yom yom be'Erez Yisra'el.* Tel Aviv, 1973.

———. "Hayei yom yom umelakhot masortiyot ba'ir ha'atikah." *Ariel* 57/58 (1988), pp. 57–58, 77–92.

Bailey, Clinton. "Bedouin Weddings in Sinai and the Negev." *Mehkerei hamerkaz leheker hafolklor* 4 (1974), pp. 105–132.

Baker, Mark. "The Voice of the Deserted Jewish Woman, 1867–1870." *Jewish Social Studies: History, Culture, Society,* new series 2/1 (1995), pp. 98–123.

Bakon, Brenda. "Benot Zelofhad vesivlah shel Rayna Batyah," in Margalit Shilo, ed., *Lihyot ishah yehudiyah,* pp. 287–293. Jerusalem, 2001.

Bar-Asher, Shalom. "The Jews of North Africa and the Land of Israel in the Eighteenth and Nineteenth Centuries: The Reversal in Attitude toward Aliyah," in Lawrence A. Hoffman, ed., *The Land of Israel: Jewish Perspectives,* pp. 297–315. Notre Dame, Ind., 1986.

Barclay, Sara Mathilda. *Hadji in Syria, or Three Years in Jerusalem.* Philadelphia, 1858.

Bar El, Yaron, and Nissim Levi. "Reshitah shel harefu'ah hamodernit be'arei haGalil, 1860–1900." *Cathedra* 54 (1989), pp. 96–106.

Barkan, Yosef. "Letoledot melon Kaminitz biYrushalayim." *Ariel* 119–120 (1997), pp. 65–72.

Barnai, Ya'akov. "Ha'edah hama'aravit biYrushalayim bame'ah ha19," in Yehudah Ben Porat, Ben-Zion Yehoshua, and Aharon Kedar, eds., *Perakim betoledot hayishuv hayehudi biYrushalayim,* pp. 129–140. Jerusalem, 1973.

———. *Yehudei Erez Yisra'el bame'ah ha19 bahasut pekidei Kushta.* Jerusalem, 1982.

Bar On, Ya'arah. *"Milhemet haminim bikehilah mikzo'it — meyalledot umeyalledim bePariz shel hame'ah hasheva esreh."* Historiyah 3 (1999), pp. 79–102.

Bartal, Yisra'el. *"Al demutah harav-adatit shel hahevrah hayehudit biYrushalayim bame'ah ha19."* Pe'amim 57 (1994), pp. 114–124.

———. *Galut ba'arez — Yishuv Erez Yisra'el beterem Ziyonut.* Essays and studies. Jerusalem, 1995.

———. *"Hayezi'ah min hahomot — hitpashetut hayashan o reshit hehadash?"* in Hagit Lavski, ed., *Yerushalayim batoda'ah uva'asiyah hazionit,* pp. 17–34. Jerusalem, 1989.

———. *"'Yishuv yashan' ve'yishuv hadash' — hadimuy vehamezi'ut."* Cathedra 2 (1977), pp. 3–19.

Bartal, Yisra'el, and Yeshayahu Gafni, eds., *Eros, erusin ve'isurin — Miniyut umishpahah bahistoriyah.* Jerusalem, 1998.

Bartal, Yisra'el, and Yosef Kaplan. *"Aliyat aniyim me'Amsterdam le'Erez Yisra'el bereshit hame'ah hasheva-esreh."* Shalem 6 (1992), pp. 175–193.

Bartlett, S. C. *From Egypt to Palestine through Sinai: The Wilderness and the South Country.* New York, 1977 [1874].

Bartura, Avraham. *Belev kashuv — Toledot R. Eliezer Bergman ish Yerushalayim.* Jerusalem, 1983.

———. *Yerushalayim be'eynei ro'eha — Toledot batei hamahaseh la'aniyim vehakhnasat orehim al Har Ziyon.* Jerusalem, 1970.

Bar-Yakar, Dov Nathan. *"A[doni] A[vi] u-M[ori] R. Ya'akov be-R. Zevi Netz Z"l."* Luach Yerushalayim, twelfth year (1952), pp. 290–301.

Barzilai, Yehoshua. *"Besha'arei Yerushalayim,"* in Yafah Berlovitz, ed., *E'eberah-na ba'arez — Masa'ot beErez Yisra'el shel anshei ha'aliyah harishonah,* pp. 81–91. Tel Aviv, 1992.

———. *"Mikhtavim me'Erez Yisra'el IV."* HaShiloah 24 (1911), pp. 270–276.

Bashan, Eliezer. *"Al yahasam shel yehudei Maroko bame'ot ha18–19 lehovat ha'aliyah leErez Yisra'el,"* in H. Z. Hirschberg, ed., *Vatikin,* pp. 35–46.

———. *"Hakesharim hamasortiyim beyn yehudei hamizrah layishuv hayehudi beErez Yisra'el."* Pe'amim 6 (1979), pp. 15–22.

———. *"Helkah shel ha'ishah hayehudiyah behayei hakalkalah shel yehudei zefon Afrikah."* Mikedem umiyam 1 (1981), pp. 67–84.

———. *Sefer mimizrah shemesh ad mevo'o: Perakim betoledot yehudei hamizrah vehaMagreb: Hevrah vekhalkalah.* Lod, 1996.

———. *"Zikatam shel yehudei haMagreb vehatikvah hameshihit bekhitvei nozerim beyn hame'ot ha17 veha20."* Bar-Ilan Yearbook 14–15 (1977), pp. 160–175.

Baskin, Judith R. *"Hinukh nashim yehudiyot vehaskalatan biymei habeynayim be'arzot ha'Islam vehaNazrut."* Pe'amim 82 (2000), pp. 31–49.

———. *"Some Parallels in the Education of Medieval Jewish and Christian Women."* Jewish History 5/1 (1991), pp. 41–51.

Be'er, Haim. *Havalim.* Tel Aviv, 1998.

Ben-Ami, Yissachar. *"Minhagei herayon veleidah bekerev haSefaradim ve'edot hamizrah."* Yeda Am 26 1995, pp. 37–49.

Ben-Arieh, Yehoshua. *Erez Yisra'el bame'ah ha19: Giluyah mehadash.* Jerusalem, 1970.

———. *"Hanof hayishuvi shel Erez Yisra'el erev hahityashvut hazionit,"* in Lissak et al., eds., *Toledot hayishuv hayehudi be'Erez Yisra'el,* pp. 122–138.

——. *Ir bir'i tekufah: Yerushalayim hahadashah bereshitah.* Jerusalem, 1979.

——. *Jerusalem in the 19th Century: Emergence of the New City* (slightly abridged English translation of previous item.) Jerusalem and New York, 1986.

——. *Jerusalem in the 19th Century: The Old City.* Jerusalem and New York. 1986.

——. *Jerusalem in the 19th Century: The Old City.* Jerusalem and New York, 1984.

Ben Arzi, Yosi. *"Ha'im shinu heker nashim umigdar et yahasenu lahavanat hahistoriyah shel ha'aliyah vehahityashevut?"* in Margalit Shilo, Ruth Kark, and Galit Hasan-Rokem, eds., *Ha'ivriyot hahadashot—Nashim bayishuv uvaZiyonut bir'i hamigdar,* pp. 26–44. Jerusalem, 2002.

——. *"Haperek hanozri betoledot Har Tuv."* Nofim 9–10 (1978), pp. 14–144.

——. *"Har Tuv—moshavah niskahah beharei Yehudah."* Ofakim bege'ografiyah 3 (1977), pp. 123–140.

Ben-Avraham, N. *Sipurim Yerushalmiyim.* Jerusalem, 1994.

Benayahu, Meir. *"Ha'aliyah leMeron,"* in Eli Schiller, ed., *Sefer Ze'ev Vilnay,* vol. 2, pp. 326–330. Jerusalem, 1987.

——. *"Hanhagot mekubalei Zefat beMeron."* Sefunot 6 (1962), pp. 11–40.

——. *"Sefer takanot leminhagim shel Yerushalayim."* Kiryat Sefer 22 (1945), pp. 262–265.

Benbassa, Esther. "Education for Jewish Girls in the East: A Portrait of the Galata School in Istanbul, 1879–1912." *Studies in Contemporary Jewry* 9 (1993), pp. 163–173.

Ben-Haggai, Y. *"Aniyim vekabzanim biYrushalayim ha'atikah milifnei dor."* Yeda Am 10 (1965), pp. 108–110.

——. *"Purim ezel benei adot hamizrah biYrushalayim."* Mahanayim 77 (1963), pp. 78–81.

——. *"Shabbat ezel adot hamizrah biYrushalayim ha'atikah."* Mahanayim 85–86 (1964), pp. 186–189.

Benjamin, Yonatan. *"Kegan elohim poreah: Ketubot me'utarot meErez Yisra'el."* Rimonim 4 (1994), pp. 44–49.

Ben Na'eh, Yaron. *"Siyu'ah shel kehilat Istanbul liyhudei Erez Yisra'el bame'ah hasheva-esreh ukshareha imam."* Cathedra 92 (1999), pp. 65–106.

Ben Petahyah, Avraham. *"Reshit hinukh haMizrahi be'Erez Yisra'el,"* in Y. L. Hacohen Maimon, ed., *Yovel haMizrahi,* pp. 189–199. Jerusalem, 1952.

Benvenisti, David. *Yehudei Saloniki badorot ha'aharonim: Halikhot hayim, masoret vehevrah.* Jerusalem, 1973.

Benvenisti, Meron. *Ir hamenuhot—Batei ha'almin shel Yerushalayim.* Jerusalem, 1990.

Ben Ya'akov, Avraham. *Minhagei yehudei Bavel badorot ha'aharonim,* 3 vols. Jerusalem, 1993.

Ben-Ya'akov, Michal. *"Olot le'Erez Yisra'el—Defusei hagirah shel nashim mizefon Afrikah leErez Yisra'el bame'ah hatesha-esreh,"* in Margalit Shilo, Ruth Kark, and Galit Hasan-Rokem, eds., *Ha'ivriyot hahadashot—Nashim bayishuv uvaZiyonut bir'i hamigdar,* pp. 63–83. Jerusalem, 2002.

Ben-Yehuda, Hemdah. *Ben Yehuda—Hayav umif'alo.* Jerusalem, 1940.

Ben-Zvi, Rahel Yanna'it. *Anu olim.* Jerusalem, 1969.

Ben-Zvi, Yizhak. *Zihkronot ureshumot mehane'urim ad 1920.* Jerusalem, 1969.

Berenson, Zevi. *"Pirkei hayyim vezikhronot,"* in Aharon Barak and Hayyim Berenson, eds., *Sefer Berenson,* vol. 1, pp. 29–81. Jerusalem, 1997.

Bergman, Eliezer and Syla. *Se'u harim shalom—Mikhtevei masa va'aliyah 1834–1836.* Jerusalem, n.d.

Berlovitz, Yaffa. *E'ebra-na ba'arez-Masa'ot beErez Yisra'el shel anshei ha'aliyah hari-shonah.* Tel-Aviv, 1992.

Berman, Shim'on. *Mas'ot Shim'on — Erez Yisra'el 1870,* trans. from Yiddish by David Niv. Jerusalem, 1980.

Bernstein, Devorah. *"Heker nashim bahistoriographiyah haYisre'elit: Nekudot moza, kivunim hadashim vetovanot shebaderekh,"* in Margalit Shilo, Ruth Kark, and Galit Hasam-Rokem, eds., *Ha'ivriyot hahadashot — Nashim bayishuv uvaZiyonut bir'i hamigdar,* pp. 7–25. Jerusalem, 2002.

——. *Ishah beErez Yisra'el: Hashe'ifah leshivyon bitkufat hayishuv.* Tel Aviv, 1987.

Berrol, Selma. "Class or Ethnicity: The Americanized German Jewish Woman and the Middle-Class Sisters in 1895." *Jewish Social Studies* 47 (1985), pp. 21–32.

Bet Halevi, Yisra'el David. *Toledot yehudei Kalish.* Tel Aviv, 1961.

Biber, Mordecai. *"Ha'almah miLudmir." Reshumot* 2 1946, pp. 69–76.

Bilu, Yoram. "The Inner Limits of Communitas: A Covert Dimension of Pilgrimage Experience." *Ethos* 16 1988, pp. 302–325.

——. *"Pulhanei kedoshim va'aliyot limkomot kedoshim ketofa'ah universalit,"* in Rivkah Gonen, ed., *El kivrei zadikim — Aliyot likvarim vehilulot be Yisra'el,* pp. 11–25. Jerusalem, 1998.

——. *"Rega dahus shel ahavah gavrit bil'adit." Haaretz,* May 23, 1997, p. D1.

Binyamin, Ben Zion, ed. *MeHodu liYrushalayim: Sipur shenei masa'ot meHodu leErez Yisra'el.* Jerusalem, 1993.

Bir, Aharon. *"Kever Shim'on hazadik biYrushalayim." Mahanayim* 116 (1968), pp. 102–105.

——. *"Mosedot torah utfilah beyn hahomot,"* in Mordechai Na'or, ed., *Harova hayehudi ba'ir ha'atikah biYrushalayim,* pp. 108–183. Jerusalem, 1987.

Blau, Moshe. *Al homotayikh Yerushalayim.* Benei Berak, 1967.

Blumberg, Arnold. *A View from Jerusalem: The Consular Diary of James and Elizabeth Ann Finn.* London and Toronto, 1980.

[Bluwstein], Rachel. *Shirei Rachel.* Tel Aviv, 1970.

Bornstein-Makovetzky, Leah. *"Hamishpahah hayehudit be'Istanbul bame'ot ha-18 veha-19 kiyhidah kalkalit,"* in Bartal and Gafni, eds., *Eros, erusin ve'isurin,* pp. 305–334.

——. *"Nisu'in vegerushin bahevrah hayehudit be'Istanbul bame'ot hashemoneh-esreh vehatesha-esreh." Michael* 14 (Tel Aviv, 1997), pp. 139–167.

——. *"Pe'ilut hamisyon ha'Amerika'i bekerev yehudei Istanbul, Izmir veSaloniki bame'ah hatesha-esreh,"* in Minna Rosen, ed., *Yemei hasahar: Perakim betoledot hayehudim ba'Imperiyah ha'Othmanit,* pp. 273–310. Tel Aviv, 1996.

Braun-Rozovski, Nizah, and Karni A. S. Gavin. *"Hayav va'avodato shel Mendel John Diness: Zalam, misyoner, metif umesaper sipurim." Cathedra* 75 (1995), pp. 69–91.

Brawer, Michael Hakohen and Avraham Ya'akov. *Zihronot av uvno.* Jerusalem, 1966.

Brayer, Menachem M. *The Jewish Woman in Rabbinic Literature: A Psychological Perspective.* Hoboken, N.J., 1986.

Bridgewood, Ann. "Dancing the Jar: Girl's Dress at Turkish Cypriot Weddings," in Joanne B. Eicher, ed., *Dress and Ethnicity,* pp. 28–51. Oxford, 1995.

Bristow, Edward J. *Prostitution and Prejudice: The Jewish Fight against White Slavery, 1870–1939.* Oxford, 1982.

Bryant, Donna M., and Richard M. Clifford. "150 Years of Kindergarten: How Far Have We Gone?" *Early Childhood Research Quarterly* 7/2 (1992), pp. 147–154.

Buchman, Z. *"Hamilhamah bamisyon." Pirkei Hapo'el Haza'ir* 12 (1938), pp. 61–63.

Burke, Peter. "History of Events and the Revival of Narrative," in idem, ed., *New Perspectives on Historical Writing*, pp. 232–248. University Park, Pa., 1991.

Burla, Miriam. "*Ha'ziyara' bekever Rahel imenu: Pirkei zikhronot.*" *Bama'arakhah* 175 (1975), pp. 14–15.

Callen, Anthea. *Angel in the Studio: Women in the Arts and Crafts Movement, 1870–1914.* Great Britain, 1979.

Carlebach, Zvi Yosef. *Mikhtavim miYrushalayim.* Jerusalem, 1996.

Carmel, Alex. "*Letoledotav shel Johannes Frutiger, bankai biYrushalayim.*" *Cathedra* 48 (1988), pp. 49–72.

———. "*Pe'ilut hama'azamot beErez Yisra'el, 1878–1914,*" in Lissak et al., *Toledot hayishuv hayehudi beErez Yisra'el*, pp. 143–213.

Carpi, Daniel, and Moshe Rinot. "*Yoman mas'oteha shel morah yehudiyah miTrieste liYrushalayim, [5]617–[5]625.*" *Kevazim letoledot hahinukh hayehudi beYisra'el uvatefuzot* 1 (1982), pp. 115–159.

Chatterjee, Partha. "Their Own Words?" in Edward Said and Michael Sprinker, eds., *A Critical Reader*, pp. 194–220. Oxford, 1992.

Chelouche, Julia. *Ha'ez vehashorashim.* N.p., 1982.

Chinsky, Sarah, "*Rokemot hataharah miBezalel.*" *Teoriya uvikoret* 11 (1997), pp. 179–201.

Cohen, Amnon. *Yehudim be'veyt hamishpat hamuslemi: Hevrah, kalkalah ve'irgun kehilati biYrushalayim ha'Othmanit, Hame'ah hashemoneh esreh.* Jerusalem, 1996.

Cohen, Erik. "Pilgrimage and Tourism: Convergence and Divergence," in Alan Morinis, ed., *Sacred Journeys: The Anthropology of Pilgrimage*, pp. 47–61. London, 1992.

Cohen, Malkah. "*Yerushalayim vekabzaneha.*" *Yeda' Am* 21 (1982), pp. 121–122.

Cohen-Reiss, Ephraim. *Mizikhronot ish Yerushalayim.* Jerusalem, 1967.

Damer, G. L. Dawson. *Diary of a Tour in Greece, Turkey, Egypt and the Holy Land*, vol. 1, London 1841.

Davidson, Ephraim. "*Malbushei Shabbat uma'akhalei Shabbat.*" *Mahanayim* 85–86 (1964), pp. 158–165.

Davis, Eli, and David A. Frankel. *Hakame'a ha'ivri: Mikra'i, refu'i, kelali.* Jerusalem, 1995.

Davis, Nanette J. "Feminism, Deviance and Social Change," in Edward Sagarin, ed., *Deviance and Social Change*, pp. 247–276. London, 1977.

Davis, Natalie. "From Popular Religion to Religious Culture," in Steven Ozment, ed., *Reforming Europe: A Guide to Research*, pp. 321–341. St. Louis: Center for Reformation Research, 1982.

Della Pergola, Sergio. "Aliya and Other Jewish Migrations: Toward an Integrated Perspective." *Scripta Hierosolymitana* 30 (1986), pp. 172–209.

Dengler, Ian C. "The Turkish Woman in the Ottoman Empire: The Classical Age," in Lois Beck and Nikki Keddie, eds., *Women in the Moslem World*, pp. 229–244. Cambridge, Mass., 1978.

Devens, Carol. "'If We Get the Girls, We Get the Race': Missionary Education of Native American Girls." *Journal of World History* 3/2 (1992), pp. 219–237.

Dinaburg, Ben Zion. "*Me'arkhiono shel hehakham-bashi R. Hayim Avraham Gagin.*" *Me'assef Zion* 1 (1926), pp. 85–121.

Dingwell, Robert, Ann Rafferty, and Charles Webster. *An Introduction to the Social History of Nursing.* London, 1988.

Dror, Yuval. "*Hagerim harusiyim baGalil bereshit hame'ah ha'esrim.*" *Cathedra* 10 (1979), pp. 34–71.

Druyanov, Alter, and Shulamit Laskov, eds. *Ketavim letoledot Hibbat Zion veyishuv Erez Yisra'el*, vol. 3. Tel Aviv, 1984.

Duben, Alan, and Cem Behar. *Istanbul Households: Marriage, Family and Fertility, 1880–1910.* Cambridge, 1991.

Efrati, Natan. *Ha'edah haSefaradit biYrushalayim, [5]600–[5]677 (1840–1917).* Jerusalem, 2000.

———. *Mimashber letikvah — Hayishuv hayehudi bemilhemet ha'olam harishonah.* Jerusalem, 1991.

———. *Mishpahat Elyashar betokhekhei Yerushalayim.* Jerusalem, 1975.

Eicher, Joanne B., ed. *Dress and Ethnicity: Change across Space and Time.* Oxford, 1995.

El'azar, Ya'akov. *Diyur uklitah bayishuv hayashan, [5]602–[5]679.* Jerusalem, 1981.

———. *Harova hayehudi biYrushalayim ha'atikah.* Jerusalem, 1975.

Elboim-Dror, Rachel. *Hahinukh ha'ivri be'Erez Yisra'el*, 2 vols. Jerusalem, 1986.

Elhanani, Avraham Hayim. "*Hayei David Yellin.*" *Shevet va'am* 7 (1973), pp. 215–233.

———. *Ish vesiho.* Jerusalem, 1966.

Eliachar, Eliyahu. *Lihyot im yehudim.* Jerusalem, 1981.

Eliachar, Rachel. *Album mishpahti.* Jerusalem, 1990.

Eliachar, Ya'akov Sha'ul. *Responsa Benei Binyamin vekerev ish*, vol. 1. Jerusalem, 1876.

———, ed. *Sefer hatakanot vehaskamot minhagim hanohagim . . . Yerushalayim.* Jerusalem, 1883 [1969].

Eliade, Myrcia. *The Myth of the Eternal Return.* New York, 1954.

Eliav, Mordechai. *Ahavat Ziyon ve'anshei Hod — Yehudei Germaniyah veyishuv Erez Yisra'el bame'ah ha19.* Tel Aviv, 1971.

———. *Bahasut mamlekhet Austria 1849–1917.* Jerusalem, 1986.

———. "'*Bizhut nashim' — mekomah shel ha'ishah bema'amazei hanizur shel hamisyon haBriti biYrushalayim.*" *Cathedra* 76 (1995o, pp. 96–115.

———. *Britain and the Holy Land, 1838–1914: Selected Documents from the British Consulate in Jerusalem.* Jerusalem, 1996.

———. *Erez Yisra'el veyishuvah bame'ah ha19 1777–1917.* Jerusalem, 1978.

———. *Hahinukh hayehudi beGermaniyah biymei hahaskalah veha'emanzipaziyah.* Jerusalem, 1961.

———. *Hayishuv hayehudi be'Erez Yisra'el bir'i hamediniyut haGermanit.* Tel Aviv, 1973.

———. "*Masa liYrushalayim bishnat 5645.*" *Sinai* 50 (1970), pp. 140–166.

———. "*Mumar, ba'al teshuvah vehozer lesuro (parashat Shim'on Rosenthal).*" *Cathedra* 61 (1992), pp. 113–132.

———. "*Parashat Sarah Steinberg: Perek bema'avak hayishuv neged hamisyon.*" *Sinai* 64 (1969), pp. 78–91.

Elior, Rachel. "*Almah yafah she'ein lah eynayim?*" in David Yoel Ariel, Maya Leibovitz, and Yoram Mazor. *Barukh she'asani Ishah?* pp. 37–56. Tel Aviv, 1999.

Ellinson, Eliakim. *Ha'ishah vehamitzvot: Yalkut hore'ot hakhamenu ufiskei halakhot.* Jerusalem, 1974.

Elmaliah, Avraham. *Harishonim leZion, toledoteyhem u-f'ulatam.* Jerusalem, 1970.

———. "*Mehayei haSepharadim.*" *Hashiloah* 24. Odessa, 1911, pp. 260–269, 348–359.

Elzet, Yehudah. "*Inyenei tena'im vahatunah.*" *Reshumot* 1 (1925), pp. 353–362.

Engel, R. Shmuel. *Responsa* (in Hebrew), vol. 3. Yaroslav, 1926.

Epstein, Barukh. *Mekor Barukh.* Vilna, 1928.

Epstein, Louis M. *Sex Laws and Customs in Judaism.* New York, 1967.

Erlich, Hagai. *Mavo lahistoriyah shel hamizrah hatikhon ba'et hahadashah.* Tel Aviv, 1987.

———. *No'ar upolitikah baMizrah haTikhon: Dorot umashberei zehut.* Tel Aviv, 1998.

Etkes, Immanuel. *Lita biYrushalayim—Ha'ilit halamdanit beLita ukehilat haperushim biYrushalayim le'or iggerot umikhtavim shel R. Shemuel miKelm.* Jerusalem, 1991.

Ettinger, Mordechai Ze'ev. *Sefer ma'amar Mordechai (Responsa).* Jerusalem, 1968 (photogr. repr. of 1852 ed.).

Even-Or-Orenstein, Shmuel. "*Hanashim bemishpahat Orenstein.*" *Leveit Avotam* 3–4 (1990), pp. 34–57; 5–6 (1990), pp. 2–32.

Everett, S. "Theory of Migration." *Demography* 3/1 (1996), pp. 51–52.

Ewing, William. *Our Jewish Missions,* vol. 1: *The Holy Land and Glasgow.* Edinburgh, 1913.

Feiner, Shmuel. "*Ha'ishah hayehudiyah hamodernit: Mikreh mivhan beyahasei hahaskalah vehamodernah.*" *Zion* 58 (1993), pp. 453–499.

Feinsod-Sukenik, Hasya. *Pirkei gan: Zikhronot uma'as.* Tel Aviv, 1966.

[Feinstein], Toive Pesil. *Sefer zikhron Eliyahu.* Jerusalem, 1895. [See also Shilo, *Hakol Hanash,* pp. 164–262.]

Feuchtwanger, Naomi. *Bet Ohel Moshe: Me'ah shanah lashekhunah ulvet hakeneset shelah.* Jerusalem, 1984.

Finn, Elizabeth Ann. *Reminiscences of Mrs. Finn.* London and Edinburgh, 1929.

Finn, James. *Stirring Times, or Records from Jerusalem Consular Chronicles of 1853 to 1856,* vols. 1, 2. London, 1878.

First Marriages: Patterns and Determinants. New York: United Nations, 1988.

Fishelov, Dov. "*Tehila aduyah bezemah, amusah be'oz: Halakhah uma'aseh befarshanut hasifrut.*" *Alpayim* 11 (1995), pp. 129–148.

Fisher Roller, Alyse. "In Their Own Words: The Literature of Ultra-Orthodox Jewish Women." M.A. thesis, Hebrew University of Jerusalem, 1996.

Frager, Ruth A. *Sweatshop Strife, Class Ethnicity and Gender.* Toronto, 1993.

Franco, Rahamim Yosef. *Responsa Sha'arei Rahamim.* Jerusalem, 1902.

———. *Sefer Sha'arei Yerushalayim.* Jerusalem, 1881.

Frankl, Ludwig August. *Nach Jerusalem! In Palästina.* Leipzig, 1858.

Freeze, ChaeRan Y. *Jewish Marriage and Divorce in Imperial Russia.* Hanover, N.H., 2002.

Freidin, Israel. "*Hevrot hesed bayishuv hayashan ha'Ashkenazi biYrushalayim bame'ah ha19.*" M.A. thesis, Hebrew University of Jerusalem, 1987.

Freiman, Susan. "*Nashim yehudiyot italkiyot keyozerot tashmishei kedushah.*" *Motar* 5 (1997), pp. 97–102.

Freimann, Avraham Hayim. *Seder kidushin venisu'in.* Jerusalem, 1964.

———. "*Takanot Yerushalayim,*" in Izhak Baer, Yehoshua Gutman, and Moshe Schwaba, eds., *Sefer Dinaburg,* pp. 206–214. Jerusalem, 1949.

Freimann, Nahum Dov. *Sefer hazikaron haYerushalmi.* Jerusalem, 1913.

Friedhaber, Zevi. "*Hamahol bayishuv hayehudi biYrushalayim lifnei milhemet ha'olam harishonah.*" *Jerusalem Studies in Jewish Folklore* 11–12 (1989–1990), pp. 139–151.

———. *Hamahol be'Am Yisra'el.* Tel Aviv, 1984.

Friedman, Menahem. *Hevrah bemashber legitimaziyah — Hayishuv hayashan haAshkenazi 1900–1914.* Jerusalem, 2001.

———. "*Yeshivot hayishuv hayashan beshilhei hatekufah haUthmanit — mosadot o batei ulpena?*" in Immanuel Etkes and Yosef Salmon, eds., *Perakim betoledot hahevrah hayehudit biymei habeynayim uva'et hahadashah*, pp. 369–378. Jerusalem, 1980.

Friedman, Menahem, eds. *Perakim betoledot hayishuv hayehudi biYrushalayim*, vol. 2. Jerusalem, 1976.

Frimmer, Dov. "*Ilot gerushin ekev hitnahagut bilti musarit . . .*" Ph.D. dissertation, The Hebrew University of Jerusalem, 1980.

Frumkin, Aryeh Leib. *Masa Even Shmuel: Masa le'erez hakodesh bishnat 5631.* Petah Tikvah, 1979.

———. "*Sipur hathalat yishuv ha'Ashkenazim hanikra'im Perushim.*" *Me'asef Zion* 2 (1927), pp. 128–149.

———. *Toledot hakhmei Yerushalayim*, 4 vols. Jerusalem, 1969.

Frumkin, Gad. *Derekh shofet biYrushalayim.* Tel Aviv, 1955.

Fuchs, Ron. "*Habayit ha'aravi be'Erez Yisra'el: Iyun mehudash.*" *Cathedra* 90 (1999), pp. 53–86.

Furst, Rachel. "Red Strings: A Modern Case of Charms," in Micha D. Halpern and Chana Safrai, eds., *Jewish Legal Writings by Women*, pp. 259–277. Jerusalem, 1998.

Gamlieli, Nissim Binyamin. *Ahavat Teiman: Hashirah ha'amamit haTeimanit: Shirat hanashim.* Tel Aviv, 1979.

———. "*Hayei ha'ishah hayehudiyah beTeiman uma'amadah hahevrati.*" *Tema* 6 (1998), pp. 133–149.

Ga'on, Moshe David. "*Moshe Montefiore veda'agato legoral benei adat hayehudim hama'aravim biYrushalayim.*" *Minhah le'Avraham* (Jerusalem, 1959), pp. 176–182.

———. *Yehudei hamizrah beErez Yisra'el*, 2 vols. Jerusalem, 1928.

Gartner, Aryeh. "*Hahagirah hahamonit shel yehudei Eiropah 1881–1914*," in Avigdor Shin'an, ed., *Hagirah vehityashevut beYisra'el uva'amim*, pp. 343–384. Jerusalem, 1982.

Gat, Ben-Zion. *Hayishuv hayehudi be'Erez Yisra'el, 1840–1881.* Jerusalem, 1963 (photogr. repr. 1974).

Gavish, Galyah. *Nizanei ta'asiyah biYrushalayim.* Brochure, Old Yishuv Museum. Jerusalem, n.d.

Gellis, Ya'akov. *Midemuyot Yerushalayim.* Jerusalem, 1962.

———. *Minhagei Erez Yisra'el halakhot vahalikhot, dinim uminhagim shenahagu lefihem benei Erez Yisra'el bekhol hadorot vehazemanim umehem hanehugim ad hayom.* Jerusalem, 1968.

———. *Shiv'im shanah biYrushalayim: Toledot hayyav shel . . . Rabbenu Shmuel Salant.* Jerusalem, 1960.

Genechovsky, Dov. *Misipurei hahevrah hagevohah ve'od me'ah sipurim yerushalmiyim.* Jerusalem, 1993.

———. *Sipurim Yerushalmiyim.* Jerusalem, 1989.

Geremek, Bronislaw. *Poverty: A History.* Oxford and Cambridge, Mass., 1994.

Gerlitz, Menahem Mendel, ed. *Sefer mara de'ar'a Yisra'el: Masekhet hayav shel haga'on hakadhosh, raban umoshi'an shel Yisra'el, Maran Yosef Hayim Sonnenfeld.* Jerusalem, 1980.

Getz, Menachem. *Kakh nifrezu hahomot, Kakh hem hayu.* Jerusalem, 1981.

——, ed. *Lesha'ah uledorot: Osef keruzim umoda'ot,* vol. 2. Jerusalem, 1971.

Gidney, W. T. *The History of the London Society for Promoting Christianity amongst the Jews (1808–1908).* London, 1908.

Gid'oni-Friedland, Alizah. *Massa'ot el he'avar.* Mahanayim, 1989.

Gilat, Yisra'el Zevi. *"Al ma'amad ha'em bezikah liyladeha—beyn dinei haTorah lamishpat hanoheg beYisra'el,"* in Aharon Barak and Menashe Shava, eds., *Minhah leYizhak.* pp. 167–188. Jerusalem, 1999.

——. *"Hayahasim shebeyn horim viyladim bamishpat ha'Ivri—zekhuyot vehovot."* Ph.D. dissertation, Bar-Ilan University, Ramat-Gan, 1994.

Ginat, Shalom. *"Pe'ilut hahevrah haLondonit lekidum hanazrut beyn hayehudim."* M.A. thesis, Haifa University, 1986.

Ginzburg, Mordechai Aaron. *Devir,* vol. 1. Warsaw, 1884.

Glambek, Ingeborg. "One of the Age's Noblest Cultural Movements: On the Theoretical Basis for the Arts and Crafts Movement." *Scandinavian Journal of Design History* 1 (1991), pp. 47–76.

Glazer, Mark. "The Dowry as Capital Accumulation among the Sephardic Jews of Istanbul, Turkey." *International Journal of Middle East Studies* 10 (1979), pp. 373–380.

Glenn, Susan A. *Daughters of the Shtetl: Life and Labor in the Immigrant Generation.* Ithaca, N.Y., 1990.

Glick, Shmuel. *Hahinukh bir'i hahok vehahalakhah.* Jerusalem, 1999.]

Glückel of Hameln. *The Life of Glückel of Hameln, 1646–1724, Written by Herself,* trans. and ed. Beth-Zion Abrahams. London, 1962.

Goitein, S. D. *A Mediterranean Society,* vol. 3: *The Family.* Berkeley, Calif., 1978.

Goldberg, Harvey E. "Family and Community in Sephardic North Africa: Historical and Anthropological Perspectives," in Kraemer, ed., *The Jewish Family.*

Goldberg, Ya'akov. *"Nisu'ei hayehudim bePolin hayeshanah beda'at hakahal shel tekufat hahaskalah."* *Gal'ed* 4–5 (1978), pp. 25–33.

Goodman, Philip and Avi. "R. Simchah Yaniver Diskin" (in Hebrew). *Ariel* 100–101 (1998), pp. 34–39.

Goodman, Philip and Hanna. *The Jewish Marriage Anthology.* Philadelphia, 1965.

Goodrich-Freer, Adela. *Inner Jerusalem.* London, 1904.

Goodwin, Godfrey. *The Private World of Ottoman Women.* London, 1997.

Goody, Jack. *The Oriental, the Ancient and the Primitive: Systems of Marriage and the Family in the Pre-industrial Societies of Eurasia.* Cambridge, 1990.

Graetz, Naomi. *Silence Is Deadly: Judaism Confronts Wife Beating.* Northvale, N.J., 1998.

Graetz, Zvi. *Darkhei hahistoriyah hayehudit.* Essays and studies, trans. from German. Jerusalem, 1969.

Grayevsky, Pinehas. *Benot Zion viYrushalayim.* Jerusalem, 2000.

—— [Ben Ya'ir]. *Eshet hayil hageveret Gitel Dinovitz.* Jerusalem, 1939.

——. *Zikhron lahovevim harishonim,* vols. 1–2. Jerusalem, 1927–1929 (repr. Jerusalem, 1992–1994).

——. *Ziyun lekever Rahel imenu—Miginzei Yerushalayim.* Jerusalem, 1932.

Greenberg, Blu. "Woman," in Arthur A. Cohen and Paul Mendes-Flohr, eds., *Contemporary Religious Thought,* pp. 1039–1053. New York and London, 1987.

Grossman, Avraham. *Hasidot umoredot: Nashim yehudiyot be'Eiropah biymei habeinayim.* Jerusalem, 2001.

———. *"Hazikah beyn halakhah vekhalkalah bema'amad ha'ishah hayehudiyah be'Ashkenaz hakedumah,"* in Menachem Ben-Sassoon, ed., *Dat vekhalkalah: Yahasei Gomelin,* pp. 139–160. Jerusalem, 1995.

Grossman, Eliezer Yehezkel. *Kovez degel hazahav, "Der Goldener Fahn."* N.p., n.d. [1991?].

Gruenbaum, Avraham. *"'Heder habanot' uvanot beheder habanim beMizrah Eiropah,"* in Rivkah Feldhai and Immanuel Etkes, eds., *Hinukh vehistoriyah,* pp. 297–303. Jerusalem, 1999.

Gurock, Jeffrey S. "Influences on the Lower East Side, 1900–1910," in Todd M. Endelman, ed., *Jewish Apostasy in the Modern World,* pp. 255–271. New York, 1987.

Hadad, Moshe David. *Sefer ma'amar Ester.* Jerba, 1946.

Hagalili, Yosef. *"Ma'amadah shel ha'ishah batenu'ah hahasidit,"* in idem, *Hashomerim laboker,* pp. 155–160. Meron, 1992.

Hakohen, Dov. *"Ha'aliyah me'Izmir bame'ah ha19."* Seminar paper, Hebrew University of Jerusalem, 1991.

Hakohen, Menachem. *Sefer hayei adam: Kelulot.* Jerusalem, 1986.

Hakohen, Mordechai. *Hakotel hama'aravi.* Ramat-Gan, 1968.

Halevi, Shoshanah. *Parashiyot betoledot hayishuv.* Jerusalem, 1989.

———. *Sifrei Yerushalayim harishonim [5]601–[5]651.* Jerusalem, 1976.

Halper, Jeff. *Between Redemption and Revival: The Jewish Yishuv of Jerusalem in the Nineteenth Century.* Boulder, Colo., 1991.

Halperin, Sarah. *"Al haperushim hasoterim lasipur 'Tehilla' leSh. Y. Agnon,"* in Dov Rapel, *Mehkarim bamikra uvahinukh mugashim liProf. Moshe Arend,* pp. 236–258. Jerusalem, 1996.

Hamburger, Hayim. *Sheloshah olamot,* vols. 1–3. Jerusalem, 1939–1946.

Hanani, Yisra'el. *"Po'alim uva'alei melakhah biYrushalayim."* *Yerushalayim* 3 (1951), pp. 160–184.

Harari, Yehudit. *Beyn hakeramim,* 2 vols. Tel Aviv, 1947.

———. *Ishah va'em beYisra'el mitekufat haTanakh ve'ad he'asor limdinat Yisra'el.* Tel Aviv, 1959.

Hareven, Tamara K. "The History of a Family as an Interdisciplinary Field," in Theodore Rabb and Robert Rothberg, eds., *The Family in History: Interdisciplinary Essays,* pp. 211–226. New York, 1973.

Harlap, Amiram. *Batei keneset beYisra'el miymei kedem ve'ad yamenu.* Tel Aviv, 1985.

Haver, Charlotte. "Vom Schtetl in die Stadt." *Zeitschrift für Geschichte und Kultur der Juden* 5 (1995), pp. 331–358.

Hayat, Shim'on. *"Te'udot hadashot al hayishuv hayehudi biYrushalayim batekufah haUthmanit."* *Sinai* 83 (1978), pp. 177–180.

Hayyim, Avraham, ed. *"Mekorot ute'udot letoledot ha'edah hasefaradit biYrushalayim ha'Uthmanit."* *Shevet va'am* 7 (1973), pp. 143–172.

———. *Te'udot min ha'osef shel Eliyahu Eliachar.* Jerusalem, 1971.

Hazan, Hayyim David. *Sefer nediv lev.* Jerusalem 1876.

Heller, Shmuel. *She'elot uteshuvot Shem miShmuel.* Jerusalem, 1979.

Heller, Zeyde Avraham. *Harav hamanhig veharofé: Toledot hayav ufo'alo shel Rabbi Shmuel Heller . . .* N.p., 1989.

Herzog, Hannah. *"Hamusagim 'yishuv yashan' ve'yishuv hadash' behe'arah soziologit."* *Cathedra* 32 (1984), pp. 99–108.

Hevron ir hakodesh: Leket misihot ume'iggerot ha'admor mi-Lyubavitch. [Israel], 1998.

Hilwani-Steinhorn, Esther. *Damesek iri.* Jerusalem, 1978.

Hirschberg, Avraham Shmuel. *Be'erez hamizrah.* Vilna, 1910 (repr. Jerusalem, 1977).

Hirshcberg, Haim Z'ew, ed. *Vatikin—Mehkarim betoledot hayishuv lezikhro shel R. Yosef Rivlin.* Ramat-Gan, 1975.

Hirschensohn, Hayyim. *Malki bakodesh,* vol. 1. Saint Louis, 1919.

——. *Sefer musegei shav veha'emet.* Jerusalem, 1932.

Horowitz, Elimelech. "'Veyihyu aniyim (hagunim) benei beitkha . . . ,'" in Menachem Ben-Sasson, ed., *Dat vekhalkalah: Yahasei Gomelin,* pp. 209–232. Jerusalem, 1995.

Hostetler, John A. *Amish Society.* Baltimore, 1963.

Hoy, Suellen. "The Journey Out: The Recruitment and Emigration of Irish Religious Women to the United States, 1812–1914." *Journal of Women's History* 6/4–7/1 (1995), pp. 64–98.

Hundert, Gershon David. "Jewish Children and Childhood in Early Modern Central Europe," in Kraemer, ed., *The Jewish Family,* pp. 81–94.

Hurwitz, Eleazar. *Mosad hayesod Yerushalayim.* Jerusalem, 1958.

Hyamson, Albert M. *The British Consulate in Jerusalem in Relation to the Jews of Palestine, 1838–1914,* 2 vols. London, 1941.

Hyman, Paula E. *Gender and Assimilation in Modern Jewish History: The Roles and Representation of Women.* Seattle, 1995.

——. "Introduction: Perspectives on the Evolving Jewish Family," in Steven M. Cohen and Paula E. Hyman, eds., *The Jewish Family: Myths and Reality,* pp. 3–13. New York, 1986.

——. "The Modern Jewish Family: Image and Reality," in Kraemer, ed., *The Jewish Family,* pp. 179–193.

——. "The Volunteer Organizations: Vanguard or Rear Guard?" *Lilith* 5 (1978), pp. 16–17, 22.

Idinopulos, Thomas A. "Sacred Space and Profane Power: Victor Turner and the Perspective of Holy Land Pilgrimage," in Bryan F. LeBeau and Menachem Mor, eds., *Pilgrims and Travellers to the Holy Land,* pp. 9–20. Omaha, Neb., 1996.

Ilan, Zvi. *Kivrei zadikim beErez Yisra'el.* Jerusalem, 1997.

Ilan-Underoizer, Yehudit. "*Helko shel Irgun haPk v.Am. me'Amsterdam behahzakatan uvekiyuman shel kehilot Zefat uTeveryah bemahalakh hame'ah ha19 uvithilat hame'ah ha20.*" M.A. thesis, Tel Aviv University, 1993.

Ish Shalom, Michael. "*Al hayishuv hayehudi beHevron lefi mekorot nozriyim.*" Sefunot 9 (1965), pp. 337–359.

——. *Mas'ei nozerim leErez Yisra'el. Reshumot ve'eduyot letoledot hayishuv hayehudi.* Jerusalem, 1979.

Jayanti, Vimala. "Women in Mea Shearim: A Different Reality." M.A. thesis, Hebrew University of Jerusalem, 1982.

Joseph, Norma Baumel. "Jewish Education for Women: Rabbi Moshe Feinstein's Map of America." *American Jewish History* 83/2 (1995), pp. 205–222.

Juhasz, Esther, ed., *Yehudei Sefarad ba'imperiyah ha'Uthmanit.* Jerusalem, 1989.

Kagan, Helena. *Reshit darki biYrushalayim.* Tel Aviv, 1982.

Kahanov, Moshe Nehemiah. *Sha'alu shelom Yerushalayim.* Odessa, 1867 (repr. Jerusalem, 1969).

Kamm, Josephine. *Hope Deferred: Girls' Education in English History.* London, 1965.

Kaniel, Yehoshua. "*Batei hadin shel ha'edot biYrushalayim bame'ah ha19,*" in Shanah beshanah, pp. 325–335. Jerusalem, 1976.

——. "*Hamunahim 'yishuv yashan' ve 'yishuv hadash' be'eynei hador (1882–1914) uve'eynei hahistoriyografiyah.*" *Cathedra* 6 (1977), pp. 3–19.

——. "*Hayahasim beyn haSepharadim veha'Ashkenazim bayishuv hayashan biYrushalayim (mehityashevut talmidei haGra ad shenot ha-80 shel hame'ah ha19).*" M.A. thesis, Bar-Ilan University, Ramat-Gan, 1970.

——. "*Hayahasim hahevratiyim beyn ha'Ashkenazim laSepharadim bayishuv hayashan biYrushalayim bame'ah ha19,*" in H. Z. Hirschberg, ed., *Vatikin*, pp. 47–65.

——. *Hemshekh utmurah: Hayishuv hayashan vehayishuv hehadash bitkufat ha'aliyah harishonah vehasheniyah.* Jerusalem, 1982.

——. "*Ma'avakim irguniyim vekhalkaliyim beyn ha'edot biYrushalayim bame'ah ha19,*" in Friedman et al., eds., *Perakim betoledot hayishuv hayehudi biYrushalayim*, vol. 2, pp. 97–126.

——. "*Memadei hayeridah min ha'arez bitkufat ha'aliyah harishonah vehasheniyah.*" *Cathedra* 73 (1994), pp. 115–138.

——. "*Miba'ayot hahinukh biYrushalayim bame'ah hatesha'-esreh,* " in H. Z. Hirschberg, ed., *Zekhor le'Avraham . . .lezekher Avraham Almaliah*, pp. 140–168. Jerusalem, 1972.

Kaplan, Marion A. "Jewish Women in Nazi Germany: Daily Struggles, 1933–1939." *Feminist Studies* 16 (1990), pp. 592–605.

Karagila, Zvi. *Hayishuv hayehudi be'Erez Yisra'el bitkufat hakibush hamizri (1831–1840).* Tel Aviv, 1990.

Kark, Ruth. "*Aliyatah shel Yafo kemerkaz hayishuv hehadash — Hebetim tarbutiyim vehevratiyim,*" in Mordechai Eliav, ed., *Sefer ha'aliyah harishonah*, vol. 1, pp. 297–318. Jerusalem, 1982.

——. *The American Colony.* Jerusalem, 1998.

——. *Yafo: Zemihatah shel ir, 1799–1917.* Jerusalem, 1985.

Kark, Ruth, and Yosef Glass. *Yazamim Sefardim be'Erez Yisra'el: Mishpahat Amzaleg, 1816–1918.* Jerusalem, 1993.

Karlin, Aryeh. *Torat even ha'ezer.* Jerusalem, 1950.

Karlinsky, Nahum. "*Hahevrah hahasidit shel Zefat bamahazit hasheniyah shel hame'ah ha19 kehevrat mehagerim — hebetim demografiyim vegibush hevrati.*" *Jerusalem Studies in Jewish Thought* 15 (1999): *Mehkerei hasidut*, ed. Immanuel Etkes, David Assaf, and Yoseph Dan, pp. 151–196.

Kass, Amalie M. "Sir Moses Montefiore and Medical Philanthropy in the Holy Land," in Manfred Waserman and Samuel S. Kottek, eds., *Health and Disease in the Holy Land*, pp. 207–229. Lewiston, N.Y., 1996.

Kassan, Shalom. *David Yellin, hamehanekh vehamanhig.* Tel Aviv, 1980.

Katz, Jacob. *Le'umiyut yehudit, Massot umehkarim.* Jerusalem, 1979.

——. "*Nisu'im vehayei ishut bemoza'ei yemei habeynayim.*" *Zion* 10 (1945), pp. 21–54.

——. "*Od al hayishuv hayashan vehayishuv hehadash.*" *Cathedra* 12 (1979), pp. 31–33.

——. *Tradition and Crisis: Jewish Society at the End of the Middle Ages*, trans. Bernard Cooperman. New York, 1993.

Katzburg, Netanel. "*Pulemus hahinukh bayishuv hayashan.*" *Shanah beshanah*, vol. 6 (1966), pp. 299–312.

Kedar, Binyamin Ze'ev. "*Hemshekhiyut vehidush bahamarah hayehudit beGermaniyah shel hame'ah hashemoneh-esreh,*" in E. Etkes and Y. Salmon, eds., *Perakim betoledot hahevrah hayehudit*, pp. 154–170. Jerusalem, 1980.

Kehilat Ya'akov. Jerusalem, 1908.

Kellner, Ya'akov. *Lema'an Zion — Hahitarevut hakelal-yehudit bimzukat hayishuv [5]630–[5]642, 1869–1882*. Jerusalem, 1977.

Kertzer, David. "Toward a Historical Demography of Aging," in David Kertzer and Peter Laslett, eds., *Aging in the Past: Demography, Society and Old Age*, pp. 363–383. Berkeley, Calif., 1995.

Kertzer, David I., and Nancy Karweit. "The Impact of Widowhood in Nineteenth-Century Italy," in David I. Kertzer and Peter Laslett, eds., *Aging in the Past: Demography, Society and Old Age*, pp. 229–248. Berkeley, Calif., 1995.

Klausner, Israel. *Behit'orer am: Ha'aliyah harishonah meRusiyah*, vol. 1. Jerusalem, 1962.

Klein, Michele. *A Time to Be Born: Customs and Folklore of Jewish Birth*. Philadelphia, 1998.

Kluger, Binyamin. *Min hamakor: Hayishuv hayashan al luah moda'ot*, 2 vols. Jerusalem, 1978, 1980.

———. *Yerushalayim shekhunot saviv lah*. Jerusalem, 1979.

Kluger, Shlomo. *She'elot uteshuvot ha'elef lekha Shlomo*, pt. 3, *Even ha'ezer*. Bilgorai, 1904.

Knappe, Sabine. "The Role of Women's Associations in the Jewish Community: The Example of the Israelitisch-humanitarer Frauenverein in Hamburg at the Turn of the Century," in *Leo Baeck Institute Year-Book*, pp. 153–178. London, 1994.

Kolatt, Yisra'el. "Miyishuv edot vekolelim leyishuv le'umi." *Cathedra* 12 (1979), pp. 34–39.

———. "Yerushalayim be'einei nezig JCA — Albert Antebi," in Yosef Katz, ed., *Hahevrah lehityashvut yehudim (JCA), me'ah shenot pe'ilut, 1891–1991*, pp. 35–44. Jerusalem, 1995.

Konrad, Franz-Michael. *Würzeln jüdischer Sozialarbeit in Palästina: Einflüsse der Sozialarbeit in Deutschland auf der Entstehung moderner Hilfesysteme in Palästina, 1890–1948*. Weinheim and München, 1993.

Kook, Shmuel Hakohen. "Moshav zekenim uzkenot me'uhad biYrushalayim." *Luah Yerushalayim* 10 (1950), pp. 235–241.

Kraemer, David, ed., *The Jewish Family: Metaphor and Memory*. Oxford, 1989.

Krammer, Johann. "Austrian Pilgrimage to the Holy Land," in Marian Wrba, ed., *Austrian Presence in the Holy Land in the 19th and Early 20th Century*, pp. 66–80. Tel Aviv, 1996.

Krausman–Ben Amos, Ilana. "Defusei hitbagrut be'Angliyah ba'et hahadashah hamukdemet: Hamikreh shel Edward Barlow," in Bartal and Gafni, eds., *Eros, erusin ve'isurin*, pp. 145–158.

Kressel, Getzel. *Mivhar kitvei Yisra'el Dov Frumkin*. Jerusalem, 1954.

———. *Potehei hatikvah: MiYrushalayim lePetah Tikvah*. Jerusalem, 1976.

Krinitzi, Avraham. *Bekhoah hama'aseh*. Tel Aviv, 1950.

Kushnir, David. "Hador ha'aharon leshilton ha'Uthmanim beErez Yisra'el, 1882–1914," in Lissak et al., *Toledot hayishuv hayehudi beErez Yisra'el*, pp. 1–74.

Lamdan, Ruth. *A Separate People: Jewish Women in Palestine, Syria and Egypt in the Sixteenth Century*. Leiden, 2000.

Landau, Bezalel. "Letoledot Rabbi Moshe Nehemiah . . . Kahanov," in R. Moshe Nehemiah Kahanov, *Siftei Yeshenim*. Jerusalem, 1968.

———. "Miminhagei yahadut Ashkenaz (Perushim) beErez Yisra'el," in Asher Wasserteil, ed., *Yalkut minhagim miminhagei shivtei Yisra'el*, pp. 82–88. Jerusalem, 1980.

Landau, Lola. *Pesah Hevroni.* Jerusalem, 1972.

Lang, Yosef. *"Itonut Eliezer Ben Yehuda ve'emdoteha be'inyenei hayishuv hayehudi vehatenu'ah hale'umit [5]645–[5]675 1884–1914."* Ph.D. dissertation, Bar-Ilan University, Ramat-Gan, 1993.

Langbaum, Shelomit. *"Hitpatehut takanot Me'ah She'arim kimshakefot tahalikhei shinuy bashekhunah 1874–1995."* Seminar paper, Hebrew University of Jerusalem, 1995.

Lavski, Avraham. *"Takanot Yerushalayim lemin tehilat hame'ah ha16 ve'ad lemahazit hame'ah ha19."* M.A. thesis, Bar-Ilan University, Ramat-Gan, 1974.

Leibowitz, Ze'ev. *Ba'aliyah uvabeniyah: Zikhronot umasot.* Jerusalem, 1953.

Lesha'ah uledorot: Osef keruzim umoda'ot, vol. 2. Jerusalem, 1971.

Levanon, Mordechai. *Toledot hayay, [5]648–[5]746.* Jerusalem, 1997.

Levi, Nissim. *Perakim betoledot harefu'ah beErez Yisra'el, 1799–1948.* Haifa, 1998.

Levin, Sabina. *"Batei hasefer ha'elementariyim harishonim liyladim benei dat Moshe beVarshah bashanim 1818–1830."* *Gal'ed* 1 (1979), pp. 63–100.

Levin-Katz, Yael. *"Nashim lamdaniyot biYrushalayim."* *Mabua* 26 (1993), pp. 98–125.

Levinsky, Yom Tov. *Sefer hamo'adim,* vol. 5: *Yemei mo'ed vezikaron.* Tel Aviv, 1954.

Lewittes, Mendel. *Jewish Marriage, Rabbinic Law, Legend and Custom.* Northvale, N.Y., 1994.

Lifshitz, Avraham Moshe. *"Haheder, tekhunato veshitato."* *Hatekufah* 7 (1923), pp. 340–352.

———. *Ketavim.* Jerusalem, 1957.

Lipman, Sonia L. *"Judith Montefiore: First Lady of Anglo-Jewry."* *Jewish Historical Society of England Transactions* 21 (1962–1967), pp. 287–303.

Lipman, Sonia, and Vivian David Lipman. *The Century of Moses Montefiore.* Oxford, 1985.

Lissak, Moshe, Gavriel Cohen, and Israel Kolatt. *Toledot hayishuv hayehudi beErez Yisra'el me'az ha'aliyah harishonah.* Jerusalem, 1990.

Litt, Jacquelyn. *"Mothering, Medicalization and Jewish Identity, 1928–1940."* *Gender and Society* 10 (1996), pp. 185–198.

Loewe, Louis, ed. *Diaries of Sir Moses and Lady Montefiore,* vols. 1–2. Facsimile of the 1890 edition. London, 1983.

Lubochinsky-Lavi, Etty. *Mishpahah Yisre'elit — Toledot Shoshanah Nehemiah Yisre'elit: Yerushalayim, London, Petah Tikvah 1858–1982.* Tel Aviv, 1995.

Luncz, Avraham Moshe. *Luah Erez Yisra'el,* vols. 1–21. Jerusalem, 1896–1916.

———. *Yerushalayim,* vols. 1–13. Vienna and Jerusalem, 1882–1919.

Luncz, Avraham Moshe, *Netivot Zion viYrushalayim — Mivhar ma'amarei Avraham Moshe Luncz,* Gedaliah Kressel, ed., Jerusalem, 1961.

Luncz[-Botin], Hannah. *"Ha'em vehabat."* *Luah Erez Yisra'el* [5]671 [1910/1911], pp. 129–138.

———. *"Hayyei avi."* *Yerushalayim* 13 (1919), pp. 329–352.

———. *Me'ir netivot Yerushalayim — Hayyei Avraham Moshe Luncz.* Jerusalem, 1968.

Lynch, William Francis. *Narrative of the United States Expedition to the River Jordan and the Dead Sea.* Philadelphia, 1849.

Magnus, Shulamit. *"'Out of the Ghetto': Integrating the Study of the Jewish Woman into the Study of 'The Jews.'"* *Judaism* 39/1 (1990), pp. 28–36.

Maimon, Ada. *Le'orekh haderekh.* Tel Aviv, 1972.

Malachi, A. R. *Perakim betoledot hayishuv hayashan.* Tel Aviv, 1971.

Malino, Frances. "Prophets in Their Own Land? Mothers and Daughters of the Alliance Israélite Universelle." *Nashim* 3 (2000), pp. 56–73.

——. "The Women Teachers of the Alliance Israélite Universelle, 1872–1940," in Judith R. Baskin, *Jewish Women in Historical Perspective*, 2nd ed., pp. 248–269. Detroit, 1998.

Mandelbaum, Simcha. *Asarah dorot be'Erez Yisra'el: Matayim shanah, 1794–1994*, 2 vols. Jerusalem, 1994–1995.

Mani, Menashe. "Bahazar hayehudim beHevron." *Shevet va'Am* 2 (1958), pp. 93–97.

——. "Bahazar hayehudim beHevron." *Shevet va'Am* 5 (1960), pp. 115–122.

——. *Hevron vegiboreha.* Tel Aviv, 1963.

Mannenberg, Eliezer. "The Evolution of Jewish Educational Practices in the sançak (eyalet) of Jerusalem under Ottoman Rule." Ph.D. dissertation, University of Connecticut, 1976.

——. "Modernization and Educational Change: A Case Study in the Transition of a Jewish Community Antedating the Israeli Society." *Jewish Social Studies* 40 (1978), pp. 293–302.

Marks, Lara. "Jewish Women and Jewish Prostitution in the East End of London." *Jewish Quarterly* 34/2 (1987), pp. 6–10.

Martin, Jane. *Women and the Politics of Schooling in Victorian and Edwardian England.* London, 1998.

Mashash, Yosef. *Otzar mikhtavim*, vol. 1. Jerusalem, 1968.

Matras, Hagit. "Ki mal'akhav yezaveh lakh lishmorkha bekhol derakhekha: Keme'ot layoledet velayeled biYrushalayim beyameinu." *Rimonim* 5 (1997), pp. 15–27.

——. "Segulot urefu'ot be'ivrit: Tekhanim umekorot." Ph.D. dissertation, Hebrew University of Jerusalem, 1998.

Matthews, Glenna. *"Just a Housewife": The Rise and Fall of Domesticity in America.* New York, 1987.

Mayer, Selma. *Hayay beSha'arei Zedek.* Jerusalem, n.d. [published by Sha'arei Zedek Hospital].

Mazor, Ya'akov, and Moshe Taube. "A Hassidic Dance: The Mitsve Tants in Jerusalemite Weddings." *Yuval: Masorot yehudiyot shebe'al peh* 10 (1994), pp. 164–224.

Melman, Billie. "Hamasa la'orient bekhitvei nashim angliyot bame'ah ha-19." *Zemanim* 24 (1987), pp. 49–61.

——. "Re'alot shekufot: Kolonializm vegender — likrat diyun histori mehudash." *Zemanim* 62 (1998), pp. 89–102.

——. *Women's Orients — English Women and the Middle East, 1718–1918: Sexuality, Religion and Work*, 2nd ed. Ann Arbor, Mich., 1995.

Menachem Mendel of Kaminetz. *Korot ha'itim liYshurun be'Erez Yisra'el.* Jerusalem, 1839.

Meyuhas, Yosef. *Bat Hayil, o torat em: Sefer mikra livnot Yisra'el*, pt. 1. Jerusalem, 1900.

Mikhlin, Hayim Michal. *Bir'i hadorot.* Tel Aviv, 1950.

Miller, Ellen Clare. *Eastern Sketches: Notes of Scenery, Schools and Life in Syria and Palestine.* Edinburgh, 1871 (repr. New York, 1977).

Mohr, Avraham Menahem Mendel. *Mevaseret Zion.* Jerusalem, 1880.

Montefiore, Judith. *Private Journal of a Visit to Egypt and Palestine.* London, 1836 (photogr. repr. Jerusalem, 1975).

[Montefiore, Moses]. *Sippur Mosheh viYrushalayim*, trans. A. Amshewitz (from the original diaries). Warsaw, 1876.

Morgenstern, Aryeh. *Ge'ulah bederekh hateva bekhitvei haGra vetalmidav.* Jerusalem, 1989.

———. *Ge'ulah bederekh hateva: Talmidei haGra beErez Yisra'el, 1800–1840, Mehkarim umkorot.* Jerusalem, 1997.

———. *Meshihiyut veyishuv Erez Yisra'el bamahazit harishonah shel hame'ah ha19.* Jerusalem, 1985.

———. "*MiBrody leErez Yisra'el vahazarah.*" *Zion* 58/1 (1992–1993), pp. 107–113.

———. "*Tik hahakirah shel Sh. Z. Plonsky vehaPerushim be'Erez Yisra'el.*" *Zion* 61 (1996), pp. 455–476.

Morinis, Alan, ed. *Sacred Journeys: The Anthropology of Pilgrimage.* Westport, Conn., 1992.

Moshayoff, Sha'ul Me'ir. *Betokhekhei Yerushalayim,* [5]646–[5]734. Jerusalem, 1978.

Myers, Jody Elizabeth. "The Myth of Matriarchy in Recent Writings on Jewish Women's Spirituality." *Jewish Social Studies* 4/1 (1997), pp. 7–11.

Naveh, Hannah. "*Leket, pe'ah veshikhhah: Hahayim mihuz lakanon,*" in Dafnah Yizre'eli, Ariella Friedman, and Henriette Dahan-Kalev, eds., *Min, migdar upolitikah,* pp. 49–106. Tel Aviv, 1999.

Navot, Orit, and Avraham Gross. "*Hamilhamah bagar'enet: Reshit beri'ut hazibur be'Erez Yisra'el.*" *Cathedra* 94 (2000), pp. 89–114.

Nayor, Gillian. *The Arts and Crafts Movement.* London, 1971.

Ne'eman, Rachel. *Yomanah shel ganenet vatikah.* Tel Aviv, 1960.

Nehama, Joseph. *Dictionnaire du Judéo-Espagnol.* Madrid, 1977.

Neiman, D. Z. *Haga'on shenishkah: R. Anshil Neiman ufrakim al aliyatam shel yehudei Hungariah le'Erez Yisra'el bereshit hithadeshut hayishuv.* Jerusalem, 1982.

Neumann, Bernhard. *Ir hakodesh veyoshevei bah,* trans. into Hebrew from German (*Die heilige Stadt und deren Bewohner* [Hamburg, 1877]) by Benzion Gat. Jerusalem, 1949.

Nissenbaum, Yizhak. *Alei heldi* [5]629–[5]689. Jerusalem, 1969.

Norman, Theodore. *An Outstretched Arm: A History of the Jewish Colonization Association.* London, 1985.

Ofrat-Friedlander, Gideon. "*Tekufat Bezalel,*" in Shilo-Cohen, ed., *Bezalel shel Schatz,* pp. 31–116.

Okkenhaug, Inger Marie. "Civilization, Culture and Education: Anglican Mission, Women and Education in the Holy Land during the Nineteenth and Twentieth Centuries," in Anthony O'Mahoney, ed., *The Christian Communities of Modern Jerusalem.* University of Wales Press, forthcoming.

Olitzky, Yosef. *400 shanim le'umanut hadefus be'Erez Yisra'el.* Ramat-Gan, 1973.

Ophir, Yehoshua. *Hoter migeza.* Jerusalem, 1998.

Ornan, Uzzi. "Hebrew in Palestine before and after 1882." *Journal of Semitic Studies* 29 (1984), pp. 225–253.

Ortner, Sherry B. "Is Female to Male as Nature Is to Culture?" in M. Z. Rosaldo and L. Lamphere, eds., *Woman, Culture and Society,* pp. 67–87. Stanford, Calif., 1974.

Otztar, Eran. "*Hamilhamah bamisyon bir'i Hamoriah.*" Seminar paper, Bar-Ilan University, Ramat-Gan, 1993.

Pappenheim, Bertha. *Leben und Schriften.* Frankfurt a/M, 1963.

Parfitt, Tudor. "The Use of Hebrew in Palestine." *Journal of Semitic Studies* 17 (1972), pp. 237–252.

Parker, Rozsika. *The subversive Stitch: Embroidery and the Making of the Feminine.* London, 1996.

Parush, Irit [Iris]. *Nashim kor'ot: Yitronah shel shuliyut.* Tel Aviv, 2001.

———. "The Politics of Literacy: Women and Foreign Languages in Jewish Society of 19th-Century Eastern Europe." *Modern Judaism* 15 (1995), pp. 183–206.

Peskowitz, Miriam. "Engendering Jewish Religious History," in Miriam Peskowitz and Laura Levitt, eds., *Judaism since Gender*, pp. 17–39. New York and London, 1997.

Peteet, Julie M. "Authenticity and Gender: The Presentation of Culture," in Judith E. Tucker, ed., *Arab Women: Old Boundaries, New Frontiers*, pp. 49–62. Bloomington, Ind., 1993.

Pilovsky, Arieh L. "*Itonut Yiddish beErez Yisra'el mitehilatah ve'ad hofa'at Neivelt (1934).*" *Cathedra* 10 (1979), pp. 72–101.

Pinkerfeld, Ya'akov. *Batei hakenesiyot beErez Yisra'el.* Jerusalem, 1946.

Porush, Eliyahu. *Zikhronot rishonim.* Jerusalem, 1963.

Porush-Glickman, Naftali. *Sheloshah dorot biYrushalayim: Pirkei Zikhronot.* Jerusalem, 1978.

Preis Horev, Yehuda, and Moshe Hayim Katzenellenbogen, eds. *Menorat haMa'or* Jerusalem, 1961.

Press, Yeshayahu. *Eleh toledot bet hasefer leha'azil levet Laemel biYrushalayim.* Jerusalem, 1936.

———. *Me'ah shanah biYrushalayim.* Jerusalem, 1964.

Preston, James J. "Spiritual Magnetism: An Organizing Principle for the Study of Pilgrimage," in Morinis, ed., *Sacred Journeys*, pp. 31–46.

Preston, Jo Anne. "Gender and the Formation of a Women's Profession: The Case of Public School Teaching," in Jerry A. Jacobs, ed., *Gender Inequality at Work*, pp. 379–407. Thousand Oaks, Calif., 1995.

Prochaska, F. K. *Women and Philanthropy in Nineteenth-Century England.* Oxford, 1980.

Quataert, Donald. "Ottoman Women, Households, and Textile Manufacturing, 1800–1914," in Nikki R. Keddie and Beth Baron, eds., *Women in Middle Eastern History: Shifting Boundaries in Sex and Gender*, pp. 161–176. New Haven, Conn., 1992.

Raab, Yehudah. *Hatelem harishon—Zikhronot 1862–1930.* Jerusalem, 1988.

Rabin, Menahem Mendel. *Masa leMeron.* Jerusalem, 1983 [1889].

Rachel. See [Bluwstein], Rachel. *Shirei Rachel.* Tel Aviv, 1970.

Rakover, Nachum, ed. *Shorashim va'anafim: Lidmutam shel Aba ve'Ima, R. Hayim veHanah Malkah (leveit Mandelbaum) Rakover.* Jerusalem, 1996.

Rakovsky, Puah. *My Life as a Radical Jewish Woman: Memoirs of a Zionist Feminist in Poland*, trans. Barbara Harshav, ed. Paula E. Hyman. Bloomington, Ind., 2002.

Ram, Chanah. *Hayishuv hayehudi beYafo ba'et hahadashah: Mikehilah Sefaradit lemerkaz Zioni.* Jerusalem, 1996.

Rappaport-Albert, Ada. "On Women's Hassidim: S. A. Horodecky and the Maid of Ludmir Tradition," in Ada Rappaport-Albert and Steven J. Zipperstein, eds., *Jewish History: Essays in Honour of Chimen Abramsky*, pp. 495–525. London, 1988.

Ravitzky, Aviezer. "*Erez hemdah vaharadah: Hayahas hadu-erki leErez Yisra'el bimkorot Yisra'el,*" in idem, ed., *Erez Yisra'el bahagut hayehudit ba'et hahadashah*, pp. 1–41. Jerusalem, 1988.

Razahbi, Yehudah. *Bo'i Teiman—Mehkarim ute'udot betarbut yehudei Teiman.* Tel Aviv, 1967.

———. "*Parashat hitnahalut yehudei Teiman biYrushalayim,*" in *Yerushalayim: Riv'on leheker Yerushalayim vetoledoteha*, vol. 1 pp. 114–126. Jerusalem, 1948.

——. "*Rishonei olei Teiman ba'aliyat 5642.*" *Mahanayim* 77 (1963), pp. 70–75.

Reicher, Moshe. *Sefer sha'arei Yerushalayim.* Lemberg, 1870.

Rein, Natalie. *Daughters of Rachel: Women in Israel.* Harmondsworth, Eng., 1980.

Reiner, Elchanan. "*Aliyah va-aliyah leregel leErez Yisra'el 1099–1517.*" Ph.D. dissertation, Hebrew University of Jerusalem, 1988.

Reinharz, Jehuda. "Old and New Yishuv: The Jewish Community in Palestine at the Turn of the Century." *Jewish Studies Quarterly* 1 (1993), pp. 154–171.

Reitze, daughter of R. Mordechai Chen Tov. *Sefer mishpahat yuhasin.* Jerusalem, 1885. [See also Shilo, *Hakol Hanashi*, pp. 126–163.]

Rimerman, Yehudah. *Hazenut vehana'arah hasotah.* Tel Aviv, 1977.

Rinot, Moshe. *Hevrat ha'ezrah liyhudei Germaniyah bayezirah uvama'avak.* Jerusalem, 1972.

Rivlin, Avraham B. *Zeh karah be'Erez Yisra'el: Eru'im ufarashiyot.* Jerusalem, 1993.

Rivlin, Binyamin. *Yizhak Zvi Rivlin.* Jerusalem 1961.

——. *Zekher av.* Jerusalem, 1992.

Rivlin (Erdos), Brachah. *Arevim zeh lazeh bagetto ha'Italki, hevrot gema"h 1516–1789.* Jerusalem, 1991.

Rivlin, Eliezer. "*Takanot hahalukah shel 'Kolel haPerushim' be'Erez Yisra'el mishenat 5583.*" *Me'asef Zion* 2 (1927), pp. 150–172.

——. "*Mikhtav me-R. Mordechai Zoref le-Aviv R. A. Sh. Zalman zef mi-shemat [5]605 [1845].*" *Me'asef Zion* (1926) pp. 71–84.

Rivlin, Julie. "'*Leyl kedoshim—Aliyah lekivrei zadikim ke'erua shel te'atron sevivati.*" M.A. thesis, Hebrew University of Jerusalem, 1997.

Rivlin, Yosef. "*Minhagei Pesah biYrushalayim.*" *Mahanayim* 44 (1960), pp. 118–125.

——. *Mivhar ma'amarim ureshimot.* Ramat-Gan, 1966.

Rivlin, Yosef Yoel. *Me'ah She'arim.* Jerusalem, 1947.

——. "*Mishpahat Rivlin beErez Yisra'el,*" in H. Z. Hirschberg, ed., *Yad Yosef Yizhak Rivlin — Sefer Zikaron*, pp. 47–77. Ramat-Gan, 1964.

——. *75 shanah le'Ezrat Nashim, 1895–1970.* Jerusalem, 1970.

——. "*Zur mahzavto shel Yosef Luriya z"l,*" in D. Kimhi, ed., *Nefesh leDr. Yosef Luriya z"l*, pp. 55–65. Jerusalem, 1938.

Robels, Arodys, and Susan Watkins. "Immigration and Family Separation in the U.S. at the Turn of the Twentieth Century." *Journal of Family History* 18/3 (1993), pp. 191–211.

Robinson-Divine, Donna. *Ottoman Palestine: The Arabs' Struggle for Survival and Power.* London, 1994.

Roche, Daniel. *The Culture of Clothing.* Cambridge, 1994.

Rodrig, Aharon. *Hinukh, hevrah vehistoriyah: "Kol Yisra'el Haverim" viyhudei agan hayam haTikhon 1860–1929.* Jerusalem, 1991.

Rogers, Mary Eliza. *Domestic Life in Palestine.* London, 1862.

Rogow, Faith. *Gone to Another Meeting: The National Council of Jewish Women, 1893–1993.* Tuscaloosa, Ala., 1993.

Rosen, Minna. *Hakehilah hayehudit biYrushalayim bame'ah ha17.* Tel Aviv, 1984.

Rosenberg, Carol. "The Female World of Love and Ritual: Relations between Women in Nineteenth-Century America." *Signs* 1/1 (1975), pp. 1–29.

Ross, Tamar. "*Ha'od mesugalot anu lehitpalel le'avinu shebashamayim?*" in Naham Ilan, ed., *Ayin tovah: Du siah upulemus betarbut Yisra'el: Sefer yovel . . . Tovah Ilan*, pp. 264–277. [Tel Aviv], 1999.

Roth, Avraham Naftali Zevi. *"Al minhag giluah sa'arot ha'ishah beleyl nisu'eha."* *Yeda Am* 16 (1972), pp. 14–21.

Rothschild, Meir Menahem. *"Hahalukah" kevituy leyahasah shel yahadut h agolah layishuv hayehudi beErez Yisra'el bashanim, 1810–1860.* Jerusalem, 1986.

Rubens, Alfred. *A History of Jewish Costume.* London, 1973.

Sabar, Shalom. *"Livhinat hashoni bayahas shel haSefaradim vehaAshkenazim le'omanut hazutit beErez Yisra'el beshilhei hatekufah haUthmanit."* *Pe'amim* 56 (1993), pp. 75–105.

Safrai, Shmuel. *"Ha'im haytah kayemet ezrat nashim beveit hakeneset batekufah ha'atikah."* *Tarbiz* 32 (1963), pp. 329–338.

Salmon, Yosef. *"Hahinukh ha'Ashkenazi be'Erez Yisra'el beyn 'yashan' le'hadash."'* *Shalem* 6 (1992), pp. 281–301.

———. *"Hayishuv ha'Ashkenazi ha'ironi beErez Yisra'el, 1880–1903,"* in Lissak, ed., *Toledot hayishuv hayehudi be'Erez Yisra'el,* pp. 539–620.

———. *"Yehiel Mikhal Pines—Demuto hahistorit,"* in *Milet: Kovez mehkarim betoledot Yisra'el,* vol. 1, pp. 261–272. Tel Aviv, 1983.

Samuel, Sydney Montagu. *Jewish Life in the East.* London, 1881.

Sapir, Sha'ul. *"Gishatah ve'ofi terumatah shel hakehilah hayehudit biBritanyah lehitpatehut hayishuv hayehudi be'Erez Yisra'el bame'ah ha-19."* Ph.D. dissertation, Hebrew University of Jerusalem, 1989.

———. *"Sheloshet mas'otav harishonim shel Moshe Montefiore leErez Yisra'el,"* in Yehoshua Ben-Arieh, Yossi Ben-Artzi, and Hayim Goren, eds., *Mehkarim bege'ografiyah historit-yishuvit shel Erez Yisra'el,* vol. 1, pp. 15–33. Jerusalem, 1988.

———. *"Terumat hevrot hamisyon ha'anglikaniyot lehitpattehutah shel Yerushalayim beshilhei hashilton ha'Uthmani."* M.A. thesis, Hebrew University of Jerusalem, 1979.

Sapir, Tehiyah. *"Ma'arekhet simanim veheksheram hatarbuti bekartisei hazmanah lahatunah beErez Yisra'el mit'hilat hame'ah ve'ad yameinu."* M.A. thesis, Hebrew University of Jerusalem, 1997.

Sarid, David. *"Mezukat hayishuv ufe'ilut hamisyon biTveryah bashanim, 1884–1914,"* *Mituv Teveryah* 2 (1983), pp. 21–32.

Sarig, Tikvah. *Ima agadah.* Tel Aviv, 1980.

Sarna, Jonathan D. *"Christian Missions and American Jews,"* in Todd M. Endelman, ed., *Jewish Apostasy in the Modern World,* pp. 232–254. New York, 1987.

Sasson, Avi. *"Masoret vege'ografiyah, megamot vetahalikhim behitkadeshut kevarim bemishor hof Yehudah,"* in Eyal Regev, ed., *Hidushim beheker mishor hahof . . . ,* pp. 97–113. Ramat-Gan, 1997.

Schatz, Boris. *Bezalel, toledotav, mahuto ve'atido.* Jerusalem, 1910.

Schechter, Tamar. *"Dyoknah shel ishah-maskilit beGalizia."* M.A. thesis, Bar-Ilan University, Ramat-Gan, 1987.

Scherer, M. A. *"A Cross-Cultural Conflict Reexamined: Annette Akroyd and Keshub Chunder Sen."* *Journal of World History* 7/2 (1996), pp. 231–257.

Schlesinger, Akiva Yosef. *Bet Yosef hehadash.* Jerusalem, 1875.

———. *Hevrah mahazirei atarah leyoshnah.* Jerusalem, 1873.

Schmelz, Uziel. *"Be'ayot musagiyot bemehkar al adot Yisra'el."* *Pe'amim* 56 (1993), pp. 125–139.

———. *"Ha'ukhlusiya ba'azorei Yerushalayim veHevron bereshit hame'ah ha'esrim."* *Cathedra* 36 (1985), pp. 123–163.

——. "*Kavim meyuhadim bademografiyah shel yehudei Yerushalayim bame'ah hate-sha-esreh,*" in Friedman et al., eds., *Perakim betoledot hayishuv hayehudi biYrusha-layim,* vol. 2, pp. 52–76.

——. *Population of Jerusalem's Urban Neighborhoods According to the Ottoman Census of 1905.* Jerusalem: Institute of Contemporary Jewry, Hebrew University of Jerusalem, 1992.

Schneller, Raphael. "*Zemihato vehitpatehuto shel hinukh habanot ba'Edah ha-Haredit,*" in Mordechai Gilat and Eliezer Stern, eds., *Mikhtam leDavid* [Memorial Volume for David Ochs], pp. 322–340. Ramat-Gan, 1979.

Schölch, Alexander. "The Demographic Development of Palestine, 1850–1882." *International Journal of Middle East Studies* 17 (1985), pp. 485–505.

——. *Palestine in Transformation, 1856–1882: Studies in Social, Economic and Political Development.* Washington, D.C., 1986.

Schreier, Barbara. "Becoming American: Jewish Women Immigrants, 1880–1920." *History Today* 44/3 (1994), pp. 25–31.

Schwake, Norbert. *Die Entwicklung des Krankenhauswesens der Stadt Jerusalem vom Ende des 18. bis zum Beginn des 20. Jahrhunderts.* Herzogenrath, 1983.

Schwartz, Shifrah. "*Histadruyot nashim lema'an imahot beErez Yisra'el . . .*" *Bitahon Soziali* 51 (1998), pp. 57–81.

Schwartz, Yehosef. *Besha'arei Yerushalayim: Te'udot letoledot Yerushalayim ve-toshaveha,* ed. Bezalel Landau. Jerusalem, 1969.

Schwartz-Seller, Maxine. "The Upbringing of the Twenty Thousand: Sex, Class and Ethnicity in the Shirtwaist Makers' Strike of 1909," in Dirk Hoerder, ed., *"Struggle a Hard Battle": Essays on Working-Class Immigrants,* pp. 254–279. DeKalb, Ill., 1986.

Seeman, Don, and Rachel Kobrin. "Like One of the Whole Men: Learning Gender and Autobiography in R. Baruch Epstein's *Mekor Barukh.*" *Nashim* 2 (1999), pp. 52–94.

Sefer ma'aseh avot: Kinus lazadikim . . . Jerusalem, 1901.

Sefer shimru mishpat va'asu zedakah: Takanat ge'onei hazeman shel adat haSe-faradim. Jerusalem, 1903.

Sefer Torat Rabenu Shmuel Salant, ed. R. Nisan Aharon Tokachinsky, 3 vols. Jerusalem, 1998.

Segal, Ya'akov. *Midemuyot Yerushalayim.* Jerusalem, 1962.

Sered, Susan Starr. "Rachel, Mary and Fatima." *Cultural Anthropology* 6 (1991), pp. 131–146.

——. "Rachel's Tomb: Societal Liminality and the Revitalization of a Shrine." *Religion* 19 (1989), pp. 27–40.

——. *The Religious Lives of Elderly Jewish Women in Jerusalem.* New York, 1992.

——. "The Synagogue as a Sacred Space for the Elderly Oriental Women of Jerusalem," in Susan Grossman and Rivkah Haut, eds., *Daughters of the King,* pp. 206–211. New York, 1992.

Sethon, Hayyim. *Sefer erez hayyim.* Jerusalem, 1982.

Shahar, Shulamit. "*Al toledot hamishpahah,*" in Bartal and Gafni, eds., *Eros, erusin ve'isurin,* pp. 15–26.

——. *Ha'ishah behevrat yemei habeynayim — hama'amad harevi'i.* Tel Aviv, 1990.

Shamir, Shim'on. "*Matay hithilah ha'et hahadashah betoledot Erez Yisra'el?*" *Cathedra* 40 (1986), pp. 138–158.

Shar'abi, Rachel. *Hayishuv haSepharadi biYrushalayim beshilhei hatekufah ha'Uthmanit, 1893–1914.* Tel Aviv, 1989.

Sharshevsky, Ben Zion. *Dinei mishpahah.* Jerusalem, 1993.

Shavit, Zohar, ed. *Beniyatah shel tarbut Ivrit be'Erez Yisra'el,* vol. 1 (vol. 3/1 in a series titled *Toledot hayishuv hayehudi be'Erez Yisra'el me'az ha'aliyah harishonah.* Jerusalem, 1999.

Shefer, Miri. "Rofe'im uvatei holim bahevrah ha'Uthmanit." *Zemanim* 62 (1998), pp. 38–48.

Shilo, Margalit. *Hakol hanashi haYerushalmi: Kitvei lamdaniyot min hame'ah ha-19.* Jerusalem, 2003.

———. "Hashekhunot hahadashot—hemshekh hayashan o reshit hehadash?" in Michael Shashar, ed., *Sefer Yeshurun,* pp. 261–269. Jerusalem, 1999.

———. "Nidbakh hadash bikhtivat toledot hayishuv." *Cathedra* 58 (1990), pp. 60–69.

———. *Nisyonot behityashevut: Hamisrad ha'Erezyisre'eli 1908–1914.* Jerusalem, 1988.

———. "Self-Sacrifice, National-Historical Identity and Self-Denial: The Experience of Jewish Immigrant Women in Jerusalem, 1840–1914." *Women's History Review* 11 (2002), pp. 201–229.

———. "Takkanot Yerushalayim kime'azvot migdar," in Tovah Cohen and Yehoshua Schwartz, eds., *Ishah biYrushalayim: Migdar, hevrah vadat,* pp. 65–77. Ramat-Gan, 2002.

———. "Women as Victims of War: The British Conquest (1917) and the Blight of Prostitution in the Holy City." *Nashim* 6 (2003), pp. 72–83.

———. "The Women's Farm at Kinneret, 1911–1917: A Solution to the Problem of the Working Woman in the Second Aliyah," in Deborah S. Bernstein, ed., *Pioneers and Homemakers,* pp. 119–143. Albany, N.Y., 1992.

Shilo-Cohen, Nurit, ed. *Bezalel shel Schatz, 1906–1929.* Jerusalem, 1983.

Shiloni, Zvi. "Hadildul ba'ukhlusiya hayehudit biYrushalayim bitkufat milhemet ha'olam harishonah," in Yehoshua Ben-Arieh, Yossi Ben-Artzi, and Hayim Goren, eds., *Mehkarim bege'ografiyah historit-yishuvit shel Erez Yisra'el,* vol. 1, pp. 128–151. Jerusalem, 1988.

Shiryon, Yizhak. *Zikhronot.* Jerusalem, 1943.

Shoham, Aya. "Almenot Yerushalayim al pi mifkad Montefiore 1839—Nituah statisti." M.A. seminar paper, Bar-Ilan University, Ramat-Gan, 2000.

Shohetman, Eliav, "Mekorot hadashim lefarashat izvono shel ha 'sar' Hayim Farhi." *Asufot* 11 (1998), pp. 281–308.

Shor, Menachem (Meni). "Bet haholim Sha'arei Zedek biYrushalayim bishnotav harishonot." Seminar paper, Bar-Ilan University, Ramat-Gan, 2000.

Shor, Natan. *Massa el he'avar, massah al h e'avar.* Jerusalem, 1998.

———. *Sefer ha'aliyah leregel le'Erez Yisra'el—Toledot ha'aliyah leregel le'Erez Yisra'el mehatekufah haBizantit ve'ad hame'ah hatesha-esreh.* Jerusalem, 1994.

———. *Sefer hanose'im le'Erez Yisra'el bame'ah ha19.* Jerusalem, 1988.

Shorter, Edward. *The Making of the Modern Family.* New York, 1975.

Showalter, Elaine. "Feminist Criticism in the Wilderness," in idem, ed., *The New Feminist Criticism: Essays on Women, Literature and Theory,* pp. 243–270. New York, 1985.

Shunari, Yonatan. "Atirot nedavah umattan lehassi kallah vehatan." *Jerusalem Studies in Folklore* 4 (1974), pp. 121–124.

Shwadron, Shalom Mordechai. *She'elot uteshuvot Maharsham,* pt. 1. New York, 1962.

Sibahi-Greenfield, Zipporah. *"Bigdei kalah yehudiyah mikefar Muswar shebeTeiman kimeshakef emunah."* M.A. thesis, Hebrew University of Jerusalem, 1993.

Sigman Friedman, Reena. "'Send Me My Husband Who Is in New York City': Husband Desertion in the American Immigrant Community, 1900–1926. *Jewish Social Studies* 44 (1982), pp. 1–18.

Silbert, Yo'av. *"Megamot behitpat'hut histadrut hamorim, 1903–1913."* Ph.D. dissertation, Tel Aviv University, 1991.

Simon, Rachel. "Jewish Female Education in the Ottoman Empire." Unpublished, n.d.

Sinkoff, Nancy B. "Educating for 'Proper' Jewish Womanhood: A Case Study in Domesticity and Vocational Training, 1897–1926." *American Jewish History* 77 (1987), pp. 572–599.

Siton, David. *"Sipurah shel shekhunah Yerushalmit."* *Shevet va'am* 6 (1971), pp. 41–54.

Siton, Shoshanah. *"Beyn feminizm leZionut: ma'avak hagananot ha'ivriyot lehakarah mikzo'it."* *Zemanim* 61 (1997), pp. 26–37.

Smilanski, Moshe. *"Nig'ei hayishuv."* *Ahiassaf, Me'asef sifruti* (1905), pp. 97–109.

Sofer-Federman, Moshe. *"Milhamtenu bamisyon haProtestanti biYrushalayim."* *Yeda Am* 10 (1965), pp. 95–96.

Spafford Vester, Bertha. *Our Jerusalem.* Jerusalem, 1950.

Spector, R. Yizhak Elchanan. *Responsa Ein Yizhak.* New York, 1965.

Sperber, Daniel. *Minhagei Yisra'el*, pt. 2, pt. 4. Jerusalem, 1991, 1994.

Spitzer, David. *Sefer takhshitei nashim.* Jerusalem, 1913.

Stahl, Avraham. *"Ahavah kegorem bivhirat ben hazug bahistoriyah, basifrut uvafolklor."* *Mehkerei Hamerkaz leheker hafolklor* 4 (1974), pp. 125–136.

———. *Minhag ha'aliyah leregel lekivrei kedoshim vehityahasut elav behadrakhat metayelim.* Har Gilo, 1981.

———. *Mishpahah vegidul yeladim beyahadut hamizrah.* Jerusalem, 1993.

———. *"Zenut bekerev yehudim ketofa'at levay lema'avar mitarbut letarbut."* *Megamot* 24 (1978–79), pp. 202–225.

Stampfer, Shaul. "Gender Differentiation and Education of the Jewish Woman in Nineteenth-Century Eastern Europe." *Polin* 7 (1992), pp. 63–87.

———. *"Hamashma'ut hahevratit shel nisu'ei boser bemizrah Eiropah bame'ah ha-19,"* in Ezra Mendelson and Chone Schmeruk, eds., *Studies on Polish Jewry: Paul Glikson Memorial Volume*, pp. 65–77. Jerusalem, 1987.

———. "Remarriage among Jews and Christians in Nineteenth-Century Eastern Europe." *Jewish History* 3/2 (1988), pp. 85–114.

———. *"Yedi'at kero ukhtov ezel yehudei mizrah Eiropah batekufah hahadashah,"* in Shmuel Almog, Israel Bartal, and Michael Graetz, eds., *Temurot bahistoriyah hayehudit hahadashah—Kovez ma'amarim shay liShmuel Ettinger*, pp. 459–483. Jerusalem, 1985.

Stanislawski, Michael. "Jewish Apostasy in Russia: A Tentative Typology," in Todd M. Endelman, ed., *Jewish Apostasy in the Modern World*, pp. 189–205. New York, 1987.

Steinman, Eliezer. *Sefer hama'alot: Parshiyot mehayei anshei shem beYisra'el: Megilot, te'udot vezava'ot.* Tel Aviv, 1956.

Stern, Bat Sheva (Margalit). *"Tenu'at hapo'alot be'Erez Yisra'el: Mo'ezet hapo'alot 1920–1939."* Ph.D. dissertation, Haifa University, 1997.

Stern, Eliezer. *Ishim vekivunim: Perakim betoledot ha'ide'al hahinukhi shel "Torah im derekh erez."* Ramat-Gan, 1987.

Stern, Shim'on. *"Te'ur harefu'ah biYrushalayim be'emza hame'ah ha19 al yedei Dr.*

Titus Tobler," in Ephraim Lev, Zohar Amar, and Joshua Schwartz, eds., *Harefu'ah biYrushalayim ledoroteha*. Tel Aviv, 1999.

———. *"Yerushalayim ke'ir mizrahit."* *Ariel* 57–58 (1988), pp. 93–104.

Stillman, Yedida K., and Nancy Micklewright. "Costume in the Middle East." *Middle East Studies Association Bulletin* 26/1 (1992), pp. 13–38.

Stone, Lawrence. *The Past and the Present Revisited*. London, 1987.

———. "The Revival of Narrative: Reflections on a New Old History." *Past and Present* 85 (1979), pp. 3–24. (repr. in idem, *Past and the Present Revisited*, pp. 74–96).

Storrs, Sir Ronald. *The Memoirs of Sir Ronald Storrs*. New York, 1937.

Szajkowski, Zosa. *Jewish Education in France, 1789–1939*. Jewish Social Sciences Monograph Series 2. New York, 1980.

Tallan, Cheryl. "The Medieval Jewish Widow: Powerful, Productive and Passionate." M.A. thesis, York University, Toronto, 1989.

Talmon-Morag, Peninah. *"Hishtalvutah shel edah vatikah behevrat mehagrim — Ha'edah haSefaradit beYisra'el."* Ph.D. dissertation, Hebrew University of Jerusalem, 1980.

Tamuz, Binyamin, Gideon Ofrat, and Dorit Levite, eds. *Sipurah shel omanut Yisra'el miymei Bezalel be1906 ve'ad yamenu*. Tel Aviv, 1991.

Taubenhaus, Ephraim. *Bintiv hayahid — Hayei lohem veholem be'ir hamekubalim*. Haifa, 1959.

Thon, Dalit. *"Batei sefer limlekhet teharim beErez Yisra'el bereshit hame'ah ha20,"* in Nina Benzur, ed., *Tahara*, pp. 18–21. Haifa [Museum for Music and Ethnology], 1994.

Thon, Rafi. *Hama'avak leshivyon zekhuyot ha'ishah: Sipur hayeha shel Sarah Thon*. Tel Aviv, 1996.

Tibawi, Abdul Latif. *British Interests in Palestine, 1800–1901: A Study of Religious and Educational Enterprise*. Oxford, 1961.

Tidhar, David. *Enziklopediyah lahaluzei hayishuv uvonav*, vol. 1. Tel Aviv, 1947.

Tobi, Yosef. *"Hareka hamedini, hakalkali vehahevrati la'aliyot miTeman bashanim [5]641–[5]678."* *Tema* 3 (1983), pp. 67–91.

———. *"Hit'aslemut bekerev yehudei Teiman tahat hashilton haZayidi — emdot hahalakhah haZayidit, hashilton ha'Umayyi vehahevrah hamuslemit."* *Pe'amim* 42 (1990, pp. 105–126.

———. *"Shorshei yahasah shel yahadut hamizrah el hatenuah haziyonit,"* in Shmuel Almog, Israel Bartul, and Michael Graetz, eds., *Temurot bahistoriyah hayehudit hahadashah — Kovez ma'amarim shay liShmuel Ettinger*, pp. 169–192. Jerusalem, 1988.

Tokacinski, Yehiel Michal. *Ir hakodesh vehamikdash*, vol. 3. Jerusalem, 1969.

Toker, Naftali. *"Eshet hayil vedarkhei kishurah leleilot Shabbat."* *Mehkerei Hag* 3 (1992), pp. 44–63.

Toledano, Henry. *"Yahadut Maroko veyishuv Erez Yisra'el . . . ,"* in M. Zohari and A. Tartakover, eds., *Hagut Ivrit be'arzot ha'Islam*, pp. 228–252. Jerusalem, 1981.

———. *"Yoman masa shel Rabbi Yizhak Toledano leErez Yisra'el."* *Mimizrah umima'arav* 3 (1981), pp. 141–157.

Toll, William. "A Quiet Revolution: Jewish Women's Clubs and the Widening Female Sphere, 1870–1920." *American Jewish Archives* 41 (1989), pp. 7–26.

Toporowski, Yehudit. *Me'ah she'arim sheli: Korot mishpahat Shalom uMalkah Azulay bishkhunat Me'ah She'arim ke'aspaklariyah lehayei hayishuv hayashan beyn hashanim 1919–1924*. Jerusalem, 1994.

Toukan, Fadwa. *Derekh hararit*, trans. into Hebrew by Rachel Halvah. N.p., 1993.

Trachtenberg, Joshua. *Jewish Magic and Superstition*. New York, 1970.

Trager, Hannah. *Pictures of Jewish Home-Life, Fifty Yeras Ago*. London, n.d.

Tristram, Henry Baker. *The Land of Israel: A Journal of Travels in Palestine*. London, 1865.

Trivaks, Yizhak, and Eliezer Steinman. *Sefer me'ah shanah — Anshei mofet vahaluzim rishonim beErez Yisra'el bemeshekh me'ah shanah vama'lah*. Tel Aviv, 1938.

Tuchman, Barbara. *Bible and Sword: England and Palestine from the Bronze Age to Balfour*. New York, 1956.

Tucker, Judith E. "Marriage and Family in Nablus, 1720–1856: Toward a History of Arab Marriage." *Journal of Family History* 13/2 (1983), pp. 165–179.

Turnbull, Colin. "Postscript: Anthropology as Pilgrimage," in Morinis, ed., *Sacred Journeys*, pp. 252–274.

Turner, Victor and Edith. *Image and Pilgrimage in Christian Culture*. New York, 1978.

Turnianski, Havah. "*Iberzetzungen un be'arbetungen fun der 'Ze'enah ure'enah*,'" in Shmuel Verses, ed., *Sefer Dov Sedan*, pp. 165–190. Jerusalem, 1977.

Twersky, Yohanan. *Habetulah miLudmir*. Jerusalem, 1949.

Valero, Victoria Vida. *Zikhronot*. Tel Aviv, 1991.

van Gennep, Arnold. *The Rites of Passage*. London, 1977.

Verses, Shmuel. "*Kol ha'ishah bashevu'on beYiddish 'Kol Mevasser*,'" *Hulyot* 4 (1997), pp. 53–82.

Vilnay, Ze'ev. *Mazevot kodesh beErez Yisra'el*, 2 vols. Jerusalem, 1985–1986.

Wahrmann, Dror. *Habukharim ushkhunatam biYrushalayim*. Jerusalem, 1992.

——. "*Hazalam haYerushalmi hamikzo'i harishon?*" *Cathedra* 38 (1985), pp. 115–120.

Walkowitz, Judith R. *Prostitution and Victorian Society: Women, Class and the State*. Cambridge, 1980.

Wallace, Edwin Sherman. *Jerusalem the Holy*. New York, 1977 [1898].

Weingarten, Ya'akov. *Ish hesed biYrushalayim: Masekhet hayav shel avi hayetomot Rabbi David Weingarten z"l*. Jerusalem, 1979.

Weiss, Avraham. *Women at Prayer: A Halakhic Analysis of Women's Prayer Groups*. Hoboken, N.J., 1990.

Weiss, Shraga. *Atarim kedoshim beErez Yisra'el*. Jerusalem, 1986.

Weiss, Yehudah Aaron. *Bish'arayikh Yerushalayim*. Jerusalem, 1959.

Weissbach, Lee Shai. "The Jewish Elite and the Children of the Poor: Jewish Apprenticeship Programs in Nineteenth-Century France." *AJS Review* 12/1 (1987), pp. 123–142.

Weissblum, Elimelech. *Havay Zefat*. Tel Aviv, 1969.

Weissler, Chava. "The Religion of Traditional Ashkenazic Women: Some Methodological Issues." *AJS Review* 12 (1987), pp. 73–94.

——. *Voices of the Matriarchs*. (Boston, 1998).

Weissman, Deborah. "Bais Ya'akov: A Historical Model for Jewish Feminists," in Elizabeth Koltun, ed., *The Jewish Woman: New Perspectives*, pp. 139–148. New York, 1976.

——. "Education of Jewish Women." *Encyclopedia Judaica Yearbook*, 1986–1987, cols. 29–36.

——. "*Hinukh banot datiyot biYrushalayim bitkufat hashilton haBriti . . .*" Ph.D. dissertation, Hebrew University of Jerusalem, 1994.

Welter, Barbara. "The Cult of True Womanhood, 1820–1860." *American Quarterly* 28 (1966), pp. 151–174.

Wenger, Beth S. "Jewish Women and Voluntarism: beyond the Myth of Enablers." *American Jewish History* 79/1 (1989–1990), pp. 16–36.

Wengeroff, Pauline. *Rememberings: The World of a Russian-Jewish Woman in the Nineteenth Century*, trans. Henny Wenkart, ed. with an afterword by Bernard D. Cooperman. Bethesda, Md., 2000.

Wilson, Elizabeth. *Adorned in Dreams: Fashion and Modernity*. London, 1985.

Witerer, Caroline. "Avoiding a 'Hothouse System of Education': Nineteenth-Century Early Childhood Education from the Infant Schools to the Kindergartens." *History of Education Quarterly* 32/3 (1992), pp. 289–314.

Wollons, Roberta. "The Black Forest in a Bamboo Garden: Missionary Kindergartens in Japan, 1868–1912." *History of Education Quarterly* 33/1 (1993), pp. 1–35.

Women in Education: Transactions of the Educational Section of the International Congress of Women. London, 1900.

Woody, Thomas. *A History of Women's Education in the U.S.*, vols. 1–2. New York, 1966 [1929].

Yaari, Avraham. *Mas'ot Erez Yisra'el shel olim yehudim*. Tel Aviv, 1946.

———. "Toledot hahilula beMeron." *Tarbiz* 31 (1962), pp. 73–101.

———. *Zikhronot Erez Yisra'el*, vols. 1–2. Ramat-Gan, 1974.

Yadler, Ben Zion. *Betuv Yerushalayim*. Benei Berak, 1967.

———. *Sefer ben yekhabed av*. Jerusalem, 1948.

Yahalom, Shalem. "Giluah harosh le'ishah nesu'ah." Seminar paper, Hebrew University of Jerusalem, 1995.

Yaniv, Bracha. "Seker batei hakeneset hasefaradiyim biYrushalayim." *Mehkerei Yerushalayim befolklor yehudi* 5–6 (1984), pp. 201–208.

Yehezkel, Yehudah Yizhak. "Kotel ma'aravi." *Me'asef Zion* 3 (1929), pp. 95–163.

Yehoshua, Ya'akov. *Sipuro shel habayit haSefaradi barova hayehudi ba'ir ha'atikah shel Yerushalayim*. Jerusalem, 1976.

———. *Yaldut biYrushalayim hayeshanah — Pirkei havay miyamim avaru*, vols. 1–5. Jerusalem, 1965–1978.

———. *Yerushalayim hayeshanah ba'ayin uvalev*. Jerusalem, 1988.

———. *Yerushalayim temol shilshom — Pirkei havay*, vols. 1–3. Jerusalem, 1977–1983.

Yellin, David. *Ketavim*, 7 vols. Jerusalem, 1972–1983.

Yellin, Ita. *Leze'eza'ay — Zikhronotay*, vols. 1–2. Jerusalem, 1938–1941.

Yellin, Yehoshua. *Zikhronot leven Yerushalayim*. Jerusalem, 1924.

Yellin, Yizhak Ya'akov. *Avoteinu — Pirkei historiyah vehavay, demuyot vesipurim mehayei bonei hayishuv harishonim*. Jerusalem, 1966.

Yizre'el, Rami. "Beyt ha'almin hasefaradi hakadum behar hazeytim." *Ariel* 122–123 (1997), pp. 9–49.

Yuhasz, Esther, ed. *Yehudei Sefarad ba'imperiyah ha'Othmanit*. Jerusalem, 1989.

Ze'evi, Dror. "Hame'ah ha'Uthmanit — Sanjak Yerushalayim bame'ah hasheva-esreh." Ph.D. dissertation, Tel Aviv University, 1991.

Zeldes, Nadya. "'Kevorahat mipnei hanahash' — hitmodedut nashim yehudiyot be-Siziliyah bedor hagerush im hamarat ba'aleihen." *Pe'amim* 82 (2000), pp. 52–63.

Zevin, Shmuel Yosef. *Hamo'adim bahalakhah*. Tel Aviv, 1957.

Zinberg, Yisra'el. *Toledot Sifrut Yisra'el*, vol. 4: *Sifrut Iddish mereshitah ve'ad tekufat hahaskalah*. Tel Aviv, 1958.

Zipperstein, Steven J. "Heresy, Apostasy and the Transformation of Joseph Rabbinovich," in Todd M. Endelman, ed., *Jewish Apostasy in the Modern World*. pp. 206–231, New York, 1987.

Zivan, Gili. *"'Barukh . . . she'asani ishah / yisre'elit'—al hazorekh hadahuf betikun haberakhah,"* in Naham Ilan, ed., *Ayin tovah: Du siah upulemus betarbut Yisra'el: Sefer yovel . . . Tovah Ilan*, pp. 278–301. [Tel Aviv], 1999.

Zobrowski, Mark, and Elizabeth Herzog. *Life Is with People.* New York, 1952.

Zohar, Zevi. *"Benei palatin shel melekh: Ta'am hahayim hayehudiyim beErez Yisra'el . . . ,"* in Ravitzky, ed., *Erez Yisra'el bahagut hayehudit ba'et hahadashah*, pp. 343–344.

Zolty, Shoshana Pantel. *"And All Your Children Shall Be Learned": Women and the Study of Torah in Jewish Law and History.* Northvale, N.J., and London, 1993.

Index

DATE DUE